THEY SAW IT HAPPEN
IN EUROPE

THEY
SAW IT HAPPEN
IN EUROPE

*An Anthology
of Eyewitnesses' Accounts of
Events in European History
1450-1600*

Compiled by

C. R. N. ROUTH

*Formerly Senior History Master
Eton College*

BASIL BLACKWELL
OXFORD

© *Basil Blackwell & Mott, Ltd., 1965*

First printed in 1965

Printed in Great Britain for BASIL BLACKWELL & MOTT, LTD.
by A. R. MOWBRAY & Co. LIMITED in the City of Oxford
and bound at the KEMP HALL BINDERY

CONTENTS

THE ITALIAN WARS

THE HOLY ROMAN EMPIRE

THE REFORMATION

FRANCE

FAMILY TREES

INTRODUCTION

THIS book is intended as a source book for the history of Europe from 1450 to 1600. It is planned along the same lines as the series *They Saw It Happen*—eyewitness accounts of the men, women and events who made up that history. The basis of the plan is the idea of Expansion. Europe was expanding culturally and intellectually in the Renaissance, notably in printing, in the arts and education, and in literature. All these facets are covered in the chapters dealing with the Italian and the Northern Renaissances. Scientifically she was expanding in medicine, astronomy, mathematics, all of which are illustrated mainly in the Northern Renaissance. Expansion (and the reaction against it) in religious thought is covered in the chapters on the Reformation and the Counter-Reformation. Physically Europe was expanding across the seas into the New World, to which a chapter is devoted to Spain and Portugal, Mexico and Peru. Politically these years saw the weaker states on the periphery succumb to the stronger states at the centre, resulting in the appearance of the nation-states. These states then tried to expand at the expense of their neighbours—hence the Franco-Italian wars and the threat to Western Europe from the Turks, to which two chapters have been given. This period also saw the last great attempt by the Papacy to play a major part in European politics; the reader will find a chapter devoted to the Popes. Economically and financially great changes were taking place; the development of capitalism and the rise of banking led to the shifting of the centres of trade, to the decline of Venice and the growth of Antwerp. There were other and less creditable features in sixteenth-century Europe—political assassinations, the spread of witchcraft, the flagrant dishonesty of the alchemists. But there were also music, practical jokes, hunting and horse-racing. These have been grouped together in a final chapter, in which one entry by a Florentine diarist in the year 1529 may provide the best laugh—'at this time men began to cut their hair short, everyone having formerly worn it long on to their shoulders, without exception'.

There is any amount of material on which to draw, but the length of the book had to be controlled and therefore there are omissions which I should like to have avoided—two in particular. I am most grateful to Mr. Ernle Bradford for his generosity in allowing me to use his translation of Balbi's account of the Turkish attack on Rhodes, but unfortunately this was not completed in time for me to include it. I also very much regret having had to abandon all lists of 'further reading'.

My best thanks are due to Mr. D. H. Merry and Mr. W. O. Hassall of the Bodleian Library for their help in finding the books I needed: to Mr. Brian Rawson and the Folio Society for the most generous breach of a rule in order to supply me with a copy of *At the Court of the Borgia*: once again I am deeply in debt to the Librarian and his staff at the Public Library of Stratford-upon-Avon: but most of all I have to thank Dr. V. H. H. Green of Lincoln College, Oxford, for having not only read the typescripts of my book and made many valuable corrections and suggestions, but also for the way in which he not only suggested new sources, but even often supplied me with typed extracts. What errors remain in the book are mine and not his. It is also my pleasure to thank Colonel Bowermann and Mr. John Cutforth of Messrs. Basil Blackwell for their unfailing patience and trouble.

THE RULERS OF EUROPE 1453-1600

THE PAPACY

Nicholas V	(Thomas of Sarzana)	1447–1455
Calixtus III	(Alfonso Borgia)	1455–1458
Pius II	(Aeneas Piccolomini)	1458–1464
Paul II	(Pietro Barbo)	1464–1471
Sixtus IV	(Francesco della Rovere)	1471–1484
Innocent VIII	(Giambattista Cibo)	1484–1492
Alexander VI	(Rodrigo Borgia)	1492–1503
Pius III	(Francesco Todeschini)	1503 (Sept.-Oct.)
Julius II	(Giulio della Rovere)	1503–1513
Leo X	(Giovanni de' Medici)	1513–1521
Adrian VI	(Adrian of Utrecht)	1522–1523
Clement VII	(Giulio de' Medici)	1523–1534
Paul III	(Alessandro Farnese)	1534–1549
Julius III	(Giovanni del Monte)	1550–1555
Marcellus II	(Marcello Cervini)	1555
Paul IV	(Pietro Caraffa)	1555–1559
Pius IV	(Gian-Angelo de' Medici)	1559–1565
Pius V	(Michele Ghislieri)	1565–1572
Gregory XIII	(Ugo Buoncompagno)	1572–1585
Sixtus V	(Felix Peretti)	1585–1590
Urban VII	(Giambattista Campagna)	1590
Gregory XIV	(Niccolo Sfondrato)	1590–1591
Innocent IX	(Gian-Antonio Fachinetto)	1591
Clement VIII	(Ippolito Aldobrandini)	1592–1605

THE HOLY ROMAN EMPIRE

Frederick III	1440–1493
Maximilian I	1493–1519
Charles V	1519–1556, abd. d. 1558
Ferdinand I	1556–1564
Maximilian II	1564–1576
Rudolf II	1576–1612

FRANCE

The House of Valois

Charles VII	1422–1461
Louis XI	1461–1483
Charles VIII	1483–1498
Louis XII	1498–1515
Francis I	1515–1547
Henry II	1547–1559
Francis II	1559–1560
Charles IX	1560–1574
Henry III	1574–1589

The House of Bourbon

Henry IV	1589–1610

SPAIN

The Catholic Kings (a title granted by Alexander VI in 1495)

Isabella of Castile	1474–1504
Ferdinand of Aragon	1479–1516

The House of Hapsburg

(Joanna of Castile	1504–1555)
(Philip I	1504–1506)
Charles V	1516–1555
Philip II	1555–1598
Philip III	1598–1621

PORTUGAL

The House of Avis

Alfonso V	1438–1481
John II	1481–1495
Manuel I	1495–1521
John III	1521–1557
Sebastian	1557–1578
Henry	1578–1580

The Spanish Kings

Philip I (II)	1580–1598
Philip II (III)	1598–1621

SWEDEN

The House of Vasa

Gustavus I	1523–1560
Eric XIV	1560–1568 dep. d. 1577
John III	1568–1592
Sigismund	1592–1604 dep. d. 1632

DENMARK AND NORWAY

The House of Oldenburg

Christian I	1513–1523 dep. d. 1559
Frederick I	1523–1533
Christian III	1533–1559
Frederick II	1559–1588
Christian IV	1588–1648

THE UNITED PROVINCES

The House of Orange

William I	m. 1584
Maurice	1584–1625

TURKEY

Mohammed II	1451–1481
Bayezid	1481–1512
Selim I	1512–1520
Suleiman I	1520–1566
Selim II	1566–1574
Murad III	1574–1595
Mohammed III	1595–1603

ENGLAND

The House of Tudor

Henry VII	1485–1509
Henry VIII	1509–1547
Edward VI	1547–1553
Mary I	1553–1558
Elizabeth I	1558–1603

THE ITALIAN RENAISSANCE
(Notes on p. 81)

HUMANISM AND CLASSICISM

In analysing so large and complex a subject as the Renaissance there is always danger of over-simplifying, but probably it is safe to see the Renaissance as passing through four stages. The first may be called the Classical Revival, which was born in Italy and therefore naturally and inevitably concerned itself with the civilization of ancient Rome. Men began to study the old Roman literature and the old Roman arts.

The second stage may be called the Humanistic, when men began to discover that the more they read Latin the more necessary it became to read Greek and to study the civilization of ancient Athens.

The third stage was the religious period, in which men became critical of the Christian Church and began to turn more and more to the original Greek sources of the Scriptures and to compare the behaviour of the Church in Western Europe with the teaching of the New Testament. These ideas, which were circulating before Luther and the Reformation, owed much to the work of Erasmus and were more influential in Northern than in Southern Europe. The criticisms of the mediæval Church, to which they afforded substantial backing, made the Reformation possible.

In the fourth stage the effects of the Renaissance were felt throughout Europe, fostering humanistic ideas and artistic ideas in Italy (and for a time stimulating small groups of like-minded thinkers in Spain), encouraging the study of Greek and Hebrew (and thus assisting the Reformation) in Germany and Northern Europe, and eventually giving rise to modern philosophy and to the evolution of modern Science. (See J. M. Thompson, *Lectures on Foreign History*, pp. 16 *sqq.*: W. K. Ferguson, *The Renaissance in Historical Thought*, 1948.)

ERASMUS

The most notable figure among the Humanists was Erasmus. The following letters illustrate both the Classical and the Humanist points of view.

Source: (a) A letter from Erasmus to Antony of Bergen, Abbot of St. Bertin at St. Omer. Written perhaps from Paris on March 16th, 1501.

B

To the most illustrious prelate Antony, Abbot of St. Bertin, greetings: . . . I have accidentally happened upon some Greek books, and am busy day and night secretly copying them out. I shall be asked why I am so delighted with Cato the Censor's example that I want to turn Greek at my age. Indeed, most excellent Father, if in my boyhood I had been of this mind, or rather if time had not been wanting, I should be the happiest of men. As things are, I think it better to learn, even if a little late, than not to know things which it is of the first importance to have at one's command. I have already tasted of Greek literature in the past, but merely (as the saying is) sipped at it; however, having lately gone a little deeper into it, I perceive—as one has often read in the best authorities—that Latin learning, rich as it is, is defective and incomplete without Greek; for we have but a few streams and muddy puddles, whilst they have pure springs and rivers rolling gold. I see that it is utter madness even to touch the branch of theology which deals chiefly with the mysteries unless one is also provided with the equipment of Greek, as the translators of the Scriptures, owing to their conscientious scruples, render Greek forms in such a fashion that not even the primary sense (what our theologians call the *literal* sense) can be understood by persons ignorant of Greek. Who could understand the sentence in the Psalms (Ps. 51. 4), *Et peccatum meum contra me est semper*,[1] unless he has read, the Greek? This runs as follows: καὶ ἡ ἁμαρτία μου ενώπιον μου ἐστι διαπαντός. At this point some theologian will spin a long story of how the flesh is perpetually in conflict with the spirit, having been misled by the double meaning of the preposition, that is *contra*, when the word ἐνώπιον refers not to conflict but to position, as if you were to say *opposite*, i.e. *in sight*; so that the Prophet's meaning was that his fault was so hateful to him that the memory of it never left him, but floated always before his mind as if it were present . . . But why do I pick out a few trifling examples from so many important ones, when I have on my side the venerable authority of the papal Curia? There is a Curial Decree still extant in the Decretals, ordaining that persons should be appointed in the chief academies (as they were then) capable of giving accurate instruction in

Hebrew, Greek and Latin literature, since, as they believed, the Scriptures could not be understood, far less discussed, without this knowledge . . .

It is my delight to set foot on the path into which Jerome and the splendid host of so many ancients summon me; so help me God, I would sooner be mad with them than as sane as you like with the mob of modern theologians. Besides, I am attempting an arduous and, so to say, Phaethontean task—to do my best to restore the works of Jerome, which have been partly corrupted by those half-learned persons, and are partly—owing to the lack of knowledge of antiquities and of Greek literature—forgotten or mangled or mutilated or at least full of mistakes and monstrosities; not merely to restore them, but to elucidate them with commentaries, so that each reader will acknowledge to himself that the great Jerome, considered by the ecclesiastical world as the most perfect in both branches of learning, the sacred and the profane, can indeed be read by all, but can only be understood by the most learned. As I am working hard on this design and see that I must in the first place acquire Greek, I have decided to study for some months under a Greek teacher, a real Greek, no, twice a Greek, always hungry,[2] who charges an immoderate fee for his lessons. Farewell.

Source: (*b*) It has to be remembered how powerfully the invention of printing affected the spread of Humanism. The following letter from Erasmus to Aldus Manutius (1449–1515), founder of the Aldine Press at Venice in 1494, illustrates the close connection between Humanism and printing.

A letter from Erasmus to Manutius, from Bologna, on October 28th, 1507. Printed in Huizinga's *Erasmus of Rotterdam*, p. 207, London, Phaidon Press, 1952.

To Aldus Manutius of Rome, many greetings.

I have often wished, most learned Manutius, that the light you have cast on Greek and Latin literature, not by your printing alone and your splendid types, but by your brilliance and your uncommon learning, could have been matched by the profit you in your turn drew from them. So far as *fame* is concerned, the name of Aldus Manutius will without doubt be on the lips of all devotees of sacred literature unto all posterity; and your memory will be—as your fame now is—not merely illustrious but loved and cherished as well, because you are engaged, as I hear, in reviving and disseminating the good authors—with extreme diligence, but not at a commensurate profit—undergoing truly Herculean labours, labours splendid indeed and destined to bring you immortal glory, but meanwhile more profitable to others than to yourself. I hear that you are printing Plato[3] in Greek types; very many scholars eagerly await the book. I should like to know what medical authors you have printed;[4] I wish you would give us Paul of Aegina.[5] I wonder what has prevented you from publishing the New Testament long since[6]— a work which would delight even the common people (if I conjecture aright), but particularly my own class, the theologians.

I send you two tragedies[7] which I have been bold enough to translate, whether with success you yourself shall judge. Thomas Linacre, William Grocyn, William Latimer, Cuthbert Tunstall, friends of yourself as well as of mine, thought highly of them . . . It has been printed by Badius, successfully as far as he is concerned, so he writes, for he has now sold all the copies to his satisfaction. But my reputation has not been enhanced thereby, so full is it all of mistakes, and in fact he offers his services to repair the first edition by printing a second. But I am afraid of his mending ill with ill, as the Sophoclean saying goes. I should consider my labours to have been immortalized if they could come out printed in your types, the most beautiful of all. This will result in the volume being very small and the business being concluded at little expense. If you think it is convenient to undertake the affair, I will supply you with a corrected copy, which I send by the bearer, *gratis*, except that you may wish to send me a few volumes as gifts for my friends . . .

If you have any rare authors in your press, I shall be obliged if you will indicate this—my learned British friends have asked me to search for them. If you decide not to print the *Tragedies*, will you return the copy to the bearer to bring back to me?

Source: (c) Charles Blount was the eldest son of Lord Mountjoy (b. 1518). He had been a pupil of Erasmus and they remained firm friends.

From the Preface to *T. Livii . . . Historiae*, Basle, Froben, 1531.
Printed in Huizinga, *op. cit.*, p. 249.

Freiburg im Breisgau, March 1st, 1531

To the noble youth Charles Mountjoy, greetings

. . . I have determined to dedicate to you Livy, the prince of Latin history; already many times printed, but never before in such a magnificent or accurate edition: and if this is not enough, augmented by five books recently discovered; these were found by some good genius in the library of the monastery at Lorsch by Simon Grynaeus,[8] a man at once learned without arrogance in all branches of literature and at the same time born for advancement of liberal studies. Now this monastery was built opposite Worms . . . by Charlemagne seven hundred years and more ago, and equipped with great store of books; for this was formerly the special care of princes, and this is usually the most precious treasure of the monasteries. The original manuscript was one of marvellous antiquity, painted in the antique fashion[9] with the letters in a continuous series, so that it has proved very difficult to separate word from word, unless one is knowledgeable, careful and trained for this very task. This caused much trouble in preparing a copy to be handed to the printer's men for their use; a careful and faithful watch was kept to prevent any departure from the original in making the copy. So if the poor fragment which came to us recently from Mainz[10] was justly welcomed by scholars with great rejoicing, what acclamation should greet this large addition to Livy's *History*?

Would to God this author could be restored to us complete and entire. There are rumours flying round that give some hope of this: men boast of unpublished Livians existing, now in Denmark, now in Poland, now in Germany. At least now that fortune has given us these remnants against all men's expectations, I do not see why we should despair of the possibility of finding still more. And here, in my opinion at least, the princes would be acting worthily if they offered rewards and attracted scholars to the search for such a treasure, or prevailed upon them to publish—if there are perchance any who are suppressing or hiding away to the great detriment of studies something in a fit state to be of public utility. For it seems perfectly absurd that men will dig through the bowels of the earth almost down to Hades at vast peril and expense in order to find a little gold or silver: and yet will utterly disregard treasures of this kind, as far above those others in value as the soul excels the body, and not consider them worth searching for.

NICCOLO DE' NICCOLI

The following extract portrays a typical Renaissance scholar and collector. Niccolo de' Niccoli transcribed with his own hand all the codices in the Library of St. Mark: he ruined himself financially by buying books, whereupon he was financed by Cosimo de Medici to go on buying books. When he died, he owned 800 books, most of them transcribed by his own hand.

Source: Life of Niccolo, by Vespasiano, *Memoirs*, Eng. ed. W. G. Waters, pp. 395 *sqq*. Vespasiano da Bisticci was himself a scholar and bibliophile. Born in 1421, he died in 1498. He was a Florentine born and bred. J. A. Symonds calls him the 'last of the mediæval scribes and at the same time the first of modern booksellers'. He acted as agent for Cosimo de Medici, Pope Nicholas V, Federigo of Urbino (whose librarian he was: see below under Federigo, p. 41), he exported MSS. to England, Hungary, Germany, Portugal (cf. J. A. Symonds, *The Renaissance in Italy*, *The Revival of Learning*, p. 221).

If he heard of any book in Greek or Latin not to be had in Florence, he spared no cost in getting it; the number of Latin books which Florence owes entirely to his generosity cannot be reckoned . . . Strangers who came to Florence at that time, if they missed the opportunity of seeing him at home, thought they had not been in Florence.

First of all, he was of a most fair presence; lively, for a smile was ever on his lips; and very pleasant in his talk. He wore clothes of the fairest crimson cloth, down to the ground. He never married, in order that he might not be impeded in his studies. A housekeeper provided for his daily needs. He was one of the most particular of men in his diet, as also in other things. When he sat at table, he ate from fair antique vases; and in like manner his table was covered with porcelain and other vessels of great beauty. The cup from which he drank was of crystal or some other precious stone. To see him at table—a perfect model of the men of old—was of a truth a charming sight. He always willed that the napkins set before him should be of the whitest, as well as all the linen. Some might wonder at the many vases he possessed, to whom I answer that things of that sort were neither so highly valued then, nor so much regarded, as they have since become; and Niccolo having friends everywhere, anyone who wished to do him a pleasure would send him marble statues, or antique vases, carvings, inscriptions, pictures from the hands of distinguished masters, and mosaic tablets. He had a most beautiful map, on which all the parts and cities of the world were marked; others of Italy and Spain, all painted; Florence could not show a house more full of ornaments than his, nor one that had in it a greater number of graceful objects: so that all who went there found innumerable things of worth to please varieties of taste.

THE LIBRARY OF FEDERIGO, DUKE OF URBINO

Source: (a) Vespasiano, Vat. Urb. MSS. 941, f. 43: quoted in Dennistoun, *Memoirs of the Dukes of Urbino*, vol. 1, p. 156 *sqq.* An almost exactly similar version occurs in Vespasiano's Memoirs, ed. in English by W. G. Waters, London, 1926. Vespasiano was the Duke's librarian. The library is now in the Vatican.

We have now to mention the high estimation in which he held all Greek and Latin authors, sacred or profane; and to him alone was given the enterprise to carry out what no one for above a thousand years past had done, by establishing a library superior to any formed during all that period. In no respect did he look to expense; and whenever he learned the existence of any desirable book in Italy, or abroad, he sent for it without heeding the cost. It is now above fourteen years since he began to make this collection, and he has ever since maintained at Urbino, Florence, and elsewhere, thirty-four transcribers, and has resorted to every means requisite for amassing a famous and excellent library— which it now is. He has, in the first place, all the Latin poets, with their best commentaries; also the entire works of Cicero, with all the orators and grammarians in that language. In history, he commissioned every known work of that or the Greek tongue, as well as the orators of the latter. In moral and natural philosophy, no author of these languages is wanting. In the faculty of theology he has been most profuse, having, besides the four doctors of the church, St. Bernard, Tertullian, Hilary, Remigius, Hugh of St. Victor, Isidore, Anselm, Rabanus, Dionysius the Areopagite, St. Basil, Cyril, Gregory of Naziarsus, John of Damascus, Eusebius, Origen, St. Thomas Aquinas, Albertus Magnus, Alexander of Alexandria, Duns Scotus, Bonaventura, Richard of Middleton, Archbishop Antonino, with all the modern doctors. There are further all the best civilians, with the lectures of Bartolomeo Capretti. He had the Bible, that best of books, written in two volumes, with the richest and most beautiful illustrations, bound in brocade of gold and lavishly ornamented with silver; and he made it be thus gorgeously adorned as the chief of all literature, and it has no equal in our time. There are also the Commentaries on the Bible in Greek and Latin, including Nicolo de Lira. He further has all the treatises on astrology, geometry, arithmetic, architecture, and military tactics, and a very curious volume with every ancient and modern military engine: also all books on painting, sculpture and music; the standard writers on civil law; the Speculum Innocentiae; in medicine, the works of Hippocrates, Galen and Avicenna; the writings of Averröes on logic, ethics and physics; a volume of early councils; the writings of Boethius on logic, philosophy and music; and those of modern authors, with Pius II at their head. There are all the works of Petrarch, Dante, Boccaccio, Colluccio, Leonardo d'Arezzo, Fra Ambrogio . . . [Vespasiano then lists 46 more authors].

On all this the Duke spent upwards of 30,000 ducats; and he made a rule that every book should be bound in crimson, ornamented with silver, from the Bible already described down to the modern authors. It is thus a truly rich display to see all these books so adorned, all being manuscripts on vellum, with illuminations, and each a complete copy—perfections not found in any other library. Indeed, shortly before he went to the siege of Ferrara, I compared the catalogue with lists of other libraries which he had procured, such as those of the Vatican, Florence,

St. Mark, Pavia, down to that of the university of Oxford in England, and found that all but his had deficiencies and duplicates.

Source: (*b*) The rules for the Librarian: Vat. Urb. MSS. No. 1248, f. 58. Quoted in Dennistoun, *op. cit.*, vol. 1, p. 159.

The librarian should be learned, of good presence, temper and manners, correct and ready of speech. He must get from the garderobe an inventory of the books, and keep them arranged and easily accessible, whether Latin, Greek, Hebrew or others, maintaining also the rooms in good condition. He must preserve the books from damp and vermin, as well as from the hands of trifling, ignorant, dirty and tasteless persons. To those of authority and learning he ought himself to exhibit them with all facility, courteously explaining their beauty and remarkable characteristics, the hand-writing and miniatures, but observant that such abstract no leaves. When ignorant or merely curious persons wish to see them, a glance is sufficient, if it be not someone of considerable influence. When any lock or other requisite is needed, he must take care that it be promptly provided. He must let no book be taken away but by the Duke's orders, and if lent must get a written receipt and see to its being returned. When a number of visitors come in, he must be specially watchful that none be stolen. All of which is duly seen to by the present courteous and attentive librarian, Messer Agabito.

THE VATICAN LIBRARY

Source: Montaigne, *Travel Journal*: trans. D. M. Frame, Hamish Hamilton, 1958, p. 949.

On March 6th [1581] I went to see the Vatican Library, which is in five or six large rooms all in a row. There are a large number of books attached on to several rows of desks; there are also some in coffers, which were all opened to me; lots of books written by hand, and especially a Seneca and the *Moral Essays* of Plutarch. Among the remarkable things I saw were the statue of the good Aristides with a handsome bald head, a thick beard, a big forehead, a look full of gentleness and majesty: his name is written on the very ancient pedestal: a book from China, in strange characters, the leaves made of some material much softer and more pellucid than our paper; and because this cannot endure the stain of ink, the writing is on only one side of the sheet, and the sheets are all double and folded at the outside edges, by which they hold together. They think it is the membrane of some tree. I also saw a bit of the ancient papyrus, on which there were unknown characters; it is the bark of a tree. I saw the breviary of St. Gregory, written by hand; it bears no evidence of the year, but they hold that it has come down from him from hand to hand. It is a missal about like ours, and was brought to the last Council of Trent to serve as a testimony of our ceremonies. I saw a book by Saint Thomas Aquinas in which there are corrections in the hand of the author himself, who wrote badly, a small lettering worse than mine. *Item*, a Bible printed on parchment, one of those that Plantin has just done in four languages, which King Philip sent to the present Pope, as is stated in the inscription on the binding; the original of the book that the King of England composed against Luther, which he sent about fifty years ago to Pope Leo X, inscribed with his own hand:

> To Leo Ten, Henry, King of the English, sends
> This work, a pledge of loyalty between two friends.

I read the prefaces, the one to the Pope, the other to the reader: he excuses himself because of his military occupations and lack of ability; for scholastic Latin it is good.

I saw the library without any difficulty; anyone can see it thus and can make whatever extracts he wants; and it is open almost every morning. I was guided through it and invited by a gentleman to use it whenever I wanted . . .

SOME MEN OF THE RENAISSANCE

BENVENUTO CELLINI

If there be such a specific creature as the 'Renaissance Man', then Benvenuto Cellini may be taken as the clearest representative of the species. John Addington Symonds wrote in the introduction to his edition of Cellini's autobiography, 'From the pages of this book the Genius of the Renaissance, incarnate in a single personality, leans forth

and speaks to us. Nowhere else, to my mind . . . do we find the full
character of the epoch so authentically stamped . . . He touched the
life of the epoch at more points than any person who has left a record
of his doings. He was the first goldsmith of his time, an adequate
sculptor, a restless traveller, an indefatigable workman, a Bohemian of
the purest water, a turbulent bravo, a courtier and companion of
princes; finally a Florentine who used his native idiom with incomparable vivacity of style.' The following extracts illustrate these
various facets of Benvenuto Cellini's character.

Source: (a) The Life of Benvenuto Cellini, written by himself, ed. by
J. A. Symonds, Macmillan, 1925, pp. 288–9.

The Salt Cellar of Francis I, now at Vienna, Kunsthistorisches
Museum. Illustrations are to be found in the Phaidon edition of the
autobiography, London, 1949, plates xiv–xvii.

On the following day he [Francis I] sent for me at his dinner
hour. The Cardinal of Ferrara was there at meat with him. When
I arrived, the King had reached his second course; he began at
once to speak to me, saying with a pleasant cheer that, having
now so fine a basin and jug of my workmanship, he wanted an
equally handsome salt-cellar to match them; and begged me to
make a design and to lose no time about it. I replied: 'Your
Majesty shall see a model of the sort even sooner than you have
commanded; for while I was making the basin, I thought there
ought to be a salt-cellar to match it; therefore I have already
designed one, and if it is your pleasure, I will at once exhibit my
conception'. The King turned with a lively movement of surprise
and pleasure to the lords in his company—they were the King of
Navarre, the Cardinal of Lorraine and the Cardinal of Ferrara—
exclaiming as he did so: 'Upon my word, this is a man to be
loved and cherished by everyone who knows him'. Then he told
me he would very gladly see my model.

I set off and returned in a few minutes; for I had only to cross
the river, that is, the Seine. I carried with me the wax model
which I had made in Rome at the Cardinal of Ferrara's request.
When I appeared again before the King and uncovered my piece,
he cried out in astonishment: 'This is a hundred times more divine
a thing than I had ever dreamed of. What a miracle of a man!
He ought never to stop working!' Then he turned to me with a

beaming countenance and told me that he greatly liked the piece, and wished me to execute it in gold. The Cardinal of Ferrara looked me in the face and let me understand that he recognized the model as the same which I had made for him in Rome. I replied that I had already told him I should carry it out for one who was worthy of it. The Cardinal, remembering my words and nettled by the revenge he thought that I was taking on him, remarked to the King: 'Sire, this is an enormous undertaking; I am only afraid that we shall never see it finished. These able artists who have great conceptions in their brains are ready enough to put the same in execution without duly considering when they are to be accomplished. I therefore, if I gave the commission for things of such magnitude, should like to know when I was likely to get them.' The King replied that if a man was so scrupulous about the termination of a work, he would never begin anything at all; these words he uttered with a certain look, which implied that such enterprises were not for folk of little spirit. I then began to say, 'Princes who put heart and courage in their servants, as your Majesty does by deed and word, render undertakings of the greatest magnitude quite easy. Now that God has sent me so magnificent a patron, I hope to perform for him a multitude of great and splendid masterpieces.' 'I believe it,' said the King, and rose from table. Then he called me into his chamber and asked how much gold was wanted for the salt-cellar. 'A thousand crowns,' I answered. He called his treasurer at once, who was the Viscount of Orbec, and ordered him that very day to disburse to me a thousand crowns of good weight and old gold.

Source: (b) op. cit., pp. 292 et sqq.

On the morning which followed these events, I made the first step in my work upon the great salt-cellar, pressing this and my other pieces forward with incessant industry. My workpeople at this time, who were pretty numerous, included both sculptors and goldsmiths. They belonged to several nations, Italian, French and German; for I took the best I could find and changed them often, retaining only those who knew their business well. These select craftsmen I worked to the bone with perpetual labour. They wanted to rival me, but I had a better constitution. Consequently, in their inability to bear up against such a continuous strain, they took to eating and drinking copiously; some of the Germans in particular, who were more skilled than their comrades, and wanted to march apace with me, sank under these excesses and perished.

While I was at work upon the Jupiter, I noticed that I had plenty of silver to spare. So I took in hand, without consulting the King, to make a great two-handled vase, about one cubit and a half in height. I also conceived the notion of casting the large model of my Jupiter in bronze. Having up to this date done nothing of the sort, I conferred with certain old men experienced in that art at Paris, and described to them the methods in use with us in Italy. They told me they had never gone that way about the business; but that, if I gave them leave to act upon their own principles, they would bring the bronze out as clean and perfect as the clay. I chose to strike an agreement with them, throwing on them the responsibility, and promising several crowns above the price they bargained for. Thereupon, they put the work in progress; but I soon saw that they were going the wrong way about it, and began on my own account a head of Julius Caesar, bust and armour, much larger than the life, which I modelled from a reduced copy of a splendid antique portrait I had brought with me from Rome. I also undertook another head of the same size studied from a very handsome girl, whom I kept for my own pleasures. I called this Fontana Belio [Fontainebleau], after the place selected by the King for his particular delight.

We constructed an admirable little furnace for the casting of the bronze, got all things ready and baked our moulds; those French masters undertaking the Jupiter, while I looked after my two heads. Then I said: 'I do not think you will succeed with your Jupiter, because you have not provided enough vents beneath for the air to circulate; therefore you are but losing your time and trouble'. They replied, that if their work proved a failure, they would pay back the money I had given on account, and recoup me for current expenses; but they bade me give good heed to my own proceedings, for the fine heads I meant to cast in my Italian fashion would never succeed . . .

Then they put their own piece into the furnace with much laughter; while I, maintaining a firm carriage, showing neither mirth nor anger (though I felt it), placed my two heads, one on each side of the Jupiter. The metal came all right to melting and we let it in with joy and gladness; it filled the mould of the Jupiter most admirably, and at the same time my two heads. This furnished them with matter for rejoicing and me with satisfaction; for I was not sorry to have predicted wrongly of their work, and they made as though they were delighted to have been mistaken about mine. Then, as the custom in France is, they asked to drink, in high good spirits . . .

At daybreak they began quite quietly to break into the pit of the furnace. They could not uncover their large mould until they had extracted my two heads; these were in excellent condition and they placed them where they could be well seen. When they came to the Jupiter and dug but scarcely two cubits, they sent up such a yell, they and their four workmen, that it woke me up. Fancying it was a shout of triumph, I set off running, for my bedroom was at the distance of more than five hundred paces. On reaching the spot, I found them looking like the guardians of Christ's sepulchre in a picture, downcast and terrified. Casting a hasty glance on my two heads, and seeing they were all right, I tempered my annoyance with the pleasure that sight gave me. Then they began to make excuses, crying: 'Our bad luck'! I retorted: 'Your luck has been most excellent, but what has been indeed bad is your deficiency of knowledge; had I only seen you put the soul[11] into your mould, I could have taught you with one word how to cast the figure without fault. This would have brought me great honour and you much profit. I shall be able to make good my reputation; but you will lose both your honour and your profit. Let then this lesson teach you another time to work, and not to poke fun at your masters.'

Source: (c) Benvenuto's brother had been killed by a soldier. Benvenuto takes vengeance, *op. cit.,* pp. 102 *et sqq.*

I also took to watching the arquebusier who had shot my brother, as though he had been a girl I was in love with ... When I saw that the fever caused by always seeing him about was depriving me of sleep and appetite, I overcame my repugnance to so low and not quite praiseworthy an enterprise, and made my mind up one evening to rid myself of the torment. The fellow lived in a house near a place called Torre Sanguigua, next door to the lodging of one of the most fashionable courtesans in Rome, named Signora Antea. It had just struck twenty-four, and he was standing at the house-door with his sword in hand, having risen from supper. With great address I stole up to him, holding a large Pistojan dagger,[12] and dealt him a back-handed stroke, with which I meant to cut his head clean off; but as he turned round very suddenly, the blow fell upon the point of his left shoulder and broke the bone. He sprang up, dropped his sword, half-stunned with the great pain, and took to flight. I followed after, and in four steps caught him up, when I lifted my dagger above his head, which he was holding very low, and hit him in the back exactly at the juncture of the nape-bone and neck. The poniard entered this point so deep into the bone that, though I used all my strength to pull it out, I was not able. For just at that moment four soldiers with drawn swords sprang out from Antea's lodging and obliged me to set hand to my own sword to defend my life. Leaving the poniard then, I made off, and fearing I might be recognized, took refuge in the palace of Duke Alessandro.

More than eight days elapsed and the Pope [Clement VII] did not send for me according to custom. Afterwards he summoned me through his chamberlain, who let me in his own modest manner understand that his Holiness knew all, but was very well inclined toward me, and that I had only to mind my work and keep quiet. When we reached the Presence, the Pope cast so menacing a glance towards me that the mere look of his eyes made me tremble. Afterwards, upon examining my work, his countenance cleared and he began to praise me beyond measure, saying that I had done a vast amount in a short time. Then, looking me straight in the face, he added: 'Now that you are cured, Benvenuto, take heed how you live'. I, who understood his meaning, promised that I would. Immediately upon this, I opened a very fine shop in the Banchi, opposite Raffaello.

Source: (d) The following extract not only records the source of the true story of how Michelangelo came by his broken nose, but it also reveals what was the contemporary opinion of one of the greatest of the Renaissance artistic experts about the relative value of two famous cartoons for pictures on the same subject, one by Leonardo da Vinci, the other by Michelangelo. Modern criticism supports Benvenuto Cellini: *op. cit.,* pp. 18–20.

About that time there came to Florence a sculptor named Piero Torrigiano;[13] he arrived from England, where he had resided many years; and being intimate with my master, he daily visited his house; and when he saw my drawing and the things I was making, he said: 'I have come to Florence to enlist as many young men as I can; for I have undertaken to execute a great work for my king[14] and want some of my own Florentines to help me. Now your method of working and your designs are worthy rather of a sculptor than a goldsmith; and since I have to turn out a great piece of bronze, I will at the same time turn you into a rich and able artist.' This man had a splendid person and a most arrogant spirit, with the air of a great soldier more than of a sculptor, especially in regard to his vehement gestures and his resonant voice, together with a habit he had of knitting his brows, enough to frighten any man of courage. He kept talking every day about his gallant feats among those beasts of Englishmen.

In the course of conversation he happened to mention Michel Agnolo Bouonarroti, led thereto by a drawing I had made from a cartoon of that divinest painter. This cartoon was the first masterpiece which Michel Agnolo exhibited in proof of his stupendous talents. He produced it in competition with another painter, Leonardo da Vinci, who also made a cartoon, and both were intended for the council-hall in the palace of the Signory. They represented the taking of Pisa by the Florentines; and our admirable Leonardo had chosen to depict a battle of horses, with the capture of some standards, in as divine a style as could possibly be imagined. Michel Agnolo in his cartoon portrayed a number of foot-soldiers, who, the season being summer, had gone to bathe in the Arno. He drew them at the very moment the alarm is sounded, and the men all naked run to arms; so splendid in the action that nothing survives of ancient or of modern art which touches the same lofty point of excellence; and as I have already said, the design of the great Leonardo was itself most admirably beautiful. These two cartoons stood, one in the palace of the Medici, the other in the hall of the Pope. So long as they remained intact, they were the school of the world. Though the divine Michel Agnolo in later life finished that great chapel of Pope Julius,[15] he never rose half-way to the same pitch of power; his genius never afterwards attained to the force of those first studies.[16]

Now let us return to Piero Torrigiano, who, with my drawings in his hand, spoke as follows: 'This Buonarroti and I used, when we were boys, to go into the Church of the Carmine, to learn drawing from the chapel of Masaccio. It was Buonarroti's habit to banter all who were drawing there; and one day, among others, when he was annoying me, I got more angry than usual, and clenching my fist, gave him such a blow on the nose that I felt bone and cartilage go down like biscuit beneath my knuckles; and this mark of mine he will carry with him to the grave.' These words begat in me such hatred of the man, since I was always gazing at the masterpieces of the divine Michel Agnolo, that although I felt a wish to go with him to England, I now could never bear the sight of him.

MICHELANGELO

Michelangelo (1475-1565) was perhaps the greatest genius of the whole company of Italian artists. Without doubt he was the most tremendous personality of all that wonderful company, both as a painter, a sculptor and an architect. The best original source for his life is that by his friend and pupil, Ascanio Condivi, published in 1553 and translated into English by Sir C. Holroyd. But Vasari also knew him well, worked as a pupil in his studio and has written with knowledge and understanding of his master in his *The Lives of the Painters, Sculptors and Architects*. (Everyman edition, 4 volumes, vol. 4.) The following first extract gives a vivid portrait of Michelangelo as a sculptor at work and reveals what has been called his *terribilità*.

C

Source: (*a*) Quoted in Mrs. Oliphant's *The Makers of Florence*, p. 385–6.

I have seen Michelangelo at the age of 60 . . . make more chips of marble fly apart in a quarter of an hour than three of the strongest young sculptors would do in an hour—a thing almost incredible to him who has not seen it. He went to work with such impetuosity and fury of manner that I feared almost every moment to see the block split in pieces. It would seem as if, inflamed by the great idea which inspired him, this great man attacked with a species of fury the marble in which his statue lay concealed.

Source (*b*) Michelangelo is probably best known to the world at large as a sculptor by his gigantic statue of David, which was originally set up in the Piazza dei Signori in Florence. It was removed to the Accademia in 1873: the statue now to be seen in the Piazza is a reproduction: Vasari, *op. cit.*, vol. 4, pp. 115 *et sqq.*

Some of Michelagnolo's friends wrote from Florence urging him to return, as they did not want that block of marble on the opera to be spoiled which Piero Soderini, then gonfaloniere for life of the city, had frequently proposed to give to Leonardo da Vinci, and then to Andrea Contucci, an excellent sculptor, who wanted it . . . Unluckily one Simone da Fiesole had begun a giant, cutting between the legs and mauling it so badly that the wardens of S. Maria del Fiore had abandoned it without wishing to have it finished, and it had rested so for many years. Michelagnolo examined it afresh, and decided that it could be hewn into something new . . . and he decided to ask the wardens and Soderini for it. They gave it to him . . . Accordingly Michelagnolo made a wax model of a youthful David holding the sling to show that the city should be boldly defended and righteously governed, following David's example. He began it in the opera, making a screen between the walls and the tables, and finished it without anybody having seen him at work. (1504.) The marble had been hacked and spoiled by Simone, so that he could not do all he wished with it, though he left some of Simone's work at the end of the marble, which may still be seen. This revival of a dead thing was a veritable miracle. When it was finished various disputes arose as to who should take it to the piazza of the Signori, so that Giuliano da Sangallo and his brother Antonio made a strong wooden frame and hoisted the figure on to it with ropes: they then moved it forward by beams and windlasses and placed it in position. The knot of the rope which held the statue was made to slip so that it tightened as the weight increased, an ingenious device, the design for which is in our book, showing a very strong and safe method of suspending heavy weights. Piero Soderini came to see it, and expressed great pleasure to Michelagnolo who was retouching it, though he said he thought the nose was too large. Michelagnolo, seeing the gonfaloniere below and knowing that he could not see properly, mounted the scaffolding and taking his chisel dexterously let a little marble dust fall on to the gonfaloniere, without, however, actually altering his work. Looking down he said, 'Look now'. 'I like it better', said the gonfaloniere, 'you have given it life'. Michelagnolo therefore came down with feelings of pity for those who wish to seem to understand matters of which they know nothing.

Source (c) The Battle of Cascina, July 28th, 1364, when the English condottiere, Sir John Hawkwood, surprised the Florentines. *Cf.* Benvenuto Cellini (d) on p. 16: Vasari, *op. cit.*, vol. 4, p. 118.

When Lionardo was painting in the Great Hall of the Council, as related in his life, Piero Soderini, the gonfaloniere, allotted to Michelagnolo a part of that hall, for he perceived his great genius, and the artist chose the war of Pisa as his subject. He was given a room in the dyers hospital at S. Onofrio, and there began a large cartoon which he allowed no one to see. He filled it with nude figures bathing in the Arno owing to the heat, and running in this condition to their arms on being attacked by the enemy. He represented them hurrying out of the water to dress, and seizing their arms to go to assist their comrades, some buckling their cuirasses and many putting on other armour, while others on horseback are beginning the fight. Among other figures is an old man wearing a crown of ivy to shade his head trying to pull his stockings on to his wet feet, and hearing the cries of the soldiers and the beating of the drums he is struggling violently, all his muscles to the tips of his toes and his contorted mouth showing the effects of his exertiob. It also contained drums and nude figures with twisted draperies running to the fray, foreshortened in extraordinary attitudes, some upright, some kneeling, some bent, and some lying, There were also many groups sketched in various ways, some merely outlined in carbon, some with features filled in, some hazy or with white lights, to show his knowledge of his art. And indeed artists were amazed when they saw the lengths he had reached in this cartoon. Some in seeing his divine figures declared it was impossible for any other spirit to attain to its divinity. When finished it was carried to the Pope's hall amid the excitement of artists and to the glory of Michelagnolo, and all those who studied and drew from it, as foreigners and natives did for many years afterwards, became excellent artists . . . Having become a school for artists, this cartoon was taken to the great hall of the Medici palace, where it was entrusted too freely to artists, for during the illness of Duke Giuliano it was unexpectedly torn to pieces[17] and scattered in many places, some fragments still being in the house of M. Uberto Strozzi, a Mantuan noble, where they are regarded with great reverence, indeed they are more divine than human.

LEONARDO DA VINCI

If Michelangelo was the most tremendous personality among the Italian artists, there can be little doubt that Leonardo da Vinci was the most beautiful, both in appearance and in mind. He was born in 1452 and he died in 1519. His fame nowadays rests upon his genius as a painter. He himself probably regarded his skill as a military engineer as his chief recommendation to his own age, naturally enough since he lived in an age in which war was endemic in his own country. The first extract illustrates the general opinion held by everybody about Leonardo as a man. It is taken from Vasari's *Lives of the Painters*. Vasari was born in 1511 and died in 1574. It is improbable that he ever met Leonardo—whose name he always spelt Lionardo—but he must have had first hand evidence from many who had known Leonardo, including Michelangelo himself: but Leonardo and Michelangelo were never friends and never saw eye to eye. The second extract illustrates Leonardo's own opinion about himself.

Source: (a) Vasari's *Lives of the Painters*, Everyman edition, vol. 2, pp. 156 et sqq.

The heavens often rain down the richest gifts on human beings, naturally, but sometimes with lavish abundance bestow upon a single individual beauty, grace and ability, so that, whatever he does, every action is so divine that he distances all other men, and clearly displays how his genius is the gift of God and not an acquirement of human art. Men saw this in Lionardo da Vinci, whose personal beauty could not be exaggerated, whose every movement was grace itself and whose abilities were so extraordinary that he could readily solve every difficulty. He possessed great personal strength, combined with dexterity, and a spirit and courage invariably royal and magnanimous, and the fame of his name so spread abroad that, not only was he valued in his own day, but his renown has greatly increased since his death.

This marvellous and divine Lionardo was the son of Piero da Vinci. He would have made great profit in learning had he not been so capricious and fickle, for he began to learn many things and then gave them up. Thus in arithmetic, during the few months that he studied it, he made such progress that he frequently confounded his master by continually raising doubts and difficulties. He devoted some time to music, and soon learned to play the lyre and, being filled with a lofty and delicate spirit, he could sing and improvise divinely with it. Yet though he studied so many different things, he never neglected design and working in relief, those being the things which appealed to his fancy more than any other. When Ser Piero perceived this, and knowing the boy's soaring spirit, he one day took some of his drawings to Andrea del Verrocchio, who was his close friend, and asked his opinion whether Lionardo would do anything by studying design. Andrea was so amazed at these early efforts that he advised Ser Piero to have the boy taught. So it was decided that Lionardo should go to Andrea's workshop. The boy was greatly delighted and not only practised his profession, but all those in which design has a part. Possessed of a divine and marvellous intellect, and being an excellent geometrician, he not only worked in sculpture, doing some heads of women smiling, which were casts, and children's heads also, executed like a master, but also prepared many architectural plans and elevations, and he was the first, though so young, to propose to canalize the Arno from Pisa to Florence. He made designs for mills, fulling machines, and other engines to go by water, and as painting was to be his profession, he studied drawing from life. He would make clay models of figures, draping them with soft rags dipped in plaster, and would then draw them patiently on thin sheets of cambric or linen, in black and white, with the point of the brush. He did these admirably, as may be seen in my book of designs. He also drew upon paper so carefully and well that no one has ever equalled him. The grace of God so possessed his mind, his memory and intellect formed such a mighty union, and he could so clearly express his ideas in discourse, that he was able to confound the boldest opponent. Every day he made models and designs for the removal of mountains with ease and to pierce them to pass from one place to another, and by means of levers, a method for cleansing ports, and to raise water from great depths, schemes which his brain never ceased to evolve. Many designs for these notions are scattered about and I have seen numbers of them. He spent much time in making a regular design of a series of knots so that the cord may be traced from one end to the other, the whole filling a round space . . .

His charming conversation won all hearts, and although he possessed nothing and worked little, he kept servants and horses of which he was very fond, and indeed he loved all animals, and trained them with great kindness and patience. Often, when passing places where birds were sold, he would let them out of their cages and pay the vendor the price asked . . .

Lionardo was placed, as I have said, with Andrea del Verrocchio in his childhood by Ser Piero, and his master happened to be painting a picture of St. John baptising Christ. For this Lionardo did an angel holding some clothes, and although quite young, he made it far better than the figures of Andrea. The latter would never afterwards touch colours, chagrined that a child should know more than he . . .

Lionardo was so delighted when he saw curious heads, whether bearded or hairy, that he would follow about anyone who had thus attracted his attention for a whole day, acquiring such a clear

idea of him that when he went home he would draw the
head as well as if the man had been present. In this way many
heads of men and women came to be drawn, and I have several
such pen-and-ink drawings in my book, so often referred to.
Among them is the head of Amerigo Vespucci,[18] a fine old man
drawn in carbon, and that of Scaramuccia, the gipsy captain . . .

For Francesco del Giocondo Lionardo undertook the portrait
of Mona Lisa, his wife, and left it incomplete after working at it
for four years. This work is now in the possession of Francis,
King of France, at Fontainebleau.[19] This head is an extraordinary
example of how art can imitate nature, because here we have all
the details painted with great subtlety. The eyes possess that moist
lustre which is constantly seen in life, and about them are those
livid reds and hairs which can not be rendered without the utmost
delicacy. The lids could not be more natural, for the way in
which the hairs issue from the skin, here thick and there scanty,
and following the pores of the skin. The nose possesses the fine
delicate reddish apertures seen in life. The opening of the mouth,
with its red ends, and the scarlet cheeks seem not colour but
living flesh. To look closely at her throat you might imagine
that the pulse was beating. Indeed, we may say that this was
painted in a manner to make the boldest artists to despair. Mona
Lisa was very beautiful, and while Lionardo was drawing her
portrait he engaged people to play and sing, and jesters to keep
her merry, and remove that melancholy which painting usually
gives to portraits. This figure of Lionardo's has such a pleasant
smile that it seemed rather divine than human, and was considered
marvellous, an exact copy of nature.

Source: (*b*) In 1482 at the age of 30 Leonardo migrated from Florence
to the court of Ludovico il Moro at Milan. Before going he wrote the
following letter: quoted in Clifford Bax, *Leonardo da Vinci*, 1932,
pp. 44–6, abridged.

Most Illustrious Lord,

Having now considered the works of those who proclaim
themselves to be skilled contrivers of instruments of war, I find
that there is nothing new or exceptional in their devices. I will
therefore try, without prejudicing any one else, to explain my

secrets to your Excellency, and will offer them for your pleasure and approbation.

I have a method of making bridges that shall be light, strong and easy of transport: others, again, which can not be destroyed by fire or battle. Also methods of burning or otherwise destroying the bridges of the enemy.

When a place is besieged I can extract water from the trenches and, in addition, can construct ladders and covered ways.

I have methods of destroying a besieged fortress, even if it is founded on a rock, without resorting to bombardment.

I can make portable mortars, designed to fling a veritable storm of stones and to confuse the enemy by the smoke which they will emit.

In respect of a naval battle, I have many machines most effective both in attack and defence, and vessels which will resist the largest guns.

I am able to lay mines noiselessly and even, if required, under a trench or a river.

I will also make covered chariots, immune from attack, which will be able to pass into the ranks of the enemy, despite the opposing artillery, and will be indestructible by even the largest body of men. Behind these the infantry could follow unhurt and unhindered.

I will make big guns, mortars and light ordnance not of the common type. In short, I can contrive various and endless means of attack and defence.

In time of peace I think I shall be able to give complete satisfaction and to produce work in architecture, alike civic and domestic, that shall equal the work of any one. Moreover, I am able to divert water from one place to another.

I can carry out sculpture in marble, bronze or clay, and paint pictures, as well as any other, no matter who he may be.

Furthermore, I am ready to undertake the construction of the Bronze Horse which is to be the immortal glory of the prince your father and of the illustrious House of Sforza.

And if any of the projects mentioned above should seem to be extravagant or impossible, I am prepared to carry out my demonstrations in your park or in any place that may please your Excellency, to whose gracious attention I most humbly recommend myself.

Source: (c) Leonardo at work on the Last Supper: Matteo Bandello (1480–1562), who produced in 1554 and 1573 a collection of *Novelle* or tales: quoted in Clifford Bax, *Leonardo da Vinci*, pp. 55–6.

//Leonardo used to go early in the morning—I myself have more than once seen him do so—and climb the scaffolding (for *The Last Supper* is placed well away from the floor), and there, from sunrise to sunset forgetting to eat or drink, he would paint without ceasing. On the other hand, he would sometime spend the next two, three or four days doing nothing to it, but staying for an hour or two each day and just looking critically at the figures and considering his work.//And again I have seen him, if the humour took him so, leave the Corte Vecchio at midday, when he was working there at the clay model of that stupendous Horse which you know about, and going straight to the monastery, mount the scaffolding, take up his brush, give one or two touches to a figure, and then, quite suddenly, come down again and go off somewhere else.

Source: (d) Leonardo as an anatomist: Not only was Leonardo a painter and a military engineer, he was also one of the greatest of the Renaissance scientists. As a generalization, it is true to say that the Italian Renaissance produced the Classical Revival and Humanism, yet the greatest Classical-Humanist was the German Erasmus. Similarly, although it was the Northern Renaissance which produced the new Natural Science, yet it was the Italian Leonardo who more than anybody else understood the anatomy of the human body. Painters like Pollaiuolo and Michelangelo had used their knowledge of anatomy to develop the art of painting: what Leonardo did was to use the art of painting (or drawing) to advance the knowledge of anatomy. He dissected in all more than thirty corpses, which put him in danger of the Canon Law—that may be the reason why so much of his scientific discoveries were noted down in his notebooks in cypher. (See also under The Advance in Medicine, p. 454.) The following extracts from Leonardo's letters are taken from Erwin Panofsky's *Artist, Scientist, Genius*, one of six essays comprised in *The Renaissance*, Harper Torchbooks, 1962, pp. 145–7. They give us Leonardo's views on how the science of anatomy should be taught and represented, that is, by the use of perspective.

. . . And you who think to reveal the figure of man in words, with his limbs arranged in their different attitudes, banish the idea from you, for the more minute your description, the more you will confuse the mind of the reader, and the more you will lead him away from the knowledge of the thing described. It is necessary therefore for you to represent and describe.

. . . And you who say that it is better to look at an anatomical demonstration than to see these drawings, you would be right, if it were possible to observe all the details shown in these drawings in a single figure, in which, with all your ability, you will not see nor acquire a knowledge of more than some few veins, while, in order to obtain a true and perfect knowledge of these, I have dissected more than ten human bodies, destroying all the various members, and removing even the very smallest particles of the flesh which surrounded these veins, without causing any effusion of blood other than the imperceptible bleeding of the capillary veins. And as one single body did not suffice for so long a time, it was necessary to proceed by stages with so many bodies as would render my knowledge complete: and this I repeated twice over in order to discover the differences.

But though possessed of an interest in the subject, you may perhaps be deterred by natural repugnance, or, if this does not restrain you, then perhaps by the fear of passing the night hours in the company of these corpses, quartered, flayed and horrible to behold; and if this does not deter you, then perhaps you may lack the skill in drawing essential for such representation; and even if you possess this skill, it may not be combined with a knowledge of perspective, while, if it is so combined, you may not be versed in the methods of geometrical demonstration or the method of estimating the forces and strength of muscles, or perhaps you may be found wanting in patience so that you will not be diligent . . .

. . . If you wish to know thoroughly the parts of a man after he has been dissected, you must either turn him or your eye so that you are examining from different aspects, from below, from above and from the sides, turning him over and studying the origin of each limb . . .

Therefore by my plan you will become acquainted with every part and every whole by means of a demonstration of each part from three different aspects; for when you have seen any member from the front with the nerves, tendons and veins which have their origin on the opposite side, you will be shown the same member either from a side view or from behind, just as though you had the very member in your hand and went on turning it from side to side, until you had a full understanding of all that you desire to know.

COSIMO DE' MEDICI, 'PATER PATRIAE'

Cosimo was born in 1389 and died in 1464. He was the head of the great Florentine banking firm of Medici: he had Europe-wide connections and was immensely wealthy. He also led the opposition to the dominant party in Florence headed by Rinaldo degli Albizzi, Palla Strozzi, and Niccoló da Uzzano. It is very likely that some of his methods of making money were not very reputable—he is said to have fomented war against Lucca for financial reasons and to have made money out of it. The war was ill-conducted and Cosimo blamed Rinaldo and his party. As a result Cosimo was exiled. But in 1434 Cosimo was recalled on the defeat of his enemies and he became the ruler of Florence. He succeeded in changing the government of Florence from an oligarchy into the rule of one man, but although he manipulated the government to his own advantage, he kept a façade of popular rule and was genuinely concerned with governing in the best interest of his people. By largely keeping in the background, by ensuring that he had a large body of adherents secured by a share in the honours of government and the profits from trade promoted by the state, Cosimo built up a strong political party: but also he ensured the support of the populace by providing for them security, food and entertainment. He was a great patron of the arts and the following extract from Machiavelli will show that Cosimo was something more than a merely shrewd politician. His private life was simple, he was an admirable father and a man who used his wealth generously and wisely. Vespasiano says that he spent so much money on charity and on the arts because 'it appeared to him that he held money not over-well acquired; and he was wont to say that to God he had never given so much as to find Him on his books as a debtor.[20] I know the humours of this city; fifty years will not pass before we are driven out: but the buildings will remain.'

Source: Machiavelli, *Storia Fiorentina*, Bk. vii, ch. 1. Eng. ed. Bohn, 1871, pp. 311 *et sqq.*

Of all who have left memorials behind them and who were not of the military profession, Cosimo was the most illustrious and the most renowned. He not only surpassed all his contemporaries in wealth and authority, but also in generosity and prudence; and among the qualities which contributed to make him prince in his own country was his surpassing all others in magnificence and generosity. His liberality became more obvious after his death, when Piero his son, wishing to know what he possessed, it appeared that there was no citizen of any consequence to whom Cosimo had not lent a large sum of money; and often, when informed of some nobleman being in distress, he relieved him unasked. His magnificence is evident from the number of public edifices he erected; for in Florence are the convents and churches of San Marco and San Lorenzo and the monastery of Santa Verdiana; in the mountains of Fiesole, the church and abbey of San Girolamo; and in the Mugello he not only restored, but rebuilt from its foundation a monastery of the Frati Minori, or Minims. Besides these, he erected splendid chapels and altars, and besides building the churches and chapels we have mentioned, he provided them with all the ornaments, furniture and utensils suitable for the performance of divine service.

To these sacred edifices are to be added his private dwellings, one in Florence, of extent and elegance adapted to so great a citizen, and four others, situate at Careggi, Fiesole, Cafaggiuolo and Trebbio, each for size and grandeur equal to royal palaces. And as if it were not sufficient to be distinguished for magnificence of buildings in Italy alone, he erected a hospital at Jerusalem for the reception of poor and infirm pilgrims. Although his habitations, like all his other works and actions, were quite of a regal character, and he alone was prince in Florence, still everything was so tempered with his prudence that he never transgressed the decent moderation of civil life: in his conversation, his servants, his travelling, his mode of living and the relationships he formed, the modest demeanour of the citizen was always evident . . .

No one of his time possessed such an intimate knowledge of government and state affairs as himself; and hence amid such a variety of fortune, in a city so given to change and amongst a people of such extreme inconstancy, he retained possession of the government for thirty-one years; for being endowed with the utmost prudence, he foresaw evils at a distance and therefore had an opportunity either of averting them or of preventing their injurious results . . .

He added to the Florentine dominions the Borgo of San Sepolchro, Montedaglio, the Casentino and Val di Bagno . . .

He was born in the year 1389 on the day of saints Cosimo and Damiano. His earlier years were full of trouble, as his exile, captivity and personal danger fully testify. But after the age of forty he enjoyed the greatest felicity, and not only those who assisted him in public business, but his agents who conducted his commercial speculations throughout Europe participated in his prosperity. Hence many enormous fortunes took their origin in different families in Florence, as in that of the Tornabuoni, the Benci, the Portinari and the Sassetti . . . He sometimes complained to his friends that he had never been able to lay out so much in the service of God as to find the balance in his own favour . . .

He was of middle stature, olive complexion and venerable aspect; not learned, but exceedingly eloquent, endowed with great natural capacity, generous to his friends, kind to the poor, comprehensive in discourse, cautious in advising, and in his speeches and replies grave and witty . . . A few hours before his death his wife asked him why he kept his eyes shut, and he said 'to get them in the way of it' . . .

Cosimo was a friend and patron of learned men. He brought Argiropolo, a Greek by birth and one of the most erudite of his time, to Florence to instruct the youth in Hellenic literature. He entertained Marsilio Ficino, the reviver of Platonic philosophy, in his own house, and being much attached to him, gave him a residence near his palace at Careggi, that he might pursue the study of letters with greater convenience and himself have an opportunity of enjoying his company . . .

Towards the close of his life he suffered great affliction, for of his two sons, Piero and Giovanni, the latter, of whom he entertained his greatest hopes, died, and the former was so sickly as to be unable to attend to public or private business. On being carried from one apartment to another after Giovanni's death, he remarked to his attendants with a sigh, 'this is too large a house for so small a family'. . . His bodily infirmities prevented him from attending to either public or private affairs, as he had been accustomed, and he consequently witnessed both going to decay, for Florence was ruined by her own citizens, and his fortune by his agents and his children. He died, however, at the zenith of his glory and in the enjoyment of the highest renown. His funeral was conducted with the utmost pomp, the whole city following his corpse to the tomb in the church of San Lorenzo, on which by public decree he was inscribed, 'Pater Patriae'.

LORENZO IL MAGNIFICO

Lorenzo de' Medici was the elder son of Piero de' Medici and grandson of Cosimo. He was born in 1449 and died in 1492. He succeeded his father as ruler of Florence in 1469 and after defeating the Pazzi conspiracy (1478) he became absolute master of Florence. His rule was very much more oligarchical than that of Cosimo and he showed less financial skill. The Medici fortunes deteriorated during his reign. Yet Guicciardini, the historian of Florence, held that 'if Florence was to have a tyrant, she could never have found a better or more pleasant one'. Grossly immoral, employing a large army of spies, he yet managed the affairs of state efficiently, if ruthlessly. His court was the most cultured, perhaps in Europe, certainly in Italy: he himself possessed exceptional intellectual powers, he was a poet of great originality, a prose writer of a high order, he understood painting, architecture, sculpture and music. He did more than anybody else to support the movement in favour of a national literature written in the national, the Italian, tongue. It was Lorenzo and all that he stood for which brought out the violent opposition of Savonarola.

Source: (a) Father Vicenzo Marchese, a Frate Predicatore of the Convent of San Marco in Florence, the author of, first, *Storia dei Pittori*

Domenicani, and later of *Storia del Convento di San Marco*, which became a main source of information about Savonarola and the Lorenzo period. Quoted in Mrs. Oliphant's *The Makers of Florence*, pp. 265–6.

The Magnifico called to him, from every part of Italy, men of genius, writers and artists of reputation, in order by their works to distract all strong and noble intelligences from thoughts of the country. So had Pericles done, and Augustus . . . Poets of every kind, gentle and simple, with golden cithern and with rustic lute, came from every quarter to animate the suppers of the Magnifico; whosoever sang of arms, of love, of saints, of fools, was welcome, or he who drinking and joking kept the company amused. First among them were Politiano, Luigi, and Luca Pulci, Bieniveni, Matteo Franco, and the gay genius of Burchiello. This troop of parasites went and came, now at the villa of Careggi, now at Poggia Cajano, now at Fiesole, now at Cafaggiolo. Lorenzo, ready for everything, now discussed with Argiropolo the doctrines of Aristotle, now with Ficino discoursed on Platonic love, or read the poem of the *Altercazione*; with Politian recited some Latin elegy, or the verses of his own *Selva di Amore*; with the brothers Pulci the *Nencia da Barberino* and, when Burchiello arrived, laid aside his gravity and, drinking and singing, recited a chapter of the *Beoni*, or some of his own carnival songs.

Sometimes a select band of painters and sculptors collected in his garden near San Marco, or under the loggia of the palace in the Via Larga, designing, modelling, painting, copying the Greek statues, and the *torsi* and busts found in Rome or elsewhere in Italy . . . And in order that the Florentine people might not be excluded from this new beatitude (a thing which was important to the Magnifico) he composed and set in order many mythological representations, triumphal cars, dances, and every kind of festal celebration, to solace and delight them: and thus he succeeded in banishing from their souls any recollection of their ancient greatness, in making them insensible to the ills of the country, in disfranchising and debasing them by means of temporal ease and intoxication of the senses. Of all these feasts and masquerades Lorenzo was the inventor and master; his great wealth aiding him in his undertakings. In the darkening of twilight it was his custom to issue forth into the city to amuse himself, with incredible pomp and a great retinue on horse and foot, more than five hundred in number, with concerts of musical instruments, singing in many voices, all sorts of canzones, madrigals, and popular songs . . . When night fell, four hundred servants with lighted torches followed, and lighted this bacchanalian procession . . . In the midst of these orgies a handful of foolish youths were educated and grew up, who made open profession of infidelity and lewdness, and laying aside all shame, gave themselves up to every kind of wickedness, emulating each other in the depths of naughtiness to which they could attain. The people, with their usual sense of what is appropriate, called them the Compagnacci.

Source: (*b*) Guicciardini, *Storia d'Italia*. Eng. ed. A. P. Goddard, i, 10.

In the year 1492 Lorenzo de' Medici was taken off by a premature death, not being quite forty-four years of age. His death was a grievous stroke to his country, which lost in him a citizen who, in point of reputation, prudence and understanding, was qualified for the greatest undertakings: a citizen who not only enjoyed himself, but communicated to those about him all those advantages which usually attend a person in his situation during the course of a long peace. His death was indeed lamented by all Italy, not only on account of his zeal and solicitude for the public good, but for his great and successful diligence in moderating and curbing the frequent jealousies and dissensions of Ferdinand and Lodovico Sforza, princes of equal ambition and power.

Source: (*c*) Machiavelli, *Storie Fiorentine*, Bk. viii, ch. 36. *The Writings of Machiavelli*, Detmold, Eng. ed. i, 418.

In peaceful times he often entertained the people with various festivities, such as jousts, feats of arms and representations of triumphs of olden times. He aimed to maintain abundance in the city, to keep the people united and the nobility honoured. He had the greatest love and admiration for all who excelled in any art and was a great patron of learning and of learned men, of which his conduct towards Cristofano Landini and Messer Demetrius the Greek furnishes the strongest proof. For this reason the Count Giovanni della Mirandola, a man of almost supernatural genius, was attracted by the magnificence of Lorenzo and preferred to establish his home in Florence rather than in any other part of Europe, all of which he had visited in his travels. Lorenzo took the greatest delight in architecture, music and poetry, and many of his own compositions, enriched with commentaries, appeared in print. And for the purpose of enabling the Florentine youths to devote themselves to the study of letters, he established a university in the city of Pisa, where he employed the most eminent men in all Italy as professors. He built a monastery for Fra Mariano da Chianozzona of the Order of St. Augustine, who was a most admirable pulpit orator. And thus beloved of God and Fortune, all his enterprises were crowned with success, whilst those of his enemies had the opposite fate. For besides the conspiracy of the Pazzi, Frescobaldi also attempted his assassination in the church of the Carmine; and Baldinatto of Pistoia tried the same at his villa. Each of these together with their accomplices suffered the most just punishment for their nefarious attempts.

Thus Lorenzo's mode of life, his ability and good fortune, were recognized with admiration and highly esteemed, not only by all the princes of Italy, but also by those at a great distance. Matthias, King of Hungary, gave him many proofs of his affection; the Sultan of Egypt sent ambassadors to him with precious gifts; and the Grand Turk gave up to him Bernardo Bandini, the murderer of his brother [Giuliano]. These proofs of regard from foreign sovereigns caused Lorenzo to be looked upon with the greatest admiration by all Italy; and his reputation was daily increased by his rare ability, for he was eloquent and subtle in speech, wise in his resolves, and bold and prompt in their execution. Nor can he be charged with any vices that would stain his many virtues, though very fond of women and even taking pleasure in puerile amusements—more so than would seem becoming to so great a man, so that he was often seen taking a part in the childish sports of his sons and daughters . . . During his latter years he was greatly afflicted with sufferings from his malady, the gout, and oppressed with intolerable pains in the

D

stomach, which increased to that degree that he died in the month of April, 1492, in the forty-fourth year of his age.

Source: (*d*) Bartolomeo Cerretani, *Storia fino all'anno* 1513, quoted by F. M. Godfrey, The Pictorial Records of the Medici, *History Today*, March, 1952, p. 169.

He spoke sparingly and walked with dignity: he loved able and distinguished men in every art; it was, however, noticed that he was somewhat vindictive and envious: he was religious, and in his government much given to the popular party rather than to the nobility. He was tall and of noble presence; he had an ugly face, short sight, dark skin and hair, sallow cheeks and an extraordinary large mouth; in speaking he gesticulated with his whole body. His gait was princely; he dressed richly and enjoyed writing verse in the common tongue and wrote them beautifully.

Source: (*e*) Niccolo Valori, *La Vita del Magnifico Lorenzo*, 1568, quoted by F. M. Godfrey, *op. cit.*

Lorenzo was of more than medium height with broad shoulders, of build strong and robust, and so agile as to be second to none; and although in the other outward gifts of the body Nature had treated him badly, in respect to the inner qualities she showed herself a most kindly mother; for his olive-coloured and ungainly face was none the less of such dignity that it induced reverence in the beholder; he was short-sighted, flat-nosed and deprived of all sense of smell, which was not only no burden to him, but he used to say that in this respect he was much beholden to Nature, since far more things were offensive to the senses than delectable. For all these defects and failings, if one can call them thus, he made up by the gifts of the mind, which he by continuous exercise and strenuous application constantly improved, whereof many of his judgements bear testimony.

Source: (*f*) Donna Clarice Orsini, Lorenzo's wife. In 1468 Lorenzo married a Roman girl, Clarice Orsini, who was later to become the mother of Pope Leo X and of that Piero de' Medici who squandered and lost Florence to the family. The following account of Clarice was written by Lucrezia Tornabuoni, Lorenzo's mother, one of the most able women of her time: F. M. Godfrey, *op. cit.*, p. 172.

The girl is above the middle height, of fair complexion and pleasant manners, and, if less beautiful than our own daughters, of great modesty, so that it will be easy to teach her manners. She is not blonde, for no one is here, and her thick hair has a reddish tinge. Her face is round in shape, but does not displease me. The neck is beautiful but rather thin, or more properly, delicately shaped; the bosom I could not see, because they cover it entirely here, but it seems to me well formed. She does not bear her head as our girls do, but inclining a little forwards, which I ascribe to the timidity that seems to predominate in her. Her hands are very long and delicate. On the whole the girl seems to be far above the ordinary type, but she is not to be compared to Maria, Lucrezia and Bianca.

THE PAZZI CONSPIRACY, 1478

A large part of the Medici strength in Florence was based on an alliance with Galleazzo Maria of Milan. When he was murdered in 1476, his heir being only three years old, the lynch-pin of Medici foreign policy was gone. The moment seemed favourable to the enemies of the Medici to try to bring about their downfall. The Pope Sixtus IV was on bad terms with Lorenzo de' Medici from whom he had filched the town of Imola to give to his nephew, Girolamo Riario. The Pope also withdrew his deposits from the Medici bank and gave them to the rival bank of the Pazzi. It was Riario and Francesco Pazzi who hatched the conspiracy against the Medici, with the full knowledge and approval of the Pope and with the active participation of Francesco Salviati, Archbishop of Pisa. Gian Battista da Montesecco was hired to carry out the murder of Lorenzo and his brother Giuliano, but at the last moment he developed scruples about adding impiety to the crime of murder, as the murder was to take place in church during the celebration of the mass. Two discontented priests were substituted for him at the last moment, while one of the oligarchs who had a personal hatred for Lorenzo, Bernardo Bandini Baroncelli, was brought in to help Francesco Pazzi to murder Giuliano. Old Jacopo Pazzi was persuaded to undertake the work of rousing the city of Florence against the Medici. After the failure of the conspiracy, Botticelli was employed to paint the effigies of the chief conspirators on the façade of the Palazzo Publico. Bandini escaped to Constantinople, and in place of an effigy Botticelli painted the words, 'Bernardo Bandini, a new Judas. Murderous traitor in a church was I. A rebel who must look for a death more cruel.' Bandini was taken by the Sultan in 1479 and handed over to the Signory in Florence. He was hanged. A young man of 26 watched the execution and made a pen and ink sketch of the corpse on the gibbet. He added a detailed description: 'small cap tan coloured, doublet of black satin, black lined jerkin, blue coat lined with the throats of foxes and the collar of the coat lined with black and white stripes of velvet. Bernardo di Bandini Baroncelli. Black hose.' The young man was Leonardo da Vinci.

Source: Machiavelli, *Storie Fiorentine*, Bk. viii, ch. 2: *The Writings of Machiavelli*, Eng. ed. Detmold, i, 374 *et sqq*.

The conspirators proceeded to Santa Reparata where the cardinal and Lorenzo had already arrived. The church was crowded and divine service had already commenced before Giuliano's arrival. Francesco de' Pazzi and Bernardo Bandini, who had been designated to kill Giuliano, went to his house and by artful persuasion induced him to go to the church. It is really a noteworthy fact that such intense hatred and the thoughts of so great an outrage could be so perfectly concealed under so much resoluteness of heart as was the case with Francesco and Bernardo; for on the way to the church and after entering it, they amused him with jests and youthful pleasantries. And Francesco even, under pretence of caressing him, felt him with his hands and pressed him in his arms so as to ascertain whether he wore a cuirass or other means of protection under his garments. Giuliano and Lorenzo were both aware of the bitter feelings of the Pazzi and their anxiety to deprive them of the government of the state, but they had no apprehensions for their lives, believing that, if the Pazzi were to attempt anything, it would be by civil proceedings and not by violence: and therefore, not being apprehensive of their personal safety, they simulated a friendly feeling for them.

The murderers thus prepared placed themselves, some close by the side of Lorenzo, which the great crowd in the church enabled them to do easily without exciting suspicion, and the others near to Giuliano. At the appointed moment Bernardo Bandini struck Giuliano in the breast with a short dagger which he had prepared for the purpose. After a few steps Giuliano fell to the ground and Francesco de' Pazzi threw himself upon him covering him with wounds, and was so maddened by the fury with which he assailed Giuliano that he inflicted a severe wound upon himself in one of his legs.

Messer Antonio and Stefano, on the other hand, attacked Lorenzo, but after many blows succeeded only in wounding him slightly in the throat; for either their resolution, or the courage of Lorenzo, who, on finding himself assailed, defended himself with his weapon, or the interference of the bystanders, defeated all their efforts to kill him, so that, becoming alarmed, they fled and concealed themselves, but being found were ignominiously put to death and their bodies dragged through the whole city.

Lorenzo, on the other hand, together with the friends he had around him, shut himself up in the sacristy of the church. Bernardo Bandini, seeing Giuliano dead, also killed Francesco Nori, a devoted friend of the Medici . . . And not content with these two murders, he rushed to seek Lorenzo, so as to make good by his courage and swiftness what the others by their cowardice and tardiness had failed to do. But Lorenzo being shut up in the sacristy, Bernardo could not carry out his intention.

In the midst of these violent and tumultuous scenes, which were so terrible that it seemed as though the church itself were falling, the Cardinal [Riario] took refuge by the altar, where he was with difficulty saved by two priests, until the alarm had somewhat abated, when the Signoria were enabled to conduct him to his palace, where he remained in the greatest apprehension until his liberation.

There happened at this time in Florence certain citizens of Perugia, whom the violence of faction had driven from their homes; these the Pazzi had drawn into their plot by promises of restoring them to their country. The Archbishop Salviati, who went to seize the palace together with Jacopo Messer Poggio and his relatives and friends, took these Perugians with him; and having arrived at the palace, he left a portion of his followers below, with orders that, upon the first noise they heard, they were at once to occupy the entrance of the palace, whilst he himself with the larger number of the Perugians rushed up the stairs, where he found the Signoria at dinner, for it was already late; but after a short time he was admitted by the Gonfaloniere of Justice, Cesare Petrucci. He entered with a few of his followers, leaving the rest outside; the greater portion of these shut themselves up in the chancelry, the door of which was so arranged that once closed it could neither be opened from the inside nor the outside without the key.

The Archbishop meantime, having entered the hall together with the Gonfaloniere, on pretence of having something to communicate on behalf of the Pope, addressed him in an incoherent and suspicious manner, so that his language and change of countenance excited such suspicion in the Gonfaloniere that he rushed out shouting, and meeting Jacopo Messer Poggio, he seized him by the hair and gave him in charge to two sergeants. The Signoria, having taken the alarm, quickly seized such arms as chance supplied them, and all those who had come upstairs with the Archbishop, most of whom were shut up in the chancelry, and the rest terror-stricken, were either slain or thrown down alive out of the palace windows, between which the Archbishop, the two Jacopo Salviati and Jacopo Messer di Poggio were hanged. Those who remained below had forced the guard and the gate and occupied the whole lower floor of the palace; so that the citizens, who upon hearing the alarm had rushed to the palace, could neither give aid nor counsel to the Signoria.

Meantime Francesco de' Pazzi and Bernardo Bandini, seeing that Lorenzo had escaped and that the one of them on whom the success of the conspiracy depended was seriously wounded, became alarmed. Bernardo, with the same promptness and courage in behalf of his own safety that he had displayed against his enemies, the Medici, saved himself by flight. Francesco, having returned to his own house, tried to mount on horseback, for it was arranged that they should ride through the city and call the people to arms and liberty; but the wound in his leg and the consequent great loss of blood prevented him. He therefore undressed, and throwing himself naked upon his bed, he begged Messer Jacopo [Pazzi] to do what he himself could not. Messer

Jacopo, though old and unaccustomed to scenes of violence, yet, by way of a last effort to save their fortunes, mounted a horse and followed by one hundred armed men gathered for this purpose, went to the Piazza, calling for help on behalf of the people and liberty. But the one having been made deaf by the wealth and liberality of the Medici, and the other being unknown in Florence, his calls remained unheeded by any one. The Signori, on the other hand, who were masters of the upper part of the palace, greeted him with stones and menaces. Whilst hesitating, Messer Jacopo was met by his brother-in-law, Giovanni Serristori, who reproved him for the riot they had occasioned and advised him to return home, as the other citizens had the people's welfare and liberty as much at heart as he. Messer Jacopo, bereft of all hope, therefore, and seeing the palace in the hands of the enemy, Lorenzo safe, and the people not disposed to follow him, and being at a loss to know what else to do, resolved if possible to save his life by flight, and with such followers as were with him in the Piazza he left Florence to go to the Romagna . . .

Francesco was dragged from his bed and led to the palace, and was there hanged by the side of the Archbishop and the others. But it was impossible either on the way there or afterwards to induce Francesco by any degree of maltreatment to say one word of what had been said or done by the conspirators; and fixedly looking in another direction he sighed in silence without one word of complaint. Guglielmo de' Pazzi, brother-in-law of Lorenzo, was saved in Lorenzo's house, both on account of his innocence and through the influence of his wife, Bianca. Every citizen, armed or not, called at Lorenzo's house on this occasion to offer him his personal service or his substance—such was the power and public favour which the house of Medici had acquired by their prudence and liberality . . .

THE REBELLION IN FLORENCE, 1494

The despotic rule of Piero de' Medici in Florence, as soon as the news of Charles VIII's arrival in Italy reached the inhabitants, led to a revolt which ousted the Medici from Florence. This revolt is typical of the revolutions in Florence at the time.

Source: Giusto, *Diario*, printed in Dennistoun's *Memoirs of the Dukes of Urbino*, vol. 1, p. 336.

On Sunday the 9th of November the people of Florence rose in arms against the *palle*, that is against Pietro de' Medici, who had so used his sway and had repaired the palace. The populace, observing this, rushed thither, crying, 'the people and liberty', the children being first in the piazza: and by God's will all Florence armed and hurried to the palace, calling out, 'People and Liberty', so that Pietro, the Cardinal, and Giuliano his brother fled. And there was a reward of 2000 florins proclaimed by the Seignory for whoever would bring the Cardinal alive or dead to the palace; and thus matters continued. Next day all the banners and pennons were set up, and such was the people's fury, at the palace, throughout the town and at the gates, day and night, that although I have four times found Florence in arms since 1458, this has been the most unanimous and extraordinary affair, from the efforts made by the lillies to erase the balls [*gigli* and *palle*, the respective arms of the republic and of the Medici]: even the children two or three years old, by a miracle, cried in the houses 'People and liberty!' and among them our little Catherine. Thus by God's grace did this community free itself from the hands of many tyrants, who, thanks to the blessed God! were expelled without bloodshed.

BALDASSARE CASTIGLIONE

Baldassare Castiglione, Italian diplomatist and writer, was born in 1478 and died in 1529. He was in the service of Lodovico Sforza from 1496 until Sforza was taken prisoner to France, when he returned to his native Mantua (1500). In 1504 he went to live at the court of Urbino, where Guidobaldo Malatesta was the Duke. In 1506 he was sent on a mission to Henry VII of England to fetch the Garter which had been awarded to Guidobaldo. Under Guidobaldo's successor, Francesco Maria della Rovere, he was given command of the papal troops. In 1524 he was sent to Spain to try to settle the dispute between Charles V and Pope Clement VII, but the capture of the Pope at the sack of Rome in 1527 revealed the perfidy of the Emperor. Castiglione was made bishop of Avila and became a naturalized Spaniard. He died in Spain. His claim to fame rests on the great book he wrote, called *Il Cortegiano* (The Courtier), in which he delineates the character of

the perfect courtier or gentleman, and describes the court of Guidobaldo, 'admittedly the purest and most elevated court in Italy'. The
Italians called this book *Il Libro d'Oro*. It was published by Aldus
Manutius at Venice in 1528 and was translated into English in 1561
by Sir Thomas Hoby. The narrative takes the form of a series of
discussions in the duchess' drawing-room between Elizabetta Gonzaga,
Pietro Bembo, Bernardo Bibbiena, Giuliano de' Medici, Emilia Pia
and Ceretino Unico. By a fiction Baldassare pretends that he was not
present and thus keeps himself out of the picture.

Source: (*a*) Federigo di Montefeltro, Duke of Urbino, was born in
1422 and died in 1482. He was an able military commander, the one
and only *condottiere* of his time who never broke his word and never
betrayed those who employed him. He was an enlightened and very
popular ruler, a great patron of the arts. His library was probably the
finest in the world (see p. 7). Its MSS. are now in the Vatican
Library in Rome:

Castiglione, *Il Cortegiano*, Hoby's Eng. ed. Everyman, Bk. I, pp. 17
et sqq. Hoby's spelling and punctuation have been retained as an
example of the total lack of consistency which characterizes the writing
of English at this time, as well as French, Italian and Spanish.

As every man knoweth, the little Citie of Urbin is situated
upon the side of the Appennine (in a manner) in the middes of
Italy, towards the Goulfe of Venice. The which for all it is placed
among hilles, and those not so pleasant as perhappes some other
that we behold in many places, yet in this point the Element hath
beene favourable unto it, that all about, the Countrey is verie
plentifull and full of fruites: so that beside the holesomnes of ayre,
it is verie aboundant and stored with all thinges necessarie for the
life of man. But among the greatest felicities that man can reckon
to have, I count this the chiefe, that now a long time it hath
alwaies bene governed with very good princes, in the common
calamities of the wars of Italie it remained also a season without
any at all.

But without searching further of this, we may make a good
proofe with the famous memorie of Duke Fridericke, who in his
daies was the light of Italy. Neither do wee want true and very
large testimonies yet remaining of his wisedome, courtesie, justice,
liberalitie, of his invincible courage and policy of warre. And of

this doe his so manye victories make proofe, chiefly his conquer-
ing of places impugnable, so sodaine readines in setting forward
to give battaile, his putting to flight sundrie times with a small
number, very great and puissant armies, and never sustained losse
in anye conflict. So that we may, not without cause, compare
him to many famous men of olde time.

This man among his other deedes praise-worthie, in the hard
and sharpe situation of Urbin buylt a Palace, to the opinion of
many men, the fairest that was to bee found in all Italie, and so
furnished it with all necessarie implementes belonging thereto,
that it appeared not a Palace, but a Citie in forme of a Palace,
and that not onelye with ordinarye matters, as Silver plate,
hangings for Chambers of very rich cloth of Golde, of Silke and
other like, but also for sightlines: and to deck it out withall,
placed there a wondrous number of aunci.ent Images of Marble
and Mettall, very excellent paintings and Instruments of Musicke
of all sortes, and nothing would he have there but what was most
rare and excellent.

To this with verie great charges hee gathered together a great
number of most excellent and rare bookes, in Greeke, Latin, and
Hebrue, the which all hee garnished with gold and silver, esteem-
ing this to be the chiefest ornament of his great Palace.

This Duke then following the course of nature, when he was
three-score and five yeares of age, as he had lived, so did he end
his lyfe with glorye.[21] And left after him a child of ten yeres
having no more male, and without mother, who hight Guidobaldo.

This childe, as of the state, so did it appeare also that he was
heire of all his father's vertues: and sodainly with a marveilous
towardnes, began to promise so much of himselfe, as a man
would not have thought possible of a man mortall. So that the
opinion of men was, that of all Duke Federickes notable deedes,
there was none greater than that he begat such a sonn. But
fortune envying this so great vertue, with all her might gainstood
this so glorious a beginning, in such wise that before Duke
Guidobaldo was xx. yeares of age, he fell sick of the goute, the
which encreasing upon him with most bitter paines, in a short

time so nummed him of all his members that hee coulde neither stand on foote, nor move himselfe. And in this manner was one of the best favoured, and towardliest personages in the world, deformed and marred in his green age. And beside, not satisfied with this, fortune was so contrarie to him in al his purposes, that verye seldome he brought to passe any thing to his mind. And for all hee had in him most wise counsaile and an invincible courage, yet it seemed that whatsoever he tooke in hand, both in feats of armes, and in everye other thing small or great, it came alwaies to ill successe.

And of this make proofe his manye and diverse calamities, which he alwaies bare out with such stoutnesse of courage, that vertue never yeelded to fortune. But with a bolde stomacke despising her stormes, lived with great dignitie and estimation among all men: in sicknesse as one that was sounde, and in adversitie as one that was most fortunate. So that for all hee was thus diseased in body he served in time of warre with most honourable entertainement under the most famous kings of Naples, Alphonsus and Ferdinande the yonger. Afterward with Pope Alexander the sixt, with the Lordes of Venice and Florence.

And when Julius the second was created Pope [1503], hee was then made General Captaine of the Church: at which time proceeding in his accustomed usage, hee set his delight above all thinges to have his house furnished with most noble and valiant Gentlemen, with whom he lived verie familiarly, enjoying their conversation . . .

At Tilt, at Tourney, in playing at all sorts of weapon, also in inventing devices in pastimes, in Musicke, finally in all exercises meete for noble Gentlemen, every man strived to shew himself such a one, as might deserve to bee judged worthie of so noble assembly.

Therefore were all the houres of the day divided into honourable and pleasant exercises, as well of the bodie as of the minde. But because the Duke used continually, by reason of his infirmitie, soone after supper to goe to his rest, everie man ordinarily, at that hour drew where the Dutchesse was, the Ladie Elizabeth Gonzaga, where also continually was the Ladie Emilia Pia, who for that shee was indued with so lively a wit and judgement, as you know, seemed the maistresse and ringleader of all that company, and that everie man at her received understanding and courage.

There was then to beee heard pleasant communications and merie conceits and in everie mans countenance a man might perceive painted a loving jocundnesse. So that this house truely might wel be called the very Mansion place of mirth and joy. And I believe that it was never so tasted in other place, what manner a thing the sweet conversation is that is occasioned of an amiable and loving company, as it was once here.

Source: (*b*) Athletic Requirements for the Perfect Courtier: *ibid.*, pp. 39 *et sqq.*

Men so huge of body, beside that many times they are of a dull wit, they are also unapt for all exercise of nimblenesse, which I much desire to have in the Courtier. And therefore will I have him to bee of a good shape, and well proportioned in his lims, and to shew strength, lightnesse and quicknesse, and to have understanding in all exercises of the bodie that belong to a man of warre.

And herein I think the chiefe point is to handle wel all kinde of weapon, both for footmen and horsemen, and to know the vantages in it. And specially to bee skilfull on those weapons that are used ordinarily among Gentlemen. For beside the use he shall have of them in warre, where peradventure needeth no great cunning, there happen often times variances between one gentleman and another, whereupon ensueth a combat. And many times it shall stand him in steade to use the weapon that he hath at that instant by his side, therefore it is a very sure [safe] thing to be skilfull.

And I am none of them who say that he forgetteth his cunning when hee cometh to the point: for sure who so looseth his cunning at that time, indeed sheweth that hee hath first lost his heart and his spirites for feare.

I think also it will serve his turne greatly to know the feat of wrastling, because it goeth much together with all weapon on foote . . .

Also men occupy their weapon oftentimes in time of peace about sundrie exercises, and gentlemen are seene in open shewes in the presence of people, women and princes. Therefore will I have our Courtier a perfect horseman for everie saddle. And beside the skill in horses, and in whatsoever belongeth to a horseman, let him set all his delight and diligence to wade in everie thing a little farther than other men, so that he may be knowne among all men for one that is excellent. As it is redde of Alcibiades, that he excelled all other nations wheresoever hee came. And everie man in the thing hee had most skill in. So shall this our Courtier passe other men, and everie man in his own profession.

And because it is ye peculiar praise of us Italians to ride well, to manage with reason, especially rough horses, to runne at the Ring, and at the Tylt, he shall be in this esteemed among the best Italians.

At Tournament in keeping a passage, in fighting at Barriers, he shall be good amongst the best Frenchmen.

At *Joce di canne*,[22] running at Bull, casting of Speares and Dartes, hee shall bee among the Spaniards excellent. But principally let him accompanie all his motion with a certaine good judgement and grace, if hee will deserve that generall favour which is so much set by.

There be also many other exercises, the which though they depend not thoroughly upon Armes, yet have they a great agreement with them, and have in them much manly activitie. And of them methinke, hunting is one of the chiefest. For it hath a certaine likenesse with warre and is truely a pastime for great men and fit for one living in Court. And it is found that it hath also beene much used among them of olde time.

It is meete for him also to have the arte of swimming, to leape, to runne, to cast the stone: for beside the profit he may receave of this in the warres, it happeneth to him many times to make proofe of him selfe in such thinges, whereby hee getteth him a reputation, especially among the multitude, unto whom a man must sometime apply him selfe.

Also it is a noble exercise, and meete for one living in Court, to play at Tenise, where the disposition of the bodie, the quicknes and nimblenesse of everie member is much perceived, and almost whatsoever a man can see in all other exercises.

And I reckon vaulting of no lesse praise, which for all it is painfull and hard, maketh a man more light and quicker than any of the rest.

And beside the profit, if that lightnes bee accompanied with a good grace, it maketh (in my judgement) a better shew than any of the rest.

If our Courtier then bee taught these exercises more than indifferently well, I believe he may set aside tumbling, climbing upon a cord, and such other matters that tast somewhat of Jugglers craft and doe litle beseeme a gentleman.

NICCOLÓ MACHIAVELLI

Machiavelli was born in Florence in 1469 of a noble family in Tuscany. He was not employed by the Medici, but in 1494 he entered the service of the Florentine Republic and in 1498 he became Secretary to the Council of Ten, an office he held until 1512. In that year his literary career began. He began and completed *Il Principe* in 1513: in that year he began the *Discorsi* (upon Livy): the *Libro dell' Arte della Guerra* was written in 1519–20: the *Istoria Fiorentina* after 1522. Machiavelli died in 1526: none of his works was published till after his death. Of his written works the *Discorsi* are by far the most important for understanding this much misunderstood political thinker. (See J. W. Allen, *Political Thought in the Sixteenth Century*, pp. 447 *et sqq.*; Butterfield, *The Statecraft of Machiavelli*, 1940).

Source: Machiavelli, *Il Principe*, the last chapter, XXVI. *World's Classics*, Grant Richards, 1903. This chapter is an appeal to Lorenzo de' Medici, grandson of Lorenzo il Magnifico, to save Italy from the state of degradation into which she had fallen during the Italian Wars, or as Machiavelli wrote, 'from the Barbarians'.

Having now considered all the things we have spoken of, and thought within myself whether at present the time was not propitious in Italy for a new prince, and if there was not a state of things which offered an opportunity to a prudent and capable

man to introduce a new system that would do honour to himself
and good to the mass of the people, it seems to me that so many
things concur to favour a new ruler that I do not know of any
time more fitting for such an enterprise. And if, as I said, it was
necessary in order that the power of Moses should be displayed
that the people of Israel should be slaves in Egypt, and to give
scope for the greatness and courage of Cyrus that the Persians
should be oppressed by the Medes, and to illustrate the pre-
eminence of Theseus that the Athenians should be dispersed, so
at the present time, in order that the might of an Italian genius
should be recognized, it was necessary that Italy should be
reduced to her present condition, and that she should be more
enslaved than the Hebrews, more oppressed than the Persians,
and more scattered than the Athenians; without a head, without
order, beaten, despoiled, lacerated, overrun, and that she should
have suffered ruin of every kind. And although before now a
spirit has been shewn by some which gave hope that he might be
appointed by God for her redemption, yet at the highest summit
of his career he was thrown aside by fortune, so that now, almost
lifeless, she awaits one who may heal her wounds and put a stop
to the rapine and pillaging of Lombardy, to the rapacity and
extortion in the kingdom and in Tuscany, and cure her of those
sores which have long been festering. Behold how she prays
God to send someone to redeem her from this barbarous cruelty
and insolence. Behold her ready and willing to follow any
standard if only there be someone to raise it. There is nothing
now she can hope for but that your illustrious house may place
itself at the head of this redemption, being by its power and
fortune so exalted, and being favoured by God and the Church,
whose leadership it now occupies. Nor will this be very difficult
to you, if you call to mind the actions and lives of the men I have
named. And although those men were rare and marvellous, they
were none the less men, and had each of them less occasion than
the present, for their enterprise was not juster than this, nor
easier, nor was God more their friend than He is yours. Here is
a just cause; for that war is just which is necessary; and those

arms are merciful where no hope exists save in them. Here is the greatest willingness, provided that the measures are adopted of those whom I have set before you as examples. Besides this, unexampled wonders have been seen here performed by God, the sea has been opened, a cloud has shown you the road, the rock has given forth water, manna has rained, and everything has contributed to your greatness, the remainder must be done by you. God will not do everything, in order not to deprive us of freewill and the portion of the glory that falls to our lot. It is no marvel that none of the before-mentioned Italians have done that which it is to be hoped your illustrious house may do; and if in so many revolutions in Italy and so many warlike operations, it always seems as if the military capacity were extinct, this is because the ancient methods were not good, and no one has arisen who knew how to discover new ones. Nothing has done so much honour to a newly-risen man than the new laws and measures which he introduces. These things, when they are well based and have greatness in them, render him revered and admired, and there is not lacking scope in Italy for the introduction of every kind. Here there is great virtue in the members if it were not wanting in the heads. Look how in duels and in councils of a few the Italians are superior in strength, dexterity and intelligence. But when it comes to armies they make a poor show; which proceeds entirely from the weakness of the leaders, for those that know are not obedient, and everyone thinks that he knows, there being hitherto nobody who has raised himself so high both by valour and fortune as to make others yield. Hence it comes about that in all this time, in all the wars waged during the last twenty years, whenever there has been an army entirely Italian, it has always been a failure, as witness first Taro, then Alexandria, Capua, Genoa, Vaila, Bologna, and Mestre. If your illustrious house, therefore, wishes to follow those great men who redeemed their countries, it is before all things necessary, as the true foundation of every undertaking, to provide yourself with your own forces, for you cannot have more faithful or truer or better soldiers. And although each one of them may be good,

they will together become better when they see themselves commanded by their prince, and honoured and supported by him.
It is therefore necessary to prepare such forces in order to be able
with Italian prowess to defend the country from foreigners. And
although both the Swiss and Spanish infantry are deemed terrible,
none the less they each have their defects, so that a third order
might not only oppose them, but be confident of overcoming
them. For the Spaniards cannot sustain the attack of cavalry, and
the Swiss have to fear infantry which meets them with resolution
equal to their own. From which it has resulted, as will be seen
from experience, that the Spaniards cannot sustain the attack of
French cavalry, and the Swiss are overthrown by Spanish infantry.
And although a complete example of the latter has not been seen,
yet an instance was furnished in the battle of Ravenna, where the
Spanish infantry attacked the German battalions, which observe
the same order as the Swiss. The Spaniards, through their bodily
agility and aided by their bucklers, had entered between and under
their pikes and were in a position to attack them safely without
the Germans being able to defend themselves; and if the cavalry
had not charged them, they would have utterly destroyed them.
Knowing therefore the defects of both these kinds of infantry,
a third kind can be created which can resist cavalry and need not
fear infantry, and this will be done not by the creation of armies
but by a change of system. And these are the things which, when
newly introduced, give reputation and grandeur to a new prince.
This opportunity must not, therefore, be allowed to pass, for
letting Italy at length see her liberator. I cannot express the love
with which he would be received in all those provinces which
have suffered under these foreign invasions, with what thirst for
vengeance, with what steadfast faith, with what love, with what
grateful tears. What doors would be closed against him? What
people would refuse him obedience? What envy could oppose
him? What Italian would rebel against him? This barbarous
domination stinks in the nostrils of every one. May your illustrious house therefore assume this task with that courage and
those hopes which are inspired by a just cause, so that under its

E

banner our fatherland may be raised up, and under its auspices
be verified that saying of Petrarch:

> Valour against fell wrath
> Will take up arms; and be the combat quickly sped!
> For, sure, the ancient worth,
> That in Italians stirs the heart, is not yet dead.

GIROLAMO SAVONAROLA, 1452-98

Although Savonarola always remained a loyal member of the
Catholic Church, much of his teaching and preaching mark him out
as an unconscious forerunner of the Reformation—e.g. his violent
indictments of the corruption in the Church and his insistence on the
supremacy of the Scriptures. As a boy he was a mystic, soon he was
crossed in love, then full of self-doubts, but after hearing a sermon at
Faenza he entered the monastery of S. Domenico at Bologna, where he
conceived his intense indignation at the corruption of the Church. In
1482 he went to the convent of San Marco in Florence. Here gradually
his tremendous powers as a preacher developed and on August 1st,
1490, he preached his first sermon in San Marco. In 1491 he became
Prior of the Convent and he refused to do the customary homage to
Lorenzo de' Medici, on the grounds that God and not Lorenzo had
appointed him Prior. Now he began to have visions and to hear
voices, now also as a result he began to preach violently against the
iniquities of the Medici rule in Florence. He foretold the arrival of
Charles VIII of France, which occurred in 1494, but soon it was clear
that Charles came as a conqueror and not as a saviour. Under the
persuasions of Savonarola the French king left Florence. All the city
now turned to Savonarola as its saviour and he became virtually the
dictator of Florence. His preaching now reached its height. But he
fell foul of political opponents inside Florence and outside of the
Pope, Alexander VI. In 1495 he was excommunicated. Then the
Medici family began to intrigue against him. He was at last brought
to trial, horribly tortured and was eventually hanged and his body
burned at the stake. His remains were thrown into the river Arno.

The cell of this Old Testament prophet is still shown to the public
in the convent of San Marco.

Source: (a) Savonarola's first sermon in San Marco, August 1st, 1490.
From the life of Savonarola by Burlamacchi, a contemporary, a
disciple and a Dominican friar, from a noble family in Lucca. This

and following English versions are taken from Mrs. Oliphant's *Makers of Florence*, Macmillan, 1883, p. 257.

The grace of God appeared in the lofty words and profound thoughts which he gave forth with a clear voice and rapid tongue so that everyone understood him. And it was admirable to see his glowing countenance and fervent and reverent aspect when he preached, and his beautiful gestures, which rapt the very soul of every one who heard him, so that wonders and amazing appearances were seen by many while he was in the act of preaching.

[It is interesting to compare this effect and description with the effect which (say) Latimer had in England between 1525 and 1553. See *Who's Who in History*, vol. 2, pp. 165 *et sqq.*]

Source: (b) The Crowds who came to hear Savonarola: Burlamacchi, *op. cit.*; Oliphant, *op. cit.*, p. 260.

The people got up in the middle of the night to get places for the sermon, and came to the door of the cathedral, waiting outside till it should be opened, making no account of any inconvenience, neither of the cold, nor the wind, nor of standing in winter with their feet on the marble;[23] and among them were young and old, women and children, of every sort, who came with such jubilee and rejoicing that it was bewildering to hear them, going to the sermon as to a wedding. Then the silence was great in the church, each one going to his place: and he who could read, with a taper in his hand, read the service and other prayers. And though many thousand people were thus collected together, no sound was to be heard, not even a 'hush', until the arrival of the children, who sang hymns with so much sweetness that Heaven seemed to have opened. Thus they waited three or four hours till the Padre entered the pulpit. And the attention of so great a mass of people, all with eyes and ears intent upon the preacher, was wonderful; they listened so that when the sermon reached its end it seemed to them that it had scarcely begun.

Source: (c) Savonarola as an Old Testament prophet.

Savonarola had foretold the coming of Charles VIII to Italy. He arrived in 1494 and Savonarola went to his camp to see him. There he told the king to enter boldly, gladly, as the avenger of Christ Himself.

Vicenzo Marchese, author of *Storia del Covento di San Marco*.
Quoted in Mrs. Oliphant's *The Makers of Florence*, p. 284. Another
fine example will be found in Villari's *Life and Times of Savonarola*,
p. 126.

Nevertheless, most Christian king, listen to my words. God's
unworthy servant, to whom this has been revealed, warns and
admonishes thee, by God's authority, that according to His
example thou shouldst shew mercy everywhere, and especially
in Florence where (though there are many sinners) He has
many servants and handmaidens, both in the world and in the
cloister, for whose sake it is thy duty to spare the city . . . In
God's name I exhort and admonish thee to help and defend the
innocents, the widows and orphans and poor, and above all
modesty and purity . . . In God's name I admonish thee to
pardon the offences of the Florentines and other people who may
have offended thee . . . Remember thy Saviour, who, hanging
on the Cross, pardoned his murderers. Which things, if thou
dost, oh king, God will increase thy kingdom and give thee
victory . . . But if thou dost forget the work for which the Lord
sends thee, He will then choose another to fulfill it, and will let
the hand of his wrath fall upon thee and will punish thee with
terrible scourgings. All this I say to thee in the name of the
Lord.

Source: (*d*) The Last Meeting of Charles VIII and Savonarola.

Trouble soon broke out between the Florentines and the French,
Piero Capponi was leader of the resistance movement and his bold
behaviour infuriated Charles, who decided to sack the city. Savonarola
had to be brought into the palace to try to frighten Charles off his
plan: Burlamacchi (see (*a*) above).

When he saw the servant of God, according to the custom of
the king of France, he rose to show him respect. But the servant
of God took out a little leaden crucifix which he carried always
about with him, and holding it up to the king, said: 'This is He
who made heaven and earth. Honour not me, but honour Him
who is King of Kings, Lord of Lords, and who makes the world
to tremble, and gives victory to princes according to His will and
justice. He punishes and destroys impious and unjust kings; and

He will destroy thee with all thy army, if thou dost not give up thy cruel purpose and annul the plan thou hast formed against this city . . . Knowest thou not that it matters little to the Lord whether He gets the victory with few or with many? Have you forgotten what He did to Sennacherib, the proud king of the Assyrians? or how, when Moses prayed, Joshua and the people overcame their enemies? So shall it be done to thee . . .' Thus spake the Padre to the king, filling him with terror, and threatening him in the name of God, always with the crucifix in his hand. And he spoke with so much power and effect that all who were present were struck with dismay and terror, and the king and his ministers were moved to tears. Then the Padre took the king by the hand and said to him, 'Sacred majesty, know that it is God's will that thou shouldst leave this city without making any other change, otherwise thou and thy army will here lay down your lives'.

Source: (*e*) A Tribute from his Enemies.

When Savonarola was excommunicated and at the command of the Pope, was arrested, examined and tortured by the Signoria of Florence, they wrote to the Pope that they could get nothing out of their prisoner: a letter from the Signoria to Pope Alexander VI, quoted in Mrs. Oliphant, *op. cit.*, p. 341.

We have had to deal with a man of the most extraordinary patience of body and wisdom of soul, who hardened himself against all torture, involving the truth in all kinds of obscurity, with the intention either of establishing for himself by pretended holiness an eternal name among men, or to brave imprisonment and death. Notwithstanding a long and most careful interrogatory, and with all the help of torture, we could scarcely extract anything out of him which he wished to conceal from us, although we laid open the inmost recesses of his mind.

Source: (*f*) The Burning of Savonarola, May 22nd, 1498: Luca Landucci, *A Florentine Diary*, trans. by A. De Rosen Jervis, Dent, 1927, pp. 142–3. In the following account the *Frate* is Savonarola, the other two *Frati* were Fra Silvestro and Fra Domenico of Pescia. The Eight were the *Otti di Guardia e Balìa*. Originally they were only appointed in times of crisis to ferret out the enemies of the government, but they came to be a permanent secret police with ever-increasing powers, until they were deposed on November 1st, 1478, but others were put in their place. *Ringhiera* was a platform consisting of three steps and a railing, which was used round the *Palagio (Palazzo Vecchio)* on the front and on the north for haranguing the populace. It was demolished in 1812 and the present one replaced it.

22nd May, 1498, it was decided that he should be put to death and that he should be burnt alive. In the evening a scaffold was made, which covered the whole *ringhiera* of the *Palagio de' Signori*, and then a scaffolding which began at the *ringhiera* next to the 'lion' and reached into the middle of the Piazza towards the *Tetto de' Pisani*; and here was erected a solid piece of wood many *braccia* high, and round this a large circular platform. On the aforesaid piece of wood was placed a horizontal one in the shape of a cross; but people noticing it said, 'They are going to crucify him'; and when these murmurs were heard, orders were given to saw off part of the wood, so that it should not look like a cross.

22nd May (Wednesday morning). The sacrifice of the three *Frati* was made. They took them out of the *Palagio* and brought them on to the *ringhiera*, where were assembled the Eight and the *Collegi*, the papal envoy, the General of the Dominicans, and many canons, priests and monks of divers Orders, and the Bishop of the *Pagagliotti* who was deputed to degrade the three *Frati*; and here on the *ringhiera* the said ceremony was to be performed. They were robed in all their vestments, which were taken off one by one, with the appropriate words for the degradation, it being constantly affirmed that Fra Girolamo was a heretic and schismatic, and on this account condemned to be burnt; then their faces and hands were shaved, as is customary in this ceremony.

When this was completed, they left the *Frati* in the hands of the Eight, who immediately made the decision that they should be hanged and burnt; and they were led straight onto the platform at the foot of the cross. The first to be executed was Fra Silvestro, who was hung to the post and one arm of the cross, and there not being much drop, he suffered for some time, repeating 'Jesu' many times whilst he was hanging, for the rope did not draw tight nor run well. The second was Fra Domenico of Pescia, who also kept saying 'Jesu'; and the third was the *Frate* called a heretic, who did not speak aloud, but to himself, and so he was hanged. This all happened without a word from one of them, which was considered extraordinary, especially by good and thoughtful people, who were much disappointed, as every one had been expecting some signs, and desired the glory of God, the beginning of righteous life, the renovation of the Church, and the conversion of unbelievers; hence they were not without bitterness and not one of them made an excuse. Many, in fact, fell from their faith. When all three were hanged, Fra Girolamo being in the middle, facing the *Palagio*, the scaffold was separated from the *ringhiera* and a fire was made on the circular platform round the cross, upon which gunpowder was put and set alight, so that the said fire burst out with a noise of rockets and crackling. In a few hours they were burnt, their legs and arms gradually dropping off; part of their bodies remained hanging to the chains, a quantity of stones were thrown to make them fall, as there was a fear of the people getting hold of them, and then the hangman and those whose business it was, hacked down the post and burnt it to the ground, bringing a lot of brushwood, and stirring the fire up over the dead bodies, so that the very least piece was consumed. Then they fetched carts, and accompanied by the mace-bearers, carried the last bit of dust to the Arno, by the Ponte Vecchio, in order that no remains should be found. Nevertheless, a few good men had so much faith that they gathered some of the floating ashes together, in fear and secrecy, because it was as much as one's life was worth to say a word, so anxious were the authorities to destroy every relic.

THE IMPACT OF SAVONAROLA ON FLORENCE

After the expulsion of the Medici from Florence in 1494 (see p. 39) Savonarola for the next four years, principally by his preaching in the Duomo, was the virtual ruler of the city. During that time he wholly changed the Florentine way of life and reorganized the government. The manners and the morals of the Florentines underwent an amazing change. The old vicious carnivals[24] disappeared and in their place were to be found the 'burnings of the vanities'. Savonarola built up an almost Puritan state.

Source: (a) Luca Landucci, Diario Fiorentino, op. cit.

And as it pleased the divine grace, such a change had come over us that instead of playing their usual pranks, the children had been asking for alms for many days before, and instead of daggers, on all sides you could see crucifixes in their pure and holy hands. And about vesper-time they collected in bands in the four quarters of Florence, and each quarter had its banner. The first was a crucifix, the second an Our Lady, and so with the others; and they came with the trumpeters and fifers, the mace-bearers and guards of the Palace, singing lauds and crying out, 'Long live Christ and the Virgin Mary our Queen!', each with a branch of olive in his hand. And truly the good and sober men amongst us were weeping tears of joy and saying: 'Truly this change is the work of God. These are the boys that will enjoy the good things that he [Savonarola] has promised us.' And it seemed as though we were looking on that crowd in Jerusalem that walked before and after Christ on Palm Sunday, crying, 'Blessed is he that cometh in the name of the Lord' . . . And I have written these things because they are true; and I saw it myself and felt some of the sweetness of it, and some of my own children were among those blessed and holy bands.

Source: (b) The Burning of the Vanities, 1497: Luca Landucci, op. cit., p. 130.

27th February, (the Carnival). There was made on the Piazza de' Signori a pile of vain things, nude statues, and playing-boards, heretical books, Morganti,[25] mirrors, and many other vain things, of great value, estimated at thousands of florins. The procession of boys was made as the year before; they collected in four quarters, with crosses and olive-branches in their hands, each quarter arranged in order with tabernacles in front, and went in the afternoon to burn this pile. Although some luke-warm people gave trouble, throwing dead cats and other dirt upon it, the boys nevertheless set it on fire and burnt everything, for there was plenty of small brushwood. And it is to be observed that the

pile was not made by children; there was a rectangular wood-
work measuring more than 12 *braccia* [about 24 feet] each way,
which had taken the carpenters several days to make, with many
workmen, so that it was necessary for many armed men to keep
guard the night before, as certain lukewarm persons, specially
certain young men called *Compagnacci*, wanted to destroy it.

Source: (c) Guicciardini. *op. cit.*

Never was seen a monk of such parts, or who gained such
authority and credit. Even his foes admitted his learning in
many sciences, especially in philosophy. For centuries there had
been none to compare with him in knowledge of the Scriptures.
In eloquence he surpassed all his contemporaries. His speech was
never artificial or constrained, but flowed simply and naturally.

How shall I judge his life? There was in it no trace of avarice,
nor of luxury, neither weakness nor passion. It was the model of
a religious life, charitable, pious, obedient to the monastic rule,
not only the externals, but the very heart of piety. On none of
these points could his enemies find the slightest fault in him,
however much they tried during his trial.

He achieved a holy and admirable work in his reforms of
morals. There was never so much religion and virtue in Florence
as in his day, and after his death the fall of piety and virtue was
kept within limits. The taverns were closed, women dressed
modestly, and children lived a life of holiness. Conducted by
Fra Buonvincini they went in bands to church, wore their hair
short and pelted with stones and insults gamblers, drunkards and
women of immodest dress.

Fra Girolamo's work in the sphere of government was no less
beneficent. After the fall of the Medici the city was divided
against itself, and the supporters of the late government were in
peril. He put a stop to violence. He founded the Grand Council
to put a curb on ambition, and by leaving the appeal to the
Signoria brought the excesses of the people within bounds. And
lastly, by proclaiming a 'universal peace', he prevented any too
close scrutiny of the past and saved the supporters of the Medici
from the vengeance which threatened them.

These measures were beyond all doubt for the good of the Republic, of victors as well as vanquished.

In short, the works of this great man were excellent. Since some of his prophecies had been fulfilled, many people continued to believe in his Divine inspiration, in spite of his excommunication, trial and death on the scaffold.

If Fra Girolamo was sincere, our age has seen in him a great prophet: if he was a rogue, a very great man.

SIGISMONDO MALATESTA

This extraordinary product of the Italian Renaissance, half genius, half devil, was the son of Pandolfo Malatesta, the perfidious general of Gian Galeazzo Visconti. He was born in 1417 and he died in 1468. He was married three times: first to Ginevra d'Este in 1434 (daughter of the Duke of Ferrara), who died in 1440, and may have been murdered by her husband: secondly, to Polissena, daughter of Francesco Sforza, in 1442, by whom he had a son, Galeotto Roberto, and whom he murdered in order to marry his mistress, Isotta degli Atti, with whom he had long been madly in love. His knowledge of antiquity was unrivalled, he was something of a genius as a soldier, and he had a genuine love and admiration for learning. He took command of the Venetian troops against the Turks in the Morea and returned in 1465, bringing with him, as the greatest trophy he could find, the bones of Gemisthus Pletho, the great Platonist scholar. These he interred in a stone sarcophagus, still outside the Tempio at Rimini. This Tempio had been the cathedral church of St. Francis. Sigismondo encased the original building in a classical exterior and converted the interior into a wonderful monument to commemorate himself and his Isotta, which is in decoration virtually a pagan temple. His two great enemies were Federigo of Urbino and Pope Pius II. He still retains the unique distinction of being the only human being who has ever been 'canonized into Hell', by the Pope. In addition he was arraigned for heresy, parricide, incest, adultery, rape, sacrilege, he was burned in effigy, deprived of all his territories, and eventually, on an almost degrading submission, he was restored 'to the bosom of the Church'. The beautiful portrait of him by Piero della Francesca, hangs in the Tempio.

Source: (a) *Memoirs of a Renaissance Pope, The Commentaries of Pope Pius II,* An Abridgement, trans. by F. A. Gragg, Capricorn Books, ed. New York, 1962, pp. 110 *et sqq.* (For Pius II see p. 84.)

Sigismondo, of the noble family of the Malatesta but illegitimate, was very vigorous in body and mind, eloquent, and gifted with great military ability. He had a thorough knowledge of history and no slight acquaintance with philosophy. Whatever he attempted he seemed born for, but the evil part of his character had the upper hand. He was such a slave to avarice that he was ready not only to plunder but to steal. His lust was so unbridled that he violated his daughters and his sons-in-law. He outdid all barbarians in cruelty. His bloody hand inflicted terrible punishments on innocent and guilty alike. He oppressed the poor, plundered the rich, spared neither widows nor ophans. No one felt safe under his rule. Wealth or a beautiful wife or handsome children were enough to cause a man to be accused of crime. He hated priests and despised religion. He had no belief in another world and thought the soul died with the body. Nevertheless he built at Rimini a splendid church dedicated to St. Francis, though he filled it so full of pagan works of art that it seemed less a Christian sanctuary than a temple of heathen devil-worshippers. In it he erected for his mistress a tomb of magnificent marble and exquisite workmanship, with an inscription in the pagan style as follows, 'Sacred to the deified Isotta'. The two wives he had married before he took Isotta for his mistress he killed one after the other with the sword or poison.

He showed himself a perjurer and traitor to Alfonso, King of Sicily, and his son Ferrante. He broke his word to Francesco, Duke of Milan, to the Venetians, the Florentines, and the Sienese. Repeatedly, too, he tricked the Church of Rome. Finally, when there was no one left in Italy for him to betray, he went on to the French, who allied themselves with him out of hatred for Pope Pius, but fared no better than the other princes. When his subjects once begged him to retire at last to a peaceful life and spare his country, which had so often been exposed to pillage on his account, he replied, 'Go and be of good courage; never while I live shall you have peace'.

Such was Sigismondo, intolerant of peace, a devotee of pleasure, able to endure any hardship, and greedy of war. Of all men who have ever lived or will live he was the worst scoundrel, the disgrace of Italy and the infamy of our times.

Source: (b) The 'Canonization' of Sigismondo Malatesta, 1460: F. A. Cragg, op. cit., The Commentaries of Pope Pius II, p. 184 et sqq.

After the storming and sack of Donidei which was reported to the Pope on October 31 when he was celebrating Vespers for All Saints, the army went into winter quarters, Alessandro at Nepi and Federigo of Urbino among the Sabines. Both went to Rome to see the Pope during the feast of the Nativity and attended him as he was drinking with the Cardinals after Vespers according to a time-honoured custom. A few days later there was a public consistory at which they were present. At this Andrea Benzi, fiscal advocate, at the Pope's bidding, delivered a long and brilliant speech in which he execrated the crimes of Sigismondo Malatesta: his robberies, arson, massacres, debauchery, adultery, incest, murders, sacrilege, betrayals, treasons and heresy. He implored the Pope to rise in vengeance on them, to give ear to the prayers of suppliants who could no longer endure the cruel yoke of the tyrant, to cleanse Italy at last of that foul and abominable monster, during whose life no good man in any of his domains could live.

When the Pope heard the accusation, he said, 'There are two states to which men go when they depart this life. One is the heavenly city of Jerusalem, the country of the blest; the other is in Hell, where is the abode of Lucifer and the prison of the damned. Our ancestors declared that in the former were enrolled many whom we revere as saints and worship with the adoration called dulia.[26] In doing this we observe the ceremony which we call canonization. Our predecessor Eugenius IV canonized Nicholas of Tolentino; Nicholas V, Bernardino of Siena; Calixtus III, Vincenzo of Valencia and the Englishman Osmund. We have been petitioned to enroll Catherine of Siena, Rose of Viterbo and Frances of Rome among the maids or widows who are the saints of Christ and to declare that they have been received into the heavenly city. And this is just, for we believe that their virtues have earned this honour. But no one of them has been so extolled by the most eloquent advocates, who have in these last days spoken in their praise, as Sigismondo Malatesta has to-day been cursed. Furthermore, what has been said about the maidens requires proof; Sigismondo's crimes are manifest and evident, and not to one or two individuals only, but they are notorious to almost all the world. Let him then take precedence and before they are canonized in Heaven, let him be enrolled a citizen of Hell. Sigismondo's crimes, unprecedented in our age, call for new and unprecedented procedure. No mortal has heretofore descended into Hell with the ceremony of canonization. Sigismondo shall be considered the first to be deemed worthy of such honour. By an edict of the Pope, he shall be enrolled in the company of Hell as comrade of the devils and the damned. Nor shall we wait for his death, if haply he may come to his senses, since he has left no hope of his conversion. While still living he shall be condemned to Orcus and perhaps while still living he shall be hurled into flames. We might at this moment pass sentence upon him, since the crimes of which he is accused can be concealed by no evasions; but we will be more merciful. We will summon the accused; if he comes in, we will hear him; we will observe the customary procedure of our courts. To you, then, our dear son, Cardinal of St. Peter in Vincoli, we entrust this case to be heard, investigated, and decided *sine debito*.'

Source: (*c*) The Burning of Sigismondo, 1461: as above, p. 232.

Meantime Pius called a consistory and ordered the Cardinal of St. Peter in Vincoli to report what he had learned about Sigismondo Malatesta. The Cardinal said that an examination of the evidence in the case made it clear that Sigismondo was a heretic who denied the resurrection of the dead, asserted that the souls of men were mortal, and had no hope of a future kingdom. Murders, outrage, adultery, incest, sacrilege, perjury, treachery, and almost countless crimes of the most degrading and frightful nature had been proved against him. There was no doubt that he deserved the severest punishment.

The cardinals were asked their opinions and voted unanimously for his condemnation. In a public trial the accused was found guilty of treason against the Pope, of presuming to make impious assertions in regard to the Christian religion, of living a life foul with every crime and infamy. He was deprived of the vicariate and all his dignities and honours and was subjected to those punishments which the laws of men have decreed for heretics and traitors.

Meantime in front of the steps of St. Peter's there was built a great pyre of dry wood, on top of which was placed an effigy of Sigismondo Malatesta, imitating the wicked and accursed man's features and dress so exactly that it seemed a real person rather than an image. But that no one should make any mistake about it, an inscription issued from the figure's mouth, which read, 'Sigismondo Malatesta, son of Pandolfo, king of traitors, hated of God and man, condemned to the flames by vote of the holy senate'. This writing was read by many. Then, while the populace stood by, fire was applied to the pyre and the image, which at once blazed up. Such was the mark branded on the impious house of Malatesta by Pius.

Source: (d) Sigismondo Surrenders, 1463: as above, p. 369.

Sigismondo Malatesta, who was shut up in Rimini with only a few fortresses in his possession, sent ambassadors to the Pope and said, 'I am beaten and sue for peace. I am ready to submit to any terms you set. The glory of the victor is to spare the vanquished. I admit I have sinned grievously against you, but neither has the punishment I have suffered been light. If I am spared, I will henceforth refrain from harming the Church'. The Pope gave orders that his terms should be drawn up. After the lawyers had approved them, he granted peace to Sigismondo on the following conditions: In the Basilica of St. Peter on a feast day during Mass Sigismondo's representatives should testify that he had confessed and acknowledged his errors savoring of manifest heresy of which he had been accused, and should recant and abjure them in his name, especially those which denied the resurrection of the dead and the immortality of the human soul. For the crimes of treason and heresy he should understand himself to be deprived of all his power and other gifts of Fortune. By the Pope's grace he should receive Rimini under the new title of vicariate and pay a yearly tribute of 1000 ducats . . .

Sigismondo's agents, who had been sorely afraid of losing Rimini, accepted the terms and the next Sunday at Mass at the altar of Holy Mary in the Basilica of the Apostles, before a large congregation in the presence of many bishops, in a loud and distinct voice, they publicly confessed Sigismondo's heresy and in accordance with the powers delegated to them abjured it. On the day appointed Sigismondo, as commanded, handed over to the Count of Teano the possession of his various towns and citadels.

SOME LADIES OF THE RENAISSANCE

ISABELLA D'ESTE

Probably Benvenuto Cellini may be taken as the most representative personality of the Renaissance in its most flamboyant form. Lorenzo il Magnifico must surely be accepted as embodying in himself in the highest degree the intellectual, the cultural, the athletic, the political, and even in some respects the spiritual (but never the moral) sides of the Renaissance. There is no doubt in the minds of the best historians of that period that Isabella d'Este is the outstanding figure among a large host of remarkable women in that period. It is not possible in a short compass of quotations to do justice to the enormous vitality of this beautiful, intelligent, clever, cultured, courageous, imperious and universally beloved lady. Her life and the society in which she lived must be read in Julia Cartwright's biography.

Isabella d'Este was the elder daughter of Ercole I of Ferrara and his wife Leonora of Aragon. She was the sister of her hardly less famous Beatrice, who married Lodovico Sforza, known as Il Moro. One characteristic of these families was their personal, family affections for each other, despite the dynastic quarrels which too often invaded their family lives.

Isabella was born in 1474, she married Francesco Gonzaga of Mantua, and she died in 1539. She was a lady of unequalled ability—she could and did govern the state when her husband was a prisoner of war. She was on intimate terms with all the great scholars of the time—she was educated by Guarino. In the course of her life she was visited by such eminent scholars as Bembo and Machiavelli; she was in perpetual correspondence with the great painters of her day—Leonardo, Raphael,

Bellini; Mantegna was employed by her father and herself: her courage was equal to her sensibility, for she fortified the house in which she was staying and lived through the sack of Rome in 1527. In times when not all women in her position remained chaste, her reputation, like that of her sister Beatrice, was unsullied. She was a faithful and devoted wife, an adoring yet wise mother. The following extracts give only a glimpse of this remarkable Renaissance lady's character. Her incessant efforts to secure paintings by and directly from the finest painters of her times met with, on the whole, not much result. The great painters were too desultory in their painting to satisfy the urgent spirit of Isabella.

Source: (a) Letter to Zorzo Brognolo, the Mantuan envoy at Venice, September 17th, 1491. Luzio e Renier, Giorn, *St. d. Lett. It.*, 1899, p. 8. Quoted J. Cartwright, *Isabella d'Este*, i, 76.

We wish you to ask all the booksellers in Venice for a list of all the Italian books in prose or verse containing battle stories and fables of heroes in modern and ancient times, more especially those which relate to the Paladins of France, and send them to us as soon as possible.

Source: (b): Lorenzo Gusnaco, *Dott. Carlo dell'Acqua*, p. 20. Cartwright, *Isabella d'Este*, vol. i, p. 130.

12th March, 1496. To Lorenzo Gusnaco da Pavia famous master of organs. M. Lorenzo da Pavia, most excellent master: We remember that you made a most beautiful and perfect clavichord for that illustrious Madonna, the Duchess of Milan, our sister, when we were last in Pavia, and since we ourselves now wish to have an instrument of the same kind, which cannot be surpassed, we are sure that there is no one in all Italy who can satisfy our wish better than you can. We therefore pray you to make us a clavichord of such beauty and excellence as shall be worthy of your high reputation and of the trust we repose in you. The only difference that we wish to see in this instrument is that it should be easier to play, because our hand is so light that we cannot play well if we have to press heavily on the notes. But you, we have no doubt, will understand our wishes and requirements. For the rest, make the instrument exactly as you choose. And the more quickly you can serve us, the better we shall be pleased, and we will take care that you shall be well rewarded, and we place ourselves at your service.

Source: (c) Luzio, I Precettori, App. Cartwright, i, 318. March 1501. To Fra Pietro da Novellara, who was preaching a course of sermons at Santa Croce, Florence.

Most Reverend Father in God—If Leonardo, the Florentine painter, is now in Florence, we beg you will inform us what kind of life he is leading, that is to say if he has begun any work, as we have been told, and what this work is, and if you think he will remain for the present in Florence. Your Reverence might find out if he would undertake to paint a picture for our studio. If he consents, we would leave the subject and the time to him; but if he declines, you might at least induce him to paint a little picture of the Madonna, as sweet and holy as his own nature. Will you also beg him to send another drawing of our portrait, since our illustrious lord has given away the one he left here? For all of which we shall be no less grateful to you than to Leonardo. Mantua, March 27th, 1501.

Source: (d) Luzio, Arch. Stor. dell'Arte, i, 181. Cartwright, i, 322. 3rd May, 1502. Isabella had heard that some vases which were once the property of Lorenzo de' Medici were coming up for sale. She wrote to her agent, Francesco Malatesta, asking him to consult Leonardo da Vinci about their value. He replied as follows.

I have shewn them to Leonardo Vinci, the painter, as Your Highness desired. He praises all of them, but especially the crystal vase, which is all of one piece and very fine, and has a silver-gilt stand and cover and Leonardo says that he never saw a finer thing. The agate one also pleases him, because it is a rare thing and of large size, and is all in one piece, excepting the stand and cover, which are silver-gilt; but it is cracked. That of amethyst, or, as Leonardo calls it, of jasper, is transparent and of variegated colours, and has a massive gold stand, studded with so many pearls and rubies that they are valued at 150 ducats. This greatly pleased Leonardo, as being something quite new and exquisite in colour. All four have Lorenzo Medici's name engraved in Roman letters on the body of the vase, and are valued at very high prices: the crystal vase at 350 ducats: the jasper vase at 240 ducats: the agate

F

vase at 200 ducats: and the jasper vase on a plain stand at 150 ducats. [The prices proved too high for Isabella.]

Source: (e) When Cesare Borgia, Duke of Valentino, seized Urbino, Isabella tried to buy two statues which she recalled having seen there. —A letter to Cardinal Ippolito d'Este, her brother, dated June 30th, 1502. Gaye, *Carteggio d'Artisti*, ii, 53. Cartwright, i, 230.

Most Reverend Father in God, my dear and honoured Brother —The Lord Duke of Urbino, my brother-in-law, had in his house a small Venus of antique marble, and also a Cupid, which were given him some time ago by His Excellency the Duke of Romagna. I feel certain that these things must have fallen into the hands of the said Duke, together with all the contents of the palace of Urbino, in the present revolution. And since I am very anxious to collect antiques for the decoration of my studio, I desire exceedingly to possess these statues, which does not seem to me impossible, since I hear that His Excellency has little taste for antiques and would accordingly be the more ready to oblige others . . . pray you of your kindness to ask him for the said Venus and Cupid . . .

Source: (f) A letter from Isabella to Francesco Malatesta, her agent. September, 1502. Braghirolli, *Notizie e Documenti ined.* intorno a P. Vannucchi, Archivio Gonzaga. Cartwright, i, 329.

Since we desire to have in our *camerino* paintings of allegorical subjects by the best painters in Italy, among whom Il Perugino is famous, we beg you to see him and find out, through the intervention of some friend, if he is willing to accept the task of painting a picture on a *storia* or invention which we will give him, with small-sized figures, such as those which you have seen in our *camerino*. You will find out what payment he requires, and if he can set to work soon, in which case we will send him the measurements of the picture with our *fantasia*. And be sure to send me a prompt answer.

Source: (g) Isabella collected a splendid library which was kept in her Grotta. Calandra, a young Mantuan scholar, acted as librarian. On July 8th, 1501, she wrote to Lorenzo da Pavia inquiring about the new edition of classical authors which was just appearing from the Aldine press in Venice. Lorenzo answered on July 26th. Luzio in *Giorn. St. d. Lett.*, vol. xxxiii, p. 18. Cartwright, ii, 21.

Most illustrious Madonna,—I saw by your last letter that you wished me to send you the three books, *i.e.*, Virgil, Petrarch and Ovid, in parchment, and so I went at once to the house of Maestro Aldo, who prints these books in a small form and in the finest italic type that you ever saw. It is he who printed the first Greek books, and he is a very dear friend of mine. At present only Virgil is to be had in parchment, so I send it you herewith. The Petrarch is not yet finished, but they tell me it will be ready in about ten days. As yet they have only printed about fifteen copies on this paper, and have already bound them. This has been owing to the dearth of parchment, as they have great difficulty in obtaining the small amount required for the Virgils as well as for the Petrarchs. But Your Signoria shall have Petrarch, which is not yet bound. M. Aldo has promised me to choose a copy for you leaf by leaf, so that yours shall be the finest of all, and the said Maestro will do this all the more gladly because he has been helped in his work by M. Pietro Bembo, who is most devoted to Your Signoria. He it is who has had these poems printed from a manuscript which Petrarch wrote with his own hand. It belongs to a Paduan and is so precious that they have printed the book letter by letter after the original with the greatest possible care. As soon as it is finished I will send it to you, as they wish yours to be the first that appears, and hold this to be of good omen, and feel sure the work will obtain a great success since Your Excellency will have the first copy. After the Petrarch, Dante will be printed in the same shape and type, and after Dante, Ovid, which I think they will begin towards the end of September, but the Dante in about twenty days; and I beg you to seek for some goat-skin paper, which should be clear and very white and fine and even, not thick in one place and thin in another, because formerly I have seen beautiful paper in Mantua. The great difficulty is to find good paper for the Dante and Ovid. They will be of the same size as the Petrarch, with the sheet whole. Your Highness may trust me to do my utmost. I mean you to have something as rare and incomparable as Your

Most Excellent Highness herself. And nothing in the world pleases me more than to obey your orders, remembering the kindness which you have ever shown me. The Virgil and Petrarch, they say, will cost no less than 3 ducats apiece. Your servant, Lorenzo da Pavia.

Source: (*h*) On June 9th, 1505, Aldus Manutius sent Isabella all the books he had in stock printed on vellum with a note giving the prices. On the 30th June, Isabella sent them all back with the following covering letter: A Baschet, *Alde Manuce.* Cartwright, ii, 26.

M. Aldo,—The four volumes on vellum which you have sent us are pronounced by every one who has seen them to be twice as dear as they ought to be. We have given them back to your messenger, who does not deny the truth of this, but excuses you, saying that your partners will not take less. All the same, when you print any more, at a fair price, and on finer paper, with more careful corrections, we shall be glad to see them and hope still to be served by you.

BEATRICE D'ESTE

Beatrice d'Este was the daughter of Ercole, Duke of Ferrara, and Leonora of Aragon. She was born on June 29th, 1475, a year after her elder sister, Isabella. She married Lodovico Sforza, known as Il Moro. She died on Monday, 2nd of January, 1497. 'And that night the sky above the Castello of Milan was all ablaze with fiery flames, and the walls of the duchess' own garden fell with a sudden crash to the ground, although there was neither wind nor earthquake. And these things were held to be evil omens.'

Source: 'l'elegantissimo' Calmeta, the *Life of Serafino Aquilano,* written in 1504, quoted in J. Cartwright, *Beatrice d'Este,* p. 142, Dent, 1903. Calmeta was Beatrice's secretary.

This duke had for his most dear wife Beatrice d'Este, daughter of Ercole, Duke of Ferrara, who, coming to Milan in the flower of her opening youth, was endowed with so rare an intellect, so much grace and affability, and was so remarkable for her generosity and goodness that she may justly be compared with the noblest women of antiquity. The duchess devoted her time to the highest objects. Her court was composed of men of talent and distinction, most of whom were poets and musicians, who were expected to compose new eclogues, comedies, or tragedies, and arrange new spectacles and representations every month. In her leisure hours she generally employed a certain Antonio Grifo [a well-known student and commentator of Dante] or some equally gifted man, to read the Divina Commedia, or the works of other Italian poets, aloud to her. And it was no small relaxation of mind for Lodovico Sforza, when he was able to escape from the cares and business of state, to come and listen to these readings in his wife's rooms. And among the illustrious men whose presence adorned the court of the duchess there were three high-born cavaliers, renowned for many talents, but above all for their poetic gifts—Niccolo da Corregio, Gaspare Visconti and Antonio di Campo Fregoso, together with many others, one of whom was myself, Vincenzo Calmeta, who for some years held the post of secretary to that glorious and excellent lady. And besides those I have named there was Benedetto da Cingoli, called Piceno, and many other youths of no small promise, who daily offered her the first-fruits of their genius. Nor was Duchess Beatrice content with rewarding and honouring the poets of her own court. On the contrary, she sent to all parts of Italy to inquire for the compositions of elegant poets, and placed their books as sacred and divine things on the shelves of her cabinet of study, and praised and rewarded each writer according to his merit. In this manner poetry and literature in the vulgar tongue, which had degenerated and sunk into forgetfulness after the days of Petrarch and Boccaccio, has been restored to its former dignity, first by the protection of Lorenzo de' Medici, and then by the influence of this rare lady, and others like her, who are still living at the present time. But when Duchess Beatrice died everything fell into ruin. That court, which had been a joyous Paradise, became a dark and gloomy Inferno, and poets and artists were forced to seek another road.

VITTORIA COLONNA, MARCHESA DI PESCARA

Vittoria Colonna (1490–1547), daughter of Fabrizio Colonna, Grand Constable of the Kingdom of Naples, and of Anna da Montefeltro, was in many estimations the most remarkable lady of the Italian Renaissance. At nineteen she married the young Marquis of Pescara, who died of wounds received during the battle of Pavia. She was a poetess of great fame in her lifetime, and her poems are still rated very highly. She was a woman of the highest character and of the highest intelligence. She was adored by the ageing Michelangelo, and she numbered among her wide circle of friends Cardinal Reginald Pole, Cardinal Bembo and Baldassare Castiglione. Her published poems ran into four editions between 1538 and 1544. The following extract describes a meeting between Vittoria and a certain Spanish miniature-painter named D'Ollanda and Michelangelo.

Source: a MS. in D'Ollanda's Journal at Lisbon, quoted in Mrs. H. Roscoe's life of *Vittoria Colonna*, London, 1868, pp. 181 *et sqq*.

Tolomei helped me to become acquainted with Michael Angelo through Blasio, the Pope's secretary. He left word that I should find him in the church of San Silvestro on Monte Cavallo: where, with the Marchesa di Pescara, he was hearing the exposition of the Epistles of St. Paul. So I started off for San Silvestro.

Vittoria Colonna, the Marchesa di Pescara, and sister of Ascanio Colonna, is one of the noblest and most famous women in Italy and in the whole world. She is beautiful, pure in conduct, and acquainted with the Latin tongue; in short, she is adorned with every grace which can redound to a woman's praise. Weary of the brilliant life which she formerly led, she has quite devoted herself, since the death of her husband, to thoughts on Christ and to study. She supports the needy of her sex and stands forth as a model of Christian piety. She was the intimate friend of Tolomei and I owe her acquaintance to him. I entered; they asked me to take a place, and the reading and exposition of the Epistles was continued. When it was ended, the Marchesa spoke, and looking at me and Tolomei, said, 'I am not quite wrong if I imagine that Messer Francesco would rather listen to Michael Angelo on painting than Fra Ambrosio upon the Pauline epistles.' 'Madam', I replied, 'your Eccelenza seems to entertain the opinion that everything which is not painting and art is foreign and un-intelligible to me. It will certainly be very agreeable to me to hear Michael Angelo speak, but I prefer Fra Ambrosio's exposition of the Epistles of St. Paul.' I spoke with some pique. 'You need not take it so seriously', said Tolomei; 'the Marchesa certainly did not mean that a man who is a good painter is not good for anything else. We Italians rank too high for that. Perhaps the words of the Marchesa were intended to intimate that besides the enjoyment we have had, the other, of hearing Michael Angelo speak to-day, is still in store for us.' 'If it be so', I replied, 'it would be after all nothing extraordinary, for your Eccelenza would only be following your usual habit of granting a thousand times more than one ventured to desire.'

The Marchesa smiled. 'We ought to know how to give', she said, 'when a grateful mind is concerned, and here especially when giving and receiving afford equal enjoyment.' One of her retinue approached at her call. 'Do you know Michael Angelo's house? Go and tell him that I and Messer Tolomei are here in the chapel, where it is beautifully cool, and the church, too, is private and agreeable; and that I beg to ask him whether he is inclined to lose a few hours here in our society, and to turn them into gain for us—but not a word that the gentleman from Spain is here.'

After a few minutes, in which neither of them spoke, we heard a knocking at the door: everyone feared it could not be Michael Angelo. Fortunately the servant had met him close by San Silvestro, as he was just on the point of going to the Thermae. He was coming up the Esquiline way, in conversation with his colour-grinder, Urbino; he fell at once into the snare and it was he who knocked at the door.

The Marchesa rose to receive him and remained standing some time till she had made him take a place betwixt herself and Tolomei. I now seated myself at a little distance from him. At first they were silent, but the Marchesa, who could never speak without elevating those with whom she conversed, began to lead the conversation with the greatest art upon all possible things without however touching even remotely on painting. She wished to give Michael Angelo assurance. She proceeded as if approaching an unassailable fortress, so long as he was on his guard.

[The Marchesa eventually drew him out.]

'Your Eccelenza has only to command and I obey', said Michael Angelo. 'Art belongs to no land, it comes from Heaven', he said, and Tolomei remarked that the Emperor Maximilian, when he pardoned an artist who had been condemned to death, had said, 'I can make earls and dukes, but God alone can make a great artist'. . .

Michael Angelo was the first to rise, and the Marchesa stood up. We accompanied them to the gates. Tolomei went with Michael Angelo, and I with the Marchesa, from San Silvestro up to the monastery, where the head of John the Baptist is preserved and where she lived.

CATERINA SFORZA RIARIO

Caterina was the illegitimate daughter of Galeazzo Sforza. She was born in 1463 and died in 1509. She was three times married: (1) a political match, to Girolamo Riario in 1477—at the age of 15. Girolamo was nephew to Pope Sixtus IV. The Riario family was common, vulgar and violent. Caterina hated, quite rightly, her first husband. He was a boor and a murderer and was himself assassinated in the palace at Forlí (1488). She was a cultured, beautiful and heroic woman. (2) She married—a love match—Giacomo Feo—in 1489. He was murdered in 1495. Caterina's revenge was swift, merciless and cruel. (3) She married Giovanni de' Medici in 1497. He was the Florentine envoy at her court at Forlí. He died in 1498. From then onwards Caterina was involved in the most dangerous political situations. These culminated in the siege of Forlí by Cesare Borgia. The following extract illustrates the indomitable physical courage of Caterina. She had to capitulate: she was imprisoned in the castle of St. Angelo in Rome for some eighteen months. She was released in 1501. She had spent more than a year in a dark, narrow cell. When D'Allègre went to release her, he did not recognize the woman whom he had seen less than two years before.

Source: Guicciardini, Storia d'Italia, Eng. ed. A. P. Goddard, ii, 358

In the beginning of this year [1500] Valentino [Cesare Borgia] took possession of the city of Forlí without opposition. The Lady Governess of the place, sending away her children and her richest effects to Florence, and abandoning the rest which she was not able to preserve, was reduced to make the best of her defence in the citadel and castle, which were well provided with men and artillery. She betook herself to the citadel, and being a woman of a brave and manly spirit, she made a resistance which redounded very much to her honour. Valentino, having tried in vain to induce her to surrender, raised a great battery against the citadel, which beat down a good part of the wall, and this drew after it much of the rampart and filled up the ditch so far as to make the breach easy to be mounted. But the besieged were so much terrified that they abandoned the defence and endeavoured to retire into the castle. The lady used her utmost effort to stop the retreat and animate her men, but was borne down by the crowd, and the enemy breaking in upon them, under the present hurry and confusion, cut most of them to pieces before the gate, and entering pell mell among the rest into the castle put all to the sword, except a few of the chief, who with the Lady retired into a tower and were made prisoners. Valentino, considering her valour more than her sex, sent her prisoner to Rome, where she was kept in the castle of St. Angelo, till at the intercession of Ivo d'Allègri, she was set at liberty.

[Some writers record that when Valentino threatened, if she did not surrender the citadel, to kill her children, she took up her clothes and showing her nakedness said, 'Here, Duke, see the same mould for casting more'.]

EDUCATION

'Without doubt the two schools for boys, organized respectively by Guarino at Ferrara and by Vittorino da Feltre at Mantua, went farther towards putting the training of the young on a new foundation than any attempt made anywhere else in Italy. While both of these great educators anchored their curriculum in the classics, they did not for that reason toss overboard the ethical and spiritual values of Christianity, but attempted rather to fuse them with the rediscovered wisdom of the ancients. Their programme was to utilize the classical authors for the enrichment of the mind without sacrificing the invaluable tradition of Christian conduct. We may think of the two schoolmasters as conservative innovators who did not believe, as did so many of their fellow-humanists, that to profit adequately from the ancients it was necessary to revert to paganism.' (Schevill, *History of Florence*, p. 410.)

It is worth noting that both these teachers believed in the value of games and athletics, as did also the Englishman, Roger Ascham and the Spaniard, Juan Luis Vives.

VITTORINO DA FELTRE

Source: Vespasiano da Bisticci, *Memoirs*, Eng. ed. W. G. Waters, London, 1920.

Vittorino da Feltre [1399–1447] came from Feltre in Lombardy, a man of good position and of sober life, learned in Greek, in Latin and all the seven liberal arts. He lived in Mantua in the time of Francesco Gonzaga and Madonna Pagola dei Malatesti, his wife, who had a large family of fair children, both boys and girls. He was known throughout Italy as a virtuous and learned man, and on this account many of the Venetian aristocracy sent their children to be under his tuition in matters of conduct as well as in polite letters. Amongst his disciples were two distinguished Florentines—Francesco de Castiglione, a man of saintly life and habits, and Susero, son of Maestro Lorenzo da Prato, a fine Greek and Latin scholar, possessed of a good style, as may be seen in his writings, especially in his life of Vittorino, which was lost at the time of his death from plague after he left Mantua. Vittorino had many pupils whom he supported and taught for love of God; and because of his benefactions to these and his almsgiving he found, at the end of the year, that in addition to his salary of 300 florins from the Signori, he had spent 300 more. When he revised his accounts and saw the amount of his debt, he went to Gonzaga and said, 'I have received 300 florins as salary and I have spent 300 more, wherefore I appeal to your Lordship to help me to pay this debt'.

Gonzaga had great affection for Vittorino: he knew his worth and honesty and liberality, and that he had put by nothing for himself, so he made a grant of money without demur.

So that his studies should not be disturbed he never married. It was said, moreover, that he had no desire for women. He was a professed Christian and recited the office every day. He fasted on all the prescribed vigils, and he directed those of his pupils who were under discipline to do the same. When he went to table, he said the benediction like a priest and returned thanks afterwards, and all the rest did the same. During the meal some one read aloud that silence might be kept. He practised confession and wished all his scholars to use the same habit. His house was a sacrarium of words and deeds. He allowed his pupils to play suitable games, and the sons of the gentry were required to learn riding, throwing the stone and the staff, to play *palla*, jumping and all exercises good for bodily training, permitting them these bodily recreations after they had learned and repeated their lessons. He lectured in various subjects appropriate to the separate classes, and would give instruction to all in the liberal arts and in Greek at various times of the day. He made an accurate time-table and never allowed an hour to be wasted. Few of the scholars ever left the house and these would always return at the appointed hour, and at evening all were obliged to be back in the house early: thus he brought them into habits of order and well-doing.

From his school came many men distinguished for their work and literary attainments. Amongst his scholars were cardinals, bishops and archbishops, as well as temporal rulers and cultured gentlemen from Lombardy, Venice, Padua, Vicenza and all the chief places of the province. In the time of Pope Eugenius many sons of Venetian gentlemen entered the Church, and on festal days, when special orations were delivered, they would always be spoken by Vittorino's pupils. Amongst these I knew Messer Gregorio, nephew of the Cardinal of Verona and of Pope Gregory, a learned and eloquent youth, who wrote good verses and was high in his praise of Vittorino as a teacher . . .

This was Vittorino's system: to give a good example in his own life; to exhort and stimulate all about him to live worthily; to show that all our actions in life should lead us to live in a fashion which would allow us to reap the fruits of our labour in the future. He was not content to give his own alms for the love of God; he was always urging others to do the same. He taught gratuitously the needy youths who came to him and supplied all their other wants; he made no profit by them, for every year he spent more than his income and was forced to beg help from others to make good his losses . . .

All teachers should be fashioned after his model, not merely to teach Latin and Greek, but also good conduct, which is the most important thing in life. I have heard of books he wrote, but I will say nothing of them, as I never saw them. He was in stature small and lean, animated and cheerful in aspect. He was dignified in carriage and somewhat taciturn, being always clad in sombre-hued garments which reached to the ground. He wore a small cap on his head with narrow opening. I saw him in Florence and spoke to him several times when he came there from Rome in the train of Madonna Pagola Malatesti. In his company was also Signor Carlo Gonzaga who had been his pupil. In their house to which they were returning the life was almost that of a monastery. This is a brief record of his life and manners.

FRANCESCO VIGILIO

Tutor to Federico Gonzaga. The following letter describes the curriculum for the education of a young prince, the son of Isabella d'Este, Marchioness of Mantua.

Source: Letter from Vigilio to Isabella, February 5th, 1515, quoted in Julia Cartwright, *Isabella d'Este*, vol. ii, 121.

During your Highness' absence, your son, my master Signor Federico, has not failed to attend my instructions twice a day. It is true that he cannot keep up his attention for more than an hour, or a little longer, but during this time he is really attentive and diligent. We have gone through the abridged history of Livy, and he has translated two books of Valerius with me at hand to help him when he seemed puzzled, and now he knows Roman history and the laws and constitution of the State so well that he can sometimes remind me of things that I have forgotten, and even find me the passage I require. I have taught him a work of Ovid, *In Ibim*, full of little-known stories and fables, and he seems particularly fond of history, which I think is especially useful for a prince. I have also read some beautiful elegies with him. He does not find verses easy, although he knows how to scan them, but he construes orations very easily. Every day I dictate some epistles to him, which he writes correctly—unless he makes an accidental slip—and every day I expound an Epistle of Cicero to him, in order that he may acquire a good style. In the grammar examination he answered my questions more quickly and better than any of the other boys. I have made him run through Petrarch, as good practice in reading, and he himself has chosen to read some books of the *Orlando*, on which he often spends as much as two hours at a time. This is our method of learning letters. As for his conduct in other ways, I see nothing in him which does not lead me to hope for a glorious and honourable career, and although the natural ardour of youth inclines him to love, his conduct in this respect persuades me that he will avoid the licence which is displeasing both to God and men. I earnestly entreat Your Excellency to condescend to help my labours with your exhortations.—Your devoted servant, Jo. Franc. Vigilius.

JUAN LUIS VIVES

He was born in 1492 in Valencia and he died in 1540. He was one of the greatest educationalists in Europe, comparable with Guarino of Ferrara, Vittorino da Feltre, and Roger Ascham in England. He travelled extensively, he was in Paris in 1509, in Bruges in 1512, in Flanders, back to Paris in 1519, in England in 1522. He was an active teacher of the young for many years: he wrote treatises on the education of women, one especially for Mary Tudor, later Mary I. He was the first man in Europe to advocate State provision for the poor, the first to write on psychology. He gave up teaching and took to writing, and among his many publications the most important were his *De Tradendis Disciplinis*, the greatest Renaissance book on education: his *Exercitatio*, the most interesting text-book for the young of his times: and his edition of St. Augustine's *De Civitate Dei*, dedicated to Henry VIII and begun in 1521. His *Dialogues* were the most original and lively method of teaching the Latin language as a language to be *spoken* as well as read and written. The following English versions are taken from Foster Watson's *Tudor School Life*, Dent, 1908.

Source: (*a*) At the Valencian Academy. *T.S.L.*, p. x.

Even the youngest scholars are accustomed never to keep silence; they are always asserting vigorously whatever comes uppermost in their minds, lest they should seem to be giving up

the dispute. Nor does one disputation or even two each day
prove sufficient, as, for instance, at dinner. They wrangle at
breakfast and they wrangle after supper ... At home they dispute,
out of doors they dispute. They wrangle over their food, in the
bath, in the sweating room, in the church, in the town, in the
country, in public, in private; at all times they are wrangling.

Source: (b) Sir Thomas More to Erasmus. T.S.L., p. xii.

Certainly, my dear Erasmus, I am ashamed of myself and my
friends who take credit to ourselves for a few brochures of a quite
insignificant kind, when I see a young man like Vives producing
so many well-digested works, in a good style, giving proof of an
exquisite erudition. How great is his knowledge of Greek and
Latin; greater still is the way in which he is versed in branches of
knowledge of the first rank. Who in this respect is there who
surpasses Vives in the quantity and depth of his knowledge? But
what is most admirable of all is that he should have acquired all
this knowledge so as to be able to communicate it to others by
instruction. For who instructs more clearly, more agreeably, or
more successfully than Vives?

Source: (c) De Tradendis Disciplinis, Bk. III, ch. 3, T.S.L. xlvii.

The scholars should first speak in their homes their mother-
tongue, which is born with them, and the teacher should correct
their mistakes. Then they should, little by little, learn Latin.
Next let them intermingle with the vernacular what they have
heard in Latin from their teacher, or what they themselves have
learned. Thus, at first, their language should be a mixture of the
mother-tongue and Latin. But outside the school they should
speak the mother-tongue, so that they should not become
accustomed to a hotch-potch of languages . . . Gradually the
development advances and the scholars become Latinists in the
narrower sense. Now must they seek to express their thoughts in
Latin, for nothing serves so much to the learning of a language as
continuous practice in it. He who is ashamed to speak a language
has not talent for it. He who refuses to speak Latin after he has
been learning it for a year must be punished according to his age
and circumstances.

Source: (d) Dedication of the School Dialogues. T.S.L., p. xxi.

Vives to Philip, son and heir to the august Emperor Charles, with all good will.

Very great are the uses of the Latin language both for speaking and thinking rightly. For that language is as it were the treasure-house of all erudition, since men of great and outstanding minds have written on every branch of knowledge in the Latin speech. Nor can anyone attain to the knowledge of these subjects except by first learning Latin . . . I have in these Dialogues written a first book of practice in speaking the Latin language as suitable as possible, I trust, to boys . . .

Source: (e) The Rules of the Game: *The School Dialogues, T.S.L.,* p. 208. Over 100 editions testify to the immense popularity of this school text-book.

The first law treats of the time of recreation (*quando ludendum*). Man is constituted for serious affairs, not for frivolity and recreation. But we are to resort to games for the refreshing of our minds from serious pursuits. The time, therefore, for recreation is when the mind or body has become wearied. Nor should otherwise relaxation be taken other than as we take our sleep, food, drink and the other means of renewal and recuperation. Otherwise it is deleterious, as is everything which takes place unseasonably . . . The fourth law is as to stakes. You ought not to play so that the game is zestless and quickly satiates you. So a stake may be justifiable. But it should not be a big one, which may disturb the mind in the very game itself, and if one is beaten, may vex and torture you. That is not a game: it is rather the rack.

AN ENGLISHMAN'S VIEW OF RENAISSANCE ITALY

The Italian view of what constituted the ideal Renaissance character and society has been set out by Baldassare Castiglione in his *Il Cortegiano* (The Courtier), in which he draws a picture of the court of Federigo, Duke of Urbino, and of the discussions which went on there on what qualities the perfect courtier ought to possess. His book does not lend itself to short extracts. It is well to remember that the brilliant Italians of the sixteenth century were not at all acceptable to the English—except to the gay peacocks who visited Italy and returned to England strutting with Italian manners and fashions, as did the Macaronies of the eighteenth century. Roger Ascham (1515–68), tutor to the princess Elizabeth and author of *Toxophilus* and of *The Scholemaster*, held very strong views on both Italianate Englishmen and the Italy which had corrupted them.

Source: Roger Ascham, *The Scholemaster*, English Reprints, ed. by Barber, 1870, p. 77 *et sqq.*, spelling modernized.

I am afraid that overmany of our travellers into Italy do not eschew the way to Circe's court, but go and ride and run and fly thither: they make great haste to come to her: they make great suit to serve her: yea, I could point out some with my finger that never had gone out of England, but only to serve Circe in Italy. Vanity and vice and any licence to ill living in England was counted stale and rude unto them. And so being mules and horses before they went, returned very swine and asses home again: yet everywhere very foxes with as subtle and busy heads, and where they may, very wolves with cruel, malicious hearts ... If you think we judge amiss and write too sore against you, hear what the Italian saith of the Englishman, what the master reporteth of the scholar, who uttereth plainly what is taught by him and what learned by you, saying,

Inglese Italianato e un diabolo incarnato.

... And now choose you, you Italian Englishmen, whether you will be angry with us for calling you monsters, or with the Italians for calling you devils, or else with your own selves, that take so much pains and go so far to make yourselves both ...

I was once in Italy myself, but I thank God my abode there was but six days; yet I saw in that little time, in one city, more liberty to sin than ever I heard tell of in our noble city of London in six years. I saw it there as free to sin, not only without all punishment, but also without any man's marking, as it is free in the City of London to choose without all blame whether a man lust to wear Shoe or Pantocle ...

NOTES

[1] And my sin is ever before me', where *contra* could be rendered as either 'before' or 'against'; the ambiguity is resolved by referring to the Greek, where ἐνώπιον = face to face.

[2] Juvenal iii, 78, *Graeculus esuriens.*

[3] Published by Aldus, 1513.

[4] Erasmus was a Dutchman by birth: this remark shows his connection with the Northern Renaissance, although of course Italy was famous for its medical schools, especially at Padua.

[5] Published by Aldus, 1528.

[6] Published by Aldus, 1518.

[7] *Euripidis . . . Hecuba et Iphigenia . . .* Paris, J. Badius Sept. 1506. Reprinted by Aldus at Venice, December, 1507 (and by Froben at Basle in 1518 and 1524).

[8] *c.* 1495–1541. Professor of Greek at Basle, 1529. He found the MS. containing Livy, Bks. 41–5 in 1527.

[9] Not 'illuminated'.

[10] The MS., now lost, containing Bks. 33, 17–49 and 40, 37–59, found in the cathedral library at Mainz, published in Mainz, J. Schoeffer, November 1518.

[11] The Italian word is *anima*, in English literally *soul*—a technical expression signifying the block, somewhat smaller than the mould, which bronze-founders insert in order to obtain a hollow, and not a solid cast from the mould which gives form to their liquid metal.

[12] Later became a cutlass.

[13] Torrigiano worked for Henry VII and his monument to that King and others of his family still exists in Westminster Abbey. He also made a fine bust of John Colet, Dean of St. Paul's, now at St. Paul's school in London.

[14] Henry VII.

[15] The Sistine Chapel in Rome.

[16] See Michelangelo (*c*), p. 19.

[17] J. A. Symonds doubts the truth of this story. See his *Life of Michelangelo*, i, 164.

[18] The man who gave his name to America.

[19] Now in the Louvre.

[20] A wittier version than that of Machiavelli's in the following quotation.

[21] He was in fact sixty.

[22] Stick-throwing, a sport introduced by the Moors into Spain and by the Spaniards into Italy.

[23] An interesting sidelight for us who visit Italy in the summer and find the marble in their cathedrals so cool and beautiful.

[24] See under Lorenzo il Magnifico, p. 31.

[25] *Il Morgante maggiore* was a heroic poem by Luigi Pulci, well known, but now little read. The subject was treated jestingly, and its style pleased Lorenzo de' Medici and his companions; the most sacred things were scoffed at, under a veil of delicate irony.

[26] In distinction from the worship *latria* to God.

THE PAPACY

Its Characteristics

The principal characteristics of the Papacy during the sixteenth century were (1) the corruption of the conclaves which elected the new Pope. By canon law any election tainted with simony was to be null and void. By that law not a single Pope from Sixtus IV (1471) to Paul IV (1555) had any right to the throne of St. Peter. (2) The nepotism of the Popes. Nearly all the Popes had children and (though in some cases before ordination) often seemed more concerned with promoting the interests of their families than those of the church. This was accomplished by marrying the children into noble and powerful families, and providing them with well-defended possessions which would form protection to the Papal states against Venice, Naples and Milan. (3) The general acceptance of this state of affairs by everybody. No one thought it wrong for the Pope to favour his own family.

Source: (a) Letter from Lorenzo Il Magnifico to Pope Innocent VIII, 1489.

Others have not waited so long as Your Holiness to play the Pope: they wasted no time on nice points of honesty. Your Holiness is not only free before God and man to act as you will, but your very restraint may be misinterpreted and used against you. Devotion and duty combine to compel me to warn Your Holiness that as man is immortal and a Pope is only what he makes himself, his personal dignity can not be bequeathed: his only patrimony is the honours and gifts he can bestow in his lifetime.

Source: (b) A letter from Pope Pius II to Rodrigo Borgia, aged 29, later Pope Alexander VI, from the baths at Petriolo, June 11th, 1460. Quoted in Gregorovius, *Lucrezia Borgia*, Phaidon edition, 1948, p. 4.

Dear Son: We have learned that your Worthiness, forgetful of the high office with which you are invested, was present from the seventeenth to the twenty-second hour, four days ago, in the gardens of Giovanni de Bichis, where there were several women of Siena, women wholly given over to worldly vanities. Your companion was one of your colleagues whom his years, if not the dignity of his office, ought to have reminded of his duty. We have heard that the dance was indulged in in all wantonness; none of the allurements of love was lacking, and you conducted yourself in a wholly worldly manner. Shame forbids mention of all that took place, for not only the things themselves, but their very names are unworthy of your rank. In order that your lust might be all the more unrestrained, the husbands, fathers, brothers and kinsmen of the young women and girls were not invited to be present. You and a few servants were the leaders and inspirers of this orgy. It is said that nothing is now talked of in Siena but your vanity, which is the subject of universal ridicule. Certain it is that here at the baths, where churchmen and laity are very numerous, your name is on every one's tongue. Our displeasure is beyond words, for your conduct has brought the holy state and office into disgrace; the people will say they make us rich and great, not that we may live a blameless life, but that we may have means to gratify our passions. This is the reason the princes and the powers despise us and the laity mock us; this is why our own mode of living is thrown in our face when we reprove others. Contempt is the lot of Christ's vicar because he seems to tolerate these actions. You, dear son, have charge of the bishopric of Valencia, the most important in Spain; you are a chancellor of the Church, and what renders your conduct all the more reprehensible is the fact that you have a seat among the cardinals, with the Pope, as advisor of the Holy See. We leave it to you whether it is becoming to your dignity to court young women, and to send those whom you love fruits and wine, and during the whole day to give no thought to anything but sensual pleasures. People blame us on your account, and the memory of your blessed uncle, Calixtus, likewise suffers, and many say he did wrong in heaping honours on you. If you try to excuse yourself on the ground of your youth, I say to you: you are no longer so young as not to see what duties your offices impose upon you. A cardinal should be above reproach and an example of right living before the eyes of all men, and then we should have just

grounds for anger when temporal princes bestow uncompli-
mentary epithets upon us, when they dispute with us the possession
of our property and force us to submit ourselves to their will. Of
a truth we inflict these wounds upon ourselves, and we ourselves
are the cause of these troubles, since we by our conduct are daily
diminishing the authority of the Church. Our punishment for
it in this world is dishonour, and in the world to come well-
deserved torment. May, therefore, your good sense place a
restraint on these frivolities, and may you never lose sight of your
dignity; then people will not call you a vain gallant among men.
If this occurs again We shall be compelled to show that it was
contrary to Our exhortation and that it caused us great pain; and
Our censure will not pass over you without causing you to blush.
We have always loved you and thought you worthy of Our
protection as a man of earnest and modest character. Therefore,
conduct yourself henceforth so that We may retain this Our
opinion of you, and may behold in you only the example of a
well-ordered life. Your years, which are not such as to preclude
improvement, permit us to admonish you paternally.

SOME RENAISSANCE POPES

POPE PIUS II

Aeneas Sylvius Piccolomini (1405–64) became Pope in 1458 under the
title of Pius II; no doubt his choice had some reference to the classical
hero, Pius Aeneas. Aeneas Sylvius was the eldest of eighteen children
and he began life on his father's farm, but at the age of 18 he was
financially helped to go to Siena as a poor student. He proved himself
to be highly intelligent, witty, devoted to humanistic studies, and also
to sensual pleasures. He moved on to Florence, where he fell under
the spell of Filelfo's teaching. His rise was rapid and highly successful,
and he travelled widely, even to England and Scotland. He became
papal secretary to Pope Felix V, and in 1442 he met Frederick III of
Germany, who made him poet laureate and his private secretary. In
the first office he proved himself capable of writing witty and immoral
poems and plays, and novels after the style of Boccaccio. As secretary
he developed great skill as a diplomatist, and his attractive personality
played a great part in his success. In 1447 he became bishop of Siena,

and on the death of Calixtus III he was elected Pope (1458) after a particularly severe struggle in the papal conclave. The following extract describing that conclave is an unrivalled piece of reporting. Aeneas Sylvius cannot be looked upon as a very spiritual Pope, but if he was as ambitious to become Pope as was the Cardinal of Rouen, if his literary productions were definitely 'Renaissance', and if he harboured as much hatred against Sigismondo Malatesta as the Malatesta harboured against him, it may still be said that Pius II recognized the evil in Malatesta, that he fought to be elected Pope by decent arguments, and that he did have at least a conventional standard of religion. It might also be possible to show that he brought considerable wisdom to the solution of the political problems with which as Pope he was confronted. Judged against the background of his times, Pius II does not come out too badly, and his reign was dominated by his zeal for promoting a Crusade against the Turks. He was also well aware of his responsibilities as the spiritual head of Christendom.

Source: The Commentaries of Pope Pius II, Eng. trans. by F. A. Gragg, an abridgement, Capricorn Paperbacks, 1962, pp. 79 et sqq.

Ten days after Calixtus's death the other eighteen cardinals entered the conclave, while the whole city waited in suspense for the outcome; though indeed it was common talk that Aeneas, Cardinal of Siena, would be pope, since no one was held in higher esteem.

The conclave was held in the apostolic palace at St. Peter's, where two halls and two chapels were set apart for it. In the larger chapel were constructed cells in which the cardinals might eat and sleep; the smaller, called the chapel of San Niccolò, was reserved for discussion and the election of the pope. The halls were places where all might walk about freely.

On the day of their entrance nothing was done about the election. On the next day certain capitulations were announced, which they agreed should be observed by the new pope, and each swore that he would abide by them, should the lot fall on him. On the third day after Mass, when they came to the scrutiny, it was found that Filippo, Cardinal of Bologna, and Aeneas, Cardinal of Siena, had an equal number of votes, five apiece. No one else had more than three. On that ballot, whether from strategy or dislike, no one voted for Guillaume, Cardinal of Rouen.

The cardinals were accustomed, after the result of the scrutiny was announced, to sit and talk together in case any wished to change his mind and transfer the vote he had given to another (a method called 'by accession'), for in this way they more easily reach an agreement. This procedure was omitted after the first scrutiny owing to the opposition of those who had received no votes and therefore could not now be candidates for accession. They adjourned for luncheon and then there were many private conferences. The richer and more influential members of the college summoned the rest and sought to gain the papacy for themselves or their friends. They begged, promised, threatened, and some, shamelessly casting aside all decency, pleaded their own causes and claimed the papacy as their right. Among these were Guillaume, Cardinal of Rouen, Pietro, Cardinal of San Marco, and Giovanni, Cardinal of Pavia; nor did the Cardinal of Lerida neglect his own interests. Each had a great deal to say for himself. Their rivalry was extraordinary, their energy unbounded. They took no rest by day or sleep by night.

Rouen, however, did not fear these men so much as he did Aeneas and the Cardinal of Bologna, toward whom he saw the majority of the votes inclining. But he was especially afraid of Aeneas, whose silence he had no doubt would prove far more effective than the barkings of the rest. Therefore he would summon now some, now others, and upbraid them as follows: 'What is Aeneas to you? Why do you think him worthy of the papacy? Will you give us a lame, poverty-stricken pope? How shall a destitute pope restore a destitute church? Or an ailing pope an ailing church? He has but recently come from Germany. We do not know him. Perhaps he will even transfer the Curia thither. And look at his writings. Shall we set a poet in Peter's seat? Shall we govern the Church by the laws of the heathen? Or do you think Filippo of Bologna is to be preferred? A stiff-necked fellow, who has not the wit to rule himself, and will not listen to those who show him the right course. I am the senior cardinal. You know I am not without wisdom. I am learned in pontifical law and can boast of royal blood. I am rich in friends and resources with which I can succour the impoverished Church.

I hold also not a few ecclesiastical benefices, which I shall distribute among you and the others, when I resign them' . . .

Many cardinals met in the privies as being a secluded and retired place. Here they agreed as to how they might elect Guillaume pope and they bound themselves by written pledges and by oath. Guillaume trusted them and was presently promising benefices and preferment and dividing provinces among them. A fit place for such a pope to be elected! For where could one more appropriately enter into a foul covenant than in the privies? . . . It now appeared that eleven were agreed, and they did not doubt that they would at once get the twelfth. For when it has come to this point, some one is always at hand to say, 'I too make you pope', to win the favour that utterance always brings. They thought therefore that the thing was as good as done and were only waiting for daylight to go to the scrutiny.

Aeneas was approached by Rouen, but refused to vote for him. He then went to the Vice-Chancellor and won him over from Rouen's side. Meeting the Cardinal of Pavia he spoke to him forthrightly about the character of Rouen, so that Pavia withdrew his support for Rouen. The Cardinal of San Marco was also persuaded not to vote for a French pope, and he told the Italian cardinals to vote for an Italian and said if they listened to him they would prefer Aeneas to all others.

All approved these words except Aeneas, who did not think himself worthy of so exalted an office.

The next day they went as usual to Mass and then began the scrutiny. A golden chalice was placed on the altar and three cardinals . . . were set to watch it and see that there should be no cheating. The other cardinals took their seats and then, rising in order of rank and age, each approached the altar and deposited in the chalice a ballot on which was written the name of his choice for pope. When Aeneas came up to put in his ballot, Rouen, pale and trembling, said, 'Look, Aeneas, I commend myself to you'—certainly a rash thing to say when it was not allowable to change what he had written. But ambition overcame prudence. Aeneas said, 'Do you commend yourself to a worm like me?' and without another word dropped his ballot in the cup and went back to his place.

When all had voted, a table was placed in the middle of the room and the three cardinals mentioned above turned out upon it the cupful of votes. Then they read aloud the ballots one after another and noted down the names written on them. And there was not a single cardinal who did not likewise make notes of those named, that there might be no possibility of trickery. This proved to be to Aeneas's advantage, for when the votes were counted and the teller, Rouen, announced that Aeneas had eight though the rest said nothing about another man's loss, Aeneas did not allow himself to be defrauded. 'Look more carefully at the ballots', he said to the teller, 'for I have nine votes'. The others agreed with him. Rouen said nothing, as if he had merely made a mistake . . .

When the result of the scrutiny was made known, it was found that nine cardinals . . . had voted for Aeneas; the Cardinal of Rouen had only six votes, and the rest were far behind. Rouen was petrified when he saw himself so far outstripped by Aeneas and all the rest were amazed, for never within the memory of man had anyone polled as many as nine votes by scrutiny. Since no one had received enough votes for election, they decided to resume their seats and try the method that is called 'by accession', to see if perhaps it might be possible to elect a pope that day. And here again Rouen indulged in empty hopes. All sat pale and silent in their places as if entranced. For some time no one spoke, no one opened his lips, no one moved any part of his body except the eyes, which kept glancing all about. It was a strange silence and a strange sight, men sitting there like their own statues, no sound to be heard, no movement to be seen. They remained thus for some moments, those inferior in rank waiting for their supporters to begin.

Then Rodrigo, the Vice-Chancellor, rose and said, 'I accede vote to the Cardinal of Siena', an utterance which was like a dagger in Rouen's heart, so pale did he turn. A silence followed and each man, looking at his neighbour, began to indicate his sentiments by gestures. By this time it looked as if Aeneas would be pope, and some, fearing this result, left the conclave, pretending physical needs, but really with the purpose of escaping the fate of that day. Those who thus withdrew were the Cardinals of Rouen and San Sisto. However, as no one followed them, they soon returned. Then Jacopo, Cardinal of Sant' Anastasia, said, 'I accede to the Cardinal of Siena'. At this all appeared even more stunned, like people in a house shaken by an unprecedented earthquake, and lost the power of speech.

Aeneas now lacked but one vote, for twelve would elect a pope. Realizing this, Cardinal Prospero Colonna thought that he must get for himself the glory of announcing the pope. He rose and was about to pronounce his vote with the customary dignity, when he was seized by the Cardinals of Nicaea and Rouen and sharply rebuked for wishing to accede to Aeneas. When he insisted in his intention, they tried to get him out of the room by force, resorting even to such means to snatch the papacy from Aeneas. But Prospero, who, though he had voted for the Cardinal of Rouen on his ballot, was nevertheless bound to Aeneas by ties of old friendship, paid no attention to their abuse and empty threats. Turning to the other cardinals, he said, 'I too accede to the Cardinal of Siena and I make him pope'. When they heard this, the courage of the opposition failed and all their machinattions were shattered. All the cardinals immediately fell at Aeneas's feet and saluted him as Pope.

POPE SIXTUS IV

Pope Sixtus IV was Francesco della Rovere. He was born of poor family at Savona in 1414. He became a Franciscan at an early age and rose to be General of the Order in 1464. In 1467 he was unexpectedly created a Cardinal by Paul II, on whose death Rovere became Pope, taking the title of Sixtus IV (1471). He was a strong nepotist: he had a hand in the Pazzi conspiracy in 1478 against Lorenzo de' Medici. He spent money lavishly on buildings and all forms of art: he instituted the Sistine choir, paid pensions to men of learning and was the second founder of the Vatican library. All this cost huge sums of money which he raised by increasing taxation and by the sale of offices, dispensations and indulgences. He died in 1484.

Source: Machiavelli, *Storia Fiorentina,* Bk. vii, ch. 4. *The Writings of Machiavelli,* Detmold, 1882, 1, 348.

Death also carried off Pope Paul II, and his successor was Sixtus IV, who had previously borne the name of Francesco da Savona, a man of the lowest origin, but who by his talents had become General of the Order of St. Francis, and afterwards Cardinal. This pontiff was the first to show the extent of the papal powers and how much of what were afterwards called errors could be concealed under the pontifical authority. Amongst his family were Piero and Girolamo, who were generally believed to be his sons, though he concealed the fact by calling them by names less compromising to his character. Piero, who was a brother of a religious order, was raised by him to the dignity of Cardinal, with the title of San Sisto. To Girolamo he gave the town of Furli, which he had taken from Antonio Ordelaffi, whose ancestors had for a long time been princes of that state. This ambitious mode of procedure made Sixtus the more influential with the princes of Italy, who all sought to gain his friendship.

POPE ALEXANDER VI

Rodrigo Borgia was the son of Isabella Borgia, niece of Pope Callixtus III by her marriage with Joffrè Lenzuoli. He took the name of Borgia when he went to Rome to be made a Cardinal. On the death of Innocent VIII Rodrigo, having bribed the cardinals at the Papal Election, was elected Pope and took the name of Alexander VI. His reign has become legendary for the vices and scandals which have been—many of them, though perhaps not the worst, rightly—attributed to him. He represents more brilliantly than any other Pope the Papacy as a secular power. His task was to reduce the overmighty subjects and to bring order out of chaos in the Papal States. He worked through his son, Cesare Borgia, who with the French troops supplied by Louis XII accomplished the task Alexander had set him. The Pope died in 1503. He remains one of the most disputed characters in history.

On the death of Pope Innocent VIII, Rodrigo Borgia was elected Pope (1492).

Source: (*a*) Guicciardini, *Storia d'Italia,* Eng. ed. A. P. Goddard, vol. v, p. 12.

To Innocent [VIII] succeeded Rodrigo Borgia of Valenza, a royal city in Spain. He was an ancient cardinal and made the best figure in Rome. His election was owing partly to the disputes that arose between the two cardinals, heads of factions, Ascanio Sforza and Giuliano of S. Pietro in Vincula, but chiefly to a simony unheard of in those days. For Borgia openly corrupted many of the cardinals, some with money, others with promises of profitable places and benefices, of which he had many at that time in his power; and they, without any regard to the precepts of the Gospel, were not ashamed of making a traffic of the sacred treasures, under the name of Divine Authority, and that in the most high and eminent seat of the Christian religion.

Cardinal Ascanio had the principal hand in this detestable work, and was employed as agent for such abominable contracts. He influenced several with hopes of preferment and also by his bad example; for his heart being corrupted by an immoderate thirst for riches, he bargained for the price of his iniquity to have the Vice-Chancellorship (the most profitable post in the Pope's disposal), the revenues of divers churches and castles, and even the Pope's own family place, with all its magnificent furniture of an immense value. But divine justice overtook him, for he became an object of scorn and hatred to all mankind, who were filled with horror at an election procured by such black and enormous artifices—especially as Borgia's impious life was everywhere notorious. The King of Naples, on hearing the news, dissembled his grief in public, but with tears (which he was not accustomed to shed at the death of his children) told his Queen that this creation would prove fatal to Italy and a scandal to Christendom— a foresight worthy of the prudence of Ferdinand.

Source: (*b*) The Cardinal of Viterbo, a contemporary of Alexander VI.

He was gifted with the most penetrating intelligence; he was clever, industrious and eloquent. He was unequalled in the dexterity of his actions, in persuasiveness, in his obstinate power of resistance. He was so great a man that he would have been a great prince, in thought, word and deed, had his natural gifts been allowed to develop and not been overlaid with so many vices. There seemed, to a witness of his speech and action, that there was nothing lacking to make him ruler of a world; he was ever ready to give up his sleep, yet was greedy for pleasure. His pursuit of it, however, never prevented him from assuming the burdens of his office, such as giving audience and appearing and speaking whenever his position made it necessary. And yet, in spite of all his qualities, his reign cannot be called auspicious. All was dark as night. We need not speak of his domestic tragedies and their background of incest and crime: but never, in the lands of the Church, were seditions more threatening, robberies more frequent, murders more cruel, the peace of the public highways more brutally disturbed, or the way of travellers more dangerous. Never was Rome in a more unhappy state. Never were seen more informers, never was the insolence of the police more unbridled, never were robbers more numerous or more daring. None dared to pass beyond the city gates, yet how could one remain in the city? It was *lése-majesté* or treason to possess gold or precious goods. A man had no security in his own house, in his own room, even in his own stronghold.

Source: (c) Ieronimo Porzio, *Commentarius*, 1493: Gregorovius, *op. cit.*, p. 5.

Alexander is tall and neither light nor dark: his eyes are black and his lips somewhat full. His health is robust and he is able to bear any pain or fatigue; he is wonderfully eloquent and a man of perfect urbanity.

Source: (d) Jason Mainus of Milan: Gregorovius, *op. cit.*, p. 5.

His elegance of figure, his serene brow, his kingly forehead, his countenance with its expression of generosity and majesty, his genius, and the heroic beauty of his whole presence.

Source: (e) Michele Ferno, a pupil of the humanist Pomponio Leto.

His Holiness rides a snow-white horse. His brow is full of brightness, his dignity strikes like lightning; the crowd acclaims him as he blesses it. His presence makes men glad and is taken as a good omen. What dignity is there in his gestures, what magnanimity in his gaze! How greatly does his imperial stature, his proud though benevolent air add to the veneration he inspires!

Source: (*f*): his teacher, Gaspare da Verona.

He is handsome—always smiling and gay: his conversation is amusing and witty. He has an amazing gift for attracting the affections of women, who are drawn to him as by a magnet.

Source: (*g*) Death of Alexander VI. Guicciardini, *Storia Fiorentina*, cap. 27.

So died Pope Alexander, at the height of glory and prosperity; about whom it must be known that he was a man of the utmost power and of great judgement and spirit, as his actions and behaviour showed. But as his first accession to the Papacy was foul and shameful, seeing he had bought with gold so high a station, in like manner his government disagreed not with this base foundation. There were in him, and in full measure, all vices both of flesh and spirit; nor could there be imagined in the ordering of the Church a rule so bad but that he put it into practice. He was most sensual towards both sexes, keeping publicly women and boys, but more especially toward women; and so far did he exceed all measure that public opinion judged he knew Madonna Lucrezia, his own daughter, toward whom he bore a most tender and boundless love. He was exceedingly avaricious, not in keeping what he had acquired, but in getting new wealth: and where he saw a way toward drawing money, he had no respect whatever; in his days were sold at auction all benefices, dispensations, pardons, bishoprics, cardinalships, and all court dignities: unto which matters he had appointed two or three men privy to his thought, exceeding prudent, who let them out to the highest bidder.

He caused the death by poison of many cardinals and prelates, even among his intimates, those namely whom he noted to be rich in benefices and understood to have hoarded much, with the view of seizing on their wealth. His cruelty was great, seeing that by his direction many were put to violent death: nor was the ingratitude less with which he caused the ruin of the Sforzeschi and Colonnesi, by whose favour he acquired the Papacy. There was in him no religion, no keeping of his troth: he promised things liberally, but stood to nought but what was useful to himself: no care for justice, since in his days Rome was like a den of thieves and murderers: his ambition was boundless, and such that it grew in the same measure as his state increased: nevertheless, his sins meeting with no due punishment in this world, he was to the last of his days prosperous.

\ While young and still almost a boy, having Calixtus for his uncle, he was made Cardinal and then Vice-Chancellor: in which high place he continued until his papacy, with great revenue, good fame and peace. Having become Pope, he made Cesare, his bastard son and bishop of Pampeluna, a Cardinal, against the ordinances and decrees of the Church, which forbid the making of a bastard Cardinal, even with the Pope's dispensation, wherefore he brought proof by false witnesses that he was born in wedlock. / Afterwards he made him a layman and took away the Cardinal's dignity from him, and turned his mind to making a realm; wherein he fared far better than he purposed, and beginning with Rome, after undoing the Orsini, Colonnesi, Savelli, and those barons who were wont to be held in fear by former Popes, he was more full master of Rome than ever had been any Pope before. With greatest ease he got the lordships of Romagna, the March and the Duchy; and having made a most fair and powerful state, the Florentines held him in much fear, the Venetians in jealousy, and the King of France in esteem. Then, having got together a fine army, he showed how great was the might of a Pontiff when he hath a valiant general and one in whom he can place faith. At last he grew to that point that he was counted the balance in the war of France and Spain. In one word, he was more evil and more lucky than ever for many ages peradventure had been any pope before.

Source: (h) Letter from Francesco Gonzaga, Marquis of Mantua, to his wife, Isabella d'Este. December 22nd, 1503.

Most illustrious and beloved Wife,

In order that you may hear the latest details which have reached us of the Pope's death, we write to inform you how, in his last illness, he began to speak and act in a way which made those about him think that he was wandering, although he retained perfect possession of his faculties. His words were: 'I will come, you are right, only wait a little longer'; and those who were in his secrets afterwards revealed that in the conclave held after the death of Innocent VIII he had made a compact with the devil and had bought the papal tiara at the price of his soul. One article of the compact was that he should sit in the papal chair for twelve years, which he actually did, as well as four more days. There are others who say that seven devils were in the room at the moment when he gave up the ghost. And when he was dead, his blood began to boil, and his mouth foamed as if he were a burning cauldron, and this lasted as long as he was above ground. His corpse swelled to such a size that it lost the very shape of the human body, and there was no difference between its breadth and length. He was carried to the grave with little honour, his body being dragged from the bed to the sepulchre by a porter, who fastened a cord to his feet, because no one would touch him, and his funeral was so miserable that the wife of the lame dwarf at Mantua had a more honourable burial. Every day scandalous inscriptions are written up over his grave . . .

PIUS III

In August 1503 Pope Alexander VI died. When the election of a new Pope began, it was 'covered' (as we should say to-day) very closely by Giustinian, the Venetian representative at Rome.

Source: (a) Giustinian, *Dispacci*, vol. ii, pp. 175–7.

The representative of the King of France has received an autograph instruction from his master to exhort all the Cardinals to consult his pleasure and make the Cardinal of Rouen Pope. Every possible blandishment, promise and inducement is employed, together with implied threats against those who may ignore the request. The message has been communicated to each Cardinal individually, and all of them are in such a state of alarm that they scarcely know whether they are on their heads or their heels. The Cardinal of Naples has spoken to me in the gravest terms about the harm which would befall the Church of God, if

the King's hope should be realized . . . and the Cardinal Adrian
has assured me that he would rather die than suffer such a thing
to come about, because he has not been the Pope's secretary for
all these years without finding out what sort of people the French
really are. The Cardinals mean to hurry on the election without
waiting for the French Cardinals to come and disturb the Conclave, but I fear lest the French ambassadors should compel them
to wait by threatening to call in their own and Cesare's troops,
whom the poor Cardinals would be powerless to resist. Venice
ought to make it plain that a canonically elected Pope will have
the protection of the Powers . . .

Before going to the funeral of the Pope to-day, I called upon
Cardinal della Rovere, who reached Rome yesterday. He is
angry with the King of France, for he says that in days gone by
the King promised to further his election, and ought not now to
favour another candidate. 'I am here', he added, 'to look after
my own interests, and not those of any one else, and I do not
mean to give my vote to the Cardinal of Rouen, unless I find
that he has so many votes that he can secure his election without
having mine; and this, I fancy, will not happen'. He wanted he
said, to be a good Italian, and, if he could not secure his own
election, to bring about the promotion of one who would be of
service to the Christian religion and to the peace and tranquility
of Italy.

Neither the Cardinal of Rouen nor Cardinal della Rovere was
able to collect enough votes to ensure his election. A compromise was
arrived at and both candidates retired in favour of Francesco Piccolomini, Cardinal of Siena, a very old man who would conveniently act
as a stop-gap. He took the title of Pius III. The election took place on
September 22nd, 1503: on that day Giustinian wrote to the Venetian
Senate.

Source: (b) Giustinian, op. cit., pp. 200–1.

Experience of the new Pope's career induces the hope that his
Pontificate will be the exact opposite of the last. He was elected
unanimously, though at the beginning he was not even considered. The pretensions of the Cardinal of Rouen were defeated
by the machinations of della Rovere, and his by those of Ascanio.

... When the Cardinal of Rouen saw that he could not succeed, he thought that, if he could not be Pope himself, he had better at all events avoid the ignominy of seeing some one elected of whom he disapproved. So, like a wise man, he went with the stream and sought the prestige of getting it to appear that the Pope was of his making. He is greatly incensed against Ascanio, for he can see that he has been taken in by him, and I think that he must regret having left France and brought Ascanio with him.

POPE JULIUS II

Giuliano della Rovere was born at Savona in 1443. He was a nephew of Pope Sixtus IV, who provided him with many preferments in the Church, the last of which was the Cardinal-bishopric of Ostia and Velletri. As legate to France he acquired a paramount influence in the college of Cardinals during the pontificate of Innocent VIII. His great rival was Roderigo Borgia, and when the latter became Pope Alexander VI, Giuliano retired to Ostia. But 1494 he was in France and it was largely he who persuaded King Charles VIII to embark on the invasion of Italy. He accompanied the King to Naples. When Alexander died in 1503, Giuliano went to Rome fully expecting to be elected Pope. He failed, but Pius III died very soon and Giuliano was elected Pope and took the title of Julius II, 1503. While he proved to be an extremely shrewd and political ruler, it is fair to add that he carried out some excellent reforms, his rule of the Papal States was on the whole excellent, he was a great patron of the arts and he laid the foundation stone of the new St. Peter's. But it cannot be said that he was in the least degree a spiritual Pope.

Source: (a) Giustinian, *Dispacci*, pp. 253–5.

All the Cardinals are busied in intrigues and some show small respect for God or their sacred office; bargains are made openly, for it seems nowadays that a refusal to bargain is regarded as unbecoming; nor do men deal in small sums, but in thousands and tens of thousands, to the shame of our religion and the dishonour of the Almighty, since now there is nothing to choose between the Papacy and the Sultanate—each is knocked down to the highest bidder. Rome is quiet, though there are many Orsini soldiers here in the Spanish service, and also some men of Baglione's, who are in the French interest. However, the Orsini

H

are now at peace with the Colonnesi and get on all right with Baglione's men ... There are three likely candidates. The Cardinal of Naples will not get many votes, however, because he is suspected of French sympathies; the Cardinal of San Giorgio is objected to on account of his age; and so the chances are in favour of della Rovere. No one talks of Ascanio or of Cardinal Colonna; nor is there any mention of the Cardinal of Rouen, [d'Amboise]; yet they are afraid of him and he is in every one's mind.

Source: (b) Guicciardini, Storia d'Italia, Eng. ed. A. P. Goddard, vol. 3, p. 251 et sqq.

[After the death of Pius III] the cardinals for some days delayed entering the Conclave, because they were willing that Rome should be first cleared of the Orsini, who remained there completing their levies, but in the meantime they agreed on their choice without doors. For the Cardinal of S. Piero in Vincula, who excelled in friends, riches and reputation, had engrossed the votes of such a number of the cardinals that those who were of a contrary party found no room for opposition. Wherefore, entering the Conclave Pope already pre-elected and established, he was, the last night in October, without shutting the Conclave, exalted to the Pontificate. An instance without precedent in the memory of man.

It was certainly a matter of great surprise to all the world that there should be so great an unanimity in electing a cardinal who was universally known to be of a very untractable temper and dreaded by everybody, and who was always of a very restless disposition and had spent his time in continual bustles and contentions, whence he must of necessity have offended multitudes and drawn upon himself the hatred and enmity of many great personages. But on the other hand there were manifest reasons for his surmounting all difficulties in making his way to the Popedom, for he had been a cardinal of long-standing, of great power and influence, and by his magnificence, in which he surpassed all others, and by his unparalleled greatness of soul, had not only acquired a great number of friends, but an inveterate and established authority in the Court of Rome, and had obtained the

name of being the principal defender of the ecclesiastical dignity
and immunities. But what more effectually pleaded in his favour
and contributed to his promotion was the immoderate and unbounded promises which he made to the cardinals, princes, barons,
and to every one that could be of service to him in his election,
of whatever they pleased to demand. He had it also in his power
to distribute sums of money and to dispose of a multitude of
benefices and ecclesiastical dignities, both of his own and of others.
For such was the fame of his magnificence as to attract multitudes
who came voluntarily to offer him the use and free disposal of
their purse, their name, their places and their benefices, without
considering that his own promises were much greater than, when
he should afterwards be a Pope, it lay in his power or was consis-
tent with his duty to perform. He had long borne the character
of a frank and open-hearted person and a speaker of the truth: even
Alexander VI, his bitter enemy, who was not wanting in exposing
his faults, would yet confess that he was a man of veracity. But
as Vincula was sensible that no man has it more in his power to
deceive others than one who is not used to and is never thought
to deceive, so, for the sake of obtaining the Pontificate, he did
not scruple to sully this amiable character.

Source: (c) Guicciardini, *Storia d'Italia*, Eng. ed. A. P. Goddard,
vol. 6, p. 111.

He was a prince of inestimable courage and constancy, but
impetuous and boundless in his conceptions, which would have
carried him headlong to his own ruin, had he not been sustained
more by the reverence of the Church, the discord of princes and
the condition of the times than by his own moderation or prudence. He would certainly have been worthy of the highest
honour, had he been a secular prince, or employed the same ardour
and vigilance with which he prosecuted the advancement of the
Church in temporal greatness by the force of arms, in promoting
her progress towards purity and spiritual perfection, by the milder
arts of peace. His memory, however, is most dear and honoured
above that of all his predecessors, especially by those who, having
lost the true names of things and confounded the distinction that

arises from weighing them in a just balance, think it more the
duty of the Pontiffs to increase the empire of the Apostolic See
by arms and the blood of Christians, than to strive and labour
by the example of a good life and by correcting and healing a
degeneracy and corruption of manners to promote the salvation
of those souls for whose benefit they boast that Christ had
constituted them His vicars upon earth.

Source: (*d*) In 1511 Julius II made the Holy League against France—
the Papacy, Venice, Ferdinand of Spain, Henry VIII, Emperor Maximilian I. The generals of the Papal army were two cardinals, with the
Pope as commander-in-chief:

Guicciardini, *Storia d'Italia*, Eng. ed. A. P. Goddard, vol. 5, pp. 146
et sqq.

On the second of January the Pope set out from Bologna,
attended by three cardinals, and arriving in the camp took up his
quarters in the house of a peasant, exposed to the fire of the
enemy's artillery, being not above two ordinary bow-shots from
the walls of Mirandola. In this station he was continually fatiguing
himself, and exercising his body no less than his mind and
authority, almost perpetually on horseback, riding now here and
now there about the lines, and pushing forward the completion
of the batteries which, as well as the other military operations,
had been hitherto greatly retarded by the extreme rigour of the
season and by the snows that fell almost without intermission,
as well as by the desertion of the pioneers, which no care was able
to prevent, for besides their sufferings from the severity of the
weather, they were greatly annoyed by the cannon of the place.
It was therefore necessary to cast up new works for covering the
men employed on the batteries and to procure a fresh recruit of
pioneers. While these preparations were making, Julius, finding
the inconveniences of the camp at that season, retired to Concordia . . .

The Pope stayed but a few days at Concordia and hurried back
to the army with the same impatience and with an ardour not to
be cooled by the heavy snow which fell all the way, nor the
severe frost, hardly supportable by the soldiery. He now took
his lodging in a little church near his artillery and nearer the walls

of the town than his first quarters were. And as he was dissatisfied with all that had been done or was now doing, he broke out into the most vehement complaints against his officers, except Marc' Antonio Colonna, whom he had newly ordered thither from Modena. In the same violent manner he hurried himself amongst the troops, now crying out on some for not doing their duty, then animating and encouraging others, and in short performing both in words and deeds the office of a general . . .

It was certainly a remarkable case, and a sight very uncommon in the eye of the world . . . to behold the High Priest, the Vicar of Christ on earth, old and infirm, and educated in ease and pleasures, now employed in person in managing a war excited by himself against Christians; and at the siege of a paltry town exposing himself to all the fatigues and dangers of a commander of armies, and retaining nothing of the Pontiff but the name and the habit.

POPE LEO X

Giovanni de' Medici was born in 1475 and died in 1521. He was the second son of Lorenzo Il Magnifico, nephew of that Giuliano who was murdered in Florence cathedral during the Pazzi conspiracy. At the age of 17 he became a cardinal and he was elected Pope in 1513. He was ordained to the priesthood and consecrated bishop after election. He took the title of Leo X. His reign was marked by the usual nepotism, by an attempt to raise a crusade against the Turkish invasion of Europe, and by the Lutheran Reformation. It was to this Pope that Henry VIII sent his book on the Seven Sacraments *contra Lutherum*, in return for which Leo conferred on Henry the title of *Fidei Defensor*. Foreign policy and preoccupation with both papal and family aggrandisement much interfered with his attitude towards Luther, not to mention his necessity for raising money with which to rebuild St. Peter's, Rome. He was a great patron of the arts.

Source: Guicciardini, *Storia d'Italia*, Eng. ed., A. P. Goddard, vol. 8, pp. 353 *et sqq.*

Leo, who brought the chief ecclesiastical dignity into the house of the Medici, and with the authority of the cardinalship so well sustained himself and that family which had fallen from the height of grandeur to so low a state of decay that it had reason to expect a vicissitude and return of prosperous fortune, was a man of consummate liberality, if it be proper to give that name to a profuseness in expenses that passes all bounds and measures. After his assumption to the Pontificate he displayed so much magnificence and splendour with a truly royal spirit as would have been surprising even in one who had descended by long succession from Kings and Emperors. Nor was he only most profuse of money, but of all favours which are at the disposal of a Pope, which he disposed so immeasurably that he brought the spiritual authority into contempt, disordered the economy of the Court, and by his excessive expenses brought himself under a necessity to raise money by extraordinary means. To this so remarkable an easiness was added a most profound dissimulation, with which he circumvented every one in the beginning of his Pontificate and made himself pass for a very good prince; I dare not say of an Apostolic goodness, for in our corrupt times the goodness of a Pontiff is commended when it does not surpass the wickedness of other men: but he was reported merciful, desirous of doing good to all and quite averse from everything that might give offence to any person.

Among other good gifts of fortune, which were very great, he was so happy as to have about him Giulio de' Medici, his cousin, whom from a Knight of Rhodes (though illegitimate) he raised to the cardinalship. For Giulio, being naturally grave, diligent, assiduous in business, averse from pleasures, temperate in everything, and having in his hands, by appointment of Leo, the management of all the important affairs of the Pontificate, restrained and moderated many disorders proceeding from his profuseness and easiness; and, which is more, not following the custom of other nephews and brothers of Popes, but preferring the honour and grandeur of Leo to the consideration of making a comfortable provision to support himself after his death, he approved himself a most faithful and obedient minister to him, in such a manner that it seemed as if he were really his second self . . .

This opinion of his merit was confirmed and increased after the death of Leo, for amidst all the opposition and difficulties with which he was surrounded, he supported his affairs with such dignity that he appeared almost like a Pope, and preserved his authority with many of the cardinals to such a degree that he entered into two Conclaves absolute master of sixteen votes, and at last, after the death of Adrian, in spite of the infinite contradictions and oppositions of the greater part of the senior members of the College, he made his way to the Pontificate not two full years from the decease of Leo, entering on his own office with such high expectations that it was the universal opinion he would be the greatest Pontiff . . .

But it was soon known what vain judgements they had formed of Leo and of him; for Clement [Giulio de' Medici] had many qualities different from what was at first imagined of him, since he had nothing of that ambitious desire of novelties, nor was endowed with that greatness of soul and inclination of mind to generous and magnanimous ends, as the public had at first believed.

[see for continuation under Clement VII.]

POPE ADRIAN VI, 1522

Pope Leo X died during the night of December 1st/2nd, 1521. The conclave held to elect a new Pope resulted in the election of a foreigner, Adrian of Utrecht, a Fleming, who had been tutor to Charles V and was at the moment of his election, the Emperor's Viceroy and Inquisitor-General in Spain. He took the title of Adrian VI.

Source: A letter from Cardinal Gonzaga to Isabella d'Este, Marchioness of Mantua. Quoted in Julia Cartwright, Isabella d'Este, vol. ii, p. 197.

To-day these excellent cardinals and myself have at length come out of the conclave where we have spent a fortnight in the greatest discomfort and fatigue, both of body and mind, owing to our endless quarrels. And after all this we have—no doubt according to the will of God, since all is ordered by Him—elected a Pope who is, as people say, a holy man. I, for one, have never seen him. As for my own disappointment, I did my best, and cannot complain that any of these cardinals deceived me. Only this unexpected event, which was never dreamt of by me or any one else, has shattered my hopes. Just when I felt sure of reaching the desired goal, the greater part of the cardinals went and gave their votes to this man, simply throwing them away, without knowing what the others were doing, and when all the votes were read out, he was found to have no less than fifteen!

POPE CLEMENT VII

Adrian VI died in September, 1523. He was succeeded by Cardinal Giulio de' Medici, son of the Giuliano de' Medici who was murdered in the Pazzi conspiracy, 1478. He took the title of Clement VII.

Source: (a) Guicciardini, Storia d'Italia, op. cit. 8, 353 (see under Leo X).

For although he was exceedingly intelligent and had a marvellous knowledge of all manner of things, nevertheless his qualities of resolution and of action were far inferior, because he was hampered not only by his natural timidity (which in him was not small) and by his dislike of spending money, but especially by a certain irresolution and perplexity which was habitual with him. Thus he always remained undecided and of two minds, the moment for decision came, on matters which he had long foreseen, often considered and practically resolved upon. Both in discussion and in carrying out what had been discussed, every minute consideration that occurred to him again, every insignificant hindrance that might arise, seemed to be enough to throw him back into the original confusion from which he suffered before the discussion, so that after deciding on one course of action it always seemed to him that the rejected course would have been best.

Source: (b) Vettori, Storia d'Italia dal 1511 al 1527, in Arch. stor. Ital. Appendix, vol. vi, 1848. Vettori was one of the chief advisers to Duke Alessandro Medici in Florence.

No doubt he entered on the Papal office when it was already ruined by Leo's wars and extravagance, and when Adrian had been unable to effect any improvement, owing to the shortness of his reign and to the fact that, being new to the Curia and to Rome, everyone cheated him. More than this, Clement was under heavy obligations to the fifteen cardinals who had stood by him in the conclave. He found Italy filled with soldiery, Christendom weakened by the loss of Rhodes and the preparations which the Turks were making against Hungary, the Church in the lowest possible repute because of the continual advance of the Lutheran sect. But human ambition is so formed that it always presses on towards the highest goal. Giulio knew very well whither he was going; he talked and thought of nothing else; yet he exerted himself to the utmost to exchange the position of a great and influential cardinal for that of a miserable, despised Pope.

Source: (c) Guicciardini, *Storia d'Italia*, Eng. ed. A. P. Goddard, 10, pp. 256 *et sqq.*

This Pope was exalted from a low degree with wonderful felicity to the Pontificate, but in it he experienced a great variety of fortune, though upon the balance his bad fortune outweighed the good. For what felicity can compare with the infelicity of his imprisonment, his having seen the sack of Rome with such horrible ravages, and his being the cause of so great a ruin to his country? He died hated by the Court, suspected by the princes, and with the character of being rather a morose and disagreeable than of a pleasant and affable temper, being reputed avaricious, hardly to be trusted and naturally averse from doing a kindness. Wherefore, though in his Pontificate he created one and thirty cardinals, he created not one for his own satisfaction, but on the contrary was always in a manner necessitated to it, except the Cardinal de' Medici, whom he created rather at the solicitations of others than of his own spontaneous choice, at a time when he laboured under a dangerous disorder, and if he died, would have left those who belonged to him beggars and destitute of all relief. He was, however, very grave and circumspect in his actions, much master of himself, and of a very great capacity, if timidity had not frequently corrupted his judgment.

THE SACK OF ROME, 1527

The Italian Wars of Charles VIII and Louis XII were continued during the dynastic rivalry of Francis I and the Emperor Charles V. On February 24th, 1525, Charles won a decisive victory over Francis I at Pavia and took Francis prisoner. The reaction against this victory in Italy was rapid. Once he was released Francis broke all his promises and vows to Charles. There was formed the League of Cognac (1526) between the Pope Clement VII, Francis I, Florence, Venice and Francesco Sforza of Milan. The Imperial troops were ironically under the command of a Frenchman, the Duke of Bourbon, who had entered Charles V's service in 1523. The main strength of Bourbon's armies lay in the wild German *landsknechts* and the Spanish. There was no money with which to pay them. But plunder could take the place of pay. The Imperial armies marched on Rome: the Pope had no money with which to buy off the enemy. May 25th, 1527, Bourbon's army was outside Rome. The sack of Rome followed.

Source: (a) Letter from Mercurino da Gattinara, Commissary of the Imperial Army during the sack of Rome. *Vat. Ottobaniana MSS. No.* 2607. English translation printed in Dennistoun, *Mem. of the D. of Urbino*, vol. iii, app. II.

Most Sacred Caesar,

I have written in Italian in another hand, being unable to do so with mine own in consequence of meeting with an accident, as I shall presently explain. I have to inform your Majesty that Monsieur di Borbone, being near Florence and Siena with his army, and understanding that the former of these cities was well fortified and contained the forces of the League ready to defend it, rendering a siege impossible, or at all events so protracted as to endanger your Majesty's troops from want of provisions and other stores, whilst the lack of pay risked their disbanding and losing all;—aware, on the other hand, that Rome had been disarmed, and that to seize and bring it and the Pontiff to great straits was to gain everything, or at all events would prove a measure so useful and advantageous as to content your Majesty;—it appeared better to him to abandon his designs upon Florence and, advancing by forced marches, to beleaguer Rome, thereby anticipating the army of the League and preventing them from succouring it, for which purpose he determined to leave his artillery at Siena. Accordingly, when this was decided, the confederates being in Florence, and we thirty miles on this side of it, we advanced with the utmost diligence, doing twenty or twenty-four miles a day, which was something quite new for the army, so numerous, so distressed by past fatigues and by recent and actual hunger. Thus, on Saturday the 4th instant, it was quartered at Isola, seven miles from Rome. M. di Borbone and his officers were astonished that the Pope and cardinals should await the army and the threatened danger, whilst Rome was incapable of defence, without submitting some proposal by envoy or letter, or even answering a despatch sent to his Holiness by M. di Borbone and the Viceroy as to the terms of agreement. Some of your Majesty's good servants suggested that, were the army under the walls, it was doubtful if they could carry them from want of artillery, in which event their own destruction would follow; on the other hand, that in case of taking the city it would be sacked, which could be no good service to your Majesty, as its plunder would occasion the army to disperse, the Spaniards and Italians straggling towards Naples, or, should they not break up, they might demand immense arrears of pay, which not being discharged from want of means, everything would fall into confusion. For these reasons they recommended Borbone so to dispose his forces as to keep matters open for arrangement with the Pope. Of this advice he openly approved, desirous of any plan which should provide pay for the army. He, however, declared that he would not abstain from annoying the enemy, nor allow them time to provide for their interests, alleging that the Admiral of France, from not having taken Rome when he could, in order to save it from a sack, was unable afterwards to do so, it being defended by the Lord Prospero Colonna: also that, on another occasion, when M. di Chaumont beleagured Bologna, Fabrizio Colonna threw in succours whilst the French general was treating with Julius II, who thereupon broke off the parley: finally, that it became a pontiff rather to seek a capitulation than to wait until it was demanded of him.

Monsieur di Borbone accordingly decided on approaching the walls, and on Sunday morning the 5th we made a lodgement beyond St. Peter's palace, hard by the monastery of S. Pancrazio. Yet he did not neglect addressing a letter to the Pontiff that morning, exhorting him to make a favourable capitulation rather than abide the unpleasant alternative. It was at the same time suggested whether it might not be well for him to repair to his Holiness; but considering that he could not go for want of a safe conduct, it seemed better for him to remain; he, however, sent the letter by a trumpet, whom the enemy did not allow to pass, the missive remaining in their hands, and we know not whether it reached the Pope; at all events, no answer ever came, which was demanded before half-past seven p.m. of that day, after which it would not be any longer possible to restrain the army. For these reasons, as evening approached, it was resolved to get the ladders all prepared for an assault the following morning on the Borgo towards the furnaces, where the wall was considered very weak. And so the assault was given on Monday morning the 6th of May 1527, when by an unlucky chance the Lord di Borbone was hit in the abdomen towards the right thigh, of which wound he presently died.[1] Yet notwithstanding this accident, which was not at once known to the army, the undertaking was carried through and the Borgo was plundered that morning. The Pope, with most of the cardinals and court, were in the palace, but on hearing what had occurred they hastily retired to the castle of S. Angelo. Meanwhile our soldiery sacked the whole Borgo and slew most of the people whom they found, taking a few prisoners. The enemy's forces then in the city are supposed not to have exceeded three thousand, unused to arms, so that it was scarcely defended; the dense fog which prevailed during that day was likewise inopportune, preventing them seeing each other; and the struggle did not in all last above two hours. We afterwards learned that the Pope and the citizens, relying upon the assurances of Renzo da Ceri, considered both Rome and the Borgo to be impregnable without artillery, and looked for support from the confederate army.

The Pontiff being thus within the castle, and such of the citizens as were armed having joined their handful of troops for defence of the bridges and of the Transtevere quarter, the Borgo was occupied by a large portion of our army, and its leaders were assembled in council, when there arrived the Portuguese ambassador to say that some Romans, his neighbours, had, with the Pope's sanction, urged him to make terms. The answer given

---

[1] Benvenuto Cellini claimed to have fired this shot.

him was that the council would be ready to treat so soon as the
Pope had placed in their hands the Ponte Molle and Transtevere,
to which proposal no reply was returned during that day. A
brigade of our troops having carried the Transtevere and possessed
themselves of the Ponte Sisto and Sta. Maria, the whole army
passed into the city early on that evening of the 6th. As the
inhabitants in general relied on its being defended, none of them
had fled or removed their property, so that no one of whatever
nation, rank, condition, age or sex escaped becoming prisoners—
not even women in the convents. They were treated without
distinction according to the caprice of the soldiery; and after
being plundered of all their effects most of them were compelled
by torture or otherwise to pay ransom. Cardinals Cesarini, della
Valle and di Siena, being imperialists, considered themselves safe
and remained in their houses, whither also there retired Cardinal . . ., Fra Giacobatio and many friends with their women and
valuables; but finding no sanctuary there, they had to compound
with certain captains and soldiers for security of their persons
and property; notwithstanding which, these houses were completely pillaged three or four days afterwards, and they had
enough to do to save their lives. Some women who had carried
all their earthly possessions to Cardinal Colonna's residence were
left with but a single cloak or shift. Cardinals S. Sisto and della
Minerva, who stayed at home, are still in the soldiers' power,
being too poor to pay their ransom. All the church ornaments
are stolen, the sacred utensils thrown about, the relics gone to
destruction—for the troops, in abstracting their precious recept-
acles, heeded these no more than as many bits of wood; even the
shrine of the *sancta sanctorum* was sacked, although regarded with
particular reverence. St. Peter's church and the papal palace from
top to bottom have been made into stables. I feel confident that
your Majesty as a Catholic and most Christian Emperor will feel
displeasure at these gross outrages and insults to the Catholic
religion, the Apostolic see and the city of Rome. In truth, everyone is convinced that all this has happened as a judgement from
God on the great tyranny and disorders of the papal court; but
however this may be, there has been vast destruction, for which

no redress can be had from your Majesty's arm and authority.
This army has no head, no divisions, no discipline, no organiza-
tion, but every one behaves according to his own fancy. The
Lord Prince of Orange and Giovanni di Urbino, with the other
leaders, do what they can, but to little purpose; for in entering
Rome the lansquenets have conducted themselves like true
Lutherans. . . . Most of the troops are enriched by the enormous
booty, amounting to many millions of gold. A majority of the
Spaniards, it is supposed, will retire to Naples with their spoil . . .

Source: (b) Vettori, Sommario della Storia d'Italia dal 1511 al 1527,
J. A. Symonds, Age of the Despots, 1875, Appendix V.

It still remained for the Imperial troops to enter the populous
and wealthy quarters; and these they had to reach by one of three
bridges. They numbered hardly more than 25,000 men, all told.
In Rome were at least 30,000 men fit to bear arms between the
ages of sixteen and fifty, and among them were many trained
soldiers, besides crowds of Romans, swaggering braggarts, used
to daily quarrels, with beards upon their breasts. Nevertheless it
was found impossible to get 500 together in one band for the
defence of one of the three bridges. The soldiers slew at pleasure;
pillaged the houses of the middle classes and small folk, the
palaces of the nobles, the convents of both sexes, and the churches.
They made prisoners of men, women, and even of little children,
without regard to age, or vows, or any other claim on pity. The
slaughter was not great, for men rarely kill those who offer no
resistance; but the booty was incalculable, in coin, jewels, gold
and silver plate, clothes, tapestries, furniture, and goods of all
descriptions. To this should be added the ransoms, which
amounted to a sum which, if set down, would win no credence.
Let anyone consider through how many years the money of all
Christendom had been flowing into Rome, and staying there in
a great measure; let him remember the Cardinals, Bishops, Prelates, and public officers, the wealthy merchants, both Roman
and foreign, selling at high prices, letting their houses at dear
rents, and paying nothing in the way of taxes; let him call to
mind the artisans, the poorer folk, the prostitutes; and he will

judge that never was a city sacked of which the memory remains, whence greater store of treasure could be drawn. Though Rome has at other times been taken and pillaged, yet never before was it the Rome of our days. Moreover, the sack lasted so long that what might not have been discovered on the first day, sooner or later came to light. This disaster was an example to the world that men proud, avaricious, envious, murderous, lustful, hypo-critical, can not long preserve their state. Nor can it be denied that the inhabitants of Rome, especially the Romans, were stained with all these vices and with many greater.

POPE JULIUS III

Source: The Travels and Life of Sir Thomas Hoby, Kt., of Bisham Abbey. Written by Himself 1547–1564, ed. by Edgar Powell, Camden Society X, 1902, p. 23 *et sqq.* Egerton MSS. B.M. 2148. Thomas's brother was the English ambassador at the court of the Emperor, 1548–58.

When we arrived in Rome we saw in St. Peter's Church very solemn masses of requiem for the Pope's death [Paul III], after the manner of Rome, sung by the cardinals, everyone sitting accord-ing to his degree in a chapel, where the image of Pope Sixtus lieth all in brass curiously wrought, with the Muses all about him.

About the latter end of November, at the certain time limited for all cardinals of the see of Rome to repair thither for the election of a new Pope, all such cardinals as were in Rome, after one solemn mass of the Holy Ghost sung among them, entered into the Conclave according to the accustomed manner: that is to say, into such rooms as are belonging unto the Pope in his palace, as the outer chambers, the hall above, the chapel and such other wide places, where every cardinal had beforehand a little cabin prepared for him, hung and separated from the rest with his own hangings, without any light at all, except so much as lets in by the pinning up of the hanging in the place where he enters into this cabin, within the which he had so much place that sufficed for a little standing court bed for himself, a pallet for two of his servants, whom he listed to have with him, one little square table and a coffer for his stuff.

When they were all entered together into this conclave, every door and window where any issue was in any place round about them was after the manner mured up, saving a little part of the very top of the windows on high, in many places out of man's reach, which to let in light was left open, and a little dresser in that great door which men used most commonly to come in and out. Through this dresser every cardinal's own provision, brought thither from his own palace by his servants, was put in and delivered unto the two servants he had within attending upon him, the assay or taste thereof first taken, whatsoever was brought thither.

In this sort remained they a good space attending [*waiting for*] eight or nine cardinals out of France, for before their arrival the Cardinal of Ferrara with the rest of the French party would go about nothing. When all were come and conveyed in among the rest, they remain thus shut up until such time as by agreement of the most part they have elected a new Pope, except they find themselves ill at ease, as three or four of them were at this time, which were permitted to go to lie at their own palaces, whereon two of them died ... The Pope that died lay buried under a heap of earth by the walls' side within St. Peter's Church, paled in, until such time as a more honourable sepulture were made ready for him which his four nephews, Cardinal Farnese, Cardinal of Saint Angelo, Duke Octavio and Duke Horatio had caused to be taken in hand for him by Michelangelo.

POPE PAUL IV

Giovanni Pietro Caraffa was Pope from 1555 to 1559. He was born in 1476 of a noble Neapolitan family. He died in 1559. He was for a time papal nuncio in England and in Spain: he was one of the founders of the Theatines (1524): Cardinal-Archbishop of Naples (1536): he became the strong advocate of reaction after the failure by Contarini to reconcile the Protestants (1541), and he saw to the setting up of the Inquisition and the censorship, and the eradication of heresy from Italy. Elected Pope in 1555, he embarked on a foreign policy which led to much strife, first in alliance with France against Spain, then with Spain against France. He aroused high feelings by his nepotism: he went to war with Spain: he set about trying to reform some of the worst abuses in the Church. His unpopularity grew and when he died the populace broke down his statue and liberated the prisoners of the Inquisition.

Source: The report of the Venetian ambassador, Navagero, in Alberi, *Relazioni degli Amb. Ven.*, series ii, vol. 3, p. 379. Trans. by C.R.N.R.

In the year 1555, on the vigil of the Ascension, in the 79th year of his life, he was made Pope, against the wishes of all the Cardinals, who feared his nature, by which he never wanted to please. The complexion of this Pope is choleric and hot: he is unbelievably serious and ostentatious in his every action, and indeed he was born to dominate. He is healthy and strong, and when he walks he seems scarcely to touch the ground. He is all sinew and very little flesh; he has in his eyes and in all his bodily movements a vigour beyond his years. Two indispositions sometimes give him annoyance, the flux and catarrh: an attack of the flux at certain times could be reckoned as being in purgatory: the catarrh he cures by eating Parmesan cheese, saying that thus it is thickened and is the more easily spat out. The quality of this Pope's mind, the which much corresponds with his complexion, is surely a matter for wonder. He is a considerable man of letters: he speaks Italian, Latin, Greek and Spanish as well, and as correctly as a man born in the middle of Greece, in the middle of Spain: and those who understand these languages admit that one could not want anything better. He has a tenacious memory which brings back to him what he has read, and that is almost everything. He knows all the Scriptures by heart and the Commentators as well, especially St. Thomas. He is as eloquent as any others that I have ever heard speak. He often speaks very well in praising one whom somebody else has blamed and in blaming where somebody else has praised, such an admirably clear vision has he, and such an understanding of many things . . . He is, as I have already said, very vehement in everything, but he is most vehement in the Inquisition.

POPE GREGORY XIII

Ugo Buoncompagno of Bologna was Pope from 1572 to 1585, under the title of Gregory XIII. He is remembered for the energy with which he tried to put into practice the reforms of the Council of

I

Trent, for his devotion to education, for his educational buildings, and for his reform of the calendar which goes by his name.

Source: The Travel Journal of Montaigne, who visited Germany, Switzerland and Italy between June 22nd, 1580 and November 30th, 1581. *The Complete Works of Montaigne*, trans. by D. M. Frame, Hamish Hamilton, 1958, p. 939. Montaigne had an audience of the Pope on December 29th, 1580.

The language of the Pope is Italian, smacking of the Bolognese patois, which is the worst idiom in Italy; and then by nature his speech is halting. For the rest, he is a very handsome old man, of middle height, erect, his face full of majesty, a long white beard, more than eighty years old, as healthy and vigorous for his age as anyone can wish, without gout, without colic, without stomach trouble, and not subject to any ailment: of a gentle nature, not very passionate about the affairs of the world; a great builder, and in that respect he will leave in Rome and elsewhere exceptional honour to his memory; a great almoner, I should say beyond all measure. Among other evidences of this, there is not a girl about to marry whom he does not aid to set up house, if she is of low estate; and in this respect they count his liberality as ready money. Besides that, he has built colleges for the Greeks, and for the English, Scots, French, Germans and Poles, and has endowed each one with more than ten thousand crowns a year in perpetuity, besides the huge expense of the buildings. He has done this to call to the Church the children of those nations, corrupted by evil opinions against the Church; and there the boys are lodged, fed, dressed, instructed, and provided with everything, without one quattrino of their own going into it for anything. The troublesome public charges he readily casts off on the shoulders of others and avoids giving himself trouble.

He gives as many audiences as one wants. His replies are short and decided, and you waste your time if you combat his reply with new arguments. In what he judges to be just he trusts himself; and even for his son, whom he loves with a frenzy, he will not stir a bit against this justice of his. He gives advancement to his relations, but without any prejudice to the rights of the Church, which he preserves inviolable. He is very lavish in public buildings and the improvement of the city's streets; and in truth, his life and his conduct have nothing very extraordinary about them one way or the other, but incline much more to the good.

ROME IN 1580

Source: Montaigne, *Travel Journal,* trans. by D. M. Frame, Hamish Hamilton, London, 1958, p. 943.

All these days he spent his time only in studying Rome. At the beginning he had taken a French guide; but when this man quit for some fancy or other, he made it a point of pride to learn all about Rome by his own study, aided by various maps and books that he had read to him in the evening; and in the daytime he would go on the spot to put his apprenticeship into practice; so that in a few days he could easily have guided his guide.

He said that one saw nothing of Rome but the sky under which it had stood and the plan of its site; that this knowledge that he had of it was an abstract and contemplative knowledge of which there was nothing perceptible to the senses; that those who said that one at least saw the ruins of Rome said too much, for the ruins of so awesome a machine would bring more honour and reverence to its memory: this was nothing but its sepulchre. The world hostile to its long domination, had first broken and shattered all the parts of this wonderful body; and because, even though quite dead, overthrown, and disfigured, it still terrified the world, the world had buried its very ruin. These little signs of its ruin that still appear above the bier had been preserved by fortune as testimony to that infinite greatness which so many centuries, so many conflagrations, and all the many conspiracies of the world to ruin that these disfigured limbs which remained were the least worthy, and that the fury of the enemies of that immortal glory had impelled them to destroy first of all what was most beautiful and most worthy; and the building of this bastard Rome which they were now attaching to these ancient ruins, although fully adequate to carry away the present age with admiration, reminded him precisely of the nest which sparrows and crows in France suspend from the arches and walls of the churches that the Huguenots have recently demolished.

PORTUGAL, SPAIN AND THE NEW WORLD
(*Notes on p. 175*)

THE PORTUGUESE EXPLORERS

HENRY THE NAVIGATOR

Prince Henry, known to the English as The Navigator, was born in 1394 and died in 1460. He was the third son of King John I of Portugal and his Queen, Philippa, daughter of John of Gaunt. By nature Henry was a Crusader and he first came into prominence in the Ceuta campaign against the Moors in 1415. The capture of Ceuta was a complete success and it drove the Moors out of their most threatening stronghold, opened the way to trade with Africa and led to the great development of Portugal as a colonial power. After Ceuta Henry devoted his whole life to exploration. He had sent out expeditions before the campaign: it was in 1415 (not 1425) that he sent out John de Castro to the Canaries, and when that captain returned and reported a strong current running between the islands, Henry sent out Gonzalo Velho to investigate the cause of this—the first scientific expedition to be carried out. In order to supervise these expeditions Henry left the Portuguese court and went to live at or near Lagos in the province of Algarve, of which King John appointed him as governor. Henry also had a house near Cape St. Vincent—thus acquiring two bases admirably suited to his work. Here he became immersed in mathematics and cosmography, selected captains and pilots, saw that his charts were continually brought up to date, and collected round him a number of Jewish doctors who, because medicine and astrology were at that time closely connected, were able to advise him on nautical astrology.

Henry's objectives were to obtain knowledge of lands beyond the Canaries and Bojador: to open up trading relations with Christian nations: to find out the limits of Islam: to find any Christian kings who would help him to fight Islam: to spread the Christian faith: and to further the prosperity of his own country by getting the trade in gold dust out of the hands of Islam and into the hands of Portugal.

Henry sponsored all the great Portuguese expeditions between 1415 and 1460. His ships went to the Canaries and the Azores: to the West coast of Africa from Bojador to Cape Verde (1421–44); a variety of voyages between 1445 and 1448 increased the knowledge of the coast of Africa from 200 leagues to 650: shortage of money put a stop to exploration from 1448 to 1455. There followed the voyages of Alvise de Cadamosto to Africa in 1455 and 1456: the discovery of the Cape Verde Islands in 1456 by Diogo Gomes and Antonio da Noli. In 1458 Henry took an active part in the attack on and capture of Alcazar. The next year (1459) Henry sent an expedition to teach Christianity to the negroes of the Gambia. He died at Cape St. Vincent on November 13th, 1460.

Source: Gomes Eannes de Azurara, MS. in Paris, pub. by Visconde da Carreira. This English version from R. H. Major's *Life of Henry the Navigator*, London, 1868, pp. 306 *et sqq.* Azurara lived with Henry.

He was large of frame and brawny, and stout and strong of limb. His naturally fair complexion had by constant toil and exposure become dark. The expression of his face at first sight inspired fear in those who were not accustomed to him, and when he was angry, which rarely happened, his look was very formidable. Stout of heart and keen in intellect, he was extraordinarily ambitious of achieving great deeds. Neither luxury nor avarice ever found a home with him. In the former respect he was so temperate that after his early youth he abstained from wine altogether, while the whole of his life was reputed to have been passed in inviolate chastity. As for his generosity, the household of no other uncrowned Prince formed so large and excellent a training school for the young nobility of the country. All the worthies of the kingdom, and still more foreigners of renown, found a general welcome in his house, and there were frequently assembled in it men of various nations, the diversity of whose habits presented a curious spectacle. None left that house without some proof of the Prince's generosity. His self-discipline was unsurpassed: all his days were spent in hard work, and it would not readily be believed how often he passed the night without sleep, so that by dint of unflagging industry he conquered what seemed to be impossibilities to other men. His wisdom and thoughtfulness, excellent memory, calm bearing and courteous language gave great dignity to his address.

He was constant in adversity and humble in prosperity, and it was impossible for any subject of any rank to show more obedience and reverence to the Sovereign. This was especially noticeable in his conduct to his nephew, Don Alfonso, even at the beginning of his reign. He never entertained hatred or ill-will towards any, however serious the offence they might have committed against him. So great was his benignity in this respect that the wiseacres said that he was deficient in retributive justice, although in other matters he was very impartial. No stronger example of this could be shown than his forgiveness of some of his soldiers who deserted him in the attack on Tangier, when he was in the utmost danger. He was devoted to the public interests of the kingdom and took great pleasure in trying new plans for the general welfare at his own expense. He gloried in feats of arms against the enemies of the Faith, but earnestly sought peace with all Christians. He was universally beloved, for he did good to all and injured none. He never failed to show due respect to every person, however humble, without lowering his own dignity. A foul or indecent word was never known to pass his lips.

He was very obedient to all the commands of Holy Church and attended all its offices with great devotion, and they were celebrated with as much solemnity and ceremony in his own chapel as they could be in any cathedral church. He held all sacred things in profound reverence and took delight in showing honour and kindness to all who ministered in them. Nearly one half of the year he passed in fasting, and the hands of the poor never went empty away from his presence. His heart never knew what fear was, except the fear of committing sin. Assuredly, I know not where to look for a Prince that shall bear comparison with this one.

KING JOHN II

He was born in 1455 and was the younger brother of Henry the Navigator, who died in 1460. He succeeded to the throne in 1481 on the death of his father, John I. His mother was Philippa, the daughter of John of Gaunt. He died in 1495. His reign of fifteen years was immensely important for Portugal. It saw an end to the power of the nobles and the establishment of absolute monarchy. It saw a long struggle with Ferdinand of Aragon and Isabella of Castile. During it John effectively occupied the west coast of Africa, known then by the comprehensive name of Guinea. He achieved a great expansion overseas and he scored a great success over Ferdinand in the Treaty of Tordesillas. His great ambition was to see his son reign over a united Peninsula, to which end he married him to the daughter of Ferdinand and Isabella, but this son died from an accident while out riding. John II was an able, masterful and ruthless man, a fine diplomatist, far seeing and ambitious, but he had many enemies among the nobility and he was the first Portuguese king to need a guard.

Source: Garcia de Resende, *Cronica de D. Jodo II*, cap. 212. This English version is taken from Edgar Prestage, *The Portuguese Pioneers*, The Pioneer Histories, A. and C. Black, 1933, p. 244 *et sqq*.

The King was in great pain and the Bishop of Tangier reminded him of many pious things very needful at such a time, and among them he touched on some from the Bible, whereupon John said, 'Bishop, do not remind me about anything of the Old Law'. The Bishop of Algarve, D. John Camello, who was also with him, though a very good man, very liberal and free with his money, was considered a bad cleric, for he never said Mass, nor troubled about the Divine offices, and the King had more than once reproved him for it and was not pleased with him; and now that he was in his last hour, he said, 'Bishop, I am going with a heavy burden on your account, for love of me live better in the future and for the service of God and give me your promise to do so'; the Bishop gave it and the King took his hand in token that he would carry it out. When they gave him for signature the bond of a rental which he had bequeathed to D. Anna de Mendonca, mother of his son D. George, and he had the pen ready in his hand, he let it fall and began to weep much, and when they comforted him, he said: 'Do not comfort me, because I have been such a bad creature, for I was never provoked that I did not bite'. Then with tears he signed the bond, and because they addressed him as Highness, according to custom, he said: 'Do not call me Highness, for I am only a sack of worms'. Then one Francisco da Cunha of the Terceira Islands approached him and asked him for the sake of the Five Wounds of Jesus Christ to grant him a favour, since he was a *fidalgo* and very poor, and the King ordered a bond for a pension of 30 *milreis* to be made out in haste and signed it and told him to take the silver he had in the house, for he had nothing else to give him; and when the man left, the King said: 'I can disclose it now, that never in my life was I asked anything in honour of the Five Wounds and refused it'. Then he sent to enquire how the tide was, and when they gave him the answer said: 'In two hours from now I shall be gone', and so it was; and as he was in anguish with great and deadly sighs, which came upon him every now and then, he said: 'I have such a bitter taste in my mouth that I cannot endure it', and the Bishop of Coimbra said to him: 'Sir, remember the vinegar and myrrh they gave to Our Lord Jesus Christ when he was on the Cross and your mouth will not be bitter'. The King answered him, 'Oh, Bishop, I thank you for this, since it was the only stage of the Passion which I had forgotten'. At this point there came upon him a very great seizure, before his soul left his body, and all thought he was dead. The Bishop of Tangier closed his eyes and his mouth, but he felt it and came to himself and said: 'Bishop, the hour has not yet come'; then speaking with many holy words and begging them all not to weep lest they disturbed him, and often kissing the figure of Our Lord and the Cross and having his eyes fixed on it and the candle in his hands, fully conscious, his senses very clear and his vision intact, without any movement, always praying with the Bishops verse by verse. And at the last, with the name of Jesu on his lips, with the greatest devotion saying *Agnus Dei qui tollis peccata mundi, miserere mei*, his soul left his flesh, when the sun was about to set, on the 25th day of October in the year of Our Lord Jesus Christ 1495 at the age of forty years and six months, of which he had been married to D. Leonor his wife twenty-five and reigned fourteen years and two months; and having been very virtuous in his life, he ended in this manner, which is greatly to be envied.

VASCO DA GAMA 1497

Vasco da Gama was born about 1460, the year in which Henry the Navigator died. Reports continually reached King John II of a great monarch 'who lived east of Benin, 350 leagues in the interior and who held both temporal and spiritual dominion over all the neighbouring kings'. John decided that an expedition should be fitted out to search for this monarch, but John died before the plans were completed and it was Manuel I who in 1497 gave the command of the expedition to Vasco da Gama. Four ships were specially built: these sailed from Lisbon on July 8th, 1497. The expedition rounded the Cape, sailed up the east coast of Africa to Malindi and then made westwards for India, arriving at Calicut about May 22nd, 1498. It remained hereabouts for eighty-eight days, sailed home on August 30th and one ship reached Lisbon on July 10th, 1499. This ship was commanded by Coelho. Vasco da Gama had gone to Terçeira with his dying brother. Da Gama made a second voyage to India in 1502, and he set out on a third voyage in 1524, but he died on Christmas Day that year at Cochin.

Source: (a) Sernigi's *First Letter to a gentleman in Florence*, written immediately after the arrival of Coelho at Lisbon, on July 10th, but not all on one day. Girolamo Sernigi was born at Florence in 1453. He was a merchant living at Lisbon when Coelho returned from India. This English version is taken from *Vasco da Gama's First Voyage*, trans. and ed. by E. G. Ravenstein, Hakluyt Society, 1898, p. 123 *et sqq.*

The most illustrious Lord Manuel of Portugal sent 3 new vessels to discover new countries, namely 2 *balonieri* (having the shape of whales) of 90 tons each, and one of 50 tons, in addition to which there was a ship of one hundred and ten tons, laden with provisions. Between them they took away cxviij men, and they left this city of Lisbon on July 9th, 1497. Vasco da Gama went as captain of this fleet.

On July 10th 1499 the vessel of 50 tons came back to this city. The Captain, Vasco da Gama, remained at the Cape Verde islands with one of the vessels of 90 tons in order to land there his brother Paulo da Gama, who was very ill. The other vessel of 90 tons was burnt, because there were not people enough to navigate and steer her. The store-ship also was burnt, for it was not intended she should return.

In the course of this voyage there died 55 men from a disease which first attacked the mouth, and thence descended to the throat; they also suffered great pain in the legs from the knee downwards.

They discovered 1800 leagues[1] (each league being equal to
4¼ of our miles) of new land beyond the cape of Good Hope,
which cape was first discovered in the time of King John. Beyond
that cape they followed the coast for about 600 leagues[2] and met
with a dense population of black people. And when they had
made these 600 leagues they discovered a large river, and at the
mouth of that river a great village inhabited by black people,
who are, as it were, subject to the Moors. These Moors live in
the interior of the country and continually make war upon the
blacks. And in this river, according to the blacks, are found
immense quantities of gold; and they told the captain that if he
would tarry a moon, that is a month, they would give him gold
in plenty. But the captain would not wait, and went about
350 leagues[3] further, and discovered a great walled city, with
very good stone houses in the Moorish style, inhabited by Moors
of the colour of Indians. There the captain landed, and the
Moorish king of this city received him with much feasting and
gave him a pilot for crossing the gulf. This city is called Melinde,
and lies at the entrance of gulf, the whole of which is peopled by
Moors . . .

This gulf is above 700 leagues[4] across, and they crossed it from
side to side, and came to a very large city, larger than Lisbon,
inhabited by Christians and called Chalichut . . .

In this city are churches with bells, but there are no priests, and
the divine offices are not performed nor sacrificial [masses] celebrated, but in each church there is a pillar holding water, in the
manner of the fonts holding our holy water, and a second pillar
with balm. They bathe once every 3 years in a river which is
near the city. The houses in this city are of stone and mortar,
in the Moorish style, and the roads laid out and straight as are
these . . .

All kinds of spices are to be found in this city of Chalichut,
such as cinnamon, pepper, ginger, frankincense, lac: and brazil-
wood abounds in the forests. These spices do not grow here, but
in a certain island[5] at a distance of 160 leagues from this city, near
the mainland. It can be reached overland in xx days and is

inhabited by Moors. All the above spices are brought to this city as to a staple . . .

There is abundance of silken stuffs, namely, velvets of various colours, satins, damask, taffetas, brocades worked in gold, scarlet cloth, brass and tin ware. In fine, all these things are to be found in abundance, and it is my opinion that the cloths worked in gold and the silks are brought from Cairo . . .

The Portuguese who returned home brought a few precious stones of little value, for in truth they had neither gold nor silver to buy any. They say that these jewels are very dear there, as also are pearls, but I believe they are to be had cheap. This is my opinion, but those they bought were in the hands of Moorish brokers, who sell at a fourfold profit. They have brought some *balasci*,[6] sapphires and very small rubies, as also many garnets. They say that the captain brings some valuable jewels, which he bought with the silver which he had at his disposal, but as he has not yet come back, it is not known what he brings.

From this city of Chalichut to Lisbon is a distance of 3,800 leagues,[7] and at the rate of $4\frac{1}{2}$ miles to the league this makes 17,100 miles, and as much again for the return journey. From this the time in which such a voyage can be made may be judged, it requiring from 14 to 16 months.

At the city of Chalichut they have some knowledge of Prester John, but not much, as he is far away. These Christians believe that Jesus Christ was born of the Virgin Mary, without sin, was crucified and killed by the Jews, and buried at Jerusalem. They also have some knowledge of the Pope of Rome, but know nothing of our faith beyond this. They have letters and a written language.

Source: (b) *The Voyage across the Arabian Sea*, October 5th, 1498 to January 2nd, 1499. *The Roteiro*, a journal kept during the voyage by an unknown author. This English version, Ravenstein, *op. cit.*, pp. 87–8. The illness described is evidently scurvy.

Owing to the frequent calms and foul winds it took us three months less three days to cross this gulf, and all our people again suffered from their gums, which grew over their teeth, so that they could not eat. Their legs also swelled, and other parts of the body, and these swellings spread until the sufferer died, without exhibiting symptoms of any other disease. Thirty of our men died in this manner—an equal number having died previously—and those able to navigate each ship were only seven or eight, and even these were not as well as they ought to have been. I assure you that if this state of affairs had continued for another fortnight, there would have been no men at all to navigate the ships. We had come to such a pass that all bonds of discipline had gone. Whilst suffering this affliction we addressed vows and petitions to the saints on behalf of our ships. The captains had held council, and they had agreed that if a favourable wind enabled us, we would return to India whence we had come.

But it pleased God in His mercy to send us a wind which, in the course of six days, carried us within sight of land, and at this we rejoiced as much as if the land we saw had been Portugal, for with the help of God we hoped to recover our health there, as we had done once before.

This happened on January 2, 1499. It was night when we came close to the land, and for this reason we put about ship and lay to. In the morning we reconnoitred the coast, so as to find out whither the Lord had taken us, for there was not a pilot on board nor any other man who could tell on the chart in what place we were. Some said that we must be among certain islands off Moçambique, about 300 leagues from the mainland;[8] and they said this because a Moor whom we had taken at Moçambique had asserted that these islands were very unhealthy, and that their inhabitants suffered from the same disease which afflicted us.

FERDINAND MAGELLAN

Magellan was born about 1480, probably at Sabrosa in Portugal and he was killed in 1521. In 1495 he entered the service of the King of Portugal, Manuel I, and between that date and 1512 he saw much military service in India and other places and he was wounded many times. In 1512 he returned to Portugal and took part in an expedition against Morocco in which he was wounded and lamed for life. He now fell into disfavour with the King and therefore he transferred

himself to the service of the King of Spain, Charles V. In 1519 he made
the greatest of all voyages when he circumnavigated the globe, passing
through the straits at the foot of South America, now known as the
Straits of Magellan. In an attempt to conquer the island of Mactan in
the Philippines for the treacherous king of Cebu, Magellan was killed
by the islanders. Compared with the violent and cruel Vasco da
Gama, Magellan was a brave, loyal and merciful man. He put down
the conspiracy against him at Port St. Julian with minimum harshness.
Judged by what he accomplished in his voyage of circumnavigation,
he must be looked on as the greatest of all the navigators.

Source: (*a*) Magellan deserts the King of Portugal: Bishop Osorio,
Chronicle of King Manoel, Lib. xi, 23. *First Voyage Round the World by
Magellan*. Lord Stanley of Alderley, Hakluyt Soc. 1884.

About this time a slight offence on the part of the king so
grievously exasperated the mind of a certain Portuguese, that,
forgetful of all faith, piety, and religion, he hastened to betray the
king who had educated him, and the country which had brought
him forth; and he risked his life amongst the greatest perils.
Ferdinand Magellan . . . was a man of noble birth and endued
with a high spirit. He had given proofs in India in warlike
affairs of courage and perseverance in no small degree. Likewise
in Africa he had performed his duties with great ardour. Formerly
it was the custom among the Portuguese that the king's servants
should be fed in the palace at the king's expense; but when the
number of these servants had become so great (because the sons
of the king's officers retained the same station, and besides, many
were admitted for their services into the king's household), it was
seen to be very difficult to prepare the food of such a multitude.
On this account it was determined by the Kings of Portugal that
the food which each man was to receive in the palace should be
provided by himself out of the king's money. Thus it was settled
that a certain sum of money was assigned per month to each
man. That money, indeed, when provisions were so cheap,
provided abundantly for the men; but now that the number of
men and the prices of commodities had increased, it happened
that the sum, which formerly was more than sufficient for their
daily expenses, was now much too small. Moreover, as all the

dignity of the Portuguese depends upon the king, this small sum of money is as eagerly sought after as though it were much more ample. And as the Portuguese think that the thing most to be desired is to be enrolled among the king's household, so also they consider the greatest honour to consist in an increase of this stipend . . . Now Magellan contended that for his services his stipend should be increased monthly by half a ducat. The king refused it him, lest an entrance should be opened to ambitious persons. Magellan, excited by the injury of the refusal of this advantage to him at that time, abandoned the king, broke his faith and brought the State into extreme danger.

Source: (b) Gaspar Correa, *Lendas da India*, tome II, p. 28. Hakluyt Soc., *op. cit.*, p. xviii.

This Fernan de Magalhães was of the king's household and came to India with the Viceroy Dom Francisco d'Almeida, and he was in the action with the Turks; and he was always much wounded in the fleets and in Calecut; in these ships he lost his small portion of property and went away poor to Portugal, and went about with claims for his services, and begged of the king a hundred reis increase in his palace stipend, which the king did not choose to grant, at which he was aggrieved and went to Castile to live at Sevile, where he married. As he had much knowledge of the art of navigation, and enterprise, and devoted himself to that, he came to an understanding with the directors of the House of Trade at Sevile, so that the emperor gave him a fleet of five ships, with which he navigated, discovering a new way to Maluco, which was in the year 1519.

Source: (c) The Death of Magellan. Pigafetta, Account of Magellan's Voyage, Hakluyt Soc., *op. cit.*, p. 99. Pigafetta was on the voyage.

Friday, the 26th of April, Zula, who was one of the principal men or chiefs of the island of Matan, sent to the captain a son of his with two goats to make a present of them, and to say that if he did not do all that he had promised, the cause of that was another chief named Silapulapu, who would not in any way obey the King of Spain, and had prevented him from doing so: but that if the captain would send him the following night one boat full of men to give him assistance, he would fight and subdue his rival. On the receipt of this message, the captain decided to go himself with three boats. We entreated him not to go to this enterprise in person, but he as a good shepherd would not abandon his flock.

We set out from Zubu at midnight, we were sixty men armed with corselets and helmets; there were with us the Christian king, the prince, and some of the chief men, and many others divided among twenty or thirty balangai. We arrived at Matan three hours before daylight. The captain before attacking wished to attempt gentle means, and sent on shore the Moorish merchant to tell those islanders who were of the party of Silapulapu, that if they would recognize the Christian king as their sovereign and obey the King of Spain, and pay us the tribute which had been asked, the captain would become their friend, otherwise we should prove how our lances wounded. The islanders were not terrified, they replied that if we had lances, so also had they, although only of reeds and wood hardened by fire. They asked, however, that we should not attack them by night, but wait for daylight, because they were expecting reinforcements and would be in greater number. This they said with cunning, to excite us to attack them by night, supposing that we were ready; but they wished this, because they had dug ditches between their houses and the beach, and they hoped that we should fall into them.

We, however, waited for daylight; we then leaped into the water up to our thighs, for on account of the shallow water and the rocks the boats could not come near the beach, and we had to cross two good crossbow shots through the water before reaching it. We were forty-nine in number, the other eleven remained in charge of the boats. When we reached land, we found the islanders fifteen hundred in number, drawn up in three squadrons; they came down upon us with terrible shouts, two squadrons attacking us on the flanks, the third in front. The captain then divided his men in two bands. Our musketeers and crossbow-men fired for half an hour from a distance, but did nothing, since the bullets and arrows, though they passed through their shields made of thin wood, and perhaps wounded their arms, yet did not stop them. The captain shouted not to fire, but he was not listened to. The islanders, seeing that the shots of our guns did them little or no harm, would not retire, but shouted more loudly, and springing from one side to the other to avoid our shots, they at the same time drew nearer to us, throwing arrows, javelins, spears hardened in fire, stones, and even mud, so that we could hardly defend ourselves. Some of them cast lances pointed with iron at the captain-general.

He then, in order to disperse this multitude and to terrify them, sent some of our men to set fire to their houses, but this rendered them more ferocious. Some of them ran to the fire, which consumed twenty or thirty houses, and there killed two of our men. The rest came down upon us with greater fury; they perceived that our bodies were defended, but that the legs were exposed, and they aimed at them principally. The captain had his right leg pierced by a poisoned arrow, on which account he gave orders to retreat by degrees; but almost all our men took to precipitate flight, so that there remained hardly six or eight of us with him. We were oppressed by the lances and stones which the enemy hurled at us, and we could make no more resistance. The bombards which we had in the boats were of no assistance to us, for the shoal water kept them too far from the beach. We went thither, retreating little by little and still fighting, and we had already got to the distance of a crossbow shot from the shore, having the water up to our knees, the islanders following us and picking up again the spears which they had already cast, and they threw the same spear five or six times; as they knew the captain, they aimed specially at him, and twice they knocked the helmet off his head. He, with a few of us, like a good knight, remained at his post without choosing to retreat further. Thus we fought for more than an hour, until an Indian succeeded in thrusting a cane lance into the captain's face. He then, being irritated, pierced the Indian's breast with his lance and left it in his body, and trying to draw his sword, he was unable to draw it more than half way, on account of a javelin wound he had received in the right arm. The enemies seeing this all rushed against him, and one of them with a great sword, like a great scimitar, gave him a great blow on the left leg, which brought the captain down on his face, then the Indians threw themselves upon him, and ran him through with lances and scimitars and all the other arms they had, so that they deprived of life our mirror, light, comfort and true guide. Whilst the Indians were thus overpowering him, several times he turned round towards us to see if we were all in safety, as though his obstinate fight had no other object than to give an opportunity for the retreat of his men. We who fought to extremity and who were covered with wounds, seeing that he was dead, proceeded to the boats which were on the point of going away. This fatal battle was fought on the 27th of April, 1521, on a Saturday; a day which the captain had chosen himself, because he had a special devotion to it. There perished with him eight of our men and four of the Indians which had become Christians; we had also many wounded, amongst whom I must reckon myself. The enemy lost only fifteen men.

He died; but I hope that your illustrious highness will not allow his memory to be lost, so much the more since I see revived in you the virtue of so great a captain, since one of his principal virtues was constancy in the most adverse fortune. In the midst of the sea he was able to endure hunger better than we. Most versed in nautical charts, he knew better than any other the true art of navigation, of which it is a certain proof that he knew by his genius and his intrepidity, without any one having given him the example, how to attempt the circuit of the globe, which he had almost completed.

SEBASTIAN DEL CANO

The fleet which set out to find the new route to India sailed from Seville on August 10th, 1519. The death of Magellan prevented him from completing the circumnavigation. The command devolved on Sebastian del Cano and he was the first captain to sail round the world. Of the five ships which set out, only *Victoria* reached home on the 6th of September, 1522.

Source: Pigafetta's account of the voyage, Hakluyt Soc., *op. cit.*, p. 162.

At last, when it pleased Heaven, on Saturday, the 6th of September of the year 1522, we entered the bay of San Lucar;

K

and of sixty men who composed our crew when we left Maluco, we were reduced to only eighteen, and these for the most part sick. Of the others, some died of hunger, some had run away at the island of Timor, and some had been condemned to death for their crimes.

From the day when we left this bay of San Lucar until our return thither, we reckoned that we had run more than fourteen thousand four hundred and sixty leagues, and we had completed going round the earth from East to West.

Monday the 8th of September, we cast anchor near the mole of Seville and discharged all the artillery.

Tuesday, we all went in shirts and barefoot, with a taper in our hands, to visit the shrine of St. Maria of Victory and of St. Maria de Antigua.

Then, leaving Seville, I went to Valladolid, where I presented to his Sacred Majesty Don Carlos, neither gold nor silver, but things much more precious in the eyes of so great a Sovereign. I presented to him among other things a book written by my hand of all the things that had occurred day by day in our voyage. I departed thence as I was best able, and went to Portugal and related to King John the things which I had seen. Returning through Spain I came to France, where I presented a few things from the other hemisphere to Madam the Regent, mother of the Most Christian King Don Francis. Afterwards, I turned towards Italy, where I established for ever my abode, and devoted my leisure and vigils to the very illustrious and noble lord, Philip de Villiers Lisleadam, the very worthy grand master of Rhodes.

THE SCURVY

This is a disease caused by a deficiency of Vitamin C. It is easily curable and prevented by a regular supply of fresh vegetables, fruit and lime juice. It was common among sailors in the sixteenth century.

Source: Vasco da Gama describes the disease among his sailors. Camões, *The Lusiads*, Penguin ed. Trans. by W. C. Atkinson, canto 5, 1962.

There befell us, in a word, a disease more dread and loathsome than any I have ever known, that proved fatal to many of our men: their bones now lie buried for ever in a strange and foreign land. It attacked first the mouth and gums, leaving them all swollen and distorted, and as the flesh swelled it rotted in a way that no one who had not seen it would believe. The stench of putrefaction poisoned the air all around. We had no skilled doctor with us, still less a practised surgeon. Those who had the slightest inkling of the art set to, cutting away the poisoned flesh as if it were dead; and well they might, for a man with the disease was as good as a corpse already.

And so we left them on that unknown shore, left them for ever, the companions who had shared our every adventure and misadventure from the beginning. What an easy thing it is to give the body burial! Any wave of the sea, any hillock in a foreign land, will serve for the bones of the greatest of men, just as it served for these.

THE NATIONAL SPIRIT OF PORTUGAL

Luis Vaz de Camões was born in 1524, the year in which Vasco da Gama died. The Camões family was related to the da Gamas, which probably stimulated Luis's interest in the discoveries. Luis was educated at Coimbra university and acquired a thorough knowledge of Latin and of Latin history and mythology. He took part in 1547 in the Ceuta expedition in which he lost one eye. From then onwards his life was stormy, passed almost wholly in exile and in quarrels with all whom he met. He returned to Lisbon in 1570 and *The Lusiads*, his great patriotic poem, was published in 1572. Luis died in 1580.

The Lusiads is the national epic poem of Portugal. Taking Virgil's *Aeneid* as his model, Camões tells the story of the great discoveries made by the Portuguese, which he regards as part of the Divine Plan to win first all Europe and then the whole world to the Christian faith. The narrator in the poem is Vasco da Gama. The following extracts are pitched in a key similar to that of the great outburst by the English Hakluyt, 'What English ships did heretofore ever anchor in the mighty river of the Plate, pass and repass the impassable (in former opinion) Strait of Magellan, range along the coast of Chile, Peru and all the backside of Nova Hispania, further than any Christian ever passed . . .'

Source: The Lusiads, Penguin edition, 1952, trans. by W. C. Atkinson, canto 5, p. 134 *et sqq.*

Consider, Your Majesty, the distance we had travelled now without ever getting away from these uncouth tribes and without ever coming by news or notion of our goal in the East. You may imagine how low our spirits were, how lost we felt, as, worn out with hunger and buffeted by tempests, we hazarded our way through strange climes and unknown waters. Wearied with hope so long deferred, and suffering under the strain of unnatural climatic conditions, we were brought to the verge of despair. Our food supplies had gone bad, so that we ate at our peril, and there was no source of comfort to which we could turn even for the illusion of hope.

Can you believe that if these men had not been Portuguese, they would ever have remained faithful as they have to their king and to me their leader? Do you think they would not have rebelled against me, if I had tried to resist, and taken to piracy, driven by hunger, rage and despair? In truth their metal has been well tested, since no trial, however great, has caused them to falter in that unshakable loyalty and obedience which is the crowning quality of the Portuguese . . .

What say you, Your Majesty? Do you think history can show any before us who have ventured forth on such a journey? Did the travels of Aeneas take him half so far, or those of the eloquent Ulysses? Has any daring explorer of the ocean deep seen an eighth part of what I, by dint of skill and enterprise, have seen and still hope to see, for all the poetry that may have been written about him?

Homer, who drank so deeply of the Aonian spring, seven cities contending for the honour of being his birthplace; Virgil, glory of all Italy, the sound of whose divinely stirring lyre, if it soothed the waters of his native Mincio to slumber, caused the Tiber to swell with pride; let them sing the praises of their more human heroes and exalt their prowess with constant hyperbole, inventing spell-binding Circes, Polyphemuses, sirens whose song lulled the unwary to sleep, despatching them under sail and oar to Thrace or to the land of the lotus-eaters, causing the pilot to fall over-board and be lost, loosing imaginary winds from bags, invoking love-sick Calypsos and harpies who foul their food, sending them down to the world of shades to hold counsel with the dead. Well may they deck out their empty fables, mere dream-stuff, with ever new refinements. The story I tell is the truth naked and unadorned and admits no comparison with such, for all their grandiloquence.

THE DEVELOPMENT OF NAUTICAL INSTRUMENTS

Up to 1484 islands far from the mainland were discovered only by accident, by a ship's being blown on to them by storms—e.g. the discovery of Porto Santo by Zarco and of the Cape Verde Islands by Antonio de Nolle and Diogo Gomez. No sailor cared to lose touch with the land. But according to the legend on Behaim's great globe, which he made in 1492, the Ilhas do Principe (originally named St. Anthony), S. Thomé (more than 50 leagues from the land) and Annobon (more than 80), were discovered in 1484 and no mention is made of any storms. It looks as if the instruments had improved so much that sailors no longer hugged the coast, but were ready to lose sight of it without losing their way.

Source: Behaim's Globe.

In the year 1484, King John of Portugal fitted out two caravels, well provided with men, provisions and munitions of war for three years, and he ordered that after passing the Straits, they should proceed southward and eastward as far as they possibly could. The vessels were laden with all sorts of merchandize for barter. There were also taken out eighteen horses with their harness for presents to the several kings, one for each, as we might find it convenient. We also took all sorts of spices to show the natives what we went in search of. We sailed from Lisbon straight to Madeira, where the Portuguese sugar grows. Passing the Canaries, we found some Moorish chiefs, with whom we interchanged presents, and afterwards came to the kingdom of Gambia, where the malaguette grows, eight hundred leagues distant from Portugal. Thence we passed twelve hundred leagues to the dominions of the King of Furfur, where grows the pepper called Portuguese pepper.[9] Far beyond that country we found the *casca de canella* [or cinnamon], where, having then sailed two thousand three hundred leagues, we turned back and reached Lisbon in the nineteenth month from our departure.

POPE ALEXANDER VI DIVIDES THE WORLD, 1493

The Portuguese were very sceptical about the results of Columbus's explorations—with good reason—and they also resented that Spain should explore at all in the Atlantic. John II was a good geographer and he decided to lay claim to all these new discoveries. Thereupon Spain appealed to the only recognized international authority, the Papacy. Alexander VI was himself a Spaniard and there would seem to be nothing in his character to suggest that he would be impartial in his decision (but see Orestes Ferrara's *The Borgia Pope*, trans. by F. J. Sheed, London, 1942, p. 132 *et sqq.*, for a more lenient view). The Pope issued three Bulls on May 3rd, 1493. In the first he 'donated' to Spain all the islands and mainland territories already discovered and all which might be discovered in the future, provided they did not belong to any Christian ruler. In the second he gave the territorial rights as had been given to Portugal by previous Popes. In the third he commanded the Spanish to teach the Christian faith to the inhabitants. None of these Bulls is the best known of the series, *Inter Cetera Divina*, by which he drew an imaginary line from north to south 100 leagues west of the Azores and Cape Verde Islands and allotted the land and sea west of that line as a Spanish monopoly for exploration. John II accepted the line of demarcation, but he asked for it to be moved 270 leagues farther west. The Spanish monarchs had been greatly deluded by the false geographical conclusions which Columbus had drawn from his discoveries and they saw no harm in agreeing with John II's request. In fact, the Treaty of Tordesillas (1494) was a victory for John II, because it left to Portugal not only the imaginary land of Antilla and the real land of Brazil, but also the true route to India.

Source: Alexander VI's Bull *Inter Cetera Divina*, dated May 4th, 1493, but it may have been issued rather later. This English version is taken from Davenport's *European Treaties bearing on the History of the U.S.*, Washington, 1917.

Alexander, bishop, servant of the servants of God, to the illustrious sovereigns, our very dear son in Christ, Ferdinand, king, and our very dear daughter in Christ, Isabella, queen of Castile, Leon, Aragon, Sicily, and Granada, health and apostolic benediction. Among other works well pleasing to the Divine Majesty and cherished in our heart, this assuredly ranks highest, that in our times especially the Catholic faith and the Christian religion be exalted and be everywhere increased and spread, that the health of souls be cared for and barbarous nations be overthrown and brought to the faith itself. Wherefore, inasmuch as by the favour of divine clemency, we, though of insufficient merits, have been called to this Holy See of Peter, recognizing that as true Catholic kings and princes, such as we have always known you to be, and as your illustrious deeds already known to almost the whole world declare, you not only eagerly desire, but with every effort, zeal and diligence, without regard to hardships, expenses, dangers, with the shedding even of your blood, are labouring to that end; recognizing also that you have long since dedicated to this purpose your whole soul and all your endeavours —as witnessed in these times with so much glory to the Divine Name in your recovery of the kingdom of Granada from the yoke of the Saracens—we therefore are rightly led, and hold it as our duty, to grant you even of our own accord and in your favour those things whereby with effort each day more hearty you may be enabled for the honour of God himself and the spread of the Christian rule to carry forward your holy and praiseworthy purpose so pleasing to immortal God. We have indeed learned that you, who for a long time had intended to seek out and discover certain islands and mainlands remote and unknown and not hitherto discovered by others, to the end that you might bring to the worship of our Redeemer and the profession of the Catholic faith their residents and inhabitants, having been up to the present time greatly engaged in the siege and recovery of the kingdom itself of Granada, were unable to accomplish this holy and praiseworthy purpose; but the said kingdom having at length been regained, as was pleasing to the Lord, you, with the wish to fulfill your desire, chose our beloved son, Christopher Columbus, a man assuredly worthy and of the highest recommendations and fitted for so great an undertaking, whom you furnished with ships and men equipped for like designs, not without the greatest hardships, dangers and expenses, to make diligent quest for these remote and unknown mainlands and islands through the sea, where hitherto no one had sailed; and they at length, with divine aid and with the utmost diligence sailing in the ocean sea,

discovered certain very remote islands and even mainlands that
hitherto had not been discovered by others, wherein dwell very
many peoples living in peace, and, as reported, going unclothed
and not eating flesh. Moreover, as your aforesaid envoys are of
opinion, these very peoples living in the said islands and countries,
believe in one God, the Creator in heaven, and seem sufficiently
disposed to embrace the Catholic faith and be trained in good
morals . . . Wherefore you have purposed with the favour of
divine clemency to bring under your sway the said mainlands and
islands with their residents and inhabitants and to bring them to
the Catholic faith . . . In order that you may enter upon so great
an undertaking with greater readiness and heartiness endowed
with the benefit of our apostolic favour, we, of our own accord,
not at your instance nor the request of any one else in your
regard, but of our own sole largesse and certain knowledge and
out of the fullness of our apostolic power, by the authority of
Almighty God conferred upon us in blessed Peter and of the
vicarship of Jesus Christ, which we hold on earth, do by tenor of
these presents, should any of said islands have been found by your
envoys and captains, give, grant and assign to you and your
heirs and successors, kings of Castile and Leon, for ever, together
with all their dominions, cities, camps, places, villages, and all
rights, jurisdictions and appurtenances, all islands and mainlands
found and to be found, discovered and to be discovered, towards
the west and south, by drawing and establishing a line from the
Arctic pole, namely the north, to the Antarctic pole, namely the
south, no matter whether the said mainlands and islands are found
and to be found in the direction of India or towards any other
quarter, the said line to be distant one hundred leagues towards
the west and south from any of the islands commonly known
as the Azores and Cape Verde. With this proviso, however, that
none of the islands and mainlands, found and to be found, discovered and to be discovered, beyond that said line towards the
west and south, be in the actual possession of any Christian king
or prince up to the birthday of our Lord Jesus Christ just past,
from which the present year one thousand four hundred and
ninety-three begins . . .

DEATH OF KING SEBASTIAN AT ALCAZAR-KEBIR, 1578

John III of Portugal died in 1557. He was succeeded by Sebastian, who was three years old. Stimulated by crusading enthusiasm he came to detest the Moors in Morocco and in 1578 he led an expedition against them which resulted in his total defeat and death.

Source: Fugger Newsletters, ed. by George T. Matthews, Capricorn Books, N.Y., 1959, p. 48.

I cannot hide from you the regrettable and unheard of disaster which befell our King and his whole army in Africa. On the third day of this month (August), our King marched forward to encounter the enemy, meaning to arrive at Alcazar on the same day. Now it happened that Mome Malucho was lying in wait for the King's forces outside Alcazar with fourteen thousand men on horseback and on foot, and he sent an advance guard of about four thousand mounted troops in order to skirmish with them. This filled our King with gladness, so that he ordered his whole army to advance. The Captains of the Germans and the Italians did not deem this wise and they came of their own accord to the King to inform him that the soldiery were in no fit condition, and, moreover, tired, because they had had naught to eat for a long time. They craved therefore that they might be allowed to entrench themselves and to wait until provisions and more fighters were brought up from the fleet. The King had in all not more than twenty-three thousand on foot and sixteen hundred on horseback. The remainder of his forces he had left behind with his fleet or had bidden them to accompany the Sheriff, Mulei Mehemed, who had marched on Masegna and whose father fell in the ensuing battle. But when the King had listened to the counsel of both commanders, he shook his head and said: 'Let us march, let us march'! He ordered such great haste to be made that the cannon, which had formerly headed the army, was finally left behind and in the end unable to come to their assistance. Thereupon the King in person, with the horsemen, began the skirmish with four thousand men. In the meanwhile more and more Turks joined in, until at last their whole army hastened on the scene in half-moon formation, surrounding our forces and taking the cannon, which fired from behind, but could hit no one but our own men.

The Portuguese nobility withstood the onslaught for an hour but they almost all fell on the battlefield. Likewise the Germans, Italians and Spaniards sold their lives dearly. But no more than ten or twelve of them came away alive. The rest were slain with their captains. But the Portuguese infantry surrendered at an early hour. Some of them shot first and then ran away, and some let their blunderbusses drop and surrendered.

Our King bore himself right bravely and, so it is said, killed many Turks with his own hands, but at last, after he had mounted the third horse, he disappeared, so that no one has found him either alive or dead until this hour.

Among the noblemen, of whom not more than sixteen are left, there is also the son of the Duke of Braganza, a young Lord, who drove in a gilt coach to meet the enemy. He had a thousand riflemen with him which his father had given him for his protection. But these were all mown down, and the young Lord was taken from the carriage, for he was believed to be the King. The Turks threw him twice into the air for joy, but he cried out that he was not the King, but the son of the Duke of Braganza, and besought them that his life might be spared, as his father would ransom him with much money. With this the Turks were well satisfied . . .

This letter has lain here until the 25th. To-day definite information arrived that our King fell in battle and was taken by the Moors to one of their cities, Alcazar by name. His adversary, the Moorish King Malucho, and the other Sheriff have also perished, therefore in one and the same battle three Kings and many noblemen on both sides were slain.

SPAIN

ISABELLA OF CASTILE

Isabella of Castile was the daughter of John II of Castile, by his second wife, Isabella, granddaughter of John I of Portugal. She was thus through both parents a descendant of John of Gaunt. She was born in 1451 and died in 1504. In 1469 she married Ferdinand of Aragon and on the death of her brother in 1474, she succeeded to the throne of Castile.

Source: Hernando del Pulgar, *Crónica de los Señores Reyes Católico*... Part II, ch. 4, from the English version printed in S. de Madariaga's *Christopher Columbus*, Hodder and Stoughton, 1939.

This Queen was of middle height, well made in her person and in the proportion of her limbs, very white and fair; her eyes between green and blue, her glance graceful and modest, the features of her face well set, her face very beautiful and gay. She was well measured in the countenance and movements of her person; she drank no wine; she was a very good woman and liked to have old women of good lineage and character beside her. She kept in her palace noble maids, daughters of the Great of her kingdoms, a custom which we have read of no other Queen in any chronicle. She loved much the King her husband and was jealous about him beyond all measure. She was both clever and sensible, which is rarely to be seen together in one person. She spoke very well and was of so excellent a mind that along with so much and arduous work as the government of her kingdoms exacted from her, she took on that of learning Latin letters and within a year attained so much knowledge of them that she was able to understand any Latin speech or writing. She was Catholic and devout; she used to leave secret alms in adequate places; she honoured houses of prayer, she would visit monasteries and houses of religion, particularly those which to her knowledge lived an honest life, and endowed them generously. She abhorred sorcerers and soothsayers and all persons of similar arts and inventions. She took pleasure in the conversation of religious persons who lived a clean life, with whom she often had private councils; though she heard their opinions and that of the other learned men who were at her call, she nevertheless handled most things according to her mind. She came out well in all that she began.

She was very much given to rendering justice, so much that it was said of her that she followed the way of rigour rather than that of truth; and this she did to arrest the great corruption of crimes which she found in the kingdom when she acceded to it . . .

This was the Queen who extirpated and uprooted the heresy which was rampant in the kingdoms of Castile and Aragon . . . In the provision of sees which fell vacant in her time, she had so strict a rule, that, putting off all personal leaning, she always applied to the Pope for generous learned and clean-living men; which we do not read of any other past King to have done so diligently . . . She was a big-hearted woman; she hid her temper and dissimulated it; and owing to this feature of hers which was well known, the Great of the Kingdom as well as other persons dreaded to fall under her indignation. By natural bent she was truthful; though, owing to the great changes due to the wars and other great happenings of her kingdom as well as to the shifting attitudes of certain persons, she did at times swerve. She was a hard worker, as will appear in this chronicle. She was firm in her decisions, from which she receded but with great difficulty. It was said of her that she was not liberal because she did not give away vassals of the royal patrimony to those who served her in those days. True, she kept the royal patrimony so carefully that we saw her give away but few towns and lands, for she found that many had been alienated. But strict as she was in the husbanding of her lands, she was liberal and lavish in the distribution of constant expenses and presents of great value which she made. She used to say that kings must hold to their lands, because by giving them away they lose the rent which enables them to favour their loved ones and they reduce their power to be feared.

She was a ceremonious woman in her attire and in the service of her person, and she would be served by men of greatness and nobility with much respect and humiliation . . . And while on this account she was held to be at fault on the ground of excessive ostentation, we understand that no ceremony in this life is so extreme as to remain below what is owed to the royal state, since such a state is unique and the highest in the realm and must be held in highest honour and splendour over all the states as having a divine authority on the earth.

Owing to this Queen's solicitude was begun, and owing to her diligence was continued, the war against the Moors, until the whole kingdom of Granada was conquered. And we tell the truth before God, that we knew some great lords and captains of her kingdoms who, tired out, had lost all hope of winning it, considering the great difficulty of waging it further; and by the great constancy of this Queen and by her labour and diligence which she put in the matter of provisions, and by other forces which with much strain on her spirit she harnessed to this endeavour, she brought to its final success the conquest which seems to have begun moved by the divine will, as will be seen anon in this chronicle.

FERDINAND OF ARAGON

Ferdinand V of Aragon was born in 1452 and died in 1516. In 1469 he married his cousin Isabella of Castile, in order to unite his own claims to the crown of Castile with hers. When the king died in 1474 Ferdinand tried to assert his claim without recognizing Isabella's, but she asserted her claim firmly and always insisted in having a share in the government of Castile. Ferdinand had a great part in establishing the royal authority in Spain, in expelling the Moors from Granada, in securing Navarre, in helping the voyages of Columbus. He carried on a long struggle with France for supremacy in Italy. The following character sketch bears very little similarity to the portrait usually drawn of this most perfidious king by modern historians.

Source: (a) *Crónica de los Señores Reyes Católicos Don Fernando y Doña Isabel de Castilla y de Aragón.* . . . By Hernando del Pulgar, Pt. II, ch. 3, from the English version printed in S. de Madariaga's *Christopher Columbus.* Hodder and Stoughton, 1939. Fernando del Pulgar was confidential secretary to Isabella of Castile.

This King was a man of middle height, well-proportioned in his limbs, his features well-composed, his eyes merry, his hair dark and straight, and of good complexion. He had an even speech, neither hasty nor slow overmuch. He was of good understanding, and very temperate in food and drink and in the movements of his person, for neither ire nor pleasure could unbalance him. He rode very well; he jousted with ease and with so much skill that no one in the kingdom did it better. He was a keen sportsman

and a man of good endeavour and of much activity at war. By
natural bent, he liked to render justice, and he was also com-
passionate and felt sympathy for miserable people whom he saw
in trouble. He had a singular grace, to wit, that all who spoke to
him at once loved him and wished to serve him, for he had a
friendly intercourse. He was also given to following advice,
especially that of the Queen, for he knew her great competence.
From childhood, he had been brought up in wars, in which he
underwent much hardship and personal danger. And as he spent
all his income in the war and was always short of money, we
can not say he was liberal. He was a truthful man, though the
narrow situations in which wars often put him, made him at
times swerve. He enjoyed all kinds of games such as ball, chess
or royal tables, and he devoted to this pleasure more time than
he ought to have done; while he loved the Queen his wife dearly,
yet he gave himself to other women. He was a man kind and
easy towards all, particularly towards his permanent servants.
This King conquered and won the Kingdom of Granada, as will
be seen in this chronicle.

Source: (*b*) Machiavelli, *Il Principe*, ch. xxi, Dacre's trans. 1640.

We have now in our days Ferdinand, King of Aragon, the
present King of Spain: he in a manner may be termed a new
Prince, for from a very weak King, he is now become for fame
and glory the first King in Christendom, and if you shall well
consider his actions, you shall find them all illustrious and every
one of them extraordinary.

He in the beginning of his reign assailed Granada, and that
exploit was the ground of his state. At first he made that war in
security and without suspicion he should be any ways hindered,
and therein held the Barons of Castiglia's minds busied, who
thinking upon that war never minded any innovation; and in this
while he gained credit and authority with them, they not being
aware of it; was able to maintain with the Church and the
people's money all his soldiers, and to lay a foundation for his
military ordinances with that long war: which afterwards gained
him exceeding much honour.

Besides this, to the end he might be able here-among to undertake greater matters, serving himself always of the colour of
religion, he gave himself to a kind of religious cruelty, chasing
and despoiling those Jews[10] of the Kingdom; nor can this example
be more admirable and rare: under the same cloak he invaded
Africk and went through with his exploit in Italy: and last of all
hath he assailed France, and so always proceeded on forwards
contriving of great matters: which always have held his subjects'
mind in peace and admiration.

Source: (c) Machiavelli, *Il Principe*, ch. xviii, World's Classics, ed.,
1903, p. 71.

A certain prince of the present time, whom it is well not to
name, never does anything but preach peace and good faith, but
he is really a great enemy to both, and either of them, had he
observed them, would have lost him both state and reputation
on many occasions.

THE CAPTURE OF GRANADA, 1491

The great invasion of Europe by the Moors in the eighth century
was halted at Tours by Charles Martel in 732. The expulsion of the
Moors out of Europe took 750 years and was completed after the fall
of Malaga in 1487. The terms of surrender by the Moors to Spain
were settled on November 25th, 1491. The news of the capture of
Granada created immense enthusiasm throughout Christendom. The
following description is taken from Hall's Chronicle.

*Source: The Union of the two noble and illustrate famelies of Lancastre
and Yorke, Kyng Henry the VII, Fol. XXIII.*

The VI daye of April this present yere (1492) the kynge com-
maunded all the nobilitie of his realme to assemble at the
Cathedral Church of Saincte Paule in London, where after Te
Deum solembly songe, the Cardinall of Caunterbury, standynge
on the steeps before the queer dore, declared to the people how
the famous citie of Granada, which many yeres had been possessed
of the Moores or Mawritane nacion, beying infideles and un-
christened people, and now of late beseeged by a great tyme of
Donfernando and Elisabeth his wyfe, kynge and quene of
Spayne, Arragon and Castell . . . And because thys victory

obteyned was to the glory of God, and to the publique wealth of all Christianite, the sayde Cardinall of Caunterbury declared to the people that the kynge had sent hym and the other nobles thether that day, not onely to notefye and declare to them the verite of the fact, but also to exhort them to geve laudes and praysinges to almighty God for delivering so goodly a cytye, so plentiful a countrey, and so notable a region out of the handes of his enemies and persecutors of his faith and religion. Which declaration ended, the Archebishop with the clergie, and the nobles with the cominaltie in moost devout manner, rendring to God for this grete acheved enterprice, glory, honour and most reverent and harty thankes.

THE EXPULSION OF THE JEWS FROM SPAIN, 1492

The undeviating Catholic orthodoxy of Ferdinand and Isabella made inevitable the expulsion of the Jews from Spain, which took place in 1492.

Source: Apud Mercatori, Rerum Ital, Script. Tom. xxiv, 531–2, by Senarega, a Genoese historian who was an eye-witness of the following events.

No one could behold the sufferings of the Jewish exiles unmoved. A great many perished of hunger, especially those of tender years. Mothers, with scarcely strength to support themselves, carried their famished infants in their arms and died with them. Many fell victims to the cold, others to intense thirst, while the unaccustomed distresses, incident to a sea voyage, aggravated their maladies. I will not enlarge upon the cruelty and the avarice which they frequently experienced from the masters of the ships which transported them from Spain. Some were murdered to gratify their cupidity; others were forced to sell their children for the expenses of the passage. They arrived in Genoa in crowds, but were not suffered to tarry there long, by reason of the ancient law which interdicted the Jewish traveller from a longer residence than three days. They were allowed, however, to refit their vessels and to recruit themselves for some days from the fatigues of their voyage. One might have taken them for spectres, so emacited were they, so cadaverous in their aspect and with eyes so sunken. They differed in nothing from the dead except in the power of motion, which indeed they scarcely retained. Many fainted and expired on the mole, which, being completely surrounded by the sea, was the only quarter vouchsafed to the wretched emigrants. The infection bred by such a swarm of dead and dying persons was not at once perceived; but when the winter broke up, ulcers began to make their appearance; and the malady, which lurked for a long time in the city, broke out into plague in the following year.

THE SUCCESSION QUESTION IN CASTILE, 1504

Ferdinand of Aragon was greatly concerned to ensure that when he died he would leave to his successor a strong and undivided empire. He was also anxious to ensure that the empire passed to a Spaniard and not to Portugal nor to a foreigner. He therefore arranged a series of diplomatic marriages for his large number of children, but deaths interfered with his plans. When Isabella of Castile died in 1504 she left the kingdom to her daughter, Juana, who was married to Philip of Burgundy. A clause in the will provided that Ferdinand should act as regent, if Juana should 'prove unwilling or unable to govern'. Clearly Isabella had doubts about Juana, who by 1503 was showing signs of going mad. Eventually she had to be shut up at Tordesillas, where she died in 1555. On Isabella's death, Ferdinand got himself accepted as regent for Juana. The following extracts describe the relationship between Ferdinand, his daughter and his son-in-law and the craftiness of Ferdinand. When Philip died in 1506 Ferdinand married Germaine de Foix, a member of the royal family in Navarre, hoping thereby to get an heir for the Spanish throne and that he would secure Navarre as well. He did have a son by Germaine, but he died in 1509. Thus it was that the Spanish Empire passed to Ferdinand's grandson, Charles, the child of Juana and Philip, when Ferdinand died in 1516.

Source: (a) The will of Isabella: Calendar of State Papers (Spain). Supplement to vols. i and ii, p. 65. Quoted by R. Merton, *Cardinal Ximenes*, London, 1934, p. 95.

It may chance that at the time when God shall summon me from this life, the Princess Doña Juana, Archduchess of Austria, Duchess of Burgundy, my very dear and much beloved . . . daughter, heiress and successor to my kingdoms, may be unwilling

L

or unable to reign and govern. The Cortes of Toledo has therefore begged me to provide for such a contingency and has nominated the king my lord [Ferdinand], in consideration of his great experience in governing.

The day Isabella died Ferdinand summoned the Cortes, announced that he had given the crown of Castile to his daughter, Juana, but that he would reign in her name as 'governor and administrator of Castile for life'. This decision was ratified by the Cortes. The grandees of Castile, however, wanted a less determined man than Ferdinand to rule over them and turned to Philip of Burgundy. Philip was very ambitious to be king of Castile and he was supported by his father, the Emperor Maximilian I. Juana herself backed her husband, Philip.

Source: (*b*) A letter from Juana to Philip's representative in Spain, de Beyre, May 3rd, 1505. *Documentos ineditos para la historia de España*, vol. 8, p. 291. Quoted, R. Merton, *op. cit.*, p. 98.

[Juana wrote that she was not mad: what looked like madness was only the result of jealousy]. Those who have evil intentions may know beyond a doubt that even if I felt as they would wish, I would not take from the king my lord and husband the government of those kingdoms and of all those in the world which are mine, nor would I abstain from giving him all the powers I could, both for the love I bear him and because I could not reasonably give to another the government of his children and mine and of all their inheritance without doing that which I ought not. I hope in God that we shall very soon be in Spain, where my good subjects and servants will see me with much pleasure.

Philip proceeded to fall out with his father-in-law, having arrested his ambassador and thrown him into prison. No love was lost between the two. The following letter was sent by Philip and Juana to certain grandees and prelates in Castile. It is a masterpiece of hypocrisy.

Source: (*c*) Simancas Archives. Quoted by R. Merton, *Cardinal Ximenes*, p. 100.

We wish to inform you that after the death of the very mighty and very Catholic Queen, our mother, of immortal memory, who is with God, we continued through letters and embassies to give complete obedience to the King of Aragon, our lord and father, for the great filial love we bear him. And we were determined to do nothing of importance in our kingdom without his counsel and will, and even to give to his highness as great a part of our revenues as it might please him to take.

Our reward for all this is that when our lord took the kingdom, he had himself sworn as regent without our knowledge and without allowing those who swore him to know what they were doing. Moreover, he sent the Bishop of Palencia here [the Netherlands] to put difficulties in the way of our going to Spain and to persuade us to take the kingdom of Naples and leave Castile to him during his lifetime . . . Which we refused as courteously as could be. And his highness, seeing that we were determined to come to Spain, published it abroad that I, the Queen, was not fit to reign, and said much in prejudice of ourselves and our royal crown. He sought ways of harassing and humiliating our servants, and seized our revenues for some years in advance, in order that we might find no money when we went to Spain. Moreover, he sent Castilian money to his own kingdom of Aragon and spent a large part of the rest in raising armies and fleets with which to intimidate our servants and prevent our coming to Spain . . .

In spite of all these things we have kept silence from duty to the said King so long as it was not known outside the royal council; and we think our silence has been more than reasonable. But now, recognizing the ancient loyalty of your house and yourself, we have thought it right, not without much pain, to inform you of these matters, and to ask and command that you should be on your guard and warn your relatives, friends and servants not to obey in any way whatever the orders of the said King of Aragon, our father, nor allow any office, benefice or reward to be given to anyone without our express command, until we come to Spain . . .

Philip had always been on good terms with Louis XII of France, Louis feared the future and the huge inheritance which would fall to Philip when the Emperor and Ferdinand were dead. He therefore broke with Philip and made an alliance with Ferdinand by the Treaty of Blois, 1505. Philip and Juana sailed for Spain in January, 1506, and were shipwrecked on the English coast. On arriving in Spain Ferdinand sent Ximenes to interview Philip and he arranged a meeting between the two kings. It had come to Ferdinand's ears that his son-in-law, the Constable of France, was planning, if no agreement was reached, to set up Juana as Queen against Philip and Ferdinand. Therefore Ferdinand made a treaty with Philip and an alliance against his daughter and Philip's wife, Juana.

Source: (d) C.S.P. (Spain). Supplement to vols. i and ii, p. 78. Quoted, R. Merton, op. cit., p. 113.

From modesty and out of consideration for the most serene Princess Doña Juana, Queen of Castile, our very dear and much beloved daughter, certain matters were not mentioned in the previous treaty, namely, that the said most serene Queen in no way wishes to occupy herself in or to understand any affair of administration or government. And even if she should wish it, the result would be the total ruin and destruction of these kingdoms, by reason of her infirmities and passions, which from modesty are not expressly mentioned here. [If Juana] should be persuaded to interfere with the government, each of us on request shall help the other against any attempt on the part of the grandees or anyone else. And this we will do in a sincere and straightforward way without guile or cunning.

Ferdinand now drew up a protest against his son-in-law Philip for having damaged the prospects of himself and Juana.

Source: (e) Ibid., p. 81. Merton, op. cit., p. 114.

A tremendous injury has been done us . . . My royal person is in notorious and manifest danger, and I have been forced to-day, June 27th, 1506, in the town of Villafáfila to sign a treaty by which I cede to King Philip the government of these kingdoms.

Moreover I have been forced to sign a document by which, if the most serene queen, his wife and my daughter, attempts to take part in the government, I am to combine with him against her . . . I sign the treaty under the irresistible influence of force and fear . . . I intend as soon as possible to help the most serene queen my daughter to recover what is hers as heiress to these kingdoms, and I intend again to hold the government which for many reasons belongs to me.

Ferdinand and Philip met again on July 5th, 1506. The following account was written by Ferdinand after the meeting.

Source: (*f*) *Documentos Inéditos,* vol. 14, p. 331. Quoted by R. Merton, *op. cit.,* p. 115.

The king my son and I met again at Renedo . . . When he came there passed between us acts of demonstration of the love we bear one another. And the king my son and I spoke alone together in one of the chapels for an hour and a half. What took place between us was substantially that I gave him much advice and instruction as to the good government of these kingdoms, and how to keep them peaceful. We spoke also of many other things, all as a true father and son might speak together. In all of which we were in fullest harmony and enjoyed a relation of great love and intimacy.

After this we admitted the Archbishop of Toledo to our conversation, and there passed in his presence matters of great love, as though we had been real father and son. And so we took our leave of one another after demonstration of love as is fitting between such princes and such close relatives.

CARDINAL XIMÉNES

Francisco Ximénes de Cisneros was born in 1436 at Torrelaguna near Madrid. He was educated at Salamanca and Alcalá for the priesthood, reading both civil and canon law. About 1460 he went for a period to Rome, he returned to Spain in 1465 and that is about all that is known of his life until 1492, when he became confessor to Isabella of Castile. He had a quarrel with Carillo, the Archbishop of Toledo, who threw him into prison for six years. He was released about 1479, left the diocese of Toledo and went to Sigüenza, where he came into contact with the Bishop, Mendoza, who recommended Ximénes to Isabella. Meantime he was vicar-general of the diocese of Sigüenza and acquired a great reputation as an administrator. He joined the Franciscan Order, where he lived a very ascetic life at Castañar for three years. In 1492 he became Isabella's confessor: he was appointed Provincial of the Franciscans and in 1495 Archbishop of Toledo. In 1506 Philip, King of Castile, died: Ximénes became Regent of Castile. In 1516 Ferdinand of Aragon died and Ximénes became Regent for the second time until Charles V landed in Spain, 1517. In that year Ximénes died.

When Ximénes became Archbishop of Toledo he continued to live the same sort of life as he had lived when Provincial of his Order—a great contrast to his predecessor, who had lived magnificently. The people did not approve of the change and their complaints came to the ears of Pope Alexander VI.

Source: (*a*) Alvaro Gómez de Castro, *De Rebus Gestis a Francisco Ximenio Cisnerio, Archiepiscopo Toletano* (Alcalá, 1569), the main source for Ximénes' life. Letter from Pope Alexander VI to Ximénes, 1496.

Dear Brother, the Holy and Universal Church, as you know, like heavenly Jerusalem, has many and diverse adornments. As it is wrong to seek them too earnestly, so it is also wrong to reject them too contemptuously. Each state of life has its appropriate conditions, which are pleasing to God and worthy of praise. Everyone therefore, especially prelates of the church, must avoid arrogance by excessive display, and superstition by excessive humility; for in both cases the authority of the Church will be weakened. Wherefore we exhort and advise you to order your life suitably to the rank which you hold; and since the Holy Father has raised you from humble station to that of Archbishop, it is reasonable that as you live in your conscience according to the rules of God, (at which we feel great joy), so in your external life you should maintain the dignity of your rank.

Source: (*b*) A letter from Pope Leo X to Ximénes, dated May 31st, 1517. Quintanilla, *Archetypo de Virtudes*, 4. 10. Quoted by R. Merton, *Cardinal Ximénes and the Making of Spain*, London, 1934, p. 257.

We have learned that though you are eighty years old and exhausted by the fatigue of church and state matters, you continue, against the advice of your doctors, not only to observe the fasts and abstinences ordained by the Church, but to practise all the austerities customary to the Order of St. Francis: that you wear the habit and the girdle, and sleep fully clothed on a hard bed, without linen and clad in a woollen tunic. Though this manner of life, my dear son, is most edifying, and though we recognize by it that in the evening of your days you are striving nobly to attain the eternal crown which the just Judge shall give you; yet, having regard to your great age and your labours, and to your irreplaceable services to the Holy Church and your country, we, in virtue of the obedience which you owe and have always shown us and under penalty of our displeasure, do of our own will order and command you to soften your manner of life during the time that is left to you, in accordance with the advice of your doctors. We order you namely to discard your habit and to sleep soft and in linen, in order that your health be maintained.

[Ximénes said to his friends] 'What advice is this! Men of the world consider it an honour to die in the habit of St. Francis; and I am ordered to discard it when I am dying, who have worn it all my life long'!

Source: (c) Talavera, Archbishop of Granada, had the catechisms, etc., translated into Arabic for the use of Moorish converts. Ximénes strongly disapproved. *De Rebus Gestis*, fol. 32, 33.

It would be throwing pearls before swine to open the Scriptures to persons in their low state of ignorance, who could not fail, as St. Paul says, to wrest them to their own destruction. The word of God should be wrapped in discreet mystery from the vulgar, who feel little reverence for what is plain and obvious. It was for this reason that our Saviour Himself clothed His doctrines in parables when He addressed the people. The Scriptures should be confined to the three ancient languages, which God with mystic import permitted to be inscribed over the head of His crucified Son: and the vernacular should be reserved for such devotional and moral treatises as holy men indite in order to quicken the soul and turn it from the pursuit of worldly vanities to heavenly contemplation.

CHRISTOPHER COLUMBUS

When Columbus set out on his first voyage in 1492, 'I thought', he wrote, 'to write down upon this voyage in great detail from day to day all that I should do and see, and encounter, as hereinafter shall be seen'. This he did and his Journal is the main source for nearly all our knowledge of Columbus. For a long time this Journal was much criticized by historians who wished to denigrate its author, but its accuracy and reliability have been established by the American historian,

S. E. Morison. The original of the Journal has been lost, probably in the Spanish archives, but a few fair copies were made of it at the time. one was possessed by Bartolomé de Las Casas who used it to write his *Historia de las Indias*, which was composed mostly between 1550 and 1563, but was not printed until 1875. Las Casas saw Columbus in Hispaniola in 1500 and his father and uncle had been shipmates and colonists under Columbus. Columbus's son, Ferdinand, wrote a biography of his father and his description of him tallies with the following account written by de Las Casas.

Source: Historia de las Indias, by de Las Casas. This extract is taken from S. E. Morison's *Christopher Columbus*, O.U.P., undated, pp. 44–6.

As regards his exterior person and bodily disposition, he was more than middling tall; face long and giving an air of authority; aquiline nose, blue eyes, complexion light and tending to bright red; beard and hair red when young but very soon turned grey from his labours; he was affable and cheerful in speaking, and, . . . eloquent and boastful in his negotiations; he was serious in moderation, affable with strangers, and with members of his household gentle and pleasant, with modest gravity and discreet conversation; and so could easily incite those who saw him to love him. In fine, he was most impressive in his port and countenance, a person of great state and authority and worthy of all reverence. He was sober and moderate in eating, drinking, clothing and footwear; it was commonly said that he spoke cheerfully in familiar conversation, or with indignation when he gave reproof or was angry with somebody: 'May God take you, don't you agree to this or that?' or 'Why have you done this or that?' In matters of the Christian religion, without doubt he was a Catholic and of great devotion; for in everything he did or said or sought to begin, he always interposed 'In the name of the Holy Trinity I will do this', or 'launch this' or 'this will come to pass'. In whatever letter or other thing he wrote, he put at the head 'Jesus and Mary be with us on the way', and of these writings of his in his own hand I have plenty now in my possession. His oath was sometimes, 'I swear by San Fernando'; when he sought to affirm something of great importance in his letters on oath, especially in writing to the Sovereigns, he said, 'I swear this is true'.

He observed the fasts of the Church most faithfully, confessed and made communion often, read the canonical offices like a churchman or member of a religious order, hated blasphemy and profane swearing, was most devoted to Our Lady and to the seraphic father St. Francis; seemed very grateful to God for benefits received from the divine hand, wherefore, as in the proverb, he hourly admitted that God had conferred upon him great mercies, as upon David. When gold or precious things were brought to him, he entered his cabin, knelt down, summoned the bystanders, and said, 'Let us give thanks to Our Lord that he has thought us worthy to discover so many good things'. He was extraordinarily zealous for the divine service; he desired and was eager for the conversion of these people [the Indians], and that in every region the faith of Jesus Christ be planted and enhanced. And he was specially affected and devoted to the idea that God should deem him worthy of aiding somewhat in recovering the Holy Sepulchre . . .

He was a gentleman of great force of spirit, of lofty thoughts, naturally inclined (from what one may gather of his life, deeds, writings, and conversation) to undertake worthy deeds and signal enterprises; patient and long-suffering (as shall appear later), and a forgiver of injuries, and wished nothing more than that those who offended against him should recognize their errors, and that the delinquents be reconciled with him; most constant and endowed with forbearance in the hardships and adversities which were always occurring and which were incredible and infinite; ever holding great confidence in divine providence. And verily, from what I have heard from him and from his own father, who was with him when he returned to colonize Hispaniola in 1493, and from others who accompanied and served him, he held and always kept on terms of intimate fidelity and devotion to the Sovereigns.

SAILING INSTRUCTIONS FOR COLUMBUS

Paolo Toscanelli, a Florentine astronomer, was regarded as the highest authority on cosmography and navigation. King Alfonso V, through Canon Fernan Martins, sought for information from Toscanelli about the westward voyage to India. Toscanelli answered on June 25th, 1474, and sent with his letter a map. Soon after Columbus also asked for his advice. Toscanelli answered and sent him a copy of his earlier letter to Martins.

Source: (*a*) Toscanelli's First Letter. *Columbus's Journal*, C. R. Markham, Hakluyt Society, LXXXVI, 1893, p. 3.

Paul, the Physician, to Cristobal Colombo greeting. I perceive your magnificent and great desire to find a way to where the spices grow, and in reply to your letter I send you a copy of another letter which I wrote some time ago to a friend and favourite of the most serene King of Portugal before the wars of Castile, in reply to another which, by direction of his Highness, he wrote to me on the said subject, and I send you another sea-chart like the one I sent him, by which you will be satisfied respecting your enquiries: which copy is as follows:

Source: (*b*) Copy of the Letter to Martins: as above, p. 4.

Paul, the Physician, to Fernan Martins, Canon at Lisbon, greeting. It was pleasant to me to understand that your health was good and that you are in the favour and intimacy with the most generous and most magnificent Prince, your King. I have already spoken with you respecting a shorter way to the places of spices than that which you take by Guinea, by means of maritime navigation. The most serene King now seeks from me some statement, or rather a demonstration to the eye, by which the slightly learned may take in and understand that way. I know this can be shown from the spherical shape of the earth, yet, to make comprehension of it easier and to facilitate the work, I have determined to show that way by means of a sailing chart. I therefore send to his Majesty a chart made by my own hands, on which are delineated your coasts and islands, whence you must begin to make your journey always westward, and the places at which you should arrive, and how far from the pole or the equinoctial line you ought to keep, and through how much space or over how many miles you should arrive at those most fertile places full of all sorts of spices and jewels. You must not be surprised if I call the parts where the spices are west, when they usually call them east, because to those always sailing west, those parts are found by navigation on the under side of the earth. But if by land and by the upper side, they will always be found to the east. The straight lines shown lengthways on the map indicate the distance from east to west, and those that are drawn across show the spaces from south to north. I have also noted on the map several places at which you may arrive for the better information of navigators, if they should reach a place different from what was expected, by reason of the wind or any other cause; and also that they may show some acquaintance with the country to the natives, which ought to be sufficiently agreeable to them. It is asserted that none but merchants live on the islands. For there the number of navigators with merchandize is so great that in all the rest of the world there are not so many as in one most noble port called Zaitun.[11] For they affirm that a hundred ships laden with pepper discharge their cargoes in that port in a single year, besides other ships bringing other spices. That country is very populous and very rich, with a multitude of provinces and kingdoms, and with cities without number, under one Prince who is called Great Kan, which name signifies *Rex Regum* in Latin, whose seat and residence is generally in the province Katay. His ancestors desired intercourse with Christians now 200 years ago. They sent to the Pope and asked for several persons learned in the faith, that they might be enlightened, but those who were sent, being impeded in their journey, went back. Also in the time of Eugenius one of them came to Eugenius, who affirmed their great kindness towards Christians, and I had a long conversation with him on many subjects, about the magnitude of their rivers in length and breadth, and on the multitude of cities on the banks of the rivers. He said that on one river there were near 200 cities with marble bridges great in length and breadth, and everywhere adorned with columns. This country is worth seeking by the Latins, not only because great wealth may be obtained from it, gold and silver, all sorts of gems, and spices, which never reach us; but also on account of its learned men, philosophers, and expert astrologers, and by what skill and art so powerful a province is governed, as well as how their wars are conducted. This is for some satisfaction to his request, so far as the shortness of time and my occupations admitted: being ready in future more fully to satisfy his royal Majesty as far as he may wish.

Given at Florence, June 24th, 1474.

First Letter to Columbus Resumed.

From the city of Lisbon due west there are 26 spaces marked on the map, each of which has 250 miles, as far as the most noble and very great city of Quinsay.[12] For it is a hundred miles in circumference and has ten bridges, and its name signifies the city of Heaven; many wonders being related concerning it, touching the multitude of its handicrafts and resources. This space is almost a third part of the whole sphere. That city is in the province of Mangi, or near the province of Katay, in which land is the royal residence. But from the island Antilia, known to you, to the most noble island of Cippangue[13] there are ten spaces. For that island is the most fertile in gold, pearls and precious stones, and they cover the temples and palaces with solid gold. Thus the spaces of the sea to be crossed in the unknown parts are not great. Many things might perhaps have been declared more exactly, but a diligent thinker will be able to clear up the rest for himself. Farewell, most excellent one.

Source: (c) Second Letter to Columbus: as above, p. 10.

Paul, the physician, to Cristoval Colombo greeting. I received your letters with the things you sent me, and with them I received great satisfaction. I perceive your magnificent and grand desire to navigate from the parts of the east to the west, in the way which was set forth in the letter I sent you, and which will be demonstrated better on a round sphere. It pleases me much that I should be well understood; for the said voyage is not only possible, but it is true, and certain to be honourable and to yield incalculable profit and very great fame among all Christians. But you can not know this perfectly save through experience and practice, as I have had in the form of most copious and good and true information from distinguished men of great learning who have come from the said parts, here in the court of Rome, and from others being merchants who have had business for a long time in those parts, men of high authority. Thus when that voyage shall be made, it will be to powerful kingdoms and cities and most noble provinces, very rich in all manner of things in great abundance and very necessary to us, such as all sorts of spices in great quantity, and jewels in the greatest abundance.

It will also go to the said Kings and Princes who are very desirous, more than ourselves, to have intercourse and speech with Christians of these our parts, because a great part of them are Christians, as well as to have speech and intercourse with men of learning and ingenuity here, as well in religion as in all the other sciences, by reason of the great fame of the empires and governments in these parts that has reached them. On account of all these things, and of many others which might be mentioned, I do not wonder that you, who have great courage, and all the Portuguese people who have always been eager for all great undertakings, should be with a burning heart and feel a great desire to undertake the said voyage.

COLUMBUS LANDS IN THE NEW WORLD

At 2 a.m. on October 12th, 1492, Rodrigo de Triana, look-out on the *Pinta's* forecastle, suddenly cried out, 'Tierra! Tierra'! The New World had been discovered. The land sighted was the island Guanahani, one of the Bahamas. Perhaps the Northmen centuries earlier had sighted the Western Hemisphere, but nobody had done so since. It was the East coast which was first seen by Columbus: it was on the west coast that Columbus landed on the beach of Long or Fernandez Bay.

Source: The Journal of Columbus, trans. and edited by C. R. Markham, Hakluyt Society, No. LXXXVI, 1893.

At two hours after midnight the land was sighted at a distance of two leagues. They shortened sail, and lay by under the mainsail without the bonnets. The vessels were hove to, waiting for daylight; and on Friday they arrived at a small island of the Lucayos, called, in the language of the Indians, *Guanahani*. Presently they saw naked people. The Admiral went on shore in the armed boat, and Martin Alonzo Pinzon and Vicente Yañez, his brother, who was captain of the Niña. The Admiral took the royal standard, and the captains went with two banners of the green cross, which the Admiral took in all the ships as a sign, with an F and a Y[14] and a crown over each letter, one on one side of the cross and the other on the other. Having landed, they saw trees very green and much water, and fruits of diverse kinds. The Admiral called to the two captains, and to the others who leaped on shore, and to Rodrigo Escovedo, secretary of the whole fleet, and to Rodrigo Sanchez of Segovia,[15] and said that they should bear faithful testimony that he, in presence of all, had taken, as he now took, possession of the said island for the King and for the Queen, his Lords making the declarations that are required, as is more largely set forth in the testimonies which were then made in writing.

Presently, many inhabitants of the island assembled. What follows is in the actual words of the Admiral in his book of the first navigation and discovery of the Indies. 'I knew', he said, 'that we might form great friendship, for I knew that they were a people who could be more easily freed and converted to our holy faith by love than by force, gave to some of them red caps, and glass beads to put round their necks, and many other things of little value, which gave them great pleasure, and made them so much our friends that it was a marvel to see. They afterwards came to the ship's boats, where we were, swimming and bringing us parrots, cotton threads in skeins, darts, and many other things; and we exchanged them for other things that we gave them, such as glass beads and small bells. In fine, they took all and gave what they had with good will. It appeared to me to be a race of people very poor in everything. They go as naked as when their mothers bore them, and so do the women, though I did not see more than one young girl. All I saw were youths, none more than thirty years of age. They are very well made, with very hand-some bodies and very good countenances. Their hair is short and coarse, almost like the hairs of a horse's tail. They wear the hairs brought down to the eyebrows, except a few locks behind, which they wear long and never cut. They paint themselves black, and they are the colour of the Canarians, neither black nor white. Some paint themselves white, others red, and others of what colour they find. Some paint their faces, others the whole

body, some only round the eyes, others only on the nose . . .
They are all of fair stature and size, with good faces and well
made . . . They should be good servants and intelligent, for I
observed that they quickly took in what was said to them, and
I believe that they would easily be made Christians, as it appeared
to me that they had no religion . . . I saw no beast of any kind
except parrots on this island . . .

Their hair is not curly, but loose and coarse, like horse hair.
In all the forehead is broad, more so than in any other people I
have hitherto seen. Their eyes are very beautiful and not small,
and themselves far from black, but the colour of the Canarians
. . . Their legs are very straight, all in one line, and no belly, but
very well formed. They came to the ship in small canoes, made
out of the trunk of a tree like a long boat, and all of one piece,
and wonderfully worked, considering the country. They are
large, some of them holding 40 to 45 men, others smaller, and
some only large enough to hold one man. They are propelled
with a paddle like a baker's shovel, and go at a marvellous rate.
If the canoe capsizes, they all promptly begin to swim and to bale
it out with calabashes that they take with them.

A STATE VISIT TO COLUMBUS

On December 6th, 1492, Columbus arrived at the island which is
now known as Hispaniola. On the 12th he took possession of the
island for Ferdinand and Isabella. The harbour where he had anchored
he named *Puerto de la Concepción*, because that day was the vigil of the
Conception of the Virgin, but the Spaniards soon changed its name to
Bahía de los Mosquitos. On December 18th, the feast of the Annuncia-
tion, the ships *Santa María* and *Niña* were dressed, banners were displayed, escutcheons were hung along the bulwarks and salutes were
fired. At about 9 a.m. a young *cacique* (an Indian ruler) paid a state
visit to Columbus's ships.

Source: Columbus's *Journal*, C. R. Markham, *op. cit.*

Without doubt, his state and the reverence with which he is
treated by all his people would appear good to your Highnesses,
though they all go naked. When he came on board, he found
that I was dining at a table under the poop, and at a quick walk

he came to sit down by me, and did not wish that I should give place by coming to receive him or rising from the table, but that I should go on with my dinner. I thought that he would like to eat of our viands, and ordered them to be brought for him to eat. When he came under the poop, he made signs with his hand that all the rest should remain outside, and so they did, with the greatest possible promptitude and reverence. They all sat on the deck, except the men of mature age, whom I believe to be his councillors and tutor, who came and sat at his feet. Of the viands which I put before him, he took of each as much as would serve to taste it, sending the rest to his people, who all partook of the dishes. The same in drinking: he just touched with his lips, giving the rest to his followers. They were all of fine presence and of very few words. What they did say, so far as I could make out, was very clear and intelligent. The two at his feet watched his mouth, speaking to him and for him, and with much reverence. After dinner, an attendant brought a girdle, made like those of Castile, but of different material, which he took and gave to me, with pieces of worked gold, very thin. I believe they get very little here, but they say they are very near the place where it is found and where there is plenty. I saw that he was pleased with some drapery I had over my bed, so I gave it him, with some very good amber beads I wore on my neck, some coloured shoes, and a bottle of orange-flower water. He was marvellously well content, and both he and his tutor and councillors were very sorry that they could not understand me, nor I them. However, I knew that they said that if I wanted anything, the whole island was at my disposal. I sent for some beads of mine, with which as a charm I had a gold *excelente*, on which your Highnesses were stamped. I showed it to him and said, as I had done yesterday, that your Highnesses ruled the best part of the world, and that there were no Princes so great. I also showed him the royal standards, and the others with a cross, of which he thought much. He said to his councillors what great lords your Highnesses must be to have sent me so far, even from Heaven to this country, without fear. Many other things passed between them which I did not understand, except that it was easy to see that they held everything to be very wonderful.

CHRISTOPHER COLUMBUS ARRIVES IN LISBON

Source: Ruy de Pina, *Crónica d'el Rei Dom Joaõ, cap.* 66, *apud Collecaõ de Livros Ineditos de Historia Portugeza*, Lisbon, 1790–93, tom. ii. Ruy de Pina was a man high in the royal confidence and an eye witness of the following event.

In the year 1493, on the sixth day of March, arrived in Lisbon, Christopher Columbus, an Italian, who came from the discovery, made under the authority of the sovereigns of Castile, of the islands of Cipango and Antila; from which countries he brought with him the first specimens of the people, as well as of the gold and other things to be found there; and he was entitled admiral of them. The king, being forthwith informed of this, commanded him into his presence; and appeared to be annoyed and vexed, as well from the belief that the said discovery was made within the seas and boundaries of his seignory of Guinea—which might give rise to disputes—as, because the said admiral, having become somewhat haughty by his situation, and in the relation of his adventures always exceeding the bounds of truth, made this affair, as to gold, silver and riches, much greater than it was. Especially did the King accuse himself of negligence in having declined this enterprise, when Columbus first came to ask his assistance, from want of credit and confidence in it. And, not withstanding the King was importuned to kill him on the spot, since with his death the undertaking, so far as the sovereigns of Castile were concerned, would cease from want of a suitable person to take charge of it; and notwithstanding this might be done without suspicion of the King's being privy to it—for, inasmuch as the admiral was overbearing and puffed up by his success, they might easily bring it about that his own indiscretion should appear the occasion of his death—yet the King, as he was a prince greatly fearing God, not only forbade this, but even showed the admiral honour and much favour, and therewith dismissed him.

M

NEWS OF THE DISCOVERY REACHES ITALY

Source: A letter from Luca Fancelli, an old architect in the service of the Gonzaga, to Francesco Gonzaga, Marquis of Mantua: July 22nd, 1493. Quoted in Cartwright, *Isabella d'Este*, vol. i, p. 94 *et sqq.*

Your Highness may have heard that we have had letters here [Florence] telling us that the King of Spain sent some ships over the seas, which, after a voyage of thirty-six days, discovered certain islands, amongst others a very big one lying east, with broad rivers and terrible mountains, and a very fertile land, inhabited by handsome men and women, who go naked or only wear a cotton leaf round the waist. This country abounds in gold, and the people are very courteous and liberal of their property, and there are quantities of palms of more than six different kinds, and some wonderfully tall trees. There are other islands, five of which have been given names, and one which is nearly as large as Italy. And the rivers there run with gold, and there is plenty of copper but no iron, and many other wonders, and you can neither see the Arctic nor the Antarctic poles.

Francesco had sent two servants, Giovanni dei Bardi and Giambattista Strozzi to Spain to buy horses. They wrote to him from Cadiz. Cartwright, *ibid.*

A Savona sailor named Columbus has landed here, bringing 30,000 ducats in gold, as well as pepper and other spices, and parrots as big as falcons and as red as pheasants. They found trees bearing fine wool and others which produce wax and linen fibres, and men like Tartars, tall and active, with long hair falling over their shoulders. They eat human flesh, and fatten men as we do capons, and are called cannibals. . . . It is certain that these sailors have brought back a great quantity of gold, sandal-wood, spices, and what I myself have seen,—sixty parrots of variegated colours, eight of them as big as falcons—as well as twelve Indians, who have been sent to the King. And in that land they found great forests in which the trees grew so thickly you could hardly see the sky, and if some men had not climbed to the top of the trees, they would never have got out again, and many other things of which I have not time to tell.

A letter from a scholar at Ferrara named Ponzone to Isabella d'Este, Marchioness of Mantua: Cartwright, *ibid.*

I hear that a man named Columbus lately discovered an island for the King of Spain, on which are men of our height but of copper-coloured skin, with noses like apes. The chiefs wear a plate of gold in their nostrils which covers the mouth, the women have faces as big as wheels, and all go naked, men and women alike. Twelve men and four women have been brought back to the King of Spain, but they are so weakly that two of them fell ill of some sickness which the doctors do not understand, and they had no pulse and are dead. The others have been clothed, and if they see any one who is richly clad, they stroke him with their hands and kiss his hands to show how much they admire him. They seem intelligent and are very tame and gentle. No one can understand their language. They eat of everything at table, but are not given any wine. In their own country they eat the roots of trees and some big kind of nut which is like pepper but yields good food, and on this they live.

HERNAN CORTES

CONQUEROR OF MEXICO

Hernán Cortés was born in 1485. On November 18th, 1518, he set out with 600 foot, 18 horses and some artillery to conquer Mexico for Spain. He founded Vera Cruz and then burned his ships behind him to prevent his men from deserting. In a short time he had conquered Mexico, but his methods in consolidating his gains were savage in the extreme. He was ungratefully treated by the Spanish authorities and died, a neglected hero, in 1547.

Source: Bernal Díaz del Castillo, *Historia verdadera de la Conquista de la Nueva España.* Bernal Díaz served with Cortés. This English version is taken from the Hakluyt Society's edition, 2nd series, xxx, vol. v, pp. 215 *et sqq.*

He was of a good height and body and well-proportioned and robust, and the colour of his face inclined to be greyish and not very bright, and had his face been longer, he would have been better looking; in his eyes and expression there was something kindly, yet grave; his beard was rather dark, scant and thin and the hair, which at that time he possessed, was of the same sort as the beard. He had a deep chest and well-shaped shoulders, and he was lean and of little belly and slightly bow-legged, with his legs and thighs well set on. He was a good horseman and skilful with all weapons on foot and on horseback and knew very well how to manage them. Above all he possessed courage and spirit, which is what matters most of all. I have heard it said that when he was a youth in the island of Hispaniola he was somewhat disso-lute about women, and that he fought with knives several times with strong and dexterous men, and always came off victorious. He had a scar from a knife-wound near his under-lip, and if one looked hard at it, he was inclined to cover it up more with his beard. This scar was given him when he indulged in those quarrels. In all of which he showed both by his appearance and in his speech and conversation, and in eating and in his dress, signs of being a great Lord.

The clothes he wore were in accordance with the time and fashion and he cared nothing for wearing many silks and damasks and satins, but dressed simply and very neatly, nor did he wear heavy gold chains, except a thin chain of gold of finest workman-ship and a small pendant with the image of Our Lady the Virgin Santa Maria, with her precious son in her arms and with a motto in Latin on our Lady's side, and on the other side of the jewel St. John the Baptist with another motto. He wore besides on his fingers a very rich ring with a diamond, and on the cap, which in those days was usually made of velvet, he wore a medal. I do not remember what design was on it, but on the medal were his initials. In the course of time he always wore a cloth cap without a medal. He was luxuriously attended, as a great Lord, by two stewards and mayordomos and many pages, and all the service of his house was very complete, with great table services of silver and gold. He dined well and he drank a good cup of wine and water which held a pint, and he also took supper, but he was not dainty nor did he care to eat of delicate and expensive dishes, except when he saw that expenditure was necessary or he was obliged to give them.

He was very affably disposed towards all his captains and comrades . . . He was a Latin scholar, and I heard it said that he was a bachelor of laws and when he spoke with educated men or Latin scholars, he answered them in Latin. He was something of a poet and made couplets both in rhyme and in prose, and in what he talked about he spoke with moderation and very good expression. He recited prayers every morning out of a book of Hours and heard mass with devoutness. He took as his especial patron saint our Lady the Virgin Mary, of whom all we faithful should take hold as our intercessor and advocate, and he also held by Senor San Pedro and Santiago and Senor St. John the Baptist. And he was charitable with alms. When he swore, he said, 'on my conscience', and when his anger was aroused by one of his soldiers who were his friends, he would say to him 'oh, evil take you'. When he was very angry, a vein in his throat swelled up and another in his forehead, and sometimes when very angry he raised a cry to heaven, but he never said a foul or injurious word to any captain or soldier.

He was most long-suffering, for there were very inconsiderate soldiers who said insolent things to him and he never answered them haughtily or unpleasantly, even though there may have been reason for it; the most he would say to them was 'be quiet' or 'God go with you and for the future be more careful what you say or it will cost you dear' . . .

He was very fond of cards and dice, and when he played he was very sociable and would use certain witty expressions which dice-players are wont to repeat: and he was addicted to women in excess and jealously guarded his own. He was most careful in all our campaigns, even by night, and many nights he went the rounds and challenged the sentinels, and he entered into the Ranchos and shelters of our soldiers, and if he found one without his arms and with his shoes off, he admonished him and said to him 'to a worthless sheep the wool seems heavy'.

THE BATTLE OF TABASCO, 1519

In February, 1519, Cortés landed at Tabasco where he found the natives very hostile. After some skirmishes an army of some thousands of Indians advanced to attack the Spaniards, who defeated them, largely owing to the panic which the strange sight of sixteen horses and riders caused among the Indians.

Source: Bernal Díaz, *True History of the Conquest of Mexico*.

Diaz accompanied Cortés's expedition and saw the events which he describes. As an old man living in Guatemala he wrote his history in reply to Gomara's *History of the Conquest of Mexico*, which he thought too laudatory of Cortés. Quoted in Kirkpatrick, *The Spanish Conquistadores*, Black, 1934, pp. 67–8.

The Indians come on like mad dogs and surround us on all sides and hurl so many arrows, javelins and stones that at the first onslaught they wounded more than seventy of us . . . and they kept on shooting and wounding. With our artillery and muskets and crossbows we fought hard . . . Mesa, our gunner, killed many of them because they were dense squadrons . . . but with all the hurts and wounds we gave them, we could not drive them away . . . All this time Cortés with his horsemen did not appear . . . and we feared some disaster had happened to them . . . When we fired, the Indians raised loud shouts and whistling and threw dust and grass in the air that we might not see their losses; and they sounded their trumpets and drums and whistlings and shouts and cried *Ala Lala*.

At this, we saw the horsemen appear; and since these dense squadrons were heedlessly intent on attacking us, they did not at once perceive the horsemen who attacked them in the rear; and since the ground was level and the horsemen were good riders and some of the horses handy and swift, they dealt with them so well, spearing them as they pleased . . . and we went so hard at them, the horsemen on one side and we on the other, that they soon turned their backs. The Indians thought the horse and rider were one creature, for they had never seen horses till then . . . they took refuge in some woods that were there . . . We buried two men who had been killed and we seared the wounds of the men and the horses with fat from a dead Indian, and we set guards and sentinels and supped and went to rest.

MONTEZUMA, AZTEC EMPEROR OF MEXICO

Montezuma II was born in 1466 and died in 1520. In 1502 he was elected Emperor. In 1518 the Spaniard, Hernán Cortés, landed in Mexico, marched on the capital and soon made Montezuma a prisoner. In June 1520 the Spaniards were attacked by the inhabitants of Mexico City. Montezuma ordered his subjects to lay down their arms, but he was set upon by the Mexicans and wounded, so that he died three days later.

Source: (a) Francisco Cervantes de Salazar: *Crónica de la Nueva España*, written about 1560, published in 1914. Bk. IV, ch. 3, p. 279. This English version is taken from Madariaga's *Hernán Cortés*, Hodder and Stoughton, 1942. The original was written about 1560.

He was a man of average stature, with a certain gravity and royal majesty which plainly showed who he was even to those who did not know him. He was thin, light-bodied, of a yellowish-brown colour, as of a parrot, in the manner of all persons of his nation; his hair was long, very black and shiny, almost down to his shoulders; he had a sparse beard, with a few black hairs some inches long; his eyes black, his glance brave, and all over his face a certain affability along with a royal majesty, such that those who looked at him felt drawn to love and revere him. He was a fairly strong man, lithe and light; he was a good archer, a good swimmer and proficient in all warlike exercises; he was good-natured, though strict as a judge, and this he did in order to be loved and dreaded, for on account both of what his predecessors had told him and of what he had learned from personal experience, he knew that his subjects were such that they could not be governed nor kept within bounds of justice otherwise than by rigorous and stern ways . . . He spoke well and wittily when there was occasion for it; yet most prudently; he was very fond of women and used to take drugs to strengthen his virility; he treated them well and enjoyed them in the utmost secrecy; he was fond of feasts and pleasures, though owing to his gravity, he was sparing in the use of them. In his religion and worship of his vain gods he was most careful and devout; in offering sacrifices most assiduous; he ordered that all laws and statutes concerning religion should be respected with the utmost rigour; for nothing was he less lenient than for an offence, however slight, to the divine worship. In the punishment of larceny and adultery, to which he saw his people especially addicted, he was so severe that no friendship nor entreaty was enough to stay the execution of a law. Towards his own people, he behaved with such majesty that, no matter how great the person, he allowed no one to sit down in his presence or to wear shoes or to look at his face, save such and such a person and they had to be great lords and of royal blood.

He went about always very polished and, in his way, richly dressed; he was marvellously clean, for every day he took two baths; he seldom left his apartment, save for meals; he did not receive many visitors; most business was transacted through the members of his council, and they or one of them came to report to him, but even this only through two or three interpreters, though they all spoke the same language. He went through his house to the sacrifices which were offered in the chief temple of Uitzilopochtli, where, at some distance from the great of his realm, he showed much devotion; he came out downcast, wrapped in thought, speaking to no one.

Source: (*b*) Bernal Díaz: *The Conquest of New Spain*, trans. J. M. Cohen, Penguin Classics, 1963, pp. 224 *et sqq.*

The great Montezuma was about forty years old, of good height, well-proportioned, spare and slight, and not very dark, though of the usual Indian complexion. He did not wear his hair long but just over his ears, and he had a short black beard, well-shaped and thin. His face was rather long and cheerful, he had fine eyes, and in his appearance and manner could express geniality or, when necessary, a serious composure. He was very neat and clean, and took a bath every afternoon. He had many women as his mistresses, the daughters of chieftains, but two legitimate wives who were *Caciques* in their own right, and when he had intercourse with any of them, it was so secret that only some of his servants knew of it. He was quite free from sodomy. The clothes he wore one day he did not wear again till three or four days later. He had a guard of two hundred chieftains lodged in rooms beside his own, only some of whom were permitted to speak to him. When they entered his presence they were compelled to take off their rich cloaks and put on others of little value. They had to be clean and walk barefoot, with their eyes downcast, for they were not allowed to look him in the face, and as they approached they had to make three obeisances, saying as they did so, 'Lord, my lord, my great lord'. Then, when they had said what they had come to say, he would dismiss them with a few words. They did not turn their backs on him as they went out, but kept their faces towards him and their eyes downcast, only turning round when they had left the room. Another thing I noticed was that when other great chiefs came from distant lands about disputes or on business, they too had to take off their shoes and put on poor cloaks before entering Montezuma's apartments; and they were not allowed to enter the palace immediately, but had to linger a while near the door, since to enter hurriedly was considered disrespectful.

THE DESTRUCTION OF MEXICO CITY, 1521

So resolutely did the Aztecs defend Mexico City that Cortés (who called it 'the most beautiful city in the world') reluctantly decided that it must be systematically and completely destroyed.

Source: Bernal Díaz, *True History of the Conquest of Mexico*, p. 99. Hakluyt Society, 2nd series, XXX, vol. iv, p. 183.

That night there was rain, thunder and lightning . . . and when Guatemoc [the Aztec King] was taken prisoner, all of us soldiers found ourselves as deaf as if one had been standing on the top of a belfry with many bells ringing and as if at the height of the ringing they had suddenly ceased to ring. And I say this purposely; for during all the ninety-three days we had been besieging this city, the Mexican squadrons both night and day were raising such shouts and cries and whistlings, preparing the troops and warriors who were to fight on the causeways; others summoning the canoes which were to fight with the brigantines and to attack us on the bridges; others marshalling those who were to drive down stakes and make breaches in the causeways and deepen the water and make breastworks; others preparing stones, javelins and arrows, and the women providing round stones for the slings; and from the temples the drums and horns and the great drum and other wailing trumpets never ceased to sound; so that night and day we had great noise such that we could not hear one another: and when Guatemoc was taken, the shouts and noise ceased: and thus I say it was as if till then we had been standing on a belfry.

DE LAS CASAS AND THE CONQUEST OF PERU

Peru was discovered by Vasco Nuñez de Balboa in 1513. It was conquered by Francisco Pizzaro who perpetrated in Peru atrocities at least as appalling as Cortés and other conquistadors had used against the Indians of the New World. De Las Casas was not the first Spaniard to protest against these evils, but he was by far the greatest. He was born in 1474 and died in 1566. He was a member of Diego Velasquez's expedition to conquer the island of Cuba (1511–12) and he tried in vain to stop the atrocities. In 1514 he began a campaign against the system known as *repartimiento*, the enslaving of Indians for forced labour. He met with great opposition, but on the death of King Ferdinand in 1516, the regent, Cardinal Ximénes, put him in charge of a commission to find out methods for relieving the Indians. He returned to Spain in 1517, dissatisfied with the caution of the rest of the commission. His plan for colonizing the Indians and importing negro slaves failed. In 1530 he obtained a royal command forbidding slavery in Peru, but the conquistadors were stronger than the royal authority. De Las Casas now wrote several books, of which the most famous is his *Short Relation of the Destruction of the Indians of the West*, 1539. In 1544 he became Bishop of Chiapas, in Southern Mexico, where he met with such opposition that he gave up his bishopric. He continued to fight for the Indians, without success, until he died in 1566.

Source: De Las Casas, *Short Relation*, trans. by F. A. MacNutt, in his *Bartholomew de Las Casas*, Putnam, 1909, p. 397 *et seqq.*

Of the countless notoriously wicked and cruel acts committed in the extirpation of these people by those who call themselves Christians, I will relate some few that a Friar of St. Francis witnessed in the beginning; and he signed depositions with his name, sending some of the copies to those regions and others to the kingdoms of Castile; and I have one of the copies in my possession with his own signature, in which he makes the following statements.

'I, Fray Marcus de Nizza of the Order of St. Francis, commissary of the Friars of the same Order in the provinces of Peru, who were among the first monks who entered the said provinces with the first Christians, speak to render truthful testimony of some of the things that I saw with my own eyes in that country; chiefly concerning the treatment of the Indians and the acquisition of property taken from the natives.

'First of all I am eye-witness, and from actual experience know, that these Indians of Peru are the most affable people that have been seen among the Indians, and were very well inclined and friendly towards the Christians.

'And I saw that they gave gold abundantly to the Spaniards, and silver and precious stones and all that was asked of them, and that they rendered them every good service; and the Indians never went forth in war fashion, but always peaceably, as long as no cruelty and ill-treatment provoked them; on the contrary, they received the Spaniards with all benevolence and honour in their towns, giving them provisions and as many male and female slaves for their service, as they asked.

'I am also witness, and I testify, that without the Indians giving them any cause or occasion, the Spaniards, as soon as they entered their country, and after the chief lord Atabaliba had paid them more than two millions of gold and had left all the country in their power, immediately burnt the said Atabaliba, who was ruler of all the country; and after him they burnt alive his captain-general Cochilimaca, who had come peacaably to the governor, accompanied by other high personages.

'Within a few days after these executions they likewise burnt Chamba, another very high lord of the province of Quito, without his giving them any cause.

'Thus too they burnt unjustly Chapera, lord of the Canarios.

'Likewise they burnt the feet of Luis, who was one of the great lords in Quito, and tortured him in many other ways, to force him to reveal the hiding place of Atabaliba's gold, of which treasure it was known that he knew nothing whatever . . .

'The Spaniards assembled a large number of Indians, and shut up as many as could enter in three large houses, which they then set on fire and burnt them all, although they had never done the slightest thing against any Spaniard, nor given the least cause.

'It once happened that, when a priest called Ocana pulled a child out of the fire in which it was burning, another Spaniard snatched it out of his hands and threw it back in the middle of the flames, where it became ashes together with the others; while the aforesaid Spaniard, who had thus thrown the Indian into the fire, was returning to his dwelling the same day, he suddenly fell dead in the road; and it was my opinion that they should not give him Christian burial.

'Moreover I affirm that I myself saw the Spaniards cut off the hands, noses and ears of the Indian men and women for no purpose whatever, but just because the fancy struck them; and in so many places and regions did this occur that it would be a long story to tell . . .

'I call God and my own conscience to witness that, as far as I can understand, the Indians only revolted on account of this ill-treatment, which sufficiently justified their action, as may be clearly seen by everybody . . .'

A SWISS VIEW OF THE CHARACTER OF THE INHABITANTS OF SPAIN, 1599

Source: (a) Thomas Platter, *Journal of a Younger Brother*, ed. and trans. by Seán Jennet, Fuller, London, 1963, pp. 227–8.

The country is more thinly inhabited and less fertile than France, and so quantities of wheat have to be brought from abroad to feed the people. Let us add, too, that the Spaniard prefers the lance to the plough and would rather find wealth in war than in the cultivation of the fields. The farmers and cultivators are mostly Frenchmen, who, ashamed to work so lowly in

their own country, where many of them once occupied honourable positions, have exiled themselves so that they do not have to
blush because they live by the work of their hands. As for the
Spaniards, they are at once so proud and so avid that they disdain
small wages and prefer to cross the seas in search of glory and
fortune in the Indies. Men of the lowest origins have thus raised
themselves to the highest ranks. As soon as they attain to riches
they dress in magnificent clothes and surround themselves with
extraordinary luxury, and give themselves the airs of a great lord,
although their father may be no more than a poor labourer. In
Barcelona the wives of simple cobblers were pointed out to me,
with whom the ladies of the nobility could scarcely compete.
They suck pride in with their milk. They are the vainest nation
I have ever seen. They have nothing but disdain for foreigners,
and as they try to lord it everywhere, they are everywhere
detested.

The Spaniard is sad by nature, taciturn, uncommunicative, slow
in his enterprise, and never takes a risk unless the profit is clear.
Always stiff and affected, he knows neither the gaiety nor the
affability of the French. Otherwise sober, especially when it is
he who has to pay, he does not drink pure wine, and accustoms
himself as well as he may to a little salad or cardoons for his
complete nourishment; but this does not prevent him from
putting a partridge claw in his hat and playing negligently with a
tooth-pick, to give the impression that he has just come from a
feast. Drunkards are never seen in the streets, for drunkenness is
regarded as a disgrace.

There are no courtesies for strangers, as there are in France.
Indeed, the Spaniards show little courtesy among themselves,
and a peasant would think twice before making way for a prince.
On the other side of the medal, however, their word is sure.
Away from home, they strive to maintain their pride, though it
be to the death. No other nation so well endures thirst, hunger,
or heat, and this is what makes them such good soldiers. Skilful
in skirmishes, cautious in combat, agile in scaling walls, because
of their slender stature, they are as prompt to attack as to retreat.
But their infantry is superior to their cavalry, despite the fact that

the latter have horses so fine and so fleet that they are called the sons of the wind. They also make incomparable seamen.

Source: (b) Seán Jennet, op. cit., p. 228.

In Spain parliaments are replaced by chambers of justice, one in Castile, one in Granada, a third in Galicia, and a fourth in Navarre. Advocates are less numerous than in France, and less eloquent. Each province has its own customs, *pragmaticas*. Barcelona in particular enjoys extraordinary privileges and recognizes the king only as count, *conditionaliter*. They are so intractable about this privilege that they would go over to the King of France rather than renounce their right. Further, as I found more than once watching their plays, Catalans and Castilians have little love for each other. The Catalans also have more prerogatives. They may wear large starched ruffs and long rapiers, whereas for others ruffs must not be more than two fingers wide, without starch, and their rapiers must not be more than a certain measure. They are forbidden to walk at night more than four persons together. If there are only two of you, you must never let anyone pass between you. There are a thousand petty regulations of this sort that expose a stranger to considerable fines.

A considerable advantage enjoyed by the Spaniards is that of the Confraternity or *Hermandad*, a kind of league formed between towns which enables them at the first signal to put thousands of armed men into the field. It is especially useful for the pursuit of malefactors, few of whom remain unpunished. As soon as a criminal is caught by the *Hermandad* he is tied to a post and killed by arrows from bows. This association renders useful service in a country full of workless men and lazy and debauched soldiers.

Notes

[1] In reality 800 along the coast of Africa and 60 in India.

[2] In reality 330.

[3] In reality about 160.

[4] In reality 682.

[5] Ceylon.

[6] Pink rubies.

[7] In fact 10,500 nautical miles, or 3,060 Portuguese leagues.

[8] Moçambique is only 60 leagues from Madagascar: 300 would carry a ship as far as the Seychelles.

[9] The name 'Grain Coast' is derived from the 'Grains of Paradise', 'Guinea Grains', or malguette pepper which is found there.

[10] Machiavelli's word is 'Marranos', a Spanish name for people of oriental origin, especially Moors.

[11] Zayton, Kwangehang-fu.

[12] Hangchow-fu.

[13] Japan.

[14] Ferdinand and Isabella.

[15] The Royal Inspector.

THE ITALIAN WARS
(*Notes on p. 209*)

CHARLES VIII AND THE ITALIAN WARS

THE CONDITION OF ITALY IN 1490

Source: Guicciardini, *Storia d'Italia*, Eng. ed. A. P. Goddard, i.

It is certain that, for above a thousand years back (at which period the Roman Empire, weakened by a change of her ancient institutions, began to fall off from that pitch of grandeur, to the attaining of which the most incredible virtue and good fortune had equally contributed) Italy had at no time enjoyed a state of such complete prosperity and repose as in the year 1490, and some time before and after.

The people too had taken advantage of this halcyon season and been busied in cultivating their lands, as well mountains as valleys; and being under no foreign influence, but governed by their own princes, Italy not only abounded with inhabitants and riches, but grew renowned for the grandeur and magnificence of her sovereigns, for the splendour of many noble and well-built cities, learned in all arts and sciences. She had also no small share of military glory, according to the knowledge and practice of arms in those days.

CHARLES VIII

He was the only son of Louis XI: born in 1470, died in 1498. He succeeded his father when he was 13 years old and was totally unfit to govern. Until 1492 he left the government to his sister, Anne of Beaujeu, but in that year he asserted himself and got rid of the Beaujeus. He set out on his disastrous plans to revive the Angevin claims to the kingdom of Naples, thereby setting in motion the Italian Wars, 1494. He entered Naples on May 12th, 1495, but a general coalition was formed against him and he was forced to return to France. He was planning a second expedition in 1498 when he died on April 8th.

Source: (*a*) Albèri, *Relazioni degli Ambasciatori Veneti al Senato*, Series I, vol. iv, pp. 15–16.

His Majesty the King of France is twenty-two years old, small and ill-formed in person, with an ugly face, large lustreless eyes which seem to be short-sighted, an enormous aquiline nose, and thick lips which are continually open; he stutters and has a nervous twitching of the hands which is unpleasant to watch. In my opinion—it may well be wrong—he is not of much account either physically or mentally; however, he is generally well-spoken of in Paris as being a good hand at tennis, hunting, and tilting—pursuits to which, whether for good or ill, he devotes much time. He is praised also in that he now desires himself to debate and decide questions which in the past he would leave to certain members of his Secret Council, and it is said that in this respect he acquits himself quite creditably.

Source: (*b*) Ludovico il Moro, as reported by Sebastian Badoer, December 3rd, 1494. *Storia documentata di Venezia*, 2nd ed., vol. v, p. 51.

The King is young, of small capacity and indifferent judgement. His counsellors are divided into two sets: one is led by M. Philippe [de Bresse], whose followers are my enemies; the other is led by M. de Saint-Malo [Briçonnet] and M. de Beaucaire [de Vesc], and is opposed in every respect to the first. Neither cares a straw for the good of the country, provided it can get the better of its rivals and secure the triumph of its own views. The real aim and object of all is the acquisition of money; they care for nothing else, and they have no sense among them. I have in my mind a picture of the King at Asti with his counsellors around him. When some question came up for discussion, some would begin to gamble, others to eat, one to do one thing, one another. Some one would express an opinion, and the King would adopt it and dispatch orders in that sense: then somebody else would come and speak with him, and the orders would be revoked. Charles is consumed by pride and ambition and respects nobody: sometimes, when we were sitting together, he would rise and go off to dinner, leaving me alone, as though I had been a dog . . . Seeing his backwardness in the common cause, his forwardness in asking for money, and the rapacity of his courtiers, who give

N

not a thought to what might be called administration, I said to him one day:—'Sire, if you wish me to give you money, I ought to know what has been done with that which you have already had, and what you purpose to do with that for which you now ask'. As his officials would not let in the light on their peculations, I was not troubled with any further demands.

WHY THE EXPEDITION WAS UNDERTAKEN

Source: P. de Commines, *Mémoires,* ed. T. Calmette, vol. iii, pp. 3 *et sqq.*

I must tell how it came about that King Charles, who is now on the throne, undertook his voyage to Italy, in which I took part . . . There was much dispute as to the likelihood of his going, for the enterprise seemed the height of folly to all wise and experienced men, and no one approved of it save himself and a certain person called Etienne de Vers, a low-born Languedocian without knowledge or experience. Another had taken a hand in it until his courage failed him, a finance minister called General Briconet, to whom the said voyage afterwards brought a Cardinal's hat and much ecclesiastical property and preferment. The other had already acquired many estates; he was Seneschal of Beaucaire and President of the Chambre des Comptes at Paris; and during the King's childhood he had served him well as a Valet de Chambre. It was he who brought the General into it, and these two were the cause of the said enterprise, for which few praised and many blamed them, since everything requisite for so great an undertaking was lacking. The King was young, feeble, self-willed, and with few wise advisers or good leaders in his company. Money was scarce, and before starting they had to borrow a hundred thousand francs from the Sauli bank at Genoa at 14 per cent. interest, and to raise several other loans elsewhere, as I will recount later. There were no tents or pavilions, yet the winter was come when they began to advance into Lombardy. One good thing they had, and that was a gallant company of young gentlemen, full of courage, but something lacking in discipline. Thus we must conclude that the expedition was conducted throughout by the hand of God, for the sense of its leaders, whom I have named, was unequal to the conduct of it. All the same, they may claim to have been the means of winning great honour and glory for their master.

THE FRENCH IN NAPLES

Charges of atrocities are always difficult to prove or disprove when they are brought against invading armies. Frightful accusations were brought by Italians against the armies of Charles VIII. More damaging to the French was the half-hearted defence made by a Frenchman, P. de Commines, who almost admitted the charges and certainly knew all the facts.

Source: P. de Commines, *Mémoires*, ed. T. Calmette, vol. iii, p. 100.

The King conferred great favours upon the people and lightened their fiscal burden; and I am certain that this people, inconstant though it was, would not for its part have turned against us, had he but done some little thing to satisfy the nobles. But he never received them, and they were insulted at his doors. Those best treated were avowed adherents of the House of Aragon; but everybody lost something, and not an office or appointment was left to them, the Angevins being even worse treated than the Aragonese. An edict, said to have been obtained by bribing the President de Ganay and the Seneschal [de Vesc], who had lately been made Duke of Nola and Grand Chamberlain of the kingdom, decreed that all holders of properties should be confirmed in their possession; the result was to make it impossible for the Angevins to recover their estates except by litigation; and those who had resumed possession on their own account, like the Count of Celano, were forcibly ejected. All offices and appointments were bestowed on Frenchmen, often two or three on the same recipient. The stores found in the castle of Naples when it was captured, which were very great, as the King was well aware, he gave away to all who asked for them . . . The conclusion is plain, that the conduct of this great affair had been no achievement of its leaders but entirely the work of God. The great faults I have mentioned, however, these were the work of men— of men made blind by glory, who did not recognize the source of their good fortune, and behaved themselves as was natural in persons of their character and experience.

The above account is borne out almost word for word by Guicciardini, *Storia d'Italia*, vol. i, pp. 114–15.

THE FRENCH ARMIES

Source: (*a*) Guicciardini, *Storia d'Italia*, vol. i, p. 150.

At this time the Kingdom of France, though very powerful in Cavalry, copiously furnished with artillery, and most expert in the use of it, was very weak in native infantry, for arms and military exercises were confined to the nobility, and the commons, devoted to peaceable interests and occupations, and long unused to war, had thus lost their former martial qualities. By reason, too, of divers conspiracies and rebellions occurring in the kingdom, several former Kings, in fear of popular violence, had set themselves to disarm the people and divorce them from military pursuits. Thus the French no longer put any confidence in their own infantry, and went to war in trepidation, if their army did not contain a band of Swiss. Always of a fierce, untameable spirit, this people within the last twenty years had much enhanced its reputation, for, when attacked in force by Charles, Duke of Burgundy, who by his power and vigour had made himself a terror to France and all his neighbours, they had in a few months inflicted upon him three defeats, in the last of which he had met his end, either in the battle itself or in flight, for the manner of his death was obscure. In view, then, of their efficiency and of the fact that with them the French had no rivalry, jealousy or competition of interests, as with the Germans, the French engaged none but Swiss infantry, and never embarked upon a serious war without their co-operation.

Source: (*b*) Machiavelli, *Ritratti delle Cose della Francia*, *Opere*, vol. vi, pp. 299–300. Bridge, *History of France 1493–1815*, vol. ii, p. 107. O.U.P., 1924.

The infantry of France is but indifferent: for as it is a long time since they were employed in any service, they must be supposed to have little or no experience. Besides, they are composed altogether of peasants and pitiful mechanics, who, having been long used to live in the most servile and abject subjection to the Noblesse, at last became dispirited and always behave like cowards and poltroons when they come to action: of which a thousand instances might be given. The King, therefore, makes little or no account of them, and seldom or never employs them. Indeed, there are some regiments of Gascon infantry in the service, who are something better than the rest; for as they live near the confines of Spain, they seem to have a little of the Spanish discipline and spirit; and yet, from what has been seen of them for many years past, they have behaved more like freebooters and marauders than good soldiers. In assaulting or defending towns, however, they make tolerable proof; but in the field they are good for nothing; in which they are very unlike the Germans and Swiss, who have no equals in open action, though they are very little esteemed when they are made use of either to storm or to defend a fortified place. The reason of which I take to be that the method of fighting and discipline is very different in these two cases; and, upon this consideration, the King of France always employs either Swiss or German infantry in the field, because his Gendarmerie can not be persuaded to put any confidence in the Gascons in time of action. But if his infantry was as good as his Gens d'Armes, he would be able to make head against all the Princes in Europe.

Source: (c) But Machiavelli saw the ill-effects of employing the Swiss. *The Prince*, ch. xii, Farneworth's trans., vol. ii, pp. 305–6. Bridge, *op. cit.*, ii, 109.

[The employment of the Swiss was] the occasion of all those dangers to which that kingdom is visibly exposed at this day; for by giving that preference to the Swiss, they have discredited and daunted their own soldiery, having entirely broken their infantry and made their cavalry so dependent upon others, by accustoming them to fight always in conjunction with the Swiss, that they are now possessed with an opinion that they can do nothing without them. From hence it came to pass that the French are no match for the Swiss; and without their assistance they make no figure in the field against any other forces. So that the French armies are at present composed of mixed troops, partly mercenary, partly national; which, however, are much better in the main than either mercenaries or auxiliaries alone; but still much inferior to national forces only.

Source: (*d*) The Artillery: Albèri, *Relazioni degli Ambas. Ven.*, Series I, vol. iv, p. 23. Bridge, *op. cit.*, ii, 111.

The Royal artillery consists of bombards with iron projectiles, which, if of stone, would weigh about one hundred pounds; they are mounted on carriages with so admirable an ingenuity that they can fire without any emplacement or other preparation. There also *spingardes*, mounted on carriages. This artillery is utilized in two ways: when the camp is pitched a rampart is made of the carriages, which renders the camp impregnable; and when some place is to be reduced, the bombards destroy the walls; this they do much more easily and quickly than our big guns could do it. It is said that when Louis took the field, thirty thousand horses were required to draw his artillery. In the present King's campaigns about twelve thousand horses have been wanted for this purpose.

Source: (*e*) The Florentine ambassadors to the Seignoria on the eve of Charles VIII's departure for Italy. Canestrini et Desjardins, *Négociations diplomatiques de la France avec la Toscane*, vol. i, pp. 401–2. Bridge, *op. cit.*, ii, 112.

The French are taking with them a numerous artillery, all on carriages. The guns are not too big, being of one hundred to three hundred pounds; the balls are of iron, which weighs more; the guns are made very heavy and strong in the breech, where the powder is put; and then they taper off into a narrowish mouth. In the centre are supports for making them fast on the carriages; each gun has its carriage, gunners and balls, with a great number of charges of powder suited to the gun. The carriages make a park when in camp . . . When they reach a place, they take the beasts from the carriages, turn the guns round, and gradually push them forward, so that in a single day they can work their way up to the walls under cover of the carriages,

without other protection; and when they come to a bombardment, thirty or forty guns open fire, with the result that the wall
is soon reduced to powder. They say that their artillery can
breach a wall eight feet thick, and although each hole may be
small, yet the number is great, for from the time they begin, they
do not stop a single moment day or night, so that the defence has
neither rest nor leisure to make repairs. They have no doubt that
they could dispose of Leghorn in one day and of Pisa in two; they
mock at Ostia and say they would be ashamed if they could not
take it in forty-eight hours; and a bombardier who has been to
spy upon Naples, is ready to stake his head on having the Castel
Nuovo in two days;[1] and though the French are by nature
braggarts, yet Francesco della Casa and other Florentines, who
have seen the guns with their own eyes, tell you things about them
that make your flesh creep.

   Source: (*f*) Guicciardini, *Storia d'Italia*, Eng. ed. A. P. Goddard, i, 138.

   At Genoa in the meantime arrived from Marseilles a great
quantity of field pieces and battering cannon, such as in Italy had
never hitherto been seen. This plague had its origin in Germany
and with great labour was brought from thence by the Venetians
about the year 1380 and made use of against the Genoese ... The
largest pieces of the artillery we are speaking of were called
bombarde, some whereof were iron, some brass. From that time
they were spread through Italy and made use of in sieges; but for
size and awkward make they were moved from place to place
with great difficulty, and for some reason were very unhandy
when placed against the walls of a town. The intervals between
the firings were so long that a great deal of time was lost, which
gave leisure to the besieged to repair the breaches. But notwithstanding all these impediments, the violence of the powder was
such that the balls of these instruments flew with a thundering
noise and did greater execution than any engines till that time
invented by Archimedes or any of the ancients.

   But now the French brought a much handier engine made of
brass and called *cannon*, which they charged with heavy iron balls,
much larger than those of stone, made use of heretofore, and

drove them with horses, not with oxen, so as to keep pace with the army. These were planted against the walls of a town with great ease and speed; the space between the shots was so little and the ball was impelled with such force that as much was done in a few hours as formerly in the like number of days. These rather diabolical than human instruments were used, not only in sieges, but also in the field, and were mixed with others of smaller size. This artillery rendered Charles's army, already formidable for the number and valour of its troops, dreadful to all Italy.

Source: (*g*) On December 31st, 1494 in the fading light of a winter's evening, Charles VIII's army entered Rome. A contemporary historian has given a detailed account of that entry, too detailed to be interesting to-day. But his account does stress the enormous impression left on his mind when he saw the artillery arriving: *Istorie del suo, trans.* L. Domenichi (1555), vol. i, pp. 53–5.

But that which above all else caused universal amazement and dread was the artillery; there were thirty-six pieces on carriages drawn by horses with incredible speed over any ground, rough or smooth. The majority were called cannons: these were eight feet long, containing six thousand pounds of bronze, and fired iron balls as big as a man's head. Then came the culverins, which were rather more than half as long, were smaller in the bore and fired smaller shot. After these came the falcons, of varying sizes; the smallest fired balls about the size of an orange. All these pieces were secured by their handles to great axles, being so disposed as to allow of adjustment for the discharge. The small ones were borne on two wheels, the large on four, of which the pair behind were detachable, to admit of greater speed. On smooth ground the gunners and drivers, urging their horses on with whip and voice, could move at the gallop and attain a wonderful speed.

POPE ALEXANDER VI AND CHARLES VIII

Source: Johann Burchard, *At the Court of the Borgia*, being an Account of the Reign of Pope Alexander VI written by his Master of Ceremonies, ed. and trans. by Geoffrey Parker, Folio Society, 1963, pp. 90 *et sqq.*

On the following Tuesday, Don Engelardo, the Pope's private secretary, summoned a number of Germans in the city, myself included, to an audience with His Holiness at seven o'clock in the evening. The Pope recounted to us what trouble the French King was causing him by his insolent behaviour in occupying the lands of the Church and approaching to besiege Rome, and stated that, although he did not anticipate a siege by the French, he nevertheless did not know what conclusions to draw about His Majesty's intentions, when he was scarcely behaving as the Most Christian King of Europe. He accordingly asked us to communicate this news to our compatriots in Rome, since he had great confidence in the German nation and wished us to stir them to the defence of Pope, Church and city alike. . . . On Thursday, December 18th, all the Pope's possessions, including even his bed and daily credence-table, were assembled for removal by road from the Vatican Palace to the Castel Sant' Angelo. The vestments from the Apostolic Chapel, all the money chests from the sacristy, the palace weapons and stores of food, and all the papal belongings were sent to the Castle, whilst the Cardinals also prepared to leave, loading packhorses and furnishing their mounts for the road . . . On Monday, December 2nd, they began to demolish the house of Dom Jacopo Magnolino, around which a ditch was then dug. During these days also, from December 19th onwards, the French troops were breaking into the city's suburbs by Monte Marco and penetrating as far as the Church of San Lazzaro and the fields close to the Castel Sant' Angelo . . . On the morning (of Wednesday, December 24th) news had reached the Pope before daybreak that the King wished to reach a peaceful settlement for his entry into Rome, and His Holiness therefore wanted him to despatch another of his officials immediately with whom he could make arrangements about the Royal arrival. On the same morning, before coming to Chapel, the Pope summoned the Cardinals to the Sala del Pappagallo (with the exception of the celebrant, Cardinal San Giorgio), and in the presence of the Duke of Calabria he told them of all the developments about Charles VIII's approach to the city.

THE NEWS OF THE FALL OF NAPLES

Charles VIII's successful and easy march through Italy, his entry into Rome, followed by the advance on Naples with the complete collapse of Spanish resistance and the occupation of Naples itself, was far from acceptable to the rest of Italy and the European powers. Most especially did Venice look askance at this challenge to her supremacy in Italy. P. de Commines was Charles VIII's representative in Venice.

Source: Commines, *Mémoires*, ed. T. Calmette, vol. iii, p. 124.

I found the Signory assembled in great numbers, somewhere about fifty or sixty, in the room of the Doge, who was sick of a colic. He told me the news with an affectation of joy, but none of the others could dissemble as he did. Some sat on footstools, their heads bowed in their hands; others were in different postures; and all showed symptoms of being sick at heart. I doubt if the Roman Senators were more amazed or taken aback when the news of Hannibal's victory at Cannae reached their city. Not a single Venetian seemed to see me; saving the Doge, not one addressed me; and I was amazed to behold them. The Doge asked me if the King would abide by his promises, which I had always confirmed. I assured him earnestly that he would, did my best in the interests of peace, and offered to serve therein to the best of my ability, hoping to allay their mistrust; and then took my leave.

THE LEAGUE OF VENICE, 1495

The immediate reaction to Charles VIII's success was the making of the League of Venice against him. The Pope, the King of the Romans, the Catholic Sovereigns, the Republic of Venice, and the Duke of Milan, banded themselves together for twenty-five years to maintain the peace in Italy, to promote the welfare of Christendom, to uphold the honour of the Papacy and of the rights of the Empire, and to protect each other against aggression from any other powers. Commines was summoned to the Signory on April 1st, 1495.

Source: (*a*) Commines, *op. cit.*, vol. iii, p. 126. Bridge, *op. cit.*, vol. ii, p. 219.

The league was concluded late one night. The next morning the Signory sent for me earlier than usual. After I had entered

and taken my seat, the Doge informed me that in honour of the
Holy Trinity they had concluded a league between our Holy
Father, the Pope, the King of the Romans, the King of Castile,
the Duke of Milan, and themselves with three objects; first, the
defence of Christendom against the Turk; secondly, the defence
of Italy; thirdly, the preservation of their states: and I was to
communicate it to the King. They were assembled in great
numbers, a hundred or more; they held their heads high and were
in great spirits, and their expressions were very different from
those which I had beheld when they had told me of the taking of
the castle at Naples. They told me further that they had written
to recall their ambassadors who were with the King . . . I was
sick at heart and very anxious for the safety of the King and all
his company, believing, as they did themselves, that matters were
more advanced than they were. I feared that they might have the
Germans ready; and in that case the King could never get out of
Italy. I made up my mind that in this predicament I would not
talk too much; but they set to work to draw me out. I told them
that already on the previous evening and on several other occasions I had advised the King of what was going on, and that, as
he told me in reply, he had heard of it also from other sources.
At this they made wry faces, for there is no people so suspicious
or secretive—indeed, they often give themselves away by their
own craftiness—and this was why I told them. I added that I had
also written to Messieurs d'Orléans and Bourbon, so that they
might look to Asti: this I said, hoping to delay their advance
upon Asti, which could not possibly be saved, had they been as
well prepared as they pretended and believed; for the place was
ill-equipped, and so for long remained.

They proceeded to tell me that the business was not aimed
against the King, but was designed for protection from him; and
they said that they could not tolerate the deception he practised
upon everyone, saying he wanted nothing but Naples and a
crusade, and then acting in a manner quite contrary, trying to
destroy the Duke of Milan and the Florentines and to seize estates
of the Church. I answered to this that the Kings of France had
augmented the Church and increased and defended her, and that

the present King was more likely to do the same than to take anything from her; that their alleged motives were not those by which in fact they were actuated; that they wished to trouble Italy for their own profit; and that they seemed quite likely to succeed. They took that a little ill, as I was told; but I spoke the truth, as is shown by the places they have gained in Apulia as a reward for helping King Ferrand against us. When I rose to withdraw, they made me be seated again, and the Doge asked me if I were not desirous of making some overture of peace, seeing that I had spoken in that sense on the previous day. That, however, had been upon the condition that they should postpone the conclusion of their league for a fortnight, so that I might send to the King and have his answer. These things being said, I withdrew to my lodging. They sent for the ambassadors one after the other; and when their council dispersed, I met the Neapolitan in a new robe and high glee; and there was reason for it, for this was great news for him.

Source: (*b*) The Venetian version of the same episode runs as follows: Malapiero, Annali Veneti, in *Archivio Storico Italiano*, Series I, vol. vii, p. 334. Bridge, *op. cit.*, vol. ii, p. 221.

On the first of April, the Doge summoned the ambassador of France and informed him that on the previous day a league and good understanding had been concluded . . . and would be published on the ensuing Palm Sunday. The ambassador was astonished: never, he said, had the Signory broken faith with any one; how could they have betrayed his King? Upon the Doge replying that peace with his King was more than ever desired, he asked: 'Then why was the league made?' He was told that it was from a desire to avoid molestation. The Frenchman retorted: 'The result is to close my King's road home'. To which the Doge responded: 'Far from that. Everyone will give him free passage; the Signory will be the first to offer it, together with victuals in their territories; and if he does not care to risk the journey, by land, we will offer him for his service fifteen, twenty, or even thirty-five galleys.' Directly the ambassador left the Palace, orders were given that joy bells should be rung throughout the Venetian territory; and for three days the rejoicings were kept up with illuminations in the customary manner.

CHARLES VIII LEAVES NAPLES

The League of Venice made it imperative that Charles should leave Naples while the going was good. He left on May 20th, 1495, leaving a garrison in Naples. The Appennines proved his most difficult obstacle, but he got across to find an army of the League under the Marquis of Mantua waiting at Fornovo on the river Taro. The King was anxious to negotiate, for his position was perilous, but the battle came on suddenly while the discussions were in progress. It lasted barely a quarter of an hour. The French succeeded in forcing their way through the enemy, but with heavy losses, and eventually they made their way out of Italy by the end of September, 1495. Back in France, Charles was planning another expedition into Italy, but he died in 1498 before he could complete his plans.

Source: The Battle of Fornovo. A letter from Francesco Gonzaga, Marquis of Mantua, the Captain of the armies of the League, to his wife, Isabella d'Este, July 7th, 1495: Luzio, *Archivio Storico Italiano*, quoted in Julia Cartwright's *Isabella d'Este*, vol. i, p. 119.

Yesterday's battle, as you will have heard from the herald, was very fiercely contested, and we lost many of our men, amongst others Signor Rodolfo and Messer Giovanni Maria, but certainly many more of the enemy were slain. And what we ourselves did is known to all, so that I need not speak of it here, and will only tell you that we found ourselves in a position of such peril that only God could deliver us. The chief cause of the disorder was the disobedience of the Stradiots, who gave themselves up to plunder, and in the hour of danger not one of them appeared. By the grace of God we and this army have been saved, but many fled without being pursued by any one, and most of the foot soldiers, so that few of these remain. These things have caused me the greatest sorrow which I have ever known, and if by ill chance our enemies had turned upon us, we must have been utterly destroyed. Some French nobles were made prisoners by our company, amongst others the Comte de Pigliano and Monsieur le Bâtard de Bourbon. The enemies departed this morning and are gone over the hill towards Borgo San Domino and Piacenza. We will watch their course and see what we have to do. If others had fought as we did, the victory would have been complete, and not a single Frenchman would have escaped. Farewell.

LOUIS XII AND THE ITALIAN WARS

Louis XII (1462–1515) was the son of Charles of Orléans, who after the battle of Agincourt spent twenty-five years in captivity in England. Louis was Duke of Orléans up to his accession in 1488. At the age of 14 he married Joan, daughter of Louis XI. After 1499 he divorced Joan in order to marry Anne of Bretagne, the widow of Charles VIII. She died in 1514 and Louis then married Mary Tudor, sister of Henry VIII. Louis died on January 1st, 1515. In 1499 Louis laid claim to the Duchy of Milan. The claim was rejected by Lodovico il Moro and by the Emperor, Maximilian I. Owing to mutual jealousies the League of Venice collapsed, Pope Alexander VI welcomed an alliance with Louis, as did also the Venetians. Louis bought off the Emperor by a gift of some towns in Artois to his son Philip, the Archduke. The French armies entered Milan on October 6th, 1499, but Lodovico, thanks to the help of the Swiss, won back his duchy in February, 1500. He then seized Novara, where the French besieged him. The Swiss at this point went over to the side of the French, the Duke escaped but was eventually found and taken prisoner. Louis imprisoned him in the chateau of Loches where he languished until he died ten years later.

LODOVICO IL MORO

Lodovico Sforza, known as Il Moro, was the son of Francesco Sforza, Duke of Milan, and his wife Bianca Maria. He was born in 1451 and he died in 1510. He succeeded his nephew Gian Galeazzo as Duke in 1494, but the general belief that he had his nephew murdered is not now accepted. His contemporary, Paolo Giovio, wrote of him that he was 'born for the ruin of Italy' because it was Lodovico who invited Charles VIII to invade Italy. He married Beatrice d'Este, sister of Isabella d'Este. He was a very great and enlightened patron of the arts, and perhaps his chief claim to fame is that he employed Leonardo da Vinci at Milan. He eventually lost his duchy to Louis XII of France, who captured him in 1500 and shut him up in the chateau of

Loches, where he died in 1510 after much suffering in miserable conditions.

Source: Guiciardini, Storia d'Italia, Eng. ed. A. P. Goddard, ii, 349.

Lodovico Sforza was without question a prince of extraordinary wit and eloquence, and of many other natural endowments, and might well deserve the appellation of gentle and merciful, had not the infamy of his nephew's death sullied that part of his character. But on the other hand it must be confessed that he was naturally vain, restless, ever full of ambitious projects, made light of his promises or a breach of his faith, and was so conceited of his wisdom that he could by no means endure to hear another commended for extraordinary prudence and sagacity, persuading himself that by his own art and industry he could dive into the thoughts and penetrate the designs of the most able politicians and bend them to his purposes.

Unless otherwise stated, the English versions dealing with Louis XII and the Italian Wars are taken from J. S. C. Bridge, A History of France, 1483–1515, Clarendon Press, 1921–36.

Source: (b) The Capture of Lodovico il Moro. Report from La Trémoille, the French commander, Chartrier de Thouars, pp. 40–1. Bridge, op. cit., vol. iii, p. 114.

I think that, had it come to a battle, we should have given them a good drubbing, but the main thing was to catch the Moor. Our search lasted for three hours. We made them all pass under a pike and at last our man was discovered. It is the best thing that has happened for a century and redounds to your honour. He gave himself up to M. de Ligny, alleging an agreement come to with him over-night. M. de Ligny had told me something about this agreement during the morning, but the Moor forfeited his safe-conduct, if he ever got one, for he tried to run away ... Sire, methinks that you should lose no time in taking the Moor into your own hands and putting him into some good, strong place, from which he cannot escape. Sire, you promised me, when I left, that as soon as your business here should be done, you would permit me straightway to come home. I beg that you will bear me in mind.

[From Louis's answer] I have a marvellous longing to see the Moor on this side of the Alps. Let Hédouville and Louvain start with 200 men-at-arms and take him to Susa, where they will find M. de Crussol, Captain of the Guard, with his archers, who will bring him in safety to me. I shall never be happy till I get him across the Alps.

Source: (c) Lodovico arrives at Lyons. Sanuto, I Diarii, vol. iii, cols. 320–2. The Venetian envoy to the Signory. Bridge, op. cit., vol. iii, p. 116.

Signor Lodovic was brought into this city yesterday. He was preceded by twelve local officials, who kept back the people, of whom there were great crowds in all the streets. Then came the governor of the city and the King's Provost of Justice on horseback, followed by a hundred archers of the Royal Bodyguard; and after these came Signor Ludovic, clad in black and with a black hat, which he carried almost continuously in his hand. He looked about in every direction, trying to conceal the mortification which he felt in so complete a change of fortune. Though newly shaved, he had the air of a sick man and he trembled in every limb. Close beside him was the Captain of the Royal Archers, and behind him came a hundred archers more. In this fashion he was led through the middle of the town to the castle, where he is being closely guarded, until the iron cage, in which he is to be lodged at night, is completed. The cage will be very strong, the iron being encased in wood, and the whole being so fashioned that it will be impossible to tamper with it. I must not omit to mention that, as Ludovic passed, the Spanish ambassador and I stood at a window to watch, and, upon having the Spanish ambassador pointed out to him, Lodovic took off his hat. When told that the Venetian ambassador was there as well, he stopped and made as if to speak. I took no notice and the Captain of the archers hurried him on. Discussing the matter with the King afterwards, I told him that I should have felt shame rather than honour in receiving any mark of good will from such a person. The King tells me that he has given up the idea of sending him to Loches, because he himself sometimes goes there to hunt, and he does not wish ever to see him or to be in the same place with him. He will send him to a place in Berry, near Bourges, where there is a very strong castle with a live moat larger than that round the castle at Milan. The place is in the very centre of France, and there will be a strong guard composed of persons devoted to His Majesty and commanded by the man who was captain of his archers, when he was Duke of Orléans. When Ludovic dismounted from his mule, he had to be lifted bodily and carried into the castle, being incapable, so it is said, of walking a step without help. Everyone feels sure that his days are numbered.

LOUIS XII LAYS CLAIM TO NAPLES. THE BATTLE OF GARIGLIANO

Having had such a success over his claim to Milan, Louis made up his mind to revive the French claim to Naples. But Ferdinand of Aragon also had his eye on Naples. A most corrupt agreement was made between them in the Treaty of Granada (1500) by which they agreed to divide the Kingdom of Naples between them—each expecting to be able to oust the other when the moment came. The conquest of Naples was achieved: then the two thieves fell out. In the end the French army was beaten by the Spanish army under Gonsalvo at the battle of Garigliano (1503).

Source: (a) Machiavelli, *Opere*, vol. iv, pp. 393-4. Bridge, *op. cit.*, vol. iii, p. 196.

The French have established themselves firmly on the Garigliano, and the Spaniards have not been able to prevent them from setting foot on the further bank, or to drive them from it afterwards. It is generally held that the Spaniards, being in inferior numbers, cannot offer battle, but must fall back on strong positions, as they did formerly . . . and have done again now on the Garigliano. Beaten on the bank of the river, they have fallen back about a mile, and there with ditches and earthworks have confronted the French with a new obstacle. The French have been prevented from advancing by the badness of the weather, for, as the country is low-lying, and marshy, and it rains incessantly, both sides have been obliged to hold only their earthworks, and to break up their armies and to quarter them in

o

neighbouring hamlets. Both sides alike have been worsted by the floods and the weather, which seemed to be mending yesterday, but to-day is hopelessly wet again, with every appearance of continued rain. Both camps suffer from want of litter and provisions, especially the French, who occupy a district which has been more thoroughly drained of supplies, and this may become serious for them, if they cannot advance; but they have an advantage in ample supplies of money, the lack of which may greatly prejudice the Spaniards. The general opinion, all things considered, is that the French have more funds and better troops, the Spaniards more skilful leadership and better luck.

Source: (*b*) Gonsalvo was reinforced by Alviano and his Italian troops. On December 27th, Alviano constructed a bridge over the river without the French discovering it. The French commander lost his head and retreated to Gaeta. Gonsalvo followed and the French army became demoralized. Gaeta surrendered without a struggle: Giustinian, *Dispacci*, vol. ii, pp. 375–6, 379. Bridge, *op. cit.*, vol. iii, p. 201.

The remnants of the French army are hourly arriving in Rome. They are despoiled and even actually naked; nor have they refuge or resting-place; and to avoid perishing of cold, they go—if I may be pardoned for mentioning such details—and bury themselves up to the heads in the dung-heaps. And of such pitiable creatures there are, not handfuls merely, but literally hundreds ... In this defeat of the French His Holiness has come out as a sympathizer with them, and in addition to other favours he has made Cardinal Colonna go off to the estates of his family to see to it that the returning French—those, I mean, who were not in the defeat, being nearer Rome—should be given lodgings and treated properly and not injured by the people living on the Colonna properties. However, the assistance comes rather late in the day, for nearly all have been robbed and plundered by the peasants, and every day they may be seen coming naked into Rome, so that the sight of them excites compassion. Yet injury does not protect them from insult, for when on their outward march to Naples they did much harm to the Romans; and the Romans, mindful of their wrongs, but unable to exact amends from the destitute, avenge themselves by abuse, so that, as soon as a Frenchman shows himself in the streets, he is pursued by derisive cries.

Source: (c) Landucci, *Diario Fiorentino*, ed. I. del Badia, pp. 265–6. Bridge, *op. cit.*, p. 201.

In this time of cold many French—as many as were able—had fled from the Regno naked and destitute. In the neighbourhood of Rome large numbers died in the ditches of cold and hunger; nor did they find any to help them, because of the cruel murders and robberies which they had committed in the city. For that cause were they suffered by Providence to die upon the dunghills of Rome, whither in their nakedness they resorted for warmth; and all would have perished, had not the Pope supplied them with cloaks and money, and put them upon vessels bound for France. Even as it was, more than five hundred died of cold and were found of a morning naked and dead upon the dunghills. In Rome they would enter the houses, wherever a door was open nor could they be induced to leave, not even by blows, for they said: 'Kill us'! Never was such destruction seen. Yet their King sent them no help and thought of them not at all. It was the judgement of Heaven upon vicious and godless blasphemers, who had come to slay and to steal.

Source: (d) Machiavelli, *Ritratti delle cose della Francia. Opere*, vol. vi, p. 300. Bridge, *op. cit.*, vol. iii, p. 203.

[Machiavelli noted an inability] to endure hardship and privation, which have the effect of disordering them so much that it becomes easy to defeat them. This was often shown in the Neapolitan wars, the most recent instance being on the Garigliano, where they were half as strong again as the Spaniards, whom they were expected hourly to swallow up; but when the winter came with very heavy rains, they went off one by one to the adjacent districts to look for more comfortable quarters; the camp was left disordered and half deserted; and the Spaniards were able to win an unlooked for victory.

GONSALVO FERNÁNDEZ DE CÓRDOBA, THE GREAT CAPTAIN

Gonsalvo was born in 1453 and he died in 1515. He was the son of the Count of Aguilar. He made his name as a soldier in the wars against Portugal and in the Spanish civil wars: but his great reputation was won in the ten years of war against the Moors in Granada. It was as the commander in the wars in Naples against Charles VIII of France that he won the title of The Great Captain. His reputation was of the highest, but he was very scurvily treated by Ferdinand of Aragon, who showed no gratitude for Gonsalvo's loyal service to enhance the prestige and success of the Spanish monarchy.

Source: (*a*) Hernando del Peréz Pulgar, *Crónicas de los Reyes Católicos.* This English version is taken from Mary Purcell's *The Great Captain*, Alvin Redman, London, 1962, p. 159. Hernando was a fellow captain and friend of Gonsalvo.

The Great Captain was of lordly bearing. In the carrying out of momentous and laudable enterprises he was of indomitable spirit. His mind was clear and serene, his glance always alert. Whether on foot or mounted, he personified the authority he represented. Though small as a child, in manhood he was not so. In hard battles he was terrible, with a voice full of fury, and mighty strength and vigour. But in peacetime he lived a quiet family life and went about with easy, modest gait. In conversation he spoke clearly but not loudly. Baldness did not prevent him from doffing his bonnet when speaking to others.

Neither lack of sleep nor hunger affected him when on his fighting campaigns, and when need required, he took upon himself the hardest tasks and greatest risks. Although not a man for jesting, being always very much in earnest, in times of danger he would crack jokes with his men to cheer them and raise their spirits. He was as competent in perfecting many affairs as he was diligent in bringing one to a successful end. Ability and diligence were so united in him that he not only defeated his foes by his great courage and vigorous efforts, but surpassed them by his intelligence and wisdom.

Source: (*b*) A letter from Bartolommeo d'Alviano to his brother after the battle of the Garigliano, 1503. Bridge, *op. cit.*, vol. iii, p. 200.

The Great Captain has treated me with the utmost honour . . . and his behaviour could not be improved on. Throughout the operations his attitude has been one of the greatest consideration and frankness, and I wish for nothing better than to fight under such a leader. He has qualities which might well be compared with those of Scipio Africanus, for he has courage, vigilance, and swiftness of decision, combined with moderation and high principles, and these are the very qualities of which one reads in Africanus. Small wonder, if he wins victories, for it seems impossible that any who fight under his banners should lose. At the same time he is a most devout observer of religious duties and a man of firm faith; and never have I seen in him, either in word or deed, aught that was not good.

Source: (c) Brantôme, *Grand Capitaines Etrangers*, à Leyde chez Sambix le Jeune, à la Sphere, MDCLXV. trans. C.R.N.R.

Now for all that this King Ferdinand made use of the Duke of Alba and was well served by the conquest of Navarre, it was Gonzalvo Hernandez of Cordova whom he employed for the conquest of Naples and he appointed him there as his Lieutenant-General: and afterwards, for his fine exploits and high achievements in arms, the Spanish gave him the name and title of The Great Captain, as in olden times it was given to Alexander and to Pompey. And indeed he has been a very great, a very good, valiant and wise Captain. But if he was going to earn such a splendid name, there wasn't much sign of it, for on his first arrival in the war for Naples, which he was bent on prosecuting to the full and on proving himself in the eyes of that brave knight, Monsieur Daubigny, who was called at that time *Le Chevalier sans reproche* and was commanding in Calabria, when the fight came hand to hand, the Chevalier and his men charged so well and furiously that, Great Captain as he was (but he had not by then acquired that name), Gonsalvo fled helter skelter as quick as he could and, as the Spanish say, *a riendas fueltas*,[2] as far as Reggio. He was lucky to reach it in the nick of time, for otherwise he was done.

The histories of his times say, and indeed there are still many of

these countries which say it, that he was captured by their fore-
fathers—see, for example, Guicciardini. On account of this failure
and blemish, in the meantime he all but died of shame: but he
plucked up his courage and reestablished his reputation by the
fine things he achieved.

The truth must be told, but one must also remember gratefully
the armies which worshipped him among our Captains and
leaders, who helped him greatly on his road to fortune in all his
battles, engagements and victories which he won for them.
Above all one must remember the death of that brave and valiant
Count d'Armagnac and how little reinforcement in men and
money was available on the French side. The disloyalty of
foreigners, too, who deserted our side against their pledged word,
the crafty and temporising Spanish, served him well. In short,
everything injured us as far as fortune and fate were concerned,
which banded themselves together against us. But to have beaten
us, hunted us and defeated us so easily, one would say was against
all the rules . . .

Now to show that Gonsalvo depended for success as much on
his craftiness as on his courage, he invented a huge cross-bow to
which people gave his name and which was cocked by pulleys
and had these words on it, 'cleverness overcomes strength'; as
much as to say that there was no splendid force which the spirit
and ingenuity of the man could not surpass. And in truth there
was no man however strong, not even a giant, who could cock
that cross-bow by hand: but with its machinery it could easily
be cocked. This invention, however, was not such a great benefit
to the Great Captain, because at last there was only gallantry
with which to crown a brave and gallant captain. It was said,
and was also written, that when the King Ferdinand went to take
possession of his kingdom of Naples, which was returned to him
in a state of complete peace by the Great Captain, seeing him so
much loved and renowned, he conceived a certain mistrust and
jealousy of him, as he the subject was the fine prince; and not
perhaps without reason, fearing that he might want to swallow
the morsel which he had carved.

He took him with him to Spain; perhaps those were the last of his glorious days, perhaps also the best; because afterwards he did not at all[3] . . . Spain and had no more means of exercising his genius, neither in war nor peace, for the King cut down his 'morsels' so much that he neither carved nor swallowed any except as the King willed.

He was with the King at Savonna at that interview between the two Kings which I have described before. He was greatly regarded and admired by everybody for his noble exploits and victories.

Above all, the King made much of him and wanted him to dine at the same table as the two Kings and the Queen of Spain, but he declined this honour. But our King besought King Ferdinand to command him to sit down. Our King took great pleasure in chatting with him and entertaining him by force. In the opinion of everybody, that day was for Gonsalvo no less glorious than that on which he entered Naples at the head of his army, victorious and triumphant after defeating our French forces, or our Partisans in Calabria, at Ceringnola . . . Now at last to end, the Great Gonsalvo died a little before King Ferdinand, having withdrawn from Court to his own discontent. Always the King was anxious, remembering his character, that he should be paid the same honours in his kingdom and in his Court, which it was the custom in Spain to pay to the greatest princes. The people loved and esteemed him: and there he is, cured and resuscitated.

THE SWISS

Although the Swiss had a great reputation as infantry soldiers, especially after Pavia (1525), they were cordially detested both for their bad behaviour and for their greed for money.

Source: (a) Guicciardini, *Storia d'Italia*, Eng. ed. A. P. Goddard, v, p. 330.

This wild and unpolished nation has gained great renown by its Union and glorious exploits in war; for the Swiss, by their natural ferocity and orderly discipline, have not only frequently defended their own country with great valour, but highly signalized their martial abilities in foreign service. And their praise would have

been incomparably greater, if they had employed that skill and
courage for the service of their own empire, which they spent
abroad for hire and for enlarging the dominions of others; and
if they had directed their views to more generous ends than to
the getting of money, by the love of which they have suffered
themselves to be corrupted and have since lost the opportunity
of being formidable to all Italy. For as they marched out of their
country only as mercenary soldiers, they acquired nothing to the
public service by their victories, being accustomed out of a greedy
desire of gain to require large subsidies and make new demands
for pay, and so become intolerable in armies, besides being
troublesome and contumacious in their behaviour and obedience
to those that paid them.

The effect of military service was brutalizing and the easily obtained
foreign gold brought with it a corruption of morals. The chronicler
Anshelm, writing about 1500, probably exaggerates the picture, but
his account of the extravagance and luxury is likely to be basically
true. He was specially hard on the women, who must have costly
dresses and ornaments. See (c) below.
Source: (b) Anshelm, Berner-Chronik (1503); Oechsli, Quellenbuch, ii,
464.

As these expensive manners have increased, so in the same
measure have increased the lust for honours and goods, trickery
and unfaithfulness, unbelief, haughtiness, pride, debauchery,
scorn, and with them all arts for gaining money, especially those
things which serve the palate and trades which are serviceable to
luxurious pride.

The above account is that of a Swiss. The following account is that
of an ambassador from Milan and gives the views of a foreigner.
Source: (c) Balcus, Descriptio Helvetiae: Oechsli, op. cit., ii, 470.

Although the Swiss are altogether unhewn barbarians, yet they
live among themselves according to certain laws which they
consider so holy that no one dare to overstep them, because it is
a crime to have broken them even in the slightest. Our civil law,
however, our good manners and honourable customs, and, what
is worse, their own laws and ordinances respecting other nations,

they do not themselves at all observe, because they are without fidelity, uprightness and humanity; but they seize rudely everything before them, building upon obstinacy, not upon wisdom.

When they start out to war they swear a solemn oath that every man who sees one of his comrades desert, or act the coward in battle, will cut him down on the spot, for they believe that the courage and persistency of warriors is greater when they, out of fear of death, do not fear death.

In peace, however, and when one citizen brings complaints against another citizen, they bind themselves also by an oath, for, if they have any business with one another and fall into strife, as it often happens, and seize their weapons or begin to curse each other, if then another party comes forward, places himself in their midst, and begs them to lay down the weapons and to talk over the matter in peace, and commands them to be peaceful, and if one of the contending parties will not hearken, the man who offers himself as peacemaker is bound by oath to kill him, and that without punishment . . .

Although accustomed to robbery, yet the people have an extravagant generosity to the poor. The scholars in the study of Latin, if there are any such, beg their living with singing. Their stately but remarkably extravagant daily meals they spin out to great length, so that they spend two or three hours at table eating their many dishes and barbarous spices with much noise and conversation. They show ill-will against those who despise this kind of table pleasure.

When princely ambassadors arrive, the heads of the city, or certain ones from the council, visit them immediately to give them greeting. At breakfast or supper there is a continual crowd around them, including not only the invited or important persons in office, but with these many insignificant people. All these the ambassadors must receive in a friendly way and feed them richly, otherwise they will be followed with perpetual hate and ill-will. In among these will creep also clowns and jugglers and whoever understands amusing arts, and one must receive this kind of people, admire their wit, and before going away must leave them some kind of present or reward for their art. Furthermore, the council is accustomed to send to every ambassador, daily, several measures of wine at the hours for breakfast and supper. The persons who bring these things are rewarded by the receiver of the gift with a small gold piece. Whereupon the whole expense is charged to public good and advantage.

Custom allows that women, who on account of the beauty of their faces and the attraction of their persons are uncommonly lovable, may be embraced and kissed anywhere and by anybody without distinction.[4] The cultivation of the intellect is rare and the noble virtues receive no honour. This low-born people, this lot of peasants, born in mountains and woods and brought up in a narrow hole, have begun to play the lord in Europe, and think nothing of enlarging the borders of their own dominion, if any one allows them the opportunity to do so . . . This little band of cowherds and shepherds, who pass the day in the drawing and thickening of milk; who are, so to speak, without law and ignorant of things human and divine; will prescribe laws for all others and sit in judgement on the affairs of princes, as though the appeal and the highest judgement belonged to them. For assumption and violent passion, the diseases which are so near to madness, they surpass all other mortal beings, but among themselves they agree so well together that as a reward and fruit of their unity they enjoy an undisturbed and continuous freedom, to which indeed the quarrels of others have given assistance.

In 1488 those lands, cities, counts, knights in Germany who felt themselves threatened by the Swiss Confederation from the south, by Burgundy in the north and Bavaria on the east, formed themselves into the Suabian League. The wars of the Suabian League followed. A German abbot, Johannes Trithemius, wrote a history of these wars and included the following description of the Swiss.

Source: (d) Johannes Trithemius, Annalium Hirsaugiensium, ii, 572 (ed. 1690): Oechsli, op. cit., i, 282.

Whether the Confederates have had a just or an unjust cause for war is not for me to decide, since I do not hold the place of a judge. But this I say, this I write and hand on in writing to the future world, which everybody knows to-day who has lived with us in Germany, and which all say, who know the manner of the Swiss, that they are a people proud by nature, enemies of princes, riotous, and for a long time have been contrary and disobedient to their overlords; filled with contempt for others and full of assumption for themselves; deceitful in war and lovers of treason; in peace never steadfast; nor do they enquire about the justice of what is due from them by law, especially when it affects the independence which they have the effrontery to assume. I say nevertheless, that they are not only bold in war, but also shrewd, and they are mutually helpful in time of need, and no one leaves another in danger, nor do the rich despise the poor.

Source (*e*) A Sumptuary Law in Zurich, 1488. Oechsli, *op. cit.*, i, 209.

In view of the marked disorder which has begun in our city among the common people on account of the costly clothing which their wives and daughters wear, and in order to prevent this, we have ordained that hereafter no woman or girl shall in any wise wear silver- or gold-plated pins, rings, or buckles, nor any silk garment or trimming on coats, shoes, neckwear, etc., except the women of the guilds of the *Rüden* and *Schnecken*. Further, no woman of the community shall have a mounted girdle, except those whose husbands possess 1000 gulden or over, and they may have one such girdle and no more to the value of about 12 gulden. These persons may also have silk borders and trimmings on their bodices with modesty, but without hooks and buckles, as above said. If any one acts contrary to this, such forbidden girdles shall be confiscated to the city, and whoever already has such girdles, whether few or many, shall sell the same, or allow their husbands to sell them for his business and necessities. As to buckles, rings and silk, everyone who disobeys this ordinance shall pay two marks of silver for each offence.

THE APPEARANCE OF SYPHILIS IN EUROPE

There is plenty of evidence that syphilis existed in a mild form among the American Indians before 1492. There is no certain evidence that it existed in Europe before 1494. In that year it appeared in a virulent form in Italy and spread rapidly. By 1520 it was generally believed that the disease had come from America, because a reputed cure for it, the guaiacum or *lignum vitae*, had been discovered there. There was no sickness on board the *Niña* in 1493, and no reason for thinking the contrary on the *Pinta*, therefore it is improbable that Columbus's men had contracted the disease by 1493. Las Casas states positively that the Indians gave it to the Spaniards. Oviedo states that it was the second voyage which brought the disease to Europe, although another Spaniard, a doctor, asserts it was the first voyage which brought it, because he had treated patients for it at Barcelona in 1493. The general belief came to be that the Spanish troops carried the disease to Italy during the Italian wars of Charles VIII. The whole question is dealt with at length in the two-volume edition of S. E. Morison's *Admiral of The Ocean Sea*. The name of syphilis was first used by the Veronese Humanist, Girolamo Fracastoro in 1530 when he published a long poem on the subject, *Syphilidis sive Morbi Gallici, libri tres*. This is the only disease to have a poetical name. See J. A. Symonds, *The Renaissance in Italy*, *The Revival of Learning*, ch. viii.

Source: Guicciardini, *Storia d'Italia*, Eng. ed. A. P. Goddard, i, 403.

In giving the history of these times, I think it ought not to be forgot that amongst all other calamities which overwhelmed Italy by this invasion of the French, or were at least attributed to it, a new and unheard of distemper broke out, by them called the Neapolitan, but by the Italians the French disease, because it showed itself first among the French whilst they were at Naples, and on their return was spread all over Italy.

This distemper, either quite new or never known before in our hemisphere, unless in its remotest parts, has made for a number of years such havoc that it deserves to be mentioned as a fatal calamity. It first discovered itself either with ugly boils, which often became incurable wounds, or with acute pains in all joints and nerves throughout the body. The unexperienced physicians applied not only improper, but often contrary medicines, which irritated the distemper and deprived of life a multitude of both sexes and of all ages.

Many became deformed, useless and subject to perpetual pains, and the best part of those who seemed to be cured relapsed into the same misery. But as some years are now elapsed, either because the celestial influence which produced it in so virulent a manner is mitigated, or that by length of time proper remedies have been found out, it has lost very much of its malignity.

However, the French ought in justice to be cleared from this ignominious imputation, for it afterwards plainly appeared that the distemper was brought to Naples from Spain: nor was it the product of that country: it was conveyed thither from those islands which, about this time, through the means of Christopher Columbus, a Genoese, began to be known in our hemisphere. But Nature has been indulgent to the inhabitants of those islands in providing an easy remedy, for by drinking the juice of a particular medicinal wood which grows among them, they are entirely cured.

THE DECLINE OF VENICE

Down to about the year 1423 in which the Doge Modenigo died, the wealth and reputation of Venice were the greatest among all the Italian states. Thence forward three things combined to bring about her decline. Between 1423 and 1457 Doge Foscari reigned 'to the great glory and the inevitable ruin of his country'. Venice expanded on to the mainland and acquired Brescia, Bergamo and Ravenna, thereby arousing the jealousy of other Italian states and ruining her own finances, at the same time bringing her into collision with Charles VIII of France when, on the death of Visconti, he laid claim to the Visconti estates. Secondly, the fall of Constantinople in 1453 brought the Turks into the Mediterranean and a series of wars with the Turks further weakened Venice. Thirdly, in 1486 Diaz discovered the Cape of Good Hope and Venice lost her monopoloy of the Mediterranean trade.

UNPOPULARITY OF VENICE

Source: Galeazzo Sforza's warning to the Venetian ambassador in Milan. Horatio Brown, *Venice, An Historical Sketch*, London, 1895, pp. 328–9.

Certes, you Venetians are wrong to disturb the peace of Italy, and not to rest content with the fine State which is now yours. If you only knew how every one hates you, your hair would stand on end and you would let other people alone. Do you

believe that these Italian princes are really friends? Oh no; it is
only their dread of you that binds them together. Everyone of
them will do his best to clip your wings. Do you think that you
have done wisely to arm all Italy like this? You would be amazed
if you knew the offers that are made to me to induce me to
declare war on you. No, no; let everyone live in peace. When
my father died, it seemed to me that he had left me a fine estate,
and so I went a-hunting and amused myself, and thought of
nothing else; but now, with this Bartolomeo[5] of yours, you have
forced me to arms, and into an alliance with my mortal enemy,
King Ferdinand of Naples. You imagine that you are acting
wisely; you will see. You are acquiring a very bad name. Everyone says you want to eat up all Italy. You have spent much and
your treasury is empty. I know the way you raise your loans,
with what difficulty. I know that you have borrowed money
from your banks and your private citizens and have not yet repaid
it. A single despot has a great advantage over a commonwealth,
for he can keep his eye on everything and has only to consult
himself, while you have to trust to others. A monarch is worth
more, and does more, with 50,000 ducats than a commonwealth
with 100,000. You are alone and all the world is against you, not
merely in Italy but also beyond the Alps. Rest assured your
enemies are not asleep. Take good counsel, for, by God, you
need it. I know what I am saying.

THE EFFECT OF THE CAPE ROUTE ON VENICE

Source: (a) Priuli, *Diarii*, Archivio Veneto, tom. 1. Brown, *Studies in
Venetian History*, 1, 353 et sqq. 1907.

All Venice was alarmed and amazed, and the wiser heads took
it for the worst news that could have reached us. For everyone
knows that Venice has reached her commanding prestige and
wealth solely by her mercantile marine, which brought in every
year great stores of spices, so that foreign merchants flocked to
buy; and their presence and their business left us a large profit.
But now by this new route the spices from the East will be
carried to Lisbon, where Hungarians, Germans, Flemish and
French will go to purchase them, as they will be cheaper there

than here. For the spices which reach Venice have to pass through Syria and the territories of the soldan, and everywhere they have to pay such exorbitant duties, that by the time they reach Venice what cost a ducat will have to be sold for eighty or a hundred ducats. The sea route, on the other hand, is free from these burdens, and the Portuguese can sell at a lower rate. While the better heads see this, others refuse to believe the news, while others again declare that the King of Portugal cannot keep up this trade to Calicut, for out of thirteen carvels which he sent out, only six have come back safe, and so the loss will exceed the gain, nor can he easily find men to risk their lives in so long and perilous a voyage; again, it is urged that the soldan, when he realizes the danger to his revenue, will take steps—and so on, and so on; seeking, as usual, to find out reasons to support their hopes and refusing to hear and believe what is reported to their own hurt.

Source (b): Brown, *op. cit.*, p. 355.

Our ancestors were brave, fierce, impatient of injuries, quick to strike, prone to fight. Now we are of milder mind, meek, long-suffering, shy of a blow, shrinking from war. And this, I take it, because in the olden times we all lived by trading and not on fixed incomes; we spent many years of our lives away from home in distant lands, where we dealt with different races and grew courageous. Most of our days were passed at sea in struggle with storm and tempest and buccaneers, and we waxed valiant and strong to strike; for those who tried to take our goods tried to rob us of our food, and with our food went our life. Now few of us live by trade. Most subsist on their incomes or on their official pay. Few leave Venice; fewer still for distant lands; and so, as we never see them close, we have come to believe that the rest of mankind are born with three hands, and thus we have grown cowards.

Source: (c) Foscarini, Venetian ambassador in England, reporting home. *Archivio di Stato*, Senato, Secreta, Dipacci, Inghilterra, December 2nd, 1611. Brown, *op. cit.*, p. 356.

It is generally thought that in a very short time the trade of the Dutch with all parts of the world will multiply, for they are content with moderate gain and are richly supplied with excellent seamen, ships, money, everything that used to belong especially to Venice when her trade was flourishing. The leading merchants here point out to me that the trade of Venice has declined, because Venetians have almost abandoned navigation, investing their money in estates. As matters now stand, there is not either in England or Holland, a ship so small that she could not outfight the biggest Venetian and weather a storm with greater security. They also attack the build of Venetian craft, which, they say, is ill-suited to face either the ocean or the pirates. They declare that twenty English sailors would show more fight than forty Venetians. Yet all these defects might be remedied; for the Venetians have a far shorter voyage to make and through a sea less infested by pirates. If they chose, they might build ships of a type that experience has approved, while the geographical position of Venice is hers and hers only.

THE CONDITION OF VENICE IN 1509

Source: Guicciardini, *Storia d'Italia*. Eng. ed. A. P. Goddard, iv, 274.

Thus were the affairs of the Venetian republic, by a violent and astonishing shock, precipitated to the lowest degree of misery, with a continual accumulation of calamity upon calamity, all hopes vanishing as soon as proposed, and no resource left by means of which it might hope at least after the loss of so much empire to preserve its own liberty. So great a catastrophe variously affected the minds of the Italians: some beheld it with the greatest pleasure, remembering the ambitious proceedings of that people, who, setting aside all regard to justice and public faith, seized upon all opportunities that offered and had openly sought means to bring all Italy in subjection to them. Such attempts rendered their name universally detested and they were still the more hated for the report, which prevailed everywhere, of their natural pride and haughtiness.

Many, on the contrary, considered the matter with more sound judgement, reflecting what a dismal and calamitous situation it must be for Italy to find itself entirely reduced under slavery to foreigners. They resented with the deepest concern and indignation that so great a city, so ancient a seat of Liberty, that diffused the splendour of the Italian name over all the world, should be driven to such extremities; that now there remained no bridle to the fury of the ultramontanes, since the most honourable member of the Italic body, which had above all others maintained the common fame and estimation, was struck dead and useless.

But the Pope, more than all the rest of the powers of Italy, began to be concerned at so great a revolution.

NOTES

[1] In the event, the bombardier was in no danger of losing his bet and his head: owing to the desertion of its commander, the castle surrendered at once.

[2] i.e. On a loose rein.

[3] MS. defective.

[4] Erasmus noted the same custom in England at the same time.

[5] The *condottiere*, Colleoni.

P

THE HOLY ROMAN EMPIRE
(Notes on p. 233)

THE HAPSBURGS

MAXIMILIAN I

Maximilian I was the son of the Holy Roman Emperor Frederick III. He was born in 1459 and died in 1519. In 1477 he married Mary of Burgundy, daughter of Charles the Bold, who had inherited Burgundy and the Netherlands. His son was Philip the Fair, who married the mad Joanna, daughter of Ferdinand of Aragon. He had incessant quarrels with the Netherlands and was on very bad terms with France. In 1482 his wife, Mary, died. The death of his father in 1493 left Maximilian the sole ruler of Germany and head of the house of Hapsburg. In 1494 he married Bianca Maria Sforza, daughter of Galeazzo Sforza, Duke of Milan. His reign was punctuated with incessant wars, he was always in chronic financial difficulties, and on the whole he was a most unsuccessful ruler. But he had many personal merits and he was liked by everybody. He did a good deal for the advance of education in Vienna, Ingolstadt and Freiburg. It was he who established the famous troops, called the *Landsknechte*, but although he carried out some constitutional reforms in the Empire, he did little more than harm to Germany. His personal appearance is preserved for us in the beautiful drawing by Dürer in Vienna. The following English versions of foreign sources are taken from R. W. Seton Watson's *Maximilian I*, Constable, 1902.

Source: (a) Pontus Heuterus, *Rerum Belgic*, lib. iii, 69.

Though still a youth, he displayed the true qualities of a man and a prince. He was magnanimous, brave and liberal, born for the good of the race. His fame was increased by a countenance of right royal dignity, the splendour of his father's majesty, the antiquity of his lineage, and the amplitude of his inheritance.

Source: (b) Letter of Wilhelm von Hovede, Aug. 23, 1477.

Mounted on a large chestnut horse, clad in silver armour, his head uncovered, his flowing locks bound with a circlet of pearls and precious stones, Maximilian looks so glorious in his youth, so strong in his manliness, that I know not which to admire the most—the beauty of his youth, the bravery of his manhood, or the promise of his future.

Source: (c) Machiavelli, *Opere,* iv, 174.

Anyone could cheat him without his knowing it . . . The Emperor is a great general; he bears fatigue like the most hardened soldiers, he is brave in danger and just in governing. When he grants an audience, he is patient and gracious, and is a pattern of many princely virtues.

Source: (d) Quirini, Venetian Ambassador, 1507: *Relazioni degli Amb. Ven.* ed. Alberi, Serie I, vol. vi, 26.

He is of excellent parts and more fertile in expedients than any of his advisers, yet he does not know how to avail himself of any single remedy at the right moment; while he is as full of ideas and plans as he is powerless to execute them. And though two or three methods lie open to him, and though he chooses one of them as the best, yet he does not pursue this, because before its fulfillment another design which he considers better has suddenly presented itself. And thus he flits from better to better, till both time and opportunity for execution are past.

Source: (e) Vettori, quoted by R. W. Seton Watson, *Maximilian I.* Constable, 1902, p. 116.

None can deny that he is wise and circumspect, skilful and untiring in war, widely experienced. He possesses the confidence of the nation more than any of his predecessors for more than a hundred years; but he is so amiable and kind-hearted that it makes him yielding and credulous.

Source: (f) Louis XII of France, quoted Seton Watson, *op. cit.,* p. 117.

What this King says at night, he does not hold to next morning.

Source: (g) Ferdinand V, Despatch of Cornero to Venice, 1508, quoted Seton Watson, *op. cit.,* p. 117.

If Maximilian thinks of a thing, he also believes it is already done.

MAXIMILIAN I AND THE PAPACY

Maximilian was a man of inordinate ambition and with a mind which conceived the most impossible and even ludicrous ideas.

Source: A letter from Maximilian to his daughter, Margaret of Austria, the Regent of the Netherlands. It is dated September 18th, without any year: it was presumably 1512. Quoted in C. Hare, *Marguerite of Austria*, Harpers, London, 1907, p. 188.

Very dear and much beloved daughter . . . we send to-morrow Monsieur de Gurce, bishop, to Rome to the Pope [Julius II] to find some way in which we can agree with him to take us as coadjutor, in order that after his death we may be assured of having the Papacy and become a priest and after that to be a saint, so that it will be necessary for you that after my death you will be constrained to adore me, of which I shall be very proud.

Upon this I send a post to the King of Aragon, to beg him that he will help us to arrive at this, with which he also is content, on condition that I resign the empire to our common son, Charles. With that also I am satisfied . . .

I begin also to work upon the cardinals, with whom two or three thousand ducats will do me a great service, with the partiality they already have.

The King of Aragon has sent word to his ambassador that he wishes to command the Spanish cardinals that they favour the Papacy for us.

I beg you to keep this matter entirely secret; although I fear that in a few days all the world will have to know it; for it is not possible to work so great a matter secretly, in which it is needful to have so many people and so much money and help and working. And to God, written by the hand of your good father MAXIMILIANUS, future Pope. September 18.

CHARLES V

Charles V was the son of Philip of Burgundy and Joanna, the daughter of Ferdinand of Aragon and Isabella of Castile. Philip was the son and heir of the Emperor Maximilian I, but he died before the Emperor. Thus Charles succeeded to all the possessions of both the Spanish and Austrian rulers, that is to say to Spain, the Spanish lands in the New World, to the Netherlands and to the Hapsburg domains in Austria. In addition, in 1519 he was elected Holy Roman Emperor. His life was one long struggle to govern his huge inheritance, to solve political and religious problems, and to defend his countries against external attacks. He had to put down a revolt in Castile; to deal with the troubles in Germany caused by Martin Luther and the Reformation; to face the French invasions into Northern Italy; to withstand the threat to Europe from the Turkish advance up the Danube; and in order to accomplish all this he was incessantly on the move, travelling from one point of his empire to another. At last in 1555 he gave up the struggle and abdicated in Brussels, then he retired to Spain where he died on September 21st, 1558.

Roger Ascham (1515–1568), the author of *Toxophilus* and *The Scholemaster*, was appointed secretary to the English ambassador to Charles V: he resided in Augsburg (he wrote the name as Augusta) from 1550 to 1552 and wrote many letters home to his friends, describing his travels and experiences. In the following extract he describes a meeting with the Emperor, Charles V.

Source: (a) A letter written by Roger Ascham to Edward Raven, Fellow of St. John's College, in Cambridge. *Lans. MS.* 98: printed as letter CXVI in Giles's edition of Ascham's works, vol. 1, part 2, p. 243: dated Augsburg, Jan. 20th, 1551. The extract is printed on pp. 267–8.

I have seen the Emperor twice; first, sick in his privy chamber, at our first coming. He looked somewhat like the parson of Epurstone. He had on a gown of black taffety, and a furred nightcap on his head, Dutch-like, having a seam over the crown, like a great cod-piece. I saw him also on St. Andrew's Day, sitting at dinner at the feast of Golden Fleece; he and Ferdinando [his brother] both under one cloth of estate; then the prince of Spain [his son], Philip; all of one side, as the Knights of the Garter do in England . . .

I stood hard by the Emperor's table. He had four courses; he had sod beef very good, roast mutton, baked hare; these be no service in England. The Emperor hath a good face, a constant look; he fed well of a capon; I have had a better from mine hostess Barnes many times in my chambers. He and Ferdinando ate together very handsomely, carving themselves where they list, without any curiosity. The Emperor drank the best that ever

I saw; he had his head in the glass five times as long as any of us, and never drank less than a good quart at once of Rhenish wine. His chapel sung wonderfully cunningly all the dinner-while. Ferdinando is a very homely man; gentle to be spoken to of any man, and now of great power and riches. The prince of Spain, I think, is not in all so wise as his father. Maximilian, Ferdinando's son, now king of Beaume [Bohemia] is a worthy gentleman, learned, wise, liberal, gentle, loved and praised of all.

Source: (*b*) Badovaro MS. Gachard: *Relationes des Ambassadeurs Venitiens.* Badovaro was the Venetian ambassador to Charles V, and describes him at the age of 55.

He is of moderate height and has a grave look. His forehead is broad, his eyes blue, with a look of energy, his nose aquiline and a little bent, his lower jaw long and projecting, so that his teeth do not meet, and one cannot hear the ends of his words distinctly. His front teeth are few and bad: he has a good colour, and a short beard, bristly and white, well-proportioned to his figure.

Source: (*c*) Guicciardini, *op. cit.* I, p. 132.

From infancy he had been weak in constitution and subject to illnesses. His stature was short and his face very ugly, if you except the dignity and vigour of his glance. His limbs were so disproportioned that he had less the appearance of a man than of a monster. Not only was he ignorant of the liberal arts, but he hardly knew his letters. Though eager to rule, he was in truth made for anything but that; for while surrounded by dependents, he exercised no authority over them and preserved no kind of majesty. Hating business and fatigue, he displayed in such matters as he took in hand a want of prudence and of judgement. His desire for glory sprang rather from impulse than from reason. His liberality was inconsiderate, immoderate, promiscuous. When he displayed inflexibility of purpose, it was more often an ill-founded obstinacy than firmness, and that which many people called his goodness of nature rather deserved the name of coldness and feebleness of spirit.

Source: The usual source in English history books is the account sent home by the English ambassador, Sir John Mason. The following account is taken from the despatch sent by the Venetian Ambassador, Federigo Badoer; this English version in *The Cloister Life of The Emperor Charles V*, Stirling-Maxwell, London, 1891.

Most Serene Prince,

Yesterday after dinner the Emperor made the cession of these states to his most serene son, the lords and deputies having petitioned His Majesty that they might be no longer kept waiting, on account of the great expense to which they were put, an expense of 12,000 florins daily among them all, and because there was now no hope of the coming of the deputies from Friesland: and the Emperor having formally declared that, as regarded the question of precedence between Brabant and Flanders, his renunciation was to be made in Brabant solely for his personal convenience, and having assured them all that the King would confirm their old privileges, keeping these on their former footing and granting them new privileges besides.

His Majesty came from his house through the park to the palace, mounted on a mule and wearing a long black dress with the Order of the Golden Fleece. Shortly before him the most serene King of England had entered on foot.[1] The Emperor took his seat in the great hall of the palace, having on his right hand the King, who also wore the Fleece, and on his left Queen Mary,[2] near whom he made the Duke of Savoy sit, and then the Knights of the Fleece, and the lords and deputies of the provinces; all, after the Duke, having their heads bare.

One of the councillors of Brabant then began to narrate the causes which had led His Majesty to make this cession, which were his age and his ill-health, and after many observations in honour of their Majesties, concluded with the formal legal phrases used in public acts of cession and renunciation. The Emperor, with a paper of notes in his hand, because he could not retain firmly in his memory all he had to say, recounted in their order the various actions of his life, the labours, hardships and dangers sustained in the course of his journeys by sea and land, and his enterprises for the defence of these states, now united with England, and of his other realms, and for the preservation of the empire and the benefit of religion, saying in each case by the grace of God so I did, or so it happened; adding, that not feeling in himself the vigour which the government of so many states required, and knowing that his son was capable of supporting weighty duties, he wished to give the remainder of his life to the service of God, and cede these states, as he had done and would do others, to the King; further informing them that it was possible that he might return afterwards to see them, and saying that in this renunciation he had the consolation of knowing that he left them to a prince worthy of the true faith and devotion which they had ever shown to himself, and to the prince, subjects worthy of his merits. Then turning to the King, he entreated him to cheer him by taking upon himself this charge with good will, exhorting him above all things to have a care for religion and justice. At these last words the King's Majesty rose up with his cap in his hand, and kneeling before the Emperor, said that his earnest desire had been that His Majesty should rule these and all his other states during the rest of his life; but that as His Majesty had firmly resolved otherwise, he for his own part swore to follow out his commands to the utmost of his power. After which the Emperor embraced him, with many tears on both sides, which caused the Queen and many others to weep also.

One of the deputies then replied in the name of the rest, that it had been the desire of them all that their lord should grant them this grace, that, as they had lived in security under the rule of the greatest prince that Christendom had known for many ages, His Majesty would continue to reign over them during the course of his life; but that, as it was the will of God that they were to undergo a change, they must render him their thanks for giving them such a ruler as the late King's Majesty. After enlarging greatly in His Majesty's praises, he concluded by saying that they would obey and serve him heartily; and by entreating him not to leave the country, for the sake both of his own service and their advantage.

The King, having said a few words, speaking, as the others had done, in French, then desired M. d'Arras to address the deputies in his name in a manner corresponding to his regard. Whereupon that most reverend lord said that the King's Majesty accepted with goodwill the burden now imposed on him, in the hope that God would grant him His grace, and assured them that he would have that care for them which was due to their loyalty and to the expectations which they had conceived of him. He was likewise confident that henceforth they would show themselves obedient and well-disposed towards his ministers and orders; using such words as were interpreted to mean that he desired to be furnished with a supply of moneys for the war.

The Queen then stood up and begged for leave to speak,— saying that if in the course of her government she had failed in anything, it arose from the weakness of her sex and not from her own will—and at some length, and with her usual masculine vigour, gave an account of her many years's administration. The deputy who had before spoken, having thanked and highly commended her in the name of the States, the Emperor at last in a few words gave the Assembly leave to depart.

This morning the States of Flanders and Brabant met in a hall in the Queen's apartments to swear fidelity to the King, when His Majesty confirmed in their posts for one year all the official personages. Tomorrow the other States are to perform the same ceremony . . .

Orders have been given by His Imperial Majesty for the quartermasters of his household to set out for Zeland for the purpose of preparing the cabins in the vessels, and of allotting them by name to the persons who are about to accompany him to Spain. Queen Mary had fixed upon taking thither 200 horses, but that number seeming to His Majesty too great, he wished, upon seeing the list, to reduce it to eighty, diminishing also the number of menial servants, by allowing none of his gentlemen more than one each. The secretary Eraso has likewise been instructed to provide money to pay the commissaries who have furnished the provisions; they having been given notice that all the necessary stores had been laid in.

Don Luis de Avila, who is general of light cavalry and chamberlain of his Imperial Majesty, wishing to follow him, has resigned his command. The servants of the Emperor have waited on the King to inform him that in consequence of His Majesty's approaching departure, they have been summoned before the tribunals and severely pressed to pay for articles both of food and clothing which it was necessary His Majesty should provide them with during the time they had been in his service; and that they were expecting with the greatest anxiety the announcement of the donations to be made to them, in order by these methods to discharge their debts. The King, having called the chief servants before him, asked, by way of counsel, their opinion as to what should be done. They advised that the people attached to the court should at once pay a third of what was due by them, and engage to pay the remainder within two years, finding security for the payment amongst the merchants of Antwerp, in hopes thus of quieting the creditors; upon which His Majesty committed the affair to their charge to be thus arranged, as a trial of their good disposition. Commending myself to the grace of your serenity; from the 26th October, 1555.

Federigo Badoer, Ambassador.

Addressed—To the Most Serene Prince, and most excellent lord, the Lord Francesco Veniero, by Divine grace Doge of Venice and my very worshipful lord.

THE FUNERAL OF THE EMPEROR CHARLES V

On the 21st September, 1558, the Emperor Charles V died. His funeral took place in Brussels on December 29th and lasted for two days.

Source: A letter written by Richard Clough to Sir Thomas Gresham, whose agent he was in the Netherlands. The letter is dated January 2nd, 1558/9. Gresham once warned Sir William Cecil that 'my servant is very long and tedious in his writing'. The lengthy and tedious sections of the letter have here been omitted. The letter is printed in J. W. Burgon's *Life and Times of Sir T. Gresham*, vol. 1, pp. 243 *et sqq.* Spelling has been modernized.

The next day after your departing, I went to Brussels about such matters as you gave me commission to do . . . where, at my being there, I saw the funeral of the late Emperor Charles, which began the 29th of the last month and dured 2 days. The order whereof was partly as here after followeth.

First, in the court [of the Palace] there was no great ceremonies of mourning, saving over the court-gate hanged about 6 yards of black cloth: and in the midst of the cloth, the whole breadth of the velvet, whereon hanged the arms of the Emperor, painted upon a table. And the like hanged before the door of the great hall within the court.

From the court to the market, or fish mart, and so from thence to the head church called Saint Golls [Gudule's] the streets were relaid on both the sides of the street—all black: and along those relays stood of the burgh of the town in black gowns; the one distant from the other about 1 *fedone;* and in every of their hands a torch of wax with the Emperor's arms upon them, which might be in number about 3000 torches.

The church was hanged all with black cloth; and above the cloth, the breadth of a velvet round about the church; whereon were made fast many scutcheons of the Emperor's arms.

There stood in the middle of the church a fair hearse, which was covered above with cloth of gold. But, by reason the candlesticks whereon the candles stood were so thick and black, the cloth of gold was little perceived: whereon might be by estimation about 2500 candles, or 3000 at the most. But round about the church there stood wonderful many: and under the hearse, the chest or coffin for the corse, covered with black cloth.

The burying began about 1 of the clock, or thereabout; and the procession came all out of the court in order as hereafter followeth. [there follow three pages of tedious detail which are here omitted.]

Next after came a ship about 24 foot long, or by estimation, of the burden of 20 tons, which was exceedingly well fashioned; and costly graven or carven, and gilted, as hereafter followeth.

This ship was carried as if it had been in a sea; which was so made and painted as if it had been in a sea indeed. The ship went in the streets by strength of men that were in it, and no man was seen.

There stood in the sea before the ship 2 strange monsters, whom had either a bridle or collar about their necks, whereunto was made fast a cord of silk, being fast unto the ship and unto them. So that it seemed that they had pulled the ship forward. Upon the ship, from the water to the shrouds, were painted all the voyages and victories that the Emperor had by water. The sea wherein the ship went, stuck full of banners of the Emperor's arms, standing upright; and amongst them, many banners of the Turks and Moors, fallen down and lying in the water. All the shrouds, or upper part of the ship, was costly carven and gilt, the shrouds and masts, sails and tops, all black. Round about the stern of the ship was painted all the arms of the kingdoms whereof Charles the Emperor was king. Above in the ship, it was stuck full of banners of all the countries whereof he was governor . . .

In the fore part of the ship sat a maid, all clothed in brown and in her hand an anchor [personifying Hope.]

Before the stool of estate sat another maid, all clothed in white and her face covered with white lampors [tiffany, or thin silk]. In her right hand a red cross, and in her left hand a chalice, with the sacrament. [She personified Faith].

In the after part of the ship stood 1 other maid, all clothed in red, and in her hand a heart branning [burning]: and at the main mast hanged a streamer with the picture of the crucifixion, with many other streamers. [there follow six pages of tedious detail, here omitted].

And the service being done, there went a nobleman to the hearse, (so far as I could understand it was the Prince of Orange), who standing before the hearse, struck with the hand upon the chest and said 'he is dead'. Then standing still awhile he said 'He shall remain dead'. And then, resting a while, he struck again and said, 'He is dead, and there is another risen up in his place greater than ever he was'. Whereupon the king's hood was taken off: and as I did learn at others who were there, the king went home without his hood. But I could not tarry so long to see it, because I had promised my Lord Cobham to meet him the next day in the morning at Antwerp.

This was the order of the burial of the Emperor, so far as I could carry away; but and if I might have tarried till the next day, I would have had all their names that carried the standards before the horses. It was sure a sight worth to go 100 miles to see it! . . . The Lord give his soul rest.

CHARLES V'S POLITICAL TESTAMENT OF 1543

The political situation which faced Charles V in 1543 was extremely dangerous. 'The Pope was a luke-warm friend, the King of England was not to be trusted, the King of France was a bitter and unrelenting enemy' (Brandi, p. 485). In order the better to cope with the dangers in central Europe, Charles decided to leave Spain for Germany and to make his son Philip, Regent in Spain. The following is the advice which Charles put into writing for Philip. Cf. Philip II's instructions to his Viceroy at Naples on p. 228.

Source: Brandi, The Emperor Charles V, trans. by C. V. Wedgwood, Jonathan Cape, 1939, pp. 485 et sqq.

My son, my departure from these kingdoms draws near. I have daily proof that I must go, for you have already sustained much wrong through my fault in this inheritance which God has entrusted to me, and worse can only be prevented by my going. Therefore I have resolved upon this experiment of leaving you to govern in my stead.

You are still young to bear so great a burden. I therefore commend you to the mercy of God and pray that you may take as examples all those who have made good in age and experience by their courage and zeal in the pursuit of honour. Then I shall have cause to thank God for giving me such a son. I for my part will do all I can to help you, and I am therefore writing to you, my son, in the faith that God will inspire my words. Be devout, fear God and love Him above all else.

Be a friend to justice, my son. Command your servants that they be moved neither by passion, nor by prejudice, nor yet by gifts. Let no man think that your decisions in anything, least of all in the administration of justice, are the fruit of passion, prejudice or anger. After the manner of our Lord, temper justice with mercy. In your bearing, be calm and reserved. Say nothing in anger. Be easy of approach and pleasant of manner; listen to good advice and take heed of flatterers as you would of fire.

To enable you the better to fulfill your part I have left you here in Spain all the members of my royal council, and given special instructions to them, which I send to you by Cobos. I beseech you to act in accordance with what I tell you. The royal council will see to the administration of justice and will care for the welfare of the land. Support them in their endeavours. Do not permit the publication of interdicts and the prohibition of worship except on the most urgent grounds, or unless the commands proceed from the Holy See itself, when you must religiously respect them, for in these times many men no longer respect the Holy See. Trust in the Duke of Alva as commander-in-chief of the army. Obey my instructions in your dealings with the Council of State, the Council for the Indies, for finance, for the Order of the Golden Fleece, and in your relations with the Inquisition. Have a special care to finance, which is to-day the most important department of the state; the treasury has a clear knowledge of the means which are at your disposal . . .

And now, my son, one word more—for your own behaviour. I entreat you to take my advice to heart. You must know that this your early marriage and your calling to the regency make you a man long before your time. But do not on that account falsely presume that study is an occupation fit only for a child. On the contrary, it is the only means by which you will gain honour and reputation. You cannot grow to early manhood merely by imagining and wishing; you must gain the knowledge and judgement which will enable you to do a man's work. Study and good company will alone help you to this. Remember how many lands you will be called upon to govern, how far apart they are, how many different languages they speak, how necessary it will be for you to know them all so that you may understand and be understood by your subjects, and you will see how needful it is for you to learn languages. Latin is indispensable, French very important. Until this time you have had boys for companions and amused yourself with the pleasures of childhood. From now on you are master of yourself and must seek the company of

experienced men. You must not altogether abandon such
pleasures as suit your age, but you must not neglect your work
for them. Don Juan will be able to advise you for the best in
this. He will know how best to deal with those flatterers who try
to become your boon companions by splintering lances with
you, riding at the ring, jousting and hunting, or who try to
tempt you to more unworthy pleasures. You would do wisely
to show no pleasure in the company of those who are for ever
making unseemly jokes.

With God's will, my son, you are soon to marry. May God be
pleased to give you grace to live soberly in this state, and to get
sons. I am convinced that you have not deceived me as to your
chastity until this time, and I am sure that you will continue so
after your marriage . . .

It is impossible to think of everything, for there are more
exceptions than rules in politics. The chief is that you should
pursue the straight path, have a good judgement and do good
works. Even older men than you need someone to keep them
constantly alive to their duty and to remind them of what has to
be done. Every man needs advice, and so I ask you to make
Don Juan de Zuñiga your watch and your alarum in all things.
I too have commanded him to do his own part therein and to
speak sharply if he must. Sleep is often sweet and an alarum is
commonly a nuisance: therefore remember that he acts only out
of devotion and duty to me, and be grateful to him . . .

May God grant, my son, that you may so live and act with
His help that He will be rightly served, and that He will receive
you at last in Paradise after your days on earth. This is the
constant prayer of your loving father.

I, THE KING.

PROSPERITY IN CASTILE

In 1520 the Communes of Castile revolted against the government
of Charles V, who in fact was outside Spain during the revolt, which
was completely suppressed. A period of great prosperity followed,
but after the abdication of Charles V in 1556 a rapid decline (of which
there had been signs even in the 1540's) took place in industry and

trade, as is proved by the following complaint made by the Cortes in 1573.

Source: Quoted by R. Trevor Davies in *The Golden Century of Spain*, Macmillan, 1954, p. 70.

When the silk and woollen industries were in progress in these places (viz. Toledo, Segovia, Cuença, Granada and Seville), there was neither man nor woman, however aged or infirm, neither boys nor girls, however young, who could not earn their board by rendering assistance, so much so that it was a memorable experience to walk about the hills around Segovia and Cuença, and to see how widespread was industry everywhere. Neither young nor old, neither male nor female lacked employment. Everyone in every house was busy with the woollen industry; and since the city of Toledo was too small to contain the multitude of its weavers, all the neighbouring villages were crowded with them—a busy, rich and contented population, consisting not only of natives of those regions, but of foreigners in large numbers; and whether foreigners or native, none was without profitable work.

PHILIP II

Philip II of Spain was born in 1527 and died in 1598. He was the son of the Emperor Charles V and his first wife, Isabella of Portugal. On October 26th, 1555, Charles V abdicated and Philip became King of Spain and the Netherlands and of the Spanish empire overseas. He was married in 1554 to Mary I, Queen of England, his second wife. She died in 1558. Philip was married twice more.

Source: (a) The Venetian Ambassador, 1559: C.S.P. Ven. 1558–80, No. 274. Quoted Kidd, *op. cit.*, p. 681.

The Catholic king was born in Spain in the month of May 1527. He passed his early days and the greater part of his youth in that kingdom, where either from custom of the country or by the will of his mother, who was a Portuguese, he was educated with all the care and respect which could become the son of the greatest Emperor who ever reigned in Christendom and the heir of possessions of such vast magnitude.

Having been brought up in this manner, his Majesty, when he first quitted Spain, passed through Italy and Germany to Flanders, and conveyed a universal impression that he was of a severe and intractable disposition, and therefore he was not much liked by the Italians, thoroughly disliked by the Flemings, and hated by the Germans. Consequently he was first warned by the Cardinal of Trent, then by Queen Mary, and even more effectually by his father, that a character for severity did not become the ruler of various nations and people of various habits and customs . . .

His efforts are directed not to increase his possessions by war, but to preserve them by peace; for at the commencement of his reign he made a truce with the king of France, notwithstanding that the Emperor refused his consent and that the Bishop of Arras publicly condemned it. He regulated the disorders of the ministers of his realms; he restored the courts of law; he expedited the grants of favours and the decrees of justice, which the Emperor was accustomed to delay; he showed liberality to all persons and never permitted any one to leave his presence dissatisfied. But when the Emperor, who had by his great reputation for prudence and experience maintained the authority of his son, departed for Spain, his Majesty was too weak to support so great a burden and soon found himself involved in serious difficulties, which might have overthrown him, had he not been aided by fortune and by the imprudence of his enemies. Then, if he had desired to imitate the Emperor, he might have done so by the strength of his power and the prosperity of his fortune, which are most formidable to the world: but although he resembles his father in his features, in his mode of speech, in his observance of religion and in his kindness and good faith, he is dissimilar in many other respects which constitute the crowning-point of the greatness of Princes. The Emperor delighted in all that pertained to war, but his Majesty has neither knowledge of warlike matters nor delight in them. The Emperor undertook great expeditions, but these the king avoids. The Emperor planned great designs and conducted them with dexterity, and to his great benefit; but the king thinks less of increasing his own power than of obstructing the power of

Q

others. The Emperor never yielded to threats or to fear, but the king under very small apprehensions has given away states.

The Emperor governed entirely according to his own views, but the king governs according to the views of others, and he has no esteem for any nation except the Spanish; he consorts only with Spaniards, and with these only he takes counsel and governs. Moreover, contrary to the custom of the Emperor, he takes no notice of Italians and Flemings, and least of all Germans, and although he retains the chief men of each nation in his kingdom, still it is observed that he declines to admit any of them to his secret councils, but keeps them only for affairs of war; and he probably acts thus, not so much because he has a good opinion of them, as to prevent their services being employed by his enemies. For this reason he has never summoned either the Duke of Savoy or the Duke Ottavio to the Council of State, but only to the Council of War, into which all the chief officers, and even the colonels, are admitted. The Duke Ottavio has nicknamed this Council the 'Council of the Populace'.

Source: (*b*) Cabrera, *Vita de Felipe Segundo, Rey de España*, lib. i, 12 and 4.

His body was but a human cage, in which, however brief and narrow, dwelt a soul to whose flight the immeasurable expanse of heaven was too contracted. His aspect was so reverend that rustics who met him alone in a wood, without knowing him, bowed down with instinctive veneration.

Source: (*c*) Giovanni Michele, Venetian Ambassador to England. MS.

In face he was the living image of his father, having the same skin and features with that mouth and the one pendulous lip overhanging the other, and all the other characteristics of the Emperor, except for his smaller stature . . . The lower lip thick: the forehead large and fine, the eyes the colour of the sky and large.

Source: (*d*) Badovaro, MS.

He wears his beard short and pointed, and its hair is light and yellow. He looks like a Fleming, but his loftiness is that of a Spaniard . . . Just as nature has given His Majesty a weak body, so has it given him as timid a spirit, and as a result of his temperament he goes in for eating a great deal, being specially addicted to pastry, which gives him pains in his stomach and sides.

The following quotations are from the English translations of Marañon's *Antonio Pérez* by C. D. Ley, Hollis & Carter 1954.

Source: (e) As a judgement on Philip II's 'prudence' a monk in the Escorial wrote about Medina Sidonia, whom Philip chose to command the Armada.

If he had known as much about war as about selling tunny-fish, he would not have turned out such a poor soldier as he did.

Source: (f) Don Rodrigo Manuel to Mateo Vázquez:

Although dilatoriness is usually bad in all things, it is sometimes incurable, as His Majesty's is beginning to be.

Source: (g) Don John of Austria to Philip II:

Leave it to the mercy of time no longer, Your Majesty, for having done so has brought us to the pretty pass we are in.

Source: (h) Pope Pius V to Philip II:

Your Majesty spends so long considering your undertakings that when the moment to perform them comes, the occasion has passed and the money has all been spent.

Source: (i) Antonio Perez said that Philip II's smile:

'cut like a sword'.

Source: (j) St. Teresa only met Philip II once. Of that meeting she said:

'I felt deeply disturbed when I began to speak to him, because his piercing glance seemed to wound me. It was one of those glances that plumb into the very soul, and he had fixed it on me. So I lowered my eyes and as briefly as I could told him what I wanted.'

Source: Lorenzo Priuli, Venetian Ambassador: Alberi, *Relazione* ...
This English version from Koenigsberger, *The Government of Sicily under Philip II*, Staple Press, N.Y., 1951, p. 69. The government was almost wholly carried out in councils which contained nothing but lawyers, the reasons being:

One, to have in his councils men completely dependent on him, who will serve him with greater loyalty, knowing their greatness to derive from him; the other, because the nobles and great lords are little qualified in this service, not having been brought up in the honourable study of letters. But this arrangement, while leaving the gentlemen and great lords ill-satisfied, does not at the same time bring forth the good effect which the King desires; for in these doctors, who have applied themselves to study primarily for the end of gain, there is not to be found that desire for the public weal which is necessary; and as persons of low birth who do not know how to use their authority with moderation, they carry out their duties with great arrogance and pride, for it seems to them that with cruelty they will acquire a great reputation for justice with the King ... and if the King's goodness and justice did not console and curb everyone, there would be danger that some disaster might one day befall.

PHILIP II'S INSTRUCTIONS TO THE VICEROY OF NAPLES

Source: B.M. MS. Add. 28. 701, fo. 86.

The first thing you must realize is that the community was not made for the Prince, but rather that the Prince was created for the sake of the community; and you will have to represent our Person and act as we would act, if we were present. Your principal object and intention must be to work for the community which is in your charge, so that it may live and rest in full security, peace, justice and quiet; to watch so that it may sleep without anxiety; and finally to take heed that you are not accepting this office to be idle or to live at your pleasure, nor for any benefit of your own, but only, as I have said, for the peace and quiet and good of the community.

PHILIP II AND THE INQUISITION

Philip II had made up his mind to suppress Calvinism in the Netherlands. A mass of correspondence on this subject exists between Philip,
the Regent, the Cardinal Granvelle, and their agents in Madrid, Rome
and Brussels.

Source: (*a*) September 29th, 1561. Philip to the Regent:

Maintain religion, chastise all who act against it; nothing gives
me greater pleasure.

Source: (*b*) September 25th, 1564:

I am grieved to learn that the people should grow angry at the
burning of a heretic.

Source: (*c*) October 4th, 1565:

I urge the Inquisitors to fresh activity; I will spare neither money
nor life to maintain the faith.

Source: (*d*) October 17th, 1565, from Segovia:

As to the Inquisition, my will is that it be enforced by the
Inquisitors, as of old and as is required by all law, human and
divine. This lies very near my heart and I require you to carry
out my orders. Let all prisoners be put to death, and suffer them
no longer to escape through the neglect, weakness and bad faith
of the judges. If any are too timid to execute the edicts, I will
replace them by men who have more heart and zeal.

Source: (*e*) July, 1566, to his ambassador in Rome:

As to the pardons publicly announced in my name, whisper in
the ear of his Holiness that I do not pretend to pardon in matters
religious. Assure his Holiness that rather than suffer the least
thing in prejudice of religion, I will lose my States and a hundred
lives, for I will not live to be a king of heretics. And if I must use
force, I will carry out my intentions myself, and neither my own
peril nor the ruin of my provinces, or even of all my dominions,
shall stop me from fulfilling my duty as a Christian prince to
maintain the Catholic faith and the Holy See now filled by a
Pope whom I love and revere. [Pius V.]

PHILIP II CHOOSES A COMMANDER FOR THE ARMADA

The first commander of the Armada was Alonzo de Bazan, Marques de Santa Cruz, but he died in February, 1584, at the age of 73. Philip chose as his successor Alonzo de Guzman, Duke of Medina Sidonia, aged 38 and wholly without naval experience. No one was more astonished and dismayed than Sidonia himself.

Source: (a) Medina Sidonia to Philip II. Froude, *The Spanish Story of the Armada,* London, 1892, p. 23 *et sqq.*

My health is bad and from my small experience of the water I know that I am always sea-sick. I have no money which I can spare. I owe a million ducats and I have not a *real* to spend on my outfit. The expedition is on such a scale and the object is of such high importance that the person at the head of it ought to understand navigation and sea-fighting, and I know nothng of either. I have not one of those essential qualifications. I have no acquaintances among the officers who are to serve under me. Santa Cruz had information about the state of things in England; I have none. Were I competent otherwise, I should have to act in the dark by the opinion of others, and I cannot tell to whom I may trust. The Adelantado of Castile would do better than I. Our Lord would help him, for he is a good Christian and has fought in naval battles. If you send me, depend upon it, I shall have a bad account to render of my trust.

Source: (b) Philip insisted on Sidonia's accepting, which he most reluctantly did. Sidonia to Philip II. Froude, *op. cit.*

Since your Majesty still desires it, after my confession of incompetence, I will try to deserve your confidence. As I shall be doing God's work, I may hope that He will help me.

Source: (c) Philip II's reply. Froude, *op. cit.*

You are sacrificing yourself for God's service and for mine. I am so anxious that, if I was less occupied at home, I would accompany the fleet myself, and I should be certain that all would go well. Take heart; you have now an opportunity of showing the extraordinary qualities which God, the author of all good, has been pleased to bestow upon you. Happen what may, I charge myself with the care of your children. If you fail, you fail; but the cause being God's, you will not fail.

THE DEATH OF PHILIP II, SEPTEMBER 13TH, 1598

Source: The Venetian Ambassador to his Government. Quoted by R. Trevor Davies, *The Golden Century of Spain*, Macmillan, 1954, p. 224.

His majesty expired at the Escorial this morning at daybreak, after having received all the sacraments of the Church with every sign of devoutness, piety and religion . . . He was a Prince who fought with gold rather than with steel, by his brain rather than by his arms. He has acquired more by sitting still, by negotiation, by diplomacy, than his father did by armies and by war . . . Profoundly religious, he loved peace and quiet. He displayed great calmness and professed himself unmoved in good or bad fortune alike . . . On great occasions . . . he never counted the cost; he was no close reckoner, but lavished gold without a thought; but in small matters in the government of his household, in his presents and rewards, he was more parsimonious than became his station . . . He held his desires in absolute control and showed an immutable and unalterable temper . . . No one ever saw him in a rage, being always patient, phlegmatic, temperate, melancholy. In short, he left a glorious memory of his royal name, which may serve as an example, not only unto his posterity and his successors, but unto strangers as well.

MADRID IN 1593

For more than six centuries from 1234 the rulers of Spain waged a futile war against the luxury and splendour in which their subjects loved to indulge. The sumptuary decrees usually took the form of a representation from the Cortes to the sovereign setting forth the abuses to be remedied and suggesting the remedies. The decree was generally confirmed by what was known as the king's 'pragmatic sanction', it was then published and had the force of law. Few of these 'pragmatics' had any success for any length of time, but they had an evil effect on the Spanish trade and industries. In 1593 Camillo Borghese was sent by the Pope to Madrid and he has left an account of the fashions which he saw there.

Source: L'Espagne au 16me and 17me siécles, par Morel Fatio, Paris, 1878, printed in M. A. S. Hume's *The Year after the Armada,* London, 1896, pp. 232–4.

The dress of this country is as follows. The men wear long breeches, with a surcoat and hat, or else a cloak and cap, as it would be a great breach of decorum with them to wear a hat and cloak together. This costume would certainly be very pretty if the breeches were not cut so long as to be disproportionate. Some men have taken to wearing hose in the Seville style, which they call galligaskins, and with these it is proper to wear a cloak and hat instead of a cap. The ladies, like the men, usually dress in black and have a veil round their faces like nuns, their heads being enveloped in their mantillas in such a way that their faces are hardly visible. Indeed, if it were not for the pragmatic issued by the King on the subject, they would still cover their faces completely, as they used to do a few years ago. When they do not wear these veils over their faces, they have on collars with enormous ruff pleats. They are naturally dark-skinned, but the use of paints is so common that they all look fair, and though small in stature, their high pattens make them look tall, so that it may truly be said that all Spanish ladies turn themselves from little and dusky to big and bright. The main street of Madrid would be fine if it were not unutterably filthy and almost impassable on foot, and the better class of ladies are always in carriages or litters, whilst the humbler ones ride on donkey-back or pick their way through the mire. They (the ladies) are naturally impudent, presumptuous and off-handed, and even in the street go up and talk with men whom they do not know, looking upon it as a kind of heresy to be introduced properly. They admit all sorts of men to their conversation and are not a bit scandalized at the most immodest proposals being made to them.

The gentlemen now rarely ride on horseback, but often go in carriages. They are preceded in the streets by a group of pages and a couple of servants they call lacqueys, the pragmatic not allowing them more, although the grandees may be attended by four. The pragmatics only allow saddle cloths to be worn from

October to March, but the rest of the year velvet saddles may be used. The one pastime of these people is to drive up and down the Calle Mayor (High Street) from midday to midnight.

NOTES

[1] i.e. Philip II.

[2] i.e. Mary, sister of Charles V, wife of Lewis of Hungary and Regent of the Netherlands.

THE REFORMATION
(Notes on p. 283)

MARTIN LUTHER

It is scarcely possible any longer to hold the view that the tremendous revolution of the sixteenth century was brought about solely by religion. No doubt the old mediaeval church had for some time been undermined by a loss of administrative efficiency, itself the result of gradual decentralization. The rise of national monarchies had encroached on the papal supremacy, and this was especially true in the Empire, which itself often had to surrender its authority into the hands of the princes and nobles. The rise of a new middle class, greatly taken up with trade, had lowered the respect for the Papacy and even for religion, and helped to bring about the dissolution of the feudal system. The peasant class was growing more and more dissatisfied with its lot (although this had in fact been much improved in the later middle ages), and was ready to revolt, which it did in Germany during the Reformation. Perhaps even more the new discoveries of Columbus and Magellan, the widening of men's horizons which these brought about, and the terrific effects of the printing press, and above all the fierce pace at which these changes were taking place, were producing a new set of conditions to which the Church was dangerously slow to accommodate itself. Yet even so, these explosive forces might have taken far longer to produce the actual upheaval if they had not found a central flash-point. That point was Martin Luther, an Augustinian monk. Thus it was that the explosion took place in the realm of religion.

Martin Luther was born in 1483 and he died in 1546. He was the son of a man of humble origin who raised himself to the position of a town councillor of Mansfeld. He gave Martin a good education in Latin in a school at Eisenach and at the University of Erfurt. In 1505 Martin became an Augustinian monk and he then began to study the Bible and later the writings of St. Augustine. He was appointed to lecture on theology at the University of Wittenberg and between 1508 and 1515 he made himself into a learned theologian, but he never became a Humanist, being very weak in Greek and Hebrew. He first noticed the abuse of Indulgences in 1513, but he did not then deny the doctrine of the *Thesaurus Meritorum*. His real revolt began in 1517

with the campaign of Tetzel, after which Martin nailed his 95 Theses
to the Castle church door at Wittenberg, condemning Indulgences.
The development of Luther's views and theology will be illustrated in
the following series of extracts from his writings. The chief events in the
Lutheran Reformation are: 1519, the Leipzig Disputation; 1520, *Appeal
to the Ruling Class of German Nobility*, in which he attacked the Papacy;
the burning of a Papal Bull at Wittenberg; 1521, his defence of his
doctrine at the Diet of Worms before the Emperor Charles V; 1522,
the Zwickau Prophets; 1523, the Rising of the Free Knights of the
Empire under Sickingen; 1525, the Peasants' Revolt; 1530, the meeting
with Zwingli at Marburg; 1525–35, the Anabaptist movement. In
1525 he married Katherine von Bora. He died in 1546 and his place
was taken by Philip Melancthon. Martin Luther must be regarded as
one of the giants in the history of Europe, and that in spite of the fact
that he was no statesman, he had no talent for organization, and he
had no power of compromise. The dissensions among the Lutherans
proves the one, the failure to come to terms with Zwingli in 1529
proves the other.

  Source: Walch ed. of Luther's works, xv, p. 1201. This English
version is taken from R. Bainton's *Here I Stand*, Hodder & Stoughton,
1951, p. 113. The name of the eyewitness is not given.

  Martin is of middle height, emaciated from care and study, so
that you can almost count his bones through his skin. He is in
the vigour of manhood and has a clear, penetrating voice. He is
learned and has the Scripture at his fingers' ends. He knows
Greek and Hebrew sufficiently to judge of the interpretations. A
perfect forest of words and ideas stands at his command. He is
affable and friendly, in no sense dour or arrogant. He is equal to
anything. In company he is vivacious, jocose, always cheerful
and gay no matter how hard his adversaries press him. Everyone
chides him for the fault of being a little too insolent in his
reproaches and more caustic than is prudent for an innovator in
religion or becoming to a theologian. Much the same can be said
of Carlstadt,[1] though in a lesser degree. He is smaller than Luther,
with the complexion of a smoked herring. His voice is thick and
unpleasant. He is slower in memory and quicker in anger. Eck[2]
is a heavy, square-set fellow with a full German voice supported
by a hefty chest. He would make a tragedian or town crier, but

his voice is rather rough than clear. His eyes and mouth and his whole face remind one more of a butcher than a theologian.

THE LUTHERAN REFORMATION

THE INDULGENCE AND PAPAL FINANCE

The Papal Bull *Liquet Omnibus*, dated January 11th, 1510, seven years later caused Luther's revolt. In it no mention was made of Repentance and Confession as a condition for gaining Indulgence. Payment of money was the only reason given. For an extra sum the sinner might choose his own confessor, and if that confessor imposed a 'salutary penance', that was to consist of a further payment towards the building of St. Peter's, Rome. Clearly, Indulgences had become one of the normal expedients of the Papacy for raising money. At the end of 1514, Pope Leo X had begun to organize collections for St. Peter's on a large scale.

At this moment the Archbishop of Mainz owed the Fugger banking family 30,000 florins which he had borrowed from them to pay the Pope for his appointment as Archbishop and for a papal dispensation to hold two other bishoprics, of which one was another Archbishopric, at the same time. To hold two Archbishoprics was most unusual, therefore the price for the dispensation went up. He hoped to recover this sum by acting as agent for the Pope in the sale of Indulgences for St. Peter's and for a crusade against the Turk. He entrusted the sales to a Dominican friar, John Tetzel (1470–1519), an able theologian and a notable preacher. Luther was infuriated at the abuse being made of Indulgences, and he was the more angry when he learned that Tetzel was visiting villages close to Wittenberg. It has been claimed that modern research has to some extent redeemed the character of Tetzel, but the following account illustrates the views and feelings of the German people at the time against the methods of the Papacy.

Source: F. Myconius, *Historia Reformationis, ap.* Gieseler, *Eccl. Hist.* v. 362, ed. 1855. This English version is taken from Kidd's *Documents Illustrative of the Continental Reformation*, Oxford, 1911, p. 19.

[Tetzel] gained by his preaching in Germany an immense sum of money, all of which he sent to Rome; and especially at the new mining works at St. Annaberg, where I, Frederick Mecum, heard him for two years, a large sum was collected. It is incredible what this ignorant and impudent friar gave out. He said that if a

Christian had slept with his mother, and placed the sum of money in the Pope's indulgence chest, the Pope had power in heaven and earth to forgive the sin, and, if he forgave it, God must do so also. Item, if they contributed readily and bought grace and indulgence, all the hills of St. Annaberg would become pure massive silver. Item, so soon as the coin rang in the chest, the soul for whom the money was paid would go straightway to heaven. The indulgence was so highly prized that, when the commissary entered a city, the Bull was borne on a satin or gold-embroidered cushion, and all the priests and monks, the town council, schoolmaster, scholars, men, women, maidens, and children, went out to meet him with banners and tapers, with songs and procession. Then all the bells were rung, all the organs played; he was conducted into the church, a red cross was erected in the midst of the church, and the Pope's banner displayed; in short, God himself could not have been welcomed and entertained with greater honour.

LUTHER'S SERMON ON INDULGENCE AND GRACE

On October 31st, 1517, Luther posted his Ninety-five Theses on the door of Castle Church in Wittenberg. He explained his action and views to the people in a sermon on *Indulgence and Grace*. He was at that moment confident that he had only to expose the scandal of the sale of indulgences to get it removed.

Source: Gieseler, *op. cit.* v, 367; Kidd, *op. cit.,* p. 29.

First, you ought to know that some modern teachers such as the Master of the Sentences,[3] S. Thomas [Aquinas] and their followers, divide Penance into three parts, namely, Contrition, Confession, and Satisfaction: and although this distinction, according to their meaning, was found to be hardly or not at all grounded upon Holy Scripture, nor upon the early Fathers of the Church, we are willing to let it stand and to speak after their fashion . . .

Sixth, it cannot be proved from any Scripture that divine justice requires or desires any other punishment or satisfaction from the sinner than his hearty and true repentance and conversion, with a resolution henceforth to bear the cross of Christ and

practise the good works before-mentioned, also imposed on him
by no man . . .

Ninth, if the Church were at this day to decide and declare that
indulgence made more satisfaction than works, still it were a
thousand-fold better that no Christian man should purchase or
desire the indulgence, but rather perform the works and suffer
loss . . .

Fourteenth, indulgence is allowed for the sake of imperfect
and slothful Christians, who will not exercise themselves indus-
triously in good works or are impatient. For indulgence improves
no man, but only tolerates and allows his imperfection. So men
should not speak against indulgence, but neither should they
persuade any one to take it.

LUTHER AND LEO X

Source: (a) The Papal Bull, *Exsurge Domine*, was issued by Leo X on
June 15th, 1520. No offer of a safe conduct ever reached Luther.

Arise, O Lord, and judge thy cause. A wild boar has invaded
thy vineyard. Arise, O Peter, and consider the case of the Holy
Roman Church, the mother of all churches, consecrated by thy
blood. Arise, O Paul, who by thy teaching and death hast illu-
mined and dost illumine the Church. Arise, all ye saints, and the
whole universal Church, whose interpretation of Scripture has
been assailed. We can scarcely express our grief over the ancient
heresies which have been revived in Germany. We are the more
downcast because she was always in the forefront of the war on
heresy. Our pastoral office can no longer tolerate the pestiferous
virus of the following forty-one errors . . . We can no longer
suffer the serpent to creep through the field of the Lord. The
books of Martin Luther which contain these errors are to be
examined and burned. As for Martin himself, good God, what
office of paternal love have we omitted in order to recall him
from his errors? Have we not offered him a safe conduct and
money for the journey? And he has had the temerity to appeal
to a future council, although our predecessors, Pius II and Julius

II, subjected such appeals to the penalties of heresy. Now therefore we give Martin sixty days in which to submit, dating from the time of the publication of this Bull in his district. Anyone who presumes to infringe our excommunication and anathema will stand under the wrath of Almighty God and of the Apostles Peter and Paul.

Dated on the 15th day of June, 1520.

Source: (*b*) The Bull reached Luther on October 10th, 1520. Luther reacted as follows. Luther's comment to Spalatin. Bainton, *op. cit.*, p. 160.

This Bull condemns Christ himself. It summons me not to an audience but to a recantation. I am going to act on the assumption it is spurious, though I think it is genuine. Would that Charles were a man and would fight for Christ against these Satans. But I am not afraid. God's will be done. I do not know what the prince should do unless to dissemble. I am sending you a copy of the Bull that you may see the Roman monster. The faith and the Church are at stake. I rejoice to suffer in so noble a cause. I am not worthy of so holy a trial. I feel much freer now that I am certain the pope is Antichrist. Erasmus writes that the imperial court is overrun with mendicants, and there is no hope from the emperor. I am on the way to Lichtenburg for a conference with Miltitz. Farewell and pray for me.

VIOLENCE AT WORMS

The Diet of Worms was about to take place (1522), but there were delays and these gave the populace opportunities for violence. Jerome Aleander was one of the two papal nuncios (Eyk was the other) who were responsible for publishing the Bull *Exsurge* throughout Germany.

Source: (*a*) Aleander's report on conditions in Worms. Bainton, *op. cit.*, p. 175. Martin is pictured with a halo and a dove above his head.

The people kiss these pictures. Such a quantity have been sold that I was not able to obtain one. A cartoon has appeared showing Luther with a book in his hand, accompanied by Hutten in armour with a sword under the caption, 'Champions of Christian Liberty'.

Another sheet portrays Luther in front and Hutten carrying a
a chest on which are two chalices with the inscription, 'The Ark
of the True Faith'. Erasmus, in front, is playing the harp as David
did. In the background is John Hus, whom Luther has recently
proclaimed his saint. In another part of the picture the pope and
the cardinals are being bound by the soldiers of the guard. I
cannot go out on the streets but the Germans put their hands to
their swords and gnash their teeth at me. I hope the pope will
give me a plenary indulgence and look after my brothers and
sisters if anything happens to me.

   Source: (*b*) A Humanist at Worms wrote to Hutten. Bainton, *op. cit.*,
p. 176.

A Spaniard tore up your edition of the Bull and trampled it in
the mud. A chaplain of the emperor and two Spaniards caught a
man with sixty copies of *The Babylonian Captivity*. The people
came to the rescue, and the assailants had to take refuge in the
castle. A mounted Spaniard pursued one of our men, who barely
escaped through a door. The Spaniard reined up so suddenly that
he fell off his horse and could not rise until a German lifted
him

THE EMPEROR, CHARLES V's VIEW, April 19th, 1521. Armstrong, I, 77.

   A single monk, led astray by private judgement, has set himself
against the faith held by all Christians for a thousand years and
more, and impudently concludes that all Christians up till now
have erred. I have therefore resolved to stake upon this cause all
my dominions, my friends, my body and my blood, my life and
soul. For myself and you, sprung from the holy German nation,
appointed by peculiar privilege defenders of the faith, it would be
a grievous disgrace, an eternal stain upon ourselves and posterity,
if, in this our day, not only heresy, but its very suspicion, were
due to our neglect. After Luther's stiff-necked reply in my
presence yesterday, I now repent that I have so long delayed
proceedings against him and his false doctrines. I have now
resolved never again, under any circumstances, to hear him.
Under protection of his safe conduct he shall be escorted home,

but forbidden to preach and to seduce men with his evil doctrines and incite them to rebellion.

GERMAN FEELING IN FAVOUR OF LUTHER

Source: Despatches of Gaspar Contarini, Venetian Ambassador. Kidd, *op. cit.,* p. 89.

[April 25th, 1521.] I cannot tell you how much favour he enjoys here [Worms], which is of such a nature that, on the Emperor's departure and the dissolution of the Diet, I suspect it will produce some bad effect, most especially against the prelates of Germany. In truth, had this man been prudent, had he restricted himself to his first propositions, and not entangled himself in manifest errors about the faith, he would have been, I do not say favoured, but adored by the whole of Germany. I was told so at Augsburg by the Duke of Bavaria and many others, and I see the same by experience.

[April 26th, 1521] Luther is a man who will not relinquish his opinion, either through argument, fear or entreaty . . . He has many powerful partisans who encourage him, and against whom none dares to proceed . . . His books are sold publicly in Worms, although the Pope and the Emperor, who is on the spot, have prohibited them.

LUTHER AND THE ARCHBISHOP OF MAINZ

Source: (a) A letter from Luther, dated December 1st 1521. Kidd, *op. cit.,* p. 95.

Your Electoral Grace has again set up the idol at Halle, which ruins poor simple Christians in wealth and soul . . . Your Electoral Grace, perhaps, thinks that I am removed from your way; that you will now be safe from me; and that you will easily crush the monk by means of the Emperor's Majesty . . . Your Electoral Grace will remember the beginning, how great a fire has risen from the little despised spark, when all the world was so secure and thought that one poor Mendicant was immeasurably too small for the Pope and was undertaking impossibilities. But God has taken up the cause. He has given the Pope with all his followers

R

enough to do. Against and above the thoughts of the world He has carried the game to a point from which the Pope will hardly bring it down again. It will grow worse with him daily, so that the work of God may be clearly recognized. The same God lives still: no man can doubt it now. He has power to withstand a Cardinal of Mainz, though four Emperors were to stand by him. He has also special pleasure in breaking the lofty cedars; and abashing the proud hardened Pharaohs ... But let not your Electoral Grace think that Luther is dead. He will glory freely and joyously in the God who has humbled the Pope, and begin a game with the Cardinal of Mainz that he did not much expect. Act together, dear Bishops! Ye may remain lordlings! But ye shall neither silence nor deafen this spirit. Such disgrace shall befall you from it as ye now little look for! So I would have you warned ...

To this I request and await a straightforward, speedy answer from your Electoral Grace, within fourteen days. For after fourteen days my book 'Against the Idol in Halle' will be published, unless a plain answer be made me.

Source: (*b*) The Elector Mainz to Luther. 21st of December, 1521. Kidd, *op. cit.*, p. 96.

Dear Sir Doctor, I have received and read your letter ... and taken it all in good part; but pardon me for saying that the cause which has moved you to write thus, has been long since done away with. I will conduct and show myself, if God will, a pious priest and Christian prince, so far as God shall give me grace, strength and understanding: for which I pray truly and will have prayers offered for me. For I can do nothing of my own self, and confess that I stand in need of the grace of God. I cannot deny that I am a poor sinful man, who can sin and err, and daily do sin and err.

LUTHERANISM AND HYMNS

One of the great reforms which Lutheranism brought about was that it introduced congregational singing. This was largely the work of Luther, who could play the lute and sing, and probably could also compose at least simple melodies, harmonize them and arrange them.

Source: (*a*) The following English version is taken from R. Bainton, *Here I Stand*, Hodder & Stoughton, 1951, p. 341.

Music is a fair and lovely gift of God which has often wakened and moved me to the joy of preaching. St. Augustine was troubled in conscience whenever he caught himself delighting in music, which he took to be sinful. He was a choice spirit, and were he living today would agree with us. I have no use for cranks who despise music, because it is a gift of God; Music drives away the Devil and makes people gay; they forget thereby all wrath, unchastity, arrogance, and the like. Next after theology I give to music the highest place and greatest honour. I would not exchange what little I know of music for something great. Experience proves that next to the Word of God only music deserves to be extolled as the mistress and governess of the feelings of the human heart. We know that to the devils music is distasteful and insufferable. My heart bubbles up and overflows in response to music, which has so often refreshed me from dire plagues.

Source: (*b*) A chronicle in the city of Magdeburg, quoted by R. Bainton, *op. cit.*, p. 346.

On the day of St. John between Easter and Pentecost, an old man, a weaver, came through the city gate to the monument of Kaiser Otto and there offered hymns for sale while he sang them to the people. The burgomaster, coming from early mass and seeing the crowd, asked one of his servants what was going on. 'There is an old scamp over there', he answered, 'who is singing and selling the hymns of the heretic Luther'. The burgomaster had him arrested and thrown into prison; but two hundred citizens interceded and he was released.

Source: (*c*) Luther wrote some thirty-six hymns of which the following is the best known, *Ein feste Burg ist unser Gott*. Kidd, *op. cit.*, p. 132.

A safe stronghold our God is still,
A trusty shield and weapon;
He'll help us clear from all the ill
That hath us now o'ertaken.
The ancient Prince of Hell
Hath risen with purpose fell;
Strong mail of Craft and Power
He weareth in this hour,
On earth is not his fellow.

With force of arms we nothing can,
Full soon were we downridden;
But for us fights the proper Man,
Whom God himself hath bidden.
Ask ye, Who is this same?
Christ Jesus is His name,
The Lord Zeboath's Son,
He and no other one
Shall conquer in the battle.

And were this world all Devils o'er,
And watching to devour us,
We lay it not to heart so sore,
Not they can overpower us.
And let the Prince of Ill
Look grim as e'er he will,
He harms us not a whit;
For why? His doom is writ,
A word shall quickly slay him.

God's word, for all their craft,
One moment will not linger,
But spite of Hell, shall have its course,
'Tis written by His finger.
And though they take our life,
Goods, honour, children, wife,

Yet is their profit small;
These things shall vanish all,
The City of God remaineth.

THE ENTRY OF CAMPEGGIO INTO NUREMBERG, MARCH 16, 1524

On November 18th, 1523, Cardinal Giulio de' Medici was elected
Pope as Clement VII. He understood the importance of the German
revolt and he appointed Cardinal Campeggio as legate in Germany
for Lutheran affairs. The following extract describes the state of things
which he found on entering Nuremberg.

Source: A letter from Friar Paolo Ziani, dated March 29th, 1524.
Kidd, op. cit., p. 134.

We arrived at Nuremberg on the Wednesday in Passion Week.
In these parts the sincere faith of Christ is utterly cancelled; no
respect is paid either to the Virgin Mary or the saints. On the
contrary, it is said that those who employ their aid sin mortally.
They deride the Papal rights and call the relics of the saints bones
of those who have been hanged. In Lent they eat meat openly,
saying they do not consider it prohibited. Confession is neglected,
as they say it should be made to God, and that auricular confession
is a buffoonery. They generally communicate under both forms.
They make a laughing-stock of the Pope and Cardinals, and other
ambassadorial ecclesiastics, by means of paintings and other
caricatures. In short, they consider Martin their illuminator, and
that until now they have been in darkness, and the indulgences
are held by them like bread sold in the market-place. In proof of
all this, the Legate, to avoid scorn, did not enter Nuremberg as
Legate ut moris est, neither did he give the blessing and absolution,
but came in as a mere horseman, though he was accompanied by
a most noble escort of all the Princes and part of the nobility,
who (with the exception of the Duke of Saxony and Palatine),
are sincere Christians. Some of the noblemen and the mass of the
merchants are all tainted, nay, obstinate and unconvertible, so
that at present neither the Legate's authority nor the will of the
Princes . . . can stem so strong a current.

Martin is not at Nuremberg, nor will he make his appearance
there; but, unless the Almighty stretch forth his arm, it will

doubtless come to pass that as the Princes and part of the nobility remain staunch Catholics, whilst the people persist in their errors, they will some day cut each other to pieces.

LUTHERANISM IN SWEDEN

On June 7th, 1523, Gustavus Vasa was elected King of Sweden by the Diet of Strengnäs. Strengnäs had since 1519 been the centre from which reforming doctrines had been propagated. John Brask, Bishop of Linköping, was the leader of the opponents of Lutheranism, but he did not get the support he hoped for from the King, who was anxious to get hold of the wealth of the Church (cf. Henry VIII in England) to pay his debts for the Danish war to Lübeck.

Source: (*a*) A letter from Brask to the King and the King's reply, dated 1524. Kidd, *op. cit.*, p. 153.

[The Bishop, 21st May, 1524.]

By the allegiance which I owe you, I deem it my duty to urge you not to allow the sale of Luther's books within the realm, nor give his pupils shelter or encouragement of any kind, till the coming council of the Church shall pass its judgement ... I know not how your Grace can better win the love of God, as well as of all Christian Kings and Princes, than by restoring the Church of Christ to the state of harmony that it has enjoyed in ages past.

Source: (*b*) *The King*, June 8th, 1524.

Regarding your request that we forbid the sale of Luther's writings, we know not by what right it could be done, for we are told that his teachings have not yet been found by impartial judges to be false. Moreover, since writings opposed to Luther have been circulated throughout the land, it seems but right that his too should be kept public, that you and other scholars may detect their fallacies and show them to the people. Then the books of Luther may be condemned. As to your charge that Luther's pupils are given shelter at our court, we answer that they have not sought it. If indeed they should, you are aware it is our duty to protect them as well as you. If there be any in our protection whom you wish to charge, bring your accusation and give names.

THE DEVELOPMENT OF LUTHER'S VIEWS

PERIOD I. THE BREAK WITH ROME

Luther's great contribution was his rediscovery of the biblical meaning of the righteousness of God. There is much debate now over the date at which Luther achieved this: perhaps it was between 1513 and 1515, or between 1518 and 1519. In the preface to the complete edition of his Latin writings, published in Wittenberg in 1545, Luther himself gives 1518 as the date, but he was writing from memory and his memory more than once played him false. The following extract is taken from that preface, because it gives Luther's own account of his 'conversion'.

Source: The English translation used by John Dillenberger in his *Martin Luther*, Anchor Paperback, Doubleday & Co., New York, 1961, pp. 10–12.

Meanwhile, I had already during that year (1519) returned to interpret the Psalter anew. I had confidence in the fact that I was more skilful, after I had lectured in the university on St. Paul's Epistles to the Romans, to the Galatians, and the one to the Hebrews. I had indeed been captivated with an extraordinary ardour for understanding Paul in the Epistle to the Romans. But up till then it was not the cold blood about the heart, but a single word in Chapter 1 (v. 17), 'In it the righteousness of God is revealed', that had stood in my way. For I hated that word 'righteousness of God', which, according to the use and custom of all teachers, I had been taught to understand philosophically regarding the formal or active righteousness, as they call it, with which God is righteous and punishes the unrighteous sinner.

Though I lived as a monk without reproach, I felt that I was a sinner before God with an extremely disturbed conscience. I could not believe that he was placated by my satisfaction. I did not love, yes, I hated the righteous God who punishes sinners, and secretly, if not blasphemously, certainly murmuring greatly, I was angry with God, and said, 'As if, indeed, it is not enough that miserable sinners, eternally lost through original sin, are crushed by every kind of calamity by the law of the decalogue, without having God add pain to pain by the gospel and also by the gospel threatening us with his righteousness and wrath'! Thus I raged with a fierce and troubled conscience. Nevertheless, I beat importunately upon Paul at that place, most ardently desiring to know what St. Paul wanted.

At last, by the mercy of God, meditating day and night, I gave heed to the context of the words, namely, 'In it the righteousness of God is revealed, as it is written, "He who through faith is righteous shall live" '. There I began to understand that the righteousness of God is that by which the righteous lives by a gift of God, namely by faith. And this is the meaning: the righteousness of God is revealed by the gospel, namely, the passive righteousness with which merciful God justifies us by faith, as it is written, 'He who through faith is righteous shall live'. Here I felt that I was altogether born again and had entered paradise through open gates. There a totally other face of the entire Scripture showed itself to me. Thereupon I ran through the Scriptures from memory. I also found in other terms an analogy, as, the work of God, that is, what God does in us, the power of God, with which he makes us strong, the wisdom of God, with which he makes us wise, the strength of God, the salvation of God, the glory of God.

And I extolled my sweetest word with a love as great as the hatred with which I had before hated the word 'righteousness of God'. Thus that place in Paul was for me truly the gate to paradise. Later I read Augustine's *The Spirit and the Letter*, where contrary to hope I found that he too interpreted God's righteousness in a similar way, as the righteousness with which God clothes us when he justifies us . . . Armed more fully with these thoughts, I began a second time to interpret the Psalter.

FREEDOM OF CONSCIENCE

Out of his doctrine of justification by faith, Luther went on to declare the Christian is a free man—freed from human authority and from all works and outward practices in which he might be tempted to find his justification. This Christian liberty he called 'freedom of conscience' which was a new expression at that time. But there is not any reason to think that by freedom of conscience Luther meant at that stage 'private judgement', e.g. of the interpretation of Scriptures.

Source: (a) Quotations from Luther in Joseph Lecler's *Toleration and the Reformation*, trans. by T. L. Westow, Longmans, London, 1960, pp. 148 *et sqq.*

(1520). Faith is enough for a Christian, he does not need any works: he is definitely freed from all commandments and all laws, and if he is freed from them, he is surely free. Such is Christian liberty, and faith alone causes it.

Source: (b) Lecler, *op. cit.*, p. 149.

It is because of this freedom and this conscience that I proclaim and proclaim loudly: laws, whether they come from angels or from men, cannot be imposed on Christians unless with their consent, for they are free in regard to all things.

Source: (c) Lecler, *op. cit.*, p. 149. (Luther, *De Votis Monasticis*, 1521.)

The freedom of conscience is that which frees our conscience from works, not in order to reject them completely, but in order to avoid putting our trust in them.

Source: (d) Lecler, *op. cit.*, p. 149. (Luther, *De Servo Arbitrio*, 1525.)

The conscience must not be bound by anything except by the Word of God.

Source: (e) In 1525 Luther seems to have been certain in his own mind that the Scriptures were absolutely clear. By 1531 he was writing as follows: Lecler, *op. cit.*, p. 150. (Luther, *Commentary on the Epistle to the Galatians.*)

If our theology achieves certainty, it is because it takes us away from ourselves and puts us outside ourselves, so that we no longer rely on our own strength, our conscience, our senses, our personality, our works, but only on what is beyond ourselves, namely the promise and truth of God who cannot deceive us.

Source: (f) In 1523 Luther, in his *Secular Authority*, wrote as follows: but later he took up a position opposed to this view. Lecler, *op. cit.*, p. 151.

In matters of faith we have to deal with a free action towards which no one can be forced. Indeed, it is a divine action in the spirit, and it is therefore out of the question that an outside power can obtain it by force. Hence the well-known saying quoted by St. Augustine: one neither can nor should compel anyone to believe.

Source: (g) What, then, about heresy? Lecler, *op. cit.*, p. 151.

Heresy is something spiritual. One cannot strike it with iron, nor burn it with fire, nor drown it in water. Only the Word of God can overcome it, for, as St. Paul has it, 'our arms are not of the flesh, yet are powerful in God'.

Source: (h) Luther was equally opposed to mob-violence and preached against it in 1522 at Wittenberg. Lecler, *op. cit.*, p. 153.

I grant that one may preach against the Mass, I grant that one may speak and write against it; but I do not wish anyone to use compulsion and violence; for the faith demands to be free and willing, and must be received without force.

Source: (j) Luther was in 1524 pretty tolerant towards the Anabaptists. Lecler, *op. cit.*, p. 153.

Do not prevent the ministry of the Word. Let them preach boldly as they like and against whom they like, because it is necessary that there are sects (cf. I Corinthians, xi, 19) and the Word of God must enter the lists and wage battle . . . Let the minds of men feel the shock of each other and fight. No doubt, some will be led astray, but so it is in all wars; where there is battle, there are dead and wounded; but he who will have seen right, will be crowned.

PERIOD II. THE ORGANIZED CHURCH

From the moment that Luther became convinced that the truth and meaning of the Scriptures were self-evident and that he himself fully understood them, he found he could no longer square the organization and government of the Church with his concept of the Church as an invisible society of all the faithful. Thus he came increasingly to rely on the authority of the secular princes. The most glaring example of his ruthlessness was when he inserted the word 'alone' after the word 'faith' in the Epistle to the Romans, iii, 28, and said, 'If your Papist worries about the word "alone", just tell him Dr. Martin Luther will have it so'. Anybody who stood out against the Gospel as Luther interpreted it was *ipso facto* opposed to God. Thus he built up much resistance to himself and to his views and this led him to look to the Princes for support against his opponents, and he came to attribute to them the duty of suppressing by force the celebration of the Mass and of compelling their subjects to hear the 'true' word of God. The heretic was not persecuted, he was simply not allowed to express his views: nobody was forced to believe, but all had to listen to the Word of God as interpreted by Luther. This was the line he pursued after 1525, but the seeds of it may be seen as early as 1520.

Source: (*a*) *An Appeal to the Ruling Class*, 1520. Quoted in *Martin Luther*, Dillenberger, Anchor Books, Doubleday & Co. Inc. 1961, pp. 408–9.

Those who exercise secular authority have been baptized like the rest of us, and have the same faith and the same gospel; therefore we must admit that they are priests and bishops. They discharge their office as an office of the Christian community and for the benefit of that community. Everyone who has been baptized may claim that he has already been consecrated priest, bishop, or pope . . .

Source: (*b*) *The Abomination of the Mass*, 1525, quoted Lecler, *op. cit.*, p. 156.

When an impudent rascal blasphemes, curses or insults God in the middle of the street, the authority who allows such an act and does not punish it severely, shares before God in that sin. If cursing and swearing are forbidden in a country, it is still more right here that the lay lords should prohibit and punish, because such blasphemy and such insults to God are as evident and public in the Mass as when a rascal blasphemes in the street . . . Therefore, dear Christians, let us avoid that abomination, and let us be so united in this matter that this blasphemy may be suppressed by the proper authority so that we have no part in the sin of others. For the authority has the duty to prohibit and to punish such public blasphemies.

Source: (c) A letter to Spalatinus, the parish priest of Altenburg, 1525. Quoted, Lecler, *op. cit.,* p. 157.

Our princes do not impose the faith and the Gospel, but they repress outward abominations. Since the canons themselves acknowledge the princes' right in outward matters, they stand self-condemned. The princes should indeed suppress public crime, perjury, and patent blasphemy of God's name, but in this they do not compel the person in any way, leaving him free to believe or not to believe, to curse God in secret or not to curse him. Our concern is only with public cursing and blaspheming, by which they insult our God.

Source: (d) A letter to John of Saxony, urging him to suppress the Mass at Altenburg, 1525. Quoted, Lecler, *op. cit.,* p. 157.

A secular prince should see to it that his subjects are not led to strife by rival preachers, whence factions and disturbances might arise, but in any one place there should be only one kind of preaching. [Cf. The formula of the Peace of Augsburg in 1555, *cujus regio, ejus religio.*]

Source: (e) A letter to Leonard Beyer, parish priest of Zwickau, in which Luther describes the practice in Wittenberg. Lecler, *op. cit.,* pp. 159–60, 1533. This foreshadows the Peace of Augsburg of 1555 by which opponents of the Prince's religion must either conform or leave his country.

By the authority and in the name of the Most Serene Prince we usually frighten and threaten with punishment and exile those who are negligent in religion and do not come to the sermons. This is the first step. If they do not improve, we instruct the priests in charge to set them a time-limit, one month or more, that they may listen to reason. After that, if they remain obstinate, they are excluded from the community and all contact with them ceases, as if they were pagans.

Source: (f) Luther was in the beginning tolerant towards the Anabaptists, but by 1530, probably under the influence of Melancthon, he came to agree that they should be put to death. In 1536 Luther put his signature, along with others, to a reply to a question asked by the

Landgrave Philip of Hesse, 'Are Christian princes bound to repress the Anabaptists . . . by the sword?' The answer was 'Yes'. Quoted by Lecler, *op. cit.*, p. 163.

Everyone is bound to prevent and repress blasphemy according to his status and function. By virtue of this commandment princes and civil authorities have the power and the duty to abolish unlawful cults, and to establish orthodox teaching and worship. The same commandment teaches them, moreover, to repress the public teaching of false doctrines and to punish the obdurate. Concerning this point the text of Leviticus applies (24. 16): 'he that blasphemeth the name of the Lord, dying let him die'.

MARTIN LUTHER AND THE PEASANTS' REVOLT, 1525

In 1525 the German peasants revolted against their Princes in what is known as the Peasants' War. The causes were long-standing grievances connected with tithes, game-laws and general exploitation by the landlords. Rising prices also added fuel to the flames. The peasants issued their Twelve Articles in March, 1525. The demands were conservative and not radical, the complaints were against the abuse of traditional services rather than any demand for reforms along new lines. The teaching of Luther had nothing to do with the original outbreak, but the new Protestant ideas on human brotherhood and the attacks on Church property suited the peasants. The revolt was violent, unplanned and crude. The princes acted swiftly and ruthlessly. At first Luther was inclined to take the line of a schoolmaster towards recalcitrant children: later he threw himself violently on to the side of the princes and urged them to crush the peasants in his bitter pamphlet *Against the murdering, thieving hordes of Peasants*. Luther was always ready to emphasize the importance of law and order, just because he was being accused of undermining it. He also saw the extreme damage which the peasants' revolt might inflict on the new Protestantism. It is fair to feel that his final attitude towards the peasants was dictated more by religious fervour than by political.

Source: (a) The Life of Luther written by himself, the English translation, London, 1898.

The demands you have drawn up are not in themselves contrary to the natural law and to equity, but they are rendered so by the violence with which you seek to force them from the hands of authority; so, too, he who prepared them is not a pious and sincere man; he has cited a great number of chapters of the Gospel without giving the verses themselves, which he has done for the purpose of seducing you from the text itself to confute him.

For I will tell you that when we come to read the chapters he has indicated, so far from their telling in favour of your enterprise, they are on the contrary against you; for they inculcate that all men should live and act as becomes Christians. He who has thus essayed to attack the Gospel by your means is assuredly a prophet of sedition and of murder, but God will resist him and preserve you from him . . .

As to your propositions respecting game, wood, feudal services, assessments of payments, etc., I refer these matters to the lawyers; I am not called upon to decide respecting these things; but I repeat to you that the Christian is a martyr and that he has no care for these things. Cease, then, to speak of the Christian law and say, rather, that it is the human law, the natural law that you assert, for the Christian law commands you to suffer all these things and to make your complaint to God alone . . .

Source: (b) Luther, May 30th, 1525: *ibid*. I have taken extracts and combined them into the following 'quotation', which is not necessarily in the exact order of Luther's writing. Every word was written by Luther.

I think that all the peasants should perish rather than the princes and magistrates, because the peasants have taken up the sword without divine authority. They have been false to the Gospel they profess to follow. No mercy, no toleration is due to the peasants; on them should fall the wrath of God and of man. The peasants are under the ban of God and of the Emperor and may be treated as mad dogs. Therefore strike, throttle, stab, secretly or openly, whoever can, and remember that there is nothing more poisonous, more hurtful, more devilish, than a rebellious man. A rebel is not worthy to receive a reasonable answer, because he will not accept it. Their ears must be opened with musket balls, so that their heads fly into the air. [Later, Luther wrote] It was I who slew all the peasants in the insurrection, for it was I who commanded them to be slaughtered; all their blood is on my head. But I throw the responsibility on our Lord God, who instructed me to give this order.

THE REFORMATION IN FRANCE

THE INFLUENCE OF CALVIN

By 1561 the influence of Calvin had spread and had become very strong in France.

Source: Report of the Venetian Ambassador in France. Kidd, *op. cit.*, p. 329.

Unless it otherwise pleases the Almighty, religious affairs will soon be in an evil case in France, because there is not one single province uncontaminated. Indeed, in some provinces, such as Normandy, almost the whole of Brittany, Touraine, Poitou, Gascony, and a great part of Languedoc, of Dauphiny and of Provence, comprising three fourths of the kingdom, congregations and meetings, which they call assemblies, are held; and in these assemblies they read and preach, according to the rites and usages of Geneva, without any respect either for the ministers of the king or the commandments of the king himself. This contagion has penetrated so deeply that it affects every class of persons, and, what appears more strange, even the ecclesiastical body itself. I do not mean only priests, friars and nuns, but even bishops and many of the principal prelates, who hitherto had not shown any such disposition; and it is only on account of the rigorous execution of the law that other persons besides the populace have not disclosed themselves, because they have restrained themselves for the time being, from fear of the loss of their property and lives. But your Serenity must learn that while the people and the populace show fervent devotion by frequenting the churches and observing the Catholic rites, all other classes are supposed to be disaffected, and the nobility perhaps more than any other class, and particularly persons of forty years of age and under. If these disaffected individuals continue to attend Mass and the Divine Offices, and externally to practise Catholic rites, they do so for show and from fear; because when they either are, or believe themselves to be, unobserved, they avoid and even fly from the Mass above all things, and also from the churches as far as they are able, and more so since it became known that by imprisonment, chastisement and burnings, no remedy was found. It has now been determined not to proceed against any disaffected persons, unless they venture to preach and to take part publicly in congregations and assemblies. All other such persons are allowed to live and some have been set at liberty and released from the prisons of Paris and of other parts of the kingdom. A great number of these last have remained in the kingdom, preaching and speaking publicly, and boasting that they have gained their cause against the Papists, as they delight to style their adversaries; so that now every one of them is assured against the fear of being questioned; and there exists thus a silent truce, because whilst formerly all suspected persons had to quit the kingdom, and to retire, some to Geneva, some to Germany, and some to England, now they not only do not leave the country, but a large number of those who had already emigrated have returned. It was told me, whilst passing through Geneva, on my way to Italy, that after the death of the king, a great number of gentlemen who had fled thither after the conspiracy of Amboise, had come back to France, and in particular M. de Mombrun, who was the author of the late disturbances in Provence and Dauphiny and who had been burnt in effigy; besides these more than fifty others, who are called ministers, were summoned from various parts of France to travel, and teach and preach the 'Word', for thus they term the Gospels, and their own doctrine. Your Serenity will hardly believe the influence which the principal minister of Geneva, by name Calvin, a Frenchman and a native of Picardy, possesses in this kingdom; he is a man of extraordinary authority, who by his mode of life, his doctrines, and his writings, rises superior to all the rest; and it is almost impossible to believe the enormous sums of money which are secretly sent to him from France to maintain his power. It is sufficient to add that if God does not interfere, there is great and imminent danger that one of two things will happen in this kingdom: either that the truce, which is desired and sought publicly, will end by the heretics having churches wherein they can preach, read and perform their rites according to their doctrine, without hindrance and in like manner as they obtained their churches by command of the late king, given at Fontainebleau at the end of August, in compliance with a petition presented to him by the Admiral; or else that we shall see an obedience to the Pope and to the Catholic rites enforced, and shall have resort to violence and imbrue our hands in noble blood. For these reasons I foresee a manifest and certain division in the kingdom and civil war as a consequence; and this will be the cause of ruin both of the kingdom and of religion, because upon a change in religion a change in the state necessarily follows.

FRANCIS I AND THE LUTHERANS

When Lutheranism first appeared in France, Francis I was not unsympathetic and declined to persecute the Lutherans. But when he went to war with the Emperor and invaded Italy (1524), because he needed to propitiate the Pope, persecution began. It continued as long as Francis was a prisoner after Pavia, in the hopes that this would influence the Emperor to release him. Once he was set free, the Lutherans might have hoped for a respite, but the sack of Rome in 1527 was put down to the German *landsknechts* who were Lutherans. The French Lutherans began to deface Catholic images and to placard Paris with attacks on Catholic doctrine. In 1530 after the peace of Cambrai, Francis felt free of any danger from the Emperor and he wrote the following letter to the Parlement of Paris.

Source: (a) Quoted by J. M. Thompson in *Lectures on Foreign History*, p. 117, where he attributes it to *Journal D'Un Bourgeois de Paris*, author unknown, ed. by Lalanne, 1854. I have been unable to find the letter in that book.

We are much annoyed and displeased because this cursed heretical sect of Lutherans flourishes in our good city of Paris, the head and capital of our realm, containing the principal University of Christendom, where many will be able to imitate it. This sect we intend to attack with all our power and authority, sparing nobody. We therefore will and intend that such and so heavy punishment may fall upon it as to correct the cursed heretics and be an example to all others.

S

Source: (b) *Journal d'Un Bourgeois de Paris,* 1515–1536, ed. by Lalanne, 1854, pp. 444 *et sqq.*

In the same year 1534, the 10th of November, seven persons were condemned by the Guenier to do a public penance in a tumbril, each holding a lighted torch in his hand, their goods to be forfeited to the crown, themselves to be burned at different places on different days. The sentence was confirmed. The first of them was Barthélemy Mollon, the son of a shoe-maker, who lived in the street between the two doorways of the law-courts. This Barthélemy through some disease was crippled in his arms and legs by paralysis. He had been involved in the matter of the placards and inscriptions and for this he was burned alive at the cemetery of St. John on the 13th of November.

The second was John du Bourg, a wealthy draper, who lived in the Rue St. Denis, at the sign of the Black Horse, a house which was his own property. This du Bourg had married the daughter of another wealthy draper named Favereau and he had himself stuck up the inscriptions and placards at the corners of the streets. For this on the next day, the 14th of November, he was dragged out to do a public penance in a tumbril in front of the church of Nôtre Dame; from there he was dragged to the Fountains of the Innocents in Rue St. Denis, where he had his hand cut off. After that to the market-place and there he was burned alive for of what he was not prepared to accuse his companions.

The third was a printer of Rue St. Jaques, who had printed and sold the works of Luther. For this he did a public penance in front of the church of Nôtre Dame, and from there he was dragged to be burned alive in the Square Maubert.

On the 18th of November was burned alive a stone-mason in front of the church of St. Catherine in the Rue St. Anthoine, after a public penance.

The next day in like manner a bookseller, who lived near the Square Maubert and bound and sold the works of Luther, did a public penance and was burned like the others in the Square Maubert . . .

On Monday the 25th of January 1535, there were summoned for three short days by the sound of a trumpet in the streets of Paris, up to the number of sixty-three Lutherans who had fled outside Paris. They were to appear in person, and if they did not appear, they would be accused, banished from the realm of France and be condemned to be burned. One of these was a priest called Caroli, the vicar of Alençon: another was a hosier who came from near the doorway of the law-courts; there was also Christopher Hérault, who lived by the law-court clock, and Master Clément Marot, and Master Girard, a doctor . . . The 10th of September following, two friends who were makers of silk ribbons and tissues, were burned alive, one in the Square Maubert, the other in the cemetry of St. John, as Lutherans, which they were. They were natives of Tours and were young men. The way they were discovered was like this. They had just returned to Paris from Germany and Flanders. One day they gave their landlord a certain Lutheran book to take care of, saying, 'Landlord, take care of this book, while we go into the town, and don't shew it to anyone'. They went into the town, but the landlord could not refrain from shewing the book to a certain priest. When the priest saw it, he at once said, 'this is a very bad and damnable book'. Then the landlord went to the *gueynier* to explain to him that he had such and such a book. The *gueynier* on the spot sent to the house of the landlord and led off the two young friends to Chatelêt. On being cross-examined by the *gueynier*, they confessed to the accusation. As a result, by sentence of the *loi-criminel*, confirmed by edict, they made a public penance in front of the church of Nôtre Dame, then they had their tongues cut out and were burned alive, but unyielding. They had at other times had business in Paris, and it was found that they had brought some books from Germany with the intention of binding them and selling them in Paris, and that they had in mind to stick up placards in the town . . .

Source: (*c*) In all, within a few months, forty Lutherans were burned in Paris. It is worth noting that the victims came from the trading and lower professional classes, from 'those educated by their business, in touch with wider interests or accustomed to the use of books'.

(Thompson, *op.cit.*) So shocked was Pope Paul III, the organizer of the Inquisition, that he wrote the following letter to Francis I. *Journal d'Un Bourgeois de Paris, op. cit.*, p. 458.

It was reported in June, 1535, that Pope Paul III, informed of the execrable and horrible justice which the King was executing on the Lutherans in his realm, wrote to say that, although he was sure that the King was acting in good faith, and using the excellent claims he had to be called the Most Christian King, yet God the Creator, when he was Himself in this world, made more use of compassion than of rigorous justice: that one ought never to use severity; and that it is cruel to burn a man alive . . . Wherefore the Pope requested and required of the King by his letters to appease the fury and rigour of his justice, by giving pardon and reprieve to the Lutherans.

THE MASSACRE OF VASSY, 1562

As long as Francis II was king the Guises controlled the government, but when he died in December, 1560, the power went into the hands of Catherine de' Medici, the Regent, during the minority of Charles IX. She was opposed by Navarre, Guise and Montmorency and she was thus driven to the side of L'Hopital and Coligny, leaders of the Huguenots. After the Colloquy of Poissy, which only emphasized the religious differences between the two sides, the Queen issued the Edict of January (1562) which gave the Protestants liberty of conscience and also liberty of worship *outside* the walls of towns. Catherine de' Medici is always remembered as responsible for the Massacre of St. Bartholomew: she ought also to be remembered for sowing the seed which flowered at the end of the century in the Edict of Nantes. She failed to prevent the First Religious War, for the Edict of January infuriated the Catholics, especially the Guises. The country was seething with violence, especially in the south. It was the so-called 'massacre' of Vassy which sparked off the Religious Wars. Francis of Guise was on his way from Zabern in Alsace to Paris. He passed through Vassy, where no Huguenot service was permitted by the Edict, Vassy being a walled town: but the Huguenots were there in strength and were actually holding a service in a barn inside the town when Guise arrived. Vassy stood on land which belonged to the Guises. Francis sent a messenger to the barn to say he wanted to speak

with some of the heretics. The messenger was refused admission: he
tried to force his way in: shots and blows were exchanged and perhaps
sixty Huguenots were killed.

Source: (*a*) The Edict of January.

We have prohibited and forbidden, and by these presents we
prohibit and forbid . . . on pain of death and without any hope
of pardon . . . any gathering inside the towns for the purpose of
preaching, whether in public or in private, either by day or by
night.

Nothing is to be preached which contravenes the pure word of
God as contained in the Nicene Creed and in the canonical books
of the old and new Testaments.

Source: (*b*) Memoires de Michel de Castelnau, Livre III, ch. 7.
Quoted by H. D. Sedgwick, *The House of Guise*, p. 139, London, 1938.

On the first day of March, which fell on a Sunday, the Duke
went to dine at Vassy,[4] where his officers, who had ridden on
ahead, found the Protestants holding their services in a grange
near the church. There may have been six or seven hundred
persons there of all ages. Then, as the Duke has often told me,
some of his officers, and others who had gone ahead, curious to
see such a meeting and the new form of worship, and with no
other purpose, went up to the door of the grange, and then an
altercation arose with rude words on both sides. Some of those
who were on guard at the door threw stones and shouted insults
at the Duc of Guise's men, calling them Papists and idolaters. At
the noise of this altercation some pages ran up, and several gentlemen as well as others of the Duke's suite, and both sides got angry
over the stones and insults. A great number of those within
rushed out and pushed back the Duke's men. Word of this was
brought to the Duke as he was about to sit down to table, and
it was said that they were killing his men. He went there in great
haste. He found them fighting with sticks and fists, and as he got
near the grange several stones were thrown at him, which he
warded off with his cloak. And then, as he advanced closer, both
to protect himself from the stones and to quell the disorder,
things got worse and, as the Duke said, to his great regret some

who were there to assist at the services were killed or wounded, as to which everybody had a different story.

THE FIRST WAR OF RELIGION, 1562–63

Source: (*a*) Theodore Beza, author of *Histoire Ecclésiastique* (first published, 1580), wrote to Calvin in 1562, the following extract from his letter: Whitehead, *Gaspard de Coligny*, gives Salomon Cyprian, i, 240 as the authority.

Nothing disturbs us more than the baseness of the Church, not to give it a harder name. I have been as far as Angers, in peril of my life, but I was able to do little or nothing. Their violence in the destruction of altars is incredible, and we have been quite unable to prevent it here. In short, all things are suddenly changed, so that I am amazed at the spectacle; for the enemy in a hundred years, even if victorious, could not restore, in this one city alone, what has been destroyed in the space of two hours.

Source: (*b*) Etienne Pasquier (1529–1615), *Lettres*, ii, 99.

It would be impossible to tell you what barbarous cruelties are committed by both sides. Where the Huguenot is master, he ruins the images and demolishes the sepulchres and tombs. On the other hand, the Catholic kills, murders, and drowns all those whom he knows to be of that sect, until the rivers overflow with them.

THE THIRD WAR OF RELIGION, 1568–70

Source: News out of France, forwarded to Croft by his kinsman from London: Brit. Mus. Titus, B. ii, 468. Spelling modernized. 1569.

But in effect the face of France is lamentable at this season, the meaner subjects spoiled everywhere, and the greater neither sure of life nor living in any place, whereby murder is no cruelty nor disobedience any offence, bathing one in another's blood, making it custom to despise religion and justice, or any more sacred bond, either of divine or human constitution. Where the victor may bewail his victory, and the natural lastly in danger to be overrun by the stranger whom he provides now for his defence. Having consumed the store of the last year and wasting that on the ground which should serve for the year to come, so as a present desperation and a piteous mourning doth invade every sort, as though their calamities should have no end, but with the end of their lives together. And that withal the dreadfullest cruelties at once of the world, plague, hunger, and the sword, which God of his goodness cease in them and preserve from us; and to this is joined an incredible obstinacy of either side, even hardening their hearts with malice and fury to the utter extermination one of another.

A FRENCH HUGUENOT ON FRANCE AFTER THE WARS OF RELIGION

François La Noue (1531–91) was known as Bras-de-Fer, because he lost an arm at the siege of Fontenay in 1570 and a mechanic of La Rochelle made him an new arm out of iron, with a hook to hold the reins. He was present at almost every notable battle between 1567 and 1580. In that year he was taken prisoner by the Spaniards and was imprisoned for five years. In prison he wrote his *Discours Politiques et Militaires*. In 1585 he was exchanged and was present at the siege of Paris with Henry of Navarre, at Ivry and at other battles. He died at Moncontour in 1591.

Source: Discours, ch. xx, pp. 502–19. The following extract is quoted by Oman in his *Art of War in the Sixteenth Century*, p. 396, Methuen, 1937.

The King of France rules a mighty state—two hundred leagues long from Metz to Bayonne, two hundred and fifty broad from Morlaix to Antibes, fertile in every product needed for human use, well peopled, with ample revenues and a most gallant noblesse. Why, then, the foreigner may ask, try to enlarge such a state by alien annexations rather than to perfect it by internal reform? . . . We French must remember that the time of great annexations is over and that it is no mean feat to keep what we have in good order. The dream of plunder and glory should come to an end. The young have been reading too many romances of reckless adventure, full of *amours déshonnêtes* and objectless fighting. The old have been reading and rereading Machiavelli, who saps all fundamental ideas of honour and justice. It is hard for a nation to settle down after so many nerve-wracking years.

THE DECLINE OF THE FIRST HUGUENOT ARMY OF 1562

Source: François La Noue (see p. above), *Premiers Troubles*, pp. 818–24, quoted by Oman, *Art of War in the Sixteenth Century*, pp. 399–401. Methuen, 1937.

When this war started there were some chiefs and captains who spoke of military discipline, but much more effective were the sermons in which we were admonished not to oppress the poor people, and the religious zeal which had brought most of us into the field. Without any constraint we tried to bridle ourselves, as no fear of punishment could have bridled us. The noblesse showed itself in these early days quite worthy of its name, marching in the open country, where the temptation to live by plundering is much more obvious than in towns, it lifted nothing, never maltreated a peasant and was content with poor fare. The leaders and those who had any money in their pockets paid honestly for everything they got. There were no complaints, the villagers did not abscond from their dwellings. If any soldier was guilty of violence he was banished or put in custody, and his own companions made no attempt to excuse him. Among such a large gathering we heard no one blaspheme the name of God; persistent swearers tried to drop the habit, and were reproved with anger if they failed. You could not have found a box of dice or a pack of cards in the camp. Women were not allowed to enter the quarters—such women as haunt the camp are always the source of debauchery. No one was allowed to quit the standards to forage for himself; the men had to be content with their rations and the small amount of pay that was forthcoming. Morning and evening, when the guards were set, there were public prayers and psalms were sung. We noted piety in many from whom it could not have been expected—old soldiers of former wars. One day my brother-in-law Teligny and I were praising the conduct of the army to the Admiral Coligny. 'Very fine', he said, 'provided that it lasts. But I have my fears that our people will shed their virtues in the course of two months, and have nothing left but their bad qualities. As an old infantry colonel I cannot but remember the proverb, "Young hermits may become old devils".' We smiled at his saying, but it was only too true.

The first disorders were at Beaugency, which was stormed by some Provençal companies. They gave themselves up to pillage and mishandled poor Protestant townsmen, who had not been able to get away, worse than the Catholic garrison. This example provoked the Gascon companies, who soon after showed that they would not be left behind in violence. But the North-French regiment of M. d'Tvoy would have got the first prize, if one were awarded for misbehaviour. Our infantry lost its original virginity and allied itself to Miss Pillage (*Mademoiselle La Picorée*) who, as the war went on, would become Princess Pillage. Indiscipline spread to the noblesse, some of whom, after the first taste of the dish of stolen goods, refused to sup on any other meat. And so the evil commenced on a small scale but became general. This was no fault of the Admiral, who tried strong measures to stop the disease. In Normandy he hanged a captain of irregular horse, who had sacked a village, with four or five of his men around him, all booted and spurred, with a pile of their plunder at their feet, and a written notice above, warning others of the same sort. The effect lasted about a month! I am bound to say that the Catholics during the first few weeks of the war also behaved with comparative decency—the gentlemen especially,—but they went the same way as our people in full sail. It sometimes made me laugh in bitterness to think how 'soldier' meant the same thing as 'brigand' in our days of the Troubles.

THE REFORMED RELIGION IN MONTPELIER, 1595

Thomas Platter was born in 1574 and died in 1614. His family lived in Basle where his father, who came from very humble origins, rose to be headmaster of a well known school. Thomas went to Montpelier to study medicine and while there he travelled widely and kept the diary from which the following extract is taken. He became the principal doctor in Basle, a post which his half-brother Felix (who was thirty-eight years older than Thomas), had also held. Montpelier was a Protestant stronghold.

Source: Thomas Platter, *The Journal of a Younger Brother*, ed. and trans. by Seán Jennet, Frederick Muller, London, 1963, p. 40.

Control of the Protestant faith is very severe. Anyone who attends mass, even once, is made to confess before the whole congregation, as if he had always been a papist, and he must ask to be reconciled. Those who have been denied communion, on account of some grave sin, are also compelled to appear before the whole assembly, if they wish to have grace, and if they do not do this, the communion is refused to them. Holy communion takes place only four times a year, at Christmas, at Easter, at Pentecost, and in September, and this makes it easy to exclude those who have been excommunicated. Anyone who wishes to come to the Lord's table must go to his pastor and get a token consisting of a letter of the alphabet made of lead. Before giving this token, the pastor will examine the candidate, if he does not know him already. As the man approaches the communion table, he puts his token into a wooden bowl held by one of the elders, who is called the intendant. After receiving the bread from the minister, the man goes to the elders' table, and there he is given a glass of red wine. Only a sip of the wine is taken, and the glass is given back.

So that everyone may communicate the same morning the service begins two or three hours before daybreak. Immediately after the sermon the communion begins, during which some chapters of the New Testament are read from the pulpit. When the men, and afterwards the women, have communicated, a grace is said, the congregation sings, and then about seven o'clock everyone leaves the church. Immediately a second congregation enters, the singing begins again, then the sermon, and then communion, as before. This goes on sometimes until eleven o'clock or midday, for time is needed to receive so many tokens. Sometimes at Montpelier four to six thousand people communicate in a single day, and the crush is such that in winter the church is as warm as if it were heated.

At the exit the elders ask for alms for the poor. During communion the elders bring the bread and wine to the poor who wait at the door.

The officers of the King each has his place in the church, and their seats are covered with tapestry ornamented with yellow fleur-de-lys.

THE REFORMATION IN SWITZERLAND

THE STATE OF THE CHURCH BEFORE 1519

Heinrich Bullinger, Zwingli's son-in-law and successor as the Protestant leader in Zurich, wrote a history of the Reformation in Switzerland. The following account of the condition of the Church is almost certainly true.

Source: Bullinger, *Reformationsgeschichte*, i, 3.

At one time during these years, when all the deacons of the Confederation were assembled together, there were found not over three who were well read in the Bible. The others acknowledged that none of them had read even the New Testament, whereby we may understand how it was with the other clergy, with whom the case was still worse. For among the clergy there was almost no studying, but their exercise was in gaming, in feeding and in the practice of all luxuries. The more earnest were accused of hypocrisy. Those who studied somewhat devoted themselves to scholastic theology and canon law. The greater part preached out of sermon books, learning by heart sermons written by monks and printed, repeating them to the people without judgement . . .

In the churches the mass had become a market and a place for bargaining; in fact, all sacraments and all things which one holds holy became venal and corrupt. The singing in parishes and monasteries was for the most part superstitious, and the monasteries had fallen into all sorts of scandals and idolatries, where no one of them observed so much as the first of its own rules, let alone God's Word. Every day new altars, endowments, and endless numbers of idolatrous pilgrimages were established, to the great pleasure of the clergy, who threw into their bottomless sacks all that the common man as well as the noble possessed. Whereupon there was great complaint on all sides.

ZWINGLI AND LUTHER

The Reformation in Switzerland began in 1522 in Zurich under the leadership of Ulrich Zwingli. It was partly moral, partly humanistic, partly patriotic, partly religious. Zwingli was a democrat, a republican, a humanist, who denounced fasting in Lent, celibacy of the clergy, monastic vows, the use of Latin in church services, and the doctrine of the Real Presence. By 1529 six of the thirteen cantons were Zwinglian Protestants. Very soon Zwingli and Luther were quarrelling, principally over the Real Presence. Philip the Landgrave of Hesse persuaded the two sides to meet for a discussion of their differences. This was the Colloquy of Marburg, 1529. The following extracts illustrate the views, the characters and the tempers of Zwingli, Luther and Melanchthon.

Source: (a) The Colloquy of Marburg, 1529. The chief men on the Swiss side were Zwingli and Œcolampadius, on the German side Martin Luther and Philip Melanchthon. These four met the day before the public debate in private in two pairs, Zwingli and Melanchthon, Luther and Œcolampadius, to enlighten each side on the views of the other. When the public debate began, Luther chalked on the table in front of him the words, 'This is My Body'. The debate went on for two days, chiefly on the meaning of these words. Melanchthon, quoted Jackson, *Huldreich Zwingli*, Putnam's, 1901, p. 316.

[At the end of the debate the Swiss asked that] Luther would take them for brethren. This Dr. Martin would not at all agree to. He even addressed them very seriously, saying that he was exceedingly surprised that they should regard him as a brother if they seriously believed their own doctrine true. But that was an indication that they themselves did not think there was much involved in the matter.

Source: (b) Luther to Jacobus, Provost of Bremen. Jackson, *op. cit.*, 316.

As to the statement the Sacramentarians[5] are casting abroad to the effect that I was beaten at Marburg, they are acting after their own kind. For they are not only liars but the very incarnation of lying, deceit, and hypocrisy, as Carlstadt and Zwingli show by their very deeds and words. But you see that in the Articles formulated at Marburg they took back the pestiferous teaching that they had been promulgating in their published books in regard to baptism, the use of sacraments, the external word and the rest. We took back nothing . . .

They professed with many words that they wished to agree with us so far as to say that the body of Christ is truly present in the Supper, but spiritually, with the sole view that we deign to call them brethren, and so feign harmony. This Zwingli begged with tears in his eyes before the Landgrave and all of them, saying, 'There are no people on earth with whom I would rather be in harmony than with the Wittenburgers'. They strove with the utmost eagerness and vigour to seem in harmony with us, and could never endure the expression I used, 'You have a different spirit from ours'. They burst into flame every time they heard it.

Source: (c) Œcolampadius, Jackson, *op. cit.,* 317.

There was no victory on either side since there was no fighting or contending.

Source: (d) Johann Brenz, Jackson, *op. cit.,* 317.

Afterwards, when the meeting had been disbanded, the Prince [Philip of Hesse] tried every possible way to secure agreement between us, speaking to each one of us by himself without witnesses, and begging, warning, exhorting, demanding that we have regard to the Republic of Christ and put away strife. We [Germans] decided with one voice that they were outside the Communion of the Christian Church and could not be recognized by us as brethren and members of the Church. This our opponents thought very hard indeed . . . But when the Prince also thought it hard, we modified our decision so far as to be willing to recognize our opponents of the Zwingli and Œcolampadius following as friends, but not as brethren and members of the Church of Christ.

Source: (e) Justus Jonas, a Lutheran: Jackson, *op. cit.,* 318.

Zwingli has something countrified about him, and at the same time arrogant; Œcolampadius has a wonderful kindness of disposition and tolerance; Hedio is as courteous as he is liberal-minded; Butzer has the craftiness of the fox, a distorted imitation of acuteness and wisdom. They are all learned beyond a doubt, and the Papalists are no opponents in comparison with them, but Zwingli seems to have gone into letters under the wrath of the Muses and the power of Minerva.

Source: (*f*) Zwingli to Vadianus, October 20th, 1529; Jackson, *op. cit.*, 319.

Grace and peace from the Lord. I will now write briefly what you desire to know. After we had been brought under the safest conduct to Marburg and Luther and his party had come, the Prince Landgrave determined that Œcolampadius and Luther, Melancthon and Zwingli, should meet two by two in private to see whether they could not find some ground of agreement upon which they could found peace. Hereupon Luther received Œcolampadius in such a way that the latter came to me complaining secretly that he had met another Eck[6]—but this is to be told to the trusty alone.

But as for Melanchthon, he was so slippery and so transformed himself after the manner of Proteus that he compelled me to seize a pen, to arm my hand and dry it as with salt and so hold him more firmly as he glided around in all sorts of shapes and subterfuges. From this I send you a few examples out of the hundreds of thousands of things said, yet under the condition that you are not to communicate them to any except the trusty, *i.e.* those who will not make a text for trouble out of them, for Philip himself has a copy of them. It was written by me while he was looking on and reading all, and sometimes dictating his own words. But I do not wish to give rise to a new quarrel. Philip and I were engaged in conversation for six hours, Luther and Œcolampadius for three. On the next day, in the presence of the Landgrave and twenty-four witnesses, Luther and Melanchthon and Œcolampadius and Zwingli went into the arena and fought there and in three other sessions. For there were four in all in which we contended successfully. For we presented to Luther as needing explanation the fact that he had propounded those thrice foolish statements: that Christ suffered in His divine nature; that the Body of Christ is everywhere; and that the flesh could not profit of itself otherwise than as he now asserted. But the fine fellow made no reply, except that in the matter of the flesh not profiting he said: 'You know, Zwingli, that as time progressed and their judgement grew, all the Fathers treated the passages of Scripture in ways different from the earlier expositions'. Then he said: 'The Body of Christ is eaten corporeally in our body, but in the meantime I will reserve this to myself, whether the Body is eaten by the soul'. And yet a little before he had said: 'The Body of Christ is eaten with the mouth corporeally, the soul does not eat Him corporeally'. He also said: 'The Body of Christ is produced by these words, "This is My Body", no matter how wicked the man who pronounces these words'. He conceded that the Body of Christ is finite. He admitted that the Eucharist can be called the sign of the Body of Christ. These and other innumerable vacillating, absurd and foolish utterances of his, which he babbled forth like pebbles on a beach, we so argued on that now the Prince himself is on our side, although for the sake of certain princes he pretended not to be. Almost all the Court of Hesse have deserted Luther. He himself grants that our books could be read without harm. Hereafter he will suffer the parties who agree with us to retain their positions. Prince John of Saxony was not present, but the Prince of Wittenberg was.

We parted with the understanding which you will see in print. Truth was so clearly superior that, if ever any one was overcome, Luther, the impudent and obstinate, was beaten, and before a wise and just judge, although meantime he was unconquered. We have effected this good, that after we shall agree in the other dogmas of the Christian religion, the Pope's party cannot entertain the hope that Luther will be their's . . .

Zurich, October 20, 1529.   Yours Huldreich Zwingli.

JOHN CALVIN

Calvin was born at Noyon in Picardy in 1509: he was thus more than twenty-five years younger than Luther. By the time he became the leader of the Protestants in Europe, it had become clear that only by discipline and organization could Protestantism survive. Calvin provided both and saved the new religion. He must be regarded as the equal of Luther in the history of Protestantism. Originally destined by his father for a clerical career, he went to Paris University to study theology. He soon gave up this objective and moved to Orleans to study law. In 1531 he was at Bourges, he returned to Paris and at some point he underwent a severe religious experience which was to result in affecting the whole history of Europe. He went to Basle and there in 1536 he published his *Institutes of the Christian Religion*. He went to Geneva for one day and stayed there two years to help the French leader of Protestantism there, Farel. At the end of two years he was driven out of the city and for the next three years lived almost entirely at Strasburg. Then he was invited back to Geneva by the Protestants. He went, not very readily. There he stayed until he died in 1564. During that time he profoundly influenced the development of the Protestant religion in Europe, and most especially in France and Switzerland. Geneva became the centre of Calvinism, and Calvinism became the Protestantism of France in the sect known as the Huguenots. The origin of this word is very obscure: probably it is corruption of the German word *Eidgenossen*, meaning Confederates.

Calvin's doctrines are to be found in his *Institutes*. The first version was published in 1536, but several editions followed, each of which revealed a development in Calvin's views over a period of twenty years. *The Institutes* are available in the modern *Library of Christian Classics*; also J. T. McNeill, 2 vols., 1961.

CALVIN AND PREDESTINATION

It is true that Luther also held this doctrine, but it is from Calvin that Protestant Europe derived this belief. Luther said he found it in St. Augustine, Calvin claimed to have found it in the Scriptures. 'I have not to my knowledge corrupted or twisted a single passage of the Scriptures.'

Source: The Institutes, Book III, ch. 21.

In conformity to the clear teaching of scripture we assert by an eternal and immutable counsel God hath once for all determined both whom He would admit to salvation and whom He would condemn to destruction. We affirm that this counsel, as far as concerns the elect, is founded on His gratuitous mercy, totally irrespective of human merit; but that to those whom He devotes to condemnation the gate of life is closed by a just and irreprehensible and incomprehensible judgement.

CALVIN AND THE STATE

Calvin's *Institutes* provided a complete and clear guide on how to live according to God's word (Book III). But it also set out how the State ought to be organized. Calvin never accepted the Zwinglian doctrine that the Church and State must be united in a single organization. Calvin held that the needs of the Church were quite different from the needs of the State. As far as the Church was concerned the ecclesiastical jurisdiction should exclude anything which was merely secular, it should be vested in an assembly of the Elders, and its final penalty should be excommunication. Secular government was just as essential as religious. He was always frightened by fanatics 'who would have men live pell-mell like rats in the straw'. Nor would he admit that the authority of the King was above that of God. He did not hold strong views on the forms of government: probably he preferred the aristocratic[9] to either monarchical or democratic.

Source: op. cit. Book IV, para. 8.

I, for my part, am far from denying that the form which greatly surpasses the others is aristocracy,[9] either pure or modified by popular government . . . This has already been proved by experience and confirmed also by the authority of the Lord himself, when he established an aristocracy bordering on popular government among the Israelites, keeping them under that as the best form until he exhibited an image of the Messiah in David.

CALVIN AND PASSIVE OBEDIENCE

Calvin held unequivocally that the subject has no right to disobey the sovereign power. Throughout all the editions of the *Institutes* he never deviated from this view. The following quotations from that book illustrate his insistence on Non-Resistance.

Source: Lanfranc, 1559, Book IV, p. 550.

It comes not of the perversity of man that kings and other lords have power upon earth: but it comes of the providence and holy ordinance of God whom it has pleased to manage in this fashion the government of men.

T

We must subject ourselves and be obedient to whatever superiors are ruling in the place where we are living.

It is impossible to resist the magistrate without resisting God.

Though there be divers forms and kinds of rulers, yet they differ not at all in this, that we must take them all as ministers ordained of God.

The form which is the least pleasing to men is particularly and above all others commended to us, that is the lordship and domination of a single man.

Assuredly, it is a vain occupation for private citizens who have no authority to run public affairs to dispute what is the right business for the police.

But some one will say that there is a mutual duty on the part of the rulers towards their subjects. Without exception, if a man wanted to argue from this that he only owed obedience to a just Lord, he would argue perversely.

[Just and unjust rulers,] both the one and the other alike possess that dignity and majesty which God has given to all lawful superiors.

Wherefore, if we are cruelly vexed by an inhuman Prince or robbed and plundered by one prodigal or avaricious, or despised and left without protection by one negligent: or even if we are afflicted for the Name of God by one sacriligious and unbelieving, let us first of all remember those our own offences against God which doubtless are chastised by these plagues. And secondly let us consider that it is not for us to remedy these evils; for us it remains only to implore the aid of God, in whose hands are the hearts of Kings and changes of kingdoms.

CALVIN AND THE IDEAL CHURCH, *i.e.* AT GENEVA

Calvin always believed that men could not exist without government. Government was necessary in order that men should be able to live, but also that they should live rightly.

Source: Lanfranc, 1559, Book IV.

[The State exists] in order that idolatry, blasphemy of the Name of God and against His truth and other scandals to religion, be not publicly set forth and broadcast among the people; that public peace be not troubled, that each be secured in what is his own, that men's intercourse may be without fraud and violence, in fine that among Christians there may be some public and visible form of religion and that humanity be settled among men.

[Administration is] to know that by the word of God boldly they dare anything and compel all glory, boldness and virtue in this world to obey and to yield to the divine majesty; that by this word they are given commandment over the whole world to build up the house of Christ and to demolish the rule of Satan; to feed the sheep and to kill the wolves: to guide by instruction and exhortation the tractable: to constrain and correct the rebellious and self-willed: to bind and unbind: to thunder and lighten: but always in the word of God.

Above all where we see the word of God to be purely preached and listened to, the Sacraments administered according to the institution by Christ, there without any shadow of doubt is the Church . . . The Church universal is the whole body of people who accept the truth of God and the doctrine of His word, however diverse be their nationalities . . . Under this universal Church, the Churches which are distributed throughout every town and village are thus reckoned, each of them, to have the title and authority of Church.

CALVIN AND SERVETUS

Michael Servetus was born about 1511 at Villanueva, near Lerida in Spain. He studied law at Toulouse and was for some time with the court of Charles V in Germany and Italy. He became acquainted with most of the leaders of the Reformation and at the age of twenty he published his first book, De Trinitatis Erroribus, in which he set out to show that the doctrine of the Trinity had no scriptural authority. The book was banned in Strasbourg and Basle. This was followed by his Dialogi De Trinitate. He then left Strasburg and for twenty years lived in France at Vienne, outwardly as a Catholic. But he was secretly preparing a new book, Christianismi Restitutio, which he published in 1553. The basis of the book was to prove that Christ was only man, but full of the power of God. He then began to bombard Calvin with letters, which infuriated Calvin.

Source: (a) Letter from Calvin to Farel, February 13th, 1553, *Calvini Opera*, t. XII, p. 283, quoted by Joseph Lecler, *Toleration and The Reformation*, trans. T. L. Westow, Longmans, 1960, p. 326.

Servetus recently wrote to me and has joined to his correspondence a long volume full of his mad ideas, adding with theatrical pomposity that I would see in that book some astounding and until then unheard of things. If I like, he will come here. But I do not want to bind myself. Because if he came, and my authority still counted for something, I would never let him leave alive.

The book was clearly heretical and it caused an uproar. A friend of Calvin, Guillaume de Trie, gave away the author's name to Antoine Arneys and sent him extracts from the book. Arneys informed the Inquisitor. Servetus denied any part in the publication. Arneys then got through de Trie some twenty letters from Servetus to Calvin and sent them to the Inquisitor. At his trial Servetus firmly maintained that de Trie had written the letters at the request of Calvin, a charge which Calvin never answered. On October 27th, 1553, Servetus was burnt at the stake at the gates of Geneva. The following letter shows clearly what was the usual point of view about punishment for heresy coupled with obstinacy.

Source: (b) A letter from Servetus to Calvin: *Calvini Opera*, t. VIII, p. 708 (ep. 27); quoted by Joseph Lecler, *op. cit.*, p. 329.

It is God's truth that the severity of the death-penalty was relaxed with the coming of Jesus Christ, if and when there is hope of amendment . . . It is true that St. Peter punished with death Ananias and Saphira, of whom he had no hope of conversion, to show more clearly his detestation of their crime, and to make them examples for all others, or because the Holy Spirit, whom they had scorned, made plain by that measure that they were incorrigible and obdurate in their wrong. This crime simply deserves death both before God and man. As to other crimes about which the Spirit has not laid down anything particular, where the evil has not taken root, and where one cannot point to deliberate obstinacy or an altogether monstrous wickedness, we should rather hope for correction by other punishments than death. Among such punishments banishment is praiseworthy as it is approved by Jesus Christ as excommunication is approved by the Church.

The above letter proves that there was little difference between the views of Servetus and Calvin and that therefore the whole blame for the trial should not be attributed to Calvin. For further discussion see Lecler, *op. cit.*

TWO DESCRIPTIONS OF GENEVA

J. T. McNeill, *The History and Character of Calvinism*, 1954, pp. 178–9.

Source: (*a*) John Knox to Mrs. Anna Clarke, December, 1556.

Geneva, where I neither fear man nor am ashamed to say that this is the most perfect school of Christ that ever was in the earth since the days of the apostles. In other places, I confess Christ to be truly preached; but manners and religion to be so sincerely reformed, I have not yet seen in any other place.

Source: (*b*) John Bale, Bishop of Ossory.

Geneva seemeth to me to be the wonderful miracle of the whole world: so many from all countries come hither, as it were in a sanctuary, not to gather riches, but to live in poverty. . . . Is it not wonderful that Spaniards, Italians, Scots, Englishmen, Frenchmen, Germans, disagreeing in manners, speech, and apparel, sheeps and wolves, bulls and bears, being coupled with the only yoke of Christ, should live so lovingly and friendly, and that monks, laymen and nuns disagreeing both in life and sect, should dwell together, like a spiritual and Christian congregation.

CALVIN'S CHARACTER

Source: Nicolas des Gallars, minister to the French congregation in London, to Crespin, publisher of Knox's *First Blast*. January 1st, 1570, from the *Preface to the Commentary on Isaiah*, opera XXI, *Prologomena* XXXVI.

When I look back upon his frankness and integrity, his affectionate benevolence towards me and the familiar intimacy which I enjoyed for sixteen years, I cannot but grieve for my separation from such a friend, or, I would say, such a father. What labours, watchings and anxieties did he endure! With what wisdom and perspicacity did he foresee all dangers and how skilfully did he go out to meet them! No words of mine can declare the fidelity and prudence with which he gave counsel, the kindness with which he received all who came to him, the cleverness and promptitude with which he replied to those who asked for his opinion on the most important questions, and the ability with which he disentangled the difficulties and problems which were laid before him. Nor can I express the gentleness with which he would console the afflicted and raise the fallen and distressed, or his courage in adversity and moderation in prosperity.

ANABAPTISTS

Just as Luther in Germany, frightened by the revolt of the peasants, stopped short of a full reformation in the Church and threw in his lot with the Princes, so did Zwingli in Zurich abandon the Scriptures as the court of appeal and decided that the city magistrates should be the final authority. Thus it was that when a radical party appeared in 1525 and insisted that nothing was to be accepted which did not have scriptural authority, the power of the magistrates was turned against them. The new party was led by Conrad Grebel, Felix Manz, Balthasar Hübmaier. The clash came over the question of infant baptism, for which there is no scriptural sanction. In the end Grebel died in prison, Manz was publicly drowned, and Blaurock was driven out of Zurich.

HÜBMAIER AND ZWINGLI

Source: Hübmaier's evidence in 1525 on Zwingli's admissions on May 1st, 1523. Kidd, *op. cit.*, p. 451.

In 1523 on Philip and James' day, I conferred with you [Zwingli] in Graben street upon the Scriptures relating to Baptism. Then and there you said I was right in saying that children should not be baptized before they were instructed in the faith; this had been the custom previously, therefore [such persons under instruction] were called catechumens. You promised to bring this out in your Exposition of the Articles, as you did in the XVIIIth Article on Confirmation. Anyone who reads it will find therein your opinion clearly expressed. Sebastian Ruckensperger of St. Gall, then Prior of Sion at Klingnau, was present. So you have also confessed in your book on the unruly spirits, that those who baptized infants could quote no clear word in Scripture ordering them to baptize them. From this learn, friend Zwingli, how your conversation, writing and preaching agree.

THE VIEWS OF GREBEL AND HÜBMAIER

Source: (*a*) A letter from Grebel to Münzer, September 5th, 1524. Kidd, *op. cit.*, p. 452.

We believe . . . that all children who have not yet come to know the difference between good and evil . . . are saved by the sufferings of Christ . . . Also that infant baptism is a silly blasphemous outrage, contrary to all Scripture . . . Since . . . you have published your protestations against infant baptism, we hope you do not act against the eternal Word, wisdom, and command of God, according to which only believers should be baptized, and that you baptize no children.

Source: (*b*) A letter of Hübmaier to Œcolampadius, January 16th, 1525. Kidd, *op. cit.*, p. 452.

We have publicly taught that children should not be baptized. Why do we baptize children? Baptism, say they, [Zwingli and Leo], is a mere sign. Why do we strive so much over a mere sign? The meaning of this sign and symbol, the pledge of faith until death in hope of the resurrection to the life to come, is more to be considered than the sign. This meaning has nothing to do with babes; therefore infant baptism is without reality. In Baptism a man pledges himself to God; in the Supper to his neighbour, to offer body and blood in his stead, as Christ for us. I believe, yea, I know, that it will not go well with Christendom until Baptism and the Supper are brought back to their original purity. Here, brother, you have my opinion; if I err, call me back. For I wish nothing so much that I will not revoke it, yea, cut it off, when I am taught better from the Word of God by you and yours. Otherwise, I abide by my opinion; for to that I am constrained by the command of Christ, the Word, faith, truth, judgement, conscience. Testify to the truth; you can in no way offend me . . . I have sent letters to Zwingli by the captain of our volunteers. Instead of baptism, I cause the Church to come together, bring the infant in, explain in German the Gospel, 'They brought little children, etc.', then a name is given him, the whole church prays for the child on bended knees and commends him to Christ that He will be gracious and intercede for him. But if the parents are still weak, and positively wish that the child be baptized, then I baptize it; and I am weak with the weak, for the time being, until they are better instructed. As to the Word, however, I do not yield to them in the least point.

THE COUNCIL ORDERS INFANT BAPTISM, January, 1525.

Source: Kidd, *op. cit.*, p. 453.

Whereas an error has arisen respecting baptism, as if young children should not be baptized until they come to years of discretion and know what the faith is: and whereas some have accordingly neglected to have their children baptized, our Lords the Burgomaster, Council and Great Council, have had a disputation held about this matter to learn what Holy Scripture has to say about it. As they have learned from it that, notwithstanding this error, children should be baptized as soon as they are born, all those therefore who have hitherto allowed their children to remain unbaptized, must have them baptized within the next week: and whosoever will not do this, must with wife and child, goods and chattels, leave our city, jurisdiction and dominions, or await what will be done with him.

ANABAPTISM BEGINS

Source: Confession of 14 imprisoned Anabaptists: February 7th, 1525.

They admitted that they had been baptized and had become 'servants, bondmen and subjects of God'; they would do whatever the Spirit of God prompted them, and not suffer themselves to be forced therefrom by any temporal magistrate. So far as they were not hindered by the Word of God, they would be my Lords' subjects . . . Rudolph Thomunn, of Zollikon, deposed that he had eaten the Last Supper with the old assistant-curate and the parson of Wytikon and had invited them to his house . . . There many had assembled, so that the room was full; there was much speaking and long readings. Then stood up Hans Bruggbach of Zumikon, weeping and crying out that he was a great sinner, and asking them to pray God for him. Whereupon Blaurock asked him if he desired the grace of God. 'Yes', said he. Manz then stood up and said, 'Who will hinder me from baptizing him'? Blaurock answered, 'Nobody'. So Manz took a bowl of water and baptized him in the name of God the Father, God the Son and God the Holy Ghost. [A former witness had said that Blaurock had 'sprinkled' Bruggbach.] Whereupon James Hottinger stood up and desired baptism; and Felix Manz baptized him also . . .

THE COUNCIL ORDERS ANABAPTISTS TO BE DROWNED, March 7th, 1526.

Source: The Council's mandate 'to be published on Sunday in the three parishes'. Kidd, *op. cit.*, p. 455.

Whereas our Lords the Burgomaster, Council and Great Council, have for some time past earnestly endeavoured to turn the misguided and erring Anabaptists from their errors; and yet several . . . to the injury of the public authority and the magistrates as well as to the ruin of the common welfare and of right Christian living, have proved disobedient; and several of them, men, women and girls, have been by our Lords sharply punished and put into prison: Now, therefore, by the earnest commandment, edict and warning of our Lords aforesaid, it is ordered that no one in our town, country or domains, whether man, woman or girl, shall baptize another: and if anyone hereafter shall baptize another, He will be seized by our Lords and, according to the decree now set, will be drowned without mercy. Wherefore everyone knows how to order himself and to take care that he bring not his own death upon himself.

THE FATE OF ANABAPTISTS

To be called an Anabaptist in the sixteenth century was just about equivalent to being called a Bolshevik in the 1920s or a Communist in the 1950s. They were the common enemy of Catholic and Protestant and they suffered the fate of all such untouchables.

Source: Menno Simons, one of their later leaders, reported thus: quoted by R. Bainton, *The Reformation of the Sixteenth Century,* Hodder & Stoughton, 1953, p. 102.

Some they have executed by hanging, some they have tortured with inhuman tyranny, and afterwards choked with cords at the stake. Some they roasted and burned alive. Some they have killed with the sword and given to the fowls of the air to devour. Some they have cast to the fishes . . . Others wander about here and there, in want, homelessness, and affliction, in mountains and deserts, in holes and caves of the earth. They must flee with their wives and little children from one country to another, from one city to another. They are hated, abused, slandered and lied about by all men.

THE MYSTIC-SPIRITUAL DAVID JORIS

David Joris was born in 1501 and he died in 1556, but that was not the end of Joris. He came from Delft in Holland, but he was born in Flanders. He grew up to be a craftsman who painted on glass. By 1528 he was a passionate Protestant, so much so that he was imprisoned at Delft and then was condemned to three years' exile for insulting behaviour towards a procession. He became an ardent Anabaptist and was soon having visions which led him to found his own sect. He proclaimed himself the third David and taught that the Rule of the Holy Spirit was the basis of everything. His sect was dedicated to peaceful behaviour, but it was bitterly persecuted from 1538 onwards. Twenty-seven of its members, including Joris's mother, were put to death at Delft. Joris hid himself and moved about from place to place. After 1544 he disappeared, but in that year there arrived in Basle a rich man with a wife and a large family. Jan van Brugge lived on at Basle until he died in 1556. This man was in fact Joris and he built up secretly another sect, continued to write and got his books published secretly. Twelve years after his arrival in Basle he died and was given a magnificent funeral. In 1559 it was discovered that this man was Joris. Thereupon his whole family and his closest friends were thrown into prison and Joris's corpse was dug up and burned at the stake.

Source: *Mémoires de Félix Platter* (a doctor in Basle), trans. by E. Fick, Geneva, 1866, p. 98. Quoted by Joseph Lecler, in his *Toleration and the Reformation*, Longmans, trans. by T. L. Westlow, 1960. Platter was an eye-witness of the event.

[The effigy of Joris and a box of his books] 'were handed over to the executioner who took them outside the town, as he was used to do with criminals. In the Franciscans' Square stood a bier with the exhumed corpse. Faggots were heaped up in front of the Steinenthor, the usual place for executions; there the executioner placed the coffin, and after breaking it up the dead man could be seen, dressed in a cheap cloak and a pointed velvet cap, trimmed with scarlet. The executioner set up the corpse, which was rather well preserved and still recognizable; the eye-sockets were hollow and the lids were closed. By its side they put the books, then the effigy was propped up against the stake, and the flames reduced all to cinders. The concourse of the people was enormous. I saw this execution in the company of Sebastian Castellio.

NOTES

[1] Andrew Bodenstein, called Carlstadt from his birthplace. Professor of theology at Wittenberg, he was at first a strong opponent of Luther. Later he became an ally.

[2] John Maier, known as Eck from his birthplace. He led the opposition to Luther at the Disputation of Leipzig, 1519.

[3] A title in use from the twelfth century onwards for Peter Lombard (*c.* 1100–60), author of *Sententiarum Libri Quatuor*, which became the standard textbook of Catholic theology in the Middle Ages. It was superseded by the *Summa* of Thomas Aquinas.

[4] In fact he dined before setting out. The accounts of the massacre vary greatly.

[5] An insulting name for the Zwinglians.

[6] A violent opponent of the Reformation.

[7] But Calvin did not use the word 'aristocracy' as we use it: he meant both a theocracy and government by the godly.

THE COUNTER-REFORMATION

By the middle of the sixteenth century Protestantism had been accepted by England, the Scandinavian countries, Switzerland, much of Germany, Poland, and the Dutch areas of the Netherlands. The Popes of the Roman Catholic Church were antagonistic to reform, their primary objects being the interests of their families. The Venetian ambassador, Luigi Movenigo, wrote that 'obedience to the Pope has almost ceased . . . the only remedy is a council summoned by the common consent of all princes'. Reform did at last come: it was prepared for by the foundation of new religious orders, such as the Oratory of Divine Love, the Capuchins, and especially The Society of Jesus, founded by Ignatius Loyola. These were followed by the Council of Trent (1545–63). The Inquisition and the Index Librorum Prohibitorum played their part.

IGNATIUS LOYOLA

Ignatius Loyola was a Spaniard, born about 1491 of a noble Basque family. He served as a soldier, but on May 19th, 1521, he was seriously wounded at the siege of Pamplona, his leg being shattered by a cannon-ball. He was immobilized for many months and during this time he began to read devotional works. When he was at last cured—he had a slight limp for the rest of his life—he had made up his mind to devote the rest of his life to the work of Christ. In a cave outside Manresa, where he lived for nine months, he underwent more than one mystical experience: he had a vision of the Holy Trinity and he was caught up into Paradise 'where he heard secret words which it is not granted to man to utter'. He went on to write *The Spiritual Exercises*, a book of devotion and also training manual which later became the basis of the training of every Jesuit. On the Feast of the Assumption in Paris, 1534, Loyola and his six companions took the vows of poverty and chastity and thus formed the nucleus of the Society of Jesus, which was officially recognized by Pope Paul III in a Bull published on September 27th, 1540.

Source: (a) Ribadeneira, *De Actis S. Ignatii, Scripta*, vol. 1, p. 376 (80 and 81). Ribadaneira became one of Loyola's followers in 1540.

Often and often we have seen him, in perfect calmness and with all the sweetness of manner that can be imagined, order someone brought before him for punishment; and when the offender came into his presence, it seemed as if he was transformed and all afire; and then, after he had finished speaking and the offender had gone, immediately, without the slightest interval of time he returned to his former serenity and blitheness of counten-ance, as if nothing had happened. It was clear that there had been no irritation whatever within, and that he had made use of that sudden look as a mask, putting it on and laying it aside at will...

And though his bodily condition had its ups and downs, for his health was inconstant, nevertheless his soul was invariably of an even temper. What I mean is that if you wished to ask for something from Father Ignatius, it made no difference whether he was on his way from mass or had had dinner, or whether he had just got out of bed, or had been at prayer, whether he had received good news or bad, whether things were quiet, or the world upside down. With him there was no such thing as *feeling his pulse*, no *taking a reckoning by the North Star*, no *steering by a sea chart*, as is the usual way of dealing with men in authority, for he was always in a state of calm self-mastery.

Source: (*b*) Ribadaneira, *op. cit.*, Book I, ch. 2.

I have often seen him, in his old age, standing out on the balcony, or on some place of vantage where he could look at the sky, fix his gaze upwards and remain motionless, lost in thought, for a long time, and then, overcome by emotion, shed tears of joy. And I have often heard him say: 'How contemptible the world seems when I look up at the sky'.

Source: (*c*) *Epistola P. Lainii de S. Ignatio*, written by Lainez, one of the original companions of Loyola, to Polanco, Loyola's secretary, June 17th, 1547.

Lainez attributes Loyola's powers of leadership to: 'great knowledge of the things of God, and great devotion to them, and the more metaphysical these matters were, and over our heads, the better he knew them; great good sense and prudence in matters of business; the divine gift of discretion; great fortitude and magnanimity in tribulation; great guilelessness in not judging others and in putting a favourable interpretation on all things; and great skill in knowing how to set himself and others to work for the service of God'.

Source: (*d*) Diary of Benedetto Palmio, in *Storia della Compagnia di Gesù in Italia*, by Tacchi Venturi, S.J., vol. i, ch. xvii.

His table was always resplendent with parsimony and frugality, but it had nevertheless a savour of gentle usages. There were two or three brothers to wait upon it, more especially when outsiders were invited to dinner. The wine glasses were served with elegance; it could not have been better done, or more attractively, in a palace.

Source: (*e*) *Scripta*, vol. i, p. 365 (58). Ribadeneira.

Father Ignatius and I were strolling about together after supper, and a good many others were walking about and talking of one thing or another at a little distance off. While we two were discussing spiritual matters, Father Ignatius paused, and stepping up to one of the brothers said: 'Go, see who those are walking over yonder'. The brother came back and said it was one of our priests talking to a novice. Ignatius called the priest up and asked, 'What were you talking about to the novice'? The priest replied: 'Father, we got on the topic of humility and mortification, and I was telling him what I had seen myself, or had heard, in those respects, about Brother Texeda [who was not a member of the Society of Jesus] in order to encourage the lad to follow his pattern'. Father Ignatius said: 'Are there no examples to be found in the Society, that you go seeking them from outsiders? Who gave you permission to talk to novices, when you have not sense enough? Go to the minister and bid him strike your name off that list, and don't speak again to a novice without leave from me.'

A SET OF RULES DRAWN UP BY LOYOLA

Next to the Jesuits' house in Rome there was a garden and also a vineyard. The novices were given the run of the garden where they used to play quoits and another similar game called *piastrelle*, which Ignatius had seen played in Paris: he had made a wax model of a *piastrella*, and he allowed no other games to be played. One day some of the young men were throwing oranges to each other and who ever dropped one was to say an *Ave Maria*. Ignatius caught them at it and imposed a severe penance. Another time he found some of them who were convalescing from some sickness playing ball: Ignatius had the balls brought into the house and thrown on the fire. Then he drew up the following rules. (Sedgwick, *Ignatius Loyola*, pp. 17 *et sqq.* London, 1923.

Source: Ignatio de Loyola, Scripta, vol. 1, pp. 239 *et sqq.*

No one shall go to the vineyard without permission of the Rector or of his deputy.

No one shall eat or touch the grapes or other fruit without permission.

No one shall eat more grapes or fruit than he is allowed, in order to prevent sickness from any excess.

No one shall leave his clothes about the vineyard, but in the prescribed place.

No one shall go into the kitchen without permission from the cook, or some one in the cook's place.

No games shall be played in the vineyard except *piastrelle*, and singing.

Neither the players nor any one else shall lean against the espaliers, nor the trellises, nor get up on them.

No one shall break twigs from the trees or vines, or make marks on them.

No one shall play *piastrelle* on the little paths that run across the width of the vineyard.

The Rector shall appoint a monitor, who shall give out the *piastrelle* whenever the young men go to the vineyard; and when the game is over, he shall count them and put them back in the closet appropriated for that purpose.

Every player shall be careful to return the *piastrella* he has played with, at the gate of the house, and hand it to the monitor. No one shall make lines or other marks on the walls of the house or the rooms, either indoors or out.

No one shall throw anything into the well.

A PRAYER FROM THE BOOK OF EXERCISES

Source: These were originally written in Spanish and translated into Latin in or before 1541. There is an English translation entitled *The Text of the Spiritual Exercises of Saint Ignatius*, translated from the original Spanish, Fourth Edition Revised, Burns and Oates, London, 1913.

Take, O Lord, and keep all my liberty, my memory, my understanding, and all my will, whatsoever I have and possess. Thou hast given all these things to me; to Thee, O Lord, I restore them: All are Thine, dispose of them all according to Thy will. Give me Thy love and Thy grace; that is enough for me.

SUBJUGATING THE FLESH

Source: De Origine et Progressu Societatis Jesu, pp. 480-1, by Father Simon Rodriguez, one of the first Fathers.

[All the extracts in the English versions have been taken from *Ignatius Loyola*, by H. D. Sedgwick, Macmillan, 1923.]

It happened that three of the Companions went to the same hospital. The beds offered them had been much used and were very dirty, the sheets were foul and badly spotted with blood. Nevertheless, two of them, one with his clothes on, the other stripped, were not afraid to get in. The third [probably Rodriguez], kept back by horror of the filth, sought another spot. But as he went, he reflected on what he had done and grieved greatly that he had shirked in the battle. He laid it to weakness, self-indulgence and delicacy of body, and mightily desired that a new occasion would offer itself in which he might retrieve the flabby act. God did not fail him. For when he and another brother arrived at the hospital of some village, the matron informed them that there was no bed except one which a patient had occupied who had died that day of the lousy disease; the sheets, she said, were clean, for the patient had not used them while alive, but they had been laid under his dead body, out of respect for the cross and for the priests who had come to the infirmary to say the last rites and bury the body. The matron did not exaggerate; the sheets had been sprinkled with holy water and were thick with great big lice which accompany that disease. The Father who had once been vanquished now saw his way to win a victory over himself, and seized the opportunity. He took off all his clothes and jumped quickly between the sheets. The lice rushed incontinently upon him, pricked and stung him all night long, and made his body smart till it sweated. Of a truth the Father conquered himself, he conquered and won the field gloriously. His companion also lay down in the same place, but kept his clothes on.

THE COUNCIL OF TRENT

Paul III became Pope in 1534. At first he was advised by the moderate Contarini, later by the aggressive Caraffa. The Papacy went on to the attack against the Reformers. The Society of Jesus (the Jesuits) was formed in 1540 and the Inquisition was set up in 1542. A meeting between the Germans and the Italians took place at Trent in 1542, and it was there seen that some minor concessions could be made without giving away anything of value. Pope Paul III, therefore, summoned the Council of Trent in 1545, and Julius III in 1551 and Pius IV in 1562. The questions discussed were those of Pluralism, absenteeism, sale of benefices—matters of Church reform on which most parties were agreed. The Protestant demands for marriage of the clergy, translation of the Bible, Communion in both kinds the Pope was prepared to grant in exceptional cases as a matter, not of right, but of privilege. The Protestant theological demands he was determined the Council should fully condemn. The question of the powers of the Papacy he hoped would never be reached. In the end the Papacy triumphed: a few unimportant concessions had been made in the reform of the Church: Protestant doctrine had been condemned and the control of the Church was more firmly in the hands of the Papacy than ever before. The following extract gives the decisions of the Council of Trent on the proper relationship between Religion and Art.

CANONS AND DECREES OF THE COUNCIL OF TRENT

Source: Session XXV, Tit. 2. This English version is from Anthony Blunt's *Artistic Theory in Italy*, Oxford, Clarendon Press, 1940, pp. 107–8.

That the images of Christ, of the Virgin Mother of God, and of the other Saints, are to be had and retained, particularly in churches, and that due honour and veneration are to be given

U

them; not that any divinity or virtue is believed to be in them on account of which they are to be worshipped; or that anything is to be asked of them; or that trust is to be reposed in images, as was done of old by the Gentiles who placed their hope in idols; but because the honour which is shown them is referred to the prototypes which those images represent; so that by the images which we kiss and before which we uncover our heads and prostrate ourselves, we adore Christ, and we venerate the Saints whose likeness they bear; as by the decrees of Councils, and especially the second Synod of Nicaea, has been defined against the opponents of images.

And the bishops shall carefully teach this: that, by means of the stories of the mysteries of our Redemption, portrayed by paintings and other representations, the people are instructed and confirmed in the habit of remembering, and continually revolving in mind the articles of faith; as also that great profit is derived from all sacred images, not only because the people are thereby admonished of the benefits and gifts bestowed upon them by Christ, but also because the miracles which God has performed by means of the Saints and their salutary examples are set before the eyes of the faithful; that they may give God thanks for those things, may order their own lives and manners in imitation of the Saints; and may be excited to adore and love God and to cultivate piety.

COLD COMFORT FOR THE JESUITS

Pope Paul III asked Ignatius Loyola to choose two of the Society of Jesus to represent the Pope at the Council of Trent as his theologians. Lainez and Salmerón were selected and they reached Trent in 1546, and in May 1551 for the third session.

Source: Lainii Monumenta, vol. i, pp. 192 *et sqq*. This English version is taken from *Ignatius Loyola*, by H. D. Sedgwick, Macmillan, 1923, p. 260.

Trent, August 11th, 1551.

To Father Ignatius Loyala:

We will inform your Reverence about what has happened to us since we came here, and about our lodgings, not to find fault with anybody, unless it be ourselves, but to let you know the facts, lest they may be reported in Rome after another fashion.

When we arrived here, the Very Reverend Legate (Cardinal Marcello Crescenzi) received us, as far as we could judge, with great cordiality, for even before we had got here he had spoken of our coming to many prelates, saying he was glad to have us; and they said nice things about us, as we know both from him and from them. He said he would lodge us both in a room in his house, and that an inn should be at once looked up, which he hoped would be near by in order the better to enjoy our society, and he also hoped that we would regularly dine with him, but if we preferred to dine in our own room, dinner should be served there. We kissed his hands and took our leave.

Our expectation was that he would speak to the Secretary of the Council, and tell him to take charge of us until an inn could be found. The Secretary took us to his own house and said that, as we were not lodged at an inn, we should come there for just that one night; and he gave us all three, for our joint apartment, a little, tiny, smoky oven of a room, with a bed in it and a truckle-bed (which when pulled out did not leave space to take two steps in the room). There was no table for us to study at, or write a letter, and as for chairs only one footstool, but there were lots of boots, belonging to him and his valet, and a big wallett, an old harp, and the valet's sword, which were kept in our *oven*. I said to Master Salmerón: 'See here, this is a little more than we bargained for; let's stay at the inn, and tomorrow on my way to the palace, I will tell the Secretary that, in order not to go changing inns, and as long as he said we were to be here for only one night, we had decided to stay at the inn'. But Salmerón thought it was better to come to the *oven* in spite of the heat, in order not to show any signs of discontent with the room, or any dissatisfaction. So Salmerón slept that night upon a chest, and John and I upon the beds; but the next day Salmerón betook himself to the house of the Bishop of Verona, which was near by, to sleep, but though I was offered the same, in order that we should not all leave the appartment, John and I continued to sleep in the *oven*. One day the Legate's Secretary came and asked if we lacked anything; and

I answered with my usual freedom, or foolishness: 'You can see; we lack everything'. And he said: 'That's so; but at the present moment, what do you need?' So I answered: 'At least we need a candle to go to bed by'. Then he asked: 'What more?' And I said, laughing all the time, 'A candle-stick to put it in'. However, the keeper of the store closet was out, so we couldn't have a candle that night: nevertheless we were the gainers, for we got a torch to go to bed by.

After about a week, having paid visits upon almost everybody, we went to the Cardinal to beg him to give us a room; for everybody was asking where we lodged, and a good many people wanted to come to see us, but we did not think that we could receive visitors where we were. He told us that they would surely give us a room; however, the owner of the house, where he wished to lodge us, was away, that as soon as he was back, he would take us in. The owner did return in three or four days and offered us rooms; but as the house was new and still unfinished, and as there were neither doors nor windows, he asked for an advance of ten ducats on the rent in order to complete the rooms. When he went to ask the Secretary of the Council for the ducats —I was present—the Secretary answered sharply that he was a dreadful man, etc. After the landlord had gone, I said to the Secretary: 'It would have been a good thing, if you had given him those ducats, for in the end they come out of the rent, and it makes little difference'. To which he said: 'What rent do you think we have to pay for those rooms per month, anyhow, that you increase the cost that we shall have to bear in hiring them?' I answered, a little indignantly: 'Well, there is some expense for everyone that comes to the Council; do you think you spend much for us? Don't you know that we don't eat our bread for nothing, but that we work as hard as the others? The Pope knows that, and that is why he sent us; and you have done a thing that has neither head nor tail in putting two priests, sent by the Pope, into your sevant's room, and such a room, that I am astonished at you. And since you are not spending your own money, you ought to spend according to the orders you receive from the Pope, and not keep us all this time where you do: Sal-merón had to sleep on a chest the first night, and hasn't been willing to sleep there again; and I should have liked to do the same, if it had not been that I didn't want to show your short-comings. But I promise you I shall tell the Cardinal how we are situated, and that I shall write it to Rome' . . .

We have wanted to write this to your Reverence, not to make a complaint of anyone, for we certainly have none; but in order that, in case complaints may have been written from here (but we don't think so) you may know the facts and be able to make use of them. And also because, in accordance with my character, I should not be at peace, if I had not advised you of this fault, so that you might correct me.

THE INQUISITION

THE INQUISITION IN VENICE

In 1573 the Dominican Fathers of SS. *Giovanni e Paolo* commis-sioned Paolo Veronese to paint a picture to replace a Last Supper by Titian which had been destroyed in a fire. Veronese produced for them the magnificent *Feast in the House of Levi*, which now hangs in the Academia in Venice. He was called to account by the Inquisition because, not only did the picture lack the central figure of St. Mary Magdalene, but it was filled with outrageous details—a man picking his teeth with a fork, dogs scrounging tit-bits, blackamore boy-servants, etc. It is difficult now to know whether the picture was intended to represent the Last Supper (at which Mary Magdalene was not present) or the Feast in the House of Levi (where the Bible says were many publicans and sinners), so confused were the titles used at the Inquisi-tion. Veronese was ordered to amend the picture, but there is no evidence that he did anything about it.

Source: Report of the Sitting of the Tribunal of the Inquisition, July 18th, 1573. Yriate, *La Vie d'Un Patricien de Venise au Seizieme Siecle*, trans. Crawford, *Gleanings from Venetian History*, 2 vols., London, 1905.

This day, the eighteenth July, 1573. Called to the Holy Office before the Sacred Tribunal, Paolo Galliari Veronese, residing in the parish of S. Samuel, and being asked his name and surname, replied as above.

Being asked as to his profession:

Answer: I paint and make figures.

Question: Do you know the reasons why you have been called here.

Answer: No.

Q. Can you imagine what these reasons may be?

A. I can well imagine.

Q. Say what you think about them.

A. I fancy that it concerns what was said to me by the reverend fathers, or rather by the prior of the monastery of *San Giovanni e Paolo*, whose name I did not know, but who informed me, that he had been here, and that your Most Illustrious Lordships had ordered him to cause to be placed in the picture a Magdalen instead of the dog; and I answered him that very readily I would do all that was needful for my reputation and for the advantage of the picture; but that I did not understand what this figure of the Magdalen could be doing here.

Q. What picture is that which you have named?

A. It is the picture representing the last supper that Jesus took with his disciples in the house of Simon.

Q. In this supper of Our Lord, have you painted any attendants?

A. Yes, my lord.

Q. Say how many attendants and what each is doing.

A. First, the master of the house, Simon; besides, I have placed below him a server, who I have supposed to have come for his own amusement to see the arrangement of the table. There are besides several others, which as there are so many figures in the picture, I do not recollect.

Q. What is the meaning of the men dressed in the German fashion each with a halberd in his hand?

A. It is now necessary I should say a few words.

Q. Say on.

A. We painters use the same license that is permitted to poets and jesters. I have placed these two halberdiers, one of them eating, the other drinking, by the staircase, but both ready to perform any duty that may be required of them: it seemed to me quite fitting that the master of such a house, who was rich and great—as I have been told—should have such attendants.

Q. And the one who is dressed like a buffoon with a parrot on his wrist—why did you introduce *him* into the canvas?

A. For ornament, as is usually done.

Q. Who are the people at the table of Our Lord?

A. The twelve Apostles.

Q. What is St. Peter doing, who is the first?

A. He is carving a lamb to send to the other end of the table.

Q. What is the one doing who comes next?

A. He is holding a plate to see what St. Peter will give him?

Q. What is he doing who is next to this last?

A. He is picking his teeth with a fork.

Q. Who do you really think were present at this supper?

A. I believe Christ and his Apostles were present; but in the fore-ground of the picture I have placed figures as ornaments, of my own invention.

Q. Were you commissioned to paint Germans and buffoons and such like figures in this picture?

A. No, my lord: but I was commissioned to ornament the picture as I thought best, which, being large, to my mind requires many figures . . .

Q. Does it not appear to you that . . . you have [not] done right in painting the picture in this manner, and that it can [not] be proved right and decent?

A. Illustrious lord, I do not defend it; but I thought I was doing right.

The judges pronounced that the aforesaid Paolo should be obliged to correct the picture within three months from the date of the reprimand according to the judgements and the decision of the said Sacred Court, and altogether at the expense of the said Paolo.

THE INQUISITION IN SPAIN, 1599

Source: Thomas Platter, *Journal of a Younger Brother,* ed. and trans. by Seán Jennet, Fuller, London, 1963, p. 207 *et sqq.* The following account deals with Barcelona.

Not far from the cathedral and next to the episcopal palace is the palace of the Inquisition. It is an enormous building and very high, with a façade ornamented with large and beautiful windows. Each time that I passed this building my thoughts turned to the cruelties which are committed there, and which are described in the great book of *Martyrs.* Any man who is suspected by his conduct or his speech of not hating the Lutherans—which is what they call the reformers in this country—or of not finding everything perfect that is Catholic, is at once denounced to the Jesuit inquisitors and promptly incarcerated in this palace, charged with heresy. After a few days, or a few months, as the fathers think fit, one of them comes to interrogate him on the reasons for his detention, or to acquaint him with them, if he does not know. If he says that he is a Catholic, they ask him his age and where he was born, and where he made his last confession and his last communion, and his answers are at once checked by the spies whom the Jesuits have everywhere. If the prisoner has lied, or if he contradicts himself during the enquiry, without further ado he is burned alive as a heretic, for having misled the Holy Office. But if he claims to belong to the reformed religion, one of two courses follows: if he refuses to be converted, he is sent to a large town to be burned on the pyre, perhaps alone, perhaps with others like him. Wearing a gown on which are pictures of devils pulling him into hell and tormenting him in a thousand ways, he is thus put to death in the most atrocious manner, and his picture is exhibited in the cathedrals to perpetuate his shame; but for the martyrs this death is glory, as indeed it is thus to suffer persecution and death for the true religion of Jesus Christ. If, on the other hand, he agrees to be converted, he is taught all the articles of the

Catholic faith, and for a long time is given weekly instruction in religion, until the time when he appears sufficiently catechized and is confirmed. Then he is allowed out of prison, but remains for two years in the palace of the Inquisition, still clothed in a long robe with pictures of devils trying to pull him down to hell, but also with angels and inquisitors trying to draw him up to heaven. In this costume he watches all the processions and all the *autos-da-fé*, so that people may know him as a convert from Lutheranism.

THE SUCCESS OF THE COUNTER-REFORMATION

Once the problem of reforming the Church was tackled thoroughly and genuinely, the Counter-Reformation was very successful. The old scandal of the Papal Conclaves was apparently cured by 1579.

Source: Cardinal de Retz on the Conclaves, 1579. Ranke, *Französische Geschichte xvi and xvii cc.* Quoted by Reddaway, *Select Documents, 1453–1714,* where the date is printed as 1679, p. 74.

I can say with truth that I have never seen, in any of the Conclaves at which I have been present, any Cardinal or member lose control of himself; I have indeed seen very few of them grow warm. It is rare to hear a raised voice or to see an angry face. I have often tried to find some difference in the look of those who had just been defeated, and I can say with truth that, with one single exception, I have never found any. So remote is even the suspicion of those revenges with which Italy is usually wrongly charged, that it is even common enough for an opponent to drink at dinner the wine which the candidate whom he has defeated that morning has just sent him. In a word, I dare say that there is nothing more wise or grand than the ordinary scene in a Conclave. I know well that the procedure practised there since the Bull of Gregory contributes greatly to regulate it; but it must be admitted that only Italians are capable of observing this order with as much decorum as is necessary.

FRANCE
(*Notes on p. 362*)

From Bayard to the Civil Wars

THE DEATH OF THE CHEVALIER BAYARD, 1524

Pierre Terrail, Seigneur de Bayard, was born in 1473 and was killed at the passage of the Sesia on April 30th, 1524. As a soldier he was one of the most skilled commanders of his time and he maintained a perfect system of reconnaissance and espionage, so that he was the best informed commander. In days when mercenary armies produced faithless and self-interested leaders, Bayard remained untainted. He was indeed to everybody of his time the perfect knight of heroic chivalry, '*sans peur et sans reproche*'.

Source: Le Loyal Serviteur (? Jacques de Maille), *La très joyeuse, plaisante, et recreative histoire . . . des faiz . . . du bon chevalier sans paour et sans reproche, le gentil seigneur de Bayart.* (1st ed. Paris, 1527: many later editions.) Quoted in M. F. Jerrold, *Vittoria Colonna, Her Friends and her Times*, Dent, 1906, pp. 18 *et sqq.*

In war there is fortune and ill-fortune more than in all other things . . . The good Knight put his soldiers in motion and retired slowly, as much at ease as if he had been in his own house; and with his face always turned towards the enemy, and brandishing his sword, he kept them more in fear than a hundred others would have done. But, as God willed it, a shot was fired from an arquebus which struck him through the loins and broke his spine. When he felt the blow, he cried out, 'Jesus'! and then 'Alas! my God, I am slain'. Then he took his sword by the cross-handle and said aloud, '*Miserere mei, Deus, secundum magnam misericordiam tuam*', and immediately he became quite pale, as though he was swooning, and almost fell; but he had strength to grasp the saddle-bow, and remained upright until a young gentleman, his steward, helped him to dismount and placed him under a tree. In a short time it was known that the Captain Bayart had been killed by a shot of artillery, whereat all those who heard the news were marvellously displeased.

When the tidings spread abroad among the two armies that the good Knight had been killed, or at least mortally wounded, even in the camp of the Spaniards, although he was one of the men in the world of whom they had most fear, gentlemen and soldiers were marvellously displeased at it for many reasons. For when during his lifetime he made assaults and took any prisoners, he was always wont to treat them so humanely as it was a marvel, and to ask so little ransom that everyone was content with him. They all agreed that by his death knighthood was greatly weakened, for, without derogating from others, he was a perfect knight in this world. Their young nobles acquired skill in warring with him, and one of their principal captains, the Marquis of Pescara, who went to see him before he rendered up his soul, said a high word in his praise, which was this: 'Would to God, gentle seigneur de Bayart, that it had cost me a quart of my blood (short of dying), and that by abstaining from flesh-meat for two years I might have kept you whole and in good health as my prisoner; for by the treatment that I would have given you, you would have known how much I have esteemed the prowess which was in you . . . Since I have borne arms, I have never seen nor heard tell of a knight who approached you in all virtues. And though I ought to rejoice to see you in this plight, being assured that my master, the Emperor, had in these wars no greater or more formidable enemy than you, yet when I consider the great loss which all chivalry sustains to-day, God aid me if I would not have given the half of all I am worth that it had befallen otherwise . . .'

FRANCIS I AND THE RENAISSANCE

Francis, Count of Angoulême, was born in 1494. He succeeded to the throne of France in 1515 on the death of his cousin Louis XII, who left no son as heir. The great victory at Marignano (1515) gave Francis Milan. The death of Ferdinand of Aragon in 1516 and of Maximilian I in 1519, and the election as Emperor of Charles V in 1519 started the rivalry between the Valois and the Hapsburg. In 1525 Francis was taken prisoner at the battle of Pavia and he was for a time imprisoned in Spain, but he was released in 1526. Between 1529 and 1535 Francis carried on a series of complicated alliances against Charles V, and at one time he succeeded in combining Henry VIII, Pope Clement VII and the Turks against the Emperor. He died in 1547. His chief claim to fame is as a splendid Renaissance figure, cultivated, brilliant, with exquisite taste, a lover of all beautiful things and a great builder. He succeeded in attracting some of the best painters, sculptors and architects to his court, including Leonardo da Vinci and Benvenuto Cellini (see pages 11, *et sqq.*). Among others were Giovanni Battista Giacopo, commonly known as Il Rosso (1494–1541), and Francesco Pimaticcio of Bologna (1504–70).

Source: (*a*) Vasari, *Lives of the Painters*, ii, 361. Dent, 1927. Vasari was born in 1511 and died in 1574. Rosso went to Paris in 1530, when Vasari was 19 years old: it is improbable that he ever met Rosso, but he must have had contacts with many Florentines who had known Rosso.

From Venice, Rosso went to France, where he was heartily welcomed by the Florentines. Having painted some pictures, which were afterwards put in the gallery at Fontainebleau, he gave them to King Francis, who was greatly delighted. The monarch was even more delighted with Rosso's bearing, conversation and habits (his ruddy complexion suited his name), his grave, serious manner and great judgement. After granting him a provision of 400 crowns and giving him a house in Paris, which Rosso used little, spending most of his time at Fontainbleau, where he had apartments and lived like a lord, the king made him chief of all structures, paintings and other ornaments of that place. Here Rosso began a gallery over the lower court, not vaulting it, but making a flat roof with open beams, beautifully partitioned. The sides he decorated with stucco and curious and fantastic panels, with several kinds of cornices carved with life-sized figures, the lower part being adorned with rich festoons in stucco, others with paintings of fruit and every sort of verdure . . . When the king saw these works, he was greatly pleased and took Rosso into high favour, giving him soon after a stall in Nôtre Dame at Paris and other revenues, so that he lived like a lord with his servants and his horses, giving banquets to his friends and acquaintances, especially to the Italians who came there . . .

Source: (*b*) Vasari, *op. cit.*, iv, 192. Francesco Primaticcio of Bologna, Abbot of San Martino, Painter and Architect. Vasari specifically states that Primaticcio was a 'great friend' of his.

Francesco was born at Bologna of the noble family of the Primaticcio . . . and was first destined for commerce. But he cared little for it, his lofty mind turning to design, for which he had a natural bent, and by means of study he soon showed great promise. Proceeding to Mantua, where Giulio Romano was engaged upon the T palace for Duke Federigo . . . he acquired such favour with the Duke that when King Francis of France, hearing of the palace, wrote asking that a youth might be sent to him who could paint and do stucco, the Duke sent Francesco in 1531. The year before Rosso had been sent to serve the King, and had done many things, notably the Bacchus and Venus, and Cupid and Psyche. However, it is said that Francesco did the first stucco and frescoes of any account in France, decorating many rooms and loggias for the King, who, liking his style, sent him to Rome in 1540 to procure marble antiquities. In this Primaticcio showed great diligence, buying in a short time one hundred and twenty-five pieces. At the same time he had the bronze horse in the Capitol, a great part of the reliefs of the column, the statue of Commodus, the Venus, the Laocoon, the Nile and Tiber, and the Cleopatra in the Belvedere modelled by Jacopo Barozzi of Vignola, to be cast in bronze.

Meanwhile the death of Rosso took place in France (1541), and as he left a long gallery unfinished Primaticcio was recalled. Packing his marble treasures and moulds he returned to France, and began by making casts of a great number of antique figures, to be placed in the Queen's garden at Fontainebleau, to the delight of the King, who there established a sort of new Rome, for they looked like original antiques . . . The King, being well pleased with his eight years' service, appointed him to be one of his chamberlains and soon afterwards, in 1544, made him abbot of St. Martin's.

Source: (c) Vasari, *op. cit.*, ii, 312. Andrea del Sarto (1486–1531). Vasari records that he saw Andrea forging a picture by copying a Raphael for Ottaviano de' Medici.

While Andrea was just maintaining himself in Florence with these works, without improving his condition, the two pictures he sent to King Francis in France were considered much the best of all that came from Rome, Venice and Lombardy. The King praised them greatly, and he was told that Andrea would readily come to France to serve him. Accordingly being paid the expenses of his journey, Andrea set out joyfully for France (1518), taking with him his pupil, Andrea Sguazzella. Arrived at the court, they were graciously welcomed by the King, and before he had been a day there Andrea experienced the liberality and and courtesy of that magnaminous King, receiving rich vestments and money. He then began to work, and was so highly favoured by the King and court that he seemed to have exchanged a very wretched condition for a most happy one. He drew among his first things a portrait of the Dauphin, then only a few months old, and took it to the King, receiving for it 300 gold crowns. Continuing, he did a Charity for the King which was much admired and valued, as it deserved. The King gave him a large pension and did everything to retain him, promising him that he should lack nothing, for he was pleased with Andrea's quickness and his satisfaction with everything. Besides this, Andrea pleased the court, doing many works for them. If he had considered his origin and the position to which Fortune had raised him, no doubt he could have attained an honourable rank, not to mention riches. But one day, as he was doing a St. Jerome in penitence for the King's mother, some letters arrived from his wife at Florence, and he began, for some cause or other, to think of returning. He asked the King's permission to go, saying that he would return when he had arranged some affairs, and that he would bring back his wife, to enable him to live more comfortably, and that he would bring back some valuable painting and sculptures. The King trusted him and gave him money, while Andrea swore on the Gospels to return in a few months. Arrived in Florence, (1519), he enjoyed his wife, his friends and the city for several months. When the time for his return to France had passed, he found that in building (a house for himself) and pleasures, without working, he had spent all his money and the King's also. But though he wished to return, the tears and entreaties of his wife prevailed more than his own needs and his promise to the King.

Francis became so angry at his faithlessness that he for a long time looked askance at Florentine painters, and he swore that if Andrea ever fell into his hands, he would have more pain than pleasure, in spite of all his ability. Thus Andrea remained in Florence, fallen very low from his high station and maintaining himself as best he could.

THE RELEASE OF FRANCIS I

On February 24th, 1525, was fought the battle of Pavia in which the Imperial armies utterly defeated Francis I and his army. Francis himself was taken prisoner and was sent to Spain, where he was imprisoned. On January 14th, 1526, there was signed the Treaty of Madrid by which Francis was released on certain conditions. As a guarantee that the terms would be fulfilled, his two eldest sons were placed as hostages in Spain.

Source: Guicciardini, quoted in *Marguerite of Austria*, C. Hare, Harpers, London, 1907, p. 299.

The French King was to come to Fontaraby, a town appertaining to the Emperor, standing near the Ocean Sea upon the frontiers of Biscay . . . and on the other side the Lady Regent was arrived with the children of France at Bayon, which is not far from Fontaraby . . . Then the 18th day of March, the French King accompanied by the Viceroy, Captain Alarcon, and fifty horse, came to the shore of the river that divideth the realm of France from the kingdom of Spain; at the same time M. de Lautrec with the King's children and the like number of horse presenting themselves on the other side. [The exchange was made in a barque in the middle of the river, and as soon as the Dauphin and his brother had been given into the care of the Spanish noble] the French King leaped out of the barque into his boat and being brought to the shore mounted suddenly on a Turkish horse of a wonderful swiftness . . . and run without stay to St. Jean de Luz, a town of his obedience four leagues from thence; and being there readily relieved with a fresh horse, he ran with the same swiftness to Bayon, where he was received with incredible joy of all the Court.

THE DEAD FRANCIS I

The body of Francis I lay unburied for forty days.

Source: Ruscelli, *Lettere di Principi*, i, 153. Letter from Casale to Pope Paul III, May 25th, 1547.

During all the time between the death and sepulture of the said King, they made of him an effigy and clothed it in fine vestments, with the crown and sceptre and other royal ornaments. And having placed it on an honoured bed, morning and evening at the accustomed hours they brought wherewith to dine and sup, with the same ceremonies and forms as they are wont with the living person of the King. And when this had been done for some days, they took away those royal vestments and clothed it in mourning. And forty-eight friars stood by, and each day and all day long chanted Mass and performed other devout offices for the safety of his soul.

A BALL AT THE COURT OF FRANCIS I, 1546

In the following account, the King is Francis I, the Dauphin is the future Henry II, his wife is Catherine de' Medici, the Admiral is Coligny, the future leader of the Huguenots.

Source: Alvarotto, Ferraran Ambassador in France, whose letters are in the archives of Modena. He was twenty years resident at the Valois court and watched not only Valois policy, but also Guise and Huguenot. Paris, January 4th, 1546. This extract gives a picture of court life under Francis I.

The King, with Madame d'Etampes on his arm, and with the Admiral following, left his apartments, which are on one side of the courtyard, and came to the banqueting chamber, which was on the other and on the ground floor. On entering, they found the Queen of France, the Dauphin and his wife, Madame Marguerite, and many other ladies. When the repast was over—it lasted a good two hours—they entered another room close by, set apart for dancing. It was hung with beautiful arras and had a stage at one end for the ladies, and a barrier running its whole length to keep the crowd from impeding the dance. There was a gallery also for the fifers and young ladies of the court wishing to see, of whom there were many. When all had entered, dancing began . . .

HENRY II

Henry II was born in 1519 and died in 1559 as the result of a blow which he received while tilting against the Count of Montgomery. He was the second son of Francis I and Claude. He succeeded to the French throne in 1547, his elder brother having died in 1536. He married Catherine de' Medici in 1533, but he was much under the influence of Diane de Poitiers. He had seven surviving children by Catherine: Elizabeth, who became Queen of Spain: Claude, Duchess of Lorraine: Francis II: Charles IX: Henry III: Marguerite, Queen of Navarre; Francis, Duke of Alençon and later Anjou.

Source: The Venetian ambassador, Contarini.

Henry is thirty-two years old and eight or nine months; he is tall and proportionately big and very well made in every part. He has black hair, a fine brow, dark expressive eyes, a large nose, mouth of medium size, and a pointed beard two inches long. All this makes a pleasant face and not lacking in royal dignity. He is physically very strong and greatly given to bodily exercises; every day from two hours after dinner till evening he spends the time playing ball or football, or with bow and arrow, or something of the sort, and he enjoys all kinds of hunting like his father, especially chasing deer, which he does two or three times a week, riding after the deer for six or seven hours, though very exhausting. He gallops through the forest at the risk of his life, and his horse often falls under him. He gets great pleasure from weapons and horses, and rides and handles all sorts of weapons as well as any one at Court. He jousts extremely well, and there is never a tournament or joust, and they are frequent, but he appears in armour like the others, and remains with his helmet on a long time, and jousts as much as or more than any of them. It is the same in all kinds of tournaments on horse or on foot. And he always does well.

As to his character, he has great natural kindness, so much so that you can not rank any prince, no matter how far back you go in the past, above him. He wants to do good and he does it;

x

he is charitable and never refuses audience to anybody. At meals there are always people about him who talk on some particular subject, while he listens or answers very politely. He is never angry, unless sometimes out hunting when somebody gets in his way, and then he never uses immoderate language. For this he is dearly loved by everybody.

He has a good mind, to judge by the experience of his reign, and he is bold in all that he does. He is temperate and he eats and drinks very moderately; and as to bodily pleasures, in comparison with his father and former kings he may be deemed very chaste. And besides that, his amorous affairs are done so quietly that nobody speaks of them, or perhaps nobody knows them, which was not King Francis's habit. So, the Court that used to be licentious is now very respectable. He is very pious, never fails to be present at Mass every day, or at vespers on feast days, or at processions in certain seasons. And on every great feast day, with extreme and devout patience, he touches a great many sick people who have scrofula, which they say is cured by the King's touch.

He has a good memory, and speaks French, Italian and Spanish, which he learned when he was hostage for his father in Spain. In letters he can only read and write; but as to a knowledge of things in general or matters of State, he knows a great deal, and that would be more manifest than it is, if he were not different from most men, in that he thinks he knows less than he does. And the reason that he, with his good mind, does not know much more about them than his father did, is that his father did not like him, and as long as he lived, not only never employed him, nor had him interested in State affairs, but never admitted him to his Cabinet. And that is why Henry puts himself into the hands of the Constable, who has control of everything and does everything. The Constable would like the King to remain in tutelage, and therefore urges him to physical exercises, saying that will prevent him from getting fat (which the King is afraid of), and to enjoy himself and let others do the work. Nevertheless one sees that the King acts more and more on his own responsibility every day. He is of a melancholy nature, reflects upon things, and usually spends the whole morning in listening to business of

State ... He is truthful; it has always been his code, even before he was King, to keep his word; and the general opinion at Court among those who know His Majesty is that he always performs what he promises. A good many people were afraid lest the influence of the Constable, by persuading him to do a thing in one way rather than another, would end in making him break faith; but there has been no clear case of that and one may even assert the contrary.

THE DEATH OF HENRY II OF FRANCE, JULY 1559

The Franco-Spanish War which broke out in 1552, involved England through Mary I's marriage to Philip II of Spain and saw for her the loss of Calais, was ended by the treaty of Cateau-Cambrésis (April 1559). The peace was celebrated in Paris with great festivities, including a tournament at which the French king, Henry II, tilted against the Count of Montgomery (in the following account he appears under the name of M. de Lorges), Captain of the Scottish Guard. The king was not satisfied with the first course and insisted on a second, in spite of the protests of his attendants and the unwillingness of Montgomery. He received a severe blow and a splinter of Montgomery's lance went into his eye. He died a few days later. Montgomery later became a Huguenot and took part in the French wars of religion. Catherine de' Medici never forgave him for the death of her husband. In 1574 he was taken prisoner and she insisted on his being executed, although the French Catholic officers tried to save him.

Source: A letter written by the English ambassador in Paris, Sir Nicholas Throckmorton, to 'The Right Honourable The Lords and Others of the Queen's Majesty's Most Honourable Privy Council. From Paris. 1 July, 1559.' Printed in *Full View of Public Transactions in the Reign of Queen Elizabeth*, ed. by Dr. Patrick Forbes, 2 vols., 1740–1, vol. i, p. 151.

The last of this present [i.e. 30th June] the Prince of Nevers, otherwise called Count d'Eu, came to tilt with his band, where I was to see them run, and none Ambassador else. Whereat it happened that the King, after he had run a good many courses very well and fair, meeting with young Monsieur de Lorges [i.e. Count Montgomery], captain of the Scottish Guard, received at the said de Lorges's hands such a counterbuff as, the blow first lighting upon the King's head and taking away the pannage which was fastened to his headpiece with iron, he did break his staff withal; and so with the rest of the staff hitting the King upon the face, gave him such a counterbuff as he drove a splint right over his eye on his right side, the force of which stroke was so vehement and the pain he had withal so great, as he was much astonished and had great ado (with reeling to and from) to keep himself on horseback; and his horse in like manner did somewhat yield. Whereupon, with all expedition, he was unarmed in the field, even against the place where I stood; and as I could discern, the hurt seemed not to be great, whereby I judge he is but in little danger. Marry, I saw a splint taken out of a good bigness, and nothing else was done to him upon the field; but I noted him to be very weak and to have the sense of all his limbs almost benumbed: so, being carried away, as he lay along, nothing covered but his face, he moved neither hand nor foot, but lay as one amazed. Whether there were any more splints entered in, as in such cases it happeneth, it was not known. There was marvellous great lamentation made for him and weeping of all sorts, both men and women. Thus your Lordships may see what God sometimes doth to shew what he is and to be known, that amongst all these triumphs, and even in the very midst and pride of the same, suffereth such mischance and heaviness to happen...

Since the writing of this before touching the French King, I do understand that the gates of the house, which is at the Turneyles, whither he was carried, are kept so strict and close as no noblemen's servants are suffered for a great distance to come near; whereupon I do guess that after the hurt was searched and that the French King was dressed, there appeared further matter than I myself was aware of before. Nevertheless, the Duke of Savoy, the Duke of Alva and the Prince of Orange were suffered to enter.

Having stayed this letter till this morning [i.e. July 1st], I understand that the Duke of Savoy, the Cardinal of Lorraine, the Constable and M. de Guise watched all night with the King, who had very evil rest, whereupon there is great lamentation at the Court. But what will follow God knoweth. And thus I beseech

God to preserve your Lordships in much honour and prosperity. From Paris, the first of July, 1559.

Your Good Lordshps humbly to command
N. Throckmorton.

THE BATTLE OF ST. QUENTIN, AUGUST 10TH, 1557

After his failure to capture Metz Charles V was inclined for peace and on February 5th, 1556, there was signed the truce of Vaucelles, which was intended to last for five years: it lasted barely one year. Henry II accepted the truce gladly: the Guises meant to ruin it. They succeeded and war broke out again in the summer of 1557. The French army was commanded by Anne of Montmorencey, the Constable of France. The Imperial troops were under Emmanuel Philibert, Duke of Savoy. The two armies met on August 10th and the French were defeated, the Constable was killed.

Source: Memoirs of Sir James Melville, ed. by A. F. Steuart, Routledge, 1929, pp. 44–7. Melville was in the service of the Constable and took part in the battle. Later he was employed by Mary, Queen of Scots, and he had a famous interview with Queen Elizabeth I (see *T.S.I.H.* vol. 2).

Now the Spanish army was led by Emmanuel, Duke of Savoy, along the frontiers of France, who at last planted his camp about the town of St. Quentin. Whither the Constable sent the Admiral of Chastillon, his sister's son, to defend the same, and lodged his camp at La Fer, five leagues from the town of St. Quentin, which was not sufficiently furnished with men and munition: wherefore he essayed the next day, in vain, to put in it more companies, under the conduct of Monsieur d'Andelot, brother to the said Admiral. After the preparation of two days, he marched forward with his whole army toward St. Quentin, carrying with him eighteen cannons, with some boats that are commonly in camps, to pass the army over rivers and waters. For there was a little loch upon the south-west side of the town, in which the said boats were set. And Monsieur d'Andelot first with 300 entered the town that way; but so soon as it was perceived, the enemy stopped the rest from entering.

But so soon as the Duke of Savoy was coming with his whole army towards us, the Constable, alleging that he had furnished St. Quentin sufficiently, drew homewards towards La Fer in good order, intending to eschew the battle if he could, the other being more powerful than he. His intention was to pass and besiege Calais; but the whole horsemen of the enemy were hard at us, against the time we had travelled four miles; where the Constable stopped a little time. At length he said that these horsemen of the enemy came to stay us till the foot were advanced. Therefore he thought best to pass forward to a narrow post betwixt a wood and a village, there to give them battle if he could not escape them.

In the meantime, Marshal St. André, a great man for that time, gave unhappy advice that all the French servants who were on horseback should retire from among the men-at-arms, lest they should be an impediment to them who were to fight, there being as many servants as there were masters. They were glad to get them out of the press, spurring their horse with speed homewards, intending to stay upon some hill to behold the combat.

The enemy perceiving so great a number of horsemen as they thought flying, in the very instant took occasion to charge upon our light-horsemen. Whereupon the Constable, being in a valley between two hills, marching towards the strait part, where he intended to stay, spurred forward up the little hill that he might see how to resist and put order to the battle; which gave an hard apprehension to others that he was flying. But when he turned on the top of the hill to behold the onset, no man would tarry with him for any command. Though he always cried, 'Return Return', their heads were homewards and their hearts also, as appeared. Then his master of the horse, bringing him a Turkey speedy horse to run away with the rest, he answered in anger, 'that it was against his profession and occupation to fly'; addressing himself fearlessly against the greatest troop of enemies, saying, 'Let all true servants to the King follow me': though only three-score gentlemen accompanied him, who were all overthrown in an instant. The Constable desired to be killed; but the master of the horse cried continually, 'It is the Constable, kill him not'.

But before he was known he was shot through the thigh, and then was taken prisoner.

I being hurt by a stroke upon the head, was again mounted by my servant upon a Scots gelding, which carried me through the enemies, who were all betwixt me and home. Two of them struck at my head with swords, because my headpiece was strucken off in the first encounter. These two were standing betwixt us and home, to catch prisoners in a narrow strait. But my horse ran through them against my will, and through the village, for the field between it and the wood was full of smoke of the culverins. There most of our foot were slain. The leaping over a dyke separated me from the two, and so being past the said village there was room enough to escape. So I came safe to La Fer, where I did meet with Mr. Henry Killigrew an English gentleman, my old friend, who held my horse till I sat down in a barber's booth to be dressed of the hurt in my head. In the meantime a proclamation was made that no man should remain within the town, but the ordinary garrison, because the governor thereof looked for a siege.

DIANE DE POITIERS, DUCHESSE DE VALENTINOIS

Diane de Poitiers was born in 1499 and died in 1566. She was the daughter of Jean de Poitiers, who came of an old family in the Dauphiné. She married Louis de Brézé, grand seneschal of Normandy. After his death in 1533 she became the mistress of the Dauphin, later Henry II. He was ten years younger than she, but his passion for her lasted all his life. When Henry came to the throne, Diane virtually became Queen and the King's wife, Catherine de' Medici, lived in obscurity. Diane set about looking after her own interests and those of her family. The King loaded her with gifts, including the crown jewels and the duchy of Valentinois. When Henry died Catherine de' Medici assumed control over the young king, drove Diane from Court and made her disgorge the crown jewels. Diane retired to her castle at Anet, where she died in 1566.

Source: Brantôme: *Le Livre des Dames.* K. P. Wormeley, Boston, 1909.

I saw Madame la duchesse de Valentinois at the age of seventy [she died at 68], as lovely of face, as fresh and as amiable as at the age of thirty ... I saw her six months before her death, still so beautiful that no heart however strong could remain unmoved, although she had at that time broken her leg in the street at Orléans. She was riding, and managing her horse with as much dexterity and agility as ever, when it slipped and fell under her. You might suppose that her beautiful face would have been changed by the fracture and the pain she suffered. Not at all; her beauty, grace, majesty, her noble mien, remained such they always were. And her complexion was still very white and with no powder or paint.

CATHERINE DE' MEDICI

Catherine de' Medici was born in 1519 and died in 1589. She was the daughter of Lorenzo II de' Medici and her uncle was Pope Clement VII. At the age of 14 she married the Duke of Orleans, later Henry II, by whom she was soon abandoned for Diane de Poitiers. She therefore led a lonely married life. Henry died in 1559 and Catherine found herself the Regent with a large family to look after. Desperately maternal, immensely ambitious, politically unscrupulous, she was also very able and very courageous, but she was a schemer rather than a stateswoman, and she was not really equal to the fearful religious and political problems with which she had to deal. There can be little doubt that she was principally responsible for the Massacre of St. Bartholomew—although Brantôme denies that. Probably it is a fair comment to say that she was a true Medici and that her Italian political instincts were not well suited to solve the French problems with which she was faced.

Source: (a) Pierre de Bourdéille, Abbé de Brantôme, *Le Livre des Dames.* Brantôme was born in 1537 and died in 1614. The following extract is taken from the English translation of his book by K. P. Wormeley, Boston, 1909. Brantôme was a courtier who paid little or no attention to his office as an Abbé. He was a great traveller and soldier, and not being a wise statesman he had rather too golden a view of Catherine de Medici. But he stresses the more personal and attractive side of this much tried woman whom he saw frequently and whom he seems to have known fairly well.

She was of rich and very fine presence; of great majesty, but very gentle when need was; of noble appearance and good grace, her face handsome and agreeable, her bosom very beautiful, white and full; her body also very white, the flesh beautiful, the skin smooth, as I have heard from several of her ladies; of a fine plumpness also, the leg and thigh very beautiful (as I have heard too from the same ladies); and she took great pleasure in being well shod and in having her stockings well and tightly drawn up.

Besides all this, the most beautiful hand that was ever seen, as I believe. Once upon a time, the poets praised Aurora for her fine hands and beautiful fingers; but I think our queen would efface her in that, and she guarded and maintained that beauty all her life. The king, her son, Henry III, inherited much of this beauty of the hand.

She always clothed herself well and superbly, often with some pretty and new invention. In short, she had many charms in herself to make her beloved . . . For the rest she was very good company and of gay humour, loving all honourable exercises, such as dancing, in which she had great grace and majesty.

She also loved hunting; about which I heard a lady of the Court tell this tale: King François, having chosen and made a company which was called 'the little band of the Court ladies', the handsomest, daintiest and most favoured, often escaped from the Court and went to other houses to hunt the stag and pass his time, sometimes staying thus withdrawn eight days, ten days, sometimes more and sometimes less, as the humour took him. Our queen (who was then only Mme. la dauphine) seeing such parties made without her, and that even Mesdames her sisters-in-law were there while she stayed at home, made prayer to the king to take her always with him, and to do her the honour to permit that she should never budge without him. It was said that she, being very shrewd and clever, did this as much or more to see the king's actions and get his secrets and hear and know all things, as from liking for the hunt.

King François was pleased with this request, for it shewed the good will she had for his company; and he granted it heartily; so that besides loving her naturally he now loved her more, and delighted in giving her pleasure in the hunt, at which she never left his side, but followed him at full speed. She was very good on horseback and bold; sitting with ease and being the first to put the leg round a pommel, which was far more graceful and becoming than sitting with the feet upon a plank. Till she was sixty years of age and over she liked to ride on horseback, and after her weakness prevented her she pined for it. It was one of her greatest pleasures to ride far and fast, though she fell many times with damage to her body, breaking her leg once, and wounding her head, which had to be trepanned. After she was widowed and had charge of the king and the kingdom, she took the king always with her, and her other children; but while her husband, King Henry, lived, she usually went with him to the meet of the stag and the other hunts.

If he played at pall-mall she watched him play, and played herself. She was very fond of shooting with a cross-bow à jalet [a ball of stone] and she shot right well, so that always when she went to ride, her cross-bow was taken with her, and if she saw any game, she shot it . . .

She passed her time in the afternoons at work on her silk embroideries, in which she was as perfect as possible. In short, this queen liked and gave herself up to all honourable exercises; and there was not one that was worthy of herself and her sex that she did not wish to know and practise . . .

When she called any one 'my friend' it was either that she thought him a fool, or she was angry with him. This was so well-known that she had a serving gentleman named M. de Bois-Fevrier, who made reply when she called him 'my friend': 'Ha! madame, I would rather you called me your enemy; for to call me your friend is as good as saying I am a fool, or that you are in anger against me; for I know your nature this long time' . . .

She wrote and spoke French very well, although an Italian; and even to persons of her own nation she usually spoke it, so much did she honour France and its language; taking pains to exhibit its fine speech to foreigners, grandees and ambassadors, who came to visit her after seeing the king. She always answered them very pertinently, with great grace and majesty, as I have also seen her do to the courts of parliament, both publicly and privately . . .

Source: (*b*) Claude Groulard, *Memoirs*, quoted in Brantôme, *op. cit.*, p. 88, in some remarks on Catherine de' Medici by Sainte-Beuve, *Causeries du Lundi*. Groulard was told by Henry IV that he was going to marry a princess from Florence, to which he answered that the Florentine house would now repair the wounds given to France by Catherine de' Medici. Henry IV replied:

'But I ask you, I ask you what a poor woman could do, left by the death of her husband, with five little children on her arms, and two families in France who were thinking to grasp the crown —ours and the Guises. Was she not compelled to play strange parts to deceive first one and then the other, in order to guard, as she has done, her sons, who have successively reigned through the wise conduct of that shrewd woman? I am surprised that she never did worse.'

How deeply Catherine de' Medici was wounded by the treatment meted out to her by her husband Henry II may be seen in the two following letters. One may guess what was the psychological effect on her, and probably on her children.

Source: (*c*) *Lettres de Catherine de' Medici*, ed. Count Hector de la Ferrière et G. Bagnerault de Puchesse (1903). Quoted G. F. Young, *The Medici*, ii, 43–4. Catherine to her daughter Elizabeth.

M'Amie, commend yourself very much to God; for you have seen me in former days as contented as you are now, and believing that I should never have any trouble but this one, that I was not loved in the way I wished by the King, your father, who doubt-less honoured me beyond my deserts; but I loved him so much that I was always afraid of offending him, as you know well enough. And now God has taken him from me . . . Therefore think of me, and let me serve as a warning to you not to trust too much in the love of your husband, the King of Spain [Philip II].

Source: (*d*) *Ibid.* G. F. Young, *op. cit.* 44. Catherine to Henry of Navarre, who had married Catherine's daughter, Margaret, to whom he was very unfaithful.

My son, I was never in my life so dumbfounded as when I heard the words which Frontenac has been reporting everywhere as being those which you ordered him to convey to your wife . . . You are not, I know, the first husband who is young and not too wise in such matters, but I believe that you are the first, and the only one, who after such events would venture on such language to his wife. I had the honour of marrying the King, my lord and your sovereign, whose daughter you have married, but the thing which vexed him most in the world was after he found out that I knew about such doings.

Catherine hated the Guises and disapproved of the way in which the Protestants were treated, believing that for political reasons toleration was the only right policy. That she was not an insensitive monster seems to appear from the following extract from a letter: *ibid*. G. F Young, *op. cit.* 79.

When I see these poor people burnt, beaten and tormented, not for thieving or marauding, but simply for upholding their religious opinions, when I see some of them suffer cheerfully, with a glad heart, I am forced to believe that there is something in this which transcendeth human understanding.

Source: (*f*) Catherine's answer to those who blamed the miseries of France wholly on her. *Ibid*. G. F. Young, *op. cit.* 120.

If things were even worse than they are after all this war, they might have laid the blame upon the rule of a woman; but if such persons are honest, they should blame only the rule of men who desire to play the part of kings [the Guises]. In future, if I am not any more hampered, I hope to show that women have a more sincere determination to preserve the country than those who have plunged it into the miserable condition to which it has been brought.

Source: (*g*) The view of a Venetian ambassador, Giovanni Correr, on Catherine's government: Baschet, *La Diplomatie Venitienne*; G. F. Young, *op. cit.* 114.

I do not know what prince would not have made mistakes in such great confusion; how much more a woman, a foreigner, without trusty friends, frightened and never hearing the truth from those about her. For my part, I have often been surprised that she did not become thoroughly confused and give way to one or other of the two parties, which would have been a final calamity for the kingdom. It is she alone who has preserved the remnant of royal majesty still to be found there. For this reason I have always pitied rather than blamed her; and she has often reminded me of it when speaking of her distresses and the woes of France.

Source: (*h*) Giovanni Correr to the Venetian Senate, 1570. Alberi, *Relazioni, degli Amb. Ven.* iv, 202–4. G. F. Young, *op. cit.*

Her Majesty entered on the 51st year of her age on April 12th. Her years, however, though many, are not attended by the signs of feebleness and old age. She has a strong and vigorous constitution, and there is no one in the court who can keep pace with her when walking. She takes a great deal of exercise, which gives her an appetite. She eats well and of all things indifferently . . . She inherits from her ancestors the desire of being remembered by her buildings, libraries, and collections of antiquities . . . As princess she is benevolent, courteous and affable to all, making it her business to see that none leave her dissatisfied, at least as far as words are concerned, of which she is very liberal. Her industry in affairs causes a general wonder and astonishment. No step, however unimportant, is taken without her. Scarcely has she time to eat, drink or sleep, so great are her harassing cares. She runs here and there between the armies, doing a man's work, without a thought of sparing herself. Yet she is beloved by no one in the land—or at least by few. The Huguenots say that she has given them fine words and feigned welcomes, while all the time she has been treating with the Catholic King and scheming their destruction. The Catholics, on the other hand, declare that if she had not exalted and favoured the Huguenots, these latter would not have been able to do what they have. Moreover, this is an age in France when every man presumes. He thinks of something, then passionately asks for it. If his request is refused, he grumbles and throws the blame on the Queen Mother. And

as she is a stranger, though she were to give all, they would only
say that she gave nothing of her own.

All resolutions taken in peace and war which have not given
satisfaction have been attributed to her, as though she governed
absolutely without the advice and counsel of others. I do not
say that the Queen is a Sybil and cannot err, and that she does
not sometimes rely too much on herself; but I do say that I
know of no other prince, whatever his wisdom and experience,
who would not have lost his head with a war on his hands in
which it was difficult to tell friend from foe, and in which, to
provide a remedy, he would have to make use of the aid and
counsel of those around him, all of whom were interested and
part not too faithful. I repeat, I know of no prince, however
prudent, who would not have been lost with so much against
him—not to speak of a woman, a stranger, without confidants,
fearful, and always kept in ignorance of the truth. Indeed, it has
been a marvel to me that she has not been confused and given
herself up altogether to one of the parties, a course of action which
would have ended in the total ruin of that kingdom. She has
thus preserved that royal majesty, small though it is, which one
sees to-day in that court. I have therefore rather pitied than
blamed her, as I told her once when I had the chance. And in
talking over the difficulties which beset her, she confirmed me in
my opinion, and has reminded me of it several times since. I
know, too, she has been seen weeping in her cabinet more than
once. Then, forcing herself, she has dried her eyes and appeared
in public with a smiling countenance. And so those who judged
how things were going from her face were not disturbed. Then
resuming her conduct of affairs, when she has not been able to
have her way, she has compromised here and there. Thus have
been arranged those ill-considered measures which have redounded
little to her honour and set all the world talking.

Source: (i) Pierre de l'Estoile, *Mémoires-Journeaux*, trans. and ed. by
N. L. Roelker, under title of *The Paris of Henry of Navarre*, Harvard
U.P., 1958, pp. 167–8.

Saturday, January 7, the news of the death of the Queen Mother arrived in Paris . . . [she] died in the Château of Blois the preceding Thursday, January 5th. She was 71 years old, and carried it well, for a plain, fat woman. She ate well, but she did not understand matters of state, although she had as great importance in them as any Queen in the world, in the thirty years since her husband died. She died in debt 800,000 crowns, being very extravagant and generous beyond any prince or princes in Christendom, a trait she inherited from her family. She was already sick when the executions of December took place. And when the King her son came to see her, saying, 'Madame, I am now sole King of France, I have no more partner', she replied . . . 'What do you think you have done? God will see you come out right. You have killed two men[1] who leave many friends behind them. But, at least, my son, have you given orders [for control] of the cities, especially Orléans? If you haven't, do it as soon as you can, otherwise it will go badly for you, and don't fail to notify the Papal Legate, Cardinal Gondi.'

After saying this, and after the King . . . had begged her to take care of herself, assuring her that everything would be all right . . . she had herself carried, sick as she was, to M. le Cardinal de Bourbon, who was also sick and a prisoner . . . When he saw her he cried with tears in his eyes, 'Ah, Madame, Madame, these are your acts . . . you will be the death of us all'. She was terribly moved by these words and replied that she wished God would damn her if, on the contrary, she were not terribly upset . . . with such regret in her soul that she would die of it. She left at once, saying, 'I can do no more, I must go to bed', as she did, and never got up again, dying January 5th, the day of Kings, fatal to her house. Alexander de' Medici was killed on that day, and Lorenzo de' Medici, and others in the history of Florence. She was mourned by some of her domestics, and a little by the King, her son, who still had some dealings with her.

Those closest to her were of the opinion that her displeasure at what the King had done shortened her days, not for friendship to the fallen princes (whom she loved à la Florentine, that is, to use them), but because [by the] act she saw her son-in-law, the King

of Navarre, established which is what she least wanted in the
world, having sworn his ruin by all means.

All the same, the people of Paris thought that she had consented
to the death of the two Lorraine princes. And the Sixteen[2] said
that if her body were brought to Paris, to be buried in the magnificent sepulchre she had had built for her late husband and herself
in St. Denis, they would . . . throw it in the river. So much for
the feeling of Paris. As for Blois, where she had been revered
and adored as the Juno of the Court, she had no sooner rendered
her last breath than they took no more notice of her than if she
had been a dead doe . . .

THE ADMIRAL COLIGNY AND PRINCE DE CONDÉ

Gaspard de Chatillon, Comte Coligny, Admiral of France and
leader of the Huguenots, the French Protestants, was born in 1519 and
was murdered at the Massacre of St. Bartholomew, in 1572. One of
his daughters married William the Silent.

Louis de Bourbon, Prince de Condé (1530–69), was the first of the
famous house of Condé. He was a brilliant soldier, a deformed but
splendidly gay human being, very badly off financially, and he became
a staunch Huguenot. He was taken prisoner at the battle of Jarnac and
was treacherously shot down by a Catholic officer, named Montesquiou,
through the head. As Coligny's nephew he was of the highest importance in the Huguenot party. The following extract gives a contemporary's views of both the Admiral and the Prince.

Source: The Papal Nuncio, Santa Croce, printed in Martène and
Durand, *Veterum Scriptorum Collectio*, v. 1478.

Yet the pursuits and talents of each are different. The Admiral
excels in counsel, the Prince in action. The strength of the latter
lies in a certain impetuosity of mind, that of the former in a steady
constancy. The one is shrewd, the other still shrewder. Just as
the Prince has a more pleasing character, the Admiral has one
more austere. The Prince, too, is a lover of racing, jumping,
exhibitions of wrestling, hunting, public shows of every kind,
every kind of armed contest, horses, sports, jests, the dancing of
girls, and the singing of women. But with the Admiral there
always seems to be a certain seriousness of thought and action.

Then again, the Prince is a most graceful speaker, while the eloquence of the Admiral is of a graver kind, since he has become familiar with the Latin tongue and devotes himself earnestly to theological pursuits. The latter, also, is zealous in state affairs and swift to punish wrongs, the former being more easy-going. And while the Admiral consults as to what must needs be done, the Prince does it. Then, too, the former gives audience to ambassadors, busies himself with supplies and finance, decides points of law, fortifies positions, draws up the line of battle, pitches the camp, reviews the army, chooses the place and time of battle, and superintends religious affairs. The Prince, on the other hand, asks for dangers and the fight; and while he is small and elegant of figure, the former uses a toothpick and has it in his mouth day and night. Yet both, by their graciousness and generosity are a power with all.

GASPARD DE COLIGNY

Source: In 1575, three years after Coligny's death, there appeared a small book of 130 pages, *Gasparis Colonii Castellonii, Magni Quondam Franciae Admiralii, Vita.* The author was almost certainly a distinguished lawyer named Hotman. He knew Coligny well. The following description is taken from that book.

As soon as he had risen from bed, which was always at an early hour, he put on his gown and, falling on his knees, made prayer and invocation to God on behalf of the whole company. And when the rest had kneeled down after his example, prayer was made in the manner usual in churches in France. When it was ended, he employed the whole time before the sermon in hearing the delegates of the churches which were sent to him, or in despatching other public business. The sermon was delivered on alternate days at a given sign and was accompanied by the singing of a psalm. Business was then resumed until dinner-time. When it was ready, all the servants, except a few who were preparing the food, assembled in the hall where the table was laid. And if there had been no sermon, a psalm was sung and the accustomed blessing was said, the Admiral standing at the board with his wife by his side. This was his constant practice, not only in his

Y

own house and when at ease, but in the camp, as innumerable Frenchmen and many German knights and captains who were often invited to dine with him can testify.

On the removal of the cloth, rising and standing with his wife and the rest of the company, he either returned thanks or called on his minister to do so. At supper-time the same order of prayer and singing of psalms was followed. And in addition, since he perceived that it would be somewhat difficult for all his servants to attend nightly prayers at bedtime, for the hour was uncertain owing to their various duties, he gave order that they should all be with him immediately after supper, when after singing a hymn prayer was made. It cannot be told how many of the French nobility began to establish this religious order in their families after his example, the more so as he used often to admonish them that, for the cultivation of true piety, it was not enough for the father of a family to be present at services and order his own private ways as piety and religion demand, unless by his example he brought his household and domestics to the same rule of life as well. And it is agreed that such was the admiration entertained for his piety and holy life, even by those of the Catholic party, that, but for the dread of tortures and massacres which followed, a far greater number of the French would have been converted to the same religion and discipline.

When the time of the Lord's Supper was at hand, he was wont to call his domestics and members of his household about him and make known unto them that he had to render an account unto God, not only of his own mode of life but of theirs. If any discord had fallen among them, they were reconciled. If any man seemed insufficiently prepared for the understanding and veneration of that great mystery, he caused him to be more diligently instructed in religion. If any seemed more stubborn, he told them openly that he would rather be alone in his house than keep a following of the wicked . . .

The Admiral lived three and fifty years, six months and eight days. He was of a middle stature, of a ruddy complexion, with regular and well-proportioned limbs. He had a calm and unclouded countenance, a soft and winning voice, though his utterance was somewhat hesitating and slow. His health was fairly good. He was graceful in gesture and bearing, especially when at home, dressed in his gown, and walking with his wife and friends. He was sparing of wine, ate and slept moderately, his rest covering at the most seven hours. Since the time of the last pacification, he let no day slip by without entering with his own hand in his diary, before going to rest, such things as had happened and were worthy of notice in the last civil wars. These memoranda, having been found after his death, were taken to the King's Council, and his calm and tranquil mind gained him the admiration even of those who hated him most.[4]

THE ATTEMPT TO MURDER COLIGNY, FRIDAY, 22ND AUGUST, 1572

In August 1572 Paris was full of young Huguenot nobles who had come to see the marriage of their leader, Henry of Navarre, to the French Princess, Margaret of Valois. On the 22nd, four days after the wedding, somebody fired a shot at Coligny as he was on his way to the house he was occupying, now the site of 144, Rue de Rivoli. One bullet smashed his right forefinger and either the same bullet or another one passed through his left wrist and came out at the elbow. Coligny was carried home and the great French doctor, Ambroise de Paré, was sent for. The following eye-witness account was written probably by a man named Cornaton. (For de Paré see p. 458.)

Source: *The Lyfe of Jasper Colighie Shatilion* (trans. 1576). Spelling modernized.

He that was witness of the thing ensuing did both see them and also held up the Admiral's arm as he lay upon his bed. The said Ambroise began his cure at the bruised finger, and did cut it off not without putting his patient to great pain. For inasmuch as his pincers were not sharp enough, he was fain to open them thrice and thrice to grip them together again. Afterwards he lanced both the sides of his left arm where the pellets had pierced through; the pain whereof the Admiral abode, not only with a stout courage, but also with a steadfast countenance. Yea, and whereas they that held up his arms and beheld this lancing were not able to forbear weeping, the Admiral, perceiving them to be dismayed, said unto them, 'Why weep ye, my friends? I think myself blessed in suffering these wounds for God's name sake.' And therewithal looking upon Merlin, a minister of God's word, 'my friends', quoth he, 'these are God's benefits. Indeed, I am full of pain, but I acknowledge this to be the will of our Lord God, and I thank His Majesty that he hath vouchsafed me so great an honour as to lay some cross upon me for His most holy name's sake. Therefore let us pray Him to grant me the gift of perseverance.' Then beholding Merlin mourning and lamenting, 'my Merlin' quoth he, 'why dost thou not rather comfort me?' 'Ye say truth, sir', answered Merlin, 'neither is there any greater or surer comfort for you than to think continually that God doth you great honour in deeming you worthy to suffer these griefs for His name and religious sake'. 'My Merlin', replied the Admiral, 'if God should handle me according to my deserts and worthiness, and deal with me according to His justice, I should have far other manner of griefs to endure. But blessed be His name for using His mercy and clemency towards me His most unworthy servant' . . .

THE MASSACRE OF ST. BARTHOLOMEW, 1572

In the summer of 1572 Catherine de Medici, the Queen Mother in France, saw with fury that the Huguenot leader, Coligny, was the trusted adviser of the young King, Charles IX, and that she was excluded from the Council. She saw also that France was heading for a war with Spain. She therefore made common cause with the Guises and determined to get rid of Coligny. Paris was full of Huguenot families who had come there for the wedding of Henry of Navarre, himself a Protestant. On August 22nd, as he was coming back to his lodging, Coligny was fired at by a hired assassin and was wounded, but not killed. Catherine saw that the inevitable inquiry into the attack would reveal the part she had played in arranging it. She decided that the only safe thing was to exterminate all the Huguenots in Paris. She persuaded her weakling son to agree. In the early hours of August 24th, 1572, there took place the Massacre of St. Bartholomew. The number of victims in Paris and the provinces was probably about 8,000.

Source: (a) The account written by the young Princess Margaret, who had just married Henry of Navarre. The English version is to be found in J. M. Thompson's *Lectures on Foreign History*, 1494–1789, p. 132. Blackwell, 1930. Doubts have been cast on this account.

For my part I was told nothing about all this. But I saw everybody agitated—the Huguenots in despair because of the attempt on Coligny, the Guises fearing they would have justice done, and all on the alert. The Huguenots suspected me as a Catholic, and the Catholics as the wife of Henry of Navarre, who was a Huguenot. One evening, at my mother the Queen's evening reception, I was sitting on a chest near my sister of Lorraine, who was looking very depressed. The Queen, who was talking to some people, saw me and told me to go to bed. When I had made my curtsey, my sister took me by the arm and said, 'For God's sake, sister, don't go'. This terrified me. The Queen noticed what had happened and called my sister and abused her, and told her she was not to say anything to me. My sister told her it was not right to send me off to sacrifice myself like that, they would certainly avenge themselves on me. The Queen answered, 'Please God, I should come to no harm: but that in any case I must go, for fear of rousing any suspicion that would spoil the plan'. I could see they were disputing, though I did not understand what they said. At last my mother told me again, roughly, to go to bed. My sister, in tears, said goodnight to me, but dared not add another word. For my part, I seemed to see everything changed and lost, without being able to imagine what there was to fear. Directly I reached my room, I prayed God to take me under His protection and to keep me safe, without knowing from what or from whom. Just then, my husband, the King, who had already gone to bed, sent for me to come to bed too. So I did, and found his bed surrounded by thirty or forty Huguenots whom I didn't yet know, having been married only a few days. All night they did nothing but talk of the attempt which had been made on the Admiral's life: they resolved that, as soon as it was day, they would ask justice from the King against M. de Guise, and that if he refused it, they would execute it themselves. For my part, I couldn't forget my sister's tears, and couldn't sleep for fear of the warning she had given me, though I didn't know what it meant.

So the night passed, without a wink of sleep. At day-break the King said he was going to play tennis till King Charles was awake, when he would at once demand justice of him. He left my room, and all his gentlemen with him. Seeing that it was daylight, and thinking that the danger of which my sister had spoken was now past, and overcome with sleep, I told my nurse to shut the door, so that I could sleep quietly. An hour later, when I was fast asleep, there came a man beating on the door with his hands and feet, crying 'Navarre! Navarre'! My nurse, thinking it was my husband the King, ran quickly to the door and opened it. It was a gentleman named M. de Léran, with a sword wound on his elbow and another from a halberd on his arm; and he was still being pursued by four archers, who all came after him into my room. To save his life, he threw himself on my bed. Feeling him clutching me, I dragged myself into the space behind the bed, and him after me, holding me all the time in front of his body. I didn't know the man at all, and had no idea whether he had come to insult me, or whether the archers were attacking him or me. We both shrieked, and each was as frightened as the other. At last, thank God, M. de Nançay, the captain of the Guard, came up, and finding me in such a position, though he was sorry enough, could not help laughing. He abused the archers for their indiscretion and got rid of them, and granted me the life of the poor man who was holding on to me. So I put him to bed and nursed his wounds in my room, till he was completely recovered. I changed my nightgown, too, because the man had covered it with his blood: and M. de Nançay told me what had happened, and assured me that my husband was in the King's room and would come to no harm. So I threw on a dressing-gown and he took me to my sister's room, where I arrived more dead than alive; for just as I reached the lobby, all the doors of which were open, a gentleman called Bourse, trying to escape from some archers who were pursuing him, was run through by a halberd-stroke three paces from me; I fell the opposite way, half fainting, into the arms of M. de Nançay, and thought that the blow had pierced us both. When I felt a little better, I went to my sister's bedroom. Whilst I was there, M. de

Mioflans, my husband's first gentleman, and Armagnac, his first footman, came to look for me, to beg me to save their lives. I went and threw myself on my knees before the King, and my mother the Queen, to ask this favour, which at last they granted.

THE MASSACRE OF ST. BARTHOLOMEW: ESCAPE OF YOUNG SULLY

Source: (*b*) There were comparatively few escapes by the Huguenots, but some got away. The young du Plessis-Mornay, destined in later life to become a distinguished financier under Henri IV and a very fine character, was lodging in the Rue Saint-Jacques at the Sign of the Golden Compass. He had heard rumours of trouble and had vainly warned Coligny's household. On the Saturday morning he had sent his mother out of Paris. In the very early hours of Sunday morning he sent his servant out to pick up what news he could. When the servant returned with news of what was happening, du Plessis-Mornay hid between the ceiling and the roof. On Monday, hearing that a search was being made, he put on a workman's suit of clothes and escaped by the skin of his teeth. The following reminiscence describes how the thirteen-year-old Duke de Sully—later to be Henri IV's great minister—saved his own life. On the Sunday morning the tocsin woke him, his tutor and his valet: these two went out to see what was happening. Sully never saw either of them again. His landlord, a Huguenot, went to Mass and tried to take Sully with him. Sully refused. *Memoirs of Maximilian de Bethune, Duke of Sully*. London, 1778, vol. i, pp. 33 *et sqq.*

I made up my mind to try to reach the *Collége de Bourgogne*, where I was a student, although it was far from my lodgings. The distance made it dangerous. I put on my student's gown and, taking a large breviary under my arm, went downstairs. As I walked out into the street I was horrified; there were madmen running to and fro, smashing down doors and shouting, 'Kill, kill, massacre the Huguenots'. Blood spattered before my eyes and doubled my fear. I ran into a clump of soldiers, who stopped me. They plied me with questions and began to jostle me about when luckily they saw my breviary. That served as my safe conduct. Twice again the same thing happened and twice again I escaped. At last I reached the *Collége de Bourgogne*, but there a greater danger awaited me. The porter refused to let me in, and

I remained out in the street at the mercy of the madmen, who kept increasing in numbers. I bethought myself of asking for the Principal of the college, a good man who was very friendly to me, and by the aid of a little money I got in. The Principal took me to his room, where two inhuman priests talked of Sicilian Vespers and tried to get me out of his hands, saying that the order was to kill every one down to babies at the breast. The Principal locked me up in an out-of-the-way closet, where I stayed for three days.

CATHERINE DE' MEDICI'S EXPLANATION FOR THE MASSACRE

Source: Letter from Catherine de' Medici to the French Ambassador in Venice. October 1st, 1572. G. F. Young, *op. cit.*

I have seen what you wrote to me of the opinion of certain persons that what has happened to Admiral Coligny and his followers was instigated by me and my son the Duc d'Anjou, and of what they have said to you of the harm it has done my son in the eyes of the Protestant princes who all desired to elect him Emperor of Germany. I therefore think it meet to inform you that I have neither done, counselled nor permitted aught but what honour, duty and the love I bear my children commanded me, because the Admiral, since the death of my lord the late King Henri, has shewn by his deeds and bearing that he desired the overthrow of this kingdom and the usurpation of the crown of my son the King, to whom, as you know, it lawfully belongs, and because he, instead of avowing himself a subject, did so establish and make himself great within this kingdom that his powers and commandments over those of his faith were equal to the King's, and so far that, being a rebel against his King, he took by force, in the presence of the King and his brother, towns which were held against him and did not hesitate to fight several battles, by which he was the cause of the death of very many people.

Furthermore, since the late peace and edict of pacification he has so grievously conspired against the persons of the King and his brother and my own person, as will soon be proved to the satisfaction of foreign princes and all others at the trial which has now commenced and will soon be decided in the Court of the Parlement of Paris, that I am certain it will be said that my son the King has only acted within his rights as a sovereign prince, and that the Admiral, strong and powerful as he was in this realm, could not otherwise be punished for his rebellion and disobedience but in the manner after which he and his party have been treated. The King is greatly troubled that in the heat of the moment certain others of the religion were slain by the Catholics, who called to mind infinite evils, robberies and other wicked acts committed upon them during the troubles; but now at last all is peaceful, so that there is recognized only one King, and one justice rendered to all alike according to duty and equity, since the King is resolved, in view of the evils caused by the diversity of religions, to suffer none but his own.

THE NEWS OF THE MASSACRE OF ST. BARTHOLOMEW REACHES POPE GREGORY XIII

Source: The Report of the Cardinal of Como. Quoted in Reddaway, *Select Documents 1453–1714*, p. 94.

Although it was still night, I immediately sent to his Holiness to free him from the tension, and so that he might rise to the wonderful grace which God had granted to Christendom under his pontificate. On that morning there was a Consistory Court... and as his Holiness had such a good piece of news to announce to the Holy College, he had the despatches read out to them. His Holiness then spoke about their contents and concluded that in these times, so troubled by revolutions, nothing better or more magnificent could have been wished for; and that, as it appeared, God was beginning to turn the eye of His mercy on us. His Holiness and the College were extremely contented and joyful at the reading of this news...

On the same morning... his Holiness with the whole College of Cardinals went to the church of St. Mark to have the *Te Deum* sung and to thank God for granting so great a favour to the Christian people. His Holiness does not cease to pray God, and

to make others pray, to inspire the Most Christian King to follow
further the path which he has opened and to cleanse and purge
completely the Kingdom of France from the plague of the
Huguenots. Also, this morning, His Holiness went in procession
to the church of St. Louis, where a solemn Mass was held with
the same intention, and next week he will proclaim a solemn
jubilee . . .

But we are still hoping that the fire will spread of its own
accord to all places, as we have already received several intimations
of what has happened in Lyons and Rouen.

HENRY III AND LES MIGNONS

The French word *mignon* means daintily small. Henry III was an
effeminate creature and a degenerate, wholly unfitted to rule. The
third son of Henry II and Catherine de' Medici, he was born in 1551
and was assassinated in 1589. He was Catherine's favourite son and
had helped her to organize the Massacre of St. Bartholomew. In 1573
he was elected King of Poland, but in 1574 his brother Charles IX died
and Henry hurried back to France to secure the throne. He had
married Louise de Vaudemont, of the House of Lorraine, a beautiful,
intelligent and healthy girl. Unfortunately there were no children.
Devoted to clothes, pet dogs, monkeys, parrots, Henry was the least
suitable man as King to cope with civil wars which were rending
France, when he came to the throne.
Source: (a) Sully, *Memoirs, op. cit.*

I shall never forget the fantastic and extravagant equipage and
attitude in which I found this prince in his cabinet: he had a sword
at his side, a Spanish hood hung down upon his shoulders, a little
cap, such as collegians wear, upon his head, and a basket full of
little dogs hung to a broad ribband about his neck.

In 1576 there appeared in Paris a body of youths who were the
favourites of Henry III, ridiculously dressed, ill-disciplined, rowdy,
sentimentally loyal to the King, quarrelsome and 'quick on the draw'.
The principal names were Maugiron, Caylus, Saint-Mégrim, D'O,
Saint-Luc, Livarrot, Mauléon, D'Arques, La Valette. Their quarrel
was always with the followers of the Guises. Only D'Arques rose to

some sort of importance as Duke of Joyeuse. The following extracts illustrate the behaviour of the King and his Mignons.

Source: (b) Pierre de l'Estoile, *Mémoires-Journeaux*, trans. and ed. by N. L. Roelker, under title of *The Paris of Henry of Navarre*, Harvard U.P., 1958, pp. 52 *et sqq*. These memoirs are a mine of information by an eye-witness of the events, who was interested in noting not only political news, but also such details as the prices in Paris at various dates and the weather each month. de l'Estoile was at heart a Royalist, but he was also strongly suspect as a *ligueur*, a supporter of the League. Roelker's introduction to his Memoirs gives a most interesting biography of this valuable diarist.

July 1576. There is beginning to be a lot of conversation about the *mignons*, who are much hated and scorned by the people, as much for their haughty manners as for their effiminate and immodest appearance, but most of all for the excessive liberalities of the King toward them. Popular opinion holds that this is the cause of [people's] ruin . . . These *mignons* wear their hair long, curled and recurled artificially, on top of [which they wear] little velvet bonnets like those of girls in the brothels; their shirts are long and loose, so that their heads look like St. John's on the platter . . . Their occupations are gambling, blaspheming, jumping, dancing, quarrelling, fornicating, and following the King around. They do everything to please him, giving no thought to honour or to God, contenting themselves with the grace of their master . . .

February, 1578. The young seigneur Quélus, accompanied by other beloved *mignons* of the King, drew his sword and charged Bussy d'Amboise, chief *mignon* of Monsieur,[5] near the gate of St. Honoré . . . Monsieur was much offended by this action . . . and threatened to leave the court of the King. It was with great difficulty that his mother changed his mind temporarily . . . Monsieur was determined to depart and commanded his men to have his carriage ready to leave for Angers. His mother and the King, fearful of what might follow, assured themselves that he was in his room . . . and seized La Chastre, Rochepôt, and Cimier, followers of the Duke. They were locked up in the Bastille. Things looked very bad until Monsieur de Lorraine reconciled the King and his brother the next day. They swore to be friends and brothers. Bussy and other favourites of the Duke likewise swore to Quélus, Saint-Luc, and other *mignons* of the King, dissimulating their feelings and putting on a good show . . .

April 27th, 1578. To finish off a quarrel begun the day before, Quélus, one of the great favourites of the King, and young Entragues, favourite of the Guises . . . met at five in the morning . . . near the Bastille, [with their friends] and there fought so furiously that young Maugiron and Chomberg were left for dead. Riberac died the next day from his wounds . . . Quélus, who received nineteen blows, lingered thirty-three days and finally died on May 29 . . . The great favour of the King did him little good, though His Majesty sat all day by his bed and promised 100,000 francs to the surgeons, if they could pull him through, not to mention another 100,000 to the fine favourite to give him the will to live. In spite of all this he passed from this world, saying with his last breath . . . 'Oh, my King, my King', with no word for God or His Mother . . . The King held his head in his arms, after he was dead, and removed the earrings he had given him with his own hand, as he had formerly put them on.

These and similar ways of behaving (unworthy of a great and magnanimous king) were the cause of the gradual contempt for this prince, and the increased hatred of his favourites, which gave a great advantage to the House of Lorraine . . . and built up their party, that is, the League.

July 21st, 1578. Young St. Mésgrin, rich, handsome, one of the frizzed *mignons* of the King, was attacked by thirty unknown men as he was leaving the Louvre about eleven at night. They left him on the street for dead, but miraculously he lived till the next day, suffering from thirty-four or thirty-five wounds, each one bad enough to be fatal. The King had him buried in the same place . . . and with the same pomp as the late Quélus, his former companion in favouritism.

February 4, 1579. The King . . . attended the fair at St. Germain . . . and had various students arrested for parading at the fair wearing long shirts and big collars made of white paper in mocking imitation of the King and his *mignons*, and shouting insolently, 'By their costumes one recognizes the beasts . . .'

Sunday, March 5th, 1581, the King, after a long fast at St. Germain-en-Laye . . . returned to Paris . . . went with his *mignons* D'Arques and La Valette[6] and various young ladies of his private acquaintance, all masked, and rioted through the city to all the houses where he would find good company.

September 7, 1581 . . . Seigneur D'Arques, first *mignon* of the King, came to the Parlement . . . where the letters were published which raised his *vicomté* of Joyeuse to the rank of a duchy and peerage.

June 19, 1582. The Duke of Joyeuse was received at the Parlement to take the oath as Admiral of France, which office was sold by the Duke of Mayenne at the King's request, for 120,000 crowns, which the King paid for his *mignon* and brother-in-law.

February, 1583. On the day of *Mardi gras* the King and his mignons went about the streets masked, going from house to house and committing a thousand insolences, up to six in the morning of Ash Wednesday. On that day most of the preachers of Paris openly blamed him for this in their sermons. This annoyed the King very much, especially the reproaches of Rose,[7] doctor of theology, whom he sent for. Rose tried to avoid going . . . but he finally appeared and received a light reprimand from the King . . . [who] not only pardoned him, but several days later sent him 400 crowns 'to buy sugar and honey, to help pass Lent and to sweeten your bitter words'.

February, 1584. On the day before Lent the King and the Duke went together through the streets of Paris, followed by all their favourites and *mignons*, mounted and masked, disguised as merchants, priests, lawyers, etc., tearing about with loose rein, knocking down people, or beating them with sticks, especially others who were masked. This was because on this day [*Mardi gras*] the King wished it to be a royal privilege to go about masked. They went to the fair in St. Germain and committed infinite insolences, rioting and disturbing the good people who were there until six o'clock in the morning.

February, 1587. In the days before Lent the King held masquerades, feasts, and ballets with ladies participating, in his accustomed manner, and enjoyed himself very much . . . continuing his devotions (which many call hypocrisy), he shut himself up with the Capuchins on the first day of Lent, doing or pretending to do penance with his *mignons*.

THE LORRAINE-GUISE FAMILY

It is easy to confuse the various members and generations of the Guise family. The first head of the family was Claude, Duke of Guise, who married Antoinette of Vendôme. They had a large family of whom the youngest daughter married James V of Scotland. Her three brothers play a part in French history in the sixteenth century: (1) Charles, Cardinal of Lorraine, died 1574; (2) Francis, Duke of Guise, Le Balafré, died 1563; (3) Louis, Cardinal of Guise, died 1578. Francis Le Balafré, had three sons: (1) Henry, Duke of Guise, also called Le Balafré, murdered by Henry III in 1588; (2) Charles, Duke of Mayenne, died, 1611; (3) Louis, Cardinal of Guise, murdered by Henry III, 1588. Their sister was Catherine, who became Madame de Montpensier.

LOUIS, CARDINAL OF GUISE
Source: Pierre de l'Estoile, *op. cit.*, p. 64.

Sunday, March 29, 1578, the [old] Cardinal of Guise died, last of the six original brothers in his generation . . . this good prelate was called the Cardinal of Bottles, because he loved them well, and concerned himself exclusively with affairs of the kitchen, which he understood very well, much better than those of state and religion.

CHARLES, CARDINAL OF LORRAINE, 1525–74
Archbishop of Rheims, 1538: Cardinal of Guise, 1547: Cardinal of Lorraine, 1550. He was much the ablest of his family.
Source: (a) Soranzo, a Venetian. Alberi, *Relazioni degli Amb. Ven.* ii, 433.

He is not well-beloved, he is insincere, and has a nature both artful and avaricious, equally in his own affairs as in those of the King.

Source: (*b*) Pierre de l'Estoile, *Mémoires-Journaux*, trans. and ed. by N. L. Roelker under title of *The Paris of Henry of Navarre*, Harvard U.P., 1958, p. 39.

Sunday, the 26th of December, 1574, at five o'clock in the morning Charles, Cardinal of Lorraine, aged 50, died of a fever and headache, which he contracted by marching in the procession with bare head and feet . . . [this is] the poison that is now being mentioned.

The day of his death and in the night following there was a great and terrible wind . . . in most of France, whose like had never been seen. The Catholic Lorrainers said it was a sign of God's wrath, and that He had removed such a great and wise prelate. The Huguenots, on the contrary, said it was the devil's sabbath, the demons being assembled to receive him . . .

To speak without partiality, the Cardinal of Lorraine was a prelate of parts, with as many graces and abilities as France has ever seen. As to whether he used them well or abused them, the judgement is up to Him before whose throne we must all appear . . .

FRANCIS, DUKE OF GUISE, LE BALAFRÉ

Francis of Lorraine was born in 1519 and he was murdered in 1563. He was the elder son of Claude of Lorraine, the first Duke of Guise. Francois was nearly killed at the siege of Boulogne in 1545 by a wound which gave him the name of Le Balafré. He married in 1548 Anne d'Este, daughter of Ercole II, Duke of Ferrara, grand-daughter of Louis XII of France. He was a very great and successful soldier: as a statesman he made many mistakes and showed much cruelty, perhaps at the instigation of his brother the Cardinal of Lorraine. These two waged a bitter war with Catherine de' Medici for political power and he must accept his share of responsibility for the wars of religion which ravaged France. He was shot by the Huguenot Jean Poltrot and died a few days later from the wound, 1563.

Source: (*a*) Dr. Ambroise Paré, who was with the French army at Boulogne, 1545. Sedgwick, *The House of Guise*, London, 1938, p. 44.

Monseigneur, the Duc de Guise,[8] Francois de Lorraine, was wounded before Boulogne by the thrust of a lance, which entered above his right eye, drove downwards towards the nose and issued out on the other side between neck and ear, with such violence that the iron tip of the lance, with a bit of the wooden shaft, was broken off and remained in the wound, so that it could not be pulled out except by main force, even with a blacksmith's pincers. Nevertheless, notwithstanding the great wrench, accompanied by fracture of bones, nerves, veins, arteries and smashing and breaking other parts, the Duke by God's grace was cured. The Duke always went into battle with his visor up, and that is why the lance went clear through.

The man who pulled out the lance was a Dr. Regnier, a surgeon from Vendôme. A third surgeon, Nicolle Lavernan, told Brantôme that it had been necessary to put his foot on Francois's head in order to pull out the shaft by main force. It was from the scar that the name of Le Balafré arose.

Source: (*b*) The great achievement of Guise's life was his defence of Metz against Charles V, 1552. His military success was remarkable: not less remarkable was the humanity he showed: Alvarotto, the Ferraran ambassador in France, January 11th, 1553. Cp. p. 460.

The Duke of Guise thereupon had all the sick brought within and placed in a hospital and nourished; while, as to the rest, he had broths and soups given them, and had them cared for till death. He has thus won for himself the reputation of being brave, wise, circumspect, careful, diligent and pious.

THE CIVIL WARS

The first three civil wars of religion covered the years 1562 to 1570. The fourth war lasted from 1572 to 1573, in which Henry, Duke of Anjou, brother of Charles IX, commanded an army at the siege of La Rochelle. The offer of the Polish throne to Henry brought about a truce by which the Huguenots gained considerably. Charles IX died in 1574 and Henry succeeded him as Henry III. The fifth civil war ended in 1576 with the *Peace of Monsieur*. Henry made great concessions to the Huguenots and this treaty foreshadowed the Edict of Nantes. There was now set in motion the Holy League, with the ostensible purpose of defending the Catholic religion, but in reality its main purpose was to secure the succession to the throne to the House of Guise. The *Monsieur* who is frequently mentioned in de l'Estoile's memoirs is the Duke of Alençon, Henry III's younger brother and heir apparent until he died, 1584. It was he whom, it was thought, Elizabeth I of England was going to marry. On his death the Huguenot, Henry of Navarre, became the heir apparent to the French throne. The Duke of Guise now used the League against Navarre and Henry III. 1585 to 1586 saw the making of the Paris League in the Corporations and the Sixteen Quarters, the leaders of which were known as the Sixteen. In 1586 there was a temporary truce between Henry III and Guise. In 1587 Henry and Guise won a joint victory over the German Protestants at Auneau in Lorraine, but because all the credit was given by the *prédicateurs*, the Paris preachers, to Guise, the hatred between the two grew. At this point Madame de Montpensier, sister of the Duke of Guise, organized the propaganda in Paris. From 1588 to 1594 the Paris League carried on its rebellion against Henry III, who forbade Guise to enter Paris. Guise came to Paris: May 12th, the *Day of Barricades*, Henry III fled, Guise became 'King of Paris'. In December, Henry III had Guise and the Cardinal of Guise assassinated: the Duke of Mayenne succeeded Guise as leader of the League. April, 1589, Henry III acknowledged Henry of Navarre as his successor to the throne and joined forces with him. August 1st, Henry III was assassinated. Henry of Navarre was acknowledged King as Henry IV by the royal armies.

HENRY OF ANJOU LEAVES POLAND FOR FRANCE

Source: Pierre de l'Estoile, *op. cit.*, p. 34.

Meanwhile the King had secretly fled the kingdom of Poland about the middle of June [1574] with eight or nine companions, to the great annoyance of the Senate and lords of that country . . . He arrived at the Austrian border about the 25th of June. He was magnificently received by the Emperor in Vienna, and was accompanied through all the imperial lands by the Emperor's two sons . . . When he arrived in Venetian territory, he was greeted by ambassadors from the Seignory, which assumed all his expenses during his visit . . . On the 18th of July he arrived

z

in the city itself, and was given the richest apparel and most elaborate welcome that even that city had ever seen . . . [He took the route] of the princes and, on August 11th, arrived at Turin where he was greeted with great joy and in high style by his aunt, the Duchess of Savoy.

HENRY III ARRIVES IN PARIS

Source: Pierre de l'Estoile, *op. cit.,* p. 35.

Tuesday, September 14th, [1574], the Court of the Parlement de Paris, the Chambre des Comptes . . . the Corporation of the city, and all the other companies, went to Nôtre Dame for a solemn High Mass and *Te Deum* as a sign of rejoicing to celebrate the King's return to his kingdom. After dinner there were fireworks set off in front of the Hotel de Ville, cannonades, trumpets, drums, magnificent inscriptions, and other signs of celebration. The bell of the clock in Paris pealed all day, and the night was turned to day by the fireworks.

CORONATION OF THE KING

Source: Pierre de l'Estoile, *op. cit.,* p. 40.

Friday, February 11, [1515], the King arrived at Rheims, where he was crowned on Sunday, the 13th of the month . . . When the crown was placed on his head, he said aloud that it hurt him, and it started to fall off twice, which was remarked as a bad omen.

ESCAPE OF MONSIEUR, THE KING'S BROTHER

Source: Pierre de l'Estoile, *op. cit.,* p. 44.

Thursday, the 15th of September, [1575] François de France, Duke d'Alençon, sole brother of the King, who had been held virtually a prisoner . . . left Paris in a coach at six in the evening . . . being joined by forty or fifty of his followers, armed and mounted . . . The King, all his court, and the people of Paris were much disturbed by this escape.

THE PEACE OF MONSIEUR, 1576

The chief terms were: (1) Henry III expressed regret for the Massacre of St. Bartholomew and promised compensation, as far as possible, to the victims. (2) The Reformed Religion might be practised anywhere except in Paris or where the Court was residing. (3) The Huguenots were given eight fortified towns. (4) All the Parlements in France were to have a new chamber added to deal with religious cases, to be made up of half Protestants and half Catholics. This Edict became the basis for the Edict of Nantes, 1599. The Huguenots by this Treaty obtained enormous advantages. Therefore the Treaty was very unpopular in Paris.

Source: Pierre de l'Estoile, *op. cit.*, p. 50.

Tuesday, May 8th, the terms of the peace were published . . . the King wished to go to Nôtre Dame and have a *Te Deum* sung . . . but the clergy and the people would have none of it, out of annoyance at the concessions made to the Huguenots by this Edict. Nevertheless the next day a solemn *Te Deum* was sung by the royal choir, in the absence of the canons and the choir of the city, who refused even to attend . . . The King attended . . . with the Parlement, and had fireworks set off in celebration in front of the Hôtel de Ville, but with a notable lack of attendance by the people, who were very angry at this so-called peace . . .

THE FORMING OF THE LEAGUE, 1576

Source: Pierre de l'Estoile, *op. cit.*, p. 53

Thursday, August 2, Their Majesties, notified of a secret League and conspiracy among various towns and seigneurs of the realm to prevent the execution of the Edict, even by force of arms, made the Duke of Guise, the Duke of Mayenne his brother, and the Duke of Nemours their father-in-law, sign and swear to support and carry out the Edict. The King did this because he had reason to believe that these three seigneurs were the chiefs of the League, which was nothing other than the beginning of a rebellion against the state . . .

The first Sunday in Lent, which was March 10, 1585. At about this time the enterprise of the Holy League began to be known. This was headed by those of the Houses of Guise and Lorraine, supported by the Pope, the King of Spain, and the Duke of Savoy, his son-in-law. It was rumoured throughout the kingdom that the Duke of Guise and his brother, the Duke of Mayenne . . . were raising men of war and armaments. At first there was considerable doubt about the true nature of this enterprise, some thinking that it was an underhand way of the King to send aid to Flanders, others that it was to join the forces of the Spaniard, the Savoyard and the Pope, who were besieging Geneva and had sworn to ruin it. Still others said that the Guises . . . wished to back up their claims to the Duchy of Brittany, the Duchy of Anjou, and the counties of Maine, Touraine and Provence, as well as other estates of the crown of France. But it soon became apparent . . . that this army was to provide teeth for their Holy League . . . under pretext of which they declared themselves protectors of the Roman, Catholic and Apostolic Religion against those of the new opinion, or pretended Reformed Religion, introduced in this realm by those who are called Huguenots and practised with the King's permission. Holy League, I say, invented by the late Charles, Cardinal of Lorraine, who, seeing the line of Valois about to expire . . . hoping to exterminate the House of Bourbon . . . because of their profession of the Protestant religion, thought by this means to take over the crown of France.

DEATH OF MONSIEUR

Source: Pierre de l'Estoile, op. cit., p. 101.

Sunday, June 19, about noon, Monsieur, brother of the King, died in Chateâu-Thierry of a great haemorrhage . . . This prince, who was only thirty-one years old when he died, was generous and warlike, French in name and character, bitter enemy of foreigners, especially the Spaniard who feared him. He was not fond of the House of Lorraine, to whom this death was a great source of encouragement. It came at a very opportune moment for them, facilitating and advancing the designs of their League, which from then on began to grow stronger and France to grow weaker.

THE CLERGY

Source: (a) Pierre de l'Estoile, *op. cit.*, p. 132.

We are not provided with good religious leaders in Paris this season . . . with the exception of seven or eight . . . they are all in the pay of the League, to take advantage of the gullibility of the people and stir up rebellion . . . Instead of the word of God they preach I don't know what bigotry and hypocrisy . . . following the catechism of the League, which has produced more atheists than Catholics, and instilled superstition and rebellion instead of religion.

Source: (b) Pierre de l'Estoile, *op. cit.*, p. 134

In the meanwhile Madame de Montpensier is the Governor of Paris for the League, and keeps her brothers in the good graces of the Parisians . . . and does more through the mouths of her preachers (by paying them to build up their reputation with the people at the expense of the King), than they with all their arms and men.

THE JOINT VICTORY AT AUNEAU, 1587

In this year a truce was patched up between Henry III and the Duke of Guise. They won a victory over the German Protestants with bad results for Henry III.

Source: Pierre de l'Estoile, *op. cit.*, p. 135.

Tuesday, November 24, 1587, the Duke of Guise . . . managed to get the captain of St. Paul . . . into the citadel of Auneau . . . All the honour and credit for this signal exploit was given to the Duke of Guise throughout France and especially Paris, where it caused great rejoicing (and to tell the truth, he deserved a large part of the glory). Thus the victory of Auneau was the theme song of the League, the joy of the clergy . . . and the cause of the King's jealousy. He knew that these laurels were heaped on Guise to diminish his own. A truly miserable thing, for a great King to be jealous of his vassal . . . The preachers cried that without the prowess and constancy of the Duke of Guise the ark would have fallen to the Philistines . . . and heresy triumphed over religion.

THE TEMPORARY TRIUMPH OF THE GUISE

Henry ordered Guise not to come to Paris.

Source: Pierre de l'Estoile, *op. cit.*, p. 145.

Thursday, May 5, 1588. The Seigneur de Bellièvre returned
from Soissons and reported to the King that he had told the Duke
of Guise not to come to Paris as commanded . . . He brought
news of haughty words of dissatisfaction from the Duke, so that
the King sent him back again with very express orders that he
was not to come to Paris, and that if he ever did come, things
being as they are, he would hold him for ever guilty and responsible for any excitement which might ensue . . . When those of
the League learned of this, they at once sent an urgent message
to Soissons to beg the Duke to come at once . . . M. de Guise
thought this over . . . and the King's specific prohibition, but
nevertheless he mounted his horse and left at nine in the evening
with eight gentlemen . . . and they arrived in Paris at noon the
next day, which was Monday, the 9th of May.

THE DAY OF BARRICADES, MAY 12TH, 1588

Source: Pierre de l'Estoile, *op. cit.*, p. 146 *et sqq.*

Tuesday, May 10, the King was told that the Duke of Guise
had brought his men of war near the city . . . and that his followers
were entering Paris in a file, and even that the Archbishop of
Lyons, the intellect of his council, was dining at the Hôtel de
Guise. The King redoubled his precautions.

Thursday May 12, in the early morning, the King brought in a
company of Swiss and one of French soldiers to the Petit Pont,
from St. Séverin to the Hôtel-Dieu; at the Pont St. Michel he
stationed a French company; at the Marché-Neuf three companies
of Swiss and one of French; and in the Place de Grève the same;
in the Cimetière des Innocents four Swiss and two French. All
the rest were around the Louvre. By this means the King tried
to carry out what he had decided with his council, namely to
seize a number of the League *bourgeois*, the most important, and
some of the Duke's partisans . . . who had signed the pact which
was known to have been made between the Parisians and the

Guisards to seize the King's person and dispose of the Crown. He hoped to have them executed . . . to make an example to other Guise adherents who had followed the Duke in good faith, deceived by the mask of religion which he used to cover his damnable and ambitious designs . . . But this plan of the King did not succeed because the people, seeing the troops in the city, began to be stirred up and feared something worse, saying that no one had ever seen a foreign garrison in Paris.

Immediately all took arms, went into the streets, took the chains and barricaded the corners and intersections. The artisan left his tools, the merchant his deals, the University its books, the procureurs their brief cases, the lawyers their hats, even presidents counsellors putting their hand to the sword. Everywhere were frightful cries and seditious words to arouse the people to white heat. And as secrets, love and wine are no good when they are aired, so the Duke of Guise, having discovered the King's secret, (as conversely the King had discovered his), fearing to be taken, sent various of his partisans *sub rosa* to each quarter to encourage the people who were rebellious but disorganized . . . to barricade and defend themselves well. The Archbishop had assured the Duke, on the part of the King, that the presence of the troops was not directed against him, if he would confine himself to his own sword . . .

All that night people were in a state of alarm and twice during the night Brissac went the rounds to encourage and further animate them, organizing the students . . . to march when it was necessary. Because all the gates except that of St. Honoré had been closed on the Day of Barricades, the next day, Friday, the 13th of May, the gates of St. Jacques, St. Marceau and St. Antoine were opened and guarded by the League . . . so that the poor King had only the false gate of the Louvre by which to escape his plight, as he did.

The King, seeing the people grow more bold from hour to hour, and the Hôtel de Ville and the Arsenal taken by the Guise partisans, and that they were even beginning to raise barricades near the Louvre . . . left on foot, a cane in his hand, as if to walk as usual in the Tuileries. He no sooner was outside the door than a *bourgeois* of Paris . . . advised him to leave at once, as the Duke of Guise was about to capture him with 1200 men. Having arrived at his stables in the Tuileries, he mounted on horseback with those of his suite who had any mounts . . . He took the road to St. Cloud . . . and the next day dined in Chartres, where he was well received by the inhabitants and where he stayed until the last day of May.

The King moved to Blois where he stayed for many months. He pretended to be reconciled with the Duke of Guise and even entertained him to dinner. But the Edict of Union (July 21st, 1588) was a complete surrender by Henry to the demands of Guise. On December 23rd, 1588, he sent for the Duke, ostensibly to discuss affairs of state. He had made up his mind to have the Duke murdered. Guise was warned, but he paid no attention. 'He will not dare', he said. Henry invited Guise into his private room where he had hidden four men to do the murder. The next day he had the Cardinal murdered. After Guise was dead the King went down the stairs to tell his mother, Catherine de' Medici. On the stairs he met the Florentine ambassador who turned back with him and saw the meeting of the King with his mother.

THE MURDER OF HENRY, DUKE OF GUISE

At Blois, Saturday, December 24th, 1588.

Source: (*a*) The Florentine Ambassador, quoted by Sedgwick, *op. cit.*, p. 298.

He went up to her with a very calm and confident expression on his face. 'Good morning, Madam, I beg you to forgive me. M. de Guise is dead; We shan't hear more of him, I have had him killed, doing no more than forestalling the similar plan he had formed against me. I could endure his insolence no more. I tried to bear with it in order not to dip my hands in blood; I put from my memory the injury done me on May 13th, the Friday when he forced me to fly from Paris; I also forgot that he had plotted against my life, my honour and my power. But as I knew, for I had continuous proofs, that he was undermining and threatening—those are his own expressions—my authority, my life and my kingdom, I resolved on this deed, which I have long considered in my mind, asking myself whether I should do it or

not. However, as I saw that my patience turned to my shame and
dishonour, and that his offences and perfidies multiplied every
day, I was finally inspired and helped by God, to whom I am
now going to render thanks in church, at the holy office of Mass.
And if any member of the League, whosoever, shall speak to me
of what has been done, I will treat him as I did M. de Guise. I
wish to alleviate the burdens of my people, I wish to hold meetings
of the State-General, but I wish them to speak as subjects and not
as sovereigns. I have no enmity against the family and house of
M. de Guise; I shall help and shew favour to the Dukes of Lorraine, Nemours, Elboeuf and Mme de Nemours, who I know
are loyal and well-disposed towards me. But I mean now to be
King and no longer a captive and a slave, as I have been from
May 13 to this hour, when I begin anew to be King and master.
I have put guards about the Prince de Joinville, and the Dukes of
Nemours and Elboeuf and Mme de Nemours, not to harm them
but for my own safety. I have done the same towards the Cardinal
de Guise, the Archbishop of Lyons and my cousin, the Cardinal
de Bourbon; I shall do him no harm, but I shall so deal with him
that he will not be able to harm me. I shall pursue ardently the
war against the Huguenots, for I wish to extirpate heresy from
my kingdom. So, Madam, I am now sole King of France, without a partner.'

Source: (b) A friend of the Guises, quoted by Sedgwick, *op. cit.*, p. 299.

This is the abominable, detestable deed, the frightful harvest
that one could expect to reap from this accursed Henry, atheist
and parricide, who perjured himself traitorously, cowardly and
vilely, and made his rogues and villains murder the prop, the
pillar, the support of our holy religion, of his kingdom and of
himself, his Court and of all France, who, by his prowess, vigour,
valour, virtues, rendered her redoubtable and fearful to all most
potent and warlike nations. O France! What honours, what
praises, what marble monuments, what jewels and precious stones
should you lay on his grave, and by this last duty eternalize the
memory of him who, while he lived, lived only for you, and
dying cared only for your repose. The most honourable tomb

that you can erect to this holy martyr is to imitate his piety, his constancy, his holy determination to die for the preservation of religion, for the liberty of the nation, and the repose of *la Patrie*, so that his sacred zeal may be engraven everlastingly on the hearts of all true Frenchmen and of all good men.

THE MURDER OF HENRY III OF FRANCE, 1589

After the murder of the Duke of Guise and of the Cardinal, 1588, in 1589 Catherine de' Medici died. Henry III was alone, powerless and without any military force. The defeat of the Spanish Armada reduced the danger to France from Spain. Even so, Henry needed an army. Only Henry of Navarre could supply that. Henry III met him at Plessis-lez-Tours and the two came to terms. The League was now dispirited and all Paris wanted to be rid of a Catholic king who had joined with the Huguenots and who had murdered their heroes, the Guises. Jaques Clément, a Dominican friar who had lately become a priest, half-witted and fanatical, determined to assassinate Henry III, which he did on August 1st, 1589, thereby leaving France open to Henry of Navarre, a Huguenot.

Source: The Fugger Newsletters, ed. by G. T. Matthews, Capricorn Books, New York, 1959, p. 170.

On the first day of the month of August [1589], a young Dominican friar betook himself to St. Cloud where the late King sojourned, with a passport from the Count de Brienne, who is kept imprisoned in Paris. On his arrival he informed the guard that he had something which he wished to communicate to the King. The King ordered that he might be permitted to deliver his message on the following day. The Provost-Marshal gave the monk quarters at the King's request and entertained him right nobly. The following day the Provost-Marshal led the monk to the King's chamber. But, as there were several persons present, the monk demanded that the King might receive him alone. He led him into his cabinet and read various scripts which the monk handed him. When the King had perused the last, he asked the monk whether he had any more. The latter thereupon replied 'Yes' and, in place of the script, drew forth from his sleeve a short knife, the width of two fingers, which he thrust into the

King's abdomen below the navel. He left it sticking in the wound. The King pulled it out himself and thus enlarged the wound. He then himself inflicted a stab upon the monk. At his calls for help several people came into the room, among them La Bastida, who helped to murder the late Guise, and he with his dagger slashed at the monk. Also one of the halberdiers thrust his halberd into the monk so that he was mortally wounded. He said that he had not hoped to come off so easily.

After his death his corpse was dragged along the streets, rent asunder by four horses, and publicly burnt. The King did not expect to die of his wound. He walked up and down his room, and showed himself to his servants and to the soldiery at the window. But at four o'clock in the evening he felt great pains and when the doctors visited him, they found the injury to be most grievous. They gave him an enema and discovered that the intestine had been injured. The wound turned black and the King was informed of his perilous condition. He did not at first believe this, because he was feeling fairly well. But by and by he became weaker and a Capuchin was sent for to comfort him. But when he arrived the King no longer spoke. He died upon the 2nd day of this month at midnight. The body has not been interred as yet and has been taken to Senlis. It is said that he has asked the King of Navarre not to take revenge for his death on the city of Paris. The story goes that the monk had delivered discourses not far from Paris and had then said that he would take the King's life. Even though he be burnt and quartered, he would take the King's life. Even though he be burnt and quartered, he would feel no pain. The King of Navarre is still in St. Cloud and is besieging Paris to the extent of his power. He has made himself King of France and is thus acclaimed by his followers. He tries all ways and means in order to win to his side both the nobility and the common people. The Council of Paris has declared the Cardinal of Bourbon, who is held a prisoner in the castle of Chion, to be King. The King of Navarre intends to go to Rheims to be crowned there and to gain possession of the three royal cities.

HENRY OF NAVARRE

Henry IV (1553–1610) was the son of Antoine de Bourbon, Duke of Vendôme, and of Jeanne d'Albret, Queen of Navarre. He was born in 1553 and was brought up as a Protestant. During the third war of religion in France (1568–70) he was introduced to Gaspard de Coligny leader of the Huguenot armies and he distinguished himself at the battle of Arnay-le-Duc in Burgundy in 1569. In 1572 he succeeded to the throne of Navarre. He now married Margaret de Valois, sister of Charles IX of France. He escaped the Massacre of St. Bartholomew by pretending to abjure the Protestant religion. But in 1576 he joined the Huguenot armies and became the governor of Guienne. In 1577 he secured the treaty of Bergerac, which foreshadowed the Edict of Nantes. On the death in 1584 of the Duke of Anjou, brother of Henry III, he became heir presumptive to the throne of France, but he was barred from succeeding by the Treaty of Nemours (1585). He therefore began the War of the Three Henries and defeated Duke of Joyeuse at Coutras in Guienne (1587). The assassination of Henry III (1589) left Henry of Navarre King of France, but it took him ten years of war against the League and Philip II before he won his kingdom. In July, 1593, he announced his conversion to Roman Catholicism ('Paris is worth a Mass'). This piece of political wisdom ended all opposition and Paris surrendered to him on March 22nd, 1594. Spain signed the Treaty of Vervins in 1598. Henry IV set about restoring the prosperity of France after the civil wars and doing as much harm as he could to the Hapsburgs short of going to war. He was murdered on May 14th, 1610, by Ravaillac. He had no children by his first marriage, but by his second wife, Marie de' Medici, he had two sons and three daughters: one son became Louis XIII, one daughter married Philip IV of Spain, and Henrietta Maria married Charles I of England.

Source: R. Dallington, View of France, 1604.

This King, then . . . is about 48 years of age, his stature small, his hair almost white, or rather grisled, his colour fresh and youthful, his nature stirring and full of life, like a true Frenchman. He is of such an extremely lively and active disposition that to whatever he applies himself to that he entirely employs all his powers, seldom doing above one thing at once. To join a tedious deliberation with an earnest and pressing affair he cannot endure: he executes and deliberates both together. But in councils which require tract of time, to say truth, he has need of help. He has an admirable sharpness of wit. In affairs of justice, of his revenues, foreign negotiations, despatches and government of the state, he credits others and meddles little himself.

He says farther that, though by his physiognomy, his fashion and manner of behaviour, you would judge him leger and inconstant, yet is no man more firmly constant than he. He confesses that it were hard for him not to be sparing, considering the profuse and lavish spoil that his predecessors made before him; yet to salve the matter, he makes this difference, 'that the other gave much to few, this gives a little to many'. If you remember, when we saw him play at dice, here in Orléans, with his Noblesse, he would ever tell his money very precisely before he gave it back again.

I will not spare in this discourse (which is only for yourself private) to speak the truth, though of a King: we are in a country where you daily hear his own subjects speak of his liberality.

And besides, his Majesty has generally this commendation, which is very laudable in a Prince, he can endure that any man should tell him the truth, though of himself.

HENRY OF NAVARRE AND HENRY III, APRIL, 1589
Source: Pierre l'Estoille, *op. cit.,* pp. 176-7. April, 1589.

About this time the King and the King of Navarre made a treaty and pact declaring themselves friends, and enemies of each other's enemies . . . and they united their forces and councils, and joined to bring to an end the Guisards and those leagued with them. At the beginning the King of Navarre made great difficulty, not daring to trust the King's promises, which for four years he hasn't kept . . . and feared that at the first chance he would fare the same fate as the Guises, knowing that it wasn't so much a matter of love as of need . . . and that Henry III might gladly send Navarre's head to the Parisians, if he wanted to make a peace with the League. Finally . . . remembering the old saying that two heads are better than one, and thinking that the war was really his own . . . he agreed, especially with the added security that those who were most against him, and particularly his mother-in-law, had fallen.

Having taken this resolution, he crossed the river Loire on Sunday, the last day of April, and went to His Majesty at Plessis-les-Tours. It was incredible with what joy this interview was received, for there was such a crowd of people that the two Kings spent a quarter of an hour holding out their hands without being able to join them, the press was so great and the voices of the people resounding exultantly, *Vive le Roi: Vive le Roi de Navarre: Vivent les Rois:* Finally meeting, they embraced very affectionately with tears, especially the King of Navarre, from whose eyes they fell as big as peas from the great joy he had in seeing the King . . .

It came about that the King, who had fought him for so long, and even furnished the League with the means to do so, was the one who took him by the hand to install him, so that he would get his great heritage, promised him by God . . . so also it was the Pope, it was the Spaniard, it was the Lorrainer, it was the Savoyard, it was the League, it was the Sixteen—in brief, it was by his greatest enemies that he was carried on their shoulders to the royal throne. Miracle of miracles in truth, which we have seen with our own eyes.

THE BATTLE OF ARQUES, SEPTEMBER 21, 1589

The death of Henry III greatly changed the face of things in France, for very many of the Catholic nobles went over to the side of Henry IV and acknowledged him as King. On August 28th, Henry was three miles outside Rouen. On September 1st the Duke of Mayenne, who had succeeded Guise as leader of the League, marched from Paris against Henry with a very large army comprising all the Leaguers of the north and also a large contingent from Flanders sent by the Duke of Parma, and a big body of Lorrainers under Henry, Marquis of Pons, eldest son of the Duke of Guise, who had his eye on the French throne. This combined force amounted to some 25,000 men, about three times that which Henry had near Rouen. Henry determined to join battle, in spite of the immense risks. He won a decisive victory, chiefly because the battle was fought in a defile so narrow that it was only

400 yards wide, which prevented Mayenne from ever being able to deploy his immensely superior numbers.

Source: Sully, *Memoirs, op. cit.* Sully[9] took part in the battle.

When the upper trench was attacked by the landsknechts, who pretended to surrender and then seized the works, the King was in no small trouble. Of the fighting where I was not present in person I do not speak. But below the road we were attacked by 800 or 900 horse in three squadrons, whom we charged and held up at the twist of the road, though there were not more than 150 in all. Then four more squadrons came on, who drove us back at more than a foot-pace as far as a little mound, where we found about 150 of our own horse under the Count of Auvergne, on whom we rallied, and all charged together, driving the enemy off—our pistols in their backs—as far as the same turn of the road; then we could see some 3000 or so of their cavalry waiting for us. They came on and beat us back as far as a point level with the Chapel, and were only checked by arquebus fire from our infantry. But the landsknechts who had taken the upper trench drove our foot away, and we had to retire to the front of our Swiss battalion (at the second trench) who stopped our pursuers. Here my horse was shot and Mr. de Maignan brought me another. The enemy then tried to turn our left by sending 500 horse through the low ground, to get round our Swiss, but they rode into a quagmire, where the chargers sank up to their girths in the marsh, and most of them had to dismount and struggle off on their legs, leaving their horses completely embogged.

THE SIEGE OF PARIS

The great victory at Arques, followed by another victory at Ivry, March 14th, 1590, greatly advanced Henry's prospects and equally depressed the spirits of the League. Many towns now began to come over to Henry's side—*e.g.* in April, Corbeil, Montereau, Lagny, which were the keys to Paris. On May 7th Henry began to march on Paris, which he intended to starve into submission.

Source: Pierre de l'Estoile, *op. cit.,* pp. 188 *et sqq.*

Saturday, May 26, the police reported on the investigation into the grain supply, which had been made at the order of the governor . . . the word was that for the number of people there were in the city there was enough wheat for about a month, if it were carefully rationed: beyond that, there was . . . barley, which could be used for bread when the wheat gave out. There were said to be more than 220,000 souls in Paris.

Friday, June 15, 1590, Don Bernardino Mendoza, Spanish Ambassador . . . in an assembly called to find a way to deal with the famine which was growing from day to day in Paris . . . made a strange proposal, the like of which had never been heard . . . namely, to put through the mill the bones of the dead in the cemetery of the Innocents, to reduce them to powder, which could be mixed with water and used for nourishment for those who had no grain and no way to get any . . . not a man in the assembly was found to oppose this suggestion . . .

Thursday, July 5, La Chapelle-Marteau, Prévost des Marchands, assembled the city officials, read to them letters which the Duke of Mayenne had written to the Parisians, in which he exhorted them to hold fast and to cheer up, promising aid at the end of the month at the latest, and if he should fail, he gave them his wife and children to do with what they would. These beautiful words served the people for bread . . .

Monday, July 9, the town of St. Denis fell to the King . . . the settlement was one of the finest and most honourable that one could hope to see . . . they could get what they wanted, import what they needed, horses were even given them to move their artillery—not a usual way to treat the vanquished. But the King held this town to be so important, both as a foothold for himself and as a threat to Paris, that he didn't care what price he paid. He called it the citadel of Paris . . .

Monday, August 6 . . . Over the portals of the butcher shops, where there are only pieces of old cow, mule, and cat, instead of the usual beef and mutton, I found the following written in capital letters. 'These are the rewards of those who pour out their lifeblood for Philip', [Philip II of Spain].

Thursday, August 16, it was announced that anyone could leave the city, because hunger was so acute. The bread made of the bones of our fathers, called the bread of Madame de Montpensier, began to be used. She praised this invention highly, though she was unwilling to try it. But it didn't last long, because those who ate it died . . .

Tuesday, August 30, the siege was lifted, having lasted since the 7th of May.

THE CONVERSION OF HENRY OF NAVARRE, 1593

Source: Pierre de l'Estoile, *op. cit.,* p. 237 *et sqq.*

Sunday, July 18, the King went to the Protestant service for the last time.

Friday, July 23, the ecclesiastics bidden to St. Denis entered into conference with the King about his conversion. The King replied so skilfully to their arguments, quoting from Scripture, that they were astonished . . . so much so that one said the next day he had never seen a heretic so well grounded in his errors, or who could defend them so well.

When they came to the prayer for the dead, he said, 'Let's skip the Requiem, I'm not dead yet and don't want to be'. As for Purgatory, he said he believed in it, not as an article of faith, but as a doctrine of the Church, which he believed as a good son of the Church. He said this to please them, as it was their bread and butter. On the adoration of the sacrament, 'You haven't satisfied me on this point . . . but look here: to-day I put my soul in your hands. I beg you take good care of it. Where I go in to-day I will not come out till death, I swear and protest to you.' As he said this, there were tears in his eyes . . .

The next day, which was Saturday the 24th, he sent for Messieurs the Premiers Présidents of Paris and Rouen and asked them if they were satisfied he had done all he could . . . He said that even so he had been asked to take strange oaths and to sign beliefs that he was sure most of them did not really believe, like the existence of Purgatory. 'Do you', he asked point blank, 'believe in that?' They didn't reply, but returning to the original

2A

question said that it was not reasonable to force His Majesty further . . . He said, 'I pray you call them off, tell them I've done enough, and that if they press me further, worse may ensue'. Chauveau, in the presence of the assembled bishops and prelates, said that the King was not a Turk or pagan . . . that he should be led gently from error to truth, and not treated as if he were wholly ignorant. In this he was seconded by the Bishop of Mans and others so that the oath of abjuration was softened and modified . . .

A bishop said to a friend of mine, on the same subject, 'I am a Catholic by life and profession and a faithful servant of the King. I will live and die as such. But I think it would have been better if he had stayed on his own religion . . . in matters of conscience there is a God on high Who judges, Who should be the considera-tion of the consciences of men, rather than kingdoms and crowns . . . I expect only bad luck from it.'

THE EDICT OF NANTES, DECEMBER 1598–JANUARY 1599

On Thursday, March 1st, 1594, Henry was crowned King at Chartres, of which event it was said in a sermon, which Pierre de l'Estoile heard, that Henry 'was no more King of France than the devil was when he offered Jesus Christ all the kingdoms of the world that he held only in imagination' (*op. cit.*, p. 253). On the 6th the Duke of Mayenne left Paris to its fate. On the 22nd Henry entered Paris. During the rest of the year he was busy restoring order in the city. The next year Pope Clement VIII gave him absolution. Brittany surrendered to him in 1598 and in May of that year he made peace with Spain. The moment had come to put into force his concessions to the Huguenots, which was done by the Edict of Nantes, which gave them virtually speaking all that they could reasonably hope for. On Thurs-day, January 7th, 1599, Henry sent for the members of the *Parlement* to come to meet him in the Louvre to verify the Edit.

Source: Pierre de l'Estoile, *op. cit.*, p. 295.

You see me in my cabinet, not in royal costume with sword and cape like my predecessors, nor like a prince parleying with foreign ambassadors, but dressed as a father of the family, in everyday clothes, who comes to talk frankly with his children.

What I have to say is that I want you to verify the Edict which I have granted to those of the Religion.[10] I have done it to bring about peace. I have made it abroad; I want it at home. You should obey me, even if there were no other consideration but my station and the obligation of subjects, but you, of my Parlement, have a special obligation. I restored their houses to some who had been exiled, their faith to others who had lost it. If obedience was due to my predecessors, it is due still more to me, as I have reestablished the state, God having chosen me to come into this heritage. The members of my Parlement would not be in office without me . . . I know the road to sedition which led to the Barricades and the assassination of the late King. I'll take care it doesn't happen again . . .

Don't throw the Catholic religion in my face. I love it more than you do; I am more Catholic than you are. I am the eldest son of the Church. You are mistaken if you think you have the Pope on your side. He is with me instead . . .

Those who don't want the Edict to pass want war . . . you are ungrateful to cause me this worry. I call as witnesses those of my council who have found it good and necessary . . . and have advised me to do it. I am the sole conserver of religion . . . I am King now, I speak as King and I will be obeyed. Indeed, justice is my right hand, but if gangrene sets in in it, the left will have to cut it off . . .

There is not one of you who doesn't find me willing when you ask me for something. Yet to me, though I'm good to you, you return evil. The other Parlements, by their refusals, have caused those of the Religion to raise their demands. I don't want still more demands because of your refusal. There's not one of these great, devout Catholics who, if I gave to this one a 2000-crown benefice and to that one 4000 in income . . . wouldn't shut his mouth . . .

The last word you'll have from me is to follow the example of M. de Mayenne. Some have tried to incite him to defy my will, but he replied that he was too much obliged to me. All my subjects are similarly under obligation, because I have saved France in spite of those who wanted to ruin her . . . And if the chief of the League speaks thus, how much more should you, whom I restored to your offices, both those who were faithful and those whom I had to win back—what should they do at that price!

Give to my prayers what you would not give to threats. You will have none from me. Do as I command, or rather, as I entreat. You will be doing it not only for me, but also for yourselves and for the sake of peace.

The Edict was verified and ended the thirty-six years of civil war in France. Henry reigned for another eleven years, in which he restored the royal power and reconstructed the economic life of the state, with the help of Sully. These years belong to the XVII century and will be dealt with in a further volume of this series.

ORDER WHICH THE KING OF NAVARRE SHOULD OBSERVE IN HIS DAILY LIFE

Philippe de Mornay, Sieur de Plessis, was born in 1549 and died in 1623. He was a French Protestant, who had studied law and jurisprudence at Heidelberg and Hebrew and German at Padua. He began his diplomatic career in 1572 when he went on an embassy to William the Silent. He escaped from the massacre of St. Bartholomew and retired for a time to England. Returning to France in 1573 he took service under Henry of Navarre and was taken prisoner in 1575. He was ransomed and gradually he came to be looked on as Henry's right-hand man. He was present at the siege of Dieppe, fought at Ivry, was at the siege of Rouen (1591–2), went on an embassy to England, but when Henry renounced Protestantism Mornay was bitterly disappointed and he gradually withdrew from court. In 1598 he published a book on the Eucharist, but he was accused of misquoting from the scriptures, fathers and schoolmen by the Bishop of Evreux. A public disputation was held and the verdict went in favour of the Bishop. Mornay was deprived of the governorship of Saumur. He died in retirement in 1623. He gave devoted service to Henry of Navarre, who treated him badly enough over the disputation.

Source: One of de Mornay's papers dated 1583. Quoted in the introduction to Lucy Crump's translation of the Memoirs of Philippe de Mornay under the title of *A Huguenot Family*, Broadway Translations, Routledge, 1924, p. 59. These memoirs were written by de Mornay's wife, Charlotte Arbaleste at Sedan, and contain a long account of how she escaped from the Massacre of St. Bartholomew.

Whoever considers the many graces with which God has endowed the King of Navarre, and the times in which He caused him to be born, will agree with me in thinking that he is destined for great things and will be filled with impatience at seeing him turn aside to petty ones. Every one acknowledges his vigorous body, his great courage, his incomparable alertness of mind. He is the stuff of which great princes are made and the only thing needed is that he should understand that he is born for greatness and so rule his life that he may serve for an example and a model. The manner in which a prince lives is of great importance to the government of a State and this is our reason for desiring that the King of Navarre should observe a certain order in his life, for without it no prince is respected.

A day is long if it is well arranged and it gives plenty of time for both serious business and for exercise and pleasure. The King of Navarre should be dressed by eight o'clock at the latest and should then send for his chaplain to conduct morning prayers. This done, he should enter his study accompanied by those to whom he entrusts the conduct of his affairs. These should form his council. He should discuss with them every affair of importance which turns up fully and without hurry, and should afterwards sign dispatches already concluded, those which require it being first read aloud. To avoid worrying the King with trivialities his council should have assembled beforehand to decide matters of small import; prepare others of great consequence so that they can be presented to the King already half digested; look through all dispatches and sift out those he need not see so that he can get through the remainder in a short hour. And if this were done every day no one will have much to do on any one day. The rest of the time until dinner could be passed in such exercise or amusement as the King likes except on sermon days. At his dinner there should be good talk in which his counsellors could share, for his hours will regulate those of his household. His afternoon should be quite free except for an hour before supper, or some other hour as he preferred, when he should go into his study with his council to see what has been the result of previous decisions and to sign necessary dispatches. If there are none waiting, the King might invent some. Some princes, for the sake of their reputation, do this without any real occasion, and, by appearing busy, enhance the estimation in which they are held. Now and then it would not be amiss to join the council which manages his household, as much to encourage each to do his duty as to countenance them.

If His Majesty dines at 10 or 11 o'clock, he could sup at 6 or 7 and could retire to his room at 9 or at the latest at 10 o'clock. His time after supper is his own till the minister arrives in his chamber to hold prayers at 9 o'clock. With his time thus arranged the King of Navarre would manage everything without being bored and with ample leisure, and his servants would have the great happiness of knowing that he knew what they did and what they were worth, so that their labour will be nothing but pleasure.

THE STATE OF RURAL FRANCE, 1528, *et sqq.*

Source: (*a*) André Novagero, 1528, in Gascony: quoted by E. C. Lodge, *Sully, Colbert and Turgot*, Methuen, 1931, p. 10.

The men and women are very gay in this country, they are different in this respect from Spaniards, one hears nothing around but laughter, songs and jokes.

Source: (*b*) Marino Cavallo, 1546, quoted Lodge, *op. cit.*, p. 11.

The King rules over provinces most favoured by nature; they are protected by the Pyrenees and the Alps, and by the rivers Saone, Meuse and Somme; Champagne, where the boundary is less secured by natural defences, has good fortifications. Within these safe provinces there is a good variety of soils and produce. Corn and wine are produced in plenty and are sent to foreign countries, whilst all sorts of fish, meat and wood abound.

Source: (*c*) Dallington, *View of France*, 1604, quoted Lodge, as above. This picture of France would seem to contradict any idea that civil wars had seriously reduced the prosperity of the country.

If there be any that will empeache the goodnesse and beauty thereof, to say that it is not fruitful, nor so pleasant, nor so well-furnished and replenished with all things that are to be desired in a flourishing Kingdom . . . he is no more able to dispute of a country than a mole or mouse of the man in the moone.

PARIS AT THE END OF THE XVI CENTURY

  Source: R. Dallington, *The View of France,* 1604.

It is reputed not only the capital city of France, but also the greatest in all Europe. It is about the walls some ten English miles; these are not very thick, the want thereof is recompensed with the depth of the ditch and goodness of the rampart, which is thick and defensible, save on the South side, which, no doubt, is the weakest part of the town, on which side, it is reported, the Lord Willoughby offered the King in four days to enter, at such time as he besieged it. Whereunto the King condescended not by the counsel of the old Marshall Biron, who told him 'It was no policy to take the bird naked, when he may have her, feathers and all' . . . The buildings of this city are of stone, very fair, high and uniform throughout the town, only upon the Port N. Dame, Our Lady's Bridge, which is, as it were, their Cheapside; their building is of brickbat, all alike notwithstanding. The fairest fabric in the town (and worthily) is the King's Castle or Palace of the Louvre at the West. It is in form quadrangular, the fourth and West quarters are new and Princelike, the other two very antique and prisonlike. They were pulled down by Francis I and begun to be rebuilt, but finished by Henry the Second. The most Christian King, Henry the Second, began to repair this time-ruined edifice.

GALLEYS AND GALLEY-SLAVES

  Source: Thomas Platter, *The Journal of a Younger Brother,* ed. and trans. by Seán Jennet, Frederick Muller, London, 1963, pp. 113–17. The harbour of Marseilles, 1597.

In the middle of the harbour, almost opposite the Hôtel de Ville, there were two splendid galleys, richly painted and gilded, which we went to visit on the 12th of February. One of them belonged to the Duc de Guise, governor of Marseilles and of Provence, and the other to the *lieutenant-viguier* or consul of the town, whose name was Libertat. There was such a noise of chains on board and of shouting that it seemed like the heart of an immense forge. I counted thirty-one banks of oarsmen on each side. Four, and sometimes five, men of various nationalities were chained to each oar. At that time most of them were Spaniards, about four hundred in number, who had been made prisoners either when the consul Casaulx attempted to deliver the town to Spain or else on board a Genoese vessel, of which I will speak presently.

Sometimes there are only twenty-four oars to each side. The men are chained in twos by the feet, with heavy chains; but as they often succeed in escaping, and can hide their fetters under a long robe (although it is forbidden for any workman to remove a convict's chains), iron collars are put on their necks, with a rod or stalk of iron, two spans long, which stands upright above the head, and cannot be hidden in any manner.

If you wish to see how much human nature can endure, you have only to visit these wretches. They are fed with biscuits, a kind of hard and thin bread, cooked in an oven and made with uncleaned wheat. These have to be soaked in water before they can be chewed. Once or twice a week the men are given meat, but their other food is appalling. They are dressed all the same, and all cropped and shaved to avoid vermin, and are confined in the galleys day and night, winter and summer, through rain, snow and heat. At night the galley is covered with an awning of thick material, and when this is removed in the morning, it is a curious spectacle to see the men at their various occupations. Some knit, some sew, some carve wood; others chat, scratch, wash, cook, wash dishes, etc. Every one of them works, for when they are at anchor, and not employed in cleaning the streets, the squares, or the port, each one works for himself in order to gain a few sous to buy wine or linen. With their savings or the money given to them by charitable people they would be able to buy their freedom, but they quarrel constantly among themselves and do not hesitate at any kind of dastardy. In general they are robust men. When they are rowing at sea they are bare to the waist, and before them and behind them is placed a man with a whistle to convey orders. If they do not obey promptly enough, they are lashed about the head and shoulders until the blood flows. Sometimes, to make an example a limb is chopped off one of them. The two guards are usually former galley slaves, and they are devoid of any sort of pity. When the wind is favourable, sails are spread to gain extra speed.

In the middle of the galley, under the bridge, are two cannons, one pointing forwards and the other astern, and there are still others in various positions. The galley has two decks, but in front of the bridge there is a raised cabin containing two rooms for the superior officers. The cargo goes in the hold and the convicts, chained to their oars, are above it. The upkeep of each galley costs nine to ten thousand crowns a year. Usually there are six of them in the harbour: the King's, that of the Duc de Guise, and that of the Intendant of Marseilles; the others belong either to the town or to the Knights of Malta.

On the 13th of February we went in a boat to see the large vessel that the duke had taken from the Spaniards, and which was at anchor near the Island. It had cost the merchants of Genoa twenty-one thousand crowns, not counting the rigging, the sails and the anchors. When it was returning from Spain with a cargo of cochineal, wine, etc., and a troop of four hundred Spanish soldiers, the wind drove it into the waters of Marseilles. The Duc de Guise was told of this and he went out with his ships and took the vessel without firing a shot. The soldiers were chained in the galleys, the goods confiscated, and the Italians of the crew released. It was one of the largest ships ever launched in the Mediterranean; it was like a great house of five stories rising from the middle of the sea. I estimated that its capacity must be at least fifteen thousand quintals. It had eight or ten sails on two masts of prodigious height, one of which I climbed by means of rope ladders. From that height I could see far and wide, including the Château d'If, which has a windmill similar to those in the town.

Notes

[1] Henry D. of Guise and his brother Cardinal of Guise.

[2] Used by l'Estoile to mean the extreme Clerical-Spanish faction of the League as opposed to the moderate French faction.

[4] These memoranda were burned by the Comte de Retz.

[5] Francis, younger brother of the King, d. 1584.

[6] D'Arques became Duke of Joyeuse and married the King's sister-in-law: La Valette became Duke of Epernon and one of the most important of the King's favourites.

[7] Bishop of Senlis, one of the founders of the Paris League. A violent League preacher.

[8] At that time he was only Comte d'Aumale.

[9] This was Maximilien de Béthune, Duc de Sully, who was to become the lifelong friend and also the great finance minister of Henry IV.

[10] The word normally used to describe the Huguenots.

THE NETHERLANDS

THE REVOLT IN THE NETHERLANDS

THE EXECUTION OF COUNT EGMONT AND COUNT HORN, 5TH OF JUNE, 1568

By 1568 armed revolt against Spanish rule did not exceed small proportions. But in May, Louis of Nassau (William the Silent's brother) defeated a Spanish force. Alva was determined to teach the rebels a lesson. He trumped up a charge of treason against two of the best known nobles, Count Egmont and Count Horn, and had them executed on June 5th at Brussels.

Source: The Fugger Newsletters, 1st series, English trans. by Pauline de Chary, Putnam, 1924: ed. by G. T. Matthews, Capricorn Books, 1959. These newsletters are not genuine eye-witness accounts. They are written by correspondents of the great banking firm of the Fugger family from all over the world, and they illustrate the way in which news and rumours were circulated in the years 1568 to 1605.

On the 4th day of June of this year 1568, Count Egmont and Count Horn were taken on a special conveyance from Ghent to Brussels. They were accompanied by twelve back. When Count Egmont beheld the town of Brussels, troops of Spaniards on foot and several hundreds on horseback, he said: 'I am in good hopes that the Duke of Alba, will of his mercy, allow me to sup with my spouse and my children this night'. They had been with him of late and had brought him consolation. But as soon as they entered the town (it was three o'clock in the afternoon), they were taken to the King's Bread-House, which stands in the market place opposite the Town Hall, and thereupon Count Egmont said: 'Now I have lost all hope'. The same evening at seven o'clock their sentence was read out to the two Counts, thereupon Egmont on that evening and during the night oft repeated: That the wrongs he had committed against His Majesty might graciously be forgiven him and his life spared in return for the services he had rendered; that he should be punished with lifelong imprisonment and be treated not as a count, but as a poor nobleman. The King should be implored thus on his behalf. The Grand Prior likewise, it is rumoured, has thrown himself on his knees before the carriage of the Duke, but it has availed him nothing. The Duke is reported to have said that the sentence of both gentlemen is to be carried out. Therefore the Bishop of Ypres has been sent to them as Confessor, and, in addition to him, the Duke's Chaplain and a Spanish priest. These remained with them until their death. In the morning a stand, which is called here a scaffold, was erected in the market-place, and on either side a pole with an iron point was nailed thereto. The said scaffold was draped with black, cloth and two black cushions were laid upon it. The market-place was guarded by the twenty troops which had come from Ghent and by ten from Brussels. At eleven o'clock Count Egmont was first brought from the King's Bread-House to the market-place. He was unbound and accompanied by the Bishop of Ypres and the two Spanish priests and the Maistre de Camp. He was attired in a black velvet doublet, cut low at the neck, wide black velvet breeches, and broodequins, or white Spanish boots. Over this he wore a red damask night-robe, and an ordinary black cloak, both edged with gold braid. He also wore a hat with black and white plumes thereon. He walked from the said Bread-House to the scaffold. He carried his cloak over his shoulder and had his hands crossed upon his breast. And so he walked in orderly fashion and with a proud face as he had formerly been wont to go to the Council.

He carried himself bravely, though his face looked melancholy and afflicted. He held his cloak before his mouth, thrown over his shoulder, and looked around him; then he laid it aside, composed himself for death and was about to unrobe himself. The Maistre de Camp, said to him: 'Oh, there's no haste, take time for reflection. Time and to spare will be given you and this vouchsafed right willingly.' Thereupon he slung the cloak once more round his shoulders and again looked round him, but without saying a word or making a sign. Only his right hand he stretched out from under the cloak and gazed upon it fixedly. Therefore the Bishop of Ypres addressed him in these words: 'Sir, do not take thought now of any worldly matters, but bethink yourself of the salvation of your soul'. At that he asked:

'Whether the salvation of his soul could prevent him from thinking of his wife and his children'? The Bishop answered: 'Nay, since our Lord Himself, as he hung upon the Cross for the remission of our sins, committed His mother to the care of John'. Thereupon the Count made reply: 'Then there is naught that troubles my heart or lies heavy on my conscience'. With these words he put down his hat, laid aside his cloak, likewise his night-robe. The Maistre de Camp once more bade him not to hurry, but the Count made answer that, as it was ordained he must die, he wished to do so. He knelt down with the Bishop and spoke privately with him for the space of two paternosters. Thereupon he himself motioned him aside with his hand, lifted a gilt cross from where it lay on the scaffold, and knelt before it. Likewise he pulled the white cap or bandage which he had on his head over his eyes, and thus remained kneeling for some time while the executioner made ready. Meanwhile the Bishop inquired of him whether he would permit his bandage to be made tight. 'Nay', he replied, 'I will die right valiantly and deport myself in seemly fashion'. Thereupon the executioner carried out his appointed task with the sword. Immediately this was done the two Spanish priests carried away the dead body and the head, and placed them under a black cloth at the side of the scaffold.

They then fetched Count Horn from the Bread-House. He also was unfettered, and when he stepped out upon the market-place he doffed his hat and bade the soldiers on both sides good-day in the Spanish tongue. These did likewise. Then he went bravely, bareheaded, hat in hand, to the scaffold. He wore his usual garments, a doublet of white linen and laced black velvet breeches, and thereover a cloak. As soon as he mounted the scaffold he spoke to all and sundry, saying how much it grieved him that he had so acted against the King and not served him better. He craved the pardon of His Majesty and of whomsoever he should have offended. This same he was willing to grant to all. He begged that everyone should say a paternoster for him. Thereupon he fell on his knees with the Bishop and thus remained the space of two paternosters, or thereabouts. The hat he held in his hands all the time. Then he arose once more, thanked every-body in a strong and manly voice and made obeisance to all the soldiers, who did likewise. Thereupon he laid aside his cloak and knelt down unbound. After this the executioner did as he was ordered. When both gentlemen had been executed, their heads were placed on two iron spikes where they remained till the after-noon at three. But the corpses were guarded by six monks who, clad in grey, and as the custom is here, bury the dead. The bodies were unrobed under a linen cloth that was spread over them and each was laid in a special chest, in which they remained for about an hour on the scaffold. Thereafter, they, as well as the heads, were carried in a four-cornered separate little box to the Church of St. Gudule. There the heads were sewn to the bodies and Count Egmont transported to St. Claire, and Count Horn to another convent. Thereafter Egmont was embalmed and buried in his own domain at Gottegem, and Horn likewise at Weert.

IMAGE BREAKING

The revolt in the Netherlands was brought about by a mixture of reasons. The introduction of the Inquisition by Charles V and the extreme severity of his *placaten*, edicts for the suppression of heresy, had infuriated the people, who detested the executions, whether they were Catholic or Protestant. The financial exactions of Philip II, his treatment of the Dutch nobility and his attacks on their political privileges roused the resentment of the aristocracy and the rich burgher class. Most especially Philip's plan for reorganizing the Netherlands Church produced a storm of opposition with which the Regent, Margaret, proved to be incapable of dealing. Her indecision and weakness and the obstinacy and dilatoriness of Philip, led to violent outbreaks in which the smashing of images was the chief characteristic. On August 20th, 1566, such an outbreak took place in Antwerp. There was residing in that town a certain Richard Clough, an Englishman, the agent of Sir Thomas Gresham. He wrote the following account to Gresham on August 21st.

Source: The Life and Times of Sir T. Gresham, by John W. Burgon, vol. ii, pp. 137 *et sqq*. London, 1839. Spelling has been modernized.

Sir,

For that I have not received any letters from your Mastership of late, I have the less to write as touching your affairs; all things being in good order hitherto (God be praised!); but how long it shall so remain, God knoweth; for that we have had here this night past a marvellous stir—all churches, chapels, and houses of religion utterly defaced, and no kind of things left whole within them, but broken and utterly destroyed; being done after such order and with so few folks, that it is to be marvelled at.

And because you shall understand how this matter began, yesterday about 5 of the clock, the priests, thinking to have sung Compline, as we call it . . .; and when they should have begun their service, there was a company began to sing psalms, at the beginning being but a company of boys; whereupon the Margrave and other of the Lords came to the church and rebuked them. But all in vain; for that as soon as they turned their backs, they do it again; and the company increased, being begun in our Lady Church: so that about 6 of the clock, they broke up the choir and went and visited all the books; whereof, as it is said, some they saved, and the rest utterly destroyed and broke.

After that, they began with the image of our Lady, which had been carried about the town on Sunday last, and utterly defaced her and her chapel; and after, the whole church, which was the costliest church in Europe; and have so spoiled it, that they have not left a place to sit on in the church. And from thence, part went to the parish churches, and part to the house of Religion, and made such dispatch as I think the like was never done in one night; and not so much to be wondered at of the doing, but that so few people durst or could do so much: for that when they entered into some of the houses of Religion, I could not perceive in some churches above x or xii that spoiled—all being boys and rascals; but there were many in the church lookers-on, (as some thought, setters-on).

This thing was done so quiet and so still, as if there had been nothing ado in the churches; all men standing before their doors in harness, looking upon these fellows passing from church to church, who as they passed through the streets, required all men to be quiet, and cried all *vivent les gueux*. So that, after I saw that all should be quiet, I, with above x thousand more, went into the churches to see what stir there was there; and coming into our Lady Church, it looked like a hell: where were above 1000 torches burning, and such a noise! as if Heaven and Earth had gone down together, with falling of Images and beating down of costly works; in such sort that the spoil was so great that a man could not well pass through the church. So that, in fine, I cannot write you in x sheets of paper the strange sight I saw there— organs and all, destroyed! and from thence I went (as the rest of the people did), to all the houses of Religion, where was the like stir—breaking and spoiling of all that there was. Yet, they that this did, never looked towards any spoil, but broke all in pieces, and let it lie underfoot. So that, to be short, they have spoiled and destroyed all the churches, so well nunneries as other; but as I do understand they neither said nor did anything to the nuns: but when all was broken, left it there, and so departed. So that, by estimation, they that spoiled, meddled with nothing, but let it lie; and before it was iii of the clock in the morning, they had done their work, and all were gone home again, as if there had been nothing done: so they spoiled this night between xxv and xxx churches.

ANTWERP AFTER OSTRAWELL

During the religious troubles in the Netherlands, in March 1567, a young gentleman of the name of Marnix Thoulouse got together a band of Protestant rebels, sailed up the Scheldt and landed at a small village, Ostrawell, about one mile from Antwerp. He had about 3,000 'raw levies, untrained vagabonds and outlaws', as Motley calls them. Philip de Lannoir, Seigneur de Beauvoir, commander of the Regent's bodyguard in Brussels, undertook to destroy this 'nest of rebels'. This he did with the greatest ease, although he had no more than 800 men, on March 13th, 1567. The massacre of Thoulouse's men was witnessed by a crowd of Protestants from the walls of Antwerp. The effect on them is described in the following account.

Source: A description written by Thomas Churchyard, the poet, printed in his *A Lamentable and Pitifull Description of the Wofull Warres in Flanders,* 1578, p. 19: reproduced by J. W. Burgon in *The Life and*

Times of Sir T. Gresham, vol. 2, pp. 201 *et sqq.* Spelling has been modernized and some punctuation.

The common people of Antwerp standing on their walls and beholding this murder and massacre, began to murmur at the matter, and so burst out in open words of malice, and swore to revenge the bloodshed they beheld of their brethren and country-men: whereupon a common cry was suddenly raised throughout the streets of *Vive le geuxe*, [and] all the people arming themselves in every part of the city, came running to the *Mear Broeg*, a wide and large street adjoining to the Bourse. When they had assembled together to the number of ten thousand shot, and armed men, they determined to march out of the town and meet Monsieur Beavoys, as he returned from Austreviel [Beauvoir, Ostrawell]. But in the market place was assembled twelve Ancients of the Regent's side, who had the keys of the gates, and so kept the people from their purpose a little season. But the multitude was so great, and the people swarmed so thick in every place, that the Regent's power in the market place were fain to draw the cannons from the walls, and gather their friends together from all parts of the city; and having a great power all in one place, they charged all their cannons and great pieces with hail shot, and did fortify themselves in the market place very strongly.

The night before, one Captain Bright, and Captain Marya an Italian, had broken all the bridges and passages that the people of the city should have gone over, or have had any passage at; which was done upon some suspicion they had of a revolt. The people being with this and other occasions made angry and brought in a rage, began furiously to go about the walls and kept together by thousands and multitudes, the number whereof could not easily be known: but they were judged in all to be five and twenty thousand able men; and yet among them they had no special captain, nor any that would take upon him to shew what was necessary to be done, in this their extreme hazard and danger.

The Prince of Orange, the Count de Horne, the Count de Hostraed, Monsier Decaerdes [and] all the nobility being afraid to

2B

offend the King with an open revolt, did persuade the Regent's power to make peace with the people; and about that persuasion they spent three long hours. But the Regent's power, being experienced soldiers, would lose no occasion to conquer their enemies. And on that point they stood so stiffly that they determined presently to give the commoners a battle and try out the matter by sword, and not by sweet persuasions. And to perform the same, they set all in order and were ready to march into the city, and meet with the people, as by fortune they might any way encounter them.

The Prince and the nobility, much grieved with this bloody resolution, repaired towards the people and told them all the matter, and willed them to go to their own houses and he would see that all things should be well ended. The people liked no whit that counsel and gave the Prince evil words, and a great number of them burst into my lodging. And because the Prince had made of me before, (and that they knew I had served in the Emperor's days), they called me forth and said I should be their leader; which thing I refused as far as I durst, alleging I was ignorant of such affairs: whereupon they bent their pikes on me in a great fury. I, beholding the extremity I was in, gave them my faith; and so came into the street amongst the rest of their company—where I was so received as few would have believed the manner thereof, but such as had seen it:—Witness Sir Thomas Gresham.

THE SPANISH FURY, 1576

On November 8th, 1576, some Spanish mutineers from Alost rushed on Antwerp, seized the town in which they were joined by some compatriots who had been trapped in the citadel and together they drove out the local guards and sacked the whole city.

Source: G. Gascoigne, *The Spoyle of Antwerp*, in the complete works of G. Gascoigne, ed. by Cunliffe, vol. ii, 1910, pp. 590-9.

They neither spared age, nor sex: time nor place: person nor country: professions nor religion: young nor old: rich nor poor: strong nor feeble: but without any mercy did tyrannously triumph, when there was neither man nor mean to resist them. They slew great numbers of young children. The rich was spoil because he had, and the poor were hanged because they had nothing: neither strength could prevail to make resistance, nor weakness more pity to refrain their horrible cruelty. And this was not only done when the chase was hot, but (as I heard said) when the blood was cold and they now victors without resistance. I refrain to rehearse the heaps of dead carcases which lay at every trench where they entered, the thickness whereof did in many places exceed the height of a man.

I forbear also to recount the huge numbers drowned in the new town. I list not to reckon the infinite numbers of poor Alamains who lay burned in their armour: some, the entrails scorched out, and all the rest of the body into the bulk and breast. I may not pass over with silence the wilful burning and destroying of the stately town-houses, and all the monuments and records of the city: neither can I refrain to tell their shameful rapes and outrageous forces presented unto sundry honest Dames and Virgins . . . and as great respect they had to the church and church-yard as the butcher has to his shambles. They spared neither friend nor foe, Portingal nor Turk: the Jesuit must give their ready coin, and all other religious houses both corn and plate. It is also a ruthful remembrance that a poor English merchant (who was but a servant), having once redeemed his master's good for three hundred crowns, was yet hanged until he was half dead, because he had not two hundred more to give them: and the halter being cut down and he come to himself again, besought them with bitter tears to give him leave to seek and to try his credit and friends in the town for the rest of their unreasonable demand. At his return, because he sped not (as indeed no mones was then to be had) they hanged him again outright, and after-wards (of exceeding courtesy) procured the Friars Minors to bury him.

Within three days Antwerp, which was one of the richest towns in Europe, had now no money nor treasure to be found therein, but only in the hands of murderers and strumpets: for every Don Diego must walk jetting up and down the streets with his harlot by his side in her chain and bracelets of gold. And the notable Bourse, which was wont to be a safe assembly for merchants, had now none other merchandise therein but as many dicing tables as might be placed round it.

DON JOHN OF AUSTRIA AND THE NETHERLANDS

When the revolt broke out in the Netherlands the Regent was the Duchess Margaret of Parma. She was replaced by the Duke of Alva in 1567. His policy of terror proved a complete failure and he was succeeded in 1573 by Don Luis de Requesens. He was killed by typhus in 1576 and his place was taken by Don John of Austria. His instructions were to put an end to the civil war. On paper he did this, but he failed to bring about a reconciliation between the rebellious northern provinces and Philip II.

Source: (*a*) Letter from Don John to Rodrigo de Mendoza, 1576. Slocombe, *Don John of Austria,* 1935, p. 269.

At last, thank God, I reached this place on the 3rd of this month and found the worst possible tidings of these Provinces; for only this one in which I am [Luxemburg] and Friesland of which Robles has charge can certainly be said to have withstood revolt. The rest are leagued together and are calling out troops and foreign aid against the Spaniards, and making and repealing laws in their own fashion, all these being done in the behalf of the King . . . I have written to the Council in general and to some of its members in particular of my having come. I know not what the reply may be, nor whether they will receive me, but am waiting to hear this and other things which Antonio Pérez will be able to tell better than I can as yet. Such is the miserable condition of things here.

Source: (*b*) After stormy meetings between Don John and the Estates, peace was theoretically made by the Perpetual Edict, signed on February 12th, 1577. Letter from Don John to Rodrigo de Mendoza, February 12th, 1577. Slocombe, *op. cit.,* p. 279.

Peace has been made in His Majesty's name between me and the States, and if the conditions of it are not such as might have been desired and as I strove to obtain, yet we have arrived at what was possible, which is the goal of kings. In fine, religion and obedience being saved, as is the case, the rest time must show you, and I hope in God it will show quickly. And with this one may account these States as recovered by chance, for if we were to attempt to carry the day by arms, the best that could happen to us would be the total and perpetual ruin of this country . . . The Spaniards are going away and they carry my soul with them, for I had rather be enchanted than see this happen. It is for God to pardon the sorcery that goes on yonder and from which springs so much evil. In the meetings which have been held between these men and me, they have driven me on so many occasions to lose my temper that, although I have kept it in countless cases, yet there have been others when I have lost it and have rated them roundly, telling them what they are and what they deserve, so that on every point we have made ourselves useless to one another. They fear me and think that I am a choleric person, and I abhor them and consider them very great scoundrels, and so it is needful now that I should go and another come in my place, for so sure as we meet it is certain a new disagreement will arise and do mischief. I have therefore written home very urgently—let this be a secret between us—that I neither can nor will remain here any longer, since I have by God's grace accomplished that for which I came, which was to put an end to the war . . .

Source: (c) Outwardly Don John exerted all his powers to win over the Dutch. Slocombe, *op. cit.*, pp. 282 *et sqq.*

Juan Beautista Tassis:
Such were the beauty and vivacity of his eyes that with a single glance he made all hearts his own.

A Courtier:
Don John surpasses Circe. No one comes before him without being transformed into a worshipper. All the lords are drunk with his good graces.

Dr. Wylson, English envoy in Brussels:
Don John useth much courtesy and familiarity to all that come unto him, as he winneth credit greatly among those that are of

least understanding. And to me he showeth himself so well disposed, with such dolce and good words, with so many such earnest and so vehement offers of his faith and service to our sovereign, as I doubt him more than others trust him, for I see his deeds contrary to his words, using concert in secrecy with Her Majesty's rebels, and especially with Stewkley, Sir Francis Englefield, the Countess [of Northumberland's] servant, and others . . . He, being a vowed Catholic and very ambitious of great things, cannot bear such a faithful goodwill to our sovereign as he pretendeth. He hath secretly charged all rebels and fugitives to absent themselves, but yet he giveth order for their pensions. I was earnest enough with him, but I could not anger him.

Source: (*d*) Don John entirely understood the situation in the Netherlands, the popularity of William the Silent and the hatred felt for Philip II: nor was he afraid to enlighten Philip in forthright terms. Slocombe, *op. cit.*, p. 287. Don John to Philip II.

[William of Orange] is the pilot who guides the bark. He alone can destroy it or save it. The greatest obstacles would be removed if he could be gained . . . The name of Your Majesty is as much abhorred and despised in the Netherlands as that of the Prince of Orange is loved and feared. I am negotiating with him and giving him every security, for I can see that the establishment of peace, as well as the maintenance of the Catholic religion, and obedience to Your Majesty, depend on him.

WILLIAM OF NASSAU, PRINCE OF ORANGE

WILLIAM THE SILENT

William the Silent (the name of Silent arose from a mistranslation of the Latin word *taciturnus*) was born in 1533 and was murdered in 1584. He was the son of William Count of Nassau and his wife Juliana of Stolberg, and was born at the castle of Dillenburg in Nassau. He was brought up as a Catholic, but in 1573 he openly declared himself a Calvinist Protestant. It is likely that he was never a deeply religious man in a doctrinal sense—he cared very little for doctrine. But like Henry IV in France, or Elizabeth I in England, he was compelled to adapt his creed to the political necessities of the times. He had an

unswerving belief in the existence and power of God. What makes
him one of the outstanding figures in the history of his times is his
hatred of persecution in any form, whether the victims were Protestants, Catholics or Anabaptists. He was the first and probably the only
man in his century to recognize that tolerance was the proper attitude
towards religions. Almost the whole of his life was a series of disastrous
disappointments, but he never lost heart and although he failed to
unite the whole of the Netherlands into one kingdom, he was in fact
the founder of the seven northern provinces which grew into the
United Provinces.

There are historians who take a less splendid view of William the
Silent. Trevor Davies in his *The Golden Century of Spain* describes him
as intending rebellion from the beginning, the master of a whole
system of spies, hopelessly in debt, largely because of the money he
spent on his enormous number of cooks—he dismissed twenty-eight
head cooks in one day as an attempt to economize. 'This coarse and
brutal materialist has often been transformed by religious and political
partisanship into an angel of light', whereas in fact his whole purpose
was to 'carve out an independent principality for himself in the
Netherlands' (pp. 155–7). That description may be taken as a corrective
to the over-laudatory account by C. V. Wedgwood in her *William
the Silent*. But even Trevor Davies ends his account of William the
Silent with this tribute, 'the heart and soul of the rebellion, the one
leader who seemed capable of keeping men of various religious bodies
side by side and of securing foreign aid for the rebellion'. Obviously,
William might have been doing this solely for his own ends, 'to carve
out an independent principality for himself'. But if that were so, could
he have won such love and admiration as inspired the epitaph printed
on page 382.

Source: Pontus Payen, *De la Guerre Civile des Pays Bas*. MS quoted
in Motley, *Rise of the Dutch Republic* and Harrison, *William the Silent*,
1897, p. 17. Pontus Payen was the Seigneur des Essarts, one of the
royal party and a strong Catholic (see Moltey, i, 169, n. 2).

Never did arrogant or indiscreet word issue from his mouth,
under the impulse of anger or other passion; if any of his servants
committed a fault, he was satisfied to admonish them gently
without resorting to menace or abusive language. He was master
of a sweet and winning power of persuasion, by means of which
he gave form to the great ideas within him, and thus he succeeded

in bending to his will the other lords about the court as he chose; beloved and in high favour above all men with the people, by reason of a gracious manner that he had of saluting and addressing in a fascinating and familiar way all whom he met.

WILLIAM HEARS OF PHILIP'S PLANS FOR EXTIRPATING HERESY IN THE NETHERLANDS

Source: Pontus Payen, quoted in Harrison, *op. cit.* 22–3.

One day, during a stag-hunt in the Bois de Vincennes, Henry, finding himself alone with the Prince, began to speak of the great number of Protestant sectaries who, during the late war, had increased so much in his kingdom to his great sorrow. His conscience, said the King, would not be easy nor his realm secure until he could see it purged of the 'accursed vermin' who would one day overthrow his government, under the pretence of religion, if they were allowed to get the upper hand. This was the more to be feared since some of the chief men of the kingdom, and even some princes of the blood, were on their side. But he hoped by the grace of God and the good understanding that he had with his new son, the King of Spain, that he would soon master them. The King talked on thus to Orange in the full conviction that he was cognisant of the secret agreement recently made with the Duke of Alva for the extirpation of heresy. But the Prince, subtle and adroit as he was, answered the good King in such a way as to leave him still under the impression that he, the Prince, was in full possession of the scheme propounded by Alva; and under this belief the King revealed all the details of the plan arranged between the King of Spain and himself for the rooting out and rigorous punishment of the heretics, from the lowest to the highest rank, and in this service the Spanish troops were to be mainly employed.

WILLIAM'S FEELINGS ON HEARING THIS NEWS

Source: William's *Apology*, quoted Harrison, *op. cit.* 23.

I confess I was deeply moved with pity for all the worthy people who were thus devoted to slaughter, and for the country to which I owed so much, wherein they designed to introduce an Inquisition worse and more cruel than that of Spain. I saw, as it were, nets spread to entrap the lords of the land as well as the people, so that those whom the Spaniards and their creatures could not supplant in any other way, might by this device fall into their hands. It was enough for a man to look askance at an image to be condemned to the stake. Seeing all this, I confess that from that hour I resolved with my whole soul to do my best to drive the Spanish vermin from the land; and of this resolve I have never repented, but believe that I, my comrades and all who have stood with us, have done a worthy deed, fit to be held in perpetual honour.

WILLIAM'S FIRST STEP

Source: Pontus Payen, quoted Harrison, *op. cit.* 24.

The Prince, having wrung his secret from the King, maintained his composure for two or three days, and then obtained leave to make a journey to the Netherlands on private business of importance. No sooner had he reached Brussels than he explained to his intimate friends what he had heard in the Bois de Vincennes, giving a sinister meaning to the excellent purposes of the two Kings, who (he said) designed to exterminate the great chiefs so as to fill their own treasuries by confiscations, and ultimately to set up an absolute tyranny under pretence of extirpating heresy. And when he left the city, he counselled them to make the withdrawal of the Spanish troops a formal demand in the States-General about to be held in Ghent.

WILLIAM THE SILENT'S RELIGION

Source: Pontus Payen, quoted Harrison, *op. cit.* 38.

As to religion, he behaved with such discretion that the most close observers could not decide which way he inclined. The Catholics thought him a Catholic; the Lutherans, a Lutheran. He heard mass daily, whilst his wife and daughter made public profession of the Lutheran heresy, even in his presence, without any objection from him. He condemned the rigidness of our theologians in maintaining the constitutions of the Church without making a single concession to the Reformers. He blamed the Calvinists as provoking sedition and strife, yet he spoke with horror of the edict of the Emperor that sentenced them to death; for he held it to be cruelty to kill any man for maintaining an erroneous opinion. He used to say that in all matters of religion, punishment should be reserved to God alone, much as the rude German who said to the Emperor, 'Sire, your concern is with the bodies of your people, not with their souls'. In short, the Prince would have liked to see established a fancy kind of religion of his own, half-Catholic, half-Lutheran, which would satisfy both sides. Indeed, if you look at his inconsistency on religious questions, as shown in his speeches and despatches, you will see that he put the State as something above the Christian religion, which in his eyes was a political invention to keep people steady to their duty by the fear of God, so that orthodoxy was to him neither more nor less than the ceremonies, divinations, and superstitions that Numa Pompilius introduced in old Rome to tame the fierce and too warlike temper of his Romans.

WILLIAM'S APPEAL TO ELIZABETH I OF ENGLAND, 1573
   Source: quoted Harrison, *op. cit.* 148.

He declared before the Almighty Majesty of God that these wars were not for ambition or gain. He had steadily refused the sovereignty himself, and he could always withdraw (if he pleased) to a quiet life in his own hereditary domain. The war was one solely in defence of religion and the freedom of the people—a cause for which he would refuse no travail or danger till the last drop of his blood were spent. The Estates pressed on the Queen to take full possession of Holland and Zealand; they were resolved, if she refused, to throw themselves on the French, who would then be masters of the Low Countries. To prevent that, let the Queen put herself at the head of a Protestant League and with the aid of the German Protestant chiefs effect some peaceful settlement of the revolted provinces. Rather than they should fall into Spanish hands, they would not only die with their country, but before they died, they would entangle the same with such a devil as should root out the name of the Spaniards for ever amongst them.

DEATH OF WILLIAM'S BROTHERS

In 1574 disaster befell William's army which was exterminated at Mook Heide, near Nijmegen. Three of his brothers were killed, but John survived. William wrote him a twelve-page letter about his plans for the future.

Source: Quoted Harrison, *op. cit.* 156–7.

If no prince or power will give us help, and for want of it we are all to perish, so be it in God's name! Yet withal we shall have the honour of having done what no nation ever yet did, of having defended and maintained ourselves, in so petty a land, against the mighty and horrid efforts of such powerful enemies, without any aid from others. And if the poor people of these parts, abandoned by all the world, still resolve to hold out as they have done till now, and as I trust they will continue to do, and if it do not please God to chastise us and utterly destroy us, it will still cost the Spaniards the half of Spain, in wealth as well as men, before they will have made an end of us.

PHILIPS II'S DECLARATION OF WILLIAM'S OUTLAWRY

In March, 1580, Philip II, who had for a long time been advocating that William ought to be murdered, issued his *Ban*.

Source: Quoted, Harrison, *op. cit.* 208.

Philip, by the grace of God, King of Castile . . . to all to whom these presents shall come. Whereas, William of Nassau, a foreigner in our realms, once honoured and promoted by the late Emperor and by ourselves, has by sinister practices and arts gained over malcontents, lawless men, insolvents, innovators, and especially those who were suspected of religion; and has instigated these heretics to rebel, to destroy sacred images and churches and profane the sacraments of God; and has promoted revolt by a long series of offences, encouraging the public preaching of heresy, and persecuting priests, monks and nuns with a view to exterminate by impieties our Holy Catholic faith; whereas he has taken a consecrated nun and abbess in the lifetime of his own lawful wife, and still lives with her in infamy; whereas he has been the head of the rebellion against our sister, the Duchess of Parma, against the Duke of Alva, and our brother Don John, and still persists in this treason, refusing all our offers of clemency and peace, and supporting the damnable League of Utrecht; whereas the country can have no peace whilst this wretched hypocrite troubles it with his insinuations (as do those whose conscience is ulcered like Cain or Judas) and, foreigner as he is, puts his whole happiness in ruining our people:

Now we hereby declare this head and chief author of all the troubles to be a traitor and miscreant, an enemy of ourselves and our country. We interdict all our subjects from holding converse with him, from supplying him with lodging, food, water, or fire under pain of our royal indignation. And in execution of this Declaration we empower all and every to seize the person and the goods of this William of Nassau, as enemy of the human race; and hereby, on the word of a King and as minister of God, we promise to any one who has the heart to free us of this pest, and who will deliver him dead or alive, or take his life, the sum of 25,000 crowns in gold or in estates for himself and his heirs; we will pardon him any crime if he has been guilty, and give him a patent of nobility, if he be not noble, and we will do the same for all accomplices and agents. And we shall hold all who shall disobey this order as rebels, and will visit them with pains and penalties. And, lastly, we give command to all our governors to have this Declaration published in all parts of our said Provinces.

WILLIAM'S DEFENCE

William in due course replied with his *Apology*, his defence of his whole life and career. The *Apology* covers more than 100 pages. It was probably written by de Villiers, a well-known Protestant divine, once an advocate and now William's chaplain. But there can be no doubt that William composed the argument and is responsible for it throughout.

Source: Quoted Harrison, *op. cit.* 209.

I take it as a signal honour that I am the mark of the cruel and barbarous proscription hurled at me by the Spaniard for undertaking your cause and that of freedom and independence; and for this I am called traitor, heretic, foreigner, rebel, enemy of the human race, and I am to be killed like a wild beast, with a price offered to my assassins. I am no foreigner here, no rebel, no traitor. My princedom, which I hold in absolute sovereignty, and all my baronies, fiefs, and inheritances in Burgundy, and in the Netherlands are mine by ancient and indisputable right, and have the sanction of my good friend the late Emperor and the public law of Europe. My ancestors were powerful Lords in the Low Countries long before the House of Austria set foot therein . . . So far back as 1039 my ancestors were reigning Counts and Dukes in Guelderland for centuries, whilst the ancestors of the King were mere Counts of Hapsburg in Switzerland. King he may be in Spain or Naples, or of the Indies, but we know no King here: we know only Duke or Count—and even our Duke is limited by our ancient privileges, to maintain which Philip has pledged his oath on his accession, though he professes to have been absolved from it by the Pope.

Traitor, he calls me, against my lawful sovereign—he himself deriving his crown through Henry, the bastard, that traitor and rebel against Pedro, his liege lord, his own father's son, whom he killed with his own hand . . . Adulterer, he calls me, who am united in holy matrimony by the ordinances of God's church to my lawful wife—Philip, who married his own niece, who murdered his wife, murdered his own son, and many more, who is notorious for his mistresses and amours, if he did not instigate Cardinal Granvelle to poison the late Emperor Maximilian! . . .

I was bred up a Catholic and a worldling, but the horrible persecution that I witnessed by fire, sword and water, and the plot to introduce a worse than Spanish Inquisition which I learned from the King of France, made me resolve in my soul to rest not till I had chased from the land these locusts of Spain . . . And of the resistance to the tyranny of Spain I take responsibility, for I view with indignation the bloodthirsty cruelties, worse than those of any tyrant of antiquity, which they have inflicted upon the poor people of this land. Has not the King seized my son, a lad at college, and immured him in a cruel prison? Does he not delight in *autos-da-fe*? ... Did he not send here the monster Alva, who swore eternal hatred to this people and boasted that he had put to death 18,000 persons innocent of everything but differing from him in religion, a man whose tyranny and cruelty surpass anything recorded in ancient or modern history? ...

ASSASSINATION OF WILLIAM

For ten years William of Orange was dogged by assassins—French, Scotch, Spanish, German, Flemish had all tried and had all failed. Dagger, pistol, poison, explosion had no success. The publication of the *Ban* hotted up the danger for William. One attempt by a young Biscayan named Jaureguy, who received absolution from a Dominican monk, Timmermann, all but succeeded. Jaureguy shot William through the neck, the palate and the cheek. As the Prince fell, he called out, 'Do not kill him: I forgive him my death'. But William recovered, and he wrote from his sick bed asking the authorities at least not to torture the victims. The shock of the attack killed William's wife, Charlotte (1582). In 1584 Balthazar Gérard succeeded in shooting William three times in the chest. As William fell, his last words were 'My God, have pity on this poor people'.

William the Silent earned and received perhaps the most beautiful epitaph known to history. Motley closed his great history with the following words, which he took from a state document.

Source: Relation fait a ceux du Magistrat de Bruxelles, 11 *Juillet*, 1584. MS. Bib. de Bourg, no. 17, 386.

As long as he lived he was the guiding star of a whole brave nation, and when he died the little children cried in the streets.

THE TURKS

The Fall of Constantinople, 1453

Mohammed II (1451–81) was the ablest of the Ottoman sultans and determined to seize Constantinople. The city was wholly unprepared to resist. Constantine XI, the last of the Christian Emperors, was a noble character who had ruled successfully in the Morea. But at Constantinople the odds were heavily against him. The Pope made a profound mistake in compelling Constantine publicly to declare the Union of the Western Catholic and the Eastern Orthodox Churches in the face of immense opposition from the Orthodox Church, whose bishops in the Turkish dominions much preferred the Sultan to the Pope. Constantine himself made a mistake in demanding a double subsidy for the detention of Orkhan, the only Ottoman prince whom the house of Osman had left alive. Mahomet II laid his plans with great ability. Constantine received from Europe hardly any help at all—a few Venetian ships and about 1000 soldiers under the command of the Genoese Giustiniani. On April 5th, 1453, the Turkish army appeared before the walls of the city from the Golden Horn to the Sea of Marmora. The Turkish fleet occupied the sea. A great chain had been thrown across the entrance of the Golden Horn harbour. The weakest part of the defences was on the landward wall which was battered by the heaviest artillery yet made. Three Genoese ships fought their way into the harbour bringing supplies, but this was all the new help that Constantine received. The first Turkish attack was launched on April 18th and was repulsed by Giustiniani and his Genoese troops. The next day a naval attack was made and this also was repulsed. On April 20th four Christian ships tried to get into the harbour. A terrific battle ensued, which Mahomet watched on horseback, frequently riding into the sea to shout at, encourage and curse his ships and men. The wind, which had fallen and made possible the battle, suddenly got up again and the four ships were swept into harbour. Mahomet now resorted to a laborious device, which proved entirely successful. He transported his ships across land and when the Christian sentries looked out at dawn on April 23rd, they saw 72 Turkish ships at anchor in the Channel of the Golden Horn.

The siege went on through almost the whole of May, the Christians repelling attack after attack. But the final assault was made on May 29th and on that day the Christian Empire, which had lasted for more than a 1000 years, was destroyed.

Source: (*a*) Nicolò Barbaro, *Giornale dell' assedio di C.*, ed. E. Cornet, 1856. Barbaro was in the city during the siege. The following English version is taken from *Byzantium, Its Triumphs and Tragedy*, by R. Guerdan, trans. by D. L. B. Hartley, Allen and Unwin, 1954.

On the eighteenth day of this same month of April a great multitude of Turks came to the walls. This took place at about two o'clock in the night and the fight lasted until six o'clock . . . after sunset, and in this combat many Turks perished. And when these Turks approached the walls it was dark, and this enabled them to approach unexpectedly without being noticed. But do not ask me with what and how many cries they flung themselves at the walls or how they were able to retain their drums so that there seemed to be many more Turks than there actually were. Their cries were heard even on the coast of Asia Minor, twelve miles from their camp. And while they were making these terrible cries the Emperor began to weep in his sorrow and anxiety that this night the Turk might make a general assault, that we were not yet sufficiently prepared. That is why the Emperor knew this great anxiety. But Eternal God would not on this occasion permit such a great abomination and at six o'clock the fight ended and quiet reigned again to the great shame and very great losses of those pagans.

300 TURKISH SHIPS ATTACKED THE CHAIN ACROSS THE GOLDEN HORN, APRIL 19TH, 1453

Source: (*a*) Critobulus, *A History of the Deeds of Mohammed II.* Critobulos of Imbros had been a Christian, but he was by 1453 a renegade on the Turkish side, therefore he writes from the Turkish point of view. He was not an eye-witness of the events, but he had first-hand evidence. The History is dedicated to Mohammed II: it exists in MS. at Constantinople: it was first published by C. Müller in the second part of vol. v of *Fragmenta Historicorum Graecorum*, 1870. The following English version is taken from R. Guerdan, *op. cit.*, p. 196. The Turkish Fleet is transported overland.

Reducing their speed when they were within range of missiles and arrows, the enemy in their turn had recourse to weapons which can be thrown from afar. One struck and one was struck. These weapons were arrows and stone bullets from guns. Then the Turkish fleet rushed as near as possible to the Greek vessels which were ranged in line behind the Chain. From the decks of their ships a party of Turkish soldiers dressed in armour and with torches in their hands tried to set fire to the Greek ships in the port. Others incessantly shot fire arrows at them. Others tried to cut the anchor ropes. Yet others with hooks and ladders climbed up the sides of the ships. Others, by means of axes, javelins and long lances, killed the Christian sailors. And all showed high spirits and extreme courage in action. The object of all this effort was to repel, to set fire to or to sink the Christian vessels in order to break the famous Chain.

The Christian crews were prepared in advance for this attack and owing to the far-sightedness of the Grand Duke Notaras, who commanded them, and of the commander of that section of the ramparts, they were supplied with the necessary equipment and they had the advantage of the superior height of their great ships. From this eminent position they covered the assailants with a continuous hail of stones, javelins, lances, darts and projectiles of all kinds. Especially those who had taken up a position on the poop or on the masts wreaked a great carnage amongst their adversaries, killing and wounding a great number. They even had vessels full of water, dependent upon long ropes, with which they extinguished fires, and enormous stones which they let fall from on high to the enemy ships, which were drawn up almost to the very sides of theirs, causing thus frightful injuries amongst the aggressors.

The ardour of the combatants was extreme and the issue always in doubt. The Turks wanted to force a way into the Golden Horn. The Christians, Greek and Italian, resisted bravely. After a fight as short as it was violent the Christian vessels, thanks to their heroic constancy, forced the Sultan's fleet to retire. The Turkish ships, abandoning on this occasion all hope of breaking the Chain, regained their anchorage at the Two Columns,

2 C

followed by insulting remarks, the jeers and the shouts of triumph of the Christian crews.

THE TURKISH FLEET IS TRANSPORTED OVERLAND

Source: Thousands of navvies were employed to make a road from the Bosphorus shore over the heights of Pera to the edge of the Golden Horn. On each side of this road lengths of timber were placed end to end, thus forming a slipway which was then greased with oils and fat. The ships were then hoisted on to the slipway by means of ropes and winches and teams of oxen, and they were hauled along by thousands of men: Nicolò Barbaro, *Giornale*, English version from R. Guerdan and D. L. B. Hartley, *op. cit.*, p. 196 *et sqq.*

The crews which followed each ship, overjoyed by what was going on and by the thought of what was to come next, boarded their craft, when at the top of the hill, as though they were at sea, and quickly travelled downhill towards the Golden Horn. Some of the sailors unfurled the sails and raised shouts of triumph, as if they were taking to the high seas, and the wind got into the sails and filled them. Others, sitting on the rowing benches, held their oars in their hands and pretended to row, while the overseers ran up and down the high wooden track spurring on their men with whistles, shouts and lashes from the whip. Thus the Turkish vessels, strange voyagers, slid across the country as if sailing the sea. While the last ones were still ascending the slope of the hill the first were already descending the steep slope to the Golden Horn, all set and with great shouts of joy. And it was, I repeat, a strange spectacle to see these vessels with all sail set, with their crews and all their armament, move across the fields as if they were on the high sea.

THE FINAL SCENES IN CONSTANTINOPLE

Source: On May 29th the city fell and there ensued the wildest scenes of butchery and destruction by the Turks. Critobulus, *op. cit.* English version from Guerdan and Halliday, *op. cit.*, p. 218.

Nothing will ever equal the horror of this harrowing and terrible spectacle. People frightened by the shouting ran out of their houses and were cut down by the sword before they knew what was happening. And some were massacred in their houses where they tried to hide, and some in churches where they sought refuge. The enraged Turkish soldiers . . . gave no quarter. When they had massacred and there was no longer any resistance, they were intent on pillage and roamed through the town stealing, disrobing, pillaging, killing, raping, taking captive men, women, children, old men, young men, monks, priests, people of all sorts and conditions . . . There were virgins who awoke from troubled sleep to find those brigands standing over them with bloody hands and faces full of abject fury. This medley of all nations, these frantic brutes stormed into their houses, dragged them, tore them, forced them, dishonoured them, raped them at the cross-roads and made them submit to the most terrible outrages. It is even said that at the mere sight of them many girls were so stupified that they almost gave up the ghost. Old men of venerable appearance were dragged by their white hair and piteously beaten. Priests were led into captivity in batches, as well as reverend virgins, hermits and recluses who were dedicated to God alone and lived only for Him to whom they sacrificed themselves, who were dragged from their cells and others from the churches in which they had sought refuge, in spite of their weeping and sobs and their emaciated cheeks, to be made objects of scorn before being struck down. Tender children were brutally snatched from their mothers' breasts and girls were pitilessly given up to strange and horrible unions, and a thousand other terrible things happened . . .

Temples were desecrated, ransacked and pillaged . . . sacred objects were scornfully flung aside, the holy icons and the holy vessels were desecrated. Ornaments were burned, broken in pieces or simply thrown into the streets. Saints' shrines were brutally violated in order to get out the remains which were then thrown to the wind. Chalices and cups for the celebration of the Mass were set aside for their orgies or broken or melted down or sold. Priests' garments embroidered with gold and set with pearls and gems were sold to the highest bidder and thrown into the fire to extract the gold. Immense numbers of sacred and profane books were flung on the fire or torn up and trampled under foot. The majority, however, were sold at derisory prices, for a few pence. Saints' altars, torn from their foundations, were overturned. All the most holy hiding places were violated and broken in order to get out the holy treasures which they contained . . .

When Mohammed saw the ravages, the destruction and the deserted houses and all that had perished and become ruins, then a great sadness took possession of him and he repented the pillage and all the destruction. Tears came to his eyes and sobbing he expressed his sadness. 'What a town this was! And we have allowed it to be destroyed'! His soul was full of sorrow. And in truth it was natural, so much did the horror of the situation exceed all limits.

MOHAMMED II (1451–1481)

Source: (a) Critoboulos, *Monum. Hung. Hist. Script.* xxi, 291, quoted in B. Miller, *The Palace School of Muhammed II*, pp. 34–5. Harvard U.P. 1941.

[In the summer of 1455, the Sultan, tired of campaigning] gave himself up to the study of philosophy, as much to that of the Arabs and Persians as to that of the Hellenes. Daily he talked with the leaders and masters of thought, of whom there were not a few with whom he had surrounded himself and with whom he was accustomed to make his studies and researches in philosophy and in the dogma of this science; above all he was pleased with those of the Peripatetics and Stoics. In the course of a study of the works of Ptolemy, who, both as scientist and philosopher, expounds the entire world and all that is therein, Muhammed desired that this exposition and the maps which went with it, which were cut and scattered, should be brought together upon one single piece of linen. He therefore charged the philosopher Georges with this task, promising royal honour and reward to one who should depict the entire habited earth upon one map . . . He also commanded a translation of the entire works of Ptolemy into Arabic.

Source: (*b*) The Turkish historian, Saad ad-Din (Khojah Effendi), *Chronica dell'origine e progressi della casa ottomana*, trans. by V. Brattuti, 1649–52, quoted by B. Miller, *op. cit.*, 28–9.

He was generally regretted by all his subjects, particularly by those who had distinguished themselves in letters and in science during his reign, because of the marks of esteem and consideration they had received from him in the shape of liberalities . . . The protection he extended to men of letters has resulted in the production of innumerable works of value, the majority of which are dedicated to him. In the manner of his ancestors he was accustomed to give alms each Friday on so generous a scale that it would be too great an undertaking to give a detailed list of the gratuities which he bestowed upon men of letters, sheikhs or other people, devoted to the cult of God and the descendants of the Prophet.

Nothing greater or more magnificent could be imagined than the mosque which he caused to be built in the city of Stamboul . . . and the eight colleges destined to teach the sciences which surround it, each college having eight apartments of several rooms each for the purpose of housing the students. There is also a soup kitchen where morning and evening abundant meats are cooked for the poor of both sexes, as also for the students who eat in a large refectory built for that purpose. In the same place may be seen a hostel for foreign travellers, equipped with a separate kitchen, stables both for their mounts and their beasts of burden and a large storehouse where is provided barley and straw with which to feed them. There is also an infirmary for the poor with a separate bath and everything else necessary to take care of them. There is even a school to teach the children how to read.

He also collected several thousand manuscripts, in most instances commentaries and exegeses on Islamic law and religion, and caused them to be distributed in each of the mosques which he had built for the use and convenience of the teachers residing in those mosques . . .

In conclusion, so great was his genius and so deeply had he gone into the sciences that the greatest scholars of the day were filled with wonder and praise. By means of the great and unusual knowledge which he acquired he reigned with a wisdom and prudence that commanded universal admiration.

DESCRIPTIONS OF THE TURKS

THE JANISSARIES

When the Turks conquered a Christian land they levied a tribute to be paid in children. These children were brought up in barracks under a strict military discipline and they were looked on as the Sultan's private property. So complete was the mental and physical training to which they were subjected that there is scarcely one known example (Scanderbeg, an Albanian, is the only notable one) of a Janissary escaping back to his own people. To begin with the number of them was small, in 1360 about 1,000, by the sixteenth century perhaps about 100,000. They formed a thing unknown in Europe, a trustworthy infantry, all skilled bowmen.

Source: (a) *The Turkish Letters of Ogier Ghiselin De Busbecq,* Imperial ambassador at Constantinople, 1554–62, trans. by E. S. Forster, Oxford, 1927, p. 8 *et sqq.*

At Buda I first came across the Janissaries, which is the name they give to their footguards. When they are at full strength, the Sultan possesses 12,000 of them, scattered throughout his empire either to garrison the fortresses against the enemy or to protect the Christians and Jews from the violence of the populace . . . In the fortress of Buda there is a perpetual garrison of Janissaries. They wear robes reaching to their ankles, and on their heads a covering consisting of the sleeve of a coat (for this is the account they give of its origin), part of which contains the head, while the rest hangs down behind and flaps against the neck. On their foreheads rises an oblong silver cone, gilded and studded with stones of no great value. These Janissaries generally visited me in pairs, and on being admitted to my dining-room, saluted me with an obeisance and then hastened, almost at a run, towards me and took hold of my garment or hand as though they would kiss it, and offered me a bunch of hyacinths or narcissi. They would then rush back again to the door at almost the same speed, taking care not to turn their backs on me; for this, according to their ideas, is unbecoming. At the door they would take up their stand silent and respectful, their hands crossed upon their breast and their eyes fixed upon the ground; you would think they were monks rather than soldiers. However, on receiving a few little coins, which was all they wanted, they would again make obeisance and utter their thanks in loud tones and depart with every kind of good wish and blessing. Really, if I had not been told that they were Janissaries, I could well have believed that they were a kind of Turkish monks or members of some kind of sacred association; yet these were the famous Janissaries who carry such terror wherever they go.

Source: (b) Ottaviano Bon, *Il Seraglio del Gransignore* (1608), trans. G. Berchet, Venice, 1865, p. 36.

The course that is pursued with the pages is not that of a barbaric people, but rather that of a people of singular virtue and self-discipline. From the time that they first enter the school of the Grand Seraglio they are exceedingly well directed. Day by day they are continuously instructed in good and comely behaviour, in the discipline of the sciences, in military prowess, and in a knowledge of the Moslem faith—in a word in all the virtues of mind and body.

Source: (c) Busbecq, *op. cit.*, p. 112.

I mentioned that baggage animals are employed on campaign to carry the arms and tents, which mainly belong to the Janissaries. The Turks take the greatest care to keep their soldiers in good health and protected from the inclemency of the weather; against the foe they must protect themselves, but their health is a matter for which the State must provide. Hence one sees the Turk better clothed than armed. He is particularly afraid of the cold, against which, even in the summer, he guards himself by wearing three garments, of which the innermost—call it shirt or what you will—is woven of coarse thread and provides much warmth. As a further protection against cold and rain tents are always carried, in which each man is given just enough space to lie down, so that one tent holds twenty-five or thirty Janissaries . . .

The armour which is carried is chiefly for the use of the household cavalry, for the Janissaries are lightly armed and do not usually fight at close quarters, but use muskets. When the enemy is at hand and a battle is expected, the armour is brought out, but it consists mostly of old pieces picked up in various battlefields, the spoil of former victories. These are distributed to the household cavalry, who are otherwise protected by only a light shield. You can imagine how badly the armour, thus hurriedly given out, fits its wearers. One man's breastplate is too small, another's helmet is too large, another's coat of mail is too heavy for him to bear. There is something wrong everywhere; but they bear it with equanimity and think that only a coward finds fault with his arms, and vow to distinguish themselves in the fight, whatever their equipment may be; such is the confidence inspired by repeated victories and constant experience of warfare.

Source: (d) Busbecq, op. cit., p. 145 et sqq.

A window was allotted me at the back of the house, looking out upon the street by which the Sultan was to leave the city. I was delighted with the view of the departure of this splendid army. The Ghourebas and Ouloufedjis rode in pairs, the Silihdars and Spahis in single file. These are the names given to the household cavalry, each forming a separate body and having its own quarters. Their total number is said to be about 6000 men . . .

The Turkish horseman presents a very elegant spectacle, mounted on a horse of Cappadocian or Syrian or some other good breed, with trappings and horse-cloths of silver spangled with gold and precious stones. He is resplendent in raiment of cloth of gold and silver, or else of silk or satin, or at any rate of the finest scarlet, or violet, or dark green cloth. At either side is a fine sheath, one to hold the bow, the other full of bright-coloured arrows, both of wonderful Babylonian workmanship, as also is the ornamented shield which is attached to the left arm and which is only suited to ward off arrows and the blows dealt by a club or sword. His right hand is encumbered by a light spear, usually painted green, unless he prefers to keep that hand free; and he is girt with a scimitar studded with gems, while a steel club hangs from his horse-cloth or saddle . . . He keeps his spear in his possession as long as possible, and when circumstances demand the use of the bow in its turn, he puts the spear, which is light and therefore easily handled, between the saddle and his thigh, in such a position that the point projects a long way behind and the pressure of the knee holds it firm as long as he thinks fit. When circumstances make it necessary for him to fight with the spear, he puts the bow into the quiver, or else fixes it across the shield on his left arm . . . On their heads they wear turbans made of the whitest and finest cotton stuff, in the middle of which rises a fluted peak of purple silk. This headdress is often adorned with black feathers.

Source: (e) Giovio, L'Histoire des Empereurs du Turquie, Paris, 1538, quoted by B. Miller, op. cit., pp. 166–7.

As to the cavalry, those called Spahi-oghlani or Spahiglani (cavalry pages), these are the flower and elite of all, because they have been reared in the place called 'The Enclosure' [Enderun] and instructed in letters and in arms in the same manner as the children of the Prince Sultan. They are put, some in the cavalry ranks, some in the infantry, and in these consists all the strength of the Turks. Also they serve the lieutenants and governors of the provinces in honourable and profitable matters, and from these are appointed the sanjak beys, who are held in such high esteem that they are married to women of the royal blood. These are the noblest and best loved by the Prince, being the best mounted and best accoutred in rich furs and skins, and the first in order of all who are with the Turk. They are one thousand in number, each of which has servants from the number of four to ten, and the said Spahis wear hats on their heads, as do the others, and cloth of gold brocade or velvet or purple or some other colour. Their office is to accompany the Grand Signor at his right side and at all times when he goes out of the city.

Source: (f) B. Miller, op. cit., p. 149 et sqq.

The Turks were in tents in the plains hard by. Here I lived for three months and had a good opportunity of visiting their camp

and acquainting myself pretty well with their system of discipline
. . . The first thing I noticed was that the soldiers of each unit
were strictly confined to their own quarters. Any one who knows
the conditions which obtain in our own camps will find difficulty
in believing it, but the fact remains that everywhere there was
complete silence and tranquility, and an entire absence of quarrelling and acts of violence of any kind, and not even any shouting
or merrymaking due to high spirits or drunkenness. Moreover,
there was the utmost cleanliness, no dungheaps or rubbish, nothing
to offend the eye or nose, everything of this kind being buried by
the Turks or else removed from sight. The men themselves dig
a pit in the ground with their mattocks and bury all excrement,
and so keep the whole camp scrupulously clean. Moreover, you
never see any drinking or revelry or any kind of gambling, which
is such a serious vice amongst our soldiers . . .

Source: (g) B. Miller, op. cit., pp. 10–11.

It would be a long task to describe the city of Buda in detail . . .
It lies in a pleasant situation in a very fertile district on sloping
ground bordered on one side by vine-clad hills: on the other side
flows the Danube with Pesth and a view of wide plains beyond.
It seems to have been purposely designed to be the capital of
Hungary. The city was formerly adorned with the splendid
palaces of the Hungarian nobles; these have now fallen in ruins,
or are only prevented from doing so by the liberal use of props.
They are inhabited by the Turkish soldiers, whose pay only
suffices for their daily needs, and does not allow them to mend the
roofs or repair the walls of these vast buildings. They care little
if the rain comes through or the walls are cracked, so long as they
can find a dry place to stable their horses and make their own
bed. The upper stories they regard as no concern of theirs, and
leave them to be overrun by rats and mice. Moreover, it is
characteristic of the Turks to avoid any magnificence in their
buildings; to care for such things is in their opinion a sign of
pride, vanity and self-conceit, as though a man expected immortality and a permanent abode upon this earth. They regard their

houses as a traveller regards an inn; if they are safe from thieves and protected from heat or cold or rain, they require no further luxuries. This is why in the whole of Turkey you would have difficulty in finding even a rich man in possession of a house of any elegance.

A FRENCH VIEW OF THE TURKS

Source: T. Wright, *Early Travels in Palestine.* De la Brocquière returning from Palestine in 1433.

They are a tolerably handsome race, with long beards, but of moderate size and strength. I know well that it is a common expression to say 'as strong as a Turk', nevertheless I have seen an infinity of Christians excel them when strength was necessary, and I myself, who am not of the strongest make, when circumstances required labour, found very many Turks weaker than I.

They are diligent, willingly rise early, and live on little, being satisfied with bread badly baked, raw meat dried in the sun, milk curdled or not, honey, cheese, grapes, fruit, herbs, and even a handful of flour with which they make a soup sufficient to feed six or eight for a day. Should they have a horse or camel sick without hope of recovery, they cut its throat and eat it. They are indifferent as to where they sleep and usually lie on the ground. Their dress consists of two or three cotton garments, thrown one over the other, which fall to their feet. Over these again they wear a mantle of felt, called a *capinat*. This, though light, resists rain, and some *capinats* are very handsome. Their boots come up to their knees and they wear side drawers, some of crimson velvet, others of silk or fustian and common stuffs. In war, or when travelling, to avoid being embarrassed by their gowns, they tuck the ends into their drawers, that they may move with greater freedom.

Their horses are good, cost little in food, gallop well and for a long time. They keep them on short allowances, never feeding them but at night and then giving them only five or six handfuls of barley with double the quantity of chopped straw, the whole put into a bag which hangs from the horse's ears.

It is the policy of the Turks to have their armies twice as numerous as those of the Christians. This superiority of numbers augments courage and allows them to form different corps, and to make their attacks on various parts at the same time. Should they once force an opening, they rush through in incredible crowds, and it is then a miracle if all be not lost . . . The Turkish lances are worth nothing: their archers are the best troops they have, and these do not shoot so strongly nor so far as ours. They have a more numerous cavalry, and their horses, though inferior in strength to ours and incapable of carrying such heavy weights, gallop better and skirmish for a longer time without losing their wind.

I must own that in my various experiences I have always found the Turks frank and loyal, and when it was necessary to show courage, they have never failed . . . Their armies I know commonly consist of 200,000 men, but the greater part are on foot and destitute of wooden shields, helmets, mallets or swords. They have besides amongst them a great number of Christians who are forced to serve—Greeks, Bulgarians, Macedonians, Albanians, Slavonians, Wallachians, Serbians and other subjects of the despots of that country. All these people detest the Turk, because he holds them in a severe subjection; and should they see the Christians, and above all the French, march in force against the Sultan, I have not the slightest doubt but they would turn against him and do him great mischief.

A TURKISH VIEW OF THE CHRISTIANS

Source: Serbian MS. trans. Mijatovich, Constantine, London, 1892, pp. 41–3. *c.* 1500. The Sultan is encouraging his Viziers and Pashas against the threat of European invasion.

You know well the unwashed Gyaours and their ways and manners, which certainly are not fine. They are indolent, sleepy, easily shocked, inactive; they like to drink much and to eat much; in misfortunes they are impatient, and in times of good fortune proud and overbearing. They are lovers of repose and do not like to sleep without soft feather-beds; when they have no women with them they are sad and gloomy; and without plenty of good wine they are unable to keep counsel among themselves. They are ignorant of any military strategems. They keep horses only to ride while hunting with their dogs; if one of them wishes to have a good war-horse, he sends to buy it from us. They are unable to bear hunger or cold, or heat, effort and menial work. They let women follow them in the campaigns, and at their dinners give them the upper places; and they want always to have warm dishes. In short, there is no good in them . . .

And then the Christians fight constantly among themselves, because everyone desires to be a king, or a prince, or the first amongst them. One says to another, 'Brother, help thou me to-day against this Prince, and to-morrow I will help thee against that one'. Fear them not, there is no concord amongst them. Everyone takes care of himself only; no one thinks of the common interest. They are quarrelsome, unruly, self-willed and disobedient. Obedience to their superiors and discipline they have none, and yet everything depends on that.

When they lose a battle they always say, 'We were not well-prepared'; or, 'This or that traitor has betrayed us'; or, 'We were too few in number and the Turks were far more numerous'; or, 'The Turks came upon us without previous declaration of war, by misleading representations and treachery. They have occupied our country by turning our internal difficulties to their own advantage.'

Well, that is what they say, being not willing to confess truly and rightly: 'God is on the side of the Turks. It is God who helps them and therefore they conquer us.'

AN ENGLISHMAN AT THE COURT OF MOHAMMED III, 1599

Source: The Diary of Thomas Dallam, ed. by J. C. Bent, Hakluyt Society, No. 87, 1893, pp. 67 *et sqq*. Little is known about Thomas Dallam before 1599. By profession he was an organ-builder. When the Levant merchants were anxious to secure special trading privileges from the Sultan of Turkey, Mohammed III, they decided to send him a present and they commissioned Dallam to build a magnificent clock. Dallam himself took the clock to Constantinople and presented it to the Sultan as a gift from Queen Elizabeth I. The Grand Signor is the Sultan. Spelling and punctuation have been modernized.

The Grand Signor, being seated in his chair of state, commanded silence. All being quiet and no noise at all, the present began to salute the Grand Signor, for when I left it, I did allow a quarter of an hour for his coming thither. First, the clock struck 22, then the chime of 16 bells went off and played a song of 4 parts. That being done, two personages which stood upon two corners of the second storey, holding two silver trumpets in their hands, did lift them to their heads and sounded a tantarra. Then the music went off and the organ played a song of 5 parts twice over. In the top of the organ, being 16 feet high, did stand a holly bush full of blackbirds and thrushes, which at the end of the music did sing and shake their wings. Divers other motions there were which the Grand Signor wondered at. Then the Grand Signor asked the Coppagawe (gatekeeper) if it would ever do the like again. He answered that it would do the like again at the next hour. Quoth he, 'I will see that'. In the meantime the Coppagawe, being a wise man, doubted whether I had so appointed it or no, for he knew that it would go of itself but 4 times in 24 hours, so he came unto me, for I did stand under the house side where I might hear the organ, and he asked me if it would go again at the end of the next hour; but I told him that it would not, for I did think the Grand Signor would not have stayed so long by it; but if it would please him, that when the clock had struck he would touch a little pin with his finger, which before I had shewn him, it would go at any time. Then he said he would be as good as his word to the Grand Signor. When the clock began to strike again, the Coppagawe went and stood by it, and when the clock had struck 23, he touched that pin and it did the like as it did before. Then the Grand Signor said it was good. He sat very near unto it, right before the keys where a man should play on it by hand. He asked why those keys did move when the organ went and nothing did touch them. He told him that by those things it might be played on at any time. Then the Grand Signor asked him if he did know any man that could play on it. He said, 'No, but he that came with it could, and he is here without the door'. 'Fetch him hither', quoth the Grand Signor, 'and let me see how he doth it'. Then the Coppagawe opened that door which I went out at, for I stood near unto it. He came and took me by the hand, smiling upon me, but I bid my dragoman ask him what I should do or whither I should go. He answered that it was the Grand Signor's pleasure that I should let him see me play on the organ. So I went with him. When I came within the door, that which I did see was very wonderful unto me. I came in directly upon the Grand Signor's right hand, some 16 of my paces from him, but he would not turn his head to look upon me. He sat in great state, but the sight of him was nothing in comparison of the train that stood behind him, the sight whereof did make me almost to think that I was in another world. The Grand Signor sat still, beholding the present which was before him, and I sat dazzling my eyes with looking upon his people that stood behind him, the which were four hundred persons in number. Two hundred of them were his principal pages, the youngest of them 16 years of age, some 20 and some 30. They were apparelled in rich cloth of gold made in gowns to the midleg: upon their heads little caps of cloth of gold, and some cloth of tissue (interwoven or variegated): great pieces of silk about their waists instead of girdles: upon their legs Cordovan buskins, red. Their heads were all shaven, saving that behind their ears did hang a lock of hair like a squirrel's tail: their beards shaven, all saving their upper lips. Those 200 were very proper men, and Christian born.

The third hundred were dumb men that could neither hear nor speak, and they were likewise in gowns of rich cloth of gold and Cordovan buskins; but their caps were of violet velvet, the crown of them made like a leather bottle, the brims divided into five peaked corners. Some of them had hawks on their fists.

The fourth hundred were all dwarfs, big-bodied men, but very low of stature. Every dwarf did wear a scimitar by his side, and they were also apparelled in gowns of cloth of gold.

I did most of all wonder at the dumb men, for they let me understand by their perfect signs all things that they had seen the present do by its motions . . .

The Grand Signor sat in a very rich chair of state, upon his thumb a ring with a diamond in it half an inch square, a fair scimitar by his side, a bow and a quiver of arrows.

He sat so right behind me that he could not see what I did, therefore he stood up and his Coppagawe removed his chair to one side where he might see my hands, but in his rising from his chair he gave me a thrust forwards, he could not do otherwise, he sat so near me; but I thought he had been drawing his sword to cut off my head.

I stood there playing such things as I could until the clock struck, and then I bowed my head as low as I could and went from him with my back towards him. As I was taking up my cloak, the Coppagawe came unto me and bid me stand still and let my cloak lie. When I had stood a little while, the Coppagawe bade me go and cover the keys of the organ. Then I went close to the Grand Signor again and bowed myself, and then I went backwards to my cloak. When the company saw me do so, they seemed to be glad and laughed. Then I saw the Grand Signor put his hand behind him full of gold, which the Coppagawe received and brought unto me forty and five pieces of gold called *chickers* (sequins), and then was I put out again where I came in, being not a little joyful of my good success.

THE GRAND TURK, SULEIMAN I. 1520–66

SULEIMAN THE MAGNIFICENT

He was one of the most able soldiers and able rulers in the sixteenth century. Under him the Ottoman Empire reached its highest pitch. 'Strong as his father, a soldier as well as a statesman, his mind was well-balanced: he felt none of Selim's grim delight in war and butchery. Perhaps no contemporary sovereign in Christendom was so unfeignedly desirous or sincerely resolute to administer even-handed justice as Suleiman' (*C.M.H.*, old series, 1, 92–3). In the realm of politics Scandinavia and Russia were hardly an integral part of Europe. Travellers were hardly aware of Scandinavia: only economically, to those in search of expanding trade, did Russia 'swim into their ken'. But the Grand Turk was an ever-present menace. Infidels they might be, but they had perhaps the finest military organization in Europe. Therefore after Pavia, when Francis I was a prisoner in the hands of Charles V, his mind turned towards an alliance with the only power militarily strong enough to suit his purpose, heretic and common enemy of Europe as the Turk might be. Francis proposed an alliance with the Turk to Suleiman I. Suleiman's answer did not commit him to anything, but it is a fine example of the Turkish royal mind.

Source: (a) C.M.H. op. cit., p. 95.

I who am the Sultan of the Sultans, the Sovereign of the Sovereigns, the distributor of crowns to the monarchs of the surface of the globe, the shadow of God on the earth, the Sultan and Padishah of the White Sea, the Black Sea, Rumelia, Anatolia, Caramania, Rum, Sulkadr, Diabeki, Kurdistan, Azerbijan, Persia, Damascus, Aleppo, Cairo, Mecca, Medina, Jerusalem, all Arabia, Yemen, and other countries which my noble ancestors (may God brighten their tombs) conquered and which my august majesty has likewise conquered with my flaming sword, Sultan Sulayman Khan, son of Sultan Selim, son of Sultan Bayazid; you who are Francis, King of France, you have sent a letter to my Porte the refuge of sovereigns . . . night and day our horse is saddled and our sword girt.

Source: (b) Marino Sanuto, Diarii, xxix, col. 391, Venice, 1879–1903. Bartolomeo Contarini, Oct. 15th, 1520. Suleiman had just come to the throne.

He is twenty-five years old, tall, but wiry, and of a delicate complexion. His neck is a little too long, his face thin and his nose aquiline. He has a faint moustache and a small beard: nevertheless, his expression is pleasant, although his skin has rather a pallor. His reputation is that of a wise lord, he is said to be studious, and everybody hopes that his rule will be good.

Source: (c) Alberi, Relazioni degli Amb. Ven. Series III, 101. Pietro Bragadino, ambassador at Constantinople, 1524–6. June 9th, 1526.

He is thirty-two years old, deadly pale, his nose aquiline, his neck long. He does not seem to have much physical strength,

2D

but his hand is very strong, as I saw when I kissed it, and he is said to bend a stiffer bow than anybody else. By nature he is melancholy, he is much given to women, generous, proud, impetuous and at the same time very gentle.

Source: (*d*) Alberi, *op. cit.* i, 28. Daniello de' Ludovisi, June, 1534.

Tall, thin, with an aquiline nose and a rather earthy complexion. He is healthy, his temperament choleric and also melancholy, he prefers ease to business, he is orthodox in his faith and his life is respectable. The general opinion is that his mind is not at all quick, nor is he as forceful and prudent as so great a prince should be, especially because he has handed over the government of his empire into the hands of his Grand Vizier Ibrahim. Neither he nor any of his court ever undertake any important business without consulting Ibrahim, and Ibrahim does everything and never consults the Grand Signior nor any other person.

Source: (*e*) Alberi, *op. cit.* i, 72. Bernardo Navagero, February, 1553.

He is above middle height, thin, his complexion is brown, and his countenance has a majestic and very sweet expression which is beautiful to see. He eats sparingly, very little meat, no wine— they say that he used to in Ibrahim's time—only good water, because of his infirmities, which are said to be the gout and a tendency to dropsy. At Constantinople he is almost every day in his yacht, crossing over to see his gardens or to hunt in Anatolia. He is specially fond of Adrianople as a residence, because he has there a seraglio which opens on to a chase, and he goes hunting pretty well every day. He is reputed to be a very just man, and when he has been briefed on the exact facts of a case, he never wrongs any man. He observes his religion and its laws more strictly than any of his house has ever done, and he boasts that he has never broken his word, and there can not be higher praise than that. Having had many years of experience, he understands his business very well and, generally speaking, he conducts his affairs admirably.

Source: (*f*) Ogier Ghiselin de Busbecq, Imperial ambassador at Constantinople, 1555–62. He may perhaps be best remembered for

having introduced into Western Europe the horse chestnut, the lilac
and the tulip. His life and letters were published by C. T. Forster and
F. H. B. Daniell, 2 vols. in London, 1881. i, 159, *et sqq*. September 1st,
1555.

His years are just beginning to tell on him . . . Considering
his years (for he is now getting on for sixty) he enjoys good
health, though it may be that his bad complexion arises from some
lurking malady. There is a notion current that he has an incurable
ulcer or cancer on his thigh. When he is anxious to impress an
ambassador who is leaving with a favorable idea of the state of
his health, he conceals the bad complexion of his face under a
coat of rouge, his notion being that foreign powers will fear him
more if they think that he is strong and well. I detected unmistak-
able signs of this practice of his; for I observed his face when he
gave me a farewell audience, and found it much altered from
what it was when he received me on my arrival.

Source: (g) Marcantonio Donini, secretary to the Venetian ambassador at Constantinople, 1559–62. Alberi, *op. cit.*, 3rd series, iii, 178.

His Majesty during many months of the year was very feeble
of body, so that he was not far off from dying, suffering from
dropsy, with swollen legs, loss of appetite, and his face swollen
and a bad colour. Last March he had four or five fainting fits,
and another one since then, so that his attendants hardly knew
whether he was alive or dead, and they scarcely thought that he
would recover. The general opinion is that he must die soon,
although his doctor has been using very powerful remedies.
Perhaps the satisfaction which he feels at the death of his sons
and grandsons may have a wonderful effect on his health, because,
when he heard of their deaths, he is said to have raised his eyes
to heaven and clasped his hands together and said, 'God be
praised that I have lived to see the Moslems freed from the
miseries which would have come upon them, if my sons had
fought for the throne; I may now pass the rest of my days in
tranquility, instead of living and dying in despair'.
But there are people who say that either the anger of God will
not let the deaths of the innocent grandchildren go unpunished,

or that Prince Selim, now that his brother is not there to contest the throne, will soon find means of bringing his father's life to an end. May God bring about that which may be of most advantage to Christendom.

Source: (*h*) Ogier Ghiselin de Busbecq, Imperial ambassador at Constantinople, 1555 to 1562. C. T. Forster and F. H. B. Daniell, *op. cit.* The following account was written by him to a friend, when he had been summoned to the Sultan in 1555. i, 152 *et sqq.*

The Sultan was seated on a very low ottoman not more than a foot from the ground, which was covered with a quantity of costly rugs and cushions of exquisite workmanship; near him lay his bow and arrows. His air, as I said, was by no means gracious, and his face wore a stern, though dignified, expression.

On entering we were separately conducted into the royal presence by the chamberlains, who grasped our arms. This has been the Turkish fashion of admitting people to the sovereign ever since a Croat, in order to avenge the death of his master, Marcus, Despot of Servia, asked Amurath for an audience and took advantage of it to slay him. After having gone through a pretence of kissing his hand, we were conducted backwards to the wall opposite his seat, care being taken that we should never turn our backs to him.

The Sultan's hall was crowded with people, among whom were several officers of high rank. Besides these there were all the troopers of the Imperial Guard, Spahis, Ghourebas, Ouloufedgis [paid troops] and a large force of Janissaries; but there was not in all that great assembly a single man who owed his position to aught save his valour and his merit. No distinction is attached to birth among the Turks; the deference to be paid to a man is measured by the position he holds in the public service. There is no fighting for precedence; a man's place is marked out by the duties he discharges. In making his appointments the Sultan pays no regard to any pretensions on the score of wealth or rank, nor does he take into consideration recommendations or popularity; he considers each case on its own merits, and examines carefully into the character, ability, and disposition of the man whose promotion is in question. It is by merit that men rise in the service, a system which ensures that posts should only be assigned to the competent. Each man in Turkey carries in his own hand his ancestry and his position in life, which he may make or mar as he will. Those who receive the highest offices from the Sultan are for the most part the sons of shepherds or herdsmen, and so far from being ashamed of their parentage, they actually glory in it, and consider it a matter of boasting that they owe nothing to the accident of birth; for they do not believe that high qualities are either natural or hereditary, nor do they think that they can be handed down from father to son, but that they are partly the gift of God, and partly the result of good training, great industry and unwearied zeal; arguing that high qualities do not descend from a father to his son or heir any more than a talent for music, mathematics or the like; and that the mind does not derive its origin from the father, so that the son should necessarily be like the father in character, but emanates from heaven and is thence infused into the human body, Among the Turks, therefore, honours, high posts and judgeships are the rewards of great ability and good service. If a man be dishonest, or lazy, or careless, he remains at the bottom of the ladder, an object of contempt; for such qualities there are no rewards in Turkey!

This is the reason that they are successful in their undertakings, that they lord it over others and are daily extending the bounds of their empire. These are not our ideas; with us there is no opening left for merit; birth is the standard for everything; the prestige of birth is the sole key to advancement in the public service. But on this head I shall perhaps have more to say to you in another place, and you must consider what I have said as strictly private.

THE CAPTURE OF RHODES BY THE TURKS, 1522

When Suleiman the Magnificent succeeded to the throne of Turkey in 1520, he realized that two places in Europe threatened the security of his country—Belgrade, which menaced its northern frontiers, and the island of Rhodes which cut its communications between Constantinople and Cairo. Belgrade fell to his arms in 1521, and in 1522 he took

Rhodes after a siege which lasted for 145 days. Rhodes was the home of the Knights Hospitallers under their Grand Master, Villiers de l'Isle Adams. After he had surrendered Rhodes the Hospitallers moved first to Crete with the right to rule Malta and Gozo, as well as Tripoli. In 1530 the Knights of St. John (the Hospitallers) moved into Malta, which in 1565 was to withstand a memorable siege by the Turks.

Source: (a) A Brief Relation of the Siege and Taking of the city of Rhodes by Sultan Suleiman the Great Turk, translated out of the French into English at the Motion of the Reverend Lord Thomas Dockway, Great Prior of the Order of Jerusalem in England, in the Year 1524.

The 25th day of the said month many of our men went out to skirmish in the field and made great murder of the Turks, and in likewise did our artillery. And it is to be noted that the 28th day of the same month the Great Turk in person passed to Fisco, a haven in the mainland, with a galley and a fust,[1] and arrived about noon where his army lay, the which day may be called unhappy for Rhodes. For his coming, his presence and continual abiding in the field is and hath been the cause of the victory he hath had. When the galley that he came in arrived, all the other ships of the host hanged banners aloft in their tops and on their sail-yards.

Soon after that the Turk was arrived, he went to land, and mounted on his horse and rode to his pavilion which was in a high place called Megalandra, four or five miles from the town out of the danger from the gun-shot. And on the morrow, as it was reported to us, he came to a Church nigh the town called St. Steven, for to view the Town and Fortress, whereas they had set up manttellets for to lay their ordinance . . .

Source: (b) Of the mines that the Turks made and how they overthrew part of the bulwark of England: ibid.

And because as it is said before, that the greatest hope that the enemies had to get the town of Rhodes was by mining, therefore now after that I have spoken of the gunshot and beatings, I shall show of the mines that the Turks made, which were in so great quantity and in so many places that I believe the third part of the town was mined: and it is found by account made that there

---

[1] The *E.E.D.* gives no suitable meaning for this word.

were about 60 mines; howbeit, thanked be God, many of them came not to effect by occasion of the countermines that they within made, and also trenches that the right prudent Lord the Great Master caused to be made deep within the ditches unto two or three feet of water. The which trenches and certain pits that he had caused in the said ditches to be wrought or [before] the host arrived, served right well since: for night and day there were men in them to watch and hearken when the enemy mined, for to meet them and to cut their way, as was done many times.

And for to speak of the mines that had effect and damaged us, it is to wit that the fourth day of September, about four hours afternoon, the enemies put fire in two mines, one was between the postern of Spain and Auvergne, which did no hurt but to the Barbican. The other was at the bulwark of England, which was so full and strong that it caused most part of the town to shake and cast down a great part of the said bulwark at the spring of the day: and by the earth and stones that fell into the ditches the enemies came upon the bulwark with their banners and fought sore and mightily with our men, not with hands but with shot of handguns. The Lord Great Master that was come 15 days or more with his succours to the said bulwark, went with his company to help them that fought. After that they had fought the space of two or three hours, the enemies, repelled and driven back by our men from the said bulwark, and beaten with ordinance on every side, withdrew then with their shame and damage. And this was the first victory that our Lord gave us, and there abode of our enemies a thousand and more.

The Check to the Turks

DON JOHN OF AUSTRIA

Don John of Austria was the illegitimate son of Charles V and Barbara Blomberg of Regensburg. He was born in 1547 (not as often asserted in 1545). He was publicly recognized by Philip II as his step-brother in 1559. Philip intended the boy to take up an ecclesiastical career, but after some difficulties Don John persuaded Philip to let him go for a military life. In 1568, he was in command of a fleet of galleys against the Algerian corsairs: 1569 to 1570 he commanded the Spanish army against the rebellious Moriscos in Granada. The height of his fame and fortune came in 1571 when he commanded the whole fleet of the Holy League and defeated the Turks in the great battle of Lepanto. After that his life was something of an anti-climax: he failed to build a kingdom out of Tunis: he had to admit the failure of his policy when he became the governor-general of the Netherlands in 1576; the popularity of the Prince of Orange was too strong for him. In 1578 he defeated William of Orange's army at Gemblours, but the victory was really due to the skill of the Prince of Parma, which Don John handsomely and publicly admitted. He died on Oct. 1st, 1578. All the following English versions are printed in Slocombe's *Don John of Austria*, Ivor Nicholson, 1935.

Source: (a) The Venetian ambassador at Naples, 1575. Slocombe, p. 242.

[Don John is] of middle stature, well made, of a most beautiful countenance and of admirable grace. He has little beard, but large moustaches of a pale colour; he wears his hair long and turned upward, which becomes him greatly; he dresses sumptuously and with such nicety that it is a marvel to see him. Active and perfectly skilful, he has no rival in the management of horses and in jousting, in all kinds of military sports and tournaments; and in the pursuit of these exercises he is unwearied, playing at tennis five or six hours together, and in that sort of game not sparing himself more than the others, but contending with all his might and not enduring defeat, however small the stakes, but thinking that even in these little things honour is in question.

Source: (b) The Treaty of the Holy League—Pope Pius V, Philip II and the Republic of Venice—was concluded against the Turks on May 25th, 1571. Don John of Austria was put in command of the whole fleet. Marc Antonio Colonna was the second in command. Sebastian Veniero commanded the Venetian fleet. The Turks had attacked and captured Nicosia and Farmagosta in Cyprus. The way to Europe by sea was open to the Infidel. Don John's responsibility was neither more nor less than to save Western Europe from the Infidel: Pope Pius V to Don John of Austria. Slocombe, 150–1.

Pope Pius to our well-loved son in Christ, health and the Apostolic benediction. Almighty God, the author of all good, has been pleased that with His divine favour the League should be concluded, which our right dear son in Christ, the Catholic King of the Spains, your brother, and the illustrious Republic of the Venetians some months ago began to negotiate against the most cruel tyrant, the Lord of the Turks; which, having come to so good an issue, it appeared to us right to congratulate Your Nobleness on the occasion, as by these letters we do, being assured that our message will be welcome and agreeable to you, on account both of your piety towards God and of your desire for the increase of the Christian world.

Greatly do we rejoice to behold you thus prosperously navigating this our sea, that together with the fleets of the other members of the League you make a beginning of the destruction of the common enemy; and therefore do we entreat and warn you in Christ our Lord, that, imitating the virtue of the Captains-General, your predecessors, you use your discretion diligently both to provide all things requisite to the success of the expedition and to avoid delay, which in affairs of war is so important and praiseworthy.

We would further urge this upon you with many reasons, did we not know that the business carries with it its reward in the common benefit of the Christian world, and your particular honour, and that you need no further exhortation from our zealous and fatherly love, being assured that Your Nobleness will never be found wanting either to the one or to the other.

Given at Rome on the 24th May, 1571.

Source: (c) Colonna sailed with 47 galleys on July 20th, 1571. He was joined by Veniero with 55 galleys in a rotten state and with only half their complement of men. Don John joined the combined fleet at Messina a month later. Ultimately the allied fleet numbered over 300 ships and 80,000 men, but the condition of the fleet was very bad: Don John to Don Garcia, August 30th, 1571. Slocombe, p. 167.

You cannot believe in what bad order both soldiers and sailors are. Arms and artillery certainly they have, but fighting is not to be done without men . . . No kind of order seems to prevail among them, and each galley appears to come and go as each captain pleases. Fine grounds indeed for their anxiety to fight!

The allied fleet sailed from Messina on September 15th, 1571. It made contact with the Turkish fleet under Ali Pasha in the Gulf of Lepanto (now the Gulf of Corinth) on October 7th. The two fleets were roughly equal in numbers, but the weight of experience and skill lay with the Turks. The battle lasted four hours and resulted in an overwhelming victory for the Christians. 25–30 thousand Turks were killed, 8,000 Christians. 12,000 Christian galley slaves were liberated from the Turkish fleet.

THE BATTLE OF LEPANTO, 1571

Source (a) A letter from a member of the Christian fleet, October 8th, 1571. Fugger-Zeitungen, *Ungedruckte Briefe an das Hans Fugger*, 1568–1605. Ed. Klarwill, Vienna, 1923: quoted Reddaway, *Select Documents, 1453–1714.*

After the Christian armada had arrived on the sixth of this month by night in the small channel in Kephalonia, the Turkish armada, which was lying in the gulf of Lepanto, immediately observed it. This is not surprising, because the pirate Caraggogia had arranged with the Turkish commanders to sight the Christian armada and to count its ships. This he did so skilfully as to escape unhurt, but perhaps . . . failed to give the number of our galleys correctly. The Turkish commander very joyfully made preparations for battle, especially as the wind was very favourable, and embarked another 12,000 men in addition to the troops whom he already had on the armada. In this way, through God's providence, contrary to naval practice, he robbed himself of an advantage. Don Juan of Austria also set out with his armada and sent out some galleys to sight the enemy, sending also six galeasses out of harbour. The galleys reported that the Turkish armada was lying ready near Kephalonia. Thereupon Don Juan put on a suit of light armour and embarked in a small ship called a frigate. With a crucifix in his hand, he put galley after galley in battle array and exhorted them to fight valiantly against the hereditary enemy of the Christian faith. Not he, he said, but Christ, who had died for us on the Cross, was the father and lord of this armada, and he hoped they would have grace from His godly help and arm. Thereupon the warriors shouted loud for joy and formed for battle. Then Don Juan re-entered his galley and rowed off to meet the Turkish armada. The sea had become quite calm and the galeasses in the van had begun a powerful bombardment which was causing the Turks great damage and fear. They were crying 'Maom, Maom', which means 'great ships, great ships with great guns'. In this way the Turkish armada, which had been sailing close together in a crescent, was broken up into three parts. The first and greatest had attacked the left wing of the Christian armada, the second the middle, and the third the right wing under Andreas Doria. At the outset Doria lost almost the entire crews of ten galleys, although they defended themselves most gallantly. It would have gone ill with him, if some galleys from the middle section had not come to his assistance, whereat his galleys took fresh heart and made the enemy retire. The left wing also fought gallantly, but it would have gone ill with this too, if it had not been reinforced by the Marquis of Santa Cruz, who attacked the foe in such a manner that the victory was completely on our side. The wind too rose, to our advantage. In this engagement Uluch Ali disappeared, whether to Africa or to the gulf of Lepanto is not known. Out of 40 great galleys, of which we captured 29, he only escaped with one. Our General, Don Juan of Austria (as I have mentioned above), encountered with his galley the galley of the Turkish commander, finally defeated it and cut off the head of the Turkish pasha with his own hand and placed it on a spike in his galley . . .

With God's help the Christians have gained the victory in five hours. Almost all the Turkish leaders with about 18,000 men were killed, 10,000 taken prisoner, and 15,000 Christians, who had been prisoners on the galleys, set free. These had done the Turks much damage during the battle.

A hasty reckoning shows on our side 20 Venetian nobles and about 1000 men killed. A hundred Turkish galleys were captured and sixty sunk.

To Almighty God and His Blessed Mother be praise and honour for ever! Amen.

Source: (*b*) Don John to Philip II. Slocombe, p. 194–5.

Your Majesty ought to give and cause to be given, in all parts, infinite thanks to Our Lord for the great and signal victory which He has been pleased to vouchsafe to this fleet. That Your Majesty may understand all that has passed, besides the report herewith despatched, I send also Don Lope de Figueroa, to the end that he, as one who has served in this galley in a way justly to entitle him to reward, should relate all the particulars which Your Majesty may be pleased to hear . . .

I desire now to follow up the good fortune which God has given us for the advantage of Your Majesty, and to see whether Lepanto can be taken, that gulf being a place of great importance; and if not, what other enterprise . . . may be attempted. This I have not as yet been able to determine, on account of much which has to be done in refitting the fleet, in which we are every day discovering fresh damage, besides other things which must be supplied before we can or ought to advance. But to-morrow night or the next night we may, please God, be free to sail. Of all that happens Your Majesty shall be informed, step by step; but that the good news may be no longer delayed I despatch Don Lope now, merely reminding Your Majesty of the opportunity God has placed within our hands of extending your power with no greater difficulty than attends at once setting about levying troops and fitting out galleys, of which there is no lack, and providing for a supply of money and munitions in the ensuing spring . . .

In this galley Don Bernardino de Cardenas has been slain, doing the duty imposed upon him at his birth. He leaves, I am informed, many debts behind him, and here in the fleet, a natural son; whereof it would be just and for the good of the service that Your Majesty should order account to be taken. Other persons there are . . . who have in truth done good service and merited reward, and this is one of the occasions, as Your Majesty very well knows, when men watch what is done for those who have distinguished themselves . . .

I am, thank God, well, the cut which I received on the ankle, I hardly know how, having turned out a mere nothing. God keep Your Majesty with all the things which I desire and of which we all stand in need.

At Petala, October 10th, 1571.

Source: (c) Don Lope de Figueroa describes to Don John his interview with Philip II. Slocombe, p. 196.

For the first half hour he did nothing but ask, 'Is my brother assuredly well?' and all sorts of conceivable questions appropriate to the case. He then ordered me to relate everything that had happened from the beginning, omitting no single particular, and while I spoke he stopped me thrice to ask for further explanations. And when I had ended, he as often called me back to ask other questions about Your Highness' care for the wounded, and how you gave away your share of the prize-money to the soldiers, at which he was not a little moved . . . The standard he received with the greatest gladness that can be conceived. He wanted to know the meaning of the inscription on it. I answered that we could not read it because of the letters shot away; but that it was registered at the Prophet's house in Mecca, where it had been blessed by the chief priests . . . Of Your Highness' wound I have spoken as you desired. Rejoicings are in preparation; what they will be like I do not know, or whether they will be like those I saw in France. In Avignon there were more processions even than the feasts in Andalusia, where in many places they have already had cave-plays on a large scale.

Source: (d) Philip II to Don John. It is noteworthy that he refused to let Don John come to Spain—he might have been too popular: Slocombe, p. 197. Written from the Escurial, November 29th, 1571.

I cannot express to you the joy it has given me to learn the particulars of your conduct in the battle, of the great valour you showed in your own person and your watchfulness in giving proper directions to others—all which has doubtless been a principal cause of the victory. So to you, after God, I am happy to make my acknowledgements for it, as now I do, and happy am I that it has been reserved for one so near and dear to me to perform this great work, which has gained so much honour and glory in the eyes of God and of the world.

As regards your coming hither this winter, you will already have been informed of the order which has been sent you to winter at Messina, and although it would delight me exceedingly to see you now and to exchange personal congratulations with you on the occasion of this great victory, I postpone this pleasure.

Source: (*e*) Pope Pius V's comment on the victory. Slocombe, p. 198.

'There was a man sent from God, whose name was John.'

Source: (*f*) Pope Pius V on Don John. Slocombe, p. 214.

That young chief has proved himself a Scipio in valour, a Pompey in heroic grace, an Augustus in good fortune, a new Moses, a new Gideon, a new Samson, a new Saul, a new David, without any of the faults of these famous men, and I hope in God to live long enough to reward him with a royal crown.

Source: (*g*) The following letter shows the generous humanity of Don John. The Turkish commander, Ali Pasha, was killed at Lepanto. The tutor of his two sons was captured and freed by Don John. In March 1573 the tutor arrived at Naples with a letter from Fatima, the sister of Said Bey and Mahomet Bey, Ali's two sons, pleading that the sons should be released. She also sent a magnificent present of jewelled swords, daggers, furs and tapestry. Mahomet Bey had died soon after the battle: Slocombe, p. 217. Don John's answer to Fatima.

When I was yet in hopes of being able to liberate both of them, to my great grief there happened to Mahomet Bey the final end of sorrows, which is death. I now restore Said Bey to liberty, as well as the other prisoners for whom he has asked it, as I would also have set free him who is dead, were he still alive. And believe me, Madam, that it is to me a peculiar pleasure to have it in my power to fulfill and satisfy, in part at least, your desire, holding as I do in high esteem the noble character you bear. The present you have sent I have not accepted, but have left it in the hands of Said Bey, not by any means because I do not value that which has come from your hands, but because it has been the custom of my great ancestors not to receive gifts from those who apply to them for aid, but to confer favours.

THE NORTHERN RENAISSANCE
(Notes on p. 440)

The most notable single fact about the Renaissance in Northern Europe is that it was essentially religious. In Spain the Inquisition, in France the wars of religion stopped the movement. In Germany the Reformation was in itself the Renaissance, so that in Germany, England, the Netherlands, Switzerland, 'the Renaissance was carried straight forward, through the channels of religion on the one hand and of a great romantic drama on the other. Luther no less than Shakespeare was the child of the new ideas . . . The ultimate expression of puritanism was Milton, who was equally the child of the Renaissance.' (Edith Sichel, *The Renaissance*, ch. vii.)

The most notable single figure in the Northern Renaissance was Erasmus, the greatest of all the Humanists (see p. 1 *et sqq.*). He combined in himself all the characteristics of the classical revival, which began in Italy, with all the characteristics of the Northern or German Humanism, which was based on the desire to revive primitive Christianity and a bitter detestation of the Monks. Erasmus, Ulrich von Hutten, and to a lesser degree Englishmen like Colet and Frenchmen like Rabelais, invented the art of serious satire. It is nothing like so easy to deal with the realm of art in Northern Europe as it is in Italy. I have arbitrarily chosen Dürer as representative of the N. European painters. Luther balances Savonarola, Rabelais balances Benvenuto Cellini, Montaigne is very much *sui generis*: at moments one sees his sympathy with the views of Machiavelli: but he was not really a classicist: it is possible to see in him the most modern 'artist' in the realm of sixteenth century literature. He is the first literary critic who relates criticism to contemporary life. He invented the essay and to some extent he may be said to have invented the autobiography. (Edith Sichel, *op. cit.*, p. 210.)

ALBRECHT DÜRER

Albrecht Dürer was born at Nuremberg in 1471 and he died in 1528. He was the second of eighteen children, brought up in a God-fearing family. He is remembered to-day in the world of art as a painter, as a draughtsman on the block for the woodcutter, and as an engraver with his own hand on copper. 'The greatest mind that ever expressed itself in this form of art' *(Ency. Brit.)*. He travelled widely and after he had acquired a European reputation, he was fêted wherever he went—notably in Venice and in the Low Countries. He wrote several books on his theories of art—these varied from essays on anatomy, proportions of the human frame (1528): on *Geometry and Perspective* (1525): and on *Fortifications* (1527).

Dürer is one of the greatest geniuses produced in the northern European Renaissance. He personified the close connection between Art, Renaissance and Reformation. He was a great admirer of Martin Luther, though the two men never met.

Source: (a) A family history written by Albrecht Dürer in the year 1524 from 'my father's papers'. Quoted by W. M. Conway in *Literary Remains of Albrecht Dürer*, C.U.P. 1889, p. 35.

This my dear Father was very careful with his children to bring them up in the fear of God; for it was his highest wish to train them well that they might be pleasing in the sight both of God and man. Wherefore his daily speech was that we should love God and deal truly with our neighbours.

And my father took special pleasure in me because he saw that I was diligent in striving to learn. So he sent me to the school, and when I had learnt to read and write he took me away from it and taught me the goldsmith's craft. But when I could work neatly my liking drew me rather to painting than to goldsmith's work, so I laid it before my father; but he was not well pleased, regretting the time lost while I had been learning to be a goldsmith. Still, he let it be as I wished, and in 1486 (reckoned from the birth of Christ) on S. Andrew's day (30 Nov.) my father bound me apprentice to Michael Wolgemut, to serve him three years long. During that time God gave me diligence so that I learnt well, but I had much to suffer from his lads . . .

When I had finished my learning, my father sent me off, and I stayed away four years till he called me back again. As I had gone forth in the year 1490 after Easter [April 11th], so now I came back again in 1494, as it is reckoned, after Whitsuntide [May 18th].

DÜRER IN VENICE

In 1505 he visited Venice. The master painter there was Giovanni Bellini, for whom Dürer had a great veneration, although he seems

2E

to have underrated his contemporaries (Bellini was born in 1428), such
as Cima and Carpaccio. Mantegna had considerable influence on
Dürer, but they never met: Mantegna died before Dürer could reach
him.

Source: Letter to his great friend Master Wilibald Pirkheimer, the
Burgher of Nuremberg. Quoted, Conway, *op. cit.*, p. 48. Dated
February 7th, 1506.

How I wish you were here in Venice! There are so many nice
men among the Italians who seek my company more and more
every day—which is very pleasing to one—men of sense and
knowledge, good lute-players and pipers, judges of painting, men
of much noble sentiment and honest virtue, and they show me
much honour and friendship. On the other hand, there are also
amongst them some of the most false, lying, thievish rascals. I
should never have believed that such were living in the world.
If one did not know them, one would think them the nicest men
the earth could show. For my own part, I cannot help laughing
at them whenever they talk to me. They know that their knavery
is no secret, but they don't mind.

Amongst the Italians I have many good friends who warn me
not to eat and drink with their painters. Many of them are my
enemies and they copy my work in the churches and wherever
they can find it; and then they revile it and say that the style is
not *antique* and so not good. But Giovanni Bellini has highly
praised me before many nobles. He wanted to have something
of mine, and himself came to me and asked me to paint something
and he would pay well for it. And all men tell me what an
upright man he is, so that I am really friendly with him. He is
very old, but still the best painter of them all . . .

Given at Venice at the 9th. hour of the night, on Saturday
after Candlemass in the year 1506 . . .

DÜRER IN BRUSSELS, AUGUST 26TH TO SEPTEMBER 3RD, 1520

Source: His diary. Quoted, Conway, *op. cit.*, p. 101. A great artist's
appreciation of 'contemporary' art.

I saw the things which have been brought to the King from
the new land of gold [Mexico], a sun all of gold a whole fathom

broad, and a moon all of silver of the same size, also two rooms full of the armour of the people there, and all manner of wondrous weapons of theirs, harness and darts, very strange clothing, beds, and all kinds of wonderful objects of human use, much better worth seeing than prodigies. These things were all so precious that they are valued at 100,000 florins. All the days of my life I have seen nothing that rejoiced my heart so much as these things, for I saw amongst them wonderful works of art, and I marvelled at the subtle *Ingenia* of men in foreign lands.

DÜRER AS A THEOLOGICAL DISPUTANT

He became a close friend of the German Protestant leader, Melancthon. One of Dürer's oldest friends in his home town of Nuremberg was Wilibald Pirkheimer, the son of a rich merchant, in whose house Dürer was born. Pirkheimer was a scholar who had studied law and the Greek language. He was an ebullient man, not very refined in character, but an ardent enthusiast for the New Learning. He was specially picked out by the Pope for excommunication.

Source: Conway, *op. cit.*, p. 133, who gives the original source, C. Pencer, *Tract. Hist. de Ph. Melans.*, Amberg, 1569, which is not quite contemporary, but near enough to count as eye-witness.

Melancthon was often, and for many hours together, in Pirkheimer's company, at the time when they were advising together about the churches and schools at Nürnberg; and Dürer, the painter, used also to be invited to dinner with them. Dürer was a man of great shrewdness, and Melancthon used to say of him that, though he excelled in the art of painting, it was the least of his accomplishments. Disputes often arose between Pirkheimer and Dürer on these occasions about the matters recently discussed, and Pirkheimer used vehemently to oppose Dürer. Dürer was an excessively subtle disputant and refuted his opponent's arguments, just as if he had come fully prepared for the discussion. Thereupon Pirkheimer, who was rather a choleric man and liable to very severe attacks of the gout, fired up and burst forth again and again into such words as these, 'What you say cannot be painted', 'Nay', rejoined Dürer, 'but what you advance cannot be put into words or even figured to the mind'. I remember hearing Melancthon often tell this story, and in relating it he confessed his astonishment at the ingenuity and power manifested by a painter in arguing with a man of Pirkheimer's renown.

A FRIEND'S OPINION OF DÜRER

Joachim Camerarius, an intimate friend of Dürer, published a Latin version of the first two books of the *Four Books of Human Proportions*. The following is taken from his preface, quoted by Conway, *op. cit.*, p. 136 *et sqq.*

Nature bestowed on him a body remarkable in build and stature and not unworthy of the noble mind it contained . . . His head was intelligent, his eyes flashing, his nose nobly formed . . . His neck was rather long, his chest broad, his body not too stout, his thighs muscular, his legs firm and steady. But his fingers—you would vow you had never seen anything more elegant.

His conversation was marked by so much sweetness and wit that nothing displeased his hearers so much as the end of it. [He was deservedly] held a most excellent man . . .

DÜRER AND LUTHER

Dürer never met Luther, but he had a tremendous admiration for him. The following extract is from Dürer's diary in the Netherlands, quoted in Conway, *op. cit.*, p. 158 *et sqq.*

On Friday (17 May) before Whitsunday in the year 1521, came tidings to me at Antwerp that Martin Luther had been so treacherously taken prisoner; for he trusted the Emperor Karl, who had granted him his herald and imperial safe-conduct . . . Oh God of Heaven pity us! . . . And if we have lost this man, who has written more clearly than any that has lived for 140 years, and to whom Thou hast given such a spirit of the Gospel, we pray Thee, oh heavenly Father, that Thou wouldest give again Thy Holy Spirit to one, that he may gather anew everywhere together Thy Holy Christian Church, that we may again live free and in Christian manner, and so, by our good works, all unbelievers, as Turks, Heathen and Calicuts may of themselves turn to us and embrace the Christian faith. . . .

Every man who reads Luther's books may see how clear and transparent is his doctrine, because he sets forth the holy Gospel. Wherefore his books are to be held in great honour and not to be burnt; unless indeed his adversaries, who ever strive against the truth and would make gods out of men, were also cast into the fire, they and all their opinions with them, and afterwards a new edition of Luther's works were prepared. Oh God, if Luther be dead, who will henceforth expound to us the holy Gospel with such clearness. What, oh God, might he not still have written for us in ten or twenty years!

SATIRE

Satire, which may be called, in the age of the Renaissance, mockery with a moral purpose, was a characteristic of that age. The two great examples are Sebastian Brant's *Narrenschiff* or *The Ship of Fools*, first published in 1494, and Erasmus's *In Praise of Folly*, written in 1509 and printed in 1511. Although certainly Erasmus owed a good deal to Brant, there are decided differences between both the authors and their books. Brant was an old-fashioned scholasticist, while Erasmus was a modern humanist. Erasmus attacked ecclesiastical abuses and was hostile to the existing authority: Brant admired and defended the traditional authorities, most especially the Holy Roman Emperor. Like Erasmus, he was deeply religious, like Erasmus he was nervous and irritable, unlike Erasmus, who was a radical, Brant was a conservative: where Erasmus criticized cheerfully and with much sense of humour, Brant was a carping critic. He looked out upon the world and was horrified at what he saw. He felt that a catastrophe was about to befall the Holy Roman Empire at the hands of the Turk, but he had no remedy to avert it.

Brant was born in 1457 or 1458 and he died in 1521.

OF THE DECLINE OF THE FAITH

Source: (a) Brant, *The Ship of Fools*, trans. by Edwin H. Zeydel, Dover Books, New York, 1964. Chapter 99, pp. 315 *et sqq.*

When I regard neglect and shame
Which everywhere appears the same
Of prince and lord, of city, land,
No wonder then the tears do stand
In these mine eyes and flow so free
That one should see disgracefully
The faith of Christians ebb, recede,
Forgive me though I have indeed
Included e'en the princes here.
Luckless it is that we must hear
That Christians' faith has met distress,
For daily it diminishes.
At first the cruel heretic
Did tear and wound it to the quick
And then Mohammed shamefully
Abused its noble sanctity
With heresy and base intent.
Our faith was strong in th'Orient,
It ruled in all of Asia,
In Moorish lands and Africa.
But now for us these lands are gone,
'Twould even grieve the hardest stone.
W've lost and see ourselves now banned
From Asia Minor, Grecian land
And all of Greater Turkey too,
Which to our faith is quite untrue.
'Twas where the seven churches were,
And John we know wrote letters there.
Such good and faithful countries fell,
One'd vow it quite impossible.
In Europe we've been forced to see
The loss but very recently
Of kingdoms, even empires two[1]
And mighty lands and cities true
Constantinople, Trapezunt,[2]
Lands known to each and every one,
So strong the Turks have grown to be

They hold the ocean not alone,
The Danube too is now their own.
They make their inroads when they will,
Bishoprics, churches suffer ill,
Now they attack Apulia,
Tomorrow e'en Sicilia,
And next to it is Italy.
Wherefore a victim Rome may be
And Lombardy and Romance land.
We have the archfoe close at hand,
We perish sleeping one and all,
The wolf has come into the stall
And steals the Holy Church's sheep
The while the shepherd lies asleep.

By God, you princes, please behold
What injury there'll be untold
If once the empire should decay,
Not even you will live for aye.
All things have more efficiency
When they exist in unity
Than when there's discord in the world,
For concord's banner, once unfurled,
Will give us strength to thrive and grow,
But where discordance seeds may sow
The greatest, noblest things are razed.

If you'll support the ship of state
It will not sink but bear its freight.
Your king is all benignity,[3]
He'll don for you knight's panoply,
Rebellious lands he will subdue,
But you must help, he needs you too.
The noble Maximilian,
He merits well the Roman crown.
They'll surely come into his hand,

The Holy Earth, the Promised Land,[4]
He'll undertake it any day
If he can trust in you and may.

THE PRAISE OF FOLLY

Erasmus, *Encomium Moriae* or *The Praise of Folly*. This was the most widely read of all the books Erasmus wrote and it gave him an international reputation. The book opens with a dedicatory epistle to Sir Thomas More.

Source: (*a*) Preserved Smith, *Erasmus*, Dover Publications, New York, 1962.

On returning from Italy . . . I chose to amuse myself with the *Praise of Folly*. What Pallas, you will say, put that into your head? Well, the first thing that struck me was your surname More, which is just as near the name of *Moria* or Folly as you are far from the thing itself, from which, by general vote, you are remote indeed. In the next place I surmised that this playful production of our genius would find special favour with you, disposed, as you are, to take pleasure in a jest of this kind, that is neither, unless I mistake, unlearned nor inept . . . For, as nothing is more trifling than to treat serious questions frivolously, so nothing is more amusing than to treat trifles in such a way as to show yourself anything but a trifler.

Source: (*b*) A satire on the scientists and natural philosophers. Erasmus, *op. cit.* Preserved Smith, *op. cit.*, p. 121.

How sweetly they rave when they build themselves innumerable worlds, when they measure the sun, moon, stars and spheres, as though with a tape to an inch, when they explain the cause of thunder, the winds, eclipses and other inexplicable phenomena, never hesitating, as though they were the private secretaries of creative Nature, or had descended from the council of the gods to us, while in the meantime Nature magnificently laughs at them and at their conjectures.

Source: (*c*) Erasmus, *op. cit.* Allen & Unwin, 1915, p. 87.

What shall I say of such as cry up and maintain the cheat of pardons and indulgences? that by these compute the time of each soul's residence in purgatory, and assign them a longer or shorter continuance, according as they purchase more or fewer of these paltry pardons and saleable exemptions? Or what can be said bad enough of others, who pretend that by the force of such magical charms, or by the fumbling over their beads in the rehearsal of such and such petitions (which some religious impostors invented, either for diversion, or what is more likely for advantage), they shall procure riches, honour, pleasure, health, long life, a lusty old age, nay, after death a sitting at the right hand of our Saviour in His kingdom; though as to this last part of their happiness, they care not how long it be deferred, having scarce any appetite toward a-tasting the joys of heaven, till they are surfeited, glutted with, and can no longer relish their enjoyments on earth. By this easy way of purchasing pardons, any notorious highwayman, any plundering soldier, or any bribe-taking judge, shall disburse some part of their unjust gains, and so think all their grossest impieties sufficiently atoned for; so many perjuries, lusts, drunkenness, quarrels, bloodsheds, cheats, treacheries, and all sorts of debaucheries, shall all be, as it were, struck a bargain for, and such a contract made, as if they had paid off all arrears and might now begin upon a new score . . .

THE RENAISSANCE IN FRANCE

FRANCOIS RABELAIS

Rabelais was born probably in 1494 and he died in 1553. The son of a well-to-do lawyer in Chinon, Touraine, Francis became a Franciscan friar perhaps earlier than 1520, but because he was persecuted for his study of Greek, he became a Benedictine, but he travelled extensively and when he went to Paris to study medicine, he abandoned the Benedictine dress. He gained a medical degree and lectured on medicine at Lyons. He visited Rome as physician to his friend, Cardinal Jean du Bellay, and obtained from the Pope absolution for having deserted the Benedictines. He published *Pantagruel* in 1532 and *Gargantua* in 1534, the Third Book in 1546, the Fourth Book in 1548, and the whole book *Gargantua and Pantagruel* in 1552. The authenticity of the Fifth Book is much disputed.

Rabelais was one of the most courageous and distinguished of all French writers. His great book reflects brilliantly the gaiety, the voluptuousness, the ambitions and the modernity of the French Renaissance, but because he attacked in the spirit of an enlightened humanist ideas and institutions which had been accepted uncritically for centuries, he was detested by the Sorbonne and by the Paris *Parlement* and he had several times to leave Paris.

Rabelais was the warmest thinker of the Renaissance. He put laughter on the map—'a certain gaiety of spirit, conceived in scorn of chance. And, if you ask me why, good people, here is the unanswerable answer: Such is the will of the All-good and Omnipotent God, in which I acquiesce . . . whose Gospel of good tidings I worship.' He possessed a universal charity and an insatiable intellectual thirst, and he had deep understanding of the Christian religion. 'I reverence that Holiest Word of Good Tidings, the Gospel, as it first stood written.' Christ is 'the Saviour King, in whom all oracles, all prophecies found an end—just as the skulking shadows vanish at the light of the clear sun'. If Rabelais disliked asceticism more than anything else, he disliked ambition almost as much. 'Let those who will dispute about happiness and sovereign good; but it is my opinion that whosoever planteth cabbages, findeth instant happiness.'

Mediaeval people tended to concentrate upon death, the chief characteristic of Rabelais was his insistence upon Life. In that he is a pure Renaissance figure, however impure much of his writings appear at first sight. In his dislike of the Classics, in his scorn for antiquity and tradition, he is not at all typical of the Renaissance. Like Leonardo, Rabelais was interested in everything: like Bacon he was a scientist: like Erasmus he was a spiritual idealist, always restrained by his unfailing common-sense.

Source: (a) How Gargantua was taught Latin by a sophist. Rabelais hits out at the mediaeval methods of education in this scathing satire. *The Histories of Gargantua and Pantagruel*, The First Book, ch. xiv. Tran. s. by J. M. Cohen, Penguin Classics, 1955.

This discourse concluded, that good man Grandgousier was beside himself with admiration, as he considered the fine sense and marvellous understanding of his son Gargantua. And he said to the governesses: 'Philip, King of Macedon, recognized the intelligence of his son Alexander by his skill in managing a horse. This horse was so fierce and unruly that no one dared mount him, since he threw all his riders, breaking one man's neck, another's legs, another's skull, and another's jawbone. When Alexander considered this problem in the hippodrome (which was the place where horses were exercised and trained), he observed that the horse's wildness was caused only by his fear of his own shadow, and, climbing on him, forced him to gallop into the sun, so that his shadow fell behind him, in this way making the beast amenable to his will. By this the father realized the boy's divine intelligence, and afterwards had him very well taught by Aristotle, who at that time was the most highly esteemed philosopher in Greece.

And let me tell you that from this single discussion which I have just held before you with my son, Gargantua, I recognize that his understanding springs from some divine source, so acute, subtle, profound and assured do I find him in his answers. He will certainly attain a sovereign degree of wisdom, if he is well taught. Therefore I wish to entrust him to some learned man who will instruct him according to his capacities, and to this end I will spare no cost.

Accordingly they appointed as his tutor a great doctor and sophist named Thubal Holofernes, who taught him his letters so well that he said them by heart backwards; and he took five years and three months to do that. Then the sophist read him Donatus, Facetus, Theodolus, and Alanus in Parabolis,[5] which took thirteen years six months to do that. But note that all this time he was teaching Gargantua to write the Gothic script, and that he copied all these books out himself, for the art of printing was not yet practised. Also, he generally carried a huge writing-desk weighing more than seven thousand hundred weight, the pencil-case of which was as big and stout as the great pillars of Ainay, while the ink-horn hung from it on great iron chains, capable of carrying a ton of merchandise.

After this the sophist read him De modis significandi[6] with the commentaries of Bang-breeze, Scallywag, Claptrap, Gualehaul, John the Calf, Copper-coin, Flowery-tongue, and a number of others; and this took him more than ten years and eleven months. And Gargantua knew the book so well that at testing time he repeated it backwards by heart, proving to his mother on his fingers that *de modis significandi non erat scientia*.

The sophist read him the *Compostum*, on which he spent sixteen years and two months, at which point his said preceptor died. In the year fourteen twenty he caught the pox.

After that he had another old wheezer named Master Jobekin Bridé, who read him Hugutio, Hebrard's *Grecismus* . . . Mumble on the Psalms . . . and several more works of the same dough; by the reading of which he became as wise as any man baked in an oven.

Source: (b) The New Renaissance Method of Education. Rabelais, *op. cit.*, ch. xxiii; Cohen, *op. cit.*, p. 86 *et sqq.*

Meanwhile his father observed that although he was really studying very well, and spent all his time at his lessons, he was making no progress at all. What was worse, he was becoming quite sawny and simple, all dreamy and doltish.

When Grandgousier complained of this to Don Philippe des Marays, Viceroy of Papeligosse, that gentleman answered that it was better for the boy to learn nothing than to study such books under such masters. For their learning was mere stupidity, and their wisdom like an empty glove; it bastardized good and noble minds and corrupted all the flower of youth.

'To prove this', said Don Philippe, 'take any young person of the present day, who has studied only two years; and if he has not a better judgement, a better command of words, better powers of speech, better manners, and greater ease in company than your son, account me for ever a boaster from La Brenne'. This proposal greatly pleased Grandgousier, and he ordered it to be carried out.

That evening Des Marays brought in to supper a young page of his, called Eudemon, so well curled, so well dressed, so well brushed, and so courtly in his behaviour, that he was more like some little angel than a human being. Then said Des Marays to Grandgousier: 'Do you see this young lad? He is not twelve yet. Now, if you will, let us see what difference there is between the knowledge of your old-time nonsensological babblers and the young people of to-day.'

The idea pleased Grandgousier, and he commanded the page to state a proposition. Then, after demanding permission of the said Viceroy, his master, with his cap in his hand, with an open countenance and ruddy lips, and with assurance in his eyes and his gaze fixed in youthful modesty on Gargantua, Eudemon rose to his feet and began to praise and extol him, first for his virtues and fine manners, secondly for his learning, thirdly for his nobility, fourthly for his physical beauty, and in the fifth place charmingly exhorted him to show his father every reverent attention for being at such pains to have him well taught. Lastly he begged Gargantua in his kindness to engage him as the least of his servants. For he desired no other gift from Heaven at that present time save that he should have the good fortune to please Gargantua by doing him some welcome service. This speech was delivered by him with such fitting gestures, with such a clear enunciation and so eloquent a voice, in such ornate language and such good Latin, that he seemed more like a Gracchus, a Cicero, or an Emilius of the olden times than a youth of this age. But Gargantua could keep no better countenance than to burst out bellowing like a cow. He hid his face in his cap, and it was no more possible to draw a word from him than a fart from a dead donkey.

Source: (c) How Gargantua was so disciplined by Ponocrates that he did not waste an Hour of the Day: Rabelais, op. cit., ch. xxiii.

When Ponocrates saw Gargantua's vicious manner of living, he decided to educate him differently . . . Therefore, to make a better beginning of his task, he entreated a learned physician of that time, Master Theodore by name, to consider if it would be possible to set Gargantua on a better road. Theodore purged the youth in due form with black hellebore, and with this drug cured his brain of its corrupt and perverse habits. By this means also Ponocrates made him forget all that he had learned from his old tutors, as Timotheus did for his pupils who had been trained under other musicians . . . After that the tutor subjected his pupil to such a discipline that he did not waste an hour of the day, but spent his entire time on literature and sound learning.

Gargantua now woke about four o'clock in the morning and, whilst he was being rubbed down, had some chapter of Holy Writ read to him loudly and clearly . . . Moved by the subject and argument of that lesson, he often gave himself up to worship and adoration, to prayers and entreaties, addressed to the good God whose majesty and marvellous wisdom had been exemplified in that reading . . .

This done Gargantua was dressed, combed, curled, trimmed, and perfumed, and meanwhile the previous day's lessons were repeated to him. Next, he himself said them by heart, and upon them grounded some practical examples touching the state of man. This they sometimes continued for two or three hours, but generally stopped as soon as he was fully dressed. Then for three full hours he was read to.

When this was done they went out, still discussing the subjects of the reading, and walked over to the sign of the Hound or to the meadows, where they played ball or tennis or the triangle game, gaily exercising their bodies as they had previously exercised their minds. Their sports were entirely unrestrained, for they gave up the game whenever they pleased, and usually stopped when their whole bodies were sweating, or when they were otherwise tired. Then they were well dried and rubbed down, changed their shirts and sauntered off to see if dinner was ready; and whilst they were waiting there they clearly and eloquently recited some sentences remembered from their lesson. In the meantime my lord Appetite came in, and when the happy moment arrived, they sat down at table.

At the beginning of the meal there was a reading of some pleasant tale of the great deeds of old, which lasted until Gargantua had taken his wine. Then, if it seemed good, the reading was continued. Otherwise, they began to converse gaily together, speaking in the first place of the virtues, properties, efficacy, and nature of whatever was served to them at table: of the bread, the wine, the water, the salt, the meats, fish, fruits, herbs and roots, and of their dressing. From this talk Gargantua learned in a very short time all the relevant passages in Pliny, Athenaeus, Discorides, Julius Pollux, Galen, Porphyrius, Oppian, Polybius, Heliodorus, Aristotle, Aelian, and others. As they held these conversations, they often had the afore-mentioned books brought to the table, to make sure of their quotations; and so well and completely did Gargantua retain in his memory what had been said that there was not a physician then living who knew half as much of this as he.

Afterwards they discussed the lessons read in the morning; and as they concluded their meal with a confection of quinces, he picked his teeth with a mastic branch, and washed his hands and eyes with good fresh water. Then they gave thanks to God by reciting some lovely canticles, composed in praise of the Divine bounty and munificence. After this cards were brought in, not to play with, but so that he might learn a thousand little tricks and new inventions, all based on arithmetic. In this way he came to love this science of numbers, and every day, after dinner and supper, whiled away the time with it as pleasantly as formerly he had done with dice and cards; and so he came to know the theory and practice of arithmetic so well that Tunstal, the Englishman who had written so copiously on the subject, confessed that really, in comparison with Gargantua, all that he knew of it was so much nonsense. And Gargantua did not only become skilled in that branch, but also in such other mathematical sciences as geometry, astronomy and music. For while they waited for his meal to be prepared and digested, they made a thousand pretty instruments and geometrical figures, and also practised the astronomical canons.

After this they amused themselves by singing music in four or five parts or on a set theme, to their throats' content. With regard to musical instruments, he learnt to play the lute, the spinet, the harp, the German flute the nine-holed flute, the viol and the trombone . . .

This done, they left their lodging in the company of a young gentleman of Touraine, named Squire Gymnaste, who taught Gargantua the art of horsemanship; and after changing his clothes, the pupil mounted in turn a charger, a cob, a jennet, a barb, and a light horse, and made each run a hundred courses, clear the ditch, leap over the barrier, and turn sharp round to the right and left . . . He was singularly skilled also at leaping from one horse to another without touching the ground—these horses were called *desultories*—at getting up from either side, lance in hand and without stirrups, and at guiding his horse wherever he would without a bridle. For such feats are helpful to military discipline . . .

Once back at the house, while supper was being prepared, they repeated some passages from what had been read, before sitting down to table. And notice here that Gargantua's dinner was sober and frugal, for he ate only enough to stay the gnawings of his stomach. But his supper was copious and large, for then he took all he needed to stay and nourish himself. This is the proper regimen prescribed by the art of sound medicine, although a rabble of foolish physicians, worn out by the wrangling of the sophists, advise the contrary . . .

When it was quite dark, they went before retiring to the most open side of the house, to view the face of the sky, and there took note of the comets, if there were any, also of the figures, situations, aspects, oppositions and conjunctions of the stars. After which Gargantua briefly ran over with his tutor, in the manner of the Pythagoreans, all that he had read, seen, learnt, done and heard in the course of the whole day. And so they prayed to God the Creator, worshipping Him, reaffirming their faith in Him, glorifying Him for His immense goodness, rendering thanks to Him for all the past, and recommending themselves to His divine clemency for all the future. This done, they went to their rest.

Source: (*d*) How Gargantua had the Abbey of Thélème built for the Monk. Rabelais shared with Erasmus an ineradicable detestation of monastic life. In the following account of founding an abbey Rabelais ridicules the evils of the mediaeval system by founding his new abbey on exactly opposite principles. Rabelais, *op. cit.*, ch. 52; J. M. Cohen, *op. cit.*, p. 149 *et sqq.*

There only remained the monk to be provided for, and Gargantua wanted to make him abbot of Seuilly, but he refused the post. He next proposed to give him the abbey of Bourgueil or of Saint-Florant, whichever would suit him better, or both, if he fancied them. But the monk answered categorically that he wanted neither charge nor government of monks.

'For how should I be able to govern others', he said, 'when I don't know how to govern myself? If it seems to you that I have done you and may in future do you welcome service, give me leave to found an abbey after my own devices.'

This request pleased Gargantua, and he offered him all his land of Thélème, beside the river Loire, to within six miles of the great forest of Port-Huault. The monk then requested Gargantua to institute his religious order in an exactly contrary way to all others.

'First of all, then', said Gargantua, 'you musn't build walls round it, for all other abbeys have lofty walls (murs)'.

'Yes', said the monk, 'and not without reason. Where there's a *mur* before and a *mur* behind, there are plenty of murmurs, envy, and mutual conspiracy.'

Moreover, seeing that in certain monasteries in this world it is the custom that, if any woman enters—I speak of chaste and honest women—they wash the place where she trod, it was ordained that if any monk or nun happened to enter here, the spot where he or she had trod should be scrupulously washed likewise. And because in the religious foundations of this world everything is encompassed, limited and regulated by hours, it was decreed that there should be no clock or dial at all, but that affairs should be conducted according to chance and opportunity. For Gargantua said that the greatest waste of time he knew was counting the hours—what good does it do?—and the greatest nonsense in the world was to regulate one's life by the sound of a bell, instead of by the promptings of reason and good sense. Item, because at that time they put no women into religious houses unless they were one-eyed, lame, hunchbacked, ugly, deformed, lunatic, half-witted and blemished, or men that were not sickly, low-born, stupid, or a burden on their family . . .

'By the way', said the monk, 'if a woman is neither fair nor good, what can you do with her?'

2F

'Make her a nun', said Gargantua.

'Yes', said the monk, 'and a sempstress of shirts'.

It was decreed that here no women should be admitted unless they were beautiful, well-built, sweet-natured, nor any men who were not handsome, well-built and of pleasant nature also.

Item, because men never entered nunneries except secretly and by stealth it was decreed that here there should be no women when there were no men, and no men when there were no women.

Item, because both men and women, once admitted into a monastic order, after their novitiate year, were compelled and bound to remain for ever, so long as they lived, it was decreed that both men and women, once accepted, could depart from there whenever they pleased, without let or hindrance.

Item, because ordinarily monks and nuns made three vows, that is of chastity, poverty and obedience, it was decreed that there anyone could be regularly married, could become rich, and could live at liberty.

With regard to the lawful age of entry, women were to be received at from ten to fifteen, and men at from twelve to eighteen.

MICHEL DE MONTAIGNE

Montaigne was born in 1533, the son of Pierre Eyquem de Montaigne, an enterprising and successful merchant family trading in fish and in wine on an international scale. Michel was the third son, but his two brothers died, leaving him as the eldest of the family of six younger brothers and sisters. His father had original ideas about education and Michel was compelled to learn and to speak in Latin before he was allowed to learn any French. At six he went to Bordeaux to the College of Guienne. At thirteen he began to study law, probably at Toulouse. In 1558 he was present at the siege of Thionville, in 1559 and 1561 at Paris, in 1562 at the siege of Rouen. His father died in 1568. In 1571 Michel retired to Montaigne, but he was in bad health and decided to devote himself to study. He was married in 1565, he lived on good terms with his wife, but he proved himself a tolerant rather than a dutiful husband. He had six children, but only one girl survived infancy. In 1569 he published his translation of Raymond de

Sabonde's *Theologia Naturalis*. Later he edited the works of his great friend Etienne de la Boétie, whose death caused him acute pain. The earliest of his *Essays* were written in 1572–4: the *Apology for Raymond de Sabonde* was written round about 1576. The first two books of the *Essays* were published in Bordeaux in 1580. He became during this time intimate with Charles IX, Henry III, and especially with Henry of Navarre. His health growing worse and being in perpetual pain from stone and gravel, he decided to travel to the baths at Lucca (1580–1) and he kept a journal of the trip which was afterwards published as *The Travel Journal* (1774). He came home in 1581 in order to be Mayor of Bordeaux. He wrote a third book of *Essays*, and he added six hundred passages to the first two books. The first edition of the Three Books of Essays was published in 1588 in Paris. Between that date and his death on September 13th, 1592, he worked at his writings, making additions in the margin of a copy of the 1588 edition, which were incorporated in a new edition in 1595—nearly one quarter of the whole work.

Montaigne was the inventor of the Essay, he was a sceptic, an unrepentant student of himself and a beautiful writer of his native language. His book of *Essays* is simply Montaigne, 'I have no more made my book than my book has made me, a book consubstantial with its author, concerned with my own self, an integral part of my life . . . Everyone recognizes me in my book and my book in me'. It has to be noted that Montaigne went on developing his philosophy, so that in the final edition especially, which included all his alterations and additions, he may appear to contradict himself, simply because he has changed his point of view. The edition of 1958 issued by Hamish Hamilton, translation by D. M. Frame, by means of superscript letters, ingeniously makes clear what is original and what are later additions to the text. He begins by being a Stoic (1572–4): he becomes a sceptic in his *Apology for Raymond de Sabonde* (*c.* 1576): he ends as an Epicurean (1578–92). He begins by admiring the heroic characters—Cato the Younger, because he is striving to find the way to meet pain and death worthily—here he is directly opposed to Rabelais, who wanted to *live* worthily: he rejects this Stoic attitude in his *Apology*: 'Who tries to play the Angel, plays the beast'. The sceptical period shows Montaigne as searching for Truth, which he sees little hope of finding. The only thing to do is to acquire as much wisdom as you can by recognizing your ignorance. In the third period Montaigne comes into his own. Even in his sceptical period he never gave up using the Lord's Prayer.

In this last period he pronounced that 'the greatest thing in the world is to know how to belong to oneself'. Or again, 'Our soul must be commanded not to draw aside, not to despise and desert the body'.

In a short introduction it is not possible to do justice to Montaigne. He was one of the highest lights of the Northern Renaissance: among other things he invented, not only the Essay, but also the Autobiography. But also he was a counter-balance to the splendid exuberance of Rabelais. Both believed that the principal purpose of man is to Live, but Montaigne argued that 'our great and glorious masterpiece is to live appropriately'.

Source: (a) Montaigne, *Essays*, Book I, 'To the Reader'. Trans. by D. M. Frame, Hamish Hamilton, 1958.

This book was written in good faith, reader. It warns you from the outset that in it I have set myself no goal but a domestic and private one. I have had no thought of serving either you or my own glory. My powers are not adequate for such a purpose. I have dedicated it to the private convenience of my relatives and friends, so that when they have lost me (as soon they must), they may recover here some features of my habits and temperament, and by this means keep the knowledge they have had of me more complete and alive.

If I had written to seek the world's favour, I should have bedecked myself better, and should present myself in a studied posture. I want to be seen here in my simple, natural, ordinary fashion, without straining or artifice; for it is myself that I portray. My defects will here be read to the life, and also my natural form, as far as respect for the public has allowed. Had I been placed among those nations which are said to live still in the sweet freedom of nature's first laws, I assure you I should very gladly have portrayed myself here entire and wholly naked.

Thus, reader, I am myself the matter of my book; you would be unreasonable to spend your leisure on so frivolous and vain a subject.

So farewell. Montaigne, this first day of March, fifteen hundred and eighty.

Source: (b) Montaigne, Book I, *Essay* 20, 1572–4. D. M. Frame, *op. cit.*, p. 56.

Cicero says that to philosophize is nothing else but to prepare for death. This is because study and contemplation draw our soul out of us to some extent and keep it busy outside the body; which is a sort of apprenticeship and semblance of death. Or else it is because all the wisdom and reasoning in the world boils down finally to this point: to teach us not to be afraid to die. In truth, either reason is a mockery, or it must aim solely at our contentment, and the sum of its labours must tend to make us live well and at our ease, as Holy Scripture says. All the opinions in the world agree on this—that pleasure is our goal—though they choose different means to it. Otherwise they would be thrown out right away; for who would listen to a man who would set up our pain and discomfort as his goal? . . . The goal of our career is death. It is the necessary object of our aim. If it frightens us, how is it possible to go a step forward without feverishness?

Source: (c) Montaigne, Book II, Essay 12, *Apology for Raymond Sebond,* 1575–6, 1578–80. D. M. Frame, *op. cit.,* p. 358 *et sqq.* [Man's Knowledge Cannot Make Him Happy].

What good can we suppose it did Varro and Aristotle to know so many things? Did it exempt them from human discomforts? Were they freed from the accidents that oppress a porter? Did they derive from logic some consolation for the gout? For knowing how this humour lodges in the joints, did they feel it less? Were they reconciled to death for knowing that some nations rejoice in it, and with cuckoldry for knowing that wives are held in common in some region? On the contrary, though they held the first rank in knowledge, one among the Romans, the other among the Greeks, and in the period when knowledge flourished most, we have not for all that heard that they had any particular excellence in their lives; in fact the Greek has a hard time to clear himself of some notable spots in his.

Have they found that sensual pleasure and health are more savoury to him who knows astrology and grammar?

And are shame and poverty less troublesome?

[Man's Knowledge Cannot Make Him Good].

O presumption, how you hinder us! When Socrates was advised that the God of Wisdom had given him the title of Sage, he was astonished; and, examining and searching himself through and through, he found no basis for this divine judgement. He knew of men as just, as temperate, as valiant, as learned as himself, and more eloquent, handsomer and more useful to their country. Finally he concluded that he was distinguished from the others, and wise, only in that he did not think himself so; and that his God considered the opinion that we possess learning and wisdom a singular piece of stupidity in man; and that his best knowledge was the knowledge of his ignorance, and simplicity his best wisdom.

Holy Writ declares those of us wretches who think well of ourselves: 'Dust and ashes', it says to them 'What hast thou to glory in?' And elsewhere: 'God has made man like the shadow, of which who shall judge when, with the passing of the light, it shall have vanished away?' In truth, we are nothing. (Ecclesiastes, x, 9: Ecclesiasticus, vi, 12.)

Source: (*d*) Montaigne, *Essays*, Book III, 13, Of Experience, the last of all the Essays; D. M. Frame, *op. cit.*, p. 856.

Let us manage our time; we shall have a lot left idle and ill spent. Our mind likes to think it has not enough leisure hours to to do its own business, unless it dissociates itself from the body for the little time that the body really needs it.

They want to get out of themselves and escape from the man. That is madness; instead of changing into angels, they change into beasts; instead of raising themselves, they lower themselves. These transcendental humours frighten me, like lofty and inaccessible places; and nothing is so hard for me to stomach in the life of Socrates as his ecstasies and possession by his daemon, nothing is so human in Plato as the qualities for which they say he is called divine. And of our sciences, those seem to me most terrestrial and low which have risen the highest. And I find nothing so humble and so mortal in the life of Alexander as his fancies about his immortalization. Philotas stung him wittily by his answer. He congratulated him by letter on the oracle of Jupiter Ammon which had lodged him among the gods. 'As far as you are concerned, I am very glad of it; but there is reason to pity the men who will have to live with and obey a man who exceeds and is not content with a man's proportions. . . .'

It is an absolute perfection and virtually divine to know how to enjoy our being rightfully. We seek other conditions because we do not understand the use of our own, and go outside of ourselves because we do not know what it is like inside. Yet there is no use our mounting on stilts, for on stilts we must still walk on our own legs. And on the loftiest throne in the world we are still sitting only on our own rump.

The most beautiful lives, to my mind, are those that conform to the common human patterns, with order, but without miracle and without eccentricity. Now old age needs to be treated a little more tenderly. Let us commend it to that god who is the protector of health and wisdom, but gay and sociable wisdom.

ARCHITECTURE

One of the features of the Renaissance in France was the building of many of the great *châteaux* of the Loire. Chambord was built during the reign of Francis I (begun in 1526), but its appearance nowadays is very different from its first appearance, so much has it been altered and mutilated. The following account gives a picture of Chambord while it was still being built.

Source: Lippomano, the Venetian ambassador in France, describes a visit there. *Documens Inédits*, v, 2, p. 300, quoted in Mrs. Mark Pattison's *Renaissance of Art in France*, London, 1879, vol. 1, p. 55.

We made a slight detour in order to visit the *château* of Chambord, or, more strictly speaking, the palace commanded by François I; and truly worthy of this great Prince. I have seen many magnificent buildings in the course of my life, but never anything more beautiful or more rich. They say that the piles for the foundations of the *château* in this marshy ground have alone cost 300,000 francs. The effect is very good on all sides . . . I counted one hundred and eighty-six steps in the spiral staircase which occupies the centre; it is constructed with such skill, and is so convenient, that a party can go up one side and down the other, six or eight abreast, at a time . . . The number of the rooms is as remarkable as their size, and indeed space was not wanting to the architect, since the wall that surrounds the park is seven leagues in length. The park itself is full of forests, of lakes, of streams, of pasture land, and of hunting grounds, and in the centre rises the *château* with its gilt battlements, with its wings covered in with lead, with its pavilions, its towers, and its corridors, even as the romancers describe to us the abode of Morgana or of Alcinöus. More than half remains to be done, and I don't believe it will ever be finished, for the kingdom is completely exhausted by war. We left much marvelling, or rather let us say thunderstruck, and we arrived that evening at Blois.

NOTES

[1] Constantinople.

[2] Trebizond.

[3] Maximilian had been elected Roman king, but he had not yet been anointed Holy Roman Emperor by the Pope.

[4] That is Palestine, which Maximilian hoped to recapture. This is one of Brant's favourite themes.

[5] The stock mediaeval text book.

[6] The stock mediaeval grammar.

SCIENCE AND MEDICINE
(*Notes on p. 466*)

THE ADVANCE IN SCIENCE

The antiquated views propounded by Aristotle, Ptolemy and Galen held the field throughout the mediaeval times, mostly because the mediaeval scholars failed to adjust their minds and to see the old ideas in a new light. (See H. Butterfield's *Origins of Modern Science*, ch. 1.) By the fifteenth century the University of Paris was beginning to question the Aristotelian theories, and there took place some advance in the understanding of mathematics. As early as the fourteenth century William of Ockham dabbled in the subject, and in the next century Cardinal Nicholas of Cusa wrote on it. The first algebraic treatise appeared in 1494, the work of Luca Pagioli de Burgo. In 1505 a Latin translation of Euclid was made in Venice. John Widman of Eger invented the plus and minus signs, and in 1545 Cardan published his *Ars Magna*, which dealt with algebra and geometry. But the four men who worked the great revolution in science were Copernicus (1473–1543), Galileo (1564–1642), Tycho Brahe (1546–1601), Johannes Kepler (1571–1630). A feature of this revolution was the intense opposition of the Catholic and Protestant Churches. Copernicus' book was dedicated to Pope Paul III, but it was put on the Index in 1616: Galileo was summoned before the Inquisition and submitted: Kepler was ejected by the Protestant professors at Tübingen.

NICHOLAUS COPERNICUS

Niklas Koppernigk was a Polish merchant from Cracow, who moved to Thorn on the river Vistula, where he married Barbara Waczenrode. There were four children by this marriage: Niklas was the youngest. He was born on February 19th, 1473. When he was 10 years old his father died and Niklas was adopted by his uncle Lucas Waczenrode, a priest, who became Bishop of Ermland. The cathedral town was Frauenburg. Niklas was sent to school in Thorn and later went to the university of Cracow. It was here that he began to study astronomy. He now Latinized his name into Nicolaus Copernicus. In 1496 he went to Italy to Bologna and Padua to study canon law at those universities. He was also at Ferrara and spent a year in teaching in Rome. 1506, he returned to Ermland and was given a canonry at

Frauenburg cathedral. For thirty years he carried out his ecclesiastical duties and devoted his leisure hours to giving free medical treatment to the poor and to the study of astronomy. In 1530 he finished his great work, *Six Books on the Revolutions of the Heavenly Bodies*, but he did not publish it until 1543 at Nuremburg. He died immediately the book had appeared. In this book Copernicus established once and for all that the earth rotates around the sun daily on its own axis, while the planets revolve in orbits around the sun. 'The amazing thing about the discoveries of Copernicus is that they were the products of pure reason, applied to facts known to the ancients and carefully noted by Pliny. The astronomer of Frauenburg, solely by the power of his own intellect, shaped these scattered observations into one harmonious whole . . .' (Funck Brentano, *The Renaissance*, p. 26).

Source: (a) The Introduction to his *De Revolutionibus*, which he dedicated to Pope Paul III.

I can well believe that, when what I have written becomes known, there will be an uproar. I myself am not so infatuated with my own ideas as to disdain all those of others, but though a philosopher's ideas may conflict with those held by the vulgar—since the philosopher seeks only truth within the bounds set by God to human intelligence—I do not believe that they should therefore be rejected out of mere prejudice. This, and the fear of the ridicule which must needs be called forth by the novelty and apparent absurdity of my system had determined me to abstain from publishing my work. The insistence of my friends, however . . . overcame my disinclination. Mgr. Giese, above all, insisted that I should print this book, which has been in preparation, not nine only, but thirty-six years.

. . . If one imagines a number of human limbs, taken from persons of different stature and appearance, and tries to construct from them a complete body, then their disproportion and their difference of shape would produce a monster rather than a normally constituted human form. But astronomy (as it was) appeared to me precisely such a monster. In endeavouring to explain the celestial motions, I constantly met with objections which destroyed all generally admitted theories. Hypotheses favourable to certain cases could not possibly cover certain others and, being now admitted and now rejected, they sowed confusion in practice and bewilderment in the mind instead of illuminating the path of reason.

They failed to convince because they turned the wondrous works of nature into a madman's dream. What was I to think of such an ill-built structure, shrouded in the mist of obscurity and falling into ruin under the weight of contradictions and difficulties? I could but think that the very foundations were unsound.

. . . Considering these [ancient] authorities, I was myself led to meditate on the motion of the earth and, though the idea may seem absurd, I thought—since others had already taken the liberty of supposing a multitude of circles to explain astronomical phenomena—that I might risk an explanation of the motions of the celestial bodies based on the hypothesis that the earth itself was in motion.

After long study I came to these conclusions: that the sun is a fixed star, surrounded by planets which revolve round it and of which it is the centre and the light: that besides the principal planets there are secondary ones revolving, as satellites, round their principals and, with them, round the sun: that the earth is a primary planet subject to a triple motion on its own axis and round the sun, by which means I explain the phenomena of diurnal and annual movement, the alternation of the seasons with all the changes of light and temperature that go with them. Further, I hold that the apparent courses of the stars are merely an optical illusion due to the actual movement of the earth and the oscillations of its axis, and finally that the motions of the planets as a whole give rise to two entirely distinct orders of phenomena, those proceeding from the movement of the earth, and those which result from the revolutions of the planets round the sun.

Source: (b) De Revolutionibus, ch. 1, *That the Universe is Spherical*, quoted in *Treasury of World Science*, ed. Dagobert D. Runes, New York, 1962.

First of all we assert that the universe is spherical; partly because this form, being a complete whole, needing no joints, is the most perfect of all; partly because it constitutes the most spacious form, which is thus best suited to contain and retain all things; or also because all discrete parts of the world, I mean the sun, the moon, and the planets appear as spheres; or because all things tend to assume the spherical shape, a fact which appears in a drop of water and in other fluid bodies when they seek of their own accord to limit themselves. Therefore no one will doubt that this form is natural for heavenly bodies.

Source: (*c*) Tycho Brahe (1546–1601), a Danish astronomer, preserved the three sticks which were the only crude instruments Copernicus had with which to work out his system. He wrote as follows:

In these centuries his like has not been seen on earth. He stayed the course of the Sun in the heavens and set the unmoving Earth in motion. He made the Moon to move about her and changed the face of the Universe. And this, all this, with three poor sticks. No memento of this great man, wooden though it be, can ever perish. Gold would envy their value, could it but know it.

TYCHO BRAHE, ASTRONOMER

Tycho Brahe (1546–1601), the great Danish astronomer, was born at Knudstrup in Scania. He studied at Copenhagen, Leipzic, Rostock and Augsburg. In 1571 he set up a laboratory in his uncle's castle at Herritzvad and it was there that on November 11th, 1572, he saw a new star, in Cassiopeia. In 1576 Frederick II gave him the island of Hveen and a pension of 500 thalers, together with a canonry in the cathedral of Roskilde and the income of an estate in Norway. That year the building was begun of the splendid observatory at Uraniborg where Brahe worked for twenty-one years. Brahe was an arrogant and difficult man and Christian IV was less tolerant of him than Frederick had been. Brahe lost his pension and property in Norway. In 1599 he arrived in Prague where Rudolph II became his patron. There Johannes Kepler joined him in January, 1600. Brahe died on October 21st, 1601.

Source: (*a*) On a New Star, not previously seen within the memory of any since the beginning of the world. Brahe's account of its first appearance in 1572, quoted in *Treasury of World Science*, ed. by Dagobert D. Runes, Philosophical Library, New York, 1962, p. 102.

Last year [1572], in the month of November, on the eleventh day of that month, in the evening, after sunset, when, according to my habit, I was contemplating the stars in a clear sky, I noticed that a new and unusual star, surpassing the other stars in brilliancy, was shining almost directly above my head; and since I had, almost from boyhood, known all the stars of the heavens perfectly (there is no great difficulty in attaining that knowledge) it was quite evident to me that there had never before been any star in that place in the sky, even the smallest, to say nothing of a star so conspicuously bright as this. I was so astonished at this sight that I was not ashamed to doubt the trustworthiness of my own eyes. But when I observed that others, too, on having the place pointed out to them, could see that there was really a star there, I had no further doubts. A miracle indeed, either the greatest of all that have occurred in the whole range of nature since the beginning of the world, or one certainly to be classed with those attested by the Holy Oracles, the staying of the Sun in its course in answer to the prayers of Joshua, and the darkening of the Sun's face at the time of the Crucifixion. For all philosophers agree, and facts clearly prove it to be the case, that in the ethereal region of the celestial world no change, in the way either of generation or of corruption, takes place; but that the heavens and the celestial bodies in the heavens are without increase or diminution, and that they undergo no alteration, either in number or in size or in light or any other respect; that they always remain the same, like unto themselves in all respects, no years wearing them away . . . Nor do we read that it was ever before noted by any one of the founders that a new star had appeared in the celestial world, except only Hipparchus, if we are to believe Pliny. For Hipparchus, according to Pliny (book II of his Natural History) noticed a star different from all others previously seen, one born in his own age.

Source: (b) From Tycho Brahe's account of the star, quoted by J. A. Gade, *Life and Times of Tycho Brahe*, Princeton U.P., 1947, p. 41.

The star was at first like Venus and Jupiter and its immediate effect will therefore be pleasant, but since it became like Mars, there will next come a period of wars, seditions, captivity, death of princes,[1] and destruction of cities, together with dryness and fiery meteors in the air, pestilence and venomous snakes. Lastly the star became like Saturn, and there will therefore finally come a time of want, death and imprisonment, and all kinds of sad things. Its brilliance surpassed that of Sirius, Vega or Jupiter, and persons with very sharp eyes could see the star in the daytime, yes, in the very middle of the day, if it was clear.

Source: (c) Brahe's *De Nova Stella*, published by Lorentz Benedict in Copenhagen, 1573, quoted in Gade, *op. cit.*, p. 46.

Moreover this star, of which I purpose chiefly to treat, albeit it were ascititious and changeable, yet because it shined forth miraculously and contrary to the laws of nature, even in the highest firmament, like to the other natural stars, and stood there fixed and immovable for the space of a whole year and more, it seemed fit that some diligent pains should be taken in considering and unfolding the circumstances thereunto . . . I have weighed the opinion of those who have either come near unto the truth or wandered from it concerning this new star. I have written so the truth might appear and shine forth more clearly . . . This star did at first in his magnitude exceed the whole globe of the earth and was three hundred times bigger than the whole circumference thereof . . . It shone forth with a jovial, clear and bright lustre . . . with a martial, fiery glittering.

FREDERICK II AND TYCHO BRAHE

One of the interesting things about the 'Renaissance', both in Italy and in Northern Europe, is the lead which the rulers gave to the new intellectual impulse. It is common knowledge that men like the Medici family provided this lead in Italy. It is much less well-known that there was a Northern European Renaissance to which the rulers contributed: Henry VII in England—e.g. in Westminster Abbey: Francis I in France in many ways: Frederick II of Denmark ought to be remembered for the part he played. The following source shows what Frederick II did towards the development of Science in the sixteenth century scientific revolution, in his patronage of Tycho Brahe in the world of science.

Source: (*a*) Ur Tycho Brahas brevväxling. Lund, 1926, quoted Gade, *op. cit.*, p. 58.

As I still lay abed early in the morning on February sixteenth [1576], thinking about my German trip and at the same time wondering how I could disappear without attracting the attention of my relatives, and considering all sides of the matter, I was informed quite unexpectedly that a royal page had arrived at Knudstrup, who had been waiting during the night to hand me a letter from the king. The page was a nobleman and a relative. The letter instructed me to come at once to the royal hunting lodge at Ibstrup, about a mile from Copenhagen, or wherever the king might be in Sjælland. The king said that he had heard from some of his courtiers that my uncle, Steen Bille, had said I intended to go to Germany, He therefore ordered me to come to him so as to get at the bottom of the matter. He stated that he knew I did not want any mark of his favour in the form of a large castle, for I did not want to have the care of it interfere with my studies. When he was recently at Elsinore, where he was building, he had looked out of the window and seen the little island of Hveen, which did not belong to any nobleman. Steen Bille, who was with him, had told him that the island and its location attracted me, so it seemed to the King it might just suit me for both astronomy and chemistry. It had no revenues, but he would take care of that. If I would settle down there, he would be glad to give it to me as a gift, and I could live there comfortably without being disturbed. He would sail across as soon as he was through with his building at Elsinore and see how I was getting along, not that he understood much about astronomy, but he would come because he was my king and I was his subject. He asked what I could accomplish abroad that I could not do here at home and said that we should rather see German learned men coming here. He told me to think it over for a few days and to let him know at Fredriksborg what I thought about it and he wished me to act freely. When I saw him, he would arrange the necessary revenues and the expenses of building, so that I need not worry, but could honour this country, my king and myself.

Source: (*b*) Frederick was as good as his word: J. L. E. Dreyer, *Tycho Brahe*, Edinburgh, 1890, pp. 86–7.

We Frederik the Second, etc., make known to all men, that We of our special favour and grace have conferred and granted in fee, and now by this open letter confer and grant in fee, to Our beloved Tyge Brahe, Otto's son, of Knudstrup, Our man and servant, Our land of Hveen, with all Our and the Crown's tenants and servants who live thereon, with all rents and duties which come therefrom, and We and the Crown give it to him to have, enjoy, use and hold, quit and free, without any rent, all the days of his life, and so long as he lives and likes to continue and follow his *studia mathematices*, but he shall keep the tenants who live there under law and right, and injure none of them contrary to the law or by any new impost or other unusual tax, and in all ways be faithful to Us and the Kingdom, and attend to Our welfare in every way and guard against and prevent danger to the Kingdom.

Actum Fredriksborg, the 23rd May, Anno 1576.

FREDERIK.

Source: (*c*) Horoscopes. On June 2nd, 1577, Frederick's wife, Sophia, gave birth to a son, the future Christian IV. The King asked Brahe to cast the child's horoscope. Brahe did not much care by this time to mix up astronomy with astrology, but he consented: he and a Holstein nobleman, Ditlev Reventlov, were the two most famous astrologers of their time. This horoscope of prince Christian can still be seen, bound in green velvet, in the Royal Library at Copenhagen. Dreyer, *op. cit.*

[Brahe foretold that] the Prince's years of infancy are to pass without danger, as Venus was favourably placed in the ninth hour, and though in the second year the opposition of Mercury to the ascending point indicates some small illness, it will be nothing serious. In the twelfth year serious illness will take place, arising from black bile. In the twenty-ninth year he will have to be very careful both as to his health and his dignity. A very critical time will arise around his fifty-sixth year, when the sun and Mars will be most unfavourable and even Venus can not help, as she will be in the eighth hour. If he successfully passes that period, he will have a happy old age. Venus will make him pleasant, courtly and valorous, fond of the arts. Mars will make him bellicose, while Mercury will add adroitness and skill to his other faculties. He will be of a sanguine temperament. As Venus and Mars were joined [at his birth], the Prince will indulge too much in sensual enjoyment. He will be healthy and not subject to illness, he will be fortunate in his undertakings and receive many honours and riches. The prospects as to marriage are not too favourable, for he will be more inclined to amours than to matrimony. He will not have many children, as Saturn, the master of the fifth house, is in a sterile sign. Venus shows that he will cause his own death by immoderate sensuality.

GALILEO GALILEI

Galileo was born at Pisa in 1564 and he died in 1642. His father, Vincenzio Galilei, was a well-known mathematician and a good musician. Galileo was educated at the monastery of Vallombrosa, near Florence, where he studied Greek, Latin and logic, but he disliked the science which he was taught. In 1581 he went to the university of Pisa to study medicine. It was in that year that he watched a lamp swinging in the cathedral of Pisa and from this he deduced the theory of the pendulum, and he then applied the new principle to the timing of the human pulse. His father wanted him to stick to medicine, but by chance Galileo overheard a lecture on geometry and from that moment he turned his whole attention to mathematics. Owing to financial difficulties he had to leave the university before he had taken a degree. In 1586 he published an essay on his invention of the hydrostatic balance, which made him well-known throughout Italy. Between 1589 and 1591 he established by a series of experiments the first principles of dynamics. It was then that he proved to the professors and students of Pisa university by dropping stones from the Leaning Tower that falling bodies of different weights fall with the same velocities. But Galileo was an ill-tempered man and he became so unpopular that he resigned his professorship in 1591 and went to Florence. In 1592 he was given the chair of mathematics at Padua university, where he remained until 1610. Early in life he accepted the Copernican view of the universe. He next invented a telescope of triple magnifying power, which he gradually increased up to 32. With his telescope he proved

2G

that the Milky Way is a collection of stars and he discovered the satellites of Jupiter. He was then appointed by the Venetian Senate to a professorship for life at a high salary.

In 1611 he went to Rome and there incautiously got himself involved in theological disputes over scriptural authority for the Copernican system. In 1615 he was warned not to deal in theology. In 1616 the Inquisition denounced the Copernican view of the universe as heretical and Galileo was commanded not to 'hold, teach or defend' the doctrine, and Galileo promised to obey. For the next seven years he lived in silent retirement at Florence. He published some erroneous theories about comets in his *Saggiatore*, which was printed at Rome and was dedicated to Pope Urban VIII, in spite of the fact that it contained some oblique references to the Copernican views. In 1632 he published his *Dialogo dei Due Massimi Sistemi del Mondo*, which was an instantaneous success. But the book was not conformable with the decree of 1616 and with Galileo's promise. Galileo was summoned to Rome, examined by the Inquisition under threat of torture, which was never intended to be carried out, nor was it. He recanted and was in the custody of the Inquisition for three days. Eventually he was allowed to go to Siena and then back to Florence where he lived in strict seclusion until he died. But he still worked on and made many more valuable discoveries. He also envisaged applying the principle of the pendulum to clockwork, which was accomplished by Huygens fifteen years later.

Source: (*a*) On the Ptolemaic and Copernican Systems: *Dialogo dei Due Massimi Sistemi del Mondo*. Runes, *op. cit.*, pp. 327–8.

Simplicius. But what great exorbitances are there in the Ptolemaic System, for which there are not greater to be found in that of Copernicus?

Salviatus. In the Ptolemaic hypothesis there are diseases, and in the Copernican their cures. And, first, will not all the sects of philosophers account it a great inconvenience that a body naturally moveable in circumgyration should move irregularly upon its own centre and regularly upon another point? Yet there are such deformed motions as these in the Ptolemaic hypothesis, but in the Copernican all move evenly about their own centres. In the Ptolemaic it is necessary to assign to the celestial bodies contrary motions and to make them all move from East to West, and at the same time from West to East. But in the Copernican all the celestial revolutions are towards one way only, from West to East. But what shall we say of the apparent motions of the planets, so irregular that they not only go at one moment swiftly and at another moment slowly, but sometimes they cease to move altogether, and then after a long time turn back again. Now, to save these apparent motions, Ptolemy introduces very large epicycles, allotting them one by one to each planet and lays down some rules of incongruous motions which are all removed with one single motion of the Earth. Would you not, Simplicius, say that it is wholly absurd, if in the Ptolemaic hypothesis, in which the particular planets have each its peculiar orb assigned to it one above another, that one should be frequently forced to say that Mars, constituted above the sphere of the Sun, descends in such a way that, breaking the solar orb, it passes under it and approaches nearer to the Earth than to the body of the Sun, and in course of time immeasurably ascends above the same? And yet this and other exorbitances are remedied by the sole and single annual motion of the Earth.

Source: (*b*) Acceleration and Laws of Falling Bodies: Galileo, *op. cit.* Runes, *op. cit.*, pp. 331–2.

Sagredus. As far as I see at present . . . uniformly accelerated motion is such that its speed increases in proportion to the space traversed; so that, for example, the speed acquired by a body in falling four cubits would be double that acquired in falling two cubits, and this latter speed would be double that acquired in the first cubit. Because there is no doubt but that a heavy body falling from the height of six cubits has, and strikes with, a momentum double that it had at the end of three cubits, triple that it had at the end of one.

Salviatus. It is very comforting to me to have such a companion in error; and moreover, let me tell you that your proposition seems so highly probable that our Author himself admitted, when I put this opinion to him, that he had for some time shared the same fallacy. But what most surprised me was to see two propositions, so inherently probable that they commanded the assent of everyone to whom they were presented, proved in a few simple words to be not only false, but impossible.

Simplicius. I am one of those who accept the proposition and believe that a falling body acquires force for its descent, its velocity increasing in proportion to the space, and that the momentum of the falling body is doubled when it falls from a doubled height. These propositions, it appears to me, ought to be conceded without hesitation or controversy.

Salviatus. And yet they are as false and impossible as that motion should be completed instantaneously; and here is a very clear demonstration of it. If the velocities are in proportion to the spaces traversed, or to be traversed, then these spaces are traversed in equal intervals of time; if, therefore, the velocity with which the falling body traverses a space of eight feet were double that with which it covered the first four feet (just as the one distance is double the other), then the time-intervals required for these passages would be equal. But for one and the same body to fall eight feet and four feet in the same time is possible only in the case of instantaneous motion; but observation shows us that the motion of a falling body occupies time, and less of it in covering a distance of four feet than of eight feet; therefore it is not true that its velocity increases in proportion to the space.

The falsity of the other proposition may be shewn with equal clearness. For if we consider a single striking body, the difference of momentum in its blows can depend only upon difference of velocity; for if the striking body, falling from a double height, were to deliver a blow of double momentum, it would be necessary for this body to strike with a double velocity; but with this double speed it would traverse a doubled space in the same time-interval; observation shows, however, that the time required for fall from the greater height is longer.

JOHANN KEPLER

Kepler was born in 1571 and he died in 1630. He had a most unhappy childhood, for his parents were thoroughly unsatisfactory people—his mother was ultimately charged with witchcraft, of which she was acquitted, but only after thirteen months imprisonment and after

examination under the threat of torture. He recovered from smallpox
at the age of four, but he was left with crippled hands and eyesight
permanently injured. His mental powers were exceptionally well
developed and he intended to take up an ecclesiastical career, but he
abandoned this and turned to the study of Copernican science. In
1600 Kepler joined Tycho Brahe at Prague, but Brahe died suddenly
in 1601, which left the way open for Kepler. His life was spent as a
teacher, as a court astrologer,[2] as a mathematician to various German
princes, but also as one of the greatest of all astronomers. His fame
depends on his Three Laws of Planetary Motion, which are generally
accepted as the starting point of modern astronomy. These formed the
basis of Newton's discoveries in later years. Kepler also began the
study of optics and his work on mathematics led to the invention of
the calculus.

Source: The Chief Points of Astronomical Learning. *Astronomia
Nova ... de Motibus Stellae Martis*. Runes, *op. cit.*, pp. 549–52.

In the beginning let my readers understand this: that the old
astronomical hypotheses of Ptolemy . . . are to be kept far from
the present enquiry and banished wholly from the mind; for
they fail to give a true account either of the arrangement of the
heavenly bodies or of the laws governing their motions.

In their place I cannot do otherwise than substitute simply
Copernicus's theory of the universe, and (were it possible) convince all men of its truth; but, since among the mass of students
the idea is still unfamiliar, and the theory that the Earth is one of
the planets and moves among the stars about the Sun, which is
stationary, sounds to most of them quite absurd, let those who
are offended by the strangeness of this doctrine know that these
harmonic speculations hold a place even among the hypotheses of
Tycho Brahe. While that author agrees with Copernicus in
regard to everything else which concerns the arrangement of the
heavenly bodies and the laws governing their motions, the annual
motion of the Earth alone, as held by Copernicus, he transfers to
the whole system of planetary orbits and to the Sun, which
according to both authors, is the centre of the system . . .

In the first place, therefore, let my readers understand that at
the present day among all astronomers it is held to be a well-
established fact that all the planets except the Moon, which alone

has the Earth as its centre, revolve around the Sun; the Moon's orbit or course, be it said, is not large enough to enable it to be drawn on the accompanying chart in proper relation to the other orbits . . .

Secondly, the following fact is also established: that all the planets revolve in eccentric orbits; that is, they alter their distances from the Sun, so that in one part of the orbit they are very remote from the Sun, while in the opposite part they come very near the Sun . . .

THE ADVANCE IN MEDICINE

Just as the views held by Aristotle (384–322 B.C.) and by Ptolemy (fl. A.D. 127–?151) on the universe were on the whole universally accepted until Copernicus refuted them in his great book on Astronomy, *Six Books on the Revolutions of the Heavenly Bodies*, published in 1543, so were the medical views of the Greek physician, Galen (c. A.D. 130–200), universally accepted until Vesalius (1514–64) in the same year, 1543, published his *De Humani Corporis Fabrica*, which revolutionized medical science by stimulating the study of anatomy (see also under Leonardo da Vinci, p. 25). The book was greeted with a storm of abuse for daring to criticize Galen. Vesalius, who was only 28 years old and was Professor of anatomy at Padua, resigned and migrated to Madrid where he became physician to Charles V and later to Philip II. Unfortunately he began a *post mortem* on a man who proved still to be alive. Such a sin could only be expiated by a pilgrimage to Jerusalem. On the return journey Vesalius was shipwrecked on the isle of Zante, where he died.

VESALIUS

Source: The Preface to *De Humani Corporis Fabrica*, addressed to The Most Great and Invincible Emperor, The Divine Charles V.

In ancient times there were three medical sects, to wit, the Dogmatic, the Empirical, and the Methodical, but the exponents of each of these embraced the whole of the art as the means to preserve health and war against disease. To this end they referred all that they individually thought necessary in their particular sects, and employed the service of a threefold aid to health: first, a theory of diet; secondly, the whole use of drugs; and thirdly, manual operation. This last, above the rest, nicely proves the saying that medicine is the addition of that which is defective and the removal of that which is in excess; as often as we resort to the art of medicine for the treatment of disease we have occasion to employ it; and time and experience have taught, by the benefits it has conferred, that it is the greatest aid to human health.

This triple manner of treatment was equally familiar to the doctors of each sect; and those who applied manual operation according to the nature of the affection expended no less care in training their hands than in establishing a theory of diet, or in learning to recognize and compound drugs.

[Vesalius goes on to argue that after the ruin spread by the Goths the art of medicine decayed, largely because the more unpleasant duties of a doctor were left to others to perform, while the doctors stood over them and watched. This decay hit most severely 'the chief branch of natural philosophy, anatomy'.]

This deplorable dismemberment of the art of healing has introduced into our schools the detestable procedure now in vogue, that one man should carry out the dissection of the human body, and another give the description of the parts. These latter are perched up aloft in a pulpit like jackdaws and with a notable air of disdain they drone out information about facts they have never approached at first hand, but which they merely commit to memory from the books of others, or of which they have the descriptions before their eyes; the former are so ignorant of languages that they are not able to explain their dissections to the onlookers and botch what ought to be exhibited in accordance with the instruction of the physician, who never applies his hand to the dissection, and contemptuously steers the ship out of the manual, as the saying goes. Thus everything is wrongly taught, days are wasted in absurd questions, and in the confusion less is offered to the onlooker than a butcher in his stall could teach a doctor. I omit all mention of those schools in which there is scarcely even a thought of opening a human body to exhibit its structure. So far had ancient medicine fallen some years ago from its pristine glory.

[Then things began to improve and Vesalius felt that he must do what he could to raise the art or science of anatomy. He could only help by taking a hand himself in dissections].

But this effort could by no manner of means have succeeded, if, when I was studying medicine at Paris, I had not myself applied my hand to this business, but had acquiesced in the casual and superficial display to me and my fellow students by certain barbers of a few organs at one or two public dissections. For in such a perfunctory manner was anatomy then treated in the place where we have lived to see medicine happily reborn that I myself, having trained myself without guidance in the dissection of brute creatures, at the third dissection at which it was my fortune ever to be present (this, as was the custom there, was concerned exclusively or principally with the viscera), led on by the encouragement of my fellow students and teachers, performed in public a more thorough dissection than was wont to be done. Later, I attempted a second dissection, my purpose being to exhibit the muscles of the hand together with a more accurate dissection of the viscera. For except for eight muscles of the abdomen, disgracefully mangled and in the wrong order, no one (I speak the simple truth) ever demonstrated to me any single muscle, or any bone, much less the network of nerves, veins and arteries.

Subsequently at Louvain, where I had to return on account of the disturbance of war, because during eighteen years the doctors there had not even dreamed of anatomy, and that I myself might acquire greater skill in a matter both obscure and in my judgement of prime importance for the whole of medicine, I did somewhat more accurately than at Paris expound the whole structure of the human body in the course of dissecting, with the result that the younger teachers of that academy now appear to spend great and very serious study in acquiring a knowledge of the parts of man, clearly understanding what invaluable material for philosophising is presented to them from this knowledge. Further more at

Padua, in the most famous gymnasium in the world, I had been charged with the teaching of surgical medicine five years by the illustrious Senate of Venice, which is far the most liberal in the endowment of the higher branches of learning. And since the carrying out of anatomical enquiry is of importance for surgical medicine, I devoted much effort to the investigation of the structure of man, and so directed my inquiries, and, exploding the ridiculous fashion of the schools, so taught the subject that we could not find in my procedure anything that fell short of the tradition of the ancients . . .

Those who followed Galen, among whom I place Oribasius, Theophilus, the Arabs and all our own writers whom I have read to date, all of them (and they must pardon me for saying this), if they handed on anything worth reading, borrowed it from him. And believe me, the careful reader will discover that there is nothing they were further from attempting than the dissection of bodies. They placed an absolute trust in I know not what quality of the writing of their chief, and in the neglect of dissection of the rest, and shamefully reduced Galen to convenient summaries, never departing from him by so much as the breadth of a nail, that is, supposing they succeed in arriving at his meaning. Nay, they place it in the forefront of their books that their own writings are pieced together from the teachings of Galen, and that all that is theirs is his. And so completely have they all surrendered to his authority that no doctor has been found to declare that in the anatomical books of Galen even the slightest error has ever been found, much less could now be found; though all the time (apart from the fact that Galen frequently corrects himself and in later books, after acquiring more experience, removes oversights that he had committed in earlier books, and sometimes teaches contradictory views) it is quite clear to us, from the revival of the art of dissection, from a painstaking perusal of the works of Galen, and from a restoration of them in several places, of which we have no reason to be ashamed, that Galen himself never dissected a human body lately dead. Nay, more deceived by his monkeys (although it is admitted that human bodies dried, and prepared as it were for an inspection of the bones, did come under his observation), he frequently wrongly controverts the ancient doctors who had trained themselves by dissecting human corpses . . .

PARÉ

Ambroise Paré was one of the greatest surgeons of his time. He was born in 1510 and he died in 1590. He was a man of noble character, courageous, humane, and without any of the bitterness which actuated so many doctors in the sixteenth century. He had as great an influence on the development of surgery as Vesalius had on anatomy. His greatest contribution was to prove that haemorrhage after an amputation should be stopped by 'the exact method of ligature and not by the blind and brutal use of a red-hot cautery'. (K. Walker, *The Story of Medicine*, Hutchinson, 1954, p. 110.) He dedicated the whole of his life to relieving human suffering.

Source: (*a*) An academic professor of medicine attacked Paré for his use of ligatures after an amputation. Paré paid no attention at the time, but years afterwards he published his *Journeys Made in Divers Places*, in which he replied to the old-fashioned professor; avoiding the usual bitter invective of the times, he employed a gentler satire. S. Paget, *Ambroise Paré*, London, 1897.

Dare you to teach me surgery? You, who have never come out of your study . . . Surgery is learned by the eye and hand . . . You, *mon petit maistre*, know nothing else but how to chatter in a chair.

Source: (*b*) Paré spent thirty years on active service in the French and Imperial wars, and most of his experience was gained from dealing with gun-shot wounds. His first campaign was at the capture of Turin: S. Paget, *op. cit.*, p. 31.

We entered pell-mell into the city . . . and in a stable where we thought to lodge our horses, we found four dead soldiers and three propped against the wall, their features all changed. They neither saw, heard nor spoke, and their clothes were still smouldering where the gunpowder had burned them. As I was looking on them with pity, there came an old soldier who asked me if there were any way to cure them. I said, NO. Then he went up to them and cut their throats, gently and without ill-will. Seeing this great cruelty, I told him he was a villain: he answered that he prayed God, when he should be in such a plight, he might find someone to do the same for him, that he should not linger in misery.

Source: (c) At Turin, almost by accident, Paré discovered how to dress gunshot wounds. S. Paget, *op. cit.*, p. 33.

The soldiers within the castle, seeing our men come on them with great fury, did all they could to defend themselves, and killed and wounded many of our soldiers with pikes, arquebuses and stones, whereby the surgeons had all their work cut out for them. Now I was at this time a freshwater soldier; I had not yet seen gun-shot wounds at the first dressing. I had read in Jean de Vigo, first book, *Of Wounds in General*, eighth chapter, that wounds made by firearms partake of venemosity, by reason of the powder, and for their cure he bids you cauterize them with oil of elders, scalding hot, mixed with a little treacle. And to make no mistake, before I would use this said oil, knowing that it was to bring great pain to the patient, I asked first, before I applied it, what the other surgeons did for the first dressing; which was to put the said oil, boiling well, into the wounds and tents and setons; wherefore I took courage to do as they did. At last my oil ran short, and I was compelled, instead of it, to apply a digestive made of yolk of eggs, oil of roses and turpentine. In the night I could not sleep, fearing some default in not cauterizing, lest I should find the wounded to whom I had not applied the said oil, dead from the poison of their wounds; which made me rise very early to visit them; where, beyond expectation, I found that those to whom I had applied my digestive medicament had but little pain and their wounds without inflammation or swelling, having rested fairly well that night. The others, to whom the boiling oil was applied, I found feverish, with great pain, and swelling about the edges of their wounds. Then I resolved never more to burn thus cruelly poor men with gun-shot wounds.

Source: (d) The Siege of Metz, 1552. War between France and the Emperor, Charles V, broke out again in 1552. The French army crossed the Meuse and captured Metz. The Emperor raised a large army and set out to recapture the city by siege. Francis, Duke of

Guise, arrived at Metz on August 17th, 1552, to command the defence.
Paré's description: S. Paget, *op. cit.*, p. 55 *et sqq.*

The Emperor having besieged Metz with more than an hundred
and twenty thousand men, and in the hardest time of winter—it
is still fresh in the minds of all—there were five or six thousand
men in the town, and among them seven princes; MM le Duc de
Guise, the King's Lieutenant, d'Enghien, de Condé, de la Montpensier, de la Roche-sur-Yon, de Nemours, and many other
gentlemen, with a number of veteran captains and officers: who
often sallied out against the enemy (as I shall tell hereafter), not
without heavy loss on both sides. Our wounded died almost all,
and it was thought the drugs wherewith they were dressed had
been poisoned. Wherefore M. de Guise, and MM the princes,
went so far as to beg the King that if it were possible I should be
sent to them with a supply of drugs, as they believed their drugs
were poisoned, seeing that few of their wounded escaped. My
belief is that there was no poison; but the severe cutlass and
arquebus wounds, and the extreme cold, were the cause why so
many died. The King wrote to M. the Marshal de Saint André
to find means to get me into Metz, whatever way was possible.
MM the Marshal de Saint André and the Marshal de Vielleville
won over an Italian captain, who promised to get me into the
place, which he did (and for this he had fifteen hundred crowns).
The King, having heard the promise that the Italian captain had
made, sent for me and commanded me to take of his apothecary,
named Daigne, so many and such drugs as I should think necessary
for the wounded within the town; which I did, as much as a
posthorse could carry. The King gave me messages to M. de
Guise, and to the princes and captains that were in Metz.

When I came to Verdun, some days after, M. the Marshal de
Saint André got horses for me and for my man, and for the
Italian captain, who spoke excellent German, Spanish and
Walloon, beside his own mother-tongue. When we were within
eight or ten leagues of Metz, we began to go by night only; and
when we came near the enemy's camp, I saw, more than a league
and a half off, fires lighted all round the town, as if the whole

earth were burning; and I believed we could never pass through these fires without being discovered, and therefore hanged and strangled, or cut in pieces, or made to pay a great ransom. To speak the truth, I could well and gladly have wished myself back in Paris, for the great danger that I foresaw. God guided our business so well that we entered into the town at midnight, thanks to a signal the captain had with another captain of the company of M. de Guise; to whom I went and found him in bed, and he received me with high favour, being right glad at my coming.

I gave him my message as the King had commanded me, and told him I had a letter for him, and the next day I would not fail to deliver it to him. Then he ordered me a good lodging and that I should be well treated, and said I must not fail next morning to be upon the breach, where I should find all the princes and seigneurs and many captains. Which I did, and they received me with great joy, and did me the honour to embrace me, and tell me I was welcome; adding they would no more be afraid of dying, if they should happen to be wounded.

M. le Prince de la Roche-sur-Yon was the first who entertained me, and inquired what they were saying at the Court concerning the town of Metz. I told him all that I chose to tell. Forthwith he begged me to go and see one of his gentlemen named M. de Magnane, now Chevalier of the Order of the King, and Lieutenant of His Majesty's Guards, who had his leg broken by a cannon-shot. I found him in bed, his leg bent and crooked, without any dressing on it, because a gentleman promised to cure him, having his name and his belt, with certain words (and the poor patient was weeping and crying out with pain, not sleeping day or night for four days past.) Then I laughed at such cheating and false promises; and I reduced and dressed the leg so skilfully that he was without pain and slept all night, and afterward, thanks be to God, he was healed and is still living now, in the King's service. The Prince de la Roche-sur-Yon sent me a cask of wine, bigger than a pipe of Anjou, to my lodging, and told me when it was drunk, he would send me another; that was how he treated me, most generously . . . Afterward I asked M. de Guise what it pleased him I should do with the drugs I had brought with me; he bade me distribute them to the surgeons and apothecaries, and principally to the poor wounded soldiers, who were in great numbers in the Hospital. Which I did, and can truly say I could not so much as go and see all the wounded, who kept sending for me to visit and dress them.

The Emperor attacked the town with forty double cannons and the powder was not spared day or night. So soon as M. de Guise saw the artillery set and pointed to make a breach, he had the nearest houses pulled down and made into ramparts, and the beams and joists were put end to end, and between them faggots, earth, beds and wool-packs; then they put above them other beams and joists as before. And there was plenty of wood from the houses in the suburbs which had been razed to the ground, for fear the enemy should get under cover of them and make use of the wood; it did very well for repairing the breach. Everybody was hard at work carrying earth to repair it, day and night MM. the princes, the seigneurs, and captains, lieutenants, ensigns, were all carrying the basket, to set an example to the soldiers and citizens to do the like, which they did; even the ladies and girls, and those who had not baskets, made use of cauldrons, panniers, sacks, sheets, and all such things to carry the earth; so that the enemy had no sooner broken down the wall than they found behind it a yet stronger rampart. The wall having fallen, our men cried out at those outside, 'Fox, fox, fox', and they vented a thousand insults against one another. M. de Guise forbade any man on pain of death to speak with those outside, for fear there should be some traitor who would betray what was being done within the town. After this order our men tied live cats to the ends of their pikes and put them over the wall and cried with the cats, 'Miaut, Miaut'.

Truly the Imperials were much enraged, having been so long making a breach at great loss which was eighty paces wide, that fifty of their front rank should enter in, only to find a rampart stronger than the wall. They threw themselves upon the poor cats and shot them with arquebuses as men shoot at the popinjay.

Our men often ran out upon them, by order of M. de Guise;

a few days ago our men had all made haste to enrol themselves in sallying-parties, chiefly the young nobility, led by experienced captains; and indeed it was doing them a great favour to let them issue from the town and run upon the enemy. They went forth always an hundred or six score men, well armed with cutlasses, arquebuses, pistols, pikes, partisans and halberds; and advanced as far as the trenches, to take the enemy unawares. Then an alarum would be sounded all through the enemy's camp, and their drums would beat *plan, plan, tatita, tatita, tou touf touf.* Likewise their trumpets and clarions rang and sounded *To saddle, to saddle, to saddle, to horse, to horse, to horse, to saddle, to horse, to horse.* And all their soldiers cried, *Arm, arm, arm, to arms, to arms, to arms, arm, to arms, arm, to arms, arm*!; like the hue and cry after wolves, and all diverse tongues, according to their nations; and you saw them come out of their tents and little lodgings, as thick as little ants when you uncover the ant-hills, to bring help to their comrades, who were having their throats cut like sheep. Their cavalry also came from all sides at full gallop, *patati, patata, patati, patata, pa, ta, ta, patata, pata, ta,* eager to be in the thick of the fighting, to give and take their share of blows. And when our men saw themselves hard pressed, they would turn back into the town, fighting all the way; and those pursuing them were driven back with cannon-shots, and the cannons were loaded with flint-stones and with big pieces of iron, square or three-sided. And our men on the wall fired a volley and rained bullets on them as thick as hail, to send them back to their beds; whereas many remained dead on the field: and our men also did not all come back with whole skins, and there were always some left behind (as it were a tax levied on us) who were joyful to die on the bed of honour . . .

[The Emperor abandoned the siege after losing some 20,000 men.]

I would return to the reason why so many of them died; which was mostly starvation, the plague, and cold. For the snow was more than two feet deep upon the ground, and they were lodged in pits below the ground, covered only with a little thatch. Nevertheless, each soldier had his camp-bed, and a coverlet all strewed with stars, glittering and shining brighter than fine gold, and every day they had white sheets and lodged at the sign of the Moon, and enjoyed themselves if only they had been able, and paid their host so well overnight that in the morning they went off quits, shaking their ears: and they had no need of a comb to get the down and feathers out of their beards and hair, and they always found a white tablecloth, and would have enjoyed good meals but for want of food. Also the greater part of them had neither boots, half-boots, slippers, hose nor shoes: and most of them would rather have none than any, because they were always in the mire up to mid-leg. And because they went bare-foot, we called them the Emperor's Apostles.

Source: (e) In 1559 Paré retired from the army and settled down in Paris. He was surgeon to at least four monarchs and was called in by many outstanding men and women in France. Among these was the Marquis d'Aurel, who had for seven months been suffering from a fractured thigh and whom everybody had given up for lost: Walker, *History of Medicine*, 1954, p. 115.

I found him in high fever, his eyes deep sunken, with a moribund and yellowish face, his tongue dry and parched, and the whole body wasted and lean, the voice low, as of a man very near death.

I found his thigh much inflamed, suppurating and ulcerated, discharging a greenish and very offensive sanies. I probed it with a silver probe, wherewith I found a large cavity in the middle of the thigh and others round the knee . . . also several scales of bone, some loose, others not . . . There was a large bed-sore; he could rest neither day nor night, and had no appetite to eat, but very thirsty . . .

Seeing and considering all these great complications, and the vital powers thus broken down, truly I was very sorry I had come to him, because it seemed to me there was very little hope he could escape death. All the same, to give him courage and good hope, I told him I would soon set him on his legs, by the grace of God and the help of his physicians and surgeons.

Having seen him, I went for a walk in a garden and prayed God to show me this grace, that he should recover, and to bless our hands and our medicaments to cure such a complication of disease. I turned in my mind what measures I must take to this end. They called me to dinner. I came into the kitchen, and there I saw, taken out of a great pot, half a sheep, a quarter of veal, three great pieces of beef, two fowls, and a very large piece of bacon, with abundance of good herbs. Then I said to myself that the broth of the pot would be full of juices and very nourishing. After dinner we began our conversation, all the physicians and surgeons together, in the presence of M. le Duc d'Ascot and some gentlemen who were with him. I began to say to the surgeons that I was astonished that they had not made incisions in the patient's thigh, seeing that it was all suppurating, and the thick matter in it very fetid and offensive, showing that it had long been pent up there; and I had found with the probe caries of the bone and scales of bone already loose. They answered me, Never would he consent to it; indeed, it was near two months since they had been able to get leave to put clean sheets on the bed, and that one scarce durst touch the coverlet, so great was his pain. Then I said, To cure him we must touch something else than the coverlet of his bed. Each said what he thought of the malady of the patient and, in conclusion, they all held it hopeless. I told them there was still some hope, because he was young, and God and Nature sometimes do what seems to physicians impossible.

This my discourse was well approved by the physicians and surgeons. The consultation ended and we went back to the patient, and I made three openings in his thigh ... Two or three hours later, I got a bed made near his old one, with clean white sheets on it; then a strong man put him into it, and he was thankful to be taken out of his foul stinking bed. Soon afterwards, he asked to sleep, which he did for nearly four hours, and everybody in the house began to feel happy, and especially his brother.

Then, when I saw him beginning to get well, I told him that he must have viols and violins, and a buffoon to make him laugh: which he did. In a month, we got him into a chair, and he had himself carried about his garden and to the door of his chateau, to watch people passing ... In six weeks he began to stand a little upon crutches, and to put on flesh and to get a good natural

2H

colour. He wanted to go to Beaumont, his brother's place, and was taken thither in a carrying-chair by eight men at a time. And the peasants in the villages through which we passed, when they knew it was M. le Marquis, fought who should carry him, and insisted that he should drink with them; and it was only beer, but they would have given him Hippocras, if there had been any, and all were glad to see him, and prayed God for him.

Source: (*f*) Some of Paré's sayings. D. Guthrie, *A History of Medicine*, Nelson, 1945, p. 148.

Je le pansait; Dieu le guérit. I dressed his wounds; God cured him.

He who becomes a surgeon for the sake of money will accomplish nothing. Mere knowledge without experience does not give the surgeon self-confidence.

A remedy thoroughly tested is better than one recently invented.

It is always wise to hold out hope to the patient, even if the symptoms point to a fatal issue.

NOTES

[1] The massacre of St. Bartholomew occurred on August 25th, 1573. This extract shows that at this stage Brahe had not rid himself of the traditional and popular belief in astrology. Even when later he was casting horoscopes at the request of Frederick II, there is good reason to believe that neither King nor Brahe paid any attention to what to them by that time had become merely conforming to a convention.

[2] He cast the horoscope of the Emperor Rudolph II and also of Wallenstein.

A MISCELLANY
(Notes on p. 499)

Capitalism and Banking

Throughout the Middle Ages the economic unit had been the guilds, both merchant and craft, which looked after the production and exchange of goods by which the towns lived. The great feature of the Renaissance period was the arrival of the 'merchant prince', or the capitalist, individual men who seized the opportunities offered by the expansion of trade to accumulate into their own hands huge sums of money which financed, not only merchant adventurers in search of trade, but also the wars of Emperors and Kings. These capitalists flourished mostly in South Germany and in North Italy. The most famous names are those of the Fugger family, the Welser, The Tucher, the Imhof, the Kleberg, among the Germans: the Frescobaldi, the Strozzi, the Medici, among the Italians. The principal centres of the financial world were Antwerp (especially), Lyons, and to some extent Venice, though here rather more in trade than in finance. The best book on this subject is *Capital and Finance in the Age of The Rennaissance*, by R. Ehrenberg, trans. by H. M. Lucas, Jonathan Cape, 1928, from which the following extracts are taken. See also M. Griece-Hutchinson, *The School of Salamanca*, O.U.P., 1952.

Source (a) The election of Charles V as King of the Romans (i.e. as heir to the Holy Roman Empire) could never have been achieved without the financial backing of the Fugger. But Charles was dilatory in repaying the huge loans. The following letter shows clearly the tremendous power of money—that a banker should be able to write thus to the Holy Roman Emperor. From Jakob Fugger, April, 1523.

Your Imperial Majesty doubtless knows how I and my kinsmen have ever hitherto been disposed to serve the House of Austria in all loyalty to the furtherance of its well-being and prosperity; wherefore, in order to be pleasing to Your Majesty's Grandsire, the late Emperor Maximilian, and to gain for Your Majesty the Roman Crown, we have held ourselves bounden to engage ourselves towards divers princes who placed their Trust and Reliance upon myself and perchance on No Man besides. We have, moreover, advanced to Your Majesty's agents for the same end a

Great Sum of Money, of which we ourselves have had to raise a large part from our Friends. It is well known that Your Imperial Majesty could not have gained the Roman Crown save with mine aid, and I can prove the same by writings of Your Majesty's Agents given by their own hands. In this matter I have not studied mine own profit. For had I left the House of Austria and been minded to further France, I had obtained much money and property, such as was then offered me. How grave a Disadvantage had in this case accrued to Your Majesty and the House of Austria, Your Majesty's Royal Mind well knoweth.

Source: (b) The following letter from the Venetian ambassador, Suriano, gives an account of the business of the Florentine financiers, 1527: Albéri, *Relazione*, Series II, vol. v, p. 420; Ehrenberg, *op. cit.*, p. 209.

The Crown of France owes private persons in Florence 600,000 ducats. In Rome the Florentines have spent 350,000 ducats on buying offices. They suffered great losses at the sack of Rome. Formerly Florence alone made a profit of 8,000 ducats a week from goods delivered to Rome, but now only 1,000 ducats or a little more, since intercourse with Rome has been forbidden for fear they should again come to depend on the Pope. Trade in commodities with Naples has been destroyed by the war; the export of silks and brocades to France has likewise been destroyed by the war and the secession of Genoa to the Emperor's side. Trade with Flanders has been stopped by the closing of the Venetian territory. These barriers are, however, circumvented, and in spite of all these losses and hindrances, the Florentines are still extremely rich. Eight or ten families have about 100,000 ducats apiece. Tomasso Guadagni is said to have 400,000 ducats, though most of it is in France; Ruberto Degli Albizzi about 250,000, Pier Salviati 200,000; the Bartolini, Antinori, Soderini, Strozzi, and others, each more than 100,000. More than eighty families have between 50,000 and 100,000, and the number with property worth less than 50,000 cannot be counted.

Source: (c) Trading in commodities in Antwerp, of which the most important were the East Indian spices, especially pepper, was extremely speculative, and pepper was the most risky. The interest of the large syndicates and the amount of new imports regulated the price of pepper on the Bourse. Both factors were incalculable and things were made worse by the frequent alternations between war and peace. It became important for business men to follow the market from hour to hour, or, if this was impossible for those abroad, they would rely on reports from agents in Antwerp. Even astrology was used in the hopes of being able to foretell the state of the market. Christopher Kurz, a man of Nuremberg, who sent regular reports to Lienhard Tucher, a well-known and respected merchant prince: Ehrenberg, *op. cit.*, p. 240. Kurz said that he had found a system for foretelling a fortnight in advance the price of pepper, ginger and saffron.

I sought it three years, but until this year found it not. I think God hath given it to me. I have observed it for the space of a year. Yet will I not boast myself of it, till I have myself observed it for yet a time longer with mine own eyes and have traced it out. Yet I doubt not it is well-founded; if it be not, I shall know ere half a year be out. In the same manner I have known how to show for the matter as touching cinnamon, nutmegs and cloves from one market to another. But as I have always seen you wary about committing yourselves with such goods, I have forgot some pieces of this experiment, as I write not of all those which I have. Still, should I hear that ye would hazard with spice dealing, there shall be no lack of such. But ye must be diligent to frequent the places where such are bought and sold, as Venetia—and wonder seized me wherefore you use not Frankfurt, which lieth near to your hand. For there is not only good gain oftentimes to be made with spices, but likewise with bills can one hap on many a good chance. As ye have often noted in my writings to you how great an alteration is there day by day in bills on Germany, Venice, or Lyons, so that in the space of eight, ten, fourteen or twenty days with other folks' money, a man may make a profit of 1, 2, 3, 4, 5, or more per cent., with such there is here each day great business on the Bourse. Of these also have I my experiment, so that I may foretell not only from week to week the *Strettezza* and *Largezza* (tightness and ease) in money, but also for each day and whether it shall be before or after midday. I have, however,

nigh forgot this again, since I found you so reluctant . . . So
bethink you that the sale lies with you and buy in with all heat at
Lyons. Truly, Honourable Sir, from such motions of the mind
you must learn wherefore I speak my judgement in part. So
soon as ye see how much hath from this year and how much
remaineth over, and that now such wares be driven so high in
every place that they, according to the store of them, cannot
come higher, what course have you then to buy as you, I wot well,
would be fain to do? But this is naught, for the upper influences
so blind the natural reason with affections and desires . . . I am
surrounded with work like a man in the ocean with water, for
our astrologers aforetime have written much, but little with
reason; wherefore I trust not their doctrine, but seek mine own
rules, and when I have them, I search in the histories whether it
hath fallen out right or wrong.

Source: (*d*) The year 1555 saw the first example of a royal financial
transaction (between Henry II of France and a combination of all his
creditors) with a sinking fund with compound interest. The loan was
effected at Lyons: Rubys, *Histoire de Lyon*, p. 378; Ehrenberg, *op. cit.*,
p. 303.

The King made a financial affair at Lyons which was called 'le
grand parti', because this loan was open to all kinds of persons,
all whosoever would lend to His Majesty. They paid in their
money to the Receiver General of Lyons and received in return
bonds. A special office was created for the payment of the
interest and the instalments of repayment, the *Reçeveur du don
Gratuit*, who received the whole amount each fair[1] from the
Financial Administration and distributed it among the persons
concerned. God knows how greed for these excessive gains,
disguised by designation as a 'free gift' (*don gratuit*) lured men on.
Every one ran to invest his money in '*le grand parti*', the very
servants brought their savings. Women sold their ornaments and
widows their annuities in order to take shares in 'le Grand Parti'.
In short people ran for it as if to see a fire.

Source: (*e*) So speculative was trading in commodities that the big
business men abandoned that and turned to trading in money. At first

the usual form was that known as the *Deposito*, 'the loan of a sum of money for a certain time at a fixed price and interest, *e.g.* according to the permit granted by the Emperor Charles V, confirmed by his son King Philip, at an annual rate of 12 per cent . . . Such transactions would be actually useful, if people would be content with reasonable interest. This, however, is not the case, and the deposit business has assumed an arbitrary and unbearable shape.' (Guicciardini.) This was purely a loan and had no connection with what we now call Deposits in a Bank.

Another method was that known as the *Ricorsa*, a single bill for a straightforward loan, or a double bill where a man wanted to borrow money in (say) Florence and then to exchange that Italian currency into French money in Lyons, so as to make a profit on the re-exchange: Davanzati, a Florentine merchant, quoted by Ehrenberg, *op. cit.*, p. 287.

If thou (A) hast money in Florence and wilt have exchange in Lyons, because thou mayst have profit from the exchange back again, so give to me (B) who need money, 64 *scudi* in Florence, if that be the exchange rate; against this I promise to have a mark of gold paid in Lyons to Tommaso Sertini (D). I give thee a bill on Salviati (C), thou sendest him to Tommaso (D) so that he may cash it and deal with the re-exchange. The letter wherein thou dost this is called the Advice or *Spaccio*. Tommaso (D) carried out thy orders. He pays thy mark of gold in Lyons to Piero (E) and receives from him a bill on Federigo in Florence (F) in accordance with which he (Federigo) has to pay thee (A) $65\frac{1}{2}$ *scudi* in so many days. Tommaso sends thee this re-exchange, and when it matures thou hast made $1\frac{1}{2}$ *scudi*. Herein, however, thou hast to run the risk of three failures, mine, Tommaso's and Piero's. Thou therefore must look with Argus eyes at the firm to whom thou shouldst give the bill, him to whom thou remittest it and him by whom this second man should have the re-exchange drawn. Wherefore those who are not in business are wont to give their money to a Bank, which deals with the transaction for a double charge: 2 per cent for the trouble and 2 per cent for the *delcredere* (security) for the quarter. The fees in Lyons (Consular fee, charges, brokerage) amount to $1\frac{1}{2}$ per cent. A man who does not employ the agency of a Bank will, after deduction of the above fees, make on an average 8 per cent. If a Banker is employed, his fees (1 and a third per cent.) are also to be deducted.

Antwerp in the XVI Century

Source: Lodovico Guicciardini, *Description of All the Low Countries,* 1581. This English version comes from a translation made in 1593 under the same title but 'gathered into an Epitomie . . . printed at London by Peter Short for Thomas Chard', pp. 25 *et sqq.* Spelling and punctuation have been modernized.

The Bourse of Antwerp took the name of the Bourse of Bruges, which was so called because it was near to the house of the family of La Bourse, as appears by their arms yet remaining upon the said house, being three purses. This name of Bourse has gained so great credit in the world that all places where merchants are to assemble together are called Bourse: yes, the Exchange in England retains yet that name, notwithstanding the alteration made by the Queen . . .

The Causes of the Great Wealth that Antwerp is grown to are three.

The first, the two Marts that are in Antwerp, the one whereof beings 15 days before Whitsuntide and is therefore called the Fair of Pentecost. The other is called the Fair of St. Remy, because it begins the second Sunday after our Lady Day in August, which is of equal distance from either of the said feasts. Each of these Marts endures six weeks, all the which time no man is subject to arrest for debt. The payments of these Marts are the 10th of August and the 10th of November. The payments also of the two Fairs that were wont to be made at Bruges, namely of the Cold Fair and of the Easter Fair, are now made at Antwerp, the one on the 7th of February, and the other the 10th of May.

There are also at Antwerp besides these Marts two great horse fairs, the one at Whitsuntide, the other at our Lady Day in September, and likewise two of leather and skins of all sorts, which follow immediately after the horse fairs.

The second cause of the wealth of Antwerp is this. In the year 1503 the Portuguese began to bring spices out of their Indias and from Calicut into Portugal, and so thence to Antwerp, which before that time were wont to be brought by the Red Sea to Barnt and thence to Alexandria and so to Venice, which (before the Portuguese voyage into the Indias) furnished all Christendom with spices. But the King of Portugal, having partly by love, partly by force, drawn all the traffic of spices into his own hands, and having brought them to Lisbon, sent his factor with spice to Antwerp, by which means it drew all nations thither to buy the spices of the said factor. Thus Antwerp by this occasion began to be greatly frequented. Afterwards in the year 1516 divers merchants—strangers, Spaniards and Italians, departed from Bruges to go and dwell at Antwerp, and after them others, and so little by little all strangers (a few excepted) left Bruges and went to Antwerp, with no less commodity to this city than discommodity to that.

The third cause of the wealth of Antwerp was the course that Monsieur de Longueville and Martin van Rossem made with a mighty army in 1542 into the Low Countries, meaning indeed to have spoiled Antwerp, by occasion whereof the citizens of Antwerp, to avoid the like peril hereafter, have since that time marvellously fortified their town, for the safety both of it and of all merchants trafficking to it . . . Further, because the suburbs were at that time burned, and that restraint has been made since not to build within 3500 feet of the town wall, a great number of wealthy men that before dwelt without the town, have been since and daily are constrained to build and dwell within the town, by means whereof since that time Antwerp is increased by 3000 houses.

POLITICAL ASSASSINATIONS

One characteristic of the sixteenth century was the appearance of a political theory that assassination was justifiable where the defence of the State demands it. This was argued in much the same way as the use of poison gas was argued in the First World War. Horatio Brown prints in his *Studies in Venetian History*, vol. ii, a paper by an anonymous author entitled *Of The Right that Princes have to compass the Lives of their Enemies' Allies*, provoked by a conspiracy to murder the Marquis of

Pescara in order to weaken his French allies. The Council of Ten in Venice had the worst reputation for political murders: they were frequent, always brought about when the Republic was in the direst danger, and nearly always were a total failure, especially where poison was the weapon.

Source: Horatio Brown, *op. cit.*, London, 1907.

October 17th, 1509. By the authority of this Council be it decreed that the chiefs of the Council be charged to inform themselves in the most cautious and secret manner possible as to the ways and means by which we can put to death, through poison or otherwise, certain bitter and implacable enemies of our state.

On the 14th December, 1513, the said Brother John of Ragusa presented himself to the Presidents of the Ten, and declared that he would work wonders in killing anyone they chose by certain means of his own invention, and therefore begs: First, that on the success of his experiment he shall receive one thousand five hundred ducats a year for life; secondly, that if the noble lords wish him to operate on anyone else, the annuity shall be raised in a sum to be agreed upon.

[The Council accepted Brother John's offer, and] . . . enjoined him to go and make his first experiment on the person of the Emperor.

[Brother John followed up his first offer with the following scale of prices.]

For the Grand Turk, 500 ducats; for the King of Spain (exclusive of travelling expenses) 150 ducats; for the Duke of Milan, 60 ducats; for the Marquis of Mantua, 50 ducats; for his Holiness, only 100 ducats. As a rule, the longer the journey, the higher would be the price.

The following letter is dated 1649, which is outside the dates set for this book, but the example is so extraordinary that it may surely be here included.

Source: Lunardo Foscolo, Provveditore Generale di Dalmazia, writes from Zara to the Inquisitors of State.

My incessant occupation in the discharge of this most laborious service never makes me forget my intent and desire to procure advantage to my country. I then, considering the perilous state of the kingdom of Candia, first treacherously invaded, and now openly occupied by the Turks, the pre-eminence of their forces, the copiousness of their soldiery, the opulence of the Turkish treasury, which will enable them to maintain the war for many years, and also being well aware that, although the public spirit of Venice yields to none in courage and magnanimity, the Republic has neither forces, men, nor money wherewith to resist much longer the attacks of its foes, and reflecting on the impossibility to meet such a heavy expenditure, have applied myself to a study of the methods whereby the Turkish power might be overcome without risk of men or burden to the exchequer, and how the kingdom of Candia might be recovered; for, after God, our hope to reacquire it is small indeed.

Now there is here a good subject of Venice, lately appointed doctor, who besides his skill in healing is also a famous distiller. His name is Michiel Angelo Salamon. He is desirous to prove himself, what he is in fact, a faithful servant of your excellencies. I explained my wishes to him, and he availed himself of the presence here of the plague to distil a liquid expressed from the spleen, the buboes and carbuncles of the plague-stricken; and this, when mixed with other ingredients, will have the power wherever it is scattered to slay any number of persons, for it is the quintessence of the plague. I considered that if this quintessence of the plague were sown in the enemies' camps at Retimo, Cannea and San Todero, and if it operates as Dr. Michiel assures me it will, this would greatly assist us to recover the kingdom of Candia. I accordingly determined not to lose the opportunity to have a vase of the poison prepared, and this jar shall be kept, with all due precautions, for the service of your excellencies. I believe, however, that some ruse must be adopted to entice the Turks into the trap, and would suggest that we should make use of the Albanian fez, or some other cloth goods, which the Turks are accustomed to buy, so that the poison may pass through as many hands as possible. The cloth should be made up in parcels as if for sale, after having been painted over with the quintessence, and then placed in separate boxes destined for the various places where we desire to sow the poison. The quintessence, well secured in several cases for the greater safety of those who have to handle and transport it, should be sent to the commander-in-chief that he may take the necessary steps for causing it to pass into the enemies' hands. This may be done either by lading several vessels with the cloth, which vessels are to be abandoned by their crews when the enemy comes in sight; or else by means of pedlars who shall hawk the cloth about the country; so that the enemy, hoping to make booty, may gain the plague and find death. The affair must be managed with all circumspection, and the operator must be induced to his work by hopes of gain and by promises, for it will be a dangerous undertaking, and when the operation is over he must go through a rigorous quarantine. While handling the quintessence, it will be of use to the operator to stuff his nose and mouth with sponges soaked in vinegar; and while poisoning the cloth he may fasten the brush to an iron rod, and when finished he must put brush and rod into the fire. Having given the Turk the plague, every care must be taken to prevent our people coming in contact with them.

The proposition is a virtuous one, and worthy of the composer of the quintessence. It is, however, a violent course, unusual and perhaps not admitted by public morality. But desperate cases call for violent remedies, and in the case of the Turk, enemies by faith, treacherous by nature, who have always betrayed your excellencies, in my humble opinion the ordinary considerations have no weight.

[It is not known if the experiment was tried.]

A Renaissance Painter and his Patron

ANDREA MANTEGNA AND FRANCESCO GONZAGA

Francesco Gonzaga, Marquis of Mantua, was the son of Federico I of Mantua, whom he succeeded in 1484. He married Isabella d'Este. He was one of the wisest and best rulers in Italy, a great soldier, an admirable husband, and a generous and intelligent patron of the arts.

He was specially good to Andrea Mantegna, a very great painter, but an irritable man. Francesco paid him fifteen ducats a month, with supplies of corn, wood, wine, and lodgings for his family. In the last year of his reign the treasury was exhausted by a long war and by an attack of the plague in Mantua.

Source: A letter from Francesco Gonzaga to Mantegna, who had complained that he was not getting his salary. Quoted in Julia Cartwright, *Isabella d'Este*, vol. i, pp. 27–8.

Andrea, we have received a letter from you which it really seems to us that you need never have written, since we perfectly remember the promises we made to you when you entered our service, neither, as it seems to us, have we failed to keep these promises or to do our utmost for you. But you can not take from us what we have not got, and you yourself have seen that, when we have had the means, we have never failed to do all in our power for you and our other servants, and that gladly and with good will. It is true that, since we have not received our usual revenues during the last few months, we have been obliged to defer certain payments, such as this which is due to you, but we are seeking by every means in our power to raise money to meet our obligations, even if we are forced to mortgage our own property, since all our jewels are already pawned, and you need not fear but that before long your debt will be paid gladly and readily.

HUNTING IN THE XV CENTURY

Source: A letter from Isabella d'Este to her husband, the Marquis of Mantua, August 27th, 1492. Luzio-Renier, in *Archivio Storico Lombardo*, xvii, 350. English version from J. Cartwright, *Beatrice d'Este*, p. 159.

To-day we went out hunting in a beautiful valley which seemed as if it were expressly created for the spectacle. All the stags were driven into the wooded valley of the Ticino, and closed in on every side by the hunters, so that they were forced to swim the river and ascend the mountains where the ladies watched them from under the *pergola* and green tents set up on the hillside. We could see every movement of the animals along the valley and up the mountain-side, where the dogs chased them across the river; but only two climbed the hillside and ran far out of sight, so that we did not see them killed, but Don Alfonso and Messer Galeazzo both gave them chase and succeeded in wounding them. Afterwards came a doe with its young one, which the dogs were not allowed to follow. Many wild boars and goats were found, but only one boar was killed before our eyes, and one wild goat, which fell to my share. Last of all came a wolf, which made fine somersaults in the air as it ran past us and amused the whole company; but none of its arts availed the poor beast, which soon followed its comrades to the slaughter. And so with much laughter and amusement, we returned home, to end the day at supper, and give the body a share in the recreations of the mind.

A XV Century Practical Joke

Source: A letter from Lodovico Sforza to his sister-in-law, Isabella Gonzaga, December 6th, 1492. Luzio-Renier, *op. cit.*, p. 361. English version from J. Cartwright, *Beatrice d'Este*, p. 163. Mariolo was a court jester.

You know what good sport we had in the wild boar hunts at which you were present last summer. Poor Mariolo, you remember, could not be there, first because he was ill at Milan, and afterwards because he was required to keep my wife company during her illness, and was much distressed to have been absent from these expeditions, when he heard that even the king's ambassador had wounded a wild boar. And he told us what great things he would have done, had he only been present. Now that my dearest wife is better and begins to be able to go out-of-doors again, I thought we would have a little fun at his expense. Some wolves and wild goats having been driven into a wood near La Pecorata, which, as you know, is about a mile from here, on the way to La Sforzesca, Cardinal Sanseverino had a common farm pig shut up in the same enclosure, and the next day we went out hunting and took Mariolo with us. While we hunted the wolves and wild goats, we left the pig to him, and he, taking it for a wild boar, chased it with a great hue and cry along the

woods. If Your Highness could only have seen him running
after this pig, you would have died of laughter, the more so that
he gallantly tried to spear it three times over, and only succeeded
in touching its side once. And seeing how proud he was of his
prowess, we said to him, 'Don't you know, Mariolo, that you
have been hunting a tame pig?' He stood dumb with astonishment and stared as if he did not know what we could mean, and
so we all came home infinitely amused, and every one asked
Mariolo if he did not know the difference between a wild boar
and a tame pig!

ALCHEMY

In origin and in the narrowest sense Alchemy meant the art of
turning gold into silver or transmuting the base metals into noble
metals. In the Middle Ages Alchemy was synonymous with Chemistry.
In the sixteenth century it was Paracelsus who was the first to apply
chemistry to medicine by studying the properties of substances and
their effects on the human body. But for the majority of people
Alchemy meant making a fortune by turning silver or a base metal
into gold—a delusion which was soon to be riotously lampooned by
Ben Jonson. The following letters describe the machinations of an
Italian alchemist. For the full story of Bragadin, see Horatio Brown,
Studies in Venetian History, vol. ii.

Source: (a) *Fugger Newsletters*, ed. by G. T. Matthews, Capricorn
Books, New York, 1959, p. 173. From Venice, the 1st day of
November, 1589.

Your Grace will no doubt have learnt from the weekly reports
of one Marco Antonio Bragadini, called Mamugnano. He is the
bastard son of a nobleman here and was born in Cyprus. He is
reported to be able to turn base metal into gold. Our government
has had him transported hither under safe escort, because the
Inquisition has put him under ban. He is forty years old and was
formerly possessed of no mean fortune, but spent it in riotous
living. Then for some time he was mint-master to the Grand
Duke, Francis. From thence he came to the late Pope Gregory,
who held him in great esteem. He thus obtained several thousand
ducats. But when these too had been spent, he became a Capuchin

and had taken his second vows. But since he could not subject himself to the strict rule of the order, he absconded without dispensation (hence the excommunication ban by the Holy Office) and betook himself to France. There he served several princes *incognito*. Latterly he has returned again to Bergamo in Italy and has exhibited his art in Valcamonica and in a short time has increased his fortune to over two hundred thousand crowns. He has expounded his craft to several persons and it had got so far that he was prevailed upon to come here of his free will. Such a host of princes and lords beleaguered him that he was scarcely safe, although he had a bodyguard of fifty archers. This man is now here in this city, holds banquet daily for five hundred people and lives in princely style in the Palazzo Dandolo on the Giudecca. He literally throws gold about in shovelfuls. This is his recipe: he takes ten ounces of quicksilver, puts it in the fire and mixes it with a drop of liquid, which he carries in an ampulla. Thus it promptly turns into good gold. He has no other wish but to be of good use to his country, the Republic. The day before yesterday he presented to the Secret Council of Ten two ampullas with this liquid, which have been tested in his absence. The first test was found to be successful and it is said to have resulted in six million ducats. I doubt not but that this will appear mighty strange to Your Grace. It verily sounds like a fairy tale, but Your Grace will surely believe us, for everything is so obvious that it cannot be doubted. The confectioning of this liquid is, however, his secret, for in his letter of safe conduct he made express demand that he be not forced to divulge this. He also craves nothing more from this our government but that it may exercise good watch over his life and person. In return he will provide them with gold in sufficiency according to their demands. He has already made known that he is amazed at the ignorance of the world, in not discovering this art before, considering that little is requisite for this achievement. This is truly marvellous and quite novel to all of us. The alchemists have taken heart of grace again and are working night and day. One hears of nothing but of this excellent man who, as already stated, has no other wish but to serve his country.

Source: (*b*) *Ibid.*, p. 174 *et sqq.* From Venice, the 8th day of December, 1589.

You have learnt latterly that the craft of the alchemist Marco Bragadini after being tested has been approved of. The tests have shown this sufficiently. The most noble personages here address him by the title 'Illustrissimo' and feast with him daily. The Duke speaks with him in the second person. By day noblemen attend upon him, by night he is guarded by armed barges. Whereas so many strange people have arrived here, the Government holds in readiness three fully equipped galleys.

Source: (*c*) *Ibid.* from Venice, the 16th day of December, 1589.

The alchemist is said to be at work now in making five thousand sequins per month at the request of our rulers. Thereafter he will make fifteen or sixteen millions more which he has promised to hand over to it. Day by day he shows himself in great pomp. He makes his friends twenty thousand and more ducats at a time. Monday last he gave a banquet in honour of the Duc de Luxembourg, the French Catholic Ambassador in Rome, which, without counting all kinds of special confectionery, cost near on six hundred crowns.

Source: (*d*) *Ibid.* from Rome, the 16th day of December, 1589.

The Venetian ambassador has solemnly besought the Pope that Mamugnano, the alchemist, who now resides in Venice, may remain there without molestation by the Holy Office, on account of his being a former Capuchin. Thereupon the Pope made answer that he was not a little surprised at the aforementioned Rulers putting so much faith in that man. Though his art might be found to be successful, yet it could only accrue unto him by the help of Satan.

Source: (*e*) *Ibid.* from Venice, the 4th day of January, 1590.

It is said of our Mamugnano that his craft for transforming quicksilver into gold does suffice for small quantities, but fails to produce larger ones. It is reported that the night before last he made two ingots in the presence of some of our patrician aldermen, each one of the weight of one pound. There no longer

21

exists any doubt in the matter. Discussion, however, is rife amongst some of this city's philosophers as to whether Mamugnano can renew the material wherewith he has made his gold, once it is used up. Some say yes, and others say no, so that it is doubtful what they really think about it.

Source: (*f*) *Ibid.* from Venice, the 19th day of January, 1590.

Mamugnano changed a pound of quicksilver into gold some days ago. But he is not satisfied with this weight, because he has been asked by several persons to produce a larger sum.

Source: (*g*) *Ibid.* from Venice, the 26th day of January, 1590.

Concerning the alchemist, Mamugnano, no one harbours doubts any longer about his daily experiments in changing quicksilver into gold. It was realized that his craft did not go beyond one pound of quicksilver, however much various persons asked him to produce more. Thus the belief is now held that his allegations to produce a number of millions have been a great fraud, in which he caused people to believe. For he who can make a small amount of gold should also be able to produce a large quantity. This is the question upon which learned professors hold dispute. Meanwhile he has cut down his expenses, also reduced his banqueting, and is seen about with a smaller suite than before. It is reported from Spain that the King has concluded an agreement with the Genoese for a loan of five millions towards the end of the months of March and April, one million during the middle of July and the last during the middle of September.

Source: (*h*) *Ibid.* from Venice, the 26th day of January, 1589.

The alchemist Mamugnano is making gold here for his needs. He is intending to hold a joyous masque in the Square of St. Stephen, this Shrovetide, for which purpose he is having sent hither six fine stallions from Mantua.

Source: (*i*) *Ibid.* from Venice, the 11th day of May, 1590.

Whereas Mamugnano, the alchemist, passed some time in a village a certain distance from here, and several persons suspected him of making gold for other people, his rooms were sealed at the request of his creditors. By order of the Signori Capitani, however, one room was unsealed again ... We have just learned that Mamugnano, the alchemist, has returned here. The Pope is said to have granted him absolution, but he had to make a donation of five thousand crowns and enter the Order of the Knights of Malta.

Source: (*j*) *Ibid.* from Venice, March 30, 1590.

A letter from Prague states that a native of Scotland has arrived there with thirty-five horses. He gives himself out as a real artist who knows how to make gold, and is not inferior to Mamugnano in Venice.

WITCHCRAFT

The worst feature of the sixteenth century was the great development which took place in a belief in witchcraft. Persecutions of witches had occurred at various times, but after the Bull of Pope Innocent VIII in 1484 which positively ordered persecutions, they became more frequent, but the result was rather to spread the disease, so that it reached its climax in the next century. Probably it was more virulent in Italy than anywhere else, but it was not by any means confined to that country. 'Science and religion imply austerity. Not so Art, and the history of the Italian Renaissance is there to prove it. For mankind reached then a nadir of immorality, yet, from the purely artistic point of view, it was truly a golden age. On the other hand, though the quattrocento and the early cinquecento stimulated scientific research, the main achievements, with the partial exception of Leonardo da Vinci, were due to foreigners.' *The Civilization of the Renaissance*, George Sarton on Science, Atlantic Paperback 1102, 1962, p. 93.

Source: (*a*) The Bull of Pope Innocent VIII, December 9th, 1484. This English version is taken from Montague Summers, *The Geography of Witchcraft*, University Books, originally published by Routledge & Kegan Paul, 1927, in the History of Civilization Series, p. 533 *et sqq.*

Innocent, Bishop, Servant of the servants of God, for an eternal remembrance.

Desiring with the most heartfelt anxiety, even as our Apostleship requires, that the Catholic Faith should especially in this Our

21*

day increase and flourish everywhere, and that all heretical
depravity should be driven far from the frontiers and bournes of
the Faithful, We very gladly proclaim and even restate those
particular means and methods whereby Our pious desire may
obtain its wished effect, since when all errors are uprooted by
Our diligent avocation as by the hoe of a provident husbandman,
a zeal for and the regular observance of Our holy Faith will be all
the more strongly impressed on the hearts of the faithful.

It has indeed lately come to Our ears, not without afflicting Us
with bitter sorrow, that in some parts of Northern Germany, as
well as in the provinces, townships, territories, districts, and
dioceses of Mainz, Cologne, Treves, Salzburg, and Bremen,
many persons of both sexes, unmindful of their own salvation and
straying from the Catholic Faith, have abandoned themselves to
devils, incubi and succubi, and by their incantations, spells,
conjurations, and other accursed charms and crafts, enormities
and horrid offences, have slain infants yet in the mother's womb,
as also the offspring of cattle, have blasted the produce of the
earth, the grapes of the vine, the fruits of trees, nay, men and
women, beasts of burthen, herd-beasts, as well as animals of other
kinds, vineyards, orchards, meadows, pasture-land, corn, wheat,
and all other cereals; these wretches furthermore afflict and torment men and women, beasts of burthen, herd-beasts, as well as
animals of other kinds, with terrible and piteous pains and sore
diseases, both internal and external; they hinder men from performing the sexual act and women from conceiving, whence
husbands can not know their wives nor wives receive their husbands; over and above this they blasphemously renounce that
Faith which is theirs by the Sacrament of Baptism, and at the
instigation of the Enemy of Mankind they do not shrink from
committing and perpetrating the foulest abominations and filthiest
excesses to the deadly peril of their own souls, whereby they
outrage the Divine Majesty and are a cause of scandal and danger
to very many . . .

Wherefore . . . We decree and enjoin that the aforesaid inquisitors be empowered to proceed to the just correction, imprisonment, and punishment of any persons, without let or hindrance,

. . . correcting, mulcting, imprisoning, punishing, as their crimes merit, those whom they have found guilty, the penalty being adapted to the offence . . .

Source: (*b*) Alexander VI in 1501 summed up the evils of witchcraft: Montague Summers, *op. cit.*, p. 537.

Inasmuch as We have been informed that in the province of Lombardy various persons of both sexes use and practise various magical arts and devilish abominations, and by their poisons and other spells have committed many heinous crimes, destroying both men and beasts and blasting fruitful fields and spreading horrid heresies so that great scandal is given, We are determined in accordance with the solemn duty of executing Our Apostolic office bestowed upon Us from on high, to crush—With the help of Almighty God—all such enormities, to put an end to these heresies and scandals.

Source: (*c*) The following letter from Schwab-Müchen, September 5th, 1589, describes a burning of witches—a common occurrence at that time: *Fugger Newsletters*, ed. by G. T. Matthews, New York, 1959, p. 171.

There again follows a confession given at Court by a monster who was burnt there yesterday. Her accomplice, who was also taken prisoner with her and who is said to be a very rich peasant woman from Bobingen, died last Saturday in prison. It is reported that she has taken neither food nor drink for four days, nor given any evidence, for her devilish paramour has forbidden her to do so. She also continually called upon him to come and fetch her. She would listen to no mention of God or other holy matters. The witch, who was condemned yesterday, made a noose out of the straw on which she was lying and tied it round her neck in order to hang herself, but when food was brought in to her this was discovered and prevented.

Rumour hath it that the late sorceress was to have been burnt with the other witch, but neither I nor others did see anything of her. She must have been led away in secret and have lain under the stake, and so both must have been burnt together. These monsters are said to have denounced many others who will in their turn meet their fate. Some one tells me that they brought another four such persons from Bobingen before dawn to imprison them. It is also rumoured that they will not spare the beautiful ones, once they have done away with the ugly and the lewd ones. One of the four brought in is said to be a wealthy widow. The Bishop has made up his mind to exterminate all this vermin from his diocese. Dillingen also shows signs of this plague. The Bishop will probably have his hands full for some time to come with burnings and in the end, perhaps, even put part of the nobility in golden chains.

The present unfortunate female, Anna Schelkl, widow of Hans Schelkl of Bobingen, who has been produced in public, has permitted herself to be shamefully imposed upon and seduced by the accursed Satan, in contravention of the commands of God. She has repeatedly yielded herself to him in fornication and thus committed adultery in a strictly forbidden and sodomitic manner, and for over thirty years she has delivered herself to accursed witchery. She has denied God and all His heavenly Hosts as well as Holy Baptism, and instead of the sign of the Lord she has allowed her body to be marked with the four signs of the Devil. She has thus beyond doubt permitted herself to be led astray from the divine mercy of God and to surrender herself to the sway of the Evil One. By means of the said witchcraft she has caused great harm and destruction and death to little children, people, horses and other animals, and she also assisted in spoiling and ruining the precious corn of the fields. Therefore the judges of this hamlet, Schwab-München, are unanimously agreed upon their verdict that Anna Schelkl be handed over to the executioner and be led by him to the common place of execution, there to be dispatched from life to death by burning on account of her loathsome and highly punishable misdeeds. Her goods and her chattels to go to the Treasury of His Honour, the Venerable Herr Marquard, Bishop of Augsburg and Provost of the Cathedral of Bamberg. Let every one beware of such horrible sin . . .

Those who wish to pursue this subject further may like to consult the long work by James Sprenger and Henry Kramer entitled *Malleus Maleficarum*, of which there is an English translation by Montagu Summers of the 1489 edition, published in 1928. Sprenger and Kramer were the two Inquisitors mentioned by Pope Innocent VIII in his Papal Bull of 1484, quoted above, to investigate 'heretical depravities' in parts of Northern Germany and in territories along the borders of the Rhine.

HORSE-RACING

Source: Luca Landucci, *A Florentine Diary*, trans. by A. D. Rosen Jervis, Dent, 1927, p. 42.

Up till now my brother Gostanzo had won twenty *palii*[2] with his Barbary horse *Draghetto*, that is, twenty races from the 8th October, 1481 to the 25th June, 1485; the first was Santa Liperata, the next Sant' Anna, and San Vittorio several. Once when he won San Vittorio, he sold the *palio* to the Aretini for 40 gold florins, and then he went to Arezzo and won it back again. And when he went to race at Siena, there was a tie between his horse and one belonging to Lorenzo de' Medici, called *La Lucciola* (Firefly), that of Gostanzo being in reality one head's length in advance of the other. And the people who were present declared that he had won, and told him to go to the magistrate, and they would bear witness. Gostanzo, however, refused to do this out of respect for Lorenzo, and as it happened, Lorenzo was declared the winner. Another year, also at Siena, a meaner trick was played on him: namely, when Gostanzo's horse was a bowshot in advance, and reached the winning-post, he dismounted and got up on the *palio*;[2] then another horse came up, and they said that Gostanzo's horse had not passed the winning-post, and that the other one had passed it. Therefore the prize was given to the other. A very great injustice, that a rider who had not won the *palio* should receive it. It was most unfortunate, as my brother had such a good horse. He rushed about so much after this Barbary horse that in the end it proved his death. He died on 12th September, 1485.

FLORENTINE FASHIONS

Source: Luca Landucci, *op. cit.*, p. 294.

In the year 1529 the custom of wearing hoods began to go out, and by 1532 not a single one was to be seen, caps or hats being worn instead. Also at this time men began to cut their hair short, everyone having formerly worn it long on to their shoulders without exception; and they now began to wear a beard, which formerly was only worn by two men in Florence, Corbizo and one of the Martigli.

At this time also hose[3] were begun to be made in two pieces, which had formerly been made all in one and without a seam; now they slashed them up everywhere, and put silk underneath, letting it project at all the slashes.

A JOURNEY TO INDIA IN 1574

An Italian Jesuit named Alexandro Valignano left Lisbon for India in March, 1574 and journeyed thence to Malacca, Macao and Japan.

Source: Quoted in *St. Francis Xavier*, by James Brodrick, S.J., Image Books, Doubleday & Co. Inc., 1957, pp. 60–1.

The perils and hardships suffered on this expedition are very extensive and terrifying. The first hardship is the lack of accommodation. True, the ships are large and powerful, but so packed with passengers, merchandise and provisions that there is little room left for anyone to move about and the ordinary people aboard, for whose comfort there is no arrangement whatever, must stand all day on deck in the blazing sun and sleep there somehow all night in the cold. On the other hand, the berths put at the disposal of noble or wealthy persons are so low, so narrow, so confined, that it is all a man can do to fit himself into them. The second hardship has to do with food and drink. Though his Highness the King provides daily rations of biscuit, meat, fish, water and wine sufficient to keep the passengers alive, the meat and fish are so salty, and the provision of utensils to collect the rations so inadequate, that the suffering on this account, especially among the soldiers, beggars description. The third hardship among the general run of the voyagers is due to their being poor and happy-go-lucky. They set out with insufficient clothing, the little they bring soon rots on their backs, and they suffer dreadfully in the lower latitudes, both from the cold and from the stench of their rags. The fourth hardship is caused by the calms off the Guinea Coast, which may last for forty, fifty or sixty days. During that time the passengers almost sweat their souls out and suffer torments from the heat beyond the power of my pen to set forth. The fifth hardship, and the worst of any, is the lack of water. During much of the voyage, the water doled out in the daily ration is so foul and malodorous that it is impossible to bear the stench of it, and the passengers have to put a piece of cloth before their mouths to filter off the corruption. This liquid is only distributed once a day, and many fail to get their portion through having no jugs in which to collect it. Others drink their entire ration at one gulp, the result being that large numbers die of thirst. The sixth hardship results from disease of every description among the passengers, who suffer a thousand miseries before dying or recovering. The King appoints a surgeon to each ship, but he and his remedies soon cease to be of any use . . .

It often happens that the majority of the passengers die, sometimes 200, sometimes 300 or 400, on a single ship, and it is the most heart-rending thing to watch each day the poor inflated bodies being committed to the sea. With all these and other perils, it is extraordinary that so many Portuguese should seek to come to India every year. Yet they do, and as cheerfully as though India was only a league from Lisbon. They embark with no other linen than the shirts on their backs, with a couple of loaves in their hands, a cheese, a pot of marmalade, and nothing else whatever.

A CHRISTIAN MISSIONARY OF THE XVI CENTURY

ST. FRANCIS XAVIER

Francis Xavier was born in 1506 and died in 1552. He was the youngest son of Juan de Jasso, councillor to the King of Navarre, and his wife, Maria de Azpilcueta y Xavier. He took his mother's surname.

In 1524 he went to the university of Paris and there he became acquainted with Ignatius Loyola. He was one of the original six persons who took the first Jesuit vows. Between 1536 and 1541 Xavier worked with the Jesuits in Italy. In 1541 he sailed from Lisbon as papal nuncio in the Indies. On his voyage he visited Mozambique, Malindi, Sokotra, Goa, the Fishery Coast, Travancore. It is untrue that he founded forty-five churches in Travancore: he did not found one. In 1544 he was in Ceylon, he went on to Malacca, Amboyna, the Moluccas, and in 1549 he arrived in Japan. His next place of call was Singapore and he arrived in China in 1552. He died in that year: his body was transferred to Malacca and thence to Goa, where it now still lies. He was canonized in 1619 and beatified in 1621. In spite of his inability to appreciate any merits in religions other than Christianity, which to some extent limited his successes, there are good grounds for regarding him as one of the greatest missionaries since the first century. All his life he remained a close friend of Ignatius Loyola. The usual English pronunciation of his name is made to rhyme with 'saviour'. The Spanish pronunciation has the sound of 'have-ee-air', with the accent on the last syllable. The following extracts are English translations of foreign sources quoted in *Saint Francis Xavier*, by James Brodrick, S.J., Image Book D. 49, Doubleday & Co. Inc., 1957.

Source: (*a*) The surgeon of the ship *Santiago* was Cosme Saraiva. He gave the following evidence at a judicial inquiry held four years after Xavier's death. Brodrick, *op. cit.*, p. 63.

I came out from Portugal on the same ship as Father Francis and I often watched him at his charitable occupations and whilst he taught Christian doctrine. He used to beg alms from other passengers for the poor and sick persons. He took personal charge of such as were ailing or prostrated by illness. From this work of mercy, and from his hearing of confessions, he allowed himself never a moment's respite, but cheerfully accomplished it all. Everybody held him for a saint, and that was my own fixed opinion. At Mozambique the Father gave himself so completely to the service of those who were taken from the five ships who were already ill, and to those who fell ill afterwards during the winter spent on the island, that only forty or forty-one of the sufferers died. Everybody regarded this as a marvellous thing, indeed as a real miracle due under God to the devotedness and goodness of the Father. He fell sick himself in consequence of his crushing labours, and I took him to my lodging to take care of him. So bad did he become that I had to bleed him nine times, and for three whole days he was out of his senses. I noticed that while in delirium he raved unintelligibly about other things, but in speaking of the things of God was perfectly lucid and coherent. As soon as he was convalescent, he resumed his former labours with all his old enthusiasm.

Source: (*b*) Manuel Teixeira, a Jesuit in India, who saw Xavier at work and wrote a sketch of him. Brodrick, *op. cit.*, p. 74–5.

He went up and down the streets and squares with a bell in his hand, crying to the children and others to come to the instructions. The novelty of the proceeding, never seen before in Goa, brought a large crowd around him which he then led to the church. He began by singing the lessons which he had rhymed and then made the children sing them so that they might become the better fixed in their memories. Afterwards he explained each point in the simplest way, using only such words as his young audience could readily understand. By this method, which has since been adopted everywhere in the Indies, he so deeply en-grained the truths and precepts of the faith in the hearts of the people that men and women, children and old folk, took to singing the ten commandments while they walked in the streets, as did the fisherman in his boat and the labourer in the fields, for their own entertainment and recreation.

A Northern European Monarch

Gustavus I Eriksson, generally known as Gustavus Vasa, was born in 1496, became king of Sweden in 1523, and died in 1560. He founded the Vasa dynasty, which governed Sweden for some three hundred years. He was the liberator of Sweden from the rule of Denmark, he was the creator of the stable kingdom of Sweden, and he was the man who carried through the Lutheran Reformation in Sweden. In the problems which faced him as King, in the political wisdom with which he faced them, in the ruthlessness with which he solved them, and in the irritability of his temper, he may well be compared with Henry

VIII of England. Had he reigned over as important a nation as England, instead of ruling an impoverished state on the periphery of Europe, he would have attracted much more attention from the historians than he has. His more brilliant grandson, Gustavus Adolphus, has stolen his thunder. In his own day contemporary European opinions about Gustavus Vasa were far from flattering. Inside Sweden his reputation among modern historians has always been very high. The following account is a contemporary reply to his critics, written by his chaplain, to show that foreign verdicts were unjust.

Source: Quoted in Hallendorff & Schuck, History of Sweden, Eng. trans. by L. Yapp, London, 1929.

[That hostile verdicts were unjust] is proven by a certain Doctor named Carolus Paludanus of France, when he thus answered one of his countrymen, who asked him what manner of man the King's Majesty of Sweden might be, for that there were strange tales abroad concerning him. The Doctor answered thus, saying: 'Dost thou ask what manner of man is my Lord the King? Know then that he is a king of the Lord's anointing.' The other said, 'Wherefore?' Thereupon the Doctor: 'For his Majesty hath a passing great understanding, and he is so sharp of wit withal, in all matters spiritual and temporal, that seldom have I known his like. For in God's word is his Majesty so well informed that he answereth rightly in spiritual things, by whomsoever he be questioned: he can correct the clergy of his realm, for he knoweth all scriptures. Moreover, in matters temporal, the king commandeth certain things to be performed, whereof no man would believe that they could prosper at any time, nevertheless, though all men misdeem them, they have good hap, and the commonwealth flourishes exceedingly, so that every man is astounded thereat.'

THE PROPHET OF SALON

At midnight, December 14th, 1503, in Salon, in Provence, was born Michael Nostradamus, who was to become perhaps to us the most remarkable figure in the sixteenth century. The family was Jewish: the name was derived from Nostra-Donna, Gallicized into Nostradame and Latinized into Nostradamus, as was the custom of those days.

Nostradamus became one of the greatest of the medical doctors, one of the most learned astrologers, he was deeply involved in the art or science of Magic, and he was to prove that he had the gift of second sight so fully developed as to be almost incredible. His prophecies dealt for the most part with French political history, but he did also deal with the history of England. The chief characteristics of his prophecies are their vividness, their astonishing detail, and the verbal obscurity in which he clothed them; evidently he feared that he might get into trouble with both lay and ecclesiastical authorities. He became intimate with the French King, Henri II, and especially with Catherine de' Medici, who was greatly interested in magic. He foretold in minute detail the events in the history of the house of Valois and of Bourbon: he foretold the French Revolution, the Restoration, the Third Republic, and some have liked to understand many of his prophecies as dealing with the events of our own times. No doubt many of these later ones are spurious, but the undoubtedly genuine prophecies, e.g. those dealing with the Valois and Bourbons, are sufficiently remarkable to give Nostradamus the name of Prophet.

Source: The following examples are all taken from his *Centuries*, first published in 1555, though he had been at work on them for some years before that. These English translations are taken from James Laver's *Nostradamus*, Penguin Books, 1942, chapters Two and Three. Further reading may be found in Edgar Leoni's *Nostradamus, Life and Literature*, New York, 1961.

> The young lion shall overcome the old,
> In warlike field in single fight:
> In cage of gold he will pierce his eyes,
> Two wounds one, then die a cruel death.

In 1559, three years after Nostradamus had published the above quatrain, Henri II was killed accidentally by Montgomery, the Captain of the Scottish Guard, while tilting against the King during the marriage celebrations of the King's younger daughter, Margaret, to the Duke of Savoy. The point of Montgomery's lance entered the King's eye, and a splinter of the lance entered his throat. The helm looked like a cage, and the King's helm was gilded.

Montgomery fled to England and lived there for fifteen years. He became a Protestant and later a leader of the Huguenots. During the Wars of Religion in France he was captured, but one of the terms of surrender was that his life should be spared. But on May 27th, 1574, nineteen years after Nostradamus had published the following quatrain, Montgomery was arrested by the orders of Catherine de' Medici, while he was in bed, by six noblemen of the royal army.

> He who in fight on martial field shall have carried
> off the prize from one greater than he, shall be
> surprized by six men by night, suddenly, naked, and
> without armour.

When Henri III died, Catherine de' Medici was left as Regent with seven children living. Nostradamus continually refers to these seven children as The House of the Seven, and he foretells that these seven Valois children will all perish violently, and thus the House of Valois will be exterminated. But he goes further and foretells the triumph of the Turks under Suleiman the Magnificent, but also the defeat of the Turks at Lepanto. The first quatrain comes from the *Présage*, not the *Centuries*: the second half-quatrain comes from the *Centuries*.

> The death of the House of the Seven
> shall come about by a series of deaths,
> Tempest, hail, fury and pestilence. A King
> Of the Orient will put the Occidentals all
> To flight and will subjugate his former conquerors.

.   .   .   .   .

> Near the shores of Cape Araxum, the House
> Of the Great Suleiman shall fall to
> Earth.

The Battle of Lepanto (October 5th, 1571) was fought near Cape Araxum (to-day Cape Papa).

One more quotation must suffice: it is probably the most remarkable of the whole series. The Cardinal Richelieu quarrelled with Cinq-Mars and had him arrested and executed, 1642. In 1555 Nostradamus had published the following:

> Old Cardinal deceived by the young man, he will
> See himself disarmed and put out of his office,
> If you do not show, Arles, so that it can be per-
> ceived, a copy of the treaty,[4]

Et Liquiduct et le Prince embausmé.

Liqueduct: can only mean 'carried by water'. *Embausmè*: can only mean 'embalmed'. Richelieu was so desperately ill after he had dealt with Cinq-Mars that he went to bed and his bed was carried up the Rhone from Tarascon to Lyons, then down the Seine from Fontaine-bleau to Paris—*Liqueduct*. On December 4th, 1642, Richelieu died. Six months later Louis XIII died. Both were embalmed.

Is the gift of second sight a mere myth?

ST. ELMO FIRE

Source: The Art of Navigation by Martin Cortes, translated by Richard Eden, published by R. Jugge, London, 1561, first edition. *The XX Chapter of the bright and shining exhalations that appear in tempests, which the mariners call Saint Elmo or Corpus Sancti.* The spelling and punctuation have been modernized. For the importance of Richard Eden see E. G. R. Taylor, *Tudor Geography*, 1485 to 1583, ch. ii.

Ignorance is the mother of errors, and therefore will I not omit to shew the natural cause hereof, although among certain simple and ignorant people it is accounted for a miracle, that in certain tempests on the sea the mariners see certain shining and bright fires which with great superstition they kneel down unto and pray unto, affirming that it is Saint Elmo that appeareth unto them. And not contented therewith, some swear they have seen drops of green ware [matter] fall down. Others affirm that this ware is of such heat that, if it fall from the top of the ship, it doth melt the resin and pitch of the hatches of the ship, with such other foolish imaginations. And therefore it shall be good briefly to speak hereof to stop the mouths of such fond and ignorant persons.

The exhalations or vapours of the gross fumes or smokes that rise from the earth are constrained or gathered together by the coldness of the night and the air, and are thickened in the first region of the air next to the earth. This may and is wont to be inflamed or kindled. And if it find a body whereunto it may cleave, it abideth in that until it is consumed. This fire is clear and shining, and yet it burneth not. The Greeks call it Polydeuces and the Latins call it Castor and Pollux. It is accustomed to appear upon the shrouds and oftentimes is seen upon the pikes of soldiers in the armies of men of war, as Pliny writeth. And this as well by reason of the continual smoke, as also by the heat of much people. Certain it is that smoke is none other thing than fire dispersed, as flame is an exhalation or evaporation that riseth in manner of a smoke from a gross or fat body, and at the time that it riseth, being gathered together, is constrained into flame investured with fire. This resplendence or shining is also oftentimes seen not only in journeying by land, but also in sailing by rivers, and when it appeareth on the land, it riseth of the smoke that is gathered together with the cold air of night: and on the banks of rivers this smoke is gathered of the exhalations of the water, and consequently, being kindled, appeareth bright and shining.

But now let us come to the ships that sail by the sea and to the mariners who are accustomed to tempests. To them, therefore, I say that that light, or such other lights as they see, is engendered of the fumes and smokes of their ships with the heat of men couched close and near together in a narrow place, and when a tempest riseth, the said smoke is thickened, pressed together and beaten down by the winds in such sort that, being tossed from one side to another, it is set on fire by moving, and taketh hold sometime on the shrouds, and sometime in the tops, and sometime also in the poop or in the foreship, so that to see this light, or the same to appear, is a natural thing and not supernatural.

When captain Bezerra was at Corron in the Emperor's navy with his company of soldiers, he chanced to be in a tempest and saw the said fire of St. Elmo, which shortly after descended so low that the captain might safely come to it, and taking it in his cloak, he found it to be a little drop of water . . .

MUSIC

GIOVANNI PIERLUIGI DA PALESTRINA

He was born at Palestrina near the Campagna Romana probably in 1525. He died in Rome in 1594 aged sixty-eight or sixty-nine. He was the greatest composer of his time of contrapuntal music for

unaccompanied chorus. The greater part of his compositions was
church music, but he also produced a quantity of madrigals. In 1537
he was a choirboy in Rome. In 1544 he was appointed organist and
choir-master at the cathedral of St. Agapit at Palestrina under Cardinal
del Monte, who in 1550 became Pope as Julius III. In 1551 he appointed
Palestrina to the post of choir-master of the Julian Choir at St. Peter's,
Rome. 1554, Palestrina published a book of masses dedicated to the
Pope. During his lifetime he held many important offices in Rome,
including that of musical director to St. Philip Neri, the originator of
the oratorio. Palestrina's unaccompanied music led on to the unaccompanied choral music of composers such as Byrd and also to the accompanied Passion music of Bach and the oratorios of Handel. His own work
comprises some 94 madrigals, 94 masses, nearly 500 motets and many
smaller pieces, mostly liturgical.

Source: (a) Palestrina's views on secular and church music. The
Preface to the fourth book of motets, published in 1584 and dedicated
to Pope Gregory XIII. Quoted in H. Coates's *Palestrina*, Master
Musicians, Dent, London, 1938, p. 4.

There exists a vast mass of love-songs of the poets, written in
a way that is entirely foreign to the profession and the name of
Christian. They are the songs of men ruled by passion, and a
great number of musicians, corrupters of youth, make them the
concern of their art and industry: and in proportion as they
flourish by praise of their skill, so do they offend good and
serious-minded men by the depraved taste of their work. I blush
and grieve to think that once I was of their number. But since I
cannot change the past, nor undo what is done, I have mended
my ways. Therefore I have already laboured on those songs which
have been written in praise of Our Lord Jesus Christ, and His
most Holy Virgin-Mother Mary; and now I have produced a
work which treats of the divine love of Christ and His Spouse the
Soul, the Canticle of Solomon.

Source: (b) Palestrina seems to have liked money and never to have
had as much as he wanted. He spent freely, partly because publishing
music was an expensive business in the sixteenth century, partly
because he lived in a fairly prosperous style. Sales were not remunera-
tive and there was no law of copyright to protect the composer against
pirated editions. The following passage from the Preface to the book

of *Lamentations* was addressed to Pope Sixtus V, 1588: Coates, *op. cit.*, p. 18.

Worldly cares of any kind, Most Holy Father, are adverse to the muses, and particularly those which arise from a lack of private means. For when the latter afford a sufficiency (and to ask more is the mark of a greedy and intemperate man) the mind can more easily detach itself from other cares—if not, the fault lies within. Those who have experienced the necessity of labouring to provide this sufficiency, according to their rank and way of life, know full well how it distracts the mind from learning, and from a study of the liberal arts.

I have certainly known this experience all my lifetime, and especially at present. But I thank the Divine Goodness, first that now the course is almost finished and the goal in sight; secondly, that in the midst of the greatest difficulties I have never interrupted my study of music: for what other interest could I have had, as a man dedicated to the profession from boyhood, and engrossed in it to the best of my ability and energies? (Would that my progress had equalled my labour and diligence!)

I have composed and published much: a great deal more is lying by me, which I am hindered from publishing because of the straitened means of which I have spoken. It would need no little expenditure, especially if the larger notes and letters are used, which church publications really require.

Meanwhile I have only been able to publish, in this smaller format, those Lamentations of the Prophet Jeremiah which are usually sung in choral form during Holy Week in the churches.

This work I offer to your Holiness with that humility due to the exalted Pastor of the Universal Catholic Church, outstanding in holiness and admirable in authority.

Source: (c) A Contemporary Opinion on Palestrina: Papal Choir book, written by Melchior Major (or Mafor). Coates, *op. cit.*, p. 76.

Palestrina flourished in the time of our fathers and was most famous for his liturgical music, both masses and motets. He was one in whom all melody and modulation resided . . . no one in our times showed such great musical gifts as our Palestrina. I declare him to be the father of music, just as Homer was the father of poetry... He was buried in the basilica with an imposing funeral attended by a great company of musicians and others.

As Do Re Mi Fa Sol La all ascend, so does thy name, O Palestrina, rise upwards to the stars.

O inevitable Death, bitter and wicked, O cruel Death, thus to rob the churches and the palaces of sweet sounds, for by striking down Palestrina thou hast taken away one who irradiated the church with harmony. And because of him, thou, O Music, rest in peace.

NOTES

[1] The large towns held four fairs a year. It was customary to date bills and bonds so that the quarterly interest was paid at the date of each fair.

[2] The original meaning was a mantle: then a race for the prize of a mantle. To 'get up on the *palio*' sounds like a mistranslation.

[3] Hose meaning short breeches, which were then still called hose.

[4] The treaty between Gaston d'Orleans and the King of Spain which had been arranged by Cinq-Mars secretly in order to bring about the downfall of Richelieu and which Richelieu received through his agent, at Arles.

THE FRENCH CLAIM TO NAPLES

CHARLES I Count of Anjou, King of Naples 1266-85

CHARLES II

Blanche══James II , King of Aragon & Sicily

Margaret══Charles of Valois

Philip VI, King of France

John, King of France

Louis, Duke of Anjou ob. 1385

Louis II

Mary══Charles VII, King of France

Louis XI ob.1483

Alfonso(V) I , King of Aragon & Sicily ob. 1458
King of Naples 1435

FERDINAND I, King of Naples 1458-94
(Ferrante)

ALFONSO II, 1494-5

CHARLES VIII ob. 1498

FERDINAND II, 1495-6
ob s.p.

Isabella══ Gian Galeazzo, Duke of Milan

MILAN

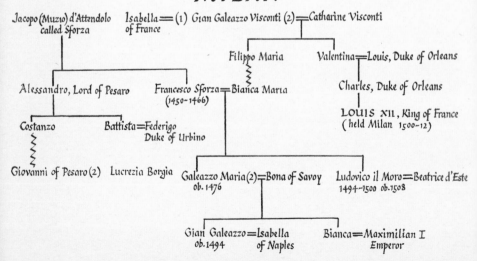

Jacopo (Muzio) d'Attendolo
called Sforza

Isabella══ (1) Gian Galeazzo Visconti (2) ══Catharine Visconti
of France

Filippo Maria

Valentina══Louis, Duke of Orleans

Charles, Duke of Orleans

Alessandro, Lord of Pesaro

Francesco Sforza══Bianca Maria
(1450-1466)

LOUIS XII, King of France
(held Milan 1500-12)

Costanzo

Battista══Federigo
Duke of Urbino

Giovanni of Pesaro (2) Lucrezia Borgia

Galeazzo Maria(2)══Bona of Savoy
ob. 1476

Ludovico il Moro══Beatrice d'Este
1494-1500 ob.1508

Gian Galeazzo══Isabella
ob.1494   of Naples

Bianca══Maximilian I
Emperor

MEDICI

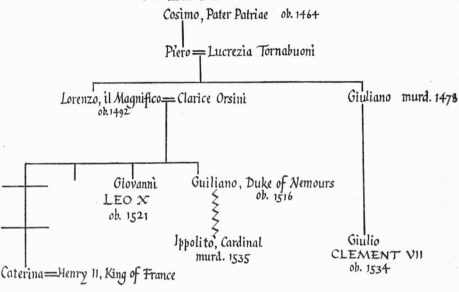

Cosimo, Pater Patriae   ob. 1464

Piero ══ Lucrezia Tornabuoni

Lorenzo, il Magnifico ══ Clarice Orsini   Giuliano   murd. 1478
   ob. 1492

Giovanni   Guiliano, Duke of Nemours
LEO X   ob. 1516
ob. 1521

Ippolito, Cardinal   Giulio
murd. 1535   CLEMENT VII
                                  ob. 1534

Caterina ══ Henry II, King of France

FERRARA AND MODENA ~ HOUSE OF ESTE

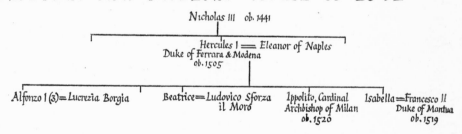

Nicholas III   ob. 1441

Hercules I ══ Eleanor of Naples
Duke of Ferrara & Modena
ob. 1505

Alfonzo I (3) ══ Lucrezia Borgia   Beatrice ══ Ludovico Sforza   Ippolito, Cardinal   Isabella ══ Francesco II
                                              il Moro   Archbishop of Milan   Duke of Mantua
                                                                    ob. 1520   ob. 1519

BORGIA

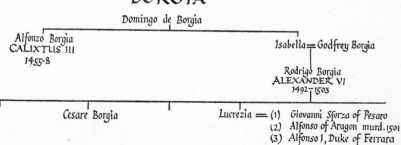

Domingo de Borgia

Alfonzo Borgia   Isabella ══ Godfrey Borgia
CALIXTUS III
1455-8   Rodrigo Borgia
                                                 ALEXANDER VI
                                                   1492 ┬ 1503

Cesare Borgia   Lucrezia ══ (1) Giovanni Sforza of Pesaro
                                                 (2) Alfonso of Aragon murd. 1501
                                                 (3) Alfonso I, Duke of Ferrara

2K

THE HOUSE OF HAPSBURG

Bianca Maria Sforza == (2) MAXIMILIAN 1 (1) == Mary, daughter of Charles the Bold
Emperor 1493–1519 — Duke of Burgundy

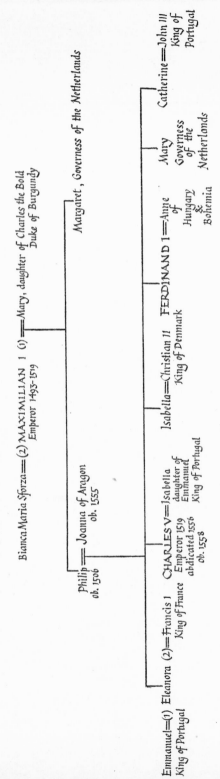

Philip == Joanna of Aragon
ob. 1506 — ob. 1555

Margaret, Governess of the Netherlands

Eleanora (2) == Francis 1
King of France

Emmanuel == (1) Eleanora
King of Portugal

CHARLES V == Isabella
Emperor 1519 — daughter of
abdicated 1556 — Emmanuel
ob. 1558 — King of Portugal

Isabella == Christian 11
King of Denmark

FERDINAND 1 == Anne
of
Hungary
&
Bohemia

Mary
Governess
of the
Netherlands

Catherine == John III
King of
Portugal

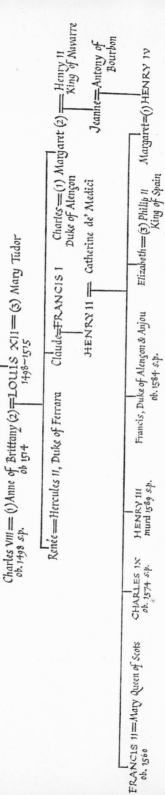

THE HOUSE OF VALOIS

Louis, Duke of Orleans ══ Valentine Visconti of Milan

Charles VIII ══ (1)Anne of Brittany (2) ══ LOUIS XII ══ (3) Mary Tudor
ob.1498 s.p.   1498–1515
                                          ob. 1514

Renée ══ Hercules II, Duke of Ferrara

Claude ══ FRANCIS I

HENRY II ══ Catherine de' Medici

Charles ══ (1) Margaret (2) ══ Henry II
Duke of Alençon   King of Navarre

Jeanne ══ Antony of
         Bourbon

Margaret ══ (1) HENRY IV

Francis, Duke of Alençon & Anjou
ob. 1584 s.p.

Elizabeth ══ (3) Philip II
             King of Spain

HENRY III
murd 1589 s.p.

CHARLES IX
ob. 1574 s.p.

FRANCIS II ══ Mary Queen of Scots
ob. 1560

INDEX